PREVENTING READING FAILURE

A Practical Approach

Richard C. Culyer, III
Coker College

Gail B. Culyer
Reading/Language Arts Consultant

UNIVERSITY
PRESS OF
AMERICA

Lanham • New York • London

Copyright © 1987 by

University Press of America,® Inc.

4720 Boston Way
Lanham, MD 20706

3 Henrietta Street
London WC2E 8LU England

British Cataloging in Publication Information Available

Library of Congress Cataloging-in-Publication Data

Culyer, Richard C.
  Preventing reading faillure.

  Bibliography: p.
  Includes index.
  1. Reading. 2. Reading—Remedial teaching.
I. Culyer, Gail B.   II. Title.
LB1050.42.C85   1987   372.4   87-14724
ISBN 0-8191-6496-8 (alk. paper)

Dedicated to

Our Parents

and First Teachers

VIRGINIA and BRICE SMITH

AGNES and the late R. D. BLAKE

and

Daughter GINGER

who, at age 11, plans to be a

fifth-grade teacher

TABLE OF CONTENTS

FOREWORD

The text you are about to read (or even better, use) is a very unique and special one in so many ways. There are a considerable number of texts devoted to the teaching of reading in the schools. Most of these books are for the most part, highly predictable. Depending upon the specific text, each represents a particular point of view with a predictable chorus of meaningless generalities designed to offend few and, unfortunately, help fewer. This text, assuredly, is not one of those.

I could begin by saying that Preventing Reading Failure: A Practical Approach is indeed a practical book. It is surely that, but it is surely so much more; it is a humane text. There are real children in it, real schools, real reading problems, real teachers and real instructional solutions. A strong cable of reality and classroom immediacy lends integrity throughout the text. It's a text about reading, about the children who come to school to learn to read and about those who teach them.

I am sure the authors, the reading scholars Richard and Gail Culyer, could find many more unique differences between their text and others. But as someone who has read it but not yet used it (as I shall) there are nine clearly apparent ones.

First, I think that in every instance the authors have stayed on the common sense side of the research literature. It is obvious they know what that literature says and just as importantly what it doesn't say. Refreshingly, they know what that empirical base means for improved classroom reading practice.

This text could easily be used as a classroom resource book because of the number of highly relevant and excellent independent and teacher directed pupil activities which are recommended for its comprehensive skills instruction program.

Thirdly, Preventing Reading Failure presents a

logical coherent methodology. The instructional procedures complement lesson objectives in a very natural way. The methodology "fits" the vocabulary, pupil text, and skills content.

Another major strength of the book is the sensible manner in which the role of phonics is explained, the teaching strategies outlined and the relevance and utility of phonics instruction detailed. The phonics position held by the authors is neither zealous nor disdained; it simply makes good sense.

Fifthly, I particularly enjoyed the many literary references which are used with the text itself as well as the excellent bibliographies of quality children and adolescent literature which follow specific chapters. The highly desirable goal of incorporating a literature strand in every school reading program is endorsed and emphasized throughout.

Another outstanding feature is the use of a "guideline" technique for both reading program content as well as for instructional application. These guidelines establish very reasonable and attainable parameters for the design of an eminent school reading program and for the teaching procedures to attain that goal.

A seventh feature of this text is the realistic and totally logical manner by which the "language of reading" content is outlined and then detailed. The sections on syllabication, homophones, and spelling patterns are three examples of how this highly structured content can be handled in a credible, intellectually acceptable manner.

Throughout the text, each philosophical or pedagogical position held by the authors is sustained by reasoned argument. The support of logic, common sense, empirical evidence, and classroom reflection sustains the reading curricula and instructional procedures which they advocate.

And finally, and most rewardingly, Preventing Reading Failure is written in a straightforward, direct and sincere manner. The authors have written from an intellectual posture but their advocacies have been tempered by the classroom experience of both success and failure. Their writing is most notably and nobly, honest writing.

If they were students of reading education, Ernest Hemingway, Beryl Markham, John Steinbeck, and Eudora Welty would have mightily congratulated the authors on their distinguished contribution to the profession. On the other hand, I would gather Joseph Conrad would still be searching for the plot.

John C. Manning
Past President
International Reading
    Association at
New Brighton, Minnesota
1987

INTRODUCTION

Christmas had come and gone, and six-year-old Terry seemed to be no closer to reading than he was in August. His perplexed first-grade teacher referred him to the school's Chapter 1 teacher, who used materials and teaching techniques focusing on diagnostic-prescriptive strategies and mastery-based instruction. One day Terry picked up some material he had seen, read it, realized what he had done, jumped up from his seat and ran shouting to his teacher, "I can read! I can read! I can read!"

When the story was told to us, it was hard to decide who was more ecstatic -- the child or the teacher.

The world is full of Terrys. Some are in kindergarten, some are in college, and many are in between. Almost every child entering school has the capacity to acquire literacy skills, and most do. However, many bright children do not approach their potentials. Many average children become mediocre learners, and many slow children leave school as illiterates or semi-literates. These situations need not exist.

Preventing Reading Failure: A Practical Approach is written with educationally disadvantaged children in the front of our minds. We consider an educationally disadvantaged child as anyone who is not making satisfactory progress in reading. Thus, a bright fifth grader who calls words at the college level but comprehends at the third-grade level is educationally disadvantaged. So is an average youngster who reads below grade level. So is the child who fills in all blanks well but still is unable to apply the information.

We believe the first academic responsibility of every teacher is to identify youngsters' needs and then provide appropriate direct instruction using the Instructional Rainbow (explanation, demonstration, guided practice, feedback, and correction). We believe teachers should use mastery teaching strategies that enhance the likelihood of pupil progress. We believe that effective teaching strategies are within the grasp of conscientious and committed teachers.

Preventing Reading Failure: A Practical Approach is the result of over two decades of work with elementary children and professional educators. We attempt to describe some specific, practical techniques that individual teachers and schools can use in helping all children learn to read (better). The ideas include those we have learned from the literature, our teachers, and the undergraduates and graduates who have been our students. Many other ideas are those we have developed in an effort to translate the research into practice. In each case we have sought to field-test our ideas in a particular sequence: with individuals, with groups, with entire classes, and finally with entire schools. This procedure has given us constant feedback and allowed us to make the necessary adaptations for meeting the needs of diverse learning situations. The ideas have been produced in mimeograph form and used in over 1000 workshops in a number of states and Canada, and further feedback has made it possible for us to add, delete, modify, and clarify. Thus the verification process has been extensive. The major strategies discussed here are used schoolwide in a number of schools, and readers who are interested in visiting and observing are invited to contact us at Coker College, Hartsville, South Carolina 29550. Constructive criticism and suggestions are also welcomed.

Several observations may prove helpful. First, we have tried to avoid the awkwardness involved in using pronouns to refer to people. While they and them are appropriate for group use, our emphasis on individuals often requires singular pronouns. We have decided to use the masculine pronouns for pupils and the feminine pronouns for teachers (except when illustrations dictate otherwise).

Second, in an effort to avoid superficial

treatment of topics, we have eliminated chapters focusing on many important aspects relating to reading: the gifted, reading teachers and remedial reading, study skills, the language arts, reading in the content areas, the library, materials evaluation, etc. Subsequent books will focus on these topics.

Third, we are deeply indebted to many educators. Dr. John Manning, past president of the International Reading Association and professor of education at the University of Minnesota, deserves special mention. His pioneering efforts in developing comprehensive coordinated programs, his erudite scholarship, his mellifluous and practical lectures and publications, and his tireless efforts have had a dramatic impact on tens of thousands of adult educators and millions of pupils. He has given freely, generously, and graciously of his time in reading the manuscript and writing the Introduction. We appreciate him as an outstanding gentleman, a good friend, and a dedicated professional.

Sara Simpson and Beth Pow are superb elementary teachers who have been our friends and shared ideas for many years. The teachers, supervisors, and administrators involved in three special long-term projects have utilized our ideas, provided valuable feedback, expanded our horizons, and compelled us to be practical and specific. In the order of our efforts, the comprehensive longitudinal projects include the Rockingham (North Carolina) County Schools with Mr. Elbert Lake as current reading supervisor; a group of schools in Lexington (North Carolina) with Dr. Athelene P. Carter as principal and co-writer of Project IRIS (Improving Reading Instruction Schoolwide); and 23 Phase I and II schools in Polk County (Florida) with Dr. Alice R. Woods as reading supervisor and Mrs. B-Annie Lewis as curriculum assistant. The latter project is midway through a six-year effort.

We also wish to acknowledge with grateful appreciation the editors of various journals who have allowed us to include some of our articles (usually revised and/or updated as appropriate). The references follow:

"Cumulative Teaching, Better Learning,"_Academic_

Therapy, XVII, No. 5 (May, 1982), 537-542.

"Guidelines for Skill Development: Comprehension," Clearing House, LV, No. 3 (November, 1981), 121-126.

"Guidelines for Skill Development: Vocabulary," Reading Teacher, XXXII, No. 3 (December, 1978), 316-322.

"Guidelines for Skill Development: Word Attack," Reading Teacher, XXXII, No. 4 (January, 1979), 425-433.

"How to Develop a Locally-Relevant Sight Word List," Reading Teacher, XXXV, No. 5 (February, 1982), 596-597.

"Interpreting Achievement Tests: Some Areas of Concern, " Clearing House, LV, No. 8 (April, 1982), 374-380.

"Project READ (Reading Encouragement and Development)," Early Years, XV, No. 9 (May, 1985), 24, 32.

"Skinny Books for Reading," Language Arts, LIII, No. 6 (September, 1975), 793-796.

Finally, we express appreciation to Dr. Joseph Wepman for permission to reproduce the Wepman Auditory Discrimination Test.

We have always tried to analyze our teaching successes and failures as ways of improving our effectiveness. Writing has required us to think more carefully and thoroughly about what we believe and how we implement practices. We recognize there is no royal road to learning. Our procedures represent but one way. We encourage you to read and think in depth, to question, and to adapt and adopt ideas from this text and from others.

You are your greatest gift to children. We hope this book will prove helpful as you work with this country's future leaders and followers.

CHAPTER 1

CHARACTERISTICS OF A DEVELOPMENTAL READING PROGRAM

Introduction

"Imagine, if you can, what your life would be like if you could not read, or if your reading skills were so meager as to limit you to the simplest of writings, and if for you the door to the whole world of knowledge and inspiration available through the printed word had never opened.

For more than a quarter of our population this is true. For them education, in a very important way, has been a failure, and they stand as a reproach to all of us who hold in our hands the shaping of the opportunity for education.

These individuals have been denied a right -- a right as fundamental as the right to life, liberty, and the pursuit of happiness -- the right to read...

From a variety of statistical information accumulated by the Office of Education regarding reading deficiences throughout the country these shocking facts stand out:

-- One out of every four students nationwide has significant reading deficiencies.

-- In large city school systems up to half of the students read below expectation.

-- There are more than three million illiterates in our adult population.

-- About half of the unemployed youth, ages 16-21, are functionally illiterate.

-- Three-quarters of the juvenile offenders in New York City are two or more years retarded in reading.

-- In a recent U.S. Armed Forces program called Project 100,000, 68.2 percent of the young men fell below Grade Seven in reading and academic ability.

The tragedy of these statistics is that they represent a barrier to success that for many young adults produces the misery of a life marked by poverty, unemployment, alienation and, in many cases, crime.

It must be recognized also, however, that for the majority who acquire the basic reading skills, there can also be a barrier which limits the fulfillment of their right to read. This barrier exists when the skill of reading is not accompanied by the desire to read. We fail, therefore, just as much in assuring the right to read when the desire is absent as when the skills are missing.

It is inexcusable that in this day when man has achieved such giant steps in the development of his potential, when many of his accomplishments approach the miraculous, there still should be those who cannot read...

Therefore, as U.S. Commissioner of Education, I am herewith proclaiming my belief that we should immediately set for ourselves the goal of assuring that by the end of the 1970's the right to read shall be a reality for all -- that no one shall be leaving our schools without the skill and the desire necessary to read to the full limits of his capability.

This is education's "moon" -- the target for the decade ahead. With the same zeal, dedication, perseverance, and concentration that made possible man's giant step of last July 20, this moon too can be reached... (4)."

Perhaps you recognize the above quotation as excerpts from an address delivered by James E. Allen, Jr., then United States Commissioner of Education, before the 1969 Annual Convention of the National Association of State Boards of Education.

Fifteen years later the National Right to Read Effort was quietly replaced by an emphasis on Basic Skills. The results of the National Assessment of Educational Progress in reading for the last two four-year cycles indicates that nine-year-olds are scoring higher but that 13- and 17-year olds remain at the same general level (290, 533). At the same time a study reveals that 23 million American adults have serious reading problems and lack the literacy required to function adequately (422). The facts stand in stark contrast to a statement of the United States Bureau of Education about 1913 that illiteracy was "doomed. A few years more and there will not be a vestige of it left (443:562)."

A recent Report of the National Commission on Excellence in Education (531) charges we have "lost sight of the basic purposes of schooling and of the high expectations and disciplined effort needed to attain them. Among its findings

4

1. Thirteen per cent of 17-year olds are functionally illiterate.
2. Functional illiteracy among minority youth may be as high as 40%.
3. "Average achievement of high school students on most standardized tests is now lower than 25 years ago when Sputnik was launched (531:n.p.)."
4. "Average tested achievement of students graduating from college is also lower(531:n.p.)."

Prior to the report 37 states had responded to an awareness of the problem by adopting high school minimum competency tests, and a majority of states required annual testing of pupils at many of the elementary grade levels. In turn these tests documented pupil weaknesses in reading as well as other areas of the curriculum.

While the causes of reading disability and failure obviously are multiple, this volume focuses on only one major aspect -- the absence in many schools and classrooms of a Developmental Reading Program. Because of the prevalence of this problem, this book attempts to focus on specific practical ways by which some of the individual needs of pupils may be met.

Let us begin by defining two terms which are heavily emphasized throughout this book. They are reading and Developmental Reading Program.

Reading -- Most educators can be generally classified by their concepts of reading. The two most frequently espoused viewpoints are those proposed by Rudolf Flesch, a journalist, and William S. Gray, who was a professor at the University of Chicago.

In his book Why Johnny Can't Read and What You Can Do About It Flesch strongly contended that reading was initially and primarily a matter of decoding (sounding out) words. A clear example of this point of view is found in his best seller:

> Many years ago, when I was about fifteen, I took a semester's course in Czech; I have since forgotten everything about the language itself, but I still remember how the letters are pronounced, plus the simple rule that all words have the accent on the first syllable. Armed with this knowledge, I once surprised a native of Prague by reading aloud from a Czech newspaper. "Oh, you know Czech?" he asked. "No, I don't understand a word of it," I answered. "I can only read it (320:27)."

5

Flesch thus considered reading as a word pronunciation process, a concept which he reiterated in his more recent book (321).

On the other hand, William S. Gray (365) conceived of reading as consisting of four components: (1) word perception, (2) comprehension of the ideas represented by the words, (3) reaction to the ideas, and (4) assimilation or integration of the ideas with previous knowledge and/or experience.

We might paraphrase Gray's components of reading to include pronunciation and meaning, understanding of the ideas, reaction in some way to the printed material, and subsequent modification of our ideas, actions, or appreciations.

Let us explore this concept more carefully. Please read the following poem:

THE SIN OF OMISSION

It isn't the thing you do;
    It's the thing you leave undone,
Which gives you a bit of heartache
    At the setting of the sun.

The tender word forgotten,
    The letter you did not write,
The flower you might have sent,
    Are your haunting ghosts tonight.

The stone you might have lifted
    Out of a brother's way,
The bit of heartsome counsel
    You were hurried too much to say.

The loving touch of the hand,
    The gentle and winsome tone,
That you had no time or thought for
    With troubles enough of your own.

The little acts of kindness,
    So easily out of mind;
Those chances to be helpful
    Which everyone may find--

No, it's not the thing you do,
   It's the thing you leave undone,
Which gives you the bit of heartache
   At the setting of the sun.

                    --Margaret E. Sangster (625)

Now analyze your thought processes. Initially you
identified the words and associated with each the
appropriate meaning. For example, you read "setting of
the sun" rather than "sitting of the sun." And you
recognized the intended meaning of "heartache" instead of
considering "heartburn" as a possibility.

While reading the passage, you recognized the
author's intent: to remind you of the importance of
being considerate. Therefore, you comprehended the
selection. The next step, reaction, required your
evaluation of the poem. Did it say anything meaningful
or personal? Did you agree with the author? Why or why
not?

This is only one kind of reaction. With other types
of printed material you might have responded in a variety
of ways: laughter (joke book or comedy), sorrow (novel),
discouragement (newspaper), horror (account of sadism or
brutality), anger or disgust (letter from a so-called
friend), intense happiness (love letter), or fear (letter
from the Internal Revenue or authority figure). Of
course, any of the types of print indicated above might
elicit a variety of responses.

The final step in the reading process involved a
change, however subtle, in your attitude, concepts, or
activities. For example, did you decide to "omit" a sin
of omission? If so, you completed the four-stage process
of reading to which Gray subscribed.

Note the difference between the viewpoints espoused
by Flesch and Gray. One conceived of reading merely as
the ability to pronounce the words of the poem. The
latter included word perception but continued much
further.

We obviously identify with the Gray point of view.
As used in this volume, reading is thinking. Reading is
understanding. Reading is action.

Developmental Reading Program -- A Developmental
Reading Program is a coordinated approach to instruction
which provides a systematic and sequential introduction,
development, mastery, and use of reading skills involving
all pupils in all academic areas at all grade levels. It
stresses the development of concepts, attitudes,
interests, and values.

7

The educational implications of this definition can hardly be exaggerated. Seven specific aspects merit comment.

First, a <u>Developmental</u> <u>Reading</u> <u>Program</u> <u>provides</u> <u>a</u> <u>systematic</u> <u>and</u> <u>sequential</u> <u>introduction</u>, <u>development</u>, <u>mastery</u>, <u>and</u> <u>use</u> <u>of</u> <u>reading</u> <u>skills</u> (626, 721). One point worth stressing here is that skills must be taught in a carefully-planned and organized manner. Unfortunately, many schools have failed to provide a continuous coordinated program in all areas of the curriculum. Observers in schools which have not provided Developmental Reading Programs often note one or more of the following undesirable practices:

A. Most or all pupils in a specified grade use identical texts. The fact that pupils may be on different pages in the same book does not alter the circumstances (224). A pupil who cannot read a grade-level book cannot read it either fast or slow. For instructional purposes a piece of material is either appropriate or inappropriate. It cannot be both.

B. Another typical practice is the presentation of skills to all members of a class or group without first determining what particular information pupils already possess. If they were used, diagnostic pretests would indicate three broad classifications of learners: (1) those who already possess the skills, (2) those who do not possess the skills, and (3) those who do not even possess the prerequisite skills. It should be obvious, therefore, that three different types of instructional provisions must be made if learning is to be systematic and sequential.

C. A third undesirable practice involves teaching skills without taking steps to assure that each child masters, at least initially, the items being presented. Teaching and learning are not considered here as identical terms.

D. A fourth practice is the tendency of some teachers simply to ignore the skills development program. Especially is this true at the intermediate levels (grades 4-8) and above when teachers assume poor readers would already have learned if they were capable of doing so.

Sometimes this practice assumes a more subtle posture. This occurs when a teacher confuses teaching with testing and merely assigns one or more exercises

8

without first providing instruction in the appropriate skills. The result often is a score which reflects the pupils' knowledge of that information when they entered the class. Those who score well usually understood the information initially, and those with poor scores failed to possess the skill either at the beginning or at the end of the "test."

Except for a few unusually competent and motivated learners, the practice of assigning most pupils to teach themselves the basic skills is both unrealistic and unacceptable. Like its fellow activities, it tends to impede learning.

Second, a Developmental Reading Program involves all pupils (95, 398, 468, 581, 717, 737). Therefore, it involves the total school staff, not just the primary personnel, and not just the language arts instructors. The important factor here is that one or two teachers cannot devise and implement a school-wide Developmental Reading Program (although they can do so within their classrooms).

A unified effort embracing the administrators, supervisors, paraprofessionals, and all faculty members is essential to initiate a program which flows smoothly and evenly from one year into the next (398). A third-grade component which is isolated from a second- or fourth-grade segment is anything but developmental. A third-grade teacher who duplicates the activities and/or materials of the preceding teacher unknowingly may cause apathy or antipathy among more proficient readers.

Still worse, a fifth-grade teacher who recognizes the fact that some of her youngsters do not possess the basic skills may still ignore the continuity of skills development and use only those books designated for her grade in order to "get them ready for next year." The end result, as we all know, is likely to be frustration -- for pupils, parents, teachers, and other professional personnel. By far the most successful instruction is that which is based on what a child needs to know today. When children learn what they need now, they become ready for tomorrow. "Reading must for the disadvantaged child, be taught throughout his entire school life, pre-kindergarten through grade twelve (467)." Other writers agree (20, 56, 487).

Third, a Developmental Reading Program is coordinated across subject areas (262, 660). Some people may find it surprising to learn that reading is not an isolated subject which occurs from 8:45 to 10:00 each morning and then disappears. Reading is the key to success in every academic area. Teachers or administrators who group youngsters for reading and consider their responsibility

9

ended are sadly mistaken. Unless we recognize and provide for individual differences in spelling, language, mathematics, social studies, science, etc., we delude ourselves when claiming to have comprehensive curricula.

Very few sights are more disheartening than seeing some first graders struggle with materials for which they are not ready or seventh graders with third-grade reading ability trying vainly to memorize spelling words they cannot read and will never use or attempting to master their sophisticated grade-level content-area textbooks.

We do not contribute to our pupils' love of learning, appreciation of school, development of adequate self-concepts, and respect for the school and its personnel when we allow them to experience frustration and failure on a consistent basis.

As educators we must assess the effectiveness of our schools at all grade levels and in all academic areas. Unfortunately the assigning of reading to an allotted period of time usually ignores the necessity for providing appropriate materials and reading-related teaching activities in the content areas. Without diminishing our efforts to improve instruction in reading per se, we still need to take steps to secure content materials which all pupils can read. This should be followed by the teaching of specific reading skills -- call them study skills if you wish -- which youngsters need to become effective readers of content materials. It is content reading, not just the basal type of material, which confronts readers every day.

Fourth, a _Developmental Reading Program is coordinated across teachers_ (626, 717). The comment has already been made that all teachers must be involved actively in planning and implementing a Developmental Reading Program. This active cooperation is essential from both a horizontal (within grade) and a vertical (between grades) point of view. When several teachers within a grade level are responsible for a group of pupils, their efforts are unlikely to result in maximum progress unless they make similar provisions for individual needs.

For example, if Mrs. Moxley provides Johnny with the necessary low-level books for some curriculum areas but Mr. Franks does not, Johnny is unlikely to practice and reinforce any skills that Mrs. Moxley may present. Maximum learning is unlikely to occur. Coordination between a special education teacher and a classroom teacher (343, 525) and a reading teacher and a classroom teacher (93) is especially important.

Likewise, when teachers in adjacent grades fail to share information about pupils on an active and planned basis, numerous opportunities for assuring continuous progress are lost. Perhaps one of the major advantages of the one-teacher school was the continuity provided by a teacher who worked with the same children year after year.

It is worth noting that a survey of 244 Wisconsin reading specialists found that over one-half identified "coordination of reading programs" as an area of deficiency in their graduate programs (661).

Fifth, a Developmental Reading Program is coordinated across grade levels (95, 102, 126, 238, 285, 286, 398, 468, 581, 588, 642). It is incorrect to assume that reading should be taught only -- or even primarily -- in the first three grades. At the high school and college levels a wide variety of reading skills must be introduced, and many items should be re-taught, reinforced, and extended. In a number of intermediate grades (4-8) and high schools, Developmental Reading Programs are either deemphasized or non-existent (93). In still other schools they exist in name only.

The irony of this fact becomes especially apparent when we consider the literature and research. They clearly indicate that the range of individual differences increases as pupils grow older (95, 271). At the seventh-grade level, for instance, reading ability within a heterogeneous class usually ranges from the first through ninth grade. Among high school students it ranges from primary to advanced college level.

Perhaps one-fourth of the pupils in our schools today operate under frustrating conditions in one or more subject areas (75). Many pupils who do not or cannot even read a daily newspaper or other simple material are expected to comprehend the subtleties of literature and highly sophisticated or technical science and social studies materials.

It is a common practice of some teachers in the intermediate grades and above to blame their pupils' poor reading ability on preceding teachers. Progress could occur if less time were spent bemoaning pupils' deficiencies and more time used in locating materials and providing appropriate instruction. Cooperative sharing of information among teachers at different grade levels might go a long way toward preventing failure, thereby eliminating the "necessity" for assessing blame. One practice is "passing the buck," the other an example of effective teaching.

Sixth, a Developmental Reading Program is coordinated across schools (423). Whenever several schools are responsible for pupils, they have a special obligation to develop and implement a continuous program which flows

11

smoothly through the elementary and high school years.

For example, if pupils in a particular attendance area are likely to attend School A in K-2, School B in grades 3-5, School C in grades 6-8, and School D in grades 9-12, the four faculties should design the framework of a Developmental Reading Program that meets the needs of all learners. It is completely unrealistic to expect that if School A institutes a comprehensive program, failure will be prevented in the other two schools. While each of the four schools must relinquish some of its traditional autonomy, the time has arrived for teachers and schools to consider the necessity for developing a carefully-planned longitudinal program for children rather than following their own individual preferences (423).

Seventh, a Developmental Reading Program is coordinated across materials (483). One of the most crucial components of academic programs is the provision of materials. Unfortunately, many people have assumed that "a wide variety of materials" will solve all problems. Two fallacies are inherent in this assumption. (1) Materials do not teach; therefore the provision of materials does not at all assure that either teaching or learning will occur. (2) An uncoordinated hodge podge of materials denies the possibility of providing systematic and sequential instruction and practice activities (79, 343, 484). What we need is not just an abundance of material but carefully-selected and coordinated materials that interrelate with each other and help coordinate a comprehensive program.

Schools that order Material A because it "looks useful" and Material B because "we have to spend this money right away" encounter two problems. The first is ordering material which will often be used regardless of its finally-determined value. Professionals often note, "Well, we have it; we may as well use it."

The second problem is reflected in the failure to develop a comprehensive plan of materials acquisition and usage which meets the needs of all children at all grade levels in all subject areas. Since materials usually comprise the bulk of the curriculum, a Developmental Reading Program is predicated on the long-term acquisition of carefully-evaluated materials resulting from the school's needs for specific items.

Only when all pupils in all subject areas at all grade levels participate in a systematic and sequential introduction, development, mastery, and use of reading competencies can a school or class claim to offer a Developmental Reading Program. It is to this end that the present book is directed.

12

Characteristics of a
Developmental Reading Program

Having established a framework as a model, let us consider characteristics of a carefully-planned and organized Developmental Reading Program. The following statements comprise our concept of the services an effective school or class provides all of its pupils:

Characteristic One: "The organization of a Developmental Reading Program is based on a comprehensive analysis of (a) the schools' success in meeting the needs of all children and (b) a determination of the competencies required by the total staff to assure the provision of a quality learning experience for all children."

Characteristic Two: "The organization of a Developmental Reading Program is preceded by a full year of a carefully-planned series of activities involving the community and all school personnel. A long-term comprehensive program development effort is initiated. In it emphasis is placed on (a) planning a coordinated approach to teaching and learning, and (b) developing the skills, concepts, and attitudes which enable teachers, paraprofessionals, and school officials to implement the program."

Characteristic Three: "Beginning with the initial efforts, the school community is actively involved, in an advisory capacity, in planning and implementing a Developmental Reading Program. Comprehensive procedures for diseminating information are utilized continuously."

Characteristic Four: "All pupils in all academic areas at all grade levels are provided initial classroom diagnosis during the first weeks of school to determine their strengths, weaknesses, and needs. Continuous diagnosis is provided throughout the year."

Characteristic Five: "Non-readers, whether at the primary or intermediate age level, are provided with a specific intensive and extensive program including oral language development and other aspects of reading readiness. This program continues without regard to rigid time limits."

Characteristic Six: "Regardless of the number of basal and supplementary materials being utilized, one series is designated as a lead basal. Except for extremely poor and highly proficient readers, all pupils are associated with some title within the lead basal series."

Characteristic Seven: "The modified Betts Criteria are utilized to determine the selection of the

13

appropriate levels of learning materials, both for instructional and independent reading. These criteria are used throughout the year to assure the continued satisfactory matching of pupils and materials."

Characteristic Eight: "An Initial Reading Inventory is used in conjunction with the modified Betts Criteria as one basis for identifying appropriate materials to be used for instructional purposes. Throughout the year informal reading inventories based on silent reading for comprehension and oral reading for word analysis are used to ensure each pupil's continuous association with the appropriate level of reading materials."

Characteristic Nine: "A comprehensive skills sequence chart is utilized by all teachers as the basis for providing further specific diagnosis and instruction at various levels. Each pupil's cumulative record includes an annotated progress form; this information is updated periodically."

Characteristic Ten: "Pupils who require additional contacts with learning materials are provided with a sufficient variety of extensive reinforcement activities to ensure their mastery and retention of information."

Characteristic Eleven: "As a corollary to the preceding guideline, emphasis is removed from completing certain lessons or units in a specified time or of finishing books. Mastery teaching is emphasized. Data about each pupil's present reading status are available in the principal's office."

Characteristic Twelve: "A variety of approaches based on pupil strengths, weaknesses, and specific needs are utilized. These approaches include basal readers, individualized instruction, language-experience, and high interest-low vocabulary programs for the types of pupils who can benefit from them.

Characteristic Thirteen: "Coordinated modality training is provided to meet the needs of pupils who learn best through auditory, visual, kinesthetic, or combined sensory channels."

Characteristic Fourteen: "For most children specific group instruction is provided rather than a dependence on materials that 'teach' or (b) pupils to teach themselves with a minimum of specific guidance."

Characteristic Fifteen: "Specific daily provision is made for every child to engage in recreational reading at school."

Characteristic Sixteen: "The school day is apportioned in such a manner as to provide additional instruction and practice time to pupils whose priority need requires an emphasis on reading."

14

Characteristic Seventeen: "Provisions similar to those in reading are used to assure the provision for individual needs in each of the content areas of the curriculum."

Characteristic Eighteen: "Materials acquisition is based upon analysis of a School-Wide Inventory of Materials, determination of specific needs, and study of materials commercially available. It is followed by specific in-service and later by evaluation of the effectiveness of material."

Characteristic Nineteen: "Procedures for evaluating and reporting pupil progress and continuing needs to them and their parents recognize each learner's growth in terms of his or her capability and progress rather than in comparison with dissimilar peers."

Characteristic Twenty: "A program development specialist provides continuing in-service assistance to teachers, paraprofessionals, and school officials rather than working with small groups of 'remedial' pupils."

Characteristic Twenty-one: "Media specialists teach weekly skills lessons designed to assist pupils and teachers in locating and using appropriate materials, both according to reading and interest levels. Media specialists are not 'bookeepers.'"

Characteristic Twenty-two: "Provisions for evaluating the effectiveness of a Developmental Reading Program are carefully planned and implemented by all school personnel. Evaluation procedures are based upon youngsters' actual programs rather than inappropriate standardized devices."

Characteristic Twenty-three: "The total school program results in daily success for all pupils and adult personnel in all subject areas at all grade levels."

These twenty-three characteristics form the basic outline for the remainder of this book as well as the companion volumes (184, 189). At this point it seems appropriate to discuss each characteristic briefly or to indicate the topics which are considered in separate chapters of the book.

Characteristic One: "The organization of a Developmental Reading Program is based on a comprehensive analysis of (a) the school's success in meeting the needs of all children and (b) a determination of the competencies required by the total staff to assure a quality learning experience for all children."

It seems safe to assume that a school which is considering the organization of a Developmental Reading Program already recognizes the importance of meeting the needs of a large number of its children. This awareness probably comes from study of achievement tests and observations by teachers, supervisors and parents.

Ideally any program being instituted in a school should result from the carefully considered study of the problem by all professionals and the community. Furthermore, the decision to pursue some particular course of action should be a group decision rather than one imposed by a well-meaning authority figure.

All too frequently we see the sad results of this course of action. A principal announces at the last faculty meeting of the year, "During the summer read some books on non-grading and team teaching. We're going to do that next year." When the innovation fails, teachers are often unjustly blamed. However, they were not involved in the decision-making and the planning. Nor did they receive adequate preparation for instituting a new program.

<u>Characteristic Two</u>: "The organization of a Developmental Reading Program is preceded by a full year of a carefully-planned series of activities involving the community and all school personnel. A long-term comprehensive program development effort is initiated. In it emphasis is placed on (a) planning a coordinated approach to teaching and learning and (b) developing the skills, concepts, and attitudes which enable teachers, paraprofessionals, and school officials to implement the program."

In recent years we have seen a plethora of innovative approaches to education. Everyone seems to have analyzed the problems of contemporary education and discovered the panacea. Thus we have those who tell us the structure of a school makes the difference. "Use team teaching, non-graded, or multi-aged grouping," they say. Others demand the immediate changes to certain specified materials or approaches. "Use Alpha One, Phonics, Language-Experience, this systems approach, or Individualized Instruction as a total program," they insist.

Research has documented the failure of many new programs (376). One reason is that too many changes have been attempted without broadly-based planning, discussion, and decision-making. When only part of a faculty knows what is involved, the whole venture is doomed. The same result occurs when administrators are not aggressively committed to the plan of action.

The problem is also present when new learning materials are being introduced. As mentioned earlier, a teacher cannot effectively utilize supplementary materials if they are suddenly presented without adequate

16

in-service related to their intended use. Likewise, unless study and planning time is available, the use of multiple learning materials may also leave much to be desired. Even on a daily basis it is difficult to teach well except when careful planning occurs. This takes time!

So does the transition from an assortment of uncoordinated efforts to a systematic and sequential plan. Any school contemplating a change from isolated and haphazard instruction to a Developmental Reading Program can expect success only if all personnel understand and subscribe to the general philosophy and actively participate in the various stages of the planning and implementation (136). Key concepts can be clarified and practices adapted or developed only if a carefully-organized, comprehensive series of practical in-service sessions is conducted at regular intervals, preferably for an entire year.

Five more years will likely be needed to develop the necessary competencies insofar as diagnosing skills knowledge, teaching strategies, classroom management, recordkeeping, and evaluation are concerned. Likewise time will be required for determining needed materials and acquiring them, promoting community understanding of the school-wide effort, and providing the necessary in-service in such a way that all school personnel (and the community as well) receive specific information in all phases of a Developmental Reading Program. In short, one summer workshop will be of little value. So too will be a professional day here and there. A carefully-planned comprehensive multi-year approach is essential. This practical approach should assist each professional -- the administrator, supervisor, teacher, media specialist, program development specialist, etc. -- in recognizing and responding to the appropriate areas of responsibility and opportunity. Careful planning and implementation should help prevent the development among teachers of "innovative fatigue" (417).

Samuels reports research suggesting that "it takes two years to get a project off the ground, two years to implement a project, and two years to produce a stable effect on student achievement scores (621:267)." Fortunately, our experience has been that it doesn't require that long to produce clear results when schools and districts make committed efforts.

One further suggestion: Because practically all professionals are drained of energy at the end of the day, it is highly desirable to conduct in-service sessions during school hours.

Characteristic Three: "Beginning with the initial efforts, the school community is actively involved, in an advisory capacity, in planning and implementing a Developmental Reading Program. Comprehensive procedures for disseminating information are utilized continuously."

Too many good ideas fail because the public is not adequately involved and informed in both the planning and production stages. We strongly recommend that all professional personnel actively cooperate with community leaders in organizing and implementing a Developmental Reading Program and in promoting an understanding of the school program -- its rationale, its structure, and its operation. Parents who are uninformed or misinformed can hardly be hearty supporters. Professionals have a responsibility to seek community involvement, to facilitate exchange of ideas, and to explain honestly and fully the classroom and total school program.

Possible ways of communicating with the public include the following:

1. Parent-Teacher Associations or Organizations

2. Parent-teacher conferences (sometimes with the pupil) and visitations

3. Teacher-pupil discussions conducted informally both within and outside the classroom

4. American Education Week type of activities conducted throughout the year

5. Open House and an Open Door policy, actively rather than passively promoted

6. Volunteers and aides

7. Maids and custodians

8. Radio and television

9. Newspapers, both local and school

10. Brochures and school newsletters placed in every barber and beauty shop, doctor and dentist office, hospital waiting room, bus terminal, launderette -- wherever people gather with time to "spare"

11. Teacher-pupil planned and -executed programs at
     meetings of civic organizations such as Kiwanis,
     Optimist, Mental Health Association, Senior
     Citizens Clubs, and any gathering where people
     need to know what is going on in the schools.

Characteristic Four: "All pupils in all academic
areas at all grade levels are provided initial classroom
diagnosis during the first weeks of school to determine
their specific strengths, weaknesses, and needs.
Continuous diagnosis is provided throughout the year."
     Perhaps you have read the following anecdote often
told about Christopher Columbus. It is said that when he
left Spain, he knew not where he was going, when he
arrived he knew not where he was, and when he returned,
he knew not where he had been.
     The parallel situation is often true in schools.
Sometimes teachers "know" where they are beginning (at
the front of grade-level books), where they are stopping
(at the end of the books), and how they will get there
(by covering two pages or one story per day).   These
teachers are in the same boat with Columbus.
     Keeping this point in mind, you will note that almost
every chapter in the remainder of this book contains
suggestions and actual examples of simple and practical
classroom diagnostic procedures to use.   It   seems
reasonable to conclude that a school whose officials
emphasize "Let's start teaching right away" or whose
teachers ignore diagnosis and plunge into instruction are
destined to fail. Effective teaching must be preceded by
careful diagnosis.   Devoting only a day or two to this
activity is nothing more than mere lip service.
     Characteristic Five: "Non-readers, whether at the
primary or intermediate age level, are provided with a
specific intensive and extensive program including oral
language development and other aspects of reading
readiness.   This program continues without regard to
rigid time limits."
     The typical kindergarten class includes children
whose language development hovers near the two- or
three-year-old level. Not only are some children unready
to learn to read, with the best of instruction, they may
still be unready after a full year of school. After all,
it is quite difficult for children to acquire two or
three or four years of oral language development and
perceptual skills in one year, especially when previous
progress rates have been only a few months per year.
     If provided an intensive and extensive program of
specific language and other readiness competencies, these
children eventually can reach the point of being able to

19

profit from reading instruction. It is essential to construct a Developmental Reading Program (DRP) on a solid base. Extended readiness for those who require it provides the appropriate foundation. Chapters 4A and 4B consider this topic.

Characteristic Six: "Regardless of the number of basal and supplementary materials being utilized, one series is designated as a lead basal. Except for extremely poor and highly proficient readers, all pupils are associated with some title within the lead basal series."

The designation and use of one series of reading books as the lead basal is recommended for providing a systematic sequential introduction, development, and mastery of reading competencies (484, 538, 593). Practically every authority in reading stresses the importance of teaching sequentially (54, 73, 74, 85, 224, 365, 392, 593, 612, 638).

Actually a series of basal readers provides for carefully organized and coordinated instruction in at least six major areas: oral language, word analysis, vocabulary, comprehension, literature, and study skills. Each book in a series continues the progression of skills in the six areas. Support of the principle of sequential learning is inherent in all basal readers as well as in series materials in other areas of the curriculum.

Although one reading series should be adopted as the lead basal series (484, 533, 593), this designation does not preclude the use of other materials, including other basals. Teachers have long recognized the need for additional sources of teaching and practice materials. When used effectively, they may enhance the value of a well-planned coordinated series of learning activities. The key factor lies in the recognition that carefully sequenced and correlated material allows pupils to build on their preceding successful experiences. This is especially true for average and below average youngsters.

Characteristic Seven: "The modified Betts Criteria (54) are utilized to determine the selection of the appropriate levels of learning materials, both for instructional and independent reading. These criteria are used throughout the year to assure the continued satisfactory matching of pupils and materials."

Over a generation ago Emmett Betts offered a series of guidelines for determining the suitability of books for instructional and independent purposes, at least insofar as reading level is concerned. As slightly modified, the Betts Criteria suggest that for instructional purposes pupils generally should be expected to pronounce correctly at least 94% of the words read orally and to comprehend at least 70% of the

material read silently. During independent reading
pupils should score at least 98% on oral reading and 90%
on silent reading. The modified Betts Criteria offer
teachers an excellent guideline for determining whether
or not pupils can read certain materials.

Because use of the modified Betts Criteria is so
closely related to success in reading, Chapter 5
considers the entire topic in detail.

Characteristic Eight: "An Initial Reading Inventory
is used in conjunction with the modified Betts Criteria
as one basis for identifying appropriate materials to be
used for instructional purposes. Throughout the year
informal reading inventories based on silent reading for
comprehension and oral reading for word analysis are used
to ensure each pupil's continuous association with the
appropriate level of reading materials."

An Informal (or Initial) Reading Inventory is highly
recommended in the literature (33, 54, 102, 113, 392,
508, 568, 572, 643). Many teachers, schools, and school
districts administer this device at the beginning of each
year and at appropriate intervals.

The device which comes closest to identifying the
actual instructional or independent level of a youngster
is the one whose material is most comparable to that
which is used in the classroom (568). Only an Initial
Reading Inventory based on the classroom series provides
this comparability. Grade-level books, achievement test
scores, and teacher judgment leave much to be desired as
far as accuracy of placement is concerned. Procedures
for constructing, administering, and interpreting an
Initial Reading Inventory are presented in Chapter 5.

Characteristic Nine: "A comprehensive skills
sequence chart is utilized by all teachers as the basis
for providing further specific diagnosis and instruction
at various levels. Each pupil's cumulative record
includes an annotated progress form; this information is
updated periodically."

One major objective of the Scope and Sequence studies
sometimes required for accreditation of schools is to
familiarize each faculty member with information
presented in materials other than grade-level texts. The
basic assumption is that knowledge and awareness of
higher- and lower- level skills will encourage and assist
teachers to make more effective provisions for the wide
range of individual needs in their classes.

Indeed, the availability of a sequential list of
skills should make it possible for teachers to determine
the lowest levels at which gaps in their youngsters'
learning first occur. For example, a first-grade teacher
may refer to a skills sequence to develop a diagnostic

21

pretest and then use the results to provide instruction and reinforcement in specific aspects of oral language, word analysis, vocabulary, comprehension, literature, and study skills. This gives the children a real "head start" in reading. Or the teacher may consult the skills sequence chart to determine what higher-level skills should be introduced to a really efficient reader.

Teachers at the upper levels should find a sequence chart especially useful. Since so many older pupils are really primary-level readers, it is absolutely essential to consult the skills sequence when preparing lessons. Because even a highly competent reader may lack certain basic skills, systematic learning experiences should be provided at grade level as well as above and below.

Whenever pupils master a skill, a teacher can place a checkmark beside the appropriate item in a group analysis chart. Because the introduction of a skill and its mastery do not necessarily occur at the same time, checkmarks should be recorded only after the latter occurs.

We recommend that kindergarten and first-grade teachers begin the process of compiling a chart for each group. At the end of the year these data should be filed in the cumulative records for use by subsequent teachers. Even though many children's reading ability regresses during the summer (19, 418, 603), reference to a group analysis chart will indicate which books have already been read and which skills were once introduced.

Cumulative records should also include copies of the Initial Reading Inventories as well as results of specific diagnostic pretests and posttests of skill development. These types of data are far more useful than achievement test scores and other information unrelated to instructional planning. They also provide a useful background for parent-teacher conferences.

Chapters 9, 10, and 11 list and discuss specific techniques for developing pupil competence in word analysis, vocabulary, and comprehension.

Characteristic Ten: "Pupils who require additional contacts with learning materials are provided with a sufficient variety of extensive reinforcement activities to ensure the mastery and retention of information."

Almost everyone agrees that some youngsters require many contacts with certain types of information before achieving mastery. In itself this is not a problem, merely a reality to be faced. Difficulty only occurs if teachers equate presentation of material with mastery (or teaching with learning).

We know, for example, that one or two contacts with a new fact or concept may be sufficient for some pupils.

22

Others may require far more instruction and practice (679). Basically the amount of learning is more closely related to the appropriateness of the material, the quality of instruction, and the extent of reinforcement than it is to the person's intelligence. This concept and related practices are considered in Chapter 8.

Characteristic Eleven: "As a corollary to the preceding guideline, emphasis is removed from completing certain lessons or units in a specified period of time or from finishing the book. Mastery teaching is emphasized. Data about each pupil's present reading status are available in the principal's office."

Some educators feel a great need to finish books. Unfortunately, they are much more capable of doing so than are some youngsters; hence, the problem.

A DRP does not expect pupils to complete tasks according to predetermined schedules. As Brown notes, "Simply moving through 'levels' does not constitute gain... (85:162)." McCormick observes that in her district, "There is no prize given to the teacher who first reaches the glossary (498:n.p.)."

Exposing pupils to skills and expecting them to achieve mastery without the necessary reinforcement creates fragmented and vague learning, frustration, and failure. At the same time, expecting pupils to skip information near the end of one book and still achieve success at the next higher grade level produces the same result. Both are inconsistent with what we know about child growth and development. If we recognize the fact that learning is sequential, we must bring our practices in line with our philosophy. If a convergence of the two is impossible, something is wrong with either the practices or the philosophy.

Characteristic Twelve: "A variety of approaches based on pupil strengths, weaknesses, and specific needs are utilized. These approaches include basal readers, individualized instruction, language-experience, and high interest-low vocabulary programs for the types of pupils who can benefit from them."

The research and the literature make it clear that there is no one best way to teach reading (71, 238, 239, 644). However, we should not indulge the fantasy that any single approach is acceptable for all pupils. Certain approaches are still more successful than others, especially with specific types of children (239, 644). We can summarize the research and professional literature by suggesting that teachers need to understand the strengths and weaknesses of several approaches and be able to utilize each wherever applicable. No one approach by itself can hope to meet the needs of every classroom. An eclectic, or combination, approach is far more likely to prove effective in providing for individual differences (238, 514, 626).

A number of chapters, especially 6 and 7, provide additional information about the two most commonly-used approaches, basal readers and language-experience. Suggestions for individualizing learning appear throughout the text.

Characteristic Thirteen: "Coordinated modality training is provided to meet the needs of pupils who learn best through auditory, visual, kinesthetic, or combined sensory channels."

While research does not support the point of view that teaching to a person's modality strength is effective (443B, 699B), teachers believe that pupils learn in different ways. For example, every primary teacher has probably encountered youngsters who did not profit from phonic instruction, perhaps because of their incomplete development of auditory discrimination. Since this ability is not fully developed in some children until the age of eight or nine (522, 570, 670, 735), it seems useful to consider visual and kinesthetic activities as components of a multi-sensory instructional process. This eclectic approach to word identification and recognition allows a child to profit from at least one sensory channel.

For some pupils it seems likely that initial reading instruction might well use a visual (i.e., look-say) technique followed by an auditory (i.e., phonic) procedure. Of course, either can be combined with a kinesthetic, or tracing, component.

At least one strong implication is present for teachers in grades three and above. Pupils who have previously failed to acquire phonic skills should not be dismissed as hopeless cases, for they may have possessed insufficient auditory discrimination in previous years to benefit from phonic instruction. There is always danger in assuming that because a child did not acquire a particular body of information at a certain grade level that the child cannot acquire it later.

Coordinated modality training is considered as an integral part of many of the instructional techniques described throughout this book.

Characteristic Fourteen: "For most children specific group instruction is provided rather than a dependence on (a) materials that 'teach' or (b) pupils to teach themselves with a minimum of specific guidance."

In many schools there is an unfortunate tendency to rely on "teacher-proof" materials for instructional purposes (660). The assumption seems to be that materials are far more effective in teaching than are the professionals.

However, there is little research to support that point of view. Pupils who are expected to work their way through an individually-prescribed and completed assignment, whether in a basal reader, manila folder, or programmed text, are far more likely either to scratch the surface of knowledge or to fill in blanks according to a pattern rather than to acquire any usable and transferable skills. We see this frequently when pupils who have completed page after page of exercises can neither read the words they have marked nor utilize the skills they supposedly have acquired.

Then, too, except for good readers, the assumption that most pupils can learn effectively without direct instruction is rejected by research (286, 322, 598, 626). If most pupils could really do so, teachers could be replaced by aides trained to select and assign materials based on the results of diagnostic pretests.

Nor is one-to-one instruction, as a total program, effective (626). First of all, it simply does not provide sufficient time to meet each individual's instructional needs. Second, by ignoring similarities of children's needs, it provides an ineffective use of the teacher's time. Third, it denies the opportunities of such socializing activities as group discussion and interaction. Finally, one-to-one instruction inhibits the development of oral language upon which comprehension is based.

One-to-one instruction has a definite place in learning, but that position is reinforcement or reteaching rather than original instruction. Because of the importance of teacher time, much of this type of activity should also be performed by aides, volunteers, and other classmates (student teachers). In essence, the younger the child, the slower the child, the less competent the child, and the less motivated the child, the more the need exists for specific group instruction.

Characteristic Fifteen: "Specific daily provision is made for every child to engage in recreational reading at school."

Obviously a program which focuses exclusively on skills cannot hope to effect the development of pupils who can and do read. Yet another aspect of a DRP is specific daily provision for the extended application of newly-acquired skills.

For many people the most difficult aspect of any activity is its initiation. Since this seems also to be the case insofar as reading books and other printed materials is concerned, every child should have a

25

definite opportunity each day to read recreationally. This activity may occur simultaneously for everyone in the class (including the teacher), or it may be used as a scheduled independent activity for those pupils not working directly with the teacher.

Since group work results in a large amount of time devoted to independent activities, thirty minutes each day can easily be made available for recreational reading purposes. This activity is best conducted if both school and classroom library or media center facilities are readily available to pupils. Chapter 8 considers specific strategies.

<u>Characteristic Sixteen</u>: "The school day is apportioned in such a way as to provide additional instruction and practice time to pupils whose priority need requires an emphasis on reading."

Tradition has decreed that each component of the curriculum should consist of a specified number of minutes. The result is that the extent of youngsters' educational progress is often determined by the artificial time allocations rather than by their specific strengths and weaknesses.

For example, a bright child who excels in science but is quite weak in mathematics obviously will find it highly advantageous to receive additional emphasis on the latter, for competence in mathematics is crucial to continuing success in science.

Likewise, pupils with a reading problem have one critical academic need. In a typical classroom they may spend much valuable time engaged in activities which do not contribute to the development of their reading ability. Much of that time could be more profitably devoted to reading instruction and practice. As Guthrie (376) has pointed out, Rosenshine's review of the literature shows that learning time is the pupil behavior most highly correlated with reading achievement. Poor readers need double or sometimes triple instructional periods daily (310). While the mere provision of additional time does not assure adequate learning, the inclusion of intensive appropriate instruction on a continuous basis should prove quite effective.

As early as 1929 Alfred Whitehead noted, "Do not teach too many subjects...What you teach, teach thoroughly...Let the main ideas which are introduced into a child's education be few and important, and let them be thrown into every combination possible (739:2-3)."

<u>Characteristic Seventeen</u>: "Procedures similar to those in reading are used to assure the provision for individual needs in each of the content areas of the curriculum."

26

In a discussion concerning ways of organizing and implementing a DRP, it may seem tangential to discuss this point. However, if we believe youngsters should be associated with reading materials they can handle, it seem only consistent to apply the same philosophy and practice to the reading of social studies, science, language, health, and mathematics. Indeed, it would appear to be the very height of inconsistency to advocate the necessity of providing for individual differences in reading and to deny or ignore them elsewhere. As Smith and Barrett comment:

> Something is amiss with a program that has students performing well with basal readers, workbooks, games, and skill development kits but doing poorly with their social studies, language arts, science, and mathematics textbooks (660:113).

Because consideration of this topic is so extensive, a companion book (184) discusses appropriate strategies in the content areas.

Characteristic Eighteen: "Materials evaluation is based upon analysis of a School-Wide Inventory of Materials, determination of specific needs, and study of materials commercially available. It is followed by specific in-service and later by evaluation of the effectiveness of the materials."

As mentioned earlier, materials acquisition and usage plays a significant role in the education of children. When materials are randomly provided either by one teacher or by teachers at successive grade levels, the results are likely to be catastrophic, especially for young and poor readers.

Materials should be selected and utilized with several questions in mind.

1. What materials of various types and levels are already available in the school?

2. What materials are needed to achieve the objectives contained in the curriculum? For example, are more decoding (word analysis) materials needed, or is information required on comprehension and study skills? Are materials needed at reading level one or five? A comparison of pupil performance data, the School-Wide Inventory of Materials, and the proposed curriculum itself should help provide answers to these types of questions.

3. What materials are available commercially? A study of catalogues housed in the media center can help supply the answer. Another source is the displays at professional conferences.

4. Of the available materials, which ones appear most likely to accomplish the school's objectives? Your classroom's objectives?

This determination is, of course, initial and tentative. One cannot be certain that specific materials will accomplish the intended objectives. Only classroom use will determine that. However, careful study can eliminate consideration of many materials because of content, poor construction, and level of difficulty, or failure to consider the specific areas in which information is being sought.

Obviously, written criteria should be developed to assist professionals in evaluating and selecting materials. After these items have been secured, attention needs to focus on two factors: (a) provision for in-service (usually via demonstration lessons) before materials are placed in the school, and (b) subsequent determination of the value of these items in achieving their intended purpose. This evaluation should be used as a reference source when considering further orders of materials.

Characteristic Nineteen: Procedures for evaluating and reporting pupil progress and continuing needs to them and their parents recognize each learner's growth in terms of his or her capability and progress rather than in comparison with dissimilar peers."

We prefer an evaluating and reporting system based on the learning sequence. If all third graders were expected to use third-grade books, it might be perfectly consistent to assign grades by determining the extent to which each pupil had mastered that material. However, if we believe children learn best when instruction is based on their present level of performance, it seems only logical to report their progress at the levels at which they are learning.

We also recommend the use of face-to-face parent-teacher conferences (sometimes with the pupil present) as well as written comments discussed first with the pupil and then communicated to the parents. A procedure recognizing the importance of communicating intelligible information helps to promote public understanding and support of the school program. Written comments make it possible to indicate a pupil's strengths, weaknesses, and specific needs. There should be much more meaning than a

28

"C" (whatever that is!) or an "N" for "needs improvement" (which surely is why children come to school!). Written comments also tend to faciliate careful thinking about a youngster's present learning status. They should be concise, objective, and unambiguous.

Regardless of the type of evaluating and reporting system being used, it should be consistent throughout the school. It should also be clearly understood by pupils, parents, teachers, and other professionals.

Characteristic Twenty: "A program development specialist provides continuing in-service assistance to teachers, paraprofessionals, and school officials rather than working with small groups of 'remedial' pupils."

The most common activity of a majority of special reading teachers involves teaching small groups of children five or more periods a day, two to five days a week. Unfortunately this practice is an ineffective utilization of the specialist's unique opportunities and (hopefully) talents and the school's specific responsibilities.

We assume reading teachers are selected because of their success in assisting poor readers to overcome their deficiencies. Furthermore, reading teachers are employed specifically because schools have large numbers of pupils who are not reading as well as they might. Principals should anticipate that the employment of reading teachers will help resolve the problem.

If this is the case, it becomes necessary to determine some of the problems. This is fairly easy to do. One major problem includes the need for all teachers to demonstrate competence in organizing their time, providing for the needs of various groups, diagnosing, teaching and reinforcing, and establishing independent activities. Because some teachers experience difficulty in one or more of these areas, and none of us is so knowledgeable or competent as to deny the need for acquiring additional competence, it seems safe to conclude that a reading teacher's special opportunity is to serve as the resident in-service teacher. Thus the role becomes one of program development.

Characteristic Twenty-one: "Media specialists teach weekly skills lessons designed to assist pupils and teachers in locating and using appropriate materials, both according to reading and interest levels. Media specialists are not 'bookkeepers.'"

In essence, a media specialist may be viewed as another teacher with responsibilities quite similar to other members of the faculty. The media specialist helps pupils locate and utilize materials and provides specific skills diagnosis, instruction, and practice in curriculum aspects related to the library or media center. And, since a variety of media are useful in fulfilling some of the objectives of a DRP, a media specialist is in an excellent position to share his or her unique expertise. Along with the classroom teacher, the media specialist is directly responsible for helping to instill in children an appreciation for good literature.

Like a special reading teacher, a media specialist is not a substitute provided to release or relieve teachers of their duties -- or their children (113). Rather the media specialist is a member of a unique team teaching venture which regularly involves every other faculty member. He or she and the classroom teacher pool their energies and efforts to guide the growth of children in living and learning in a multi-media world.

Characteristic Twenty-two: "Provisions for evaluating the effectiveness of a Developmental Reading Program are carefully planned and implemented by all school personnel. Evaluation procedures are based upon youngster's actual programs rather than inappropriate standardized devices."

Because publishers of standardized tests recognize such devices do not provide accurate information for individuals, it seems essential to supply professional personnel with data regarding the proper use of test results. A second area for investigation might be that of using standardized tests organized in levels. The tests to be administered to youngsters would depend on their level of learning rather than their grade level (117, 392). However, the use of criterion-referenced tests accompanying many sets of basal materials is superior to either of the first two possibilities.

Unfortunately, the results of standardized tests are often used in such a way as to provide little assistance to teachers, parents, or administrators. Two examples may suffice. Although state history is taught at various grade levels, standardized tests do not include items about the topics. What conclusions should we draw if a class records no "measurable" progress in social studies during the year? A second example: What happens when we teach a fifth grader second-grade material but administer a fifth-grade achievement test?

Unless tests are appropriately selected and then carefully interpreted, educational decisions may be made without any justifiable basis. The more the curriculum of a school or class or individual differs from the content of a test, the more invalid is the score and the more likely is the possibility of misinterpretation and misuse of the results. Indeed, Saily reports that a study by the Institute for Teaching at Michigan State

University showed that 30-40% of the questions on the most commonly-used standardized achievement tests "are not covered by major commercial textbooks at the same grade level (617:12)."

As a result, we should give serious consideration to a number of informal measures designed to parallel the curriculum. Some possibilities include the following:

1. Initial Reading Inventory
2. Diagnostic pretests
3. Criterion-referenced tests based on the material being studied
4. Attitude inventory
5. Data on dropouts
6. Data on attendance
7. Survey of discipline problems
8. Survey of pupil opinions
9. Survey of teacher opinions
10. Survey of opinions of specialized personnel
11. Survey of community opinions
12. Survey of the use of the media center

Both pre- and post-measures should be employed, for it is important to know to what extent we have accomplished our objectives. Consequently, it is essential that initial planning be conducted carefully. Decisions made under pressure of imminent deadlines are likely to be haphazard and hazardous.

Characteristic Twenty-three: "The total school program results in daily success for all pupils and adult personnel in all subject areas at all grade levels."

"Nothing succeeds like success," we are told, and this seems to be true. The more success we experience in the performance of an activity, the more likely we are to continue it (635). The pupil who does spelling homework first probably finds that subject easiest. And we can guess why the same pupil always saves social studies until last. Both school and home assignments should be carefully provided so every pupil has an opportunity to be successful in the activities.

Indeed, we must exert every effort to structure the learning experiences of all children in such a way as to assure that they have the opportunity to achieve success in every subject every day. When this happens, we can honestly claim to have a Developmental Reading Program for all children.

Summary

This book and this chapter advocate the initiation of a Developmental Reading Program as one major approach to the eradication of illiteracy. We agree with The Report of the National Commission on Excellence in Education (531) that

all, regardless of race or class or economic status, are entitled to a fair chance and to the tools for developing their individual powers of mind and spirit to the utmost. This promise means that all children by virtue of their own efforts, competently guided, can hope to attain the mature and informed judgment needed to secure gainful employment and to manage their own lives, thereby serving not only their own interests but also progress of society itself.

Guaranteeing every child an opportunity to learn to read is not a simple task. It will not yield to quick and easy solutions. Nor can it be accomplished through recourse to bandwagon techniques pursued by those willing to pay lip service only to an idea which requires careful planning and concerted action on a long-term basis.
To provide some initial indication of possible solutions to a few of the most urgent problems, we have identified 23 characteristics of a Developmental Reading Program and briefly considered a rationale for the inclusion of each factor. With this orientation in mind, we are now ready to begin considering ways of preventing reading failure at the primary and intermediate grade levels.

FOR FURTHER READING

Anderson, Richard C., et al., Becoming a Nation of Readers. The Report of the Commission on Reading. Washington, D.C.: National Institute of Education, 1985.

Betts, Emmett A., Foundations of Reading Instruction with an Emphasis on Differentiated Guidance. New York: American Book, 1957.

Clark, David L., Linda S. Lotto, and Martha M. McCarthy, "Factors Associated with Success in Urban Elementary Schools," Phi Delta Kappan, LXI, No. 7 (March, 1980), 467-470.

Donovan, David L., "Schools Do Make a Difference," Michigan School Board Journal, XXIX (July-August, 1982), 8-11.

Hoover, Mary Rhodes, "Characteristics of Black Schools at Grade Level: A Description," Reading Teacher, XXXI, No. 7 (April, 1978), 757-762.

Lezotte, Lawrence W., "Characteristics of Effective Schools and Programs for Realizing them," Citizen Actions in Education, IX (June, 1982), 1, 10-11.

Purkey, Stewart C., and Marshall S. Smith, "Effective Schools: A Review," Elementary School Journal, LXXXIII, No. 4 (March, 1983), 428-452.

Rauch, Sidney J., "Administrators' Guidelines for More Effective Reading Programs," Journal of Reading, XVII, No. 4 (January, 1974), 297-300.

Samuels, S. Jay, "Characteristics of Exemplary Reading Programs," in Comprehension and Teaching: Research Reviews, pp. 255-273, ed. John T. Guthrie. Newark, Delaware: International Reading Association, 1981.

What Works: Research About Teaching and Learning. Washington, D.C.: United States Department of Education, 1986.

Woods, Alice R., and Mary H. Topping, "The Reading Resource Specialist: A Model," Journal of Reading, XXIX, No. 8 (May, 1986), 733-738.

CHAPTER 2

PREVENTING READING FAILURE

Introduction

"His folks ought to keep Buddy home for another year. He's not ready for school."
"Do you know it's January, and Louis still can't read a thing?"
"Bobby misses every other word when he reads."
"Margaret can pronounce most of the words, but she doesn't know a thing she has read."

Have you heard a first-grade teacher make any of the above comments? If so, have you stopped to ponder the problems facing these teachers and their six-year-olds?

Over the past several decades, we have heard numerous discouraged comments similar to those mentioned above. Because the problems to which the teachers refer are certainly real and all too common, let us review some background factors.

1. An expectation that all first-grade youngsters will possess typical middle-class values, aspirations, and language-experience backgrounds and therefore be ready to learn soon after school begins.
2. A general pattern of teaching which tends to provide even the least academically-inclined pupils with reading books after six weeks or by Thanksgiving.
3. A rigid curriculum which tends to expect youngsters to complete at least one readiness book, three preprimers, a primer, and a first reader during the first grade.
4. A common practice of overemphasizing an isolated phonic strategy in word analysis with resultant word calling rather than comprehension.
5. An attitude that educationally disadvantaged youngsters need to be challenged, that they can do much better if they will just work harder on the tasks we assign.

We have long been concerned about the rigidity of curriculum and practices at all levels and the corresponding inflexibility of some academic attitudes. Accordingly, this book is based on three broad contentions.

34

1. Schools that are satisfied with their present status represent one of the causes of reading and learning failures. Whenever we put into practice less than we know merely because of the time and effort involved, our preoccupation with the status quo, our insistence on the same standards for all, or some other equally mundane factor, we consciously contribute to reading and learning failure.

2. Teachers, supervisors, and administrators can prevent most reading and learning failures by rethinking their philosophy, revising their objectives, restructuring the curriculum and learning experiences, and acquiring new competencies. While remediation must not be ignored, the major effort should focus on developmental and preventive programs (95, 400, 630).

3. Teachers, supervisors, and administrators should recognize one fairly simple fact: If past and present practices have either caused or permitted some children to fail, we should search actively for more efficient and effective ways of helping these youngsters achieve success -- academic, social, and emotional. At the same time we should not abandon procedures which have proved successful.

Professionals have the awesome power (and the concomitant opportunity) to determine the possibility and extent of each pupil's success or failure merely by the type of instruction that is provided. While this statement obviously applies to all stages of education, it is especially crucial at the primary and intermediate levels. In fact, it may truly be said that we circumscribe the range of success and failure by the various materials we assign and the expectations we make of pupils during the first days of the school year.

If we provide pupils with books they can read and from which they can learn, the odds are vastly in favor of their learning. If, on the other hand, we distribute books with which our pupils are unable to cope, we cause -- indeed, we force -- them to fail. Academic failure is often little more than a pupil's inability to deal with specific instruction in the manner in which it is presented.

To be more specific, school-caused failure during the primary and intermediate years may usually be considered the result of one or more of these practices:

1. Associating pupils with materials and providing formal reading experiences before they are ready.

2. Associating pupils with materials they cannot read efficiently and effectively.

3. Pacing pupils through materials with so little reinforcement they are unable to acquire and master the words as well as the word analysis, vocabulary, comprehension, literature, and study skills.

4. Providing materials almost completely devoid of interest.

5. Expecting pupils to teach themselves to read, often by working their way through programmed materials, dittoed sheets, various books, or kits.

6. Using inappropriate instructional strategies.

Philosophy

Alternatives to the practices described above are considered in various chapters of this book. At this point, however, it seems appropriate to share a series of statements of our educational philosophy. As a careful reader you should decide the extent to which you agree with each of the statements.

This we believe:

1. That almost every child (including children classified as educable mentally handicapped and learning disabled) can learn to read, write, and compute; that it is our responsibility as educators to open doors and to enable children to walk through or, if necessary, to take their hands and lead them gently but firmly down the road to learning.

2. That, because it is the school's responsibility to try to make it possible for every child to achieve to the fullest limits of his or her ability, decisions should be made with the welfare of children as the first priority.

3. That teaching and the ministry are the two most awesome of callings; one relates to eternal life, and the other to the quality of present life. Like Henry Adams, grandson of one president and great-grandson of another, we believe that "a teacher affects eternity. He never knows where his influence will end (1)."

4. That learning is sometimes minimized by the priorities we establish as educators: (a) facts, (b) skills, and (c) attitude development. We believe the items in the list should be stressed in the reverse order.

5. That education should be concerned not only with the formal curriculum (as important as it is) but also with provisions for meeting each child's unique social,

36

emotional, physical, and psychological needs.

6. That educators should consult the research and the literature before making decisions. Those who contend that "you can prove anything with research" forget the value of research summaries. These compilations of studies related to a topic either demonstrate the superiority or inferiority of a particular procedure or indicate that there is not yet a definitive answer to the reviewer's question.

7. That for disadvantaged youngsters it is not necessarily a teacher who makes the permanent difference but a succession of teachers working together to provide continuity of teaching and learning. Even great teachers have children whom they are unable to help on a long-term basis.

8. That pragmatism is important in program development. While we believe that a Developmental Reading Program is an excellent way of opening the doors to learning, there are alternative philosophies and practices. Whatever program is adopted should be implemented completely.

9. That problems which did not develop overnight will not be corrected overnight. Just as there is no royal road to learning, so there is no easy path to pupil progress. If we hitch our wagons to a star called progress for all children, we will experience "sweat, toil, and tears" on the road to success.

10. That it is better to make a commitment to a great cause and fall short than to commit ourselves to a mediocre cause and succeed or, even worse, never to make a commitment at all. Horace Mann wrote, "Be ashamed to die until you have done some great deed for mankind." Changing the lives of thousands of children and succeeding generations is a deed of the greatest magnitude. Likewise, we believe it is better to prevent undesirable situations than to correct those which never should have been allowed to occur.

11. That the "total immersion" model advocated by child psychologist Uri Bronfenbrenner (81) is the key to enabling disadvantaged children to enter the mainstream of society. All community resources must be martialed in a coordinated effort to help youngsters approach their potentials.

12. That teaching and learning are not synonymous. The concept of mastery teaching/learning requires that we recognize the difference and create conditions under which pupils can and do learn. Furthermore, we believe children should be expected, encouraged, and enabled to learn from their mistakes. Thus the school should be viewed as an institution in which children make progressively higher levels of mistakes and profit from these experiences. Finally, we believe children should be evaluated on their progress rather than on their entry or exit levels of performance.

13. That parents and the community, teachers, students, administrative/supervisory personnel, and governmental officials share an accountability for the enrichment of the lives of children. A comprehensive plan embracing efforts by all segments of society is necessary if all children -- be they bright, average, or slow -- are to achieve their birthright.

14. That disadvantaged children -- the slower learners, the poor, the racial minorities -- can achieve literacy. For example, longitudinal research showing that black children from low socio-economic backgrounds in Lexington, N. C., made one or more years of progress in reading for each of five consecutive years encourages us to believe that similar breakthroughs are in sight for other disadvantaged groups. We believe minority children should tend to make an average of a year's progress annually just as majority children should.

15. That we sometimes set our sights too low. The Rosenthal-Jacobson studies (602) and their successors convince us that if we expect little, we get little. If Thomas Edison was right when he said that genius was 2% inspiration and 98% perspiration (and we believe he was), we have accepted hamburgers when we might have had steak.

16. That the development of moral and ethical values should not be left to chance and totally to the home; that daily living (of which school is a considerable part) is the field upon which the game of life is played. We are responsible for seeing that children acquire personal habits of self-respect and concern for and consideration of the rights of others. While children need not like all of their peers, they must never do anything that makes it difficult for others to enjoy life, liberty, and the pursuit of happiness.

17. That "nothing is so unequal as the equal

treatment of unequals." Respect for the individual requires that identical curricula and materials be replaced with differentiated strategies, approaches, and time frames.

18. That a philosophy, regardless of how grandiose it may appear on paper, is like a "sounding brass or a tinkling cymbal" unless the philosophy possesses the person rather than the person possesses the philosophy.

This book and its companion volumes attempt to outline a program based on the philosophy described above. Thus all children -- the advantaged as well as the disadvantaged -- should have equal access to long-term quality learning opportunities.

The Educationally Disadvantaged

Although the term has not been defined thus far, it should be apparent that one of our major concerns is providing appropriate learning experiences for the educationally disadvantaged pupil, especially during the primary and intermediate years. As used here, the term educationally disadvantaged refers to all people for whom formal academic opportunities are presently inadequate. It includes children from depressed socio-economic backgrounds as well as those from more affluent homes. Any child who is not presently progressing satisfactorily may be considered as educationally disadvantaged.

Certainly the failure of our educational system to provide meaningful learning experiences for all children has created not only a host of psychological and physical dropouts, it has intensified the development of negative social and emotional characteristics by frustrated pupils. The term educationally disadvantaged should not be construed to refer primarily to black youngsters or members of other minority groups. After all, there are far more educationally disadvantaged whites (on a numerical basis) than there are blacks. It is important to keep this fact in mind.

Who are the educationally disadvantaged? Their characteristics may include the following:

1. Below average measurable intelligence and achievement (3, 58, 245, 597)

2. Experiential backgrounds inappropriate to support formal learning (437, 478, 586)

39

3.   Development   in oral language and other readiness
skills   insufficient   and/or   inappropriate   to   support
formal learning (39, 437, 476, 586)

4.   Little   or   no   familial   or   peer   support   and
encouragement (3, 58, 361, 597, 633)

5.   Physical,   social,   psychological,   or   economic
handicaps (245, 368, 586, 695)

Several observations may clarify key concepts related
to the preceding characteristics.
1. <u>Below</u> <u>average</u> <u>measurable</u> <u>intelligence</u> <u>and</u> <u>achieve-
ment</u>.
        Standardized   achievement   and   intelligence   tests
simply   are   not appropriate for use   with   educationally
disadvantaged   youngsters   (117, 444).   For that   matter,
group   tests   based   on reading are not very   helpful   in
establishing   the   intelligence levels of   poor   readers.
Except   for   lucky guessers, their use often   results   in
depressed   scores,   especially   when   administered   under
timed   conditions.   Such   speed   tests   merely   provide
another   hurdle   which,   in effect, discriminates   against
the educationally disadvantaged pupil.
        How   many   teachers,   one   wonders,   have   said   to
themselves   after   seeing   the   results   of   a   group
intelligence   test,   "No wonder Charles doesn't read well.
His   I.Q. is lower than I thought.   There's not much   use
in   my   spending   a lot of time with him."   Many   pupils
possess   backgrounds   of   language and   experience   which
preclude   their   functioning   well   on   a   standardized
middle-class   instrument.   And poor   readers   invariably
score   low   on group achievement and   intelligence   tests
simply because they are unable to read the material.   Yet
many   of   these pupils are regularly identified,   tagged,
and   pigeon-holed with reduced expectations and subsequent
under-achievement.
2. <u>Experiential</u> <u>backgrounds</u> <u>inappropriate</u> <u>to</u> <u>support</u>
<u>formal</u> <u>learning</u>.
        The   term <u>inappropriate</u>   is relative.   It refers   to
the   degree   which schools presently accept and   actively
utilize   the   experiences of youngsters when they come   to
school.   All   pupils have had experiences which   do   not
contribute   directly   to   their formal   academic   growth.
Even though these experiences may be quite useful -- even
necessary   for   social survival in some cases -- if   they
fail   to enhance formal educational development, they may
be   considered   inappropriate   insofar   as   schools   are
presently organized and conducted.

3. Development in oral language and other readiness skills insufficient and/or inappropriate to support formal learning.

Deprivation in oral language and other readiness skills is considered to encompass weaknesses in the areas of listening, speaking, following directions, auditory and visual discrimination, auditory and visual memory, word boundaries, left-to-right and top-to-bottom progression, vocabulary and concept development, oral and picture comprehension, oral context, and (possibly) knowledge of letter-sound associations.

Until and unless these areas are developed sufficiently to provide pupils with a firm foundation for the subsequent acquisition of written language, instruction in the latter can never be effective. Two years of inappropriate kindergarten or first-grade experiences are no more useful to "repeaters" than one year of misplaced emphasis. The end result is the same.

Fortunately, a three-year study (720) comparing the progress of kindergarten retainees with that of children who were recommended for retention but who were promoted showed that the retained group scored significantly higher than the should-have-been-retained group in both reading and mathematics in grade one (eight months higher in reading and seven months higher in math). Another finding; Pupils who repeated grade one, two, or three tended to be those for whom kindergarten retention had been recommended but rejected.

4. Little or no familial or peer support and encouragement.

Family support and later peer approval determine in large measure the degree of receptivity with which each potential learner greets new activities. If reading is not seen as an important part of home living; if standard grammar is considered poor taste; if intellectual curiosity is neither rewarded, stimulated, nor satisfied, our traditional middle-class assumptions about a child's felt need for certain types of learning become totally irrelevant.

5. Physical, psychological, or social handicaps.

These problems may occur in multiples to inhibit or prevent academic progress and success. The little fellow who can't sleep at night because part of his family stays up, comes in, or goes out late can hardly keep his eyes open and his mind alert long enough to learn during the day. If he has not eaten breakfast, his insistent stomach muscles may occupy his attention and preclude learning.

A visual problem overlooked because only the Snellen chart is used may hinder learning (95, 342, 400, 673).

Incidentally, since the Snellen indicates a person's ability to see while driving a car rather than while reading at near-point, we should either abandon use of the Snellen as leading to a highly deceptive conclusion or provide an additional screening device for near-point vision. Either the Ortho-Rater (Rochester, N.Y.: Bausch and Lomb Optical Company) or Telebinocular (Meadville, Pa.: Keystone View Company) is acceptable.

A hearing problem, chronic colds, illness, asthma, emotional immaturity, lack of friends, inappropriate or inadequate clothing, assorted fears -- whether realistic or fantastic -- may contribute to a youngster's inability to learn effectively.

This leads us to the inevitable question: "What normally happens to educationally disadvantaged children in school?"

1. They receive formal reading instruction before prerequisite attitudes, skills, and abilities are sufficient to support the new learning.

2. They experience immediate and continuous frustration and failure.

3. They develop or intensify psychological problems.

4. They develop (or extend) poor self-concepts based on prolonged academic failure.

5. They drop out of school, either physically (at ages 16 and 17) or psychologically (at age six or older).

To summarize, educationally disadvantaged pupils usually are forced into formal reading before they are capable of achieving success (634). Often their teachers feel they should stay home for another year, not realizing, we suppose, that one reason the youngsters operate at their present level is the fact that they have been at home.

Schools must become places where pupils are accepted as they are and assisted in reaching the points where they can be (223, 727). As one teacher noted, "It's not where you are that counts in the class, it's where you go from where you are now that's important (49:234)." While it may be quite acceptable to wish the home had provided all the experiences necessary for children to become highly successful academic learners, this should not prevent our providing realistic activities for the youngsters in our care.

Likewise, while we may recognize the fact that a great deal of language-experience may well be included in Head Start, Follow Through, and kindergarten programs (if they are provided), the lack of such programs should not be used to excuse our failure to provide the appropriate types of instruction. Two failures, two omissions, do not produce a success.

Six-year-olds who are forced into frustration and faced with daily failure can hardly develop an appreciation for their teachers, an interest in school, a love for learning, and positive self-concepts. We find it difficult to believe that six-year-olds are sometimes considered failures.

Several years ago the senior author conducted a study (197) to determine the characteristics of probable dropouts at the primary and intermediate levels. The study consisted of two phases. The first was a survey of the literature to learn what had been done in this area. Results were meager indeed, for most of the research and literature centered around the high school levels and youngsters who had already dropped out.

Using what little data were available, we devised a questionnaire encompassing the academic, intellectual, social, civic, ethnic, economic, and physical character-istics of children in grades 1-8 and their families. Many of the items were orally presented to the pupils during hour-long individual interviews; the answers to other questions were gleaned from school records.

Armed with multiple copies of the interviewing forms, we asked teachers in a number of schools to send or bring us those members of their classes they designated as probable dropouts. The direction of response was quite unexpected. We had anticipated that the majority of referred pupils would be overgrown males at the fifth-through eighth-grade levels. And these did appear in abundance. However, the surprise came when teachers of grades one and two recommended as high a proportion of children as did the seventh- and eighth-grade teachers! Apparently even six-year-olds can be identified as probable dropouts.

Analysis of the interviews, involving over 100 chil-dren, resulted in the drawing of at least one important conclusion and the development of one major recommen-dation. We discovered the most common characteristic of the children identified by their teachers as probable dropouts was their inability to read the books they were utilizing in class. The fact that almost 99% experienced this difficulty led the senior author to conclude that a probable dropout may be nothing more than a child for whom the school is providing inadequate educational experiences.

Under these circumstances it seems mandatory for us to initiate immediate plans to prevent any school-controlled circumstances which seem to accompany or cause reading failure. The billions of dollars of

43

federal, state, and local monies provided for remediation can be utilized far more effectively if prevention rather than cure becomes major priority. So far there is little evidence that federally-funded programs emphasizing remediation have had a significant impact (49, 291). And a Rand Corporation study suggested that more money was "not likely to improve" achievement very much (521).

Furthermore, Urie Bronfenbrenner's review of the research (81) on the effectiveness of early intervention of various types concludes:

1. For preschool programs conducted in a school setting outside the home for children ages one through six, (a) the children made dramatic cognitive gains during the first year, (b) cognitively-structured programs produced greater gains than play-oriented programs, (c) after leaving the program, pupils regressed to the problem range, and (d) the pupils who regressed the most represented the most disadvantaged backgrounds.

2. For home-based tutoring programs for age one through elementary, (a) the children made considerable gains in cognitive ability, (b) three years after participating, the gains were still evident, (c) the one- and two-year-olds made the greatest gains, and (d) children with the greatest disadvantage made the least progress.

3. For "ecological" intervention (i.e., working with the total environment of the parent and child), (a) children with retarded mothers were not "doomed to inferiority", and (b) increases of 25 to 28 I.Q. points were possible.

The implication of this summary of research is that permanent gains require early, concentrated, and continued effort. Preventive efforts should include, at one end of the spectrum, instruction related to "parenting" before pupils graduate or drop out of school. Simultaneously, comprehensive programs should be implemented for very young children and their parents.

Repairing damaged products rarely produces results equal to the original. Sometimes damaged merchandise is too badly mutilated to be repaired. Intensive, coordinated efforts devoted to preventing damage and destruction seem more likely to prove effective than frantic "crash" efforts to put Humpty Dumpty together again.

A philosophy which contends that prevention takes precedence over cure (400, 588) forms the foundation for this book. While we refer periodically to various types of educationally disadvantaged children, it is important that we avoid labeling youngsters (10), for that sometimes serves as an excuse for not teaching them (396). Indeed, one writer contends, "These students don't need labels; they need teaching. They need a teacher with enough knowledge and skills to diagnose their learning problems and help them overcome those problems (636:n.p.)."

Preventing Reading Failure

With these thoughts in mind, let us consider areas in which recognition, response, and action can help to prevent reading failure for primary and intermediate youngsters and to limit, in large measure, the number of pupils who become failures at subsequent levels.

1. Becoming aware of many types of individual differences
2. Comparing pupil performance and ability
3. Conducting diagnosis
4. Increasing the learning rate through mastery teaching -- Chapter 3
5. Developing reading readiness -- Chapters 4A and 4B
6. Selecting appropriate reading materials -- Chapter 5
7. Initiating beginning reading instruction -- Chapter 5
8. Using basal readers -- Chapters 7A, 7B, and 7C
9. Providing extensive reinforcement -- Chapter 8
10. Using the language-experience approach -- Chapter 6

The first three topics are discussed briefly below. Diagnosis is also considered throughout the text. Topics 4-10 are considered in the designated chapters.

1. Becoming Aware of Many Types of Individual Differences
As classroom teachers we are well aware of the many individual differences which characterize pupils. We know that they are unique, that they differ in at least ten significant ways.

A. Reading Achievement or Readiness Readiness. Regardless of the "grade" which we teach, a rather wide range of individual differences exists (9, 95). While some few children enter school able to sing or recite the alphabet and read a few words or simple books, others arrive without possessing the basic skills, concepts, attitudes, and learnings essential for successfully encountering a multitude of learning tasks. Efforts to teach these children to read will simply prove frustrating to both the teacher and the students.

While the range of individual differences is quite broad at grade one, it becomes even more so as one ascends the educational ladder (392). At the fifth-grade level, for example, a typical class may contain pupils with almost no reading ability as well as some operating well into the high school level. The range, then, of general reading ability is seven years in this class.

The range of achievement in a typical heterogeneous class is approximately two-thirds of the age of the children (95). Thus a group of fifth graders are approximately ten to eleven years old, and we should normally expect the seven-year differentiation indicated above.

B. <u>Native Ability</u> (<u>Intelligence</u>). But pupils differ in more than reading achievement or reading readiness. They exhibit a similarly wide range of intelligence. At all levels of our schools it is common to find classes whose pupils register intelligence quotients encompassing or surpassing the range from 70 to 130. Obviously many children at the upper end of the scale are able to absorb, retain, and utilize information far more rapidly and effectively than their less intellectually-endowed peers. And obviously such a wide variation presents a dilemma to the classroom teacher.

If we remember that a youngster with an I.Q. of 75 learns far less than three-fourths as rapidly and effectively as the so-called "average" youngster (measured intelligence quotient of approximately one hundred), and that the youngster with an I.Q. of 125 learns far more than one and one-fourth times as easily as his "average" counterpart, the range resulting from individual differences in intelligence is more clearly brought into focus. The end-points of pupil knowledge and competency are magnified, of course, as they grow older. Each year a slow learner will fall farther behind (526). An eighth grader with an actual I.Q. of 75 will achieve, under maximally desirable conditions, at a level somewhat below an average sixth grader. Similarly, an eighth grader with an actual I.Q. of 125 may reasonably be expected to achieve at a level somewhat above an average tenth grader.

C. Language and Experiential Background. Here again the range of individual differences is rather extreme. At one end of the spectrum are youngsters who have neither traveled beyond their communities nor developed an awareness of the structures and interrelationships of their immediate surroundings. These pupils are the culturally different; they possess impoverished or "different" vocabularies, poor "formal learning" skills, and inadequate and inaccurate academic concepts.

On the other hand, some of their classmates may possess a rather sophisticated knowledge of the linguistic structure of formal language. These children typically speak in complete standard sentences and verbally communicate with their peers and any number of adults on a variety of topics. Their parents read and talk to them and expose them to a variety of cultural experiences, both vicariously and directly. It should be mentioned that some children who live in the midst of potentially favorable environments may not possess experiential backgrounds commensurate with the possibilities if systematic provisions are not made to take advantage of these opportunities. Overprotected youngsters often fit into this category. Whether rural or urban, black or white, rich or poor -- a child may be isolated within his environment.

D. Interests. Experience is one way of building interests. Since the range of individual differences in experiential backgrounds is so extensive, we should expect a correspondingly wide range of interests.

Certainly pupils whose experiential backgrounds are impoverished will have fewer occasions to develop intensive and extensive personal interests. Instead, their major concerns may be based primarily on the day-to-day essentials for survival.

At the same time, however, some children lead lives filled with multiple opportunities for developing and extending significant interests. The lives of these children are filled with meaningful observations and joyful participation in their society. Because they arrive at school with vast reservoirs of information and interests, these pupils are apt to be more efficient and effective in acquiring skills, concepts, and attitudes necessary for effective living.

E. Motivation. Teachers also realize a tremendous gap exists insofar as the degree of motivation is concerned. Once again some children arrive at school without purpose, without concern for the intellectual, social, ethical, and physical objectives of the school.

47

For them school may be just another grievance to be stoically endured until the time when state statutes allow a long-awaited reprieve.

Yet our classes also contain youngsters who are highly motivated to achieve and who do so on their own power. For them, a teacher serves not as a goad or potential source of punishment, not as an adult to please by diligently applying themselves, but as a resource person who helps provide direction and guidance and then fades into the shadows.

It may very well be that the range of individual differences in motivation is much wider and far more significant than any of the other categories discussed so far.

F. Self-Concept. One of the most significant and overlooked differences in people is that of self-concept. Much of what youngsters learn or fail to learn may be influenced by their self-concepts. Pupils who have become accustomed to succeeding and who feel academically competent tend to experience success in a variety of scholastic activities. Those who have become accustomed to failing and who feel academically incompetent tend to experience failure in scholastic endeavors. Interestingly enough, these youngsters tend to perform as they have done in the past, and what may be more significant, they tend to accept their performances as inevitable.

People typically reflect the concepts others have of them. Research indicates that when teachers and fellow classmates consider a child in a positive manner, he tends to develop self-confidence and react as he thinks the group expects (602).

Conversely, when teachers and fellow classmates consider a pupil in a negative manner, he begins to mirror their prejudices and react in the way they expect. Thus we have the spiral which is often referred to as a self-fulfilling prophecy.

G. Intellectual Curiosity. Partly because of the influence of several of the preceding factors, pupils exhibit a wide range of individual differences in degree and direction of intellectual activity, often indicated by their question "Why?" Others appear to react vaguely to stimuli (television and instruction, for example) or to be completely unaware of them.

Certainly the problems of how to develop, utilize, and provide for the range of individual differences in this area are among the most important a teacher must face. After all, little learning of any type occurs without some active attention by the potential learner.

48

H. _Preferred Approach or Technique_. We have already mentioned (in Chapter 1) the necessity of recognizing the instructional approach or approaches by which individuals learn best. We listed the lead basal, high interest-low vocabulary, individualized (one-to-one) instruction, and the language-experience approach.

Likewise teaching techniques must be adapted to accommodate the learning patterns of girls and boys. We hear much today of the value of the discovery technique, and textbooks often exhort teachers to incorporate it into the instructional program. Doing so may have adverse effects, however, if only this technique is employed. Try as we may, there are some people who simply do not learn by discovery. The telling or demonstrating technique then becomes more appropriate as it does when time, danger, and correction are concerned.

So long as our classrooms provide multiple modes, multiple approaches, and multiple techniques, we may reasonably expect to prevent many types of reading failures. When we fail to provide an eclectic program, the children lose.

I. _Need for Extensive Reinforcement_. We have already suggested that some pupils acquire information after one or two exposures. Others fail to understand and cope with it until repeated experiences have been provided. Interestingly, almost every youngster of normal intelligence may possess several areas in which his competence and interest are sufficiently developed to assimilate information easily and quickly. Likewise even bright youngsters sometimes experience learning difficulties in specific areas.

J. _Rate of Learning_. By far the lion's share of attention in some professional books has been focused on merely one individual difference, that of learning rate. While teachers should be well aware of the fact that the usual wide disparity exists in typical classes, it is unfortunate that some educators seem to have acquired the idea that rate of learning is the one major area in which children differ. They seem to reason that any procedure which allows pupils "to progress at their own rates" will automatically guarantee effective learning.

Few misconcepts have proved more disastrous, for rate is a secondary function emanating from many of the previously-mentioned individual differences. Rate of learning is _a_ factor, not the only factor to be considered.

Perhaps we can summarize the ten ways in which individuals differ by suggesting that a DRP must recognize and provide for all of these aspects and avoid the temptation to overemphasize a single area. In addition, we need to recognize the fact that the wide range of differences in each of the above areas necessitates a definite decision on our parts. Consider the following two-part question:

Shall we content ourselves with bemoaning the problems created and magnified by the many types of individual differences?

or

Shall we develop programs in our schools and classrooms to recognize, accept, and provide for these differences?

We consider the second alternative as the only viable reaction to the heterogeneity of our society. You too must choose.

2. Comparing Pupil Achievement and Ability. Now that we have considered a number of ways in which pupils differ, we can address the issue related to the extent to which a child's achievement, both past and present, compares with his potential. Without this kind of information we lack a basis for determining how well a pupil is doing for him.

Several formulas have been devised to express the expected reading level for pupils with various measured intelligence quotients. Probably the most common is the one developed by Bond and Tinker (72). They state that the Expected Reading Grade equals the I.Q./100 times the number of years the pupil has been in school, with a 1.0 being added to the product of the first two numbers. Thus, ERG = (I.Q./100 x Years in School) + 1.0. The "years in school" figure is obtained by subtracting 1.0 from the grade level (except for "repeaters"); thus a beginning fourth grader has been in school 3.0 years. The final 1.0 is added to account for the fact that written materials begin at the 1.0 level of difficulty rather than the 0.0 level.

The Bond and Tinker formula assumes that a youngster with a measured I.Q. of 80 will learn 80% as rapidly and retain information 80% as well as a pupil with a 100 I.Q. Neither classroom nor clinical experience supports this assumption. Gates (338) found, for example, that the number of repetitions required for first graders to learn words increased as their intelligence decreased. It seems far more logical to expect that children whose I.Q.s deviate from the mean (100) will reflect a much greater difference in learning power than will be shown by a simple percentage of increase or decrease.

A more accurate way to estimate a youngster's annual anticipated progress is to square his measured I.Q. (183). While progress in any given year may vary considerably, particularly when huge gaps exist between a child's potential and his actual performance, the year-after-year expectation may be expressed as the following formula: Progress Anticipated in Reading (PAR) = $(I.Q./100)^2$

CHART 2-1
PROGRESS ANTICIPATED IN READING
FOR CHILDREN WITH DIFFERENT
MEASURED INTELLIGENCE QUOTIENTS

IQ(as decimal)	PAR(school yrs)	PAR(in months, years)
.70	.49	5 months
.80	.64	6 months
.90	.81	8 months
1.00	1.00	1 year
1.10	1.21	1 year, 2 months
1.20	1.44	1 year, 4 months
1.30	1.69	1 year, 7 months

A study of Chart 2-1 shows that a child with a measured I.Q. of 70 can be expected to make only one-half as much progress as his classmate with a measured I.Q. of 100. A resulting implication is that the distance between the former child's achievement and his grade level will increase every year, even if he always makes maximum progress for him.

To convert the annual growth expectations into projected reading levels for each grade, we can use the following formula:

Expected Reading Level=$(IQ/100)^2$ x Years in School)+1.0

The number of years in school should not include the one spent in kindergarten. Chart 2-2 presents the expected reading levels for pupils at different grade levels and measured intelligence quotients.

CHART 2-2
EXPECTED READING LEVELS FOR CHILDREN
WITH DIFFERENT MEASURED INTELLIGENCE QUOTIENTS
- CULYER FORMULA

Beginning of Grade	Intelligence Quotient						
	70	80	90	100	110	120	130
2	1.5	1.6	1.8	2.0	2.2	2.4	2.7
3	2.0	2.3	2.6	3.0	3.4	3.9	4.4
4	2.5	2.9	3.4	4.0	4.6	5.3	6.1
5	3.0	3.6	4.2	5.0	5.8	6.8	7.8
6	3.5	4.2	5.1	6.0	7.1	8.2	9.5
7	3.9	4.8	5.9	7.0	8.3	9.6	11.1
8	4.4	5.5	6.7	8.0	9.5	11.1	12.8
9	4.9	6.1	7.5	9.0	10.7	12.5	14.5
10	5.4	6.8	8.3	10.0	11.9	14.0	16.2
11	5.9	7.4	9.1	11.0	13.1	15.4	17.9
12	6.4	8.0	9.9	12.0	14.3	16.8	19.6

Several points should be noted in conjunction with the study of Chart 2-2. First, it assumes that children come to first grade with the reading readiness competencies which serve as prerequisites for acquiring the school's curriculum. However, some youngsters will not have had home and/or kindergarten experiences which facilitate school learning.

Second, a small number of youngsters enter both kindergarten and first grade able to read. Information on the right side of the chart reflects the expectation that they will progress at a pace considerably different from many of their classmates and retain their initial advantage rather than lose much of it due to undifferentiated assignments, as Durkin (265) has found. In any case there is no use for the formula in grade one.

Third, many textbooks are written at levels considerably more difficult than the grades for which they are designated. The fact that a small number of pupils can cope with those materials is evidence that highly competent readers can function at the levels indicated in Chart 2-2.

Fourth, even a youngster with a measured I.Q. of 70 can learn to read at the sixth-grade level if he receives twelve years of appropriate instruction. However, he will never be able to use any of the traditionally-available books provided at the high school levels.

Fifth, to increase the accuracy of the formula, a person's I.Q. should be derived from an individual rather than a group test. Although there are no intelligence tests that adequately measure the intellectual capacities of youngsters with non-standard cultural backgrounds and experiences, an individual non-reading test is preferable to one involving reading requirements.

Sixth, if a range of expected reading levels is preferred to a single score, the figures to the left and right of the designated I.Q. can be used. Thus, the expected reading level of a fourth grader with a measured I.Q. of 100 (which is probably within ten points of his actual intelligence) should fall within the range of 3.4 to 4.6. A student who scores above the upper limit probably has an actual I.Q. higher than the figure yielded by the test. A figure below 3.4 indicates that a pupil probably has a greater opportunity to make abundant progress than a classmate whose reading level falls within the range. Computational data for three hypothetical pupils are provided below. Chart 2-2 serves as a base for checking the accuracy of the figures.

1. <u>Percival Pester</u>, beginning second grader, I.Q.=100

$$\text{Expected Reading Level (ERL)} = (\text{I.Q.}/100)^2 \times \text{Years in School} + 1.0$$
$$= (1.0 \times 1) + 1.0$$
$$= (1.0) + 1.0$$
$$= 2.0$$

2. <u>Jezebel Jenkins</u>, beginning fourth grader, I.Q.=80

$$\text{ERL} = (\text{I.Q.}/100)^2 \times \text{Years in School} + 1.0$$
$$= (.64 \times 3) + 1.0$$
$$= (1.92 + 1.0$$
$$= 2.92 \text{ or } 2.9$$

3. <u>Philip Fidget</u>, beginning ninth grader, repeater, I.Q.=70

$$\text{ERL} = (\text{I.Q.}/100)^2 \times \text{Years in School} + 1.0$$
$$= (.49 \times 9) + 1.0$$
$$= (4.41) + 1.0$$
$$= 5.41 \text{ or } 5.4$$

Use of the formula for computing a pupil's reading expectancy can be useful if the following points are kept in mind:

A. The procedure described here expects more of brighter pupils and less of slower ones than does the Bond and Tinker formula. However, the proposed expectations appear to be more in line with reality.

B. The expected reading level may be compared with a pupil's results on an Initial (or Informal) Reading Inventory to indicate the extent to which he approaches his potential.

C. Since series of basal readers differ in difficulty, interpretation of a youngster's score on an Initial Reading Inventory -- See Chapter 5 -- should reflect this fact. Thus a pupil using Brand X (a series with a carefully controlled vocabulary) may score much higher than an equally competent pupil using a loosely controlled series.

D. The figures assume a quality school-wide program from kindergarten through the twelfth grade. This suggests the need for careful program development efforts by each school.

3. Conducting Intensive Diagnosis. As mentioned in Chapter 1, intensive diagnosis forms a part of all instruction and can hardly be factored out of effective classroom procedures. This is as it should be, for maximum learning is dependent on initial and continuing diagnosis.

Indeed, it seems somewhat paradoxical that teaching is the only profession known to modern society in which a decision is made prior to the collection and analysis of data. Doctors attempt to discover disabilities and their causes before prescribing specific types of medicines, lawyers seek information about a particular problem before dispensing advice. Football coaches and quarterbacks analyze a given situation before determining the next play.

Unfortunately too many teachers and administrators assume the responsibility of prescribing specific learning experiences even before the children arrive. What lawyer would dare to be so presumptuous? And what doctor would ever breeze into the waiting room and distribute duplicated prescriptions for red and white capsules to all of the patients?

Yet how often on the first day of school are teachers asked to secure thirty copies of all grade-level texts (or an average of 7 1/2 copies each of four different texts if multiple adoptions are used) and haul them to their rooms? And how often are we guilty of compounding one horrendous error with another by distributing these books during the first week (or even the first day) of school without regard for the specific strengths,

54

weaknesses, and needs of each individual?
Why should books be assigned during the first week of school? Why not utilize the time to become sufficiently familiar with the pupils and their needs? Certainly the administration and interpretation of some diagnostic items should tell us where to begin instructing. While some of the diagnostic activities require individual administration, they must be done if we are to acquire reasonably accurate information about each pupil as soon as possible. Several activities may be begun independently by individuals, and others may be handled on a group basis. Some of the diagnostic devices may be administered in more than one way.

Parents and other interested adults, aides, and older pupils can help if proper instructions are given and observations are made of their first attempts to provide assistance. For example, even an average ten-year-old should be able to check individual second graders on some diagnostic items. Certainly the determination of a youngster's strengths, weaknesses, and needs provides a firm foundation on which to initiate an effective instructional program.

Summary

This chapter considered school-based causes of reading problems and noted our responsibility for helping children achieve success. We presented our philosophy of education, briefly considered some characteristics of the educationally disadvantaged, and attempted to answer the question: "What normally happens to these children in school?"

We also discussed ten categories of individual differences, presented a procedure for comparing a pupils's performance with his ability, and indicated ten areas in which schools could prevent reading failure. The point of view permeating this chapter and the entire book is the urgent need for programs designed to prevent reading problems rather than to remedy situations which never should have developed in the first place.

FOR FURTHER READING

Alm, Richard S., "The Educational Causes of Reading Difficulties," Journal of Research and Development in Education, XIV, No. 4 (Summer, 1981), 44-49.

Glazzard, Peggy, "Adaptations for Mainstreaming," Teaching Exceptional Children, XIII, No. 1 (Fall, 1980), 26-29.

CHAPTER 3

INCREASING THE LEARNING RATE
THROUGH MASTERY TEACHING

Introduction

When the history of the last quarter of the twentieth century is written, it is entirely possible that the chapter on education will characterize the schools as being concerned with the development and implementation of mastery teaching techniques. Like all major changes in education in recent years, the movement toward mastery teaching has occurred from forces outside the educational structure. Business leaders have complained that many of their employees cannot read, write, or figure, and several studies have indicated the extent to which student achievement meets the demands of a technological society. It may be instructive to look at some of the data.

In 1975 the National Assessment of Educational Progress compared achievement test data for 9-, 13-, and 17-year-old students with their 1971 peers. The research indicated that 1975's nine-year-olds did somewhat better than their earlier agemates. However, Roy H. Forbes, director of the National Assessment, observed, "It is alarming to see the gaps remain at ages 13 and 17 (352:15)." As noted earlier, the same pattern was repeated four and eight years later.

Even more disconcerting is the realization that if the final score (17-year-olds) remains the same while the initial score (9-year-olds) increases, the implication is that pupils between the ages of nine and seventeen are actually learning _less_ than did their counterparts four years earlier.

Foshay observes:

"Reading in the elementary school improved steadily from the twenties through the fifties and sixties, if one can believe the results of restandardizing of reading tests. Arthur Gates pointed out that children in 1957 in grades four through six were reading, on the average, about half a year better than their parents in 1937. The National Assessment reports a similar finding up to about 1965, when reading skill began to level off (325:623)."

Finally, Project LONGSTEP, a three-year study commissioned by the United States Office of Education, found that the higher a student advanced in school, the lower was the increase of achievement. Furthermore, "...no evidence could be found that either of the major instructional variables -- level of innovation or degree of individualization -- was substantially and positively related to posttest performance (362:708)."

It is useful to remember that accountability is a multi-faceted concept embracing responsibilities of professional educators as well as the community (administrators, supervisors, teachers, governmental bodies, parents, pupils, etc.). It is a responsibility of the professional to recognize the expectations of each category of person or agency rather than to meekly allow the "monkey" to be placed on the back of the teacher.

A teacher is responsible for the following:

"1. conducting initial and on-going diagnosis

2. Providing appropriate materials, in terms of content, reading level, skill development, and interests

3. providing instruction (i.e., explanation, correction, guided practice, feedback, demonstration, etc.)

4. using recommended mastery teaching strategies

5. providing appropriate reinforcement activities (i.e., independent class assignments, homework, and recreational reading)

6. using recommended psychological/motivational strategies on a continuous basis (178:1-2)."

Teachers who discharge these responsibilities fulfill their accountability factor -- even if pupils do not learn! For example, research conducted by the National Education Association indicates that the greatest cause of poor reading ability among pupils is associated with absenteeism. Superb instruction by a teacher cannot overcome a child's (or parent's) failure to assume his own accountability factor. Nor can the school be held accountable for the child who comes sick or sleepy or determined not to learn. While the school should be concerned about these problems and attempt to remedy them, teachers cannot -- and should not -- be held accountable when pupils do not learn under these conditions.

There are many other conditions for which the school

is accountable. It is those situations over which the school does exercise control that professional accountability is required and in which mastery teaching techniques are the cornerstone.

Some years ago Benjamin Bloom (63) contended that pupils could learn more if instructional procedures required that they achieve mastery. He believed that over 90% of the pupils could learn what was presented if the appropriate strategies were employed. Manipulation of the amount of time provided for learning was a crucial variable. More recent research supports this point of view. The already-mentioned Project LONGSTEP found that, "...The most significant correlate with reading success in grade two was the amount of time students spent on language arts -- 113 minutes as opposed to 85 minutes for lower achievers (362:710)."

James Block (61) has summarized the research of mastery teaching procedures employed at all levels on instruction and in almost all subject areas. His conclusion is that the top 75% of a class can acquire the information typically acquired by the top 25% of a class if mastery teaching techniques are utilized. It is difficult but delightful to imagine the tremendous impact on pupil achievement that could occur if all teachers used mastery teaching techniques in all subject areas at all grade levels.

Characteristics of the Effective Application of
the Mastery Teaching Concept

Almost all children can learn more than they are presently doing. In fact, Bloom condemns the 'normal curve' distribution of achievement and grades and contends that 95% of students can achieve a high level of learning if the appropriate procedures are used (60:50).

Certain conditions must be present for mastery teaching to occur. Some of the major components we find to be essential are discussed below (178):

1. Task Analysis. Those who believe in the systematic and sequential development of learning have no difficulty accepting the importance of task analysis. Unfortunately, instruction is often provided without sufficient regard for the various types of complexity of learning experiences. The result, particularly for the bottom one-half of a typical class, is a considerable amount of wasted time, decreased amounts of achievement, and resulting frustration and lack of motivation. Task analysis consists of several important aspects:

58

A.   Identification of the task and consideration of
its effectiveness. While this aspect seems obvious, it
is often ˙ ignored. Thus we have unacceptable practices
such as: (1) Geometric shapes presented as a reading
readiness activity in visual discrimination when in fact
the ability to distinguish between non-print shapes does
not facilitate a pupil's development of reading
readiness, (2) spelling bees used to teach or test
spelling when they do not use appropriate words for all
of the children and do not either teach or test, and
(3) use of fill-in-the-blank exercises to test children's
ability to use is or are (for example) when such
true-false isolated practices do not result in either
better speaking or better writing.

     It should be quite apparent that some tasks provided
for potential learners are of little or no educational
value insofar as their stated purposes are concerned.
Task analysis begins, then, with a review of the tasks
provided for pupils. This analysis focuses on the
question, "Does the task contribute to a pupil's
development of specified skills, facts, concepts, habits,
attitudes, or values?" Tasks which either empirically,
intuitively, or demonstrably without formal research
contribute to the development of reading or some other
aspect of the curriculum should be emphasized. Other
tasks should either be omitted (as tracing in the air to
foster handwriting) or provided for an alternate purpose
(as coloring and scissors usage for gross motor training
rather than reading readiness).

     B.   Identification of the various aspects of
complexity of the task. Most behaviors consist of a
number of stages of difficulty. If potential learners
are to derive maximum benefit from their school
experience, they must receive systematic and sequential
instruction. Let us consider an example of complexity in
terms of specific skills. Chart 3-1 presents a sample
task analysis of some aspects of complexity involved in a
person's acquiring competence in identifying main ideas
at the reading stage.

CHART 3-1

SAMPLE CATEGORIES OF COMPLEXITY
MAIN IDEAS AT THE READING STAGE

Main ideas of sentences

1. Simple sentences
2. Compound sentences
3. Complex sentences

Main ideas of paragraphs

1. Initial position
2. Final position
3. Medial position
4. Implied

Main ideas of selections reflecting various types of writing

1. Literature (plays, poems, fables, satire, etc.)
2. Social studies and science
3. Newspaper
4. Mathematics

Since pupil competence in one aspect of main ideas does not necessarily lead to competence in another aspect, a pupil who can identify a literal main idea in the initial position of a paragraph will not necessarily be able to identify an implied main idea in a paragraph, much less identify the main idea of a different style of writing (expository in the content areas an opposed to fictional narrative).

C. Sequencing the components of a task according to their complexity. If tasks consist of various aspects, it seems likely that certain instructional sequences will be more appropriate than others. The sequence may be determined by sub-skill as in a basal reader's outline of letter-sound associations or by level of difficulty and usage as in the comprehension of main ideas.

D. Development and organization of lesson plans and supporting material for each component. After conducting item analysis to identify and validate the various skills, we are ready to develop or purchase and organize instructional and practice material. Many volumes could be written to elaborate on this aspect. From the standpoint of lesson plans, we have presented elsewhere (179-182) a series of models for lesson plans for various aspects of reading, reading readiness, spelling, written language, and social studies. Furthermore, we have created materials for developing phonics, vocabulary, and comprehension skills (209-215). Finally, we have presented criteria for evaluating eight types of material (191-193).

2. Diagnosis. The first step toward good teaching is thorough and continuous diagnosis. This includes the determination of pupil performance related to topics such as:

A. Instructional level (that point at which a pupil can pronounce at least 94% of the words read orally and comprehend at least 70% of the material read silently)

B. Independent level (that point at which a pupil can pronounce at least 98% of the words read orally and comprehend at least 90% of the material read silently)

C. Skills needed in reading readiness, vocabulary, word analysis, comprehension, study, and literature

D. Learning modality (visual, auditory, vocalic, kinesthetic, combined)

E. Instructional approach (basal, individualized, language-experience, high interest-low vocabulary, eclectic)

F. Interests, both present and potential

3. Specific Instruction. For years there was a seemingly endless controversy over the merits of direct rather than "informal" methods. We can now dispose of the issue since recent research provides strong support for a direct instruction model with various types of children of different ages and in a variety of settings.
As early as 1966 Albert J. Harris and Blanche L. Serwer (390), in one of the much-publicized 27 U.S. Office of Education First-Grade Studies, reported that in the first grade there was a significant relationship between the amount of time teachers spent daily on direct reading instruction and the average achievement of their pupils.

In the follow-up study completed two years later, Harris and his associates (391) found that teachers who spent the major portion of their time on direct reading instruction tended to get better results than teachers who focused on supportive activities.

A monograph on early childhood education programs commissioned by the United State Office of Education reported that, "The program which emphasizes skill development and knowledge acquisition (Englemann- Becker, DARCEE) shows more promising data regarding the program's effectiveness. In contrast, the programs that focus on affective development (Bank Street, Tucson, EDC) have little or no available data to show that these programs work (122:8-9)."

In his study of Follow-Through compensatory education programs, Stallings (677) found achievement in reading, mathematics, problem solving and creativity was significantly higher at the end of grade three in structured programs. Structured programs were models that provided practice, or application, time.

In 1977, the United States Office of Education issued a 500-page report (15) comparing the effectiveness of seventeen program models for disadvantaged Follow-Through children. According to John Guthrie (378), former research director of the International Reading Association, pertinent findings include the following:

A. When models were rank ordered in terms of effectiveness with the top models generally being superior to their control groups and the bottom models generally being inferior to their control groups, the programs that consistently fell in the top one-half were Direct Instruction, Parent Education and Bilingual Education. Programs that consistently fell in the bottom one-half were Tucson Early Education, Cognitive Curriculum and Open Education. "The Tucson model operates in an 'open classroom environment' while the Cognitive Curriculum model is 'based heavily on the learning theory of Piaget (378:242)'."
B. The only program that was considered "most effective" for both low income and high income schools was Direct Instruction.

The National Schools Public Relations Association (534) found that successful compensatory education programs were often characterized by clear written objectives, attention to individual needs, flexible grouping and structured sequential instruction. In a later study, Wargo (731) included high intensity treatment and directly relevant instruction as some of the key components in his study of effective compensatory education programs.

In 1978, a study by Educational Testing Service of achievement in grades two and five found that "the critical elements in effective practices were direct instruction by the teacher and direct interaction between the teacher and the pupil (322:9)."

Indeed, Rosenshine's (601) summary of studies considering the relationship between time and achievement suggests that time is important only when it is used for direct instruction structured and supervised by a teacher. This is true for low-income (677) and middle-class (664) families.

The research on the teaching of vocabulary reveals similar findings. Tomas' (711) review noted that any direct approach appears to produce higher vocabulary gain than does an incidental approach. One study cited in the Tomas review was conducted by Gray and Holmes. The control group in social studies read extensively while the experimental group received direct vocabulary study. The experimental group scored significantly higher than the control group.

In England the well-known Bennett study found that British teachers with formal or combination methods produced 3-5 months more annual progress in reading than did teachers using informal methods. Bennett concluded that "the effect of teaching style is statistically and educationally significant in all attainment areas tested (50:152)."

Guthrie elaborates:

"Most educational researchers would agree on at least one generalization about teaching. Formal teaching styles are more effective in teaching basic skills of reading and mathematics than informal teaching styles...(In formal education) the curriculum is highly planned and structured, a number of assessments of children's progress are conducted, extrinsic motivation is used frequently, and social interaction in the classroom is curtailed. Informal teaching, on the other hand, leans toward integration of subject matters, allowance of pupil choice of study, almost no assessment in the form of tests or grading, and reliance on the intrinsic motivations of exploration, discovery, and self-direction (378:468)."

Guthrie concludes:

"What we have learned from the illustrious investigation of Bennett and his colleagues is that basic skills of reading and math are best taught by formal teaching styles, that a mixed style (formal and informal) is often effective, and that informal schooling (open classroom) is least beneficial (378:470)."

What does the bulk of the research mean? It suggests that:

A. teachers should use direct rather than indirect instructional methods;

B. schools and teachers should provide structured as opposed to unstructured programs;

C. educationally disadvantaged children tend to show significant progress as a result of directly relevant instruction;

D. the provision of systematic and sequential instruction is an effective way of fostering pupil progress;

E. a program should be able to demonstrate pupil progress in the academics.

"Instruction" is here defined as the dialogue between a teacher (whether adult or pupil) and a potential learner. The strong implication to be derived from this comment is that instruction does not include the use of activities involving:

A. Kit programs

B. Manila folders with piles of purple papers, regardless of whether the material is differentiated for each person

C. Progression of all pupils through the same or different materials with rate of movement being the major factor

We have seen no body of research that suggests that most pupils can learn on their own with a minimum of teacher direction. Unfortunately, many pupils who would typically experience difficulty achieving competence instructionally are expected to do so independently.

"Specific" instruction focuses on whatever is to be taught and learned. Thus a teacher may state that her children are learning to decode new words beginning with the /b/ sound, identify cause-effect actions in a science selection, or use punctuation marks as a type of contextual clue to word meaning. These specifics are in contrast to the "general" teaching of phonics, comprehension, and vocabulary.

Specific instruction implies prolonged rather than passing attention to particular educational outcomes. The actual teaching act itself begins with the initial presentation of information. In skills instruction, for example, this presentation may include examples presented on a floor or wall chart (as in phonics or syllabication), on transparencies or spirit masters for longer elements (as in comprehension and study skills), or orally (as in auditory discrimination and many other reading skills). The presentation of material is accompanied by explanation, either by a teacher or pupil or both, of a number of items.

Initial pupil practice is provided under direct teacher guidance. Usually this activity takes place one example at a time with pupil practice followed by checking, clarification, further explanation and elaboration, and the assignment of additional practice items. Eventually pupils solve two or more problems at a time as they acquire increasing confidence and competence.

When it appears that pupils are acquiring instructional proficiency, the teacher administers a test of four items. Children who can correctly answer at least three of the items are assumed to possess initial instructional competence. They then engage in independent activities, either in class (at their desks, tables, or learning centers) or at home. Pupils who do not demonstrate initial instructional competence require and receive additional instruction and practice before attempting to perform independently.

Since specific instruction usually is prolonged as opposed to brief, certain types of activities do not qualify. For instance, returning a writing assignment and going over a large number of mistakes (whether individual or class) may not be instructionally specific if there are too many items to make it likely that a pupil will acquire the information being "taught." Nor does asking pupils questions following silent reading qualify as specific instruction. The variety of types of questions still do not provide pupils with instruction and practice in a small number of types of questions.

Another characteristic of specific instruction is that it involves teaching as well as testing. All too frequently we see testing activities incorrectly identified as teaching components. Consider the following examples. Which ones are teaching, and which ones are testing or practice exercises?

A. A spirit master sheet asks pupils to print the missing letters. In the first example, the picture shows a sun and the letters un.

B. A comprehension exercise provides ten questions -- three literal, three implied, three vocabulary, and one creative -- based on a silent reading selection.

C. A game provides instructions. Roll the dice. Subtract the two numbers and move your marker that many spaces on the board.

The answers: None of the above is a teaching exercise. Each number illustrates a follow-up activity that involves the practice component. Stated another way, a teacher who assigns testing and practice exercises can hardly expect pupils to acquire the information because the key component -- instruction -- is omitted. Some children spend far too much of their school day taking tests and far too little in receiving instruction.

4. Mental Involvement of Pupils. Donald D. Durrell (278) has discussed the relationship between pupil involvement in the learning process and the amount of achievement. This relationship is to be expected, and most teachers can verify the accuracy of the research.

Children are not involved in learning under a wide range of circumstances including the following:

A. They are absent, whether in sickness or in health.

B. They are asleep, either with eyes closed or open.

C. They are experiencing emotional turmoil (excessive anger, fear, loneliness, anxiety, etc.).

D. They are physically distressed (sick with a cold, headache, toothache, hungry, etc.).

E. They are required to stand in the hall (perhaps for misbehavior).

F. They are daydreaming.

G. They are asked to participate in instruction and practice which is either well above their instructional level or is too easy.

Some of the factors are beyond a teacher's control. Others are amenable to classroom intervention. For instance, pupils who misbehave can be placed in a time-out booth with materials available for study. A child who declines to "think about" his behavior has the option of doing something rather than nothing. The child who is sent outside the room should have a table and chair or desk and some study materials. Hall detention is probably not an effective procedure if the pupils appear frequently.

One of the major ways of increasing pupil involvement is through the use of Every-Pupil Response techniques (278). The basis for the strategy is the assumption that a pupil who is mentally involved in a lesson learns more than he would do otherwise. The following procedures represent techniques for providing Every-Pupil Response:

A. Pupils display YES, NO, and ? cards.

B. Pupils raise their thumbs stomach-high to indicate they know an answer.

C. Pupils raise two fingers for NO, three fingers for YES.

D. Pupils cross their fingers if two words sound alike, separate them if the words sound different (or cross if synonyms, separate for antonyms, etc.).

E. Pupils use individual slates or strips of paper to record answers in phonics, mathematics, and spelling especially.

F. Pupils display cards containing long and short vowel letters and diacritical marks.

G. Pupils display numbers to indicate the number of syllables, the number of the accented syllable, answer to a multiple-choice question.

Every-Pupil Response can be used in a variety of circumstances. Consider the following possibilities.

A. Pupils solve problems as the teacher presents them during initial instruction.

B. Pupils read orally in pairs, one person reading the left page followed by the second person reading the right page. All fifteen pairs of pupils read orally simultaneously in this dyadic reading activity (278).

C. All pupils reading at the 2-1 level or above answer written questions prior to a discussion.

D. Pupils answer in unison. This is especially appropriate for questions involving facts and skills. It is not appropriate for implied and creative questions. A teacher should ask such questions twice to provide all pupils with time to think before responding.

E. The teacher asks a question before calling on a person to respond. A very common practice involves the following dialogue pattern: "Kellie, why did...?" When a person is named before a question is raised, some pupils "tune out" temporarily. This explains the request that often occurs when the first person answers incorrectly, and another pupil is asked to respond. Many pupils ask, "Would you repeat the question?" to compensate for their earlier failure to pay attention. The most defensible use of a pupil's name before the question is to jolt a daydreamer back to reality.

F. The teacher provides wait-time. Mary Budd Rowe (605) found in her research study that teachers often allow too little time for pupils to provide answers to questions. Indeed, the slower the pupil, the less time teachers tend to allow for responses. Increased wait-time (quiet time giving pupils time to think) produced a number of beneficial results:

1. The length of student responses increased.
2. The number of unsolicited but appropriate responses by students increased.
3. Failures to respond decreased.
4. Pupil confidence and self-assurance increased.
5. Speculative thinking increased.
6. Teacher-centered show-and-tell decreased, and child-child comparing increased.
7. Inferences which were supported with evidence increased.
8. Questions asked by children increased, as did the number of experiments they proposed.
9. Contributions by slow learners increased.
10. Disciplinary moves decreased.

G. The children use individual chalkboards (580) for a variety of types of questions. For several reasons it is generally an ineffective strategy to send pupils to the board. First, pupils who can't solve the problem are publicly embarrassed. Second, many pupils sit at their desks and do nothing, even when they are directed to solve the problems. Because others have been sent to the board, the remaining pupils do not feel a compulsion to involve themselves mentally.

H. The teacher uses written comprehension questions as soon as possible. One advantage lies in the application of handwriting, spelling, and composition skills. A second advantage is the opportunity it provides for each pupil to think about every question. While oral discussion should never be discontinued or deemphasized, it alone does not assure that pupils will think about the ideas being presented.

Written comprehension questions can be provided as early as the traditional 2-1 reading level. While it is true that youngsters usually experience difficulty in answering questions on paper, this is no excuse to delay the use of written questions. As we grow, everything is difficult.

I. The teacher uses questions requiring production rather than recognition responses. Because it is easier to grade multiple-choice questions, teachers and publishers tend to favor this recognition-response format. Unfortunately, the information derived from such exercises is of limited value. After all, on a four-item multiple-choice test, "25% of the students can be expected to mark each (item) correctly on the basis of random guessing alone (576:309)," even if pupils are non-readers (172). Edward Fry (330) refers to the resulting score as the orangoutang score, since a monkey that could fill in one blank in each row would automatically receive credit for a large number of correct responses.

Multiple-choice items are common to standardized achievement tests as well as to commercial practice material and teacher-developed exercises. Despite their constant use (and acceptance by a wide variety of people), there is abundant evidence to question the value of the multiple-choice format.

J. The teacher uses questions that are passage dependent (i.e., require the person to read the selection in order to answer the questions correctly). Several writers have conducted studies that found children could answer some questions on standardized tests even without seeing the reading passage (88,575). These questions are therefore not passage dependent and do not provide accurate measures of comprehension, vocabulary, spelling, math, etc.

Furthermore, commercial practice materials often display the same problem. For instance, Axelrod (35) identified a variety of ways in which commercial materials were deficient. These included ridiculous alternative answers and grammatical construction of the questions. In another article, Pyrczak and Axelrod (577) further analyzed the passage dependence of reading comprehension exercises and recommended that questions avoid common knowledge, items which answer each other, and distinctive characteristics (i.e., unusual length or preciseness of one answer).

Examples of questions that lack passage dependence are listed below.

Type	Example
Common knowledge	1. Who discovered America? 2. Where is the nation's capital?
Questions which answer each other	1. What was the boy's name? 2. What did Harold like to do after school? 3. What position did Harold play on the baseball team?
Unusual length	Question: What is a parallelogram? Answers: 1. A circle. 2. A triangle. 3. Any four-sided figure with two pairs of parallel lines.

```
Grammatical          Question: Mary saw a
construction         Answers:  1. apple
                               2. boat
                               3. elephant

Ridiculous           Question: How did Mary get
alternatives                   to school each
                               day?
                     Answers:  a. by train
                               b. by air
                               c. by car
```

While short-answer tests are more difficult to grade, they do provide much more accurate information.

K. The teacher avoids practices which limit the opportunities for pupils to be mentally involved. Some activities are of dubious value, despite their widespread appeal to children and teachers. Examples of questionable activities include the following:

1. spelling bees -- Spelling is almost never done orally. In spelling bees the average pupil performs only 1/30 of the time, and those who spell least well receive even less practice. Furthermore, there is no evidence to indicate that pupils learn to spell more than one word -- if that -- during a 45-minute spelling bee.
2. "go fish" -- One child uses a magnet to pick up a card whose word he must pronounce. Meanwhile everyone else waits and wastes time. Once again, there is no reason to believe that "go fish" games contribute to learning.
3. round robin oral reading -- One child reads orally while the others supposedly follow along. The many teacher comments - "Pay attention,""Follow along," etc. - provide clues to the ineffectiveness of the practice. Ranson notes, "One technique which is totally ineffective for building comprehension -- or for any other purpose -- is round robin oral reading... It kills interest; it develops habits of inattention rather than thinking (580:327).

5. Feedback and Correction. While every-pupil involvement is helpful in maximizing learning, mastery teaching requires a related component. That is information regarding the accuracy of the previous response and a correction of the error. It is a sad commentary on the educational system that teachers

preclude further pupil learning by unintended but nevertheless unfortunate practices. The most common is the tabulation and recording of scores, either expressed as numerals or letters.

Consider, for example, a person's preparation for a quiz. Depending upon his age, motivation, familiarity with the content, previous experiences of success and failure, and time, a pupil will spend a certain amount of time studying and learning. However, after papers are checked and grades recorded, pupils stop learning. The existence of this phenomenon strongly suggests that the sequence of teaching/learning activities should be revised.

Chart 3-2 presents two teaching/learning sequences -- one for traditional procedures and one for mastery teaching procedures.

CHART 3-2

A COMPARISON OF TWO TEACHING/LEARNING STRATEGIES

Traditional Procedures	Mastery Teaching Procedures
The teacher presents information.	The teacher presents information.
	The teacher checks to be certain pupils can perform instructionally before assigning an independent activity.
	The teacher and/or a pupil provides additional help as needed.
The teacher assigns independent activities.	The teacher assigns independent activities.
The pupils complete the independent activities.	The pupils complete the independent activities.
The teacher and/or pupils check the papers.	The teacher and/or pupils check the papers.

CHART 3-2
(cont.)

The teacher and/or pupils
provide additional in-
struction as necessary.

Pupils rework their papers,
correcting their errors.

Pupils do additional independent activities.
After reaching the cri-
terion(70%, 80%, etc.),
pupils rework the missed
items.

The teacher and/or pupils
check the papers.

The teacher records grades.	The teacher records grades.
Pupils stop learning without initial mastery.	Pupils stop learning with initial mastery.

It should be noted that when teachers return papers, many pupils typically look at their grades, crush the papers, and toss them in the trash container. As noted above, learning ceases. Unfortunately, pupils with errors on their papers have not (fully) learned the material. With grades assigned, there is no incentive for pupils to continue to acquire competence. (Like it or not, the knowledge that grades will appear on papers does encourage pupils to work and learn.)

The grading process should not occur until pupils appear likely to have mastered the objective initially. We do not need pupils -- nor can our nation afford adult citizens -- who are 25% or 40% or 50% competent. We can and must do better.

Now let us consider some possible applications of a feedback strategy. Chart 3-3 presents questionable and recommended practices. Questionable procedures are often employed when the assignments involve spirit master worksheets, writing activities, term papers, and final examinations.

CHART 3-3

A COMPARISON OF TWO TYPES OF FEEDBACK PROCEDURES

Questionable Procedures	Recommended Procedures
The teacher does not collect papers.	The teacher collects almost all sets of papers.
The teacher collects papers only sporadically.	
The teacher collects papers but rarely returns them.	The teacher collects papers and usually returns them on the same school day.
The teacher returns papers long after instruction has been provided.	
The teacher returns papers without grades or comments.	The teacher returns papers with comments.
The teacher returns papers with grades.	
The teacher (re)checks papers, returns them with grades, and does not provide further teaching.	The teacher (re)checks papers, returns them without grades, and provides further teaching.
The teacher provides further teaching but no incentive for pupils to engage in further learning.	The teacher provides further teaching and allows pupils additional opportunities to learn the material.
The teacher uses X's to note errors.	The teacher uses checkmarks to denote accurate responses.

It can readily be seen that pupils cannot learn efficiently unless they receive feedback. Thus a continuous feedback strategy must be employed both for independent and instructional activities. Such a strategy must, of course, be used differentially if it is to have any positive effect. Consider the following situations:

A. After an oral reading session a teacher says to a group, "You certainly didn't read well today. I'm disappointed with you." Does she mean everyone? If she doesn't, someone who really read well receives inaccurate feedback.

B. After all pupils in a group display their response cards to a question, the teacher says, "That's right." Did everyone answer correctly? If not, the teacher reinforced an incorrect response for one or more pupils.

C. The teacher says to her class, "Since you've been good today, we'll stay outside an extra ten minutes today." Once again, was everyone good?

Feedback must be accurate to be effective. It can then be combined with opportunities for pupils to correct their mistakes and thus facilitate mastery teaching.

As noted earlier, traditional feedback and correction procedures often discourage further learning. Consider the following comments:

A. "You didn't do very well on this quiz, Billy. You'll have to start doing better."
B. "It's too bad that you failed this quiz. If you'll do better next time, you can pull up your grade."
C. "Anthony, you've failed six pages in a row. What's wrong?"

As alternatives we might consider practices such as the following:

A. For homework assignments such as mathematics -- Pupils solve the problems, correct the papers (or have them corrected), receive additional instruction as needed, rework the errors, and, if the original score was below the designated criterion (perhaps 70% or 80%), do a similar activity. Grading comes after the criterion figure is reached.

B. For class activities such as comprehension -- Pupils answer the questions, participate in the discussion, check their papers (or have them checked), and correct the errors by referring to the text. Pupils receive two grades -- the first indicates whether or not the material is instructionally appropriate (assuming the child did his best); the second should be 100% and reflects rework.

C. For class activities such as spelling and vocabulary -- Pupils take the quiz. If the score is unacceptable, pupils take the quiz (or, in the case of meaning vocabulary, an alternate form) over. If the score is acceptable, it is recorded. Even pupils who pass the original quiz may take it over. They rework the missed items each time.

It should be noted that the rework concept does not apply to final (summative) evaluations. The time eventually comes when teachers must report to the parents. If feedback and correction are provided for quizzes (formative evaluations), pupils have far more opportunities to learn than they would under traditional procedures. It is possible, of course, for pupils to do well daily and still do poorly on comprehensive examinations because the teacher did not provide sufficient cumulative review and practice, the pupil did not learn to study regularly and review previous learning, or the test did not reflect the content being studied.

As long as society requires summative evaluations at fixed points in time, it will be necessary to terminate the rework process at some point. In the meantime, steps should be taken to avoid these three problems.

6. Extensive Reinforcement. This term refers to the amount of instruction, practice, and cumulative review provided for various pupils.

At the school level extensive reinforcement might include instructional strands providing for both horizontal and vertical learning. For instance, many bright youngsters are able to proceed vertically through a series of materials (readers, spellers, English, or mathematics books) without undue difficulty. Not so with slower children. For these youngsters the volume of new words and skills makes a vertical progression ineffective. We see the sad results at all levels up through the twelfth grade. Poor readers and slower

76

learners have almost always been subjected to the rigor of a vertical program, despite their obvious inability to cope with this strategy. The exclusive or extensive use of grade-level books is a result of total commitment to vertical instruction.

The alternative to vertical instruction is a horizontal strategy. Using this procedure, a child might read as many as five or more books at a specified level before advancing to the next higher level. A horizontal strategy has several advantages. First, it decreases the number of new words a pupil must master. Because the overlap of words between any two basal texts usually ranges from one-third to one-half, a horizontal move produces only one-half to two-thirds as many new words as a vertical move. Second, use of additional material makes it possible for pupils to encounter basic sight words more frequently without as much interference raised by the introduction of new words. Third, the use of horizontal instruction decreases the number of new skills while simultaneously providing additional opportunities for pupils to master the ones that have been presented.

Other types of horizontal strategies can be employed within the classroom. For instance, recognizing the fact that some children may require 45 or 55 contacts with certain new words (338), a teacher may provide extensive reinforcement of these items. This practice may come in the form of word cards, duplicating masters, workbooks, or games.

Extensive reinforcement may come in the form of cumulative teaching/cumulative testing (152). This technique provides the alternate use of teaching and review of past information. As pupils thoroughly master the items, the old skills are dropped while new ones are constantly added. Beginning readers, slower learners, poor readers, and children in learning disability and emotionally disturbed classes can use the cumulative teaching/cumulative testing procedure to good advantage.

Unfortunately, very few commercial materials employ the strategy in the form shown here. It is far more common to see a number of skills, perhaps four or six or more, taught before review occurs. If pupils can cope with this modification, there is no problem. For other pupils, teachers will need to insert more frequent review sessions. Extensive Reinforcement is discussed in Chapter 8.

7. <u>Charting</u>. In order to provide mastery teaching, we must know which pupils should receive certain aspects of instruction. At this point a Class Analysis Chart is

required. Although there are dozens of variations, the basic format includes names of pupils down the left side, skills listed by number and/or item across the top, and rows and columns of boxes comprising the vast majority of the page. We find one-half inch squares convenient in size.

A Class Analysis is first used after diagnostic devices are administered. Pupil performance is recorded by means of symbols identifying either the positive or negative aspects. Thus pupil errors may be featured by recording X's or -'s in the appropriate boxes. A teacher can then use a completed Class Analysis Chart to identify (a) the pupils with the greatest deficiency (horizontal interpretation), (b) the skills most frequently missed (vertical interpretation), or (c) the pupils who should receive instruction on a particular skill (vertical instruction). Thus a Class Analysis Chart becomes a skills grouping device.

After teaching all of the items included on a Class Analysis Chart, a teacher should administer the same or a different form of a diagnostic pretest (depending on the content) and update the chart. X's may be changed to circled X's and -'s to +'s. Now a Class Analysis Chart can serve several additional functions: (d) identify pupils and skills requiring additional attention, or (e) serve as a basis for parent-teacher conferences.

Besides its use as a device to display the results of diagnostic pretesting, a Class Analysis Chart can also portray the results of diagnostic teaching. If several columns are devoted to literal, implied, and creative questions, a teacher can note pupil performance during an oral discussion of a reading selection. A plus or minus can be used each time a pupil is asked a question. During oral reading a teacher might note the frequency of pupil errors under categories such as "Basic Sight Words," "Nonsense Substitutions," "Sensible Substitutions," "Word-By-Word Reading," "Omissions," etc.

It is important to note that a Class (or Group) Analysis Chart is not an Individual Analysis Chart. The use of separate record sheets for pupils is not only extremely time-consuming, it is most frustrating. Teachers sometimes spend huge chunks of both school and home time trying to keep individual charts up-to-date. This time could be far better spent designing, developing, and delivering instruction. (Individual charts can be compiled at the end of a year.)

8. <u>Manipulation</u> <u>of</u> <u>Time</u>. It should be obvious that the strategies presented thus far are time consuming. It takes time, for example, for pupils to receive horizontal instruction and finish two, three, four, or five books at one level before advancing to the next. It takes time to conduct both initial and on-going diagnosis. It takes time to provide specific instruction. It takes time to correct errors.

It takes time to do these things just as it takes time to engage in practices of dubious value. For instance, it takes time to conduct a spelling bee. It takes time to teach something far too difficult and have to go over it three or four times. It takes time to read a social studies chapter to pupils who can't understand or retain the concepts even when presented orally.

There are probably two important facts for us to remember. One, research demonstrates that at the primary levels high pupil achievement is associated with an increased amount of time devoted to reading and the other language arts (362). Studies of effective schools report the same thing (259, 464, 618), as do studies of Chapter I effectiveness (691).

Second and more important, pupil achievement is associated with the way pupils and teachers use their time (51, 604, 621). We might ask ourselves questions such as these:

A. How much time do children who arrive at school early waste?
B. How much time do children who leave school early waste?
C. How much time do teachers waste in the lounge (sometimes while complaining about how hard they have to work)?
D. How much time do teachers and pupils waste waiting for the bell to ring, for other pupils to return from a special class, etc.?
E. How much time do pupils waste waiting for their teachers to put information on the board, distribute papers, or get ready to teach?
F. How much time do children waste waiting for instructions about what to do next?

The more we observe in classrooms, the more concerned we become about the huge chunks of wasted time that seem to characterize many classrooms. The management of time is essential for facilitating pupil progress. Although everyone has an equal amount of it, some people with similar circumstances seem to accomplish far more than do

79

others. Self-discipline by teacher and pupils may very well be the key to increased pupil achievement.

9. A Succession of Teachers Utilizing Mastery Teaching Techniques. In recent years we have witnessed a tendency of some schools to democratically encourage teachers to "do their own thing." While the idea sounds fine in theory, it is detrimental in practice, for a variety of mini-programs each unrelated to the other and maybe even incompatible with the other can hardly provide the continuity and consistency that characterize a comprehensive systematic and sequential curriculum.

Singer contends:
"Although a classroom teacher can make a difference in students' reading achievement in the classroom during the year, what makes a cumulative difference in a school is not the classroom teacher alone but a schoolwide approach to improving reading development. Essentially, we have to modify the hypothesis that the teacher alone makes the difference in reading instruction and substitute a broader hypothesis for improving a school's reading achievement (642:67)."

He continues:
"While particular teachers might be successful, if each teacher at successive grade levels in a school used a different program, the overall achievement of the school would not likely be high. The reason for this apparent paradoxical conclusion is that students in the school would not have a cumulative program that would pace them appropriately and provide for their individual differences in aptitude and in time needed for learning. Indeed, in case studies of three schools which had different programs but were alike in faculties trained and committed to the same instructional program, reading achievement in all three schools was significantly above average. Hence, the modified hypothesis for schoolwide achievement is that while a teacher can make the difference in reading achievement in a given year, what makes for a cumulative difference in a school's reading achievement is a coherent and systematic program throughout the grades to which the faculty is committed (642:67)."

John Manning appears to have been a pioneer in the area of school or district-wide development of coherent curricular programs. In a cogent commentary, Manning describes "The Minneapolis Story." As part of an effort to build a district-wide systematic and sequential reading program, Manning and his associates "did not attempt to further confuse the reading methods issue by 'letting teachers make up their own minds about which instructional methods to use'(484:22)." Furthermore, "The Reading Task Force (felt) that reading programs (were) aggravated when different programs (were) used in remedial settings even with the best of teacher motive and intention (484:26)." In other words, pupils failing in one program should not be expected to succeed in two programs!

The senior writer recently completed a three-year research project designed to implement a schoolwide approach to curriculum development and pupil progress. Project IRIS (Improving Reading Instruction Schoolwide) was based in a low-income school (Southwest Elementary School, Lexington, North Carolina) with a median pupil IQ of 93 and a 37% minority population.

Prior to the project the median schoolwide gain on the Vocabulary sub-test of the Stanford Achievement Test was .2 year. During the three project years the schoolwide gain always equalled or exceeded 1.0 years annually.

Growth in Comprehension, as measured by the Paragraph Meaning sub-test of the Stanford, increased from .8 year before Project IRIS to 1.2 years annually during the formal study. Total Reading increased from .7 year to 1.3 years.

During the second and third project years, a similar school with a highly competent principal was used as a control group. In both years Project IRIS gains were considerably higher than gains registered by the control school.

It is worth noting that the median progress rate of Project IRIS's black pupils on Total Reading was 1.0 year annually (or 3.0 years during the project). This finding is completely at variance with national and state assessment data that find Black pupils gaining considerably less than one year of progress annually.

Also significant are the results of pupil gains in other area of the curriculum. According to the California Achievement Test battery, schoolwide gains (always including EMH, TMH, and LD children) ranged from 1.2 years in Language and Study Skills to 1.5 years in Spelling. Apparently schoolwide approaches can be highly effective in meeting the needs of disadvantaged children.

Four years have passed since Project IRIS released its three-year report. The data for seven years show that every year the pupil population has averaged at least one year in growth, and scores have been above grade level for the past two years. Research data are reported elsewhere (187).

Specifics for instituting schoolwide approaches are far too voluminous to be considered here. Interested readers should consult the appropriate titles related to Strategies, Roles, and Initiating Development Reading Programs (173-175, 190, 196).

Summary

Underlying all of the comments contained on the previous pages are two important and related beliefs. The first is that the use of mastery teaching techniques can significantly increase the achievement levels of all types of pupils at all grade levels and in all areas of the curriculum. The research supports this point of view, and we are firmly committed to the concept.

Second, mastery teaching procedures can be implemented only when professionals truly believe that all children can learn (not at grade level, of course, but at levels commensurate with their ability). A teacher who truly believes that almost every child can learn to read is likely to expend the energy and effort needed to help her youngsters learn during that year. At the other end of the spectrum, a teacher who believes some of her youngsters can't learn or can't learn much is unlikely to help the children achieve at levels at which they are capable. One reason for the present emphasis on mainstreaming is that research indicated Special Education children really achieved more in regular classrooms than they did in Special Education classrooms. Does this suggest that some Special Education teachers often expected little and got just what they asked for? Sara Simpson, whose book Ways to Insure Mastery Teaching (65) is a valuable contribution of practical ideas for primary and elementary teachers, says it this way, "I want all of my children to learn and to love learning. However, if they don't love learning, they'll have to learn anyhow." We wholeheartedly concur with that attitude.

Not all learning can be fun. We cannot wait for children to decide when they are ready to learn. We cannot expect children to engage in tie-dyeing activities all morning and learn to do anything more than dye ties. While such activities are fun and have a place in education, they cannot replace the different subjects

82

that require a lot of hard work by both teacher and pupil. "Teaching is, indeed, an act of loving; but love alone does not guarantee achievement (542:9)."

Fourth graders do not have to read at first-grade levels. High school students do not have to read at fourth-grade levels. Adults do not have to be illiterate. Attention is increasingly being drawn to the home and the relationship between family income and school achievement. This fact should never be used to justify the failure of professionals to commit themselves to mastery teaching. As noted in Chapter 1, the nation that put a man on the moon can surely teach its citizens to read.

FOR FURTHER READING

Block, James H., Mastery Learning: Theory and Practice. New York: Holt, 1971.

Bloom, Benjamin, "New Views of the Learner: Implications for Instruction and Curriculum," Educational Leadership, XXXV (1978), 563-576.

Gagne, Robert M., Expectations for School Learning. Bloomington, Indiana: Phi Delta Kappa, 1973.

Purkey, William W., and John Novak, Inviting School Success, Second Edition. Belmont, Cal.: Wadsworth, 1984.

Samuels, S. Jay, and Patricia R. Dahl, "Relationships Among I.Q., Learning Ability, and Reading Achievement," in Literacy for Diverse Learners: Promoting Reading Growth at All Levels, pp. 31-38, ed. Jerry L. Johns. Newark, Del.: IRA, 1974.

Simpson, Sara, Ways to Insure Mastery Teaching. Kings Mountain, N.C.: By the Author, 1974.

84

DEVELOPING READING READINESS

LANGUAGE DEVELOPMENT

Introduction

A majority of the states require that students pass a competency test as a prerequisite for high school graduation (453). As a logical corollary, many state and local education agencies have developed guidelines for promoting pupils from one level to the next.

Emphasis on the "basics" (and particularly reading, language arts, and mathematics) is having a major impact on two levels of education -- the primary school and the high school. Recently the emphasis on early childhood education has resulted in a closer study of (a) the relationship between kindergarten and the first grade and (b) the cognitive component of the kindergarten curriculum.

The late 1970's and early 1980's witnessed an increased emphasis in kindergarten on the reading and mathematics readiness skills and a coordination of the kindergarten and first-grade curricula. The purpose of Chapters 4A and 4B is to provide information about activities that can be used either in kindergarten or grade one (and in other grades as well for youngsters with special needs) to help pupils acquire the reading readiness skills. Special emphasis here is placed on the first-grade level.

At this point it might be helpful to define some key terms.

Readiness is here considered as the state of being actively willing and able to acquire a concept, skill, or attitude. It should be noted: willing and able. The implications are two-fold and interdependent. A potential learner must be motivated to learn (249, 294) or have his motivation captured (53). He must also possess the appropriate prerequisite skills. Both characteristics are essential, for mere motivation itself will not suffice if the appropriate background competencies do not exist. Similarly, the ability to learn is also insufficient unless desire is present. It should be obvious, therefore, that willingness and ability must work in tandem if learning is to be facilitated.

Perhaps two examples will help clarify this point. A pupil who is motivated to learn how to divide by three-place numbers so he can compute the current batting averages of his heroes will be unsuccessful if he is deficient in the prerequisite skills of multiplication and subtraction. No amount of desire will overcome this lack of readiness for division. Specific lower-level instruction and learning must first occur.

Or take the opposite side of the coin. Another child who does possess the appropriate background may fail completely to master the procedures involved in division due to lack of interest. In this situation, no amount of prerequisite competency will overcome the lack of an active interest in learning. The coin of the realm of learning may thus be said to possess two sides. One is tempted to say "heads" represents ability and "tails" stands for motivation. But that might lead to some false conclusions and indefensible practices.

In any case, readiness as used here focuses on the ability factor as it relates to competencies which pre-schoolers, kindergarten youngsters, and first grade pupils must possess in order to profit from the use of printed materials.

A second definition of readiness which is of crucial importance at all levels (including the primary) is well beyond the range of the present discussion. This second type recognizes the fact that all learning provides readiness for subsequent experiences (126, 271, 487).

The reading readiness stage is defined as the stage at which youngsters acquire concepts, skills, and attitudes related to reading. A variety of reading readiness skills are considered in Chapters 4A and 4B. Listening, following directions, and oral vocabulary and comprehension are examples of skills developed during the reading readiness stage. Pupil competence in these areas directly enhances subsequent growth in reading.

Reading readiness skills are skills which directly contribute to the subsequent development of reading. For example, distinguishing between the /b/ and /p/ sounds is a reading readiness skill. Distinguishing between animal sounds is not a reading readiness skill even though it involves auditory discrimination.

Pre-reading skills are defined as learnings that do not directly enhance subsequent growth in reading despite the fact that they are usually developed before reading skills are introduced. Pre-reading skills tend to fall into two categories:

A. skills which do not have a corresponding level of reading readiness competence. Examples include naming the colors and cutting with scissors.

B. skills which do have a corresponding level of reading readiness competence. Examples include the following:

Pre-reading Skill	Reading Readiness Skill
1. identifying animal sounds or other environmental non-speech sounds	1. identifying differences and likenesses in speech sounds
2. matching geometric shapes or pictures	2. matching letters or words

Pre-reading skills may be important for their own sake (as in Category A) or useful in developing background for reading readiness skills (as in Category B). However, pre-reading skills do not directly prepare a child to learn to read. One does not have to be able to name the colors in order to learn to read. Nor must one be able to identify animal sounds to learn to read.

A teacher of pre-school, kindergarten, or first-grade children can justify instruction and practice in the pre-reading skills so long as she recognizes and emphasizes development of the appropriate reading readiness skills.

Extended reading readiness is here defined as a prolonged period of intensive and extensive learning experiences lasting approximately one school year (113) and providing instruction and practice for children with considerable formal language-experience needs.

The provision of extended reading readiness opportunities (and the delay in initiating reading instruction) does not interfere with pupils' achievement in reading. Spache, et al., found, for example, from their study of the effectiveness of an extensive and intensive reading readiness program on first-grade achievement that "the experimental readiness program was of significant value to Negro pupils and that the achievement in the experimental control groups was quite similar, despite the delay in the introduction to formal reading of the majority of experimental pupils (674:583)."

Furthermore, a longitudinal study of a prekindergarten through second-grade curriculum emphasizing language and cognitive development and methods of reading

87

readiness instruction for disadvantaged children proved
beneficial, especially when specific, structured
cognitive activities were utilized (225).

The reading readiness needs of youngsters entering
first-grade can be classified into three general areas:

A. very little or none -- one week of orientation,
diagnosis, and review to approximately one month.
This might be referred to as minimal reading
readiness.

B. several months to a semester or more.

C. approximately a year -- This is referred to here
as extended reading readiness. As Ware notes, "A
typical basal reading readiness program (for the
large majority of children in large-city schools)
sometimes requires three to four times as much time
as is expected for the mythically 'average' child
(730:535)."

Any competent kindergarten or first-grade teacher can
quickly determine, at least on a tentative basis, those
youngsters who require little or no reading readiness as
well as those whose needs cannot be met in less than an
extended period of time. Subsequent continuous diagnosis
should indicate a number of specific categories of
activities appropriate for various pupils.

On the basis of our experiences, it seems rather
clear that a majority of kindergarten pupils require
extended reading readiness. Furthermore, many first-
graders require extended reading readiness even if they
have had a full year of kindergarten. These youngsters,
the educationally disadvantaged, have consistently
frustrated and foiled our determined efforts to provide
effective reading instruction.

Probably most first-grade teachers will agree that a
distressing number of their pupils do not learn to read
(comprehend) during the first year. This problem occurs
despite the fact that these youngsters usually receive a
disproportionate share of the teachers' time and energy.

The high failure rates as well as the large numbers
of very poor readers transferred or reluctantly promoted
to the second grade and subsequently failed should point
out the obvious. Many of our pupils lack background
skills, concepts, and attitudes which in turn preclude
their successful encounter with reading experiences.

Educators once thought the first graders were rather
homogeneous and that school-based learning experiences

would make them heterogeneous as they progressed through the program. While the latter assumption certainly is correct, the initial contention is recognized as grossly inaccurate.

For example, many kindergarten and first-grade classes have one or more children who can call words in sentences or even comprehend materials at the first grade level or higher at the beginning of the year. Indeed, one of the authors diagnosed a five-year-old who could call words with 99% accuracy from a seventh-grade book. His comprehension level, however, was a "mere" 3-2.

Likewise, we worked with a child who was referred by her teacher during the first week of kindergarten. The youngster could call words and comprehend at the third-grade level. The recommendation was that she be allowed to participate in group reading readiness instruction if she wished (to promote socialization) but also have access to trade (library) books during her independent learning time. The following year the child entered the first-grade reading (comprehending) at the sixth-grade level.

These youngsters and others like them need little or no assistance in general reading readiness development. They may, however, need help in a specific reading readiness skill such as, for example, following directions. Furthermore, they may have needs related to socialization, psychomotor coordination, or arithmetic readiness.

At the other end of the spectrum, there are some kindergarten and first-grade children who function at the language level of a typical two- or three-year-old. Except in unusual circumstances, these youngsters do not learn to read during the first-grade year.

It must be emphasized that reading is comprehension rather than simply calling words. Thus a youngster who can pronounce every word but who cannot demonstrate knowledge of the information has not really read the selection. To illustrate, while consulting with a group of primary teachers, one of us was told of a girl who "finally" had finished one of the preprimers. The teacher invited the consultant to "hear her read." Being familiar with the children, the consultant knelt on the floor and asked the girl to read a page from the book she had just finished. The page contained four sentences, and the girl pronounced each word correctly.

The consultant then asked her to read another page to herself and "pay attention because I'm going to ask you some questions." Because first graders often make as much noise during silent reading as they do during oral

89

reading, the consultant knew when she was finished. Four questions were asked.

A. What was the name of the little girl in the story?
B. What was the name of the little boy in the story?
C. Where were they going?
D. How were they going to get there?

To her teacher's chagrin, the child was unable to answer a single question. The youngster could call words, but she couldn't read (comprehend). Did she lack significant reading readiness skills? On checking, we discovered her performance was inadequate in several important areas. Hopefully this anecdote illustrates the point that while the child can be taught to recognize words, she is unlikely to learn to read until she acquires competence in the reading readiness skills related to thinking about meaning.

Not all youngsters are ready to learn to read at age six. Some will already have been reading for a year or more while others will not be ready until age seven (67, 113), and a few at eight (87, 535, 668, 692). And, incidentally, we are not referring exclusively to pupils with recorded intelligence quotients below 70.

Clements has noted that first-grade teachers "often begin teaching reading to children who do not have readiness skills sufficient for effective mastery of the process, creating a downward spiral often with lifetime negative effects (127:29)." It seems only realistic to suggest that instead of submitting educationally disadvantaged children to a reading curriculum from which they cannot effectively and efficiently profit, we should develop and implement programs which reflect and provide for their needs.

Two additional points: First, although the provision of an extended reading readiness program is merely one step of the development of a sound program for the educationally disadvantaged, it is the initial prerequisite. Second, kindergarten, Head Start, and Follow Through all serve useful purposes, but one should not assume these programs are sufficient and satisfactory. A number of weaknesses inhibit the effectiveness of such programs.

A. There is often no more coordination between these "special programs" and the first grade than there is between the first and the second grades or the fourth and

90

the fifth. The typical kindergarten, Head Start, or Follow Through teacher has only a superficial knowledge of the specific program, philosophy, teaching procedures, and expectations of the first-grade teacher; furthermore, the reverse is also true. Subsequently, any systematic sequential development of skills, concepts, and attitudes is purely coincidental. Coordination of the kindergarten program with the rest of the school program is essential (550).

B. Many of these programs seem to follow the philosophy that a little help is better than none at all. While this may be true for the marginal learner, there is certainly no evidence to support the idea that a little help makes any real difference for severely disadvantaged youngsters (479). Indeed, there is longitudinal research for disadvantaged youngsters showing that while immediate gains are produced by various types of programs, these advantages are often wiped out two, three, or four years later. Thus, for example, Head Start children tend to do better in kindergarten and grade one than other youngsters eligible for Head Start but not receiving these services. A look at the achievement test data several years later, however, often shows that gains have been eroded. Both groups remain outside the mainstream and fall farther behind their more advantaged classmates each year. Fortunately, recent studies (106) are beginning to document the long-term effectiveness of many Head Start programs. As noted earlier, Bronfenbrenner (81) contends severely disadvantaged children require a comprehensive developmental program on a long-term basis. We concur.

C. Many of these special programs seem to function without any real awareness, concern, or provision for the types of activities which might enhance the development of readiness for reading. While no one will deny the importance of building social relationships and motor coordination, the absence or deemphasis of instruction and practice in a number of language-related areas does seem most unfortunate. For this reason we oppose isolated summer programs for the disadvantaged except for teacher training purposes. Summer Head Start programs, for example, do not "lastingly improve children's education," according to a national evaluation of Head Start (122). Instead, we need to develop year-around classes with strong instructional components which actually have the opportunity to make a difference for disadvantaged youngsters.

The following list of reading readiness skills should be considered for inclusion at home and in pre-school, kindergarten, and first-grade programs. It should be noted that the areas to be mentioned include only cognitive skills related to the development of the ability to read. They are presented in two categories: (A) language skills, and (B) perceptual skills.

A. Language Skills

    1. Listening
    2. Following directions
    3. Speaking
    4. Oral vocabulary and concept development
    5. Context usage
    6. Oral and picture comprehension

B. Perceptual Skills

    1. Visual discrimination
    2. Visual memory
    3. Left-to-right sequence
    4. Top-to-bottom sequence
    5. Word boundaries
    6. Auditory Memory
    7. Auditory Discrimination
    8. Letter-sound Associations

In addition, one pre-reading skill (letter-name knowledge) is also included. The remaining pages of this chapter present a number of suggested activities for developing the various reading readiness skills in the language category. Chapter 4B considers reading readiness activities related to the perceptual skills, activities for developing letter-name knowledge, and guidelines for skill development.

1. Listening

A. Talk to pupils -- as a class, in groups, as individuals. Speak softly, slowly, and clearly. Be careful that your sentence structure, vocabulary, and actual content are not too complex for the children to understand. Long drawn-out comments are confusing. Furthermore, it is dangerously easy to use "simple" words that children do not understand. Examples include same, different, beginning sound, letter, sentence, paragraph. Youngsters who do not understand what we say can hardly be faulted for not listening.

Whenever possible, sit at or near the children's eye level. This is especially important when working with small groups and individuals. Look the children in the eye. If they are not listening,

1. briefly flick the lights to get attention

2. touch those who are nearby

3. call their names as a casual part of the lesson (i.e., "Now, Ben will find this interesting" or "In a minute I'm going to ask Ben to show (tell) you how to...")

4. use the Every-Pupil Response (278) so every child must frequently respond to what you're saying by

    a. holding up a Yes-No (smiling face-sad face) card to questions
    b. selecting the letter to which you refer and holding it up
    c. raising a thumb stomach-high to indicate he knows the answer to a question

B. <u>Read</u> <u>to</u> <u>the</u> <u>class</u> <u>at</u> <u>least</u> <u>thirty</u> <u>minutes</u> <u>per</u> <u>day</u>. If necessary provide three ten-minute periods rather than a large block of time. Try to schedule this activity right after an activity such as break, lunch, or physical education. Children tend to be much better listeners during a story period than during other activities. Planned reading to young children results in higher achievement levels (90, 323, 424, 425).

Provide a balanced program of outstanding literature as well as concept- and content-oriented books. The literary selections should include but not be limited to the following categories:

1. Bible stories. If "religious" instruction is frowned upon, use of the stories can still be justified for their contribution to literature. In later years pupils will be expected to understand references to

       the Mosaic law
       the patience of Job
       strong as Samson
       the handwriting on the wall
       a land flowing with milk and honey
       as old as Methuseleh
       as wise as Solomon

2. Children's classics such as the Caldecott winners and runners-up. An excellent source of books which have received various awards is Children's Books: Awards and Prizes (135). Consult the latest edition.

3. Short classical selections such as fables, nursery rhymes, poems, talking animal stories, fairy tales, and songs.

We never cease to be amazed at how little awareness many kindergarten and first-grade children have about Bible stories, children's classics, and genres such as fables, nursery rhymes, fairy tales, etc.

4. Concept- and content-oriented books. These non-fiction books provide information to children. One excellent series consisting of approximately 200 titles, is the True Book series (Chicago: Children's Press). Many of these books can be used for a variety of purposes, including listening development.

Older children who need practice in oral reading can profit by practicing with easier materials, ostensibly for the purpose of reading to primary pupils. You should be certain, of course, that the oral reader is well prepared. As an alternative, highly competent oral readers in the upper grades can engage in these activities. The use of several pupils of each type should preclude any negative reaction or resentment on the part of older poor readers. Incidentally, the use of older pupils as oral readers will free you for small-group work.

One writer (458) conducted a study to identify the qualities which enhance the effectiveness of reading orally to young children. Effective teachers

a. involved the children in the story through activities such as choral reading of refrains, predicting outcomes, etc.

b. had much eye contact with the youngsters

c. read with expression

d. had voices of good quality, neither too loud nor too soft and pitched neither too high nor too low

e. pointed at things, either words or pictures, in the book

94

f. were obviously familiar with their books

g. provided selections with quality illustrations, especially size and color

h. grouped children in such a way that they could both hear the story and see the pictures

i. highlighted key factors such as rhyme scheme, unusual vocabulary, etc.

Fitzgerald (312, 313) has developed a list of kindergarten books. Eastland (288) has identified books to read aloud to primary children.

C. Use "Simon Says." This activity also includes the element of following directions.

D. Use "Kim's Game." Say, "Listen...What did I just say?" Pupils should list the items or ideas in a sequence or identify as many as they can. This activity also helps to build auditory memory.

It may be worth noting that a Kim's Game is any activity that relates to sensory awareness. The name is derived from a character in Kipling's Jungle Book. You can make up your own Kim's Games.

One caution: When answering a pupil's questions, some teachers have a tendency to move toward the youngster and lower their voices. This presents several problems. First, the other youngsters may not have heard the question and may therefore find the answer of little value. Second, if the teacher lowers her voice while moving toward the questioner (and this tends to happen), the other children may be unable to hear the response. As a general procedure, it is best to either remain stationary or move away from a pupil asking a question or to respond loudly enough for all to hear (assuming the question is a public rather than a private communication).

E. Use a variation of "Kim's Game." Say, "Listen...What did Alan say?" or omit the instruction "Listen." Use regularly throughout the day to emphasize the need for careful listening. The activity is usually quite difficult. The main reasons seem to be the following:

1. Many children think that a teacher's comments are the only ones to which they should listen. Consequently, they typically "tune out" questions or responses of other

95

classmates. Children should understand that their comments are also important and they should listen to the lesson-related statements of their peers.

2. The seating arrangement of many classes makes it difficult for pupils to hear each other, much less listen. A semi-circle or circle is the best seating format for developing the habit of listening to one's peers. In these arrangements all pupils can, with minimum effort, see and listen to each other.

3. Many youngsters speak so softly that their peers find it difficult to hear and listen to them. We have sometimes found it effective to place the very soft-spoken child near the middle of the group (class) and the "loudmouth" near the front.

4. Some teachers have a habit of repeating every word a child says. Thus we have this type of exchange:

Teacher: What did the man have for sale?

Ginger: A cap.

Teacher: That's right, a cap. And what did the man say as he went from place to place?

Josh: "Caps for sale."

Teacher: Okay, "Caps for sale." Now what happened one bright sunny day?

One can easily note the problem: If the teacher repeats each of the answers, why should pupils listen to their peers? Furthermore, why should pupils speak loudly and clearly enough for their classmates to hear and listen? The solution is to (a) develop pupils' speaking skills, (b) ask pupils to listen to the contributions of their classmates, and (c) avoid the habit of repeating answers whenever possible. Of course there are times when this last recommendation cannot be implemented: (1) when children have colds and are not physically up to par, or (2) when there is considerable internal noise (talking via group work, learning centers, interruptions, etc.) or external distractions (lawnmower, traffic, etc.). Ask a pupil who speaks too softly to repeat the comment or answer loudly enough so all can hear.

F. **Tell or read (part of) a story or dictate a sentence.**
Place two, three or four pictures cut from a discarded
basal reader or magazine on a sentence strip holder or
the chalkboard ledge. Number the mounted pictures.
Present a sentence or story (part) and ask pupils to
record on their individual slates or Every-Pupil Response
cards the number of the picture that refers to the oral
presentation. (The other pictures can be used for
subsequent activities of the same type.) As an initial
procedure provide several pictures; later ask pupils to
locate pictures in books. Other sources of material for
this activity include the weekday and Sunday comic pages,
reading readiness workbooks, and magazines such as Wee
Wisdom and Jack and Jill.

G. **Tell or read a story and have a pupil repeat it or
draw either a representative picture or a series of
pictures.** This activity can also be used for sequencing.
It is worth noting that upper-grade teachers sometimes
misinterpret activities they see in kindergarten and
first-grade classrooms. What appears to be idle drawing
and coloring may actually be the follow-through component
of a directed listening activity.

Arthur Gates (339) found that the ability of a child
to supply a reasonable ending to an orally-presented
story was the best predictor of success in learning to
read.

H. **Use the "I Went to town" technique.** The first child
may say, "I went to town and took an apple." The second
person should repeat the comment and add an object
beginning with the letter (or sound) b . If someone
forgets, other pupils merely supply the information, the
child repeats the entire sequence, and the practice
continues without any person's being omitted. You should
participate too.

Several variations may be appropriate. You can "skip
around" instead of calling on pupils by their seating
arrangement, or you can have them name objects without
regard for the sequence of letters in the alphabet. The
use of the alphabetical sequence will be inappropriate
until the later stages of readiness. This activity also
involves a great deal of auditory memory.

It has been our experience that if the teacher begins
by saying "apple," many of the pupils automatically follow through by naming foods. Furthermore, youngsters
tend to look at each other as an aid in remembering the
names of objects. The "I went to Town" technique works
best when pupils are seated in a circle or semi-circle.

I. Use commercial listening materials. A set developed by Dorothy Kendall Bracken (Chicago: Science Research Associates) appears to be the most effective commercial material available for this purpose. Another good source is the listening material that accompanies the Multi-Level Reading Kits (also SRA). These selections are designed to be read by the teacher while the children use pictures in a Listening Book.

J. Teach directed listening lessons. Several facts about listening are quite interesting. First, people's listening skills are generally poor (438) and they tend to get worse with age (459). Second, listening skills can be taught; specific instruction in listening results not only in increased pupil scores on listening tests but also improvement on reading achievement tests (607, 700). Third, listening is the major way children acquire information about language and learning how to read (463).

In view of these points it seems imperative to provide directed listening lessons.

1. Development of vocabulary and concepts
2. Development of background
3. Development of purpose for listening
4. Listening to the story
5. Discussion and simultaneous informal evaluation of pupil performance
6. Extended and related activities

These are, of course, the same as the steps of a developmental lesson plan in reading. They can be used with any books that are read to children.

K. In general, ask pupils to listen for a specific purpose. This practice tends to channel their thinking. For instance, "Listen to this story to find out what to do next." Providing a specific purpose is far better than the standard comment which is often made, "Listen!"

Some examples of purpose questions and books are listed below.

"Listen to this story to find out what happened to Sylvester when he made a wish on the pebble."

Steig, William, Sylvester and the Magic Pebble. New York: Simon and Schuster, 1969.

"Listen to this story to find out where Katy found her eggs."

Milhous, Katherine, The Egg Tree. New York: Charles Scribner's Sons, 1950.

"Listen to the story to find out who the little boy's friends are."

de Regniers, Beatrice Schenk, May I Bring a Friend? New York: Atheneum, 1968.

"Listen to the story to find out why Peter wanted to learn to whistle."

Keats, Ezra Jack, Whistle for Willie. New York: Viking, 1965.

"Listen to this story to find out what the big cheese was."

Garrison, Christian, Flim and Flam and the Big Cheese. New York: Bradbury, 1976.

L. **Establish rules for good listening.** Involve the pupils as much as possible in developing classroom procedures. Sample statements might include the following:

When someone is speaking, I will
1. sit or stand quietly
2. look at the speaker
3. listen to the speaker
4. try to remember what the speaker says
5. wait until the speaker finishes before I say anything

To help pupils remember these rules, ask each of five persons to learn one statement. Each day invite the five pupils to stand before the group and say the rules. After a few days the group will be able to say them. If necessary add a gesture for each rule (i.e., stand at attention for rule one, point to eyes for two, point to ears for three; put palm on forehead for four, and cover mouth with hand for five). The use of the team approach provides an interesting way of reviewing rules and helps pupils remember the information.

M. Create a learning environment that avoids numerous distractions. For example, mobiles, while attractive, can be highly distracting, especially when there is a breeze or when they are in or near the line of vision between a pupil and the teacher, flannel board, chalkboard, etc. Seating pupils so they face the windows or an open door often leads to unnecessary distractions. Open-space schools are particularly susceptible to this problem.

Brilliantly colored displays on bulletin boards are highly distracting to some children. Thus seating patterns need to reflect a consideration for elements that will avoid distraction, poor listening, and inadequate learning.

N. When groups of pupils are engaged in a formal listening/speaking situation (i.e., show and tell), ask the speaker to hold a bean bag. The other pupils must wait their turn. At the end of the sharing, the speaker can pass the bean bag to a classmate who wishes to make a comment or ask a question. This procedure is especially helpful for pupils who frequently interrupt a speaker.

O. Recognize and reward good listening habits and especially the development of such proficiency. If the development of competence in listening is an important educational objective, youngsters should see a sufficient reason to "pay attention." Unfortunately this is not always the case. Many teachers have noted that their pupils seem to listen less well than did children in previous years. This observation may be a reflection of one or more of several factors:

1. the working mother. Over one-half of United States women with children work (321b). With almost as many women as men in the labor force, women, who have traditionally assumed responsibility for developing children's reading readiness skills, may have fewer opportunities to provide such instruction. Furthermore, some women may lack the physical stamina or the opportunity (because of conflicts between the mother's work schedule and the child's sleep schedule) to provide sufficient learning opportunities.

2. the mobility factor. Over 25% of the population of the United States moves each year. This makes it much less likely that grandparents or retired relatives will be readily available to provide babysitting services. The extended family once made it possible for children to receive highly individualized instruction on a continuous basis.

100

3. the one-parent family. With the national divorce rate at approximately 35%, there are large numbers of youngsters who grow up in one-parent households. Indeed, "one-sixth of children under 18 live in single-parent homes (321b)." Furthermore, it is expected that 45% of all children born in 1976 will live with a single parent at some time prior to reaching age 18 (535). This circumstance drastically decreases the amount of time the adults have to work with children.

4. the television generation. The typical pre-schooler watches approximately five hours of television each day. For primary children the figure slightly exceeds three hours daily of watching. Note the use of the word watching. The young child does not necessarily listen to a program, for the content is often far too sophisticated. Even the supposedly juvenile Saturday morning cartoons that are so appealing to children contain numerous expressions that only an adult can appreciate. Why, then, can children who are unable to wake up during the week suddenly be able to rise bright and early on Saturday and spend hours in front of the screen? Is it the words, or is it the action (i.e., a screeching roadrunner, a train chugging toward a damsel tied to the tracks, three bandits lambasting each other with pillows)?

Because many youngsters have acquired poor listening habits, a kindergarten or first-grade teacher has a difficult job. She must help children break a bad habit, replace it with a good habit, and, at the same time, provide content instruction. (Listening is a process and therefore a means to an end rather than the end in itself.)

Like adults, children need feedback about their behavior. Feedback, which comes in the form of recognition and reward, can be provided in several ways.

1. Provide social reinforcers such as (a) a pat on the back or a hug, (b) a public comment to the child (Have you noticed that Andy is listening so much better today?), (c) a private comment to the child who is too shy or too independent to respond appropriately to a public statement, (d) applause by the group, or (e) status symbols (line leader, captain of a dodge ball squad, eating with the teacher, erasing the board, etc.).

2. Provide academic reinforcers. One of the advantages of the use of academic reinforcers is that they reinforce academics with more academics. On both sides of the coin, academics become associated with good things. Sample academic reinforcers include the following:

a. free books from volumes contributed to the school or from the bonus titles supplied by companies with kindergarten and first-grade book clubs. If pupils can't read their books, parents, older siblings, or neighbors can provide the service. We can even meet this need ourselves.

b. pencils, erasers, or paper (especially scented or decorated stationery)

c. extra time to look at new library books, materials from a picture file, or Single Concept Cards (pictures of single objects)

d. extra time to use the headphones of a listening center or to use cards with the Bell and Howell Language Master. Notice this reinforcer uses a listening activity to reward growth in listening!

e. extra time to play learning games

f. extra time to listen to the teacher read. As a class reward, say, "You have listened so well today that I'm going to read an extra story to you."

g. the right to select the next book to be read to the class. The pupil should usually choose from a group display of books (which assures quality and avoids the frustration of trying to select from a multitude of texts). Possible comment: "Tommy, do you remember how I once had to say everything to you three times? Now you almost always listen the first time. As your reward for doing so well, I'm going to let you select from this table the next book for me to read to the class.

3. Provide tangible reinforcers (if social reinforcers prove ineffective). We may as well accept the fact that different pupils respond in different ways. What is appealing to one child is distasteful to another. The evidence indicates that tangible reinforcers can prove effective if used carefully. Indeed, tangible reinforcers work extremely well with adults. We call them paychecks. Except for volunters in the schools,

102

tangible reinforcers are far more effective than social reinforcers with adult educators.

Examples of tangible reinforcers include the following:

a. stars posted on a class progress chart. Stars "went out" in the 1920's but are back "in" now.

b. race tracks and ladders on which pupils place their names as they progress

c. pasteboard clowns (for example) which children dress piece by piece as they accumulate points for exhibiting desired behavior (good listening, in this case)

d. junk toys collected from banks, cereal boxes, yard sales, and spring house-cleaning ventures

e. certificates to the child. Many companies produce mini-certificates from "Good Listener" to the "scratch and sniff" delights. Children should attach these certificates to the walls of their rooms.

f. notes or calls to the parent(s) telling some good news

g. Happy Faces or one of their offspring stamped on children's papers or on their hands

h. symbols (construction paper worms or October pumpkins, November turkeys, etc., on which children print their names before attaching to a hall wall or taking to the principal). These symbols can be duplicated on spirit masters and cut out by volunteers who prefer to stay at home rather than come to school on a regular basis.

i. Tokens (for example, strips of colored construction paper) which can be exchanged for objects the child desires.

2. Following Directions

Because this skill is rather closely allied with listening, you should also refer to the preceding section.

A. Use "Simon Says." Be sure pupils know the meanings of the directions you give. For instance, it seems unreasonable to ask youngsters to raise their right hands unless they already have learned to distinguish right from left. Those who respond incorrectly should continue to participate in the activity. Children who experience the greatest difficulty certainly require the most practice. To deprive them of this experience while continuing "the game" with others who are more competent merely to establish a winner is undesirable. "Simon Says" is a practice exercise rather than a game; therefore, we do not need a winner. Instead we should note the youngsters whose responses are inaccurate and provide additional help (on left-right orientation, for instance).

Several more comments seem appropriate. First, use Simon Says at different levels. At the lowest level ask pupils to follow your oral directions when no visual signals are given. At this level, pupils must respond correctly, either by listening or by looking at their classmates. Note the pupils who either respond incorrectly or who respond late (after getting consensus from their peers). While it is possible to avoid the looking problem by having pupils close their eyes, some kindergarten and first-grade pupils have difficulty maintaining their balance in this condition.

A higher level of Simon Says involves the teacher's simultaneous use of gestures. At this point pupils must avoid the tendency to look rather than to listen (as is also true in television watching).

As a second comment, note that Simon Says can be used to teach and/or practice recognition of body parts. For example, can pupils touch their forehead, chin, calf of leg, wrist, palm of hand, nostrils, jaw, heel, index finger, thigh, etc.? Third, position pupils throughout the room to avoid the physical contact that sometimes interferes with the learning aspect of the activity.

B. Give pupils one direction, later progressing to two and three directions. For example:

One-step direction: Bring me the kickball.

Two-step directions: Would you please get the kickball and take it to Mrs. Smith?

Three-step directions: Let's put the books on the third shelf under the window.

Obviously a child must master one direction before he

can handle two or three. The task is not as simple as it might seem. Have you ever asked for directions to a particular place and been given three or four steps? Trying to remember them is quite difficult. The same is true for children.

C. Teach terms for essential concepts and for test-taking. Examples include the following:

1. Position: left, right, up, down, over, under, below, above, between, on, beside, among, around, through, forward, back(ward), front, back, top, middle, center, bottom, near, far, close, first, second, third, next to the last, next one, row, column

2. Time: before, after, during, until, minute, hour, today, yesterday, tomorrow

3. Number: some, several, few, many, most, all, none

4. Size: big, bigger, biggest, large, larger, largest, little, littler, littlest, small, smaller, smallest, tall, taller, tallest, short, shorter, shortest, long, longer, longest

5. Shape: square, circle, ring, block, box, triangle, rectangle, X, cross(mark)

6. Testing: same, different, color and the names of colors, draw, write, print, underline, start, stop, begin, beginning, end, finish

Different strategies must be employed to help children acquire competence in these areas. For example, many of the words listed above can be taught through the use of a set of sixteen simple pictures mounted on a sheet of 18 X 24 inch tagboard in four rows of four columns or displayed on a flannel board. It now becomes a matter of providing instruction and practice with questions such as the following:

1. (using the whole chart) Which picture has something red (yellow, etc.) in it?

2. Name a big animal in one of the pictures. Name a bigger (smaller) animal in one of the pictures.

105

3. Which animal is the smallest (littlest, biggest, tallest, shortest, longest) of all?

4. Which picture is the biggest (etc.)? (It is difficult for young children to distinguish between the size of the picture and the size of the object shown in the picture.)

5. Put your hand on (over) the rabbit.

6. Touch the front (back) of this poster.

7. Name some (several, few, most, all, none) of the pictures.

8. Which picture comes first (next, second, third, last, next to last) using a row (or column) procedure.

9. (Using one of the four center pictures) Which picture is to the right (left) of this one? Which picture is above (below, under) it?

10. Go up (down) from this picture. What do you see?

11. Which pictures are around (beside, near, between) these?

12. (using pictures on the end columns or the end rows) Which pictures are between these pictures?

13. Which pictures are in the top (bottom) row (column) ?

Instruction and practice with questions of this type will obviously require considerable time. The important point is not time but the pupil's development of competence.

A followup technique for developing some test-taking concepts involves the use of duplicated pupil worksheets, with different pictures arranged in a 4 X 4 array. As you ask questions similar to those above, pupils might place a finger on the answer and hold the paper up (a difficult task for many children), circle the answers by placing a mason jar lid over them, and cover the answer with a two-inch square block of colored construction papers.

If the sheets are laminated, pupils can mark on them and erase after each question. Furthermore, laminated sheets work even better than plain duplicated sheets for an additional type of practice in following directions. Provide instruction and practice involving directions of the following type:

14. Draw a <u>circle</u> (<u>ring</u>, <u>square</u>, <u>block</u>, <u>triangle</u>) around the _____. First practice just with <u>circles</u>, being certain pupils can draw the figure. Be sure they understand that <u>circle</u> and <u>ring</u> are synonyms for this purpose. Then add <u>squares</u> (<u>blocks</u>, <u>boxes</u>) and review both shapes before proceeding to <u>triangle</u>. After review, add <u>X</u> and <u>cross</u>(<u>mark</u>).

15. Make an <u>X</u> (<u>cross</u>, <u>crossmark</u>) <u>on</u> (<u>over</u>) the _____. In the preceding sentence the word <u>over</u> can be interpreted in two ways: (a) on top of (and therefore defacing the object) or (b) above (and therefore occupying the white space above the picture or even covering the object shown on the row above the picture being discussed). Usually the direction "put an <u>X</u> over the <u>cow</u>" means "put an <u>X</u> through the <u>cow</u>". Pupils need to understand this expectation and have sufficient practice to acquire competence in using this direction.

Some concepts are best developed in other ways. Divide a spirit master into rows and draw a simple symbol (table, chair, hat, tree, bed) in the left margin beside each column. Draw rows of balls, hearts, apples, etc., with the bottom row containing several different shapes. After copies are duplicated (and possibly laminated), provide instruction and practice involving the following types of questions:

16. In the row beside the table, put an <u>X</u> on <u>all</u> (<u>several</u>, <u>some</u>, <u>most</u>, <u>many</u>) of the balls.

17. In the row beside the chair, <u>ring</u> a <u>few</u> of the hearts.

18. In the last (bottom) row, <u>underline</u> <u>all</u> of the hearts and balls but <u>none</u> of the apples.

19. <u>Color</u> the <u>first</u> ball <u>red</u>, the <u>second</u> ball <u>green</u>, etc. Start with the <u>left</u> ball.

20. Raise your hand when you <u>finish</u>.

21. On the back of your paper (or another sheet), draw two things that are the same (different). Now draw two different things that are the same color (size, shape, etc.)

Use well-chosen pictures to develop still other concepts. Provide instruction and practice involving questions of the following types:

22. In this picture, what is up front (back)?

23. What is in the middle (center) of the picture?

24. What is at the top (bottom) of the picture?

25. What animals are around (near, far away from, beside, close to) the woman?

Books (catalogs, comics, trade books, etc.) can be used to help pupils acquire certain concepts. Instruction and practice might consider questions such as those shown below:

26. Beginning here, turn one page forward (backward).

27. Beginning here, turn back (forward) one page.

28. Turn to the next page.

29. Which page comes before (after) this one?

30. What is at the top of the next page?

31. Draw a line down to the bottom of the next page.

Use a clock or stopwatch for other instruction and practice.

32. Look at your books for one minute. I will tell you when to begin and when to stop. Are you ready? Begin...stop. Provide practice opportunities on different days.

33. Look at your books during the next minute. Look at them until I say STOP.

34. Explain that two regular television programs equal one hour of time. One physical education period is one-half of an hour.

D. <u>Review directions with pupils before they begin work-ing independently.</u> We find the following sequence helpful:

1. Distribute the worksheet, game, etc.

2. Explain the purpose. "This will help you learn to..."

3. Explain the directions one step at a time, saying, "Step 1 -- do..., Step 2 -- do..."

4. If appropriate, ask pupils to do the first example (roll of dice, matching of letters, grouping of animals, etc.).

5. Discuss their responses and provide additional instruction and guided practice as needed to the group or to individuals.

6. Ask pupils to complete the activity independently if they have a reasonable possibility of succeeding. Circulate through the group resolving difficulties before they reach the disaster stage. Alternately, ask an aide or volunteer to provide the appropriate assistance.

E. <u>Provide logical consequences for pupils who fail to follow directions.</u> That is, expect pupils to assume the responsibilities being taught or be gently but firmly penalized. Of course, if our expectations regarding responsibilities are unreasonable, then we should abandon the requirements. If what we ask is realistic, we should provide conditions that encourage pupils to acquire responsibility.

Let us look at some opportunities for helping children learn to follow directions. The question often arises, "What should I do if the child does the work right but does not follow the directions?" The answer depends on whether we believe people should develop the habit of following directions (if not for immediate activities, for subsequent ones). We suggest that you:

1. Tell pupils that if they do something right but do not follow directions, they must do it over. Explain that following directions is a habit and an attitude. They should try to develop good habits and good attitudes (i.e., do it right the first time).

2. When a child underlines items when you said to circle the pictures, give the pupil another sheet and have him do the assignment again. That way he is penalized only for failing to follow directions. Caution: Do not allow a child to copy his work from one sheet to another. That partially destroys the value of the rework.

3. When a child "forgets" to put his name on his paper (after one or two reminders), ask him to do it over. He has not followed directions.

4. When a child forgets to put away the puzzles, games, blocks, etc., or does so in a messy manner, deny him this activity the next time he asks. This assumes, of course, that the child knows how to put away his materials.

5. When a child forgets his milk money for a number of days, let him drink water. While "petting" him seems more humane, it actually fosters the habit of irresponsibility.

F. Use active rather than passive voice. For example, say, "Put your blocks (papers) right here" rather than "Blocks (papers) should be put here." It is easier for people to understand active voice constructions.

G. Use positive rather than negative statements. Whenever possible, tell a child what he should do rather than what he should not do. For example, if you say, "Don't put your papers on my desk," the child may forget the word don't and put his papers on your desk. Furthermore, this direction still doesn't tell him where to put his papers.

H. After establishing your classroom routines, try to repeat directions only once. When a pupil becomes confused, ask him what he thinks the directions are. Whenever desirable, allow another pupil to supply the correct information. Praise the second without criticizing the first.

I. Teach a variety of directions. At first glance this recommendation seems to be educationally unsound. We should remember, however, that the habit of following directions cannot be developed unless a variety of procedures is used. Pupils sit in a circle for one activity, in a semi-circle for another activity, in a nebulous clump for another reason. Sometimes youngsters should raise their hands to answer a question; at other times they might hold their thumbs stomach-high; and at still other times they might respond without the formality. Sometimes pupils may talk quietly, and sometimes they may not talk at all. As situations change, so must the directions.

J. Establish a model for good listening. For instance, look at the children as they speak to you. Sometimes teachers try to "save time" by doing two things simultaneously (i.e., listening to a child and filling in a report). Unfortunately, children believe that we are not listening when we are not looking. Our three-year-old daughter, for instance, did not allow us to read the newspaper or a book while she was talking. Thus, she demanded, "Mommy (Daddy), look at my face when I talk." We did. It is usually an excellent idea to use the following sequence:

1. Decide the behavior we want children to demonstrate.

2. Demonstrate it.

3. Ask who noted the behavior and compliment anyone who responds correctly.

4. Demonstrate it again.

5. Ask pupils to demonstrate it.

6. Give them opportunities to do so.

7. Provide feedback.

K. Check each person's hearing. A general survey may be conducted by having four or five pupils stand side-by-side. Stand behind them and whisper the name of some object. Repeat this several times. Pupils should raise their hands if they can identify the information. Those who raise their hands late or not at all should be observed carefully and referred to school health personnel for screening using an audiometer.

3. Speaking

In terms of language development, speaking follows listening and precedes reading and writing. Speaking is important, for it is one of the major ways that humans

111

communicate. Inability to speak (well) can result in a
host of social-emotional problems. Edwards lists "oral
language facility (in terms of both production and
comprehension (294:359)" as prerequisites to success in
beginning reading. Durkin concurs, "Reading is an
extension of the earlier abilities of listening and
speaking. To the extent that there is proficiency in
these prior abilities, we can also expect proficiency and
richness in reading (267:33)." Perez (562) recommends
that oral English skills be stressed in all primary and
elementary grades for Mexican-American children.
Research (142) also demonstrates that teachers who stress
oral language development increase the achievement levels
of their black children.
     The following activities are designed to help young
children acquire competence in speaking.

A. Use the Show and Tell technique. When carefully
planned, this activity can involve all pupils, not just
the ones whose need for such experiences is minimal.
Show and Tell can also be used, along with many of the
following activities, to enhance the development of
listening ability. (For older children who need this
practice, use the term "Bring and Brag" rather than "Show
and Tell.")
     First explain and model the types of information
which might be presented through Show and Tell. You may
even find it useful to read to the children Janice Udry's
What Mary Jo Shared (Chicago: Albert Whitman, 1966) or
Rebecca Caudill's A Pocketful of Cricket (New York: Holt,
1964). Insist that pupils who wish to share something
practice their presentations beforehand in order to make
their contributions interesting to the others. This
practice can be done either individually or with a small
group. For shy children use Show and Tell in small
groups (sometimes with friends they select as the
audience). Gradually extend the size of the group.
     One other organizational idea: Divide the children
into several groups and let the speakers share their
information several times. Not only does this strategy
provide additional speaking opportunities, the small
group size also facilitates listening and learning by the
other pupils.
     Encourage children to stand straight, speak clearly
and loudly, establish and maintain eye contact, and talk
without rambling. While perfection is not the goal, good
communication should be. Unless the speaking component
is satisfactory, good listening habits cannot be
practiced and developed by the "audience." (Since most

youngsters have experienced few opportunities to speak formally, you will want to use common sense in your expectations.)

B. Use the Touch and Tell technique. You need a box with a small hole cut in the top. Sew the top of a sock around the hole, cut out the toes, and ask a youngster to plunge his hand through the sock into the box. Ask him either (1) to identify the hidden object or (2) to describe it so his peers can identify it. The success of Touch and Tell depends in large measure on the objects and textures placed in the box.

Draw items from the children's vocabulary. Possible materials include the following: sponge, bar of soap, orange, sand, leaf, napkin, tube of toothpaste, eraser, door knob, hinges, screw, screw driver, pin cushion (without pins), diaper pin, cork from a bottle cap, small flag, candle, peanut, beret, piece of a puzzle, spool of thread, sea shell, key, pair of glasses, scouring pad, pine cone, lock, yo-yo, clothes pin, and sandpaper. On the other hand, a syringe, thermometer, and faucet might be inappropriate unless they are in the children's oral language. Use Touch and Tell items to build concepts about size, shape, and texture and to develop vocabulary for the youngsters rather than serve merely as items to be identified by someone. One caution: The child who is describing an object should emphasize any quality except function, for this "gives away" the item.

We find the following strategies helpful:

1. Place only one object in the box when the activity is being initiated. Later include four or five objects.

2. Use the same objects on subsequent days to reinforce the first day's descriptive efforts.

3. Ask reluctant speakers to describe objects in terms of opposites. Pose questions such as the following.

      a. Is it long or short?
      b. Is it soft or hard?
      c. Is it rough or smooth?
      d. Is it big or little?

4. Ask children to review the above by describing the object.

C. Use descriptions. A pupil can describe a classmate or himself (or a place, a game, etc.) and ask others to identify what he describes. Examples of places might include: bank, hardware store, post office, telephone company, court house, park, drug store, radio station, bottling plant, and florist. People can include school personnel, community helpers, or well-known people.

At a more advanced level, descriptions can be used to help pupils travel from one place to another. In each case the starting and ending points should be well-known to all children. Simple descriptions can be school-based (going from the classroom to the media center) or community-based (going from the school to the post office).

Descriptions should begin with teacher models so pupils can acquire the concepts involved. Note the examples below. Read one sentence at a time and ask pupils to hold their thumbs at their stomachs as soon as they think they know the answer. This should retard "blurting" and provide children with more thinking time.

1. Person: This person helps you when you are sick. She takes your temperature with a thermometer. She gives you medicine and sometimes she even gives you a shot to help you get better. Who is she? nurse

2. Place: This place is really a fun place for children. There are swings and a sliding board, and usually this place has some monkey bars. Children may go to this place after school and on Saturdays. What is this place? park

3. Game: For this game you need two teams. You will also need a ball, bat, and four bases. Someone who hits the ball hard enough might run around all of the bases and score a home run. What is this game? baseball or softball

Pupils should practice ahead of time (with a teacher, aide, parent, volunteer, friend or older child) to make the presentation more meaningful. It is worth noting that simple speaking activities at the pre-school and primary grade levels serve as a foundation for the development of informal "public speaking" competence. Thus children should receive assistance in overcoming such bad habits as winding their T-shirts around their elbows, mumbling, swaying from side to side, and playing with their hair.

D. Ask pupils to describe a picture or discuss the action shown in a picture sequence. They can do the same with a story sequence. Children's magazines are especially useful for this purpose.

One excellent source of sequence pictures that can be used for helping pupils acquire speaking skills is wordless books. A wordless book is a volume that contains no words or includes only a few words, none of which are essential to the pupil's ability to "read" the story. An example of the former is Mercer Mayer's Frog, Where Are You? An example of the latter is John Peterson's Tulips, which lists the names of the months at the upper left-hand corner of each two-page spread.

Wordless books are to be distinguished from picture books, which usually present a story in both illustration and print. Although all wordless books are picture books, not all picture books are wordless. Indeed, most are not.

Like other types of material, wordless books are valuable only to the extent to which they are used appropriately. The following procedures (203) which represent one way in which wordless books can be used, are outlined in two phases: (1) teacher modeling and (2) pupil application.

TEACHER MODELING

1. Select several wordless books to "read" to children. Over 100 wordless books are annotated at the end of this chapter.

2. "Read" each story several times to yourself. Select a book with a logical plot and sequence of events. Give careful consideration to the level of sophistication of the material.

3. "Read" the story to the children using the following guidelines:

a. Sit near the children's eye level. Hold the book at the same height so that it faces the children.

b. "Read" slowly but with expression.

c. As appropriate, point to clues that pupils may not note. Elaborate as necessary.

d. After reading the book, ask the children to make up a title for the story.

115

4. As a second "reading," ask one or more pupils to "read" the same story, one page at a time.

5. Repeat this activity on subsequent days with different books. When pupils appear to "get the idea," progress to the second phase.

PUPIL APPLICATION

1. Display the first picture from the chosen book. Ask questions such as the following:

a. Who (or what) are in the picture? (probably the major characters)

b. Where are they? (setting)

c. What are they doing? (action-beginning of the plot)

d. Who will tell me in one or two sentences what is happening? (This question is designed to help pupils to summarize the information in complete sentences. A summary is a type of main idea.)

2. Turn the page and display the next picture. Ask:

a. What are they doing now? (unfolding of plot)

b. Why are they doing it? (usually cause-effect)

c. How?

d. Where?

e. Who will tell me in one or two sentences what is happening now? (This provides initial practice in sequencing ideas.)

f. What do you think will happen next? Why? (predicting outcomes)

3. Proceed in like manner through the book, involving every child if possible. Encourage children to use complete sentences. At the end of the discussion, remind them to make up a title.

4. After children have developed the concept of "reading" wordless books, encourage them to do so in

116

pairs.   This paired activity for learning (PAL)   enables
each   child to bridge the gap between teacher guidance in
a   group setting and individualized recreational reading.
Each member of the pair can take turns telling the story,
or they can do it together.

5. As PALs become able to read the   stories,   keep
them   in pairs but let each one select a different   book.
Either show children how to locate wordless books or make
the   titles   readily available to them.   After   reading
their choices, each child tells the story to his partner.
Small-group story-telling provides speaking practice in a
non-threatening   environment   and   also   encourages
listening. The children then exchange books.

6. Periodically ask children to name their favorite
books   and give reasons for their preferences.   Obviously
there is no right or wrong answer to such questions.

7. Tape   record some of the children's oral readings
and   transcribe   them   for   use   as   language-experience
stories.   Use   these peer-produced materials to   develop
concepts (word,   sentence, capital letter), sight   words,
synonyms,   names   of   objects in the   pictures,   sentence
expansion,   feelings,   spatial   concepts (in,   under,
behind), and sentence patterns (241).

We   have   heard it said that one picture is   worth   a
thousand   words.   However, there is evidence that Western
Nigerian   children   tend to name objects in pictures   in
wordless   books   rather than tell a story, despite   their
oral   storytelling heritage (551).   This   fact   suggests
that   "reading" wordless books (and assumedly other
sequential   visuals   such as comics) does not develop
naturally   and that there is a need for helping   children
learn   to   interpret wordless books.   Helping   children
"read" wordless books prepares them for the following:

a. to interpret visual media

b. to turn the pages of a book one at a time

c. to speak in complete sentences

d. to participate actively in an oral language
reading readiness experience

e. to organize ideas and information

f. to evaluate books

117

g. to value books

h. to share information with others

i. to develop storytelling abilities

j. to think divergently

Like other kinds of books on the market, wordless
books range in quality from superb to of questionable
merit. This genre also has its own key author-
illustrators who in turn have their distinctive styles of
"writing"-illustrating. Mercer Mayer is probably the
most distinguished member of the group. Ruth Carroll,
John Goodall, and Fernando Krahn also deserve special
mention. List A at the end of the chapter annotates over
100 wordless books, sometimes suggesting a particular use
and/or grade level. Where appropriate, we have
recommended titles for purchase and for use in
classrooms. When housed in media centers or classroom
libraries, these books should be displayed in such a way
that they can be located readily by children.

E. Ask pupils to compose stories and tall tales and to
share some of their own experiences. These can be tape
recorded for future listening use with individuals and
groups as they evaluate their speaking performances.

Since many pupils contend they "can't think of a
story," it is helpful to remind them of stories they have
heard. These stories might come from children's literature (nursery rhymes, etc.) or be original compositions
shared by their classmates. You may find it helpful to
use some "story starters" such as the following:

A Time When I Was Really Scared

How I learned to _____

Retelling of a television program

Something Funny Happened on the School Bus

Our Trip to the Zoo (Dairy, Lake, Mountains, etc.)

or lead sentences:

The other day I heard thunder and saw lightning. At
first...

For Christmas I got a bicycle but I didn't...

Last week I saw Popeye on television. He was...

The funniest thing happened on the school bus. My friend Bill...

We had a good time at the zoo. First we...

F. Ask one person to begin a story. After one or more sentences, stop him and point to a classmate who should continue the story. Or you may wish to start the story with, "Once upon a time there lived a...." Competence in composing individual stories is normally a prerequisite for success here.

Keeping in mind the fact that speaking practice for one child provides listening opportunities for others, you might want to remind pupils that they should try to remember the story. After three or four youngsters have offered their contributions, stop and ask pupils to identify in order the speakers and their comments. Not only is this practice good for listening development, it also fosters auditory memory.

G. Use the Voxcom Card Reader (Tapecon, Inc.). This little machine has numerous uses for individuals and pairs of pupils. Ask a reluctant speaker to dictate one sentence and let the machine record it. Replay the card so the pupil can receive feedback. Because the Voxcom is so simple to operate, even a kindergarten pupil can practice saying and hearing sentences. Incidentally, the child who can speak but never (or rarely) does so in school sometimes overcomes his phobia by using the Voxcom.

Obviously the Voxcom can be used for helping pupils practice standard language patterns. For example, tape five or ten sentences on consecutive cards to illustrate a particular standard language usage. After teaching a particular usage and providing initial guided practice, offer additional study opportunities. Give a pair of pupils a set of five or ten cards and ask them to do the following:

1. Listen to each card.

2. Listen to the card a second time and say the sentence simultaneously.

3. Say the sentence without using the Voxcom.

4. Listen to the Voxcom to determine if they were right.

119

Develop five or ten sentences for each type of language pattern that needs instructional focus. There are huge numbers of possibilities. Five sample types are listed below.

We <u>did</u> our work.

We <u>have</u> <u>done</u> our work.

I <u>am</u> <u>working</u> today.

The <u>cats</u> <u>are</u> playing.

She <u>has</u> a new toy.

If a Voxcom is not available, a Language Master (Bell and Howell) can be used. However, it does not tape as much information on a card. As a third alternative, sentences can be presented by an aide, volunteer, or older pupil. A tape recorder is not very useful for this particular activity unless an adult is available to locate the correct tape position.

H. <u>Respond</u> <u>to</u> <u>a</u> <u>child's</u> <u>non-standard</u> <u>language</u> <u>by</u> using standard language. For example:

<u>If</u> <u>the</u> <u>child</u> <u>says</u>	<u>You</u> <u>say</u>
I ain't ready.	I'm not ready. What about you?
We done it.	Who did it?
Was the books gone?	Were the books gone?

In each case encourage the child to repeat his statement using standard language. Do not over-emphasize the corrections to the point that communication is impaired. A number of language patterning activities drawn from the literature are discussed and illustrated by the junior author (144).

I. <u>Provide</u> "<u>oral</u> <u>bombardment</u>" (14), <u>using</u> <u>a</u> <u>model</u> <u>sentence</u> <u>followed</u> <u>by</u> <u>similar</u> <u>ones</u> <u>developed</u> <u>by</u> <u>children</u>. Encourage reluctant speakers to expand their sentences. Consider the following dialogue.

Child: I seen the boy.

Teacher: Who saw the boy?

Child: I saw the boy.

Teacher: Can you make your sentence longer?
          Where was the boy?

Child: In the yard.

Teacher: Okay, put it all together. I...

Child: I saw the boy in the yard.

Teacher: When did you see him?

Child: Yesterday night.

Teacher: Last night? Say that.

Child: Last night.

Teacher: Now say the whole thing. I saw...

Child: I saw the boy in the yard last night.

Sentence elaboration practice can involve and (a low level expansion which many children overuse), adjectives (pretty, blue flowers), adverbs (sometimes she plays quietly), prepositional phrases, and subordinate conjunctions (because, since, while, when, etc.).

J. Teach everyone how to dictate an experience story of the following types: group and individual. Stories can be dictated to a teacher, an aide, a parent volunteer, a pupil from a higher grade level who makes frequent short visits, or to a tape recorder.

The language-experience story can be based on classroom experience (e.g., a class hamster), a person (e.g., teacher or child with a birthday), display of pictures (e.g., art prints, photographs, post cards), event in everyday life (e.g., circus) or a creative idea.

K. Teach pupils how to greet visitors to a class. A great deal of orientation and practice will be required. Discuss what should be done when a visitor (the principal, perhaps) arrives. A procedure similar to the following might be recorded in pictures on a floor chart.

1. I invite the visitor to come in and welcome him to the class.

2. I tell my name and ask the visitor to do the same. (It may be necessary or desirable to have him sign his name on a 3 X 5 card.)

3. I lead the visitor to a seat.

4. I tell him what we are doing.

5. I ask for any questions he may have.

6. I excuse myself and return to my activities.

This service should be rotated among all pupils. Too often the few whose need for practicing speaking skills is relatively minor engage in the largest number of activities designed to facilitate growth in that area. It is always desirable to remember that an educational activity should facilitate the development of those whose backgrounds are weak, not those who are already competent. One procedure for teaching pupils how to greet guests is outlined below.

First, discuss with the class the various activities which must be conducted upon the arrival and during the visit of the guest. Second, select several pupils to role play a series of procedures. The "visitor" should leave the room and knock on the door. Third, discuss the role play and ask pupils to comment on things which were done well and some ways they might change other parts. Fourth, select another group of pupils to conduct a second role playing session and then critique it. Fifth, assign one pupil to serve as greeter for the first week. Seat him next to the door. Whoever is designated for duty the following week should be close at hand to observe techniques and serve if the greeter is either absent or otherwise occupied (participating in a teacher-directed lesson, for example).

We have found it useful to begin with a competent speaker; follow through with three or four less secure children, and return to another self-assured child. This procedure assures a widespread observation of techniques to those who lack facility in this area. The "greet the guest" procedures should be sufficiently well developed that the class is not disturbed when visitors enter the room. Young children can learn not to be distracted by quiet visitors.

L. Ask pupils to be responsible for "answering the door" when you are occupied. Children should do so in such a way as to release you from the burden of interrupting your lesson except in emergency situations. If children are worried about forgetting this information, they can ask the person to record the message on a 3 X 5 card.

M. Provide opportunities for pupils to deliver oral messages whenever possible. While this procedure does require more time and practice, it promotes listening and auditory memory as well as speaking ability. Once again, it is useful to remember the pupils who can benefit from this practical experience and those for whom the chore is merely a busywork type of activity.

As an initial precaution against the transmission of incorrect or inadequate data, you might wish to send the oral information and an envelope containing the identical written material. The receiver can write "yes" or "no" on the card to indicate whether or not the oral message was delivered accurately. Messages might be sent to the principal, custodian, media specialist, another teacher, school secretary, guidance counselor, etc.

N. Have daily news and weather reports, rotating announcers. The role-playing procedure for this activity may be quite similar to the one used for greeting visitors. For homework ask pupils to listen to the news and weather report on radio or television and practice devising information based on their own experiences. For example, a news report might focus on whose cat had kittens, what a group is doing, who visited the class, etc.

To report on the weather pupils can select visual cut-outs for each type of weather condition and post them on a large calendar each day to represent weather conditions. For pupils who can read, sentence strips can be used to summarize the data. Examples of written comments can include the following:

It is snowing (raining, windy, warm, cool, hot, cold, thundering and lightning).

Both the daily news and the weather reports can be tape recorded to provide feedback.

O. As a general rule, encourage pupils to use complete sentences. However, do not let this stifle their participation in oral communication. Even adults sometimes use incomplete sentences. It is worth remembering that "sentence speaking is a prerequisite for sentence reading (381:284)."

Except with reluctant speakers, avoid over-using questions which can be answered with "yes" or "no." Instead begin with questions such as (1) "How old are you?" (2) "What color is your shirt?" (3) "Who do you want to play with you?" When a pupil responds with a one-word answer, ask him to make up a whole sentence. In (1) above, say, "I...(if necessary) I am..." The pupil should say, "I am six years old." In (2), "My...(if necessary) My shirt..." The pupil should say, "My shirt is blue."

P. Teach telephone usage and etiquette. Most Bell Telephone systems loan classes a tele-trainer which includes two telephones and a control box. With this equipment, you can easily conduct role-playing exercises. Activities should include appropriate responses to the problems some communities face with undesirable telephone calls. For example, (1) If asked by an unknown caller, "Who is speaking?" the correct response is "Who are you calling?" (2) To the question "What number is this?" the answer is, "What number are you calling?" (3) To the question, "Is your mother or daddy here?" (and neither is) the reply is, "They're busy now. Can you call back later?" (Notice that this response is not a lie.) (4) Children should never indicate to strangers the absence of all adults in the home. Nor should they provide their street address or their parents' names. (5) If the party appears drunk or gets angry, the child should say, "Excuse me" and hang up quickly. (6) Because many young children are unable to print the numerals, it is usually easier to teach them to ask for the name of the person who wishes for the parents to return the call. They should repeat the name to the caller to assure both accuracy and retention.

Q. Use puppets. The Peabody Language Development Kits (Circle Pines, Minnesota: American Guidance Service) include a number of useful ideas and the puppets Peabo and Peabella. Many otherwise-restrained youngsters are able to express themselves through the anonymity provided by puppetry. Incidentally, if funds are limited, you may wish to purchase just the manual. It is an excellent compilation of 180 daily lessons. Levels P and 1 can be used with kindergarten and first-grade pupils.

The following materials may also be helpful:

1. Brown, Bob, and Judy Brown, <u>Puppets</u> <u>from</u> <u>Junk</u>. N.P.: Graded Press, 1975.

   This material includes 10 posters on how to make various types of puppets, a record, and a leader's guide containing some open-ended scripts. The information was prepared by the United Methodist Church.

2. Dotts, M. Franklin, and Maryann J. Dotts, <u>Clues</u> <u>to</u> <u>Creativity</u>: <u>Providing</u> <u>Learning</u> <u>Experiences</u> <u>for</u> <u>Children</u>, Volumes 1-3. New York: Friendship Press, 1975.

   Pages 116-123 of volume 3 discuss ways of making and using puppets as well as the rationale for using puppetry. (The three-volume series is an excellent resource guide.)

3. Gates, Freida, <u>Glove</u>, <u>Mitten</u>, <u>and</u> <u>Sock</u> <u>Puppets</u>. New York: Scholastic Book Services, 1978.

   This paperback provides written directions and illustrations for making thirteen different puppets. Very few materials are needed.

4. Stanchfield, Jo M., <u>Stanchfield</u> <u>Alphabet</u> <u>Puppets</u>. Mt. Gilead, NC: North Carolina Council of the International Reading Association, n.d. (Route # 3, Box 80, Mt. Gilead, NC, 27306).

   This book contains patterns for developing 27 puppets to help children learn the letters of the alphabet.

R. <u>Use</u> <u>choral</u> <u>speaking</u> <u>activities</u>. These experiences enable youngsters to practice directed speaking without the overt audience. Begin with a group of pupils, using the following procedure:

   1. Select a well-known nursery rhyme or poem. For example, use "One, Two, Buckle My Shoe." Be sure the pupils can say it.

   2. Tell the group you are going to help them learn to speak together (in unison).

3.   Provide a model illustrating the desired behavior (i.e., a tape recording of two or more teachers speaking chorally or, preferably, two or more pupils doing so).

4.   Ask pupils to stand and say the rhyme with you. If necessary, use your hands to portray visually the speaking pattern. For example, position your hands as if holding a coconut. When saying, "One,"slightly raise and then sharply lower your hands. Repeat the pattern to your left (the children's right) for the second word, "Two." For line two (Buckle My Shoe), repeat the procedure three times, from your right to left. Continue to the end of the rhyme.

5.   After pupils master this practice, divide the group into two parts. One group will say the odd lines, the other group the even lines.

6.   Proceed to selections with longer lines (i.e., "This Little Pig Went to Market," "Little Miss Muffett," "Brown Bear, Brown Bear," "Humpty Dumpty").

As pupils acquire competence, decrease the size of the group so individuals and pairs can practice and present favorite rhymes and poems.

S. Use finger plays. Young children are especially fond of imitating gross and fine-motor gestures. Finger plays provide excellent opportunities for them to concentrate so much on finger movements that they forget their fear of speaking. Helpful materials include the following:

1.   Eliason, Claudia Fuhriman, and Loa Thomson Jenkins, A Practical Guide to Early Childhood Curriculum. Elgin, Illinois: David C. Cook Publishing Company, 1977.

Pages 282-284 list finger plays for use with young children.

2.   Gode, Marguerite, and Bertha Kerry (illus.), Hayes Finger Fun: Finger Plays for Kindergarten and Primary With Songs and Poems. Wilkinsburg, Pennsylvania: Hayes School Publishing Company, 1973.

Words are accompanied both by written directions and by pictures illustrating the action.

126

T. __Provide__ __role-playing__ __experiences__. Children are accustomed to role-playing activities. At age two they are spanking the baby doll or driving a car or truck. At age three they are playing nurse and doctor, mother or father, or teacher. All of these activities involve speech in some form, ranging from "R-r-r-r-r" (for the truck driver) to "You've been a bad girl. Now you must go to bed" to imaginary telephone conversations.

Role-playing can be especially valuable if specific situations are provided. Without this guidance many children are likely to role play the same experiences over and over without ever achieving an extensive repertoire of speaking opportunities. Consider the following samples:

1. hospital-related experiences (as a patient or visitor)

2. contact with handicapped person (variety of handicaps -- intellectual, physical, social, emotional)

3. people of different races and/or nationalities

4. confrontation with a bully

5. helping someone who has been hurt

6. helping someone whose feelings have been hurt

7. using good manners (variety of situations)

8. riding on a train or in an airplane

9. showing appreciation to loved ones (variety of situations)

10. vocational choices

Some role-playing activities are creative while others require either direct or indirect experiences. A conversation taking place during an airplane flight is enhanced if the participants have flown or have had one or more vicarious experiences involving airplanes. Field trips, television, pictures, guest speakers, etc., can provide valuable background for role-playing opportunities.

U. __Note__ __possible__ __speech__ __defects__. Refer questionable cases to a speech therapist. About 5% of the population is estimated to have some type of speech disorder (442).

Common production errors as w for l (wittle for little) and w for r (wed for red), omission of y (ellow for yellow) are developmental and are usually corrected without special help.

The child's use of dialect does not dictate the need for speech therapy. Thus a child who says wif for with, aks for ask, and dat for that does not require help from specialized personnel. On the other hand, stuttering and other gross differences in language production do indicate a need for special evaluation.

One caution: Do not draw attention to a speech problem (stuttering, for instance). Focusing on this type of situation is likely to exacerbate it.

V. Expect children to express themselves verbally rather than through gestures. So long as people can have their needs fulfilled without language, they have little incentive to learn to speak (better).

W. Make leaders of reluctant speakers. For instance, designate a child as the captain of a team. The pupil must talk to choose the members. Or ask particular youngsters to perform certain duties. (feed the fish, transport a group of picture books from the library) and tell you when they have finished. One caution: The leadership opportunity should be informal (as in being the captain). A formal leadership activity such as leading the pledge of allegiance should come later.

4. Oral Vocabulary and Concept Development

Language and vocabulary development can be considered in terms of their components: listening, speaking, reading, writing, and thinking. This section addresses itself to vocabulary development involving thinking via listening (and experiencing) and speaking.

In recent years there has been widespread recognition that vocabulary is a key factor in comprehension development (273). Furthermore, there is abundant evidence that children's rate of progress often begins to slow down around grade three or four. This may occur because pupils' reading vocabularies approach their oral vocabularies about this time. When textbooks contain large numbers of new words, children are required to add new vocabulary and concepts in their listening, speaking, reading, writing, and thinking vocabularies simultaneously. Unfortunately this expectation is often totally unrealistic. To prevent impoverished vocabularies in the middle grades and above, parents and schools must provide continuous programs of oral language development.

There is disagreement among researchers as to the size of children's vocabularies when they enter school. At least part of the problem lies in the failure of writers to distinguish between the listening and speaking vocabularies. Thus we see estimates for six-year-olds of "understands ... 2500 to 2800 (465) but speaks 2500 (653), 3300-plus (684), 7500 (111), or 12,000 (637, 654)."

In any case there is evidence that "many educationally disadvantaged children have less than half the meaningful vocabulary possessed by typical middle-class children (384)." This fact is especially unfortunate in light of the finding that "Vocabulary development has been recognized as closely predictive of intellectual ability and school success... (666:262-263)."

At least six types of instructional experiences can be used to develop and extend concepts and vocabulary:

A. Realia, or real objects
B. field trips
C. films, filmstrips, and television
D. community and other guest speakers
E. pictures, photographs, and art prints
F. teacher reading

The following suggestions should help you to think of dozens of additional ideas:

A. Realia. The use of carefully-selected real objects brought to class by you or your pupils can stimulate much growth of vocabulary and concepts. Unusual foods, fabrics, building materials, tools, collections, animals, and items from days gone by can provide numerous opportunities for verbal growth. Discuss these items by name, synonym, description (size, shape, color, texture), components, function, and classification. Some items may have several names, i.e., spade and shovel or faucet and spigot. Note that several words may stand for the same thing. Give pupils many opportunities and much encouragement to use these new terms in the most realistic and practical situations possible. Then provide positive reinforcement.

The suggestion has already been made that we remember which pupils require specific learning activities. Because those who have the least knowledge have the most to learn, we should expect them to appear to progress more slowly, even if their innate characteristics and motivation are advanced. For instance, a youngster whose vocabulary is two years below another's may make a tremendous amount of progress and still remain far behind his more advantaged peers. If the highly verbal child simultaneously advances as he should, it may even appear that a slower child is learning very little. This conclusion may be far from accurate. Certainly the precocious youngster who "knows it all" should not be used as the pacesetter for assessing progress in learning or for selection of activities for the class.

B. Field trips. These experiences can be used as ways of relating the school to the community. Practically every lesson plan, regardless of its topic, has potentially useful and highly-relevant material beyond the school walls. Children might visit:

1. businesses such as a furniture company, mill, factory, dairy or truck farm, restaurant, or bank

2. governmental facilities such as a post office, fire department, police station, or city hall

3. communication and transportation centers such as a railway depot, bus station, airfield, printing office, or radio or television station

4. historical sites or museums

5. animal centers such as a zoo, circus, pet shop, fair, or a veterinarian's office

6. nature areas for the study of plants and wildlife, rocks and minerals, soil and water erosion and conservation, and pollution

Carefully-planned and -conducted field trips can be effectively used in developing extensive diversified vocabularies. A valuable by-product of such experience is the orientation it provides toward understanding the world of work, an area our guidance people tell us is often virtually ignored at the primary levels (451). Knapp offers 12 tips for parents and teachers and 66 activities classified into 13 categories for use on field trips.

C. Films, filmstrips, and television. Vicarious experiences of this type should be used when realia and field trips, both direct experiences, are unavailable or inappropriate. In either case, however, it is extremely important that the basic steps of a good reading lesson plan be followed. Slightly modified to reflect the differences in visuals, they include the following:

1. Preview the item. Determine its relevance, interest, and level of sophistication.

2. Develop the background.

3. Develop vocabulary and concepts.

4. Establish a purpose for viewing.

5. Present the material, stopping for discussion and clarification whenever necessary.

6. Follow through with appropriate extended and related activities, which might include a second viewing of the material.

While visuals can be used to introduce, extend, or culminate a unit, it is highly unlikely that they will promote the educational objectives of our programs when selected and presented as busy-work or rewards or used without the same careful planning which should accompany other learning experiences.

D. Community and other guest speakers. In addition to employees mentioned under Field Trips, you might consider a hobbyist, school custodian or dietician, doctor, nurse, guidance counselor, ranger, missionary, principal, or writer. You should, of course, be selective in securing speakers and in coordinating the content of their presentations. Potential speakers need guidance about the time factor, the types of information to present, and useful ways and appropriate levels of communicating. Many presentations of this type have been completely unsatisfactory because speakers were unable to communicate with their audiences. Careful planning can prevent this type of occurrence.

E. Pictures, photographs, and art prints. If it is true that one picture is worth a thousand words, we can immediately grasp the potential significance of visual items. Examples of these can be located in newspapers, magazines, catalogs, travel folders, seed books, Green and Gold Stamp books, discarded encyclopedias and library books, calendars, and dictionaries. Practically all

131

types of material can be used -- pictures of people, animals, food, clothing, occupations, recreation, inventions, communication and transportation, actions, feelings, and emotional attitudes.

Begin with single concept pictures, those which identify one major object only, such as a highway or faucet. Later use these same pictures to teach several terms representing the same object, such as street and highway or sofa and couch. At a more advanced level use multiple concept pictures, those portraying more than one object, such as a baseball game or life on a farm. Picture dictionaries are one source of material for use in building oral vocabulary concepts. The following titles are recommended:

Bricker, Harry, and Yvonne Beckwith, Words to Know. Chicago: Standard Education Corporation, n.d.

Brown, Amy, et al., Dictionary 1 and Dictionary 2 . N.P.: Pyramid, n.d.

Cater, Elizabeth, ABC Words: A Coloring Dictionary. Racine, Wisconsin: Western, 1971.

McNaught, Harry, 500 Words to Grow On. New York: Random House, 1973.

Monroe, Marian, and Cabell Greet, My Little Pictionary of Words I Know or Want to Know. Chicago: Scott, Foresman and Company, n.d.

Ogle, Lucille, and Tina Thoburn, I Spy: A Picture Book of Objects in a Child's Home Environment. New York: American Heritage Press, 1970.

Scarry, Richard, Best Word Book Ever. Racine, Wisconsin: Western, n.d.

Willford, Robert E., and Ronald E. Reed, A Knowledge Aid Picture Dictionary. Niles, Illinois: Knowledge Aid, 1969.

1. Teach children the names of objects in pictures. A child who has never seen an elephant -- or perhaps has seen an elephant without having its name mentioned -- can extend his oral vocabulary by naming the objects portrayed in a picture dictionary. To achieve this purpose, pair pupils with dissimilar oral vocabularies. One child identifies the picture, receiving help only

132

when he falters. Teach the second child (the word consultant) to use a technique similar to the following:

a. When the child misses the first word, tell him the name of the picture and an important characteristic. Example -- "That's a <u>raisin</u>. It's a dried grape." or "That's a <u>scooter</u>. You put your hands on these bars (pointing), one foot on the floorboard, and push with one foot."

b. Ask the child to repeat the word and tell you something about it.

c. When the child misses the second word, follow Steps <u>a</u> and <u>b</u> .

d. Now ask the child to tell you about both words.

e. Continue with the cycle -- learn a word, review, learn another word, review, etc., until the child masters five words.

The following day review the previous day's words before beginning another list. Either proceed page by page through the picture dictionary or according to pre-determined categories, such as vegetables.

2. To construct and use individual Single Concept Cards for oral vocabulary and concept development, you may want to utilize the following procedure:

a. Locate select, cut and paste pictures onto a 3 X 5, 4 X 6 or 5 X 8 inch cards. For full-sized items use tagboard or construction paper. At a later point, the pupils themselves may carry out this sequence of events with teacher-provided materials.

b. Place a number of cards, perhaps five or ten, in an envelope and label it by category (food, clothing, animals, etc.). You may also wish to label the envelope numerically for purposes of storage. It is helpful to code the contents by level of difficulty. For example:

Sets 1-99   Easy   (apple, orange, banana)

Sets 100-199   Average   (plum, tangerine, canta-
                           loupe)

Sets 200-299   Advanced   (zucchini, avocado, mango)

c. Divide youngsters into groups of three (one person who is relatively proficient in the planned exercise and two who need help).

d. Ask the group to discuss the pictures. The members should study the names of objects, description (size, shape, color, texture), synonyms (if any), function, special parts, and class.

e. Encourage each youngster to learn as much about each object as he can in small-group discussions. Say, "Try to see how many new things you can learn about these pictures."

f. As a follow up activity, ask pupils to locate additional pictures related to the same topic or bring to class the real objects discussed. (Whenever possible, it is best to have the real object available before the lesson begins.) Provide a review of information previously developed in the same group. The discussion should be lead by someone other than the most proficient member. The child might name an object and ask another member of the group some questions. If the Single Concept Cards are related to foods, the following questions might be used.

1. What shape is a _____?

2. How big is a _____?

3. What color(s) can a _____ be?

4. When is a _____ this color?

5. How does a _____ feel?

6. What do we call the outside? (peel, husk, rind, crust)

7. How do you eat it? (raw, cooked, either; with a fork, spoon, knife, fingers)

8. What kind of food is it? (fruit, vegetable, meat, etc.)

9. How does it grow? (vine, tree, bush, underground, plant, etc.)

134

g. Encourage pupils to present their sets of cards and discuss their newly-acquired knowledge with other classmates. This activity serves not only to reinforce their own new learning but also to develop other language-related skills such as listening and speaking.

h. Meanwhile, encourage more advanced pupils to read the words representing the pictured objects. These words can be printed on both sides of the card, once below the picture and once on the reverse side of the card.
Pictures with plurals (apples, grasshoppers) or two or more words (football helmet, bushel of potatoes) can also be used as Single Concept Cards.
Depending on the group, the following teaching procedure might be used:

1. Present information on the first picture.

2. Ask pupils to repeat as much of the information as possible, ticking off the items on their fingers. (a) Ask a question (i.e., What colors can this food be?), (b) give pupils an opportunity to think and raise their thumbs -- stomach-high -- to indicate readiness to respond, and (c) call on one or more pupils.

3. Present information on the second picture.

4. Review the information for both pictures.

5. Proceed in like manner to additional pictures.

As Brown notes, "It has been said that if a person uses a word in his speaking ten times, it becomes a permanent part of his speaking vocabulary (86:8)."

F. _Teacher_ _reading_. Read stories, poems, and plays (or have other students or adults do this sometimes) to the class or to a group. The pupils and teacher, in that order, should share the contents of the books. Miller (512) lists books with stories to read or tell to children, and Ellinger (297) suggests titles to use in Head Start classes. Trelease (718) has an excellent book of recommendations for reading aloud and annotated children's books.
One cannot overemphasize the importance of reading to children. Evidence from studies of children at age one

135

(425), two (323), and three (103) demonstrates the positive effect that (for instance) reading to children has on their language and vocabulary development. Research with disadvantaged second graders indicates that reading to them daily results in significant gain on both comprehension and vocabulary (129).

It is recommended that each parent and teacher read to children thirty minutes each day. Because of the attention span of some youngsters, this thirty minutes can be provided (for example) in three ten-minute segments. Oral reading sessions are especially helpful after periods of intensive physical activity or movement (i.e., after physical education or after returning from the cafeteria or media center).

Additional activities for developing vocabulary deserve mention. Among the more productive strategies are the following:

1. Teach the meanings of words in songs and nursery rhymes. For example, does the child know the meaning of the following underlined words?

broke her <u>crown</u>	<u>naughty</u> kittens
<u>fetch</u> a <u>pail</u>	down the <u>lane</u>
Jack be <u>nimble</u>	The sheep are in the <u>meadow</u>.

Children who identify words they usually use for the underlined items are studying synonyms.

Sometimes vocabulary items do not lend themselves to synonym substitutes as in the examples shown below.

Can she bake a cherry pie, <u>charming</u> Billy?

While angels watched their <u>flocks</u> by night.

Little Tommy Tinker got burned with a <u>clinker</u>.

In these cases a child needs specific description and explanation of the meaning. The same is true if the item's synonym is outside the range of the child's direct and vicarious experience (as in <u>clinker</u>).

2. Present and reinforce new vocabulary each day. This activity requires that vocabulary development be more than an accidental occurrence. Specific planned experiences are required. While the actual terms to be

introduced will vary according to the vocabulary competence of the group of children, the basic strategy remains the same.

While still at a pre-school age, Todd Hatley was exposed to many new words. The dialogue frequently followed this pattern:

Writer: Todd, do you hear that canine barking out there?

Todd: Huh?...Oh, Uncle Richard, you mean dog.

Writer: Yes, do you hear the canine barking?

Todd: Yeah.

Writer: Can you say, "The canine is barking"?

Todd: The canine is barking.

Writer: Good...(later, several times) Todd, what's a canine?...What does a canine do? (after satisfactory responses) Todd, what's another name for dog?

Todd: Canine

Writer: Good....(later), Do you hear that feline meowing out there? (Same followup pattern for this word as well as for <u>portals</u>, from George Beverly Shea's "When They Ring Those Golden Bells for You and Me.")

Todd: (sometime later) Uncle Richard, come here and see the canine chase the feline through the portals!" (a spontaneous usage)

On other days Todd remarked, "I'll sure be glad when we leave this secondary road and live on a macadamized one." And, "Mother, I have internal troubles."

At age three Ginger said she was famished. She liked canines. The floor of the car was filthy. A child does not have to be a candidate for Mensa (association for people with high I.Q.'s) to develop an extensive vocabulary. One does require, however, an enriched environment, either at school or at home (and preferably both).

137

3. Develop the vocabulary pupils will encounter in their basal reading selections. We mentioned earlier the problem caused when children's speaking vocabularies approached their reading vocabularies. Fortunately, this problem can be minimized if there is a continuous oral vocabulary development program. The strategies outlined below should be helpful.

a. Secure copies of the basals children will use in grades one, two, and three.

b. Beginning with the lowest level of book and using the word list at the back, identify the words which your pupils might not know. Note the way these words are used. It makes a difference, for example, whether coast refers to going down a hill or to part of a country. Some third-grade books do not contain (complete) word lists. In this case, you will need to look at each lesson in the manual or request a copy of the word list from the publisher.

c. Introduce several new words each day, using them as often as possible. On subsequent days present additional words while reviewing those used previously.

d. Encourage the children to note the occasions on which you use the new terms. The major purpose is to foster a sensitivity to the language. For example, they might clap when they recognize a new word and can tell what it means or use it in a sentence.

e. Recognize and reward children who adopt the new vocabulary. When pupils expand their vocabularies, encourage their classmates to note the change. Call attention to this with a note to the parents.

Dear _____.

_____ has been using some new words lately. I am very proud of him.

Teacher (Aide)

Date

138

While it is best to write such notes by hand, the form can be duplicated. Whenever possible, the words should be listed on the note. This makes the note more precise and enables parents to provide opportunities for their children to perform.

One additional comment: While our discussion has focused on words contained in basal readers, there are other excellent sources from which new vocabulary can be drawn. These include the following:

mathematics books	-- set, triangle, square
social studies, science, health books	-- community, experiment -- decay, cavity
library	-- words from books to be read to children -- new (oral) vocabulary from wordless books -- words from stories told to the group

When pupils retell or dramatize stories, encourage them to use the new words presented in the original. Thus they should refer to a <u>wicked</u> old witch rather than a <u>mean</u> old witch and a <u>cottage</u> rather than a <u>house</u>.

4. Call objects by their names. Avoid the tendency to point to something and say, "Please bring <u>it</u> to me" or "Please bring me <u>that</u> <u>thing</u>." Encourage pupils to identify objects, actions, or attributes.

5. Dramatize new words, especially action verbs, adjectives, and prepositions. For instance, <u>waddle</u>, <u>punished</u>, and <u>pouted</u> can be illustrated. The common "elephant walk" activity should illustrate the verb <u>lumber</u>. Descriptions (adjectives) can be illustrated using words such as <u>shocked</u>, <u>disgusted</u>, and <u>delighted</u>. Many prepositions (<u>over</u>, <u>under</u>, <u>around</u>, <u>through</u>, <u>near</u>, <u>beside</u>, <u>between</u>, <u>etc.</u>) can be dramatized. These are best done in a multi-purpose room or on the playground so the children can participate in the activity.

6. At the end of each day ask pupils to tell something they have learned. They may respond in various ways depending upon the information they have acquired. One technique is to ask selected children (on a rotating basis) to use a newly-learned word in a sentence (preferably an original sentence).

5. Context Usage

Important as they are, very few language skills can be considered as valuable in terms of long-range success in reading and learning as is the ability to utilize context. Indeed, unless children learn to anticipate meaning from the sense of a sentence or paragraph, they can never be adequately prepared for any meaningful formal learning. The following kinds of activities can be used to develop proficiency in the use of context:

A. Read or dictate a sentence but omit the key word. Ask pupils to supply the term. The seven examples below are representative of one level of difficulty, that of having only one logical answer:

1. John fell down, and his nose began to _____.

2. I ate too much supper. Now I have a stomach _____.

3. Mother bought me a truck for my _____.

4. The man was tall, dark, and _____.

5. The big dog began to _____ at me.

6. Why don't you lie down and take a _____?

7. Have you seen my marbles? I think I have _____ them.

Another level of difficulty involves sentences for which several words might appropriate.

1. Jill had a cold and began to _____ (sneeze, cough).

2. I ate too much supper. Now my stomach is _____ (hurting, aching, growling).

3. The children will _____ play quietly (always, sometimes, never).

4. Did you really find that _____ (ball, toy, game, etc.)?

5. I get _____ cents a week for my allowance (twenty-five, fifty, etc.).

140

B.   Read poems to the class. Stop at the end of rhyming
lines and allow pupils to supply the missing words. The
Dr. Seuss books (New York: Random House) and those by
Bill Martin, Jr. (New York: Holt) are very useful.
   Appropriate   materials should contain   sufficient
context so that a child who thinks can usually provide
the word. Poems, of course, offer the added advantage of
providing a rhyming clue. For example, use the selection
below, deleting the underlined words and encouraging
children to chime in with the responses.

The Three Bears: Revisited

Richard Culyer

Quite early one morning three curious bears
Walked into my house, and they came up the <u>stairs</u>.

The first little bear had a nose that was red.
He opened my door, and he crawled in the <u>bed</u>.

The next little bear had two eyes that were brown.
He opened his book, and he softly sat <u>down</u>.

The third little bear had big teeth shining bright.
He reached for the lamp, and he turned on the <u>light</u>.

I quickly awoke, and I saw in my bed
A bear with the covers up over his <u>head</u>.

I looked to the left; do you know what I saw?
A lamp and a shade in another bear's <u>paw</u>.

And there to my right I saw one more brown bear
Quite happily holding a book in my <u>chair</u>.

Now what could I do when my arms and legs shook?
I just didn't know 'til I saw the bear's <u>book</u>.

It showed a young girl with her long golden hair,
First eating some porridge, then breaking a <u>chair</u>,

Then falling asleep in the Baby Bear's bed.
She only awoke when she heard what he <u>said</u>.

And now I know why the three bears are up here.
I also know I now have nothing to <u>fear</u>.

The bears have now done what they wanted to do:
Repaying a visit from "You can guess who".

Now all of us need to learn never to go
Into someone's house unless someone says so.

C. Conduct the same activity with orally-presented stories and plays. Since the missing words will not be in rhyme, they represent a more difficult level involving awareness of context. Stories that contain repeating elements ("This is the House that Jack Built," "Little Orphan Annie," "The Three Little Pigs," "Nobody Listens to Andrew," etc.) are especially useful beginning selections for involving children. Before reading, tell the children to chime in just as soon as they know what you are going to say next.

At a higher level use selections which provide good context opportunities for pupils to supply appropriate responses. To illustrate:

Once upon a _____, a long time _____, there lived a king and a _____ in a great big _____ at the very top of a tall hill. Now the king and the _____ had two sons and three _____. The sons were good boys, but they were very much afraid of a dragon that lived in the forest. Now this _____ had fire coming out of his _____ and _____.

Note that sometimes there is only one obvious answer (time, ago); at other times there are several possibilities (castle or palace, nose or mouth). Either set of responses is acceptable, for each indicates the use of contextual thinking.

D. Use the Peabody Language Development Kits already mentioned. The manuals contain lessons which are especially effective in developing fluency in context.

E. At a later stage, provide practice and instruction in using context to recognize words used in the pupils' oral language. This activity bridges the gap between oral context and beginning reading context. The fact that language-experience stories reflect situations with which children are familiar facilitates the development of a thinking (context) approach to reading.

6. Oral and Picture Comprehension

While concern for comprehension development historically has focused on understanding the printed word, there has been increasing emphasis in recent years on listening comprehension (162, 220, 519, 726). This development is significant because "levels attained in language comprehension place limits on levels of attainment in reading comprehension (111)." Others concur (439). Furthermore, "Kindergarten children can make judgments, predictions, and comparisons with information they see and hear (697)." Contrary to popular opinion, they can learn to listen critically (460).

Picture interpretation has not received adequate attention (162), despite the fact that research has long demonstrated the difficulty many pupils experience in this area (513). Furthermore, there appears to be little recognition of the contribution picture interpretation can make to academic growth. One way to develop children's oral comprehension abilities is to pose questions at various levels of difficulty. To illustrate, let us consider the following example:

Harry, Barry, and Larry blew out the candles and then told their mother to turn on the light.

Literal:

a. What were the children's names?

b. What two things did they do?

Implied:

a. What kin are these people (probably triplets, although most children say three twins)

b. Why do you think so? (their names rhyme)

c. What are they having? (a birthday party)

d. When does the story take place? (about what time?) (probably at night since they have to turn on the light)

e. How old are the children? (probably between two and ten; they must be able to talk and still young enough to depend on the mother to turn on the light)

Creative:

a. How many people do you think were there? Who were they?

b. What do you think the boys got for their birthday?

c. What do you think the people did while they were together?

While many teachers find it difficult to develop a variety of question types without specific in-service assistance, this skill can be acquired. We recommend that kindergarten and first-grade teachers provide one or two such exercises daily for their pupils. When the youngsters acquire competence at the sentence level, teachers can introduce paragraphs. Eventually the focus will be on developing levels of comprehension with longer selections.

A second way of helping pupils acquire competence in oral and picture comprehension is through instruction and practice in at least seven major specific skill areas.

A. main ideas
B. major supporting details
C. classification (categorization)
D. sequence
E. predicting outcomes
F. compare-contrast
G. cause-effect

The end product, of course, is the pupil's application of these skills while using visual or auditory media.

The following suggestions are offered as possibilities. Once again, you may be able to think of many additional techniques to enhance the development of comprehension at the oral and pictorial stages.

A, B. Main Ideas and Major Supporting Details

Provide instruction and practice in identifying major supporting details either prior to or at the same time as main ideas. Obviously the vocabulary and concepts represented in the pictures or oral experiences must be familiar if pupils are to recognize major supporting details successfully. Therefore the Single Concept Cards referred to earlier must be presented first. Note: Topics are related to main ideas.

1. Present a picture and ask pupils to tell the main idea or to decide on a title. Calendars, pictures, and the pupils' own drawings are useful here.

2. Using the same materials, ask pupils to name the features which enabled them to identify the main idea of a picture. These features represent the major supporting details. For instance, the presence of an elephant, zebra, hippopotamus, and rhinoceros may lead someone to recognize the topic of a picture as the zoo. The individual animals comprise the major supporting details.

3. Use pictures which portray emotions (i.e, fear, anger, love) and attitudes (i.e., greed, courtesy). Many young children seem to go no further than describing someone as good or bad or as feeling happy or sad. Not only is character interpretation important, it can be developed through specific teaching. We find the following steps helpful:

a. Present a laminated picture portraying a particular characteristic (i.e., thoughtfulness). Lead a discussion of how thoughtfulness is shown in the picture.

b. Present a second picture showing thoughtfulness. Once again lead a discussion.

c. Present a series of pictures one at a time. With each one, ask pupils to tell whether or not the person is thoughtful and (if so), how the trait is shown. Between 1/2 and 2/3 of the pictures should show the trait.

d. Ask pupils to try to locate examples of thoughtful people (in materials you provide). Discuss any pictures that are submitted.

e. Ask pupils to note examples of thoughtfulness they see in others or any ways they themselves are thoughtful. The lessons can thus serve both an academic and a social purpose.

4. Ask pupils to identify the words in a sentence that tell the main idea. For example:

"On the first day of school Laura lost her lunch money on the playground." (Main idea: Laura lost money.)

5. Ask pupils to identify the sentence that tells the main idea of a paragraph. Because main ideas can occupy various positions of a paragraph, children need specific instruction, practice, and feedback on the different placements. Note the following examples.

a. (Beginning sentence)   Jeff likes to go to the beach.   He plays in the water when it's warm.   He builds castles out of the sand. He picks up sea shells and funny rocks. He watches the people as they swim.

b. (Ending sentence)   The sun had gone down.   Lights were coming on in the houses. Mother said she was beginning to get cold.   It was getting hard for us to see how to play ball. We decided it was time to go into the house.

c. (Middle sentence)   Bobby was outside building a snowman.   Carol was in the house making snow cream. Jack did not have to go to school today because this was such a big snow.   The snow plows could not clear the roads.   My mom could not go to work. She said she would help us find our sleds in a little while.

d. (Implied)   First I drank a small glass of orange juice.   Then I ate a bowl of cereal.   When I finished, Mother gave me an egg and some bacon.

It is helpful to use the following procedure when introducing main ideas in paragraphs:

a. Present and discuss paragraphs with main ideas at the beginning until pupils can readily identify them.

b. Present and discuss paragraphs with main ideas at the end until pupils can readily identify them.

c. Present and discuss paragraphs, some of which have their main ideas at the beginning and some at the end.

d. Present and discuss paragraphs with implied main ideas.

e. Present and discuss paragraphs, some of which have main ideas at the beginning, some at the end, and some implied.

146

f. Present and discuss paragraphs with main ideas in the middle.

g. Present and discuss paragraphs with main ideas in all four positions.

While these activities will obviously require time as well as specially-developed materials, they are quite important, for pupils cannot learn to comprehend long units of information unless they first understand shorter units.

6. Help pupils recognize the fact that titles of songs, nursery rhymes, poems, and stories either are main ideas or reflect the content of the composition. Consider the following samples:

a. (song)   Three Blind Mice, Three Blind Mice.
See how they run, See how they run.
They all ran after the farmer's wife.
She cut off their tails with a carving knife.
Did you ever see such a sight in your life
As three blind mice?

Question: What is the song about?
(the title, of course)

b. (nursery rhyme) Humpty Dumpty

c. (story) Caps for Sale by Esphyr Slobodkina (New York: William R. Scott, Inc., 1977)

d. (poem) "The Purple Cow" by Ogden Nash

7. Ask pupils to choose a title for a language-experience story that has been dictated by an individual or group. Lead them to understand that the title should relate to all of the sentences in the story. (While a title is not necessarily a main idea, it does reflect the focus of the selection.)

8. Encourage youngsters to tell why they selected certain titles for the nursery rhymes, poems, stories, songs, or language-experience stories. This activity enables you to discover valuable information relative to their thinking and reasoning processes.

147

C. Classification (Categorization)

1. Mount approximately fifteen pictures of simple objects in three diverse categories (i.e., dogs, chairs, and clothes). Show pupils how to classify them. Thus a high chair, sofa, ottoman, and stool are members of the chair family.
Label the pictures by sets and laminate them, for young children tend to eat their instructional materials. You may wish to make the materials self-scoring. For three groups, draw, for example, a happy face, a sad face, and a neutral face on the reverse sides.

2. Follow the same procedure with three parallel categories (i.e., cats, dogs and horses). Thus a tiger and a lion are in the cat family, and a zebra is in the horse family. If these concepts are too sophisticated, restrict pictures to less demanding possibilities.

3. If a simple dictionary is organized by topics, call attention to the natural groupings (animals, foods, toys, etc.) and ask pupils to name other objects which fit in the categories. If the picture dictionary is organized alphabetically, ask each pupil to take each word/picture or page and list other word/pictures that comprise the same group. Thus if apple, ape, arm, and ax are on one page, pupils must locate other word/pictures of foods, animals, parts of the body, and tools or weapons. They may copy these words on long strips of cardboard or on lined paper.

4. Ask pupils to classify pictures or objects of various topics. For example, a series of pictures related to the foods might be categorized into any of the following areas:

a. served hot -- served cold -- both

b. breakfast -- dinner -- supper -- snacks -- several of these

c. summertime -- wintertime -- both

d. grown on stalks -- grown on vines -- grown underground -- grown on trees -- came from animals

e. meats -- vegetables -- fruit -- milk products -- bread products -- desserts -- other

f. served raw -- served cooked -- both

148

5. After reading various types of selections to children, ask them to classify the material by genre. Which are talking animal, fairy tales, poems, nursery rhymes, etc.? You may find it advantageous to follow a procedure somewhat similar to the following:

a. (For several days) Read selections illustrating one genre, perhaps nursery rhymes. Discuss characteristics of nursery rhymes.

b. (For several days) Read selections illustrating a somewhat different genre, perhaps talking animal stories. Discuss characteristics of talking animal stories.

c. Read selections of both types. Ask pupils to identify the genre.

d. Add another genre and discuss its characteristics.

e. Read selections of three types, asking pupils to identify the genre.

Note: This activity should be a natural outgrowth of a carefully-planned literature-development program.

D. <u>Sequence</u>

1. Locate picture sequences in reading readiness workbooks and ask pupils to arrange the frames in the right order. These materials normally contain no more than three or four frames.

2. Introduce several pictures showing the stages of a person's growth or the construction of a home. Ask pupils to place the frame in order.

3. Use the Sequent-a-Sets (Dexter and Westbrook). Each pack consists of ten sets of four pictures each. Ask children to arrange the pictures in sequential order.

4. Ask pupils to sequence comic strips without words ("Henry," for example) and advertisements frequently found in ladies' magazines (steps in making pizza from a mix, for instance). An excellent source of wordless comic strips is "Life with Lucky" in the <u>National Enquirer</u>.

Several comments are appropriate here. First, be

certain pupils can sequence a small number of frames (daily newspaper comics) before asking them to sequence longer units (Sunday comics).

Second, avoid comics that include crime or other undesirable models of behavior. Third, if one frame is confusing, you may wish to eliminate it from the set. Try to include only sets that have clearly identifiable sequences.

Fourth, encourage pupils to work together with each one sharing information about the suggested sequence and the reasons for the proposed choice. Fifth, ask pupils to check their work. One child should point to each picture in turn while telling the story. The next child can either do the same or take the lead with the next set of comic strips.

5. Encourage an understanding and use of sequence by having members of the class listen to and retell stories such as "The Three Little Pigs," "Goldilocks and the Three Bears," "The Three Billy Goats Gruff," and "Cinderella."

6. Discuss, in order, the directions for going somewhere or making something. Science experiments and directions for visiting the most important parts of the school are quite useful in building proficiency in this area.

7. Help pupils sequence ideas they plan to use in developing a language-experience story, Show and Tell session, discussion of a television program, or other oral presentation.

8. Fold a piece of newsprint into thirds. Paste a picture in the center third and ask the children to draw what they think happened before the picture and after it. Then ask the children to tell their stories to the class.

9. Provide frequent opportunities for youngsters to explain directions orally. Most young learners are not very familiar with the practice.

10. At a later stage, ask the children to sequence the letters of the alphabet and the numerals, both orally and on paper.

E. Predicting Outcomes

1. Ask pupils to tell what they think will happen next in a picture. The last page of old _Life_ magazines is often useful for this purpose.

2. From your own oral reading to a group, encourage pupils to decide what they think will happen next, and why. For example, read Aileen Fisher's _Sing_, _Little Mouse_ (New York: Crowell, 1969). At the bottom of page 19, ask the children to answer the question: "Can you guess what I saw in my very own house?" Then ask them to tell why.

3. Read appropriate stories from children's magazines. For example, read the first fourteen paragraphs of Nancy Garber's "Angelina and the Cat" (_Wee Wisdom_, LXXV, No. 6 (January 1974), 4-8) and ask the youngsters to decide how they would solve the problem.

4. Encourage pupils to read the pictures of a book or story to decide what it is all about. They may also use the first few pictures of a story to decide the possible outcome and then uncover the next picture, modifying their predictions if necessary. As subsequent pictures are revealed, ask children to indicate the main characters, their personality types, and the setting of the story. As adults, we do this every day when we read the comics in the newspaper or follow the daily news events. Soap operas are also built with this same potential. Television programmers have thoughtfully provided commercials to allow us time to decide what might occur next.

As a pre-schooler, Todd enjoyed having a wide variety of books read to him. During each session Todd was exposed to a number of books in the True Book series (Chicago: Children's Press). He was always asked to select one of the books, "read" the pictures, and predict the content of the story before it was actually read to him. The use of this procedure helped Todd develop the ability to identify main ideas and major supporting details, and to predict outcomes. He even learned to use the Table of Contents. One day an initial study of one book completely baffled him. "I don't know what this one is about," he announced, "but it must be the True Book of something or other."

F. Compare-Contrast

The ability to compare and contrast depends upon an understanding of "alike" and "different" (or their equivalents), recognition of either a large or small category which characterizes an object or idea, experiential background, and specific instruction and practice in noting similarities and differences.

1. Present buttons or other objects of various shapes, sizes, colors, and texture. Ask pupils, "How are they alike? How are they different?"

2. Using pictures from Sunday comic pages, ask pupils to tell how the two differ. A number of objects will be missing in the second picture. (This feature is commonly found in a number of Sunday papers, sometimes under the name "Hocus Focus.")

3. Present two or more members of a class of objects. Ask, "How are a _____ and a _____ alike?" Present, for example a piece of chalk, a crayon, a pen, a pencil, and a magic marker. Or, use items such as a book and newspaper, flashlight and candle, clock and calendar, house trailer and nest, box and pocket, harmonica and trumpet, cocoon and banana peel, church bell and siren, yardstick and odometer.

4. As a more difficult activity, ask pupils how certain objects are different. Some of the writing implements listed above are liquid, some solid; also the situations in which they are used are different. A pen is appropriate for writing a letter, a piece of chalk for writing on the board, etc.

Differences might also be noted among several pencils (in color, shape, size, lead strength, etc.), books, coats, holidays, games, community helpers, etc.

5. Ask pupils to compare pictures of homes, people, automobiles, animals, tools, clothing, musical instruments, etc.

6. For art, ask pupils to compare illustrations in children's books. They might consider examples by Symeon Shimin, Ezra Jack Keats, Dr. Seuss, and Brian Wildsmith.

7. Ask pupils to compare two objects advertised in a catalog, newspaper, or magazine. For example, pupils might compare two models of minibikes or watches.

8. Ask how two pupils are alike and different. Consider physical differences as well as interests.

9. Ask pupils to compare two television programs or movies. You might use this strategy:

a. Ask pupils to name several television programs.

b. Ask them to name two that are somewhat alike.

c. Ask them to tell how the two are alike.

d. Ask them to name two television programs that are not much alike.

e. Ask them to tell how the programs are different.

f. Ask them to tell which program they prefer and why.

g. Point out that the stating of a preference means they have compared and contrasted two or more programs. All preferences result from a compare and contrast situation, whether they involve food (desserts are sweeter than vegetables -- contrast), clothing (those shoes are too small; my other ones feel better), friends, pets, etc.

10. Read two paragraphs to pupils. Use a monotone in one presentation and a voice filled with intonation in the other. Ask pupils to compare the two presentations.

11. Read two versions of the same story. There are numerous versions of such favorites as "Cinderella," "Little Red Riding Hood," and "The Three Pigs." Ask pupils to note how they are alike and how they differ (in plot and language, for instance). Also compare and contrast the illustrations.

G. Cause-Effect

1. Present two pictures. Ask pupils to decide which one caused the other.

2. Ask pupils to notice situations which are likely to create safety or health hazards (poor wiring, blockaded doors, unsanitary conditions, glass on the playground, etc.).

3. Ask a pupil to tell something he did and why he did it. The other pupils should then attempt to identify both the cause and the effect.

4. Discuss cause-effect situations in real life. For example, suppose pupils are too noisy in the cafeteria. Then the principal or the teacher requires that everyone must eat in silence for a designated period of time. Ask, "What is the cause? What is the effect?" You may prefer to go even further and discuss the question, "How can you avoid the effect?"

5. When two pupils get into a fight or have some other type of disagreement, ask them or the class to identify the cause-effect relationships. For example:

> Tom was lying in his seat with his feet in the aisle. Bob tripped over them. When Tom laughed, Bob tried to kick his feet out of the aisle. This made Tom mad, and he called Bob a name. Bob in turn pushed Tom. Tom then punched Bob in the chin. Pupils should note that each cause led to an effect which in turn became a cause for the next effect.

6. Read a story to the class. Ask, "Why did _____ happen?" This involves the identification of the cause. Or, working in the reverse fashion, say, "The story says _____ happened. What do you think caused that?" An excellent book to use is Charlotte Zolotow's Quarreling Book (New York: Harper and Row, 1963).

Regardless of the activity being used, keep these points in mind. First, develop the items used for initial presentations. These materials will serve as models for subsequent reference. Later encourage pupils to develop appropriate materials.

Second, encourage the use of PALs (Paired Activities for Learning). It is much more enjoyable to learn when someone is working with us than when we are expected to study alone. Since pupils learn so much outside of school -- think about that if you will -- it seems only sensible to maximize their potential teaching talent within the classroom.

Third, emphasize teaching rather than testing. As pupils work and learn together, they acquire much information which is not really "testable" from a group point of view. While informal observations or teacher-prepared evaluational devices will be needed at times to ascertain whether real learning is taking place, emphasis on teaching should never be eclipsed by testing procedures.

Fourth, provide feedback regarding correct or possible responses almost immediately. We have found it useful for two or three sets of pupils to work with the same materials at different times and then compare their responses. Usually the majority response is correct and can be preserved for subsequent reference. Areas of strong disagreement, of course, need to be discussed rather carefully. Sometimes we even <u>vote</u> on the correct answers!

Fifth, review each child's performance. The use of a set of self-checking materials does not release us from the responsibility of following through to determine the specific strengths, weaknesses, and continuing needs of various individuals. Perhaps the most unfortunate result of the use of readiness workbooks, as well as those of other levels, has been the failure of some teachers to assist pupils in learning from their mistakes and to provide subsequent learning activities based on performance with the assigned materials. Certainly more work of the same is not necessarily valid for a pupil whose completed assignment indicates a definite lack of proficiency. What he may need, more than anything else, is instruction, not just practice. <u>Practice makes perfect only if we know what we're doing.</u> Stated another way, <u>the mere working of exercises is not necessarily highly correlated with learning.</u>

Sixth, materials for learning are not primarily games, and it is inappropriate to think of them as such. While we have identified several Kim's Games as useful for learning, they should be considered as learning activities rather than fun-time experiences.

Games can be delightful busy-work activities. However, they justify their use by serving an educational function. Unfortunately, many games pit unequals against each other with obvious results or provide practice for pupils who either already know the skills or words or don't know them at all. The ideas presented here should not be considered and presented as games to be used "if you are really good today."

Seventh, comprehension skills may be taught through

155

three general stages: listening, pictures, and reading. Even pre-schoolers and the disadvantaged can therefore develop competency in comprehension if we provide opportunities at appropriate stages.

Summary

This chapter has considered six reading readiness skills in the language categories of listening, following directions, speaking, oral vocabulary and concept development, oral context, and oral and picture comprehension. Specific activities and strategies for using them are provided, and cautions are included whenever needed.

FOR FURTHER READING

Blanton, William E., "Books for Preschool Children," in A Teacher's Guide to Preschool Reading, PREP Report 40. Washington, D.C.: United States Department of Health, Education and Welfare, 1972.

Carlson, Ruth Kearney, Speaking Aids Through the Grades. New York: Teachers College Press, 1975.

Gonzalez, Phillip C., "How to Begin Language Instruction for Non-English Speaking Students," Language Arts, LVII, No. 2 (February, 1981), 175-180.

King, Ethel M., "Prereading Programs: Direct Versus Incidental Teaching," Reading Teacher, XXXI, No. 5 (February, 1978), 504-510.

Olilla, Lloyd (editor), Handbook for Administrators and Teachers, Reading in the Kindergarten. Newark, Delaware: International Reading Association, 1980.

Russell, David H., and Elizabeth F. Russell, Listening Aids Through the Grades. New York: Teachers College Press, 1959.

List A
WORDLESS BOOKS

Alexander, Martha, Bobo's Dream. New York: Dial Press, 1970.

A black boy takes his dog and a bone to the park. When a big dog steals the bone, the boy retrieves it for his happy pup. In turn it dreams of helping the boy and, when the big dog tries to recapture the bone, the little dog fends for itself. Recommended.

Allen, Laura Jean, Mr. Jolly's Sidewalk Market. New York: Holt, Rinehart and Winston, Inc., 1963.

Each picture shows the weather and/or season and how the sidewalk market looks at that time of the year. The only printed words are the months, one for each two-page spread. Recommended for teaching concepts.

Ames, Lee J., Draw Animals. New York: Doubleday and Company, 1976.

This is a different kind of wordless book. Each page show the step-by-step development leading to a finished drawing. Recommended for middle graders.

_____, Draw 50 Boats, Ships, Trucks, and Trains. New York: Doubleday and Company, 1976.

Like the preceding title, this book shows the step-by-step development of a finished picture. Recommended for middle graders.

Amoss, Berthe, By the Sea. New York: Parents' Magazine Press, 1969.

Each picture portrays several centers of action, all of which change from page to page. Many of the separate scenes are related to each other. This book is more sophisticated and should be used at upper primary or lower elementary levels.

Arnosky, Jim, Mud Time and More Nathaniel Stories. Reading, Massachusetts: Addison-Wesley, 1979.

Four clever stories involving Nathaniel are entitled "Mud Time," "The Weather Vane," "Gathering Eggs," and "Picking Apples." Highly recommended.

Asch, Frank, *The Blue Balloon*. New York: McGraw-Hill Book Company, 1971.

A boy and his balloon encounter trouble when different hazards appear.

_____, *In the Eye of The Teddy*. New York: Harper and Row, Publishers, Inc., 1973.

A boy explores phantasmagoria in the eye of a teddy bear.

Barton, Byron, *Elephant*. New York: Seabury Press, 1971.

This series of pictures of elephants a girl either sees or dreams about is intended for primary pupils. There is no story plot.

Baum, Willi, *Birds of a Feather*. Reading, Mass.: Addison-Wesley Publishing Company, 1969.

A bird spies a feathered hat and steals the plumage. A man captures the bird and plans to sell it until it sheds its artificial finery. Recommended.

Bollinger-Savelli, Antonella, *The Knitted Cat*. New York: Macmillan Publishing Company, Inc., 1971.

A knitted cat begins to unravel at the tail until a benefactor ties a knot and a girl finishes knitting it.

Briggs, Raymond, *The Snowman*. New York: Random House, 1978.

A lad builds a snowman that becomes his friend, exploring the house one night and taking the boy on a quick trip. This "warm" story is highly recommended for primary pupils. Encourage children to note the snowman's reaction to heat-producing objects.

Burton, Marilee Robin, *The Elephant's Nest*. New York: Harper and Row, Publishers, 1979.

Four stories about elephants, lions, kangaroos, and mice.

Carle, Eric, I See a Song. New York: Thomas Y. Crowell Company, 1973.

A violinist paints his music.

_____, 1, 2, 3, and the Zoo. New York: William Collins and World Publishing Company, 1968.

Cages of animals numbered from one to ten are placed on separate flat railroad cars.

Carroll, Ruth, The Chimp and the Clown. New York: Henry Z. Walck, Inc., 1968.

A monkey escapes from the clown and encounters a series of frightening but funny experiences before being rescued. Recommended for oral language development.

_____, What Whiskers Did. New York: Henry Z. Walck, Inc., 1965.

A puppy breaks away from his owner, tries to follow an animal's tracks, is chased by a fox, and crawls underground into a rabbit's home. Appropriate and recommended for primary use.

_____, The Witch Kitten. New York: Henry Z. Walck, Inc., 1973.

A kitten swipes and rides the witch's broom and has some hair-raising experiences. Recommended for upper primary and lower-elementary levels.

_____, and Latrobe Carroll, The Christmas Kitten. New York: Henry Z. Walck, Inc., 1970.

When a boy tries to give away a kitten, a mother refuses to accept it. Each time she takes it outside, it manages to find a way back in. Clever and highly recommended.

Curro, Evelyn M., The Great Circus Parade. New York: Holt, Rinehart and Winston, Inc., 1963.

The circus procession comes to town.

Degan, Bruce, Aunt Possum and the Pumpkin Man. New York:
Harper and Row, Publishers, 1977.

Aunt Possum and her cat are temporarily frightened by
a ghost with a pumpkin head, but a protruding tail
destroys the disguise, and the fearless lady
"handles" the situation. Recommended, especially
near Halloween, for oral language development and
drawing conclusions.

DeGroat, Diane, Alligator's Toothache. New York: Crown
Publishers, Inc., 1977.

A delightful story of an alligator with his
toothache. The illustrations are clever. Highly
recommended.

Delton, Judy, Two Good Friends. New York: Crown
Publishers, Inc., 1977.

A duck with an immaculate but foodless house is
friendly with a bear with a dirty house that is full
of food. They share their strengths. After page 26
ask, "What do you think will happen next?" Highly
recommended.

de Paolo, Tomie, Sing, Pierrot, Sing: A Picture Book in
Mime. New York: Harcourt Brace Jovanovich,
Publishers, 1983.

A court jester falls in love with a fair young damsel
who loves another. The jester sorrows until the
neighborhood children show their love to him.
Recommended for primary grades.

Eitzen, Allen, Birds in Wintertime. New York: Holt,
Rinehart and Winston, Inc., 1963.

Different birds chase each other away from the
feeding grounds.

Elzbieta, Little Mops and the Moon. New York: Doubleday
and Company, Inc., 1972.

Line drawings show an animal chasing a butterfly.
Coming across a shoe, it discovers the owner, a worm
with many legs. The worm accepts the shoe and, after
they both take a nap, becomes a butterfly.
Recommended for primary use.

_____, _Little Mops at the Seashore_. New York: Doubleday and Company, Inc., 1972.

A bear (?) captures and then returns a duck's egg and finally accompanies the mother duck and her baby on their flight.

Emberly, Ed, _A Birthday Wish_. Boston: Little, Brown, and Company, 1977.

A rather sophisticated and circuitous account of a series of cause-effect actions by which a mouse gets a birthday wish. (The few words are of a labeling nature and do not impinge on the story.)

_____, _Ed Emberly's ABC_. Boston: Little, Brown, and Company, 1978.

Emberly outdoes himself in this superb book. Each page displays the series of steps necessary to form a letter of the alphabet. For example, to represent one letter's formation, a lizard drops his line in the water where a lobster hooks it perpendicularly to make the letter L. Pupils can trace the letters with their fingers, copy them on a sheet of paper, and try to identify other words containing the same sound. Highly recommended.

Fraser, Betty, _Name and Know Books_. N.P.: Macmillan Company, 1969.

This paperback shows scenes of people and is intended to be used as a way of teaching oral vocabulary to young or severely disadvantaged children.

_____, _What's For Lunch?_ N.P.: Macmillan Company, 1969.

A boy accompanies his mother to the grocery store. Acceptable for very young or disadvantaged children.

Fromm, Lilo, _Muffel and Plums_. New York: Macmillan Company, 1972.

A lion and a rabbit are engaged in nine funny episodes. From two to fourteen frames similar to the comics are presented on each page. The material is useful for teaching cause-effect.

Fuchs, Erich, _Journey to the Moon_. New York: Delacorte Press, 1969.

This book is probably intended to be shown to children. The first two pages present paragraphs for an adult to read or summarize to children who are studying the pictures. Intended for primary or lower intermediate use.

Gilbert, Elliott, _A Cat Story_. New York: Holt, Rinehart and Winston, Inc., 1963.

A mother cat teaches her kittens what to do and what not to do. Recommended.

Ginsburg, Mirra, _Three Kittens_. New York: Crown Publishers, Inc., 1973.

Three kittens appear to change colors as they chase a mouse through some flour and a frog through a stovepipe. On the page showing a toad near the entrance to a stovepipe, ask, "What do you think will happen next?" Highly recommended.

Giovannetti, _Max_. New York: Atheneum, 1977.

A series of comic-like line drawings cartoons featuring a hamster-like comedian. This book is far more appropriate for adults than for children. Some of the episodes are clever.

Goodall, John S., _The Adventures of Paddy Pork_. New York: Harcourt Brace and World, Inc., 1968.

Paddy Pork sets out to join the circus, encounters a wolf, is rejected by a circus family, and, like the prodigal, returns home. Each alternate page is a half-sheet. Recommended.

_____, _Ballooning Adventures of Paddy Pork_. New York: Harcourt Brace and World, Inc., 1969.

Paddy Pork, aloft in a balloon, spies a pig in distress and rescues it from some cannibal apes. During a storm the pigs falls out of the balloon cage and is rescued by some bears. Alternate sheets are half-pages. Appropriate for primary and lower intermediate pupils.

_____, An Edwardian Christmas. New York: Atheneum, 1978.

A charming description of events during an English upper class family's Christmas at the turn of the century. This wordless book is most appropriate for middle graders.

_____, An Edwardian Summer. New York: Atheneum, 1976.

This picture book attempts to present visual information about life during the 1901-1910 reign of King Edward in England. The scenes are loosely related to events in the daily life of a girl and boy. Recommended for middle graders.

_____, Jacko. New York: Harcourt Brace Jovanovich, Inc., 1971.

An organ grinder's monkey creates havoc wherever he goes. He and a parrot abandon a wrecked ship and find animal companions on a tropical island. Every alternate page is a half-sheet. For primary or intermediate use.

_____, The Midnight Adventures of Kelly, Dot, and Emeralda. New York: Atheneum Books, Inc., 1972.

A bear, mouse, and doll climb into a painting at midnight and have some harrowing adventures. Each alternate sheet is half-page.

_____, Naughty Nancy. New York: Atheneum, 1975.

A naughty mouse interferes in every imaginable way to the wedding of Mr. and Miss Mouse.

_____, Paddy's Evening Out. New York: Atheneum, 1973.

While attending the theatre, Paddy inadvertently becomes entangled in the on- and back-stage activities and eventually receives the audience's applause for his misadventures.

_____, Paddy Pork's Holiday. New York: Atheneum, 1976.

This book delightfully portrays the misadventures of Paddy Pork during his holiday outing. Highly recommended for primary use. Especially useful for building sequence skills.

_____, _Shrewbettina's Birthday_. New York: Harcourt Brace Jovanovich, Inc., 1970.

Shrewbettina has a busy day preparing for her birthday celebration. Half-pages are on alternate right-hand sheets. Recommended.

_____, _The Surprise Picnic_. New York: Atheneum, 1977.

A mother cat and her kittens encounter an hilarious series of harrowing experiences during a pleasure day at the beach. Alternate pages are one-half as wide as the adjacent sheets, and the watercolor illustrations on the abbreviated sheets fit nicely with both joining pages. Recommended for oral language development.

Hamberger, John, _A Sleepless Day_. New York: Scholastic Book Services, 1973.

Trying to find a safe place to sleep, an owl encounters a lot of problems before finding a fellow owl and safety in a heart-shaped tree cavity. Highly recommended.

Hartelius, Margaret A., _The Birthday Trombone_. Garden City, New York: Doubleday and Company, Inc., 1977.

A monkey receives a trombone for his birthday and promptly annoys all the jungle animals. After being forbidden to blow the trumpet, the monkey disobeys to protect the animals from a snake. Recommended.

_____, _The Chicken's Child_. Garden City, New York: Doubleday and Company, Inc., 1975.

A chicken hatches an alligator egg and then tries to keep the growing creature from destroying all of the farmer's property. Highly recommended.

Heller, Aaron, _Let's Take a Walk_. New York: Holt, Rinehart and Winston, Inc., 1963.

Although there are some words ("milk" on the milk-truck, "fire alarm" on the box), they do not detract from the picture story. Double-page pictures show different scenes along an 11-block highway through the city. Useful for teaching number sequence (the buildings are numbered 202, 204, 206, etc.) and for oral language descriptions of the activities.

Hoban, Tana, _Dig-Drill-Dump-Fill_. New York: William
   Morrow and Company, Inc., 1975.

This wordless book of photographs portrays heavy
machinery in action. The last three pages identify
the machines and provide brief descriptions of their
functions. Recommended for vocabulary development in
the middle grades.

_____, _Look Again_! New York: Macmillan Company, 1971.

This interestingly designed book has a two-inch
square cut out of the middle of every alternate
right-hand page. The "reader" can guess what the
full photograph portrays and then turn the page to
see a more complete picture. A similar photograph is
produced on the reverse side of the sheet. Details
include a zebra, snail, turtle, cut pear, and fish.
Appropriate and highly recommended for almost any
age.

Hogrogian, Nonny, _Apples_. New York: Macmillan
   Publishing Company, Inc., 1972.

Two-page illustrations depict various people and
animals picking and eating apples.

Hutchins, Pat, _Changes, Changes_. New York: Macmillan
   Publishing Company, Inc., 1971.

Two wooden dolls change building blocks to conform to
problems that confront them, such as a fire.

Krahn, Fernado, _April Fools_. New York: E.P. Dutton and
   Company, Inc., 1974.

This clever pen-and-ink illustrated book records the
adventures of two boys who make a monster's neck and
head out of a long board, cloth, and paint. They
proceed to display it in pieces such as the window of
a two-story house, a chimney, a river, and a tall
tree in the forest. After crowds comb the forest and
discover the hoax, the boys carry the "monster"
through the city streets in a parade. Appropriate
for use with primary and lower elementary pupils,
especially for developing oral language.

_____, A _Flying Saucer Full of Spaghetti_. New York: E.P. Dutton and Company, Inc., 1970.

Some elves see a poor woman sitting at an empty table and a rich girl being served some unwanted spaghetti. They fly the saucer of spaghetti across town to the hungry woman, shocking the onlookers in the streets. Recommended for primary and lower elementary use.

_____, _How Santa Claus Had a Long and Difficult Journey Delivering His Presents_. New York: Delacorte Press, 1970.

Santa experiences all sorts of problems when the traces of his sleigh break and his reindeer bound away. A delightful story that is highly recommended for oral language development.

_____, _Journeys of Sebastian_. New York: Delacorte Press, 1968.

A set of stories. In the first story a boy travels by bee-copter. In the second story a boy daydreams in front of a mirror that he is king. In the third a boy captures a monster, rides it to victory in a race, and watches as the monster disappears into the victor's cup.

_____, _Robot-Bot-Bot_. New York: E.P. Dutton, 1979.

A clever story about a homecoming present from daddy. The robot does wonderful things until the little girl destroys it. Then it plays havoc with the family until Daddy comes to the rescue. Highly recommended.

_____, _Who's Seen the Scissors?_ New York: E.P. Dutton and Company, Inc., 1975.

A tailor's scissors wreaks havoc as it flies through the air. Recommended.

Lunchbox Library Preprimer: Chicago: Science Research Associates, 1977.

Each of sixteen eight-page wordless books presents a simple plot. Topics include a magician's tricks (Poof), a tug-of-war (Tug), a knight and his marshmallows (Dragon), etc. Materials can be used as a source for dictated language-experience stories.

166

Maestro, Betty, and Gierlio Maestro, Busy Day: A Book of
   Action Words. New York: Crown Publishers, 1978.

   Each page has a picture and an "ing-word" identifying
   it. The words are not essential. There is no story,
   but the pictures reflect circus events. This book
   could be used as a series of Single Concept Cards.

Mayer, Mercer, Ah-Choo. Pine Brook, New Jersey: Dial
   Press, 1976.

   In one of his funniest books, Mayer portrays the
   hilarious events occurring during an elephant's
   sneezing fits. Highly recommended.

_____, A Boy, A Dog, and A Frog. New York: Dial Press,
   1967.

   A boy and his dog set out to fish but decide to
   capture a frog instead. They fail miserably, but
   delightfully, and the frog follows them home. Many
   pictures can be used for predicting outcomes. Highly
   recommended for primary or intermediate use.

_____, Bubble, Bubble. New York: Parent's Magazine
   Press, 1973.

   A boy blows bubbles with a magic mixture and creates
   animals that threaten him. Each time he creates an
   animal to protect him from the present danger, it
   turns on him. A cyclical story that is recommended
   for primary grades.

_____, Frog Goes to Dinner. New York: Scholastic Book
   Services, 1974.

   A boy with a frog hidden in his coat accompanies his
   family to a restaurant. The frog escapes and creates
   havoc by hopping into a salad, a glass of wine, and a
   clarinet. The frog and finally the family are tossed
   out of the restaurant. Appropriate for primary and
   intermediate grades.

_____, Frog on His Own. New York: Dial Press, 1973.

   The frog escapes from his owner and causes trouble
   wherever he goes. Some of the pages can be used for
   predicting outcomes. Appropriate for use with
   primary pupils.

_____, _Frog_, _Where_ _Are_ _You?_ New York: Dial Press, 1969.

A cute little story of a boy who loves his pet frog. The boy and his dog experience a number of hilarious episodes including being dumped by a deer into a stream where they find the frog. Many pictures can be used for predicting outcomes. Appropriate and highly recommended for primary or lower intermediate use.

_____, _The_ _Great_ _Cat_ _Chase_. New York: Four Winds Press, 1974.

Children in grown-ups' clothes chase a cat. Delightful and highly recommended.

_____, _Hiccup_. New York: Dial Press, 1976.

This book has two words: _hiccup_ and _boo_. A male hippopotamus takes a lady friend on a boat ride and mistreats her while trying to cure her case of the hiccups. Then he gets the hiccups and she gets revenge. Highly recommended.

_____, and Marianna Mayer, _One_ _Frog_ _Too_ _Many_. New York: Dial Press, 1975.

When a boy receives a pet frog, his regular frog becomes jealous and tries to get rid of the interloper. Highly recommended.

_____, _Two_ _More_ _Moral_ _Tales_. New York: Four Winds Press, 1974.

The first half of the book is entitled "Just a Pig at Heart." Turn the book over, and the first half of the other side is "Sly Fox's Folly." In one story two pigs spruce up for a party but "return to the earth" when their car becomes mired in mud. In the second tale a fox tries to cheat two women shoppers, but they discover the duplicity and retrieve their money. Highly recommended.

McMillan, Bruce, <u>Here</u> a <u>Chick</u>, <u>There</u> a <u>Chick</u>. New York: Lothrop, Lee, and Shepard Books, 1983.

Full-page photographs show a newly-hatched chick. Each page has a special concept word at the bottom, but one need not be able to read the word to follow the sequence of the story. Indeed, the child can often use the photographs to identify the words.

McNaught, Harry, <u>Trucks</u>. New York: Random House, 1976.

This is a different kind of wordless book. It has very thick pages with no plot, just scenes.

Meyer, Renate, <u>Hide-and-Seek</u>. New York: Bradbury Press, 1969.

Two children play hide-and-seek. Illustrations are in semi-psychedelic colors.

_____, <u>Vicki</u>. New York: Atheneum, 1969.

First printed in England, this book portrays children being accepted or rejected.

Mordillo, Guillermo, <u>The</u> <u>Damp</u> <u>and</u> <u>Daffy</u> <u>Doings</u> <u>of</u> a <u>Daring</u> <u>Pirate</u> <u>Ship</u>. Holland: Harlin Quist, Inc., 1971.

The title beautifully expresses the content of the story. After destroying one ship and slaying a water monster, the pirate ship sinks, and the crew begins rebuilding. Highly recommended.

Orgel, Doris, <u>Merry</u>, <u>Merry</u>, <u>FIBruary</u>. New York: Parents's Magazine Press, 1977.

This book contains a series of opposites that could occur only in February. The reader must possess much background information to understand this book. Examples: Aida, The Met, pistachio.

Peterson, John, <u>Tulips</u>. New York: Holt, Rinehart and Winston, Inc., 1963.

This science story portrays the life cycle of tulips from the time they are planted as bulbs in the fall until they bloom in the spring and finally "go underground" again. A two-page spread portrays each month's change in a family's activities and the tulip's growth as seen from a cross-sectional view beginning below ground level. Appropriate and recommended for primary pupils.

Pierce, Robert, <u>Look</u> <u>and</u> <u>Laugh</u>. New York: Golden Press, 1964.

A series of delightful sequence and predicting outcome pictures. Recommended.

Polushkin, Maria, <u>Who</u> <u>Said</u> <u>Meow</u>? New York: Crown Publishers, Inc., 1975.

A puppy encounters a number of unhappy experiences before learning that it was the cat that said <u>meow</u>. Recommended.

Richter, Mischa, <u>Quack</u>. New York: Harper and Row, Publishers, 1978.

A lovely duck quacks his way through a host of common animals trying to find another quacker. Although the animal sounds (bzzz, cock-a-doodle-do, etc.) are recorded in print, they can usually be identified by a youngster who associates the animals and their sounds. Recommended.

Schweninger, Ann, <u>A</u> <u>Dance</u> <u>for</u> <u>Three</u>. New York: Dial Press, 1979.

This book contains three stories. While the illustrations are delightful, the stories are quite sophisticated.

Shimin, Symeon, <u>A</u> <u>Special</u> <u>Birthday</u>. New York: McGraw-Hill Book Company, 1976.

Yards of ribbon surround a sleeping girl about to celebrate her birthday.

Simmons, Ellie, <u>Wheels</u>. New York: David McKay Company, Inc., 1969.

A little boy sees wheels used in many types of transportation.

Synder, Agnes, <u>The Old Man on the Block</u>. New York: Holt, Rinehart and Winston, Inc., 1964.

Some children invite a lonely old man to join them in their day's activities and brighten his life -- and theirs. Recommended for oral language development and for developing an appreciation of senior citizens.

Spier, Peter, <u>Noah's Ark</u>. Garden City, New York: Doubleday and Company, Inc., 1977.

A pictorial story of the Great Deluge, this book has a multitude of detail and subtle humor: the mule has to be forced into the ark, numerous rabbits leave the ark, and the snails are the last. Highly recommended for K-8. Older pupils might transform the events into Noah's diary.

Stoddard, Darrell, <u>The Hero</u>. Provo, Utah: Aro Publishing Company, 1974.

A little boy fails as a football and basketball player and a runner. Finally he rescues a drowning lad, carries him to the hospital, and becomes a hero. An "I Can Read Underwater Book" printed on waterproof paper. Recommended.

Tafuri, Nancy, <u>Early Morning in the Barn</u>. New York: Greenwillow Books, 1983.

A rooster crows, and three chicks wake up and survey the scenes of the barnyard. The only words are the animal sounds.

Turkle, Brinton, <u>Deep in the Forest</u>. New York: E.P. Dutton and Company, 1976.

A delightful reverse of <u>The Three Bears</u>, this story portrays a bear cub's visit to Goldilocks' home. Use it to consider the comprehension skill of compare/contrast. Highly recommended for primary grades.

171

Ueno, Noriko, <u>Elephant Buttons</u>. New York: Harper and Row, Publishers, 1973.

An elephant with buttons on its tummy springs apart, and a horse jumps out. Next a lion emerges, and the sequence follows until only a mouse is left. An elephant then appears to complete the cycle.

Ungerer, Tomi, <u>Snail, Where Are You</u>? New York: Harper and Row, Publishers, Inc., 1962.

A series of pictures, apparently without a plot.

Ward, Lynd, <u>The Silver Pony: A Story in Pictures</u>. Reston: Houghton Mifflin, Company, 1973.

A boy imagines himself flying over the world on a magic horse. Intended for middle graders.

Watson, Aldren A., <u>The River</u>. New York: Holt, Rinehart and Winston, Inc., 1963.

This book depicts scenes along a river in the wintertime. There is no plot beyond the river's meanderings.

Webber, Helen (ill.), <u>What is Sour? What is Sweet</u>? New York: Holt, Rinehart and Winston, Inc., 1967.

This book of opposites is based on a good idea, but the illustrations are inferior.

Wezel, Peter, <u>The Good Bird</u>. New York: Harper and Row, Publishers, 1964.

A bird befriends a goldfish.

Whitman, Tom, <u>The Helper</u>. New York: American Book Company, 1966.

A little girl goes to the store for her mother and experiences difficulty carrying the heavy bag of groceries. Good for developing sequencing skills.

_____, <u>I Did</u>. New York: American Book Company, 1966.

A dog throws a rock into a neighbor's house and, after seeing a boy get the blame, admits his act. Recommended.

_____, _Just_ _Ask_. New York: American Book Company, 1966.

A creature that tries to get into a group discussion finally learns that all he has to do is ask. Recommended.

_____, _Just_ Something. New York: American Book Company, 1966.

An animal with human attributes becomes scared while going home in the dark. Recommended.

_____, _Me_ First. New York: American Book Company, 1966.

A freckle-faced boy who wants to be first pushes his classmates and others out of the way and ends up playing by himself. Good for teaching patience and cooperation.

Wildsmith, Brian, _Brian_ Wildsmith's Circus. New York: Franklin Watts, Inc., 1970.

This book has one sentence, one-half on the first page and one-half on the last page. The pictures portray circus sights. Useful for dictating Single Concept Card Sentences or Language-Experience paragraphs.

Winter, Paula, _The_ Bear and the Fly. New York: Crown Publishers, Inc., 1976.

In an absolutely hilarious story, Papa Bear destroys his family and himself trying to kill a bee. At the end it calmly flies out the same window through which it entered. Highly recommended.

Wondriska, William, A Long Piece of String. New York: Holt, Rinehart and Winston, Inc., 1963.

A long piece of string goes from an alligator on the first page to a zipper on the last, with twenty-four other words, one for each letter of the alphabet, in between. This book could be used for teaching Single Concept Cards since the printed words are listed at the end of the book. Recommended.

DEVELOPING READING READINESS

PERCEPTUAL DEVELOPMENT

Introduction

Chapter 4A discussed procedures for developing six types of language skills. This chapter considers activities and strategies for the pre-reading skill of letter-name knowledge as well as for seven reading readiness skills related to perceptual development: visual discrimination and memory, left-to-right and top-to-bottom sequence, word boundaries, auditory memory and discrimination, and letter-sound associations (phonics). The final section presents some general guidelines for developing reading readiness skills.

Letter-Name Knowledge: A Pre-Reading Skill

Knowledge of letter-names is highly correlated with reading achievement (281, 741) and has been viewed by some as the best predictor of first-grade progress (71, 281, 282, 409, 445, 506).

While the ability to name the letters when they are presented is helpful in understanding instruction ("Today we're going to study the sound n stands for."), letter-name knowledge simply doesn't increase reading ability (494, 622). Careful thinking explains why this is true. The fact that a child can identify the letters h-a-r-p does not help him pronounce the word harp. Conversely, a child may very well recognize words without being able to identify the names of all of the letters. Thus by age three some children can recognize a number of words without knowing the name of a single letter.

While sitting at the typewriter one child pointed to the A and announced "That's Amy (a cousin)...That's Todd (another cousin)...That's Me-Ma (grandma)...That's King (a dog)." Shortly thereafter she began to note letters inside words. "There's a doughnut in Todd and snowman."

Aside from the fact that letter-name knowledge can facilitate beginning reading instruction, it is also associated with "growing up." We can, therefore, justify the inclusion of letter-name knowledge as a pre-reading skill. The following activities may prove helpful:

A. Use a game format to reinforce letter-name knowledge.
One possibility is "Say and Play," an original game with
directions for constructing and playing included below.
To construct the game:

1. Divide the outer edge of each side of a spirit
master into one-inch blocks. Model 4B-1 on the next page
demonstrates the concept in a condensed form.

2. Draw arrows on the inside of the rectangle of
blocks to show that pupils proceed clockwise.

3. Duplicate the necessary copies.

4. For the first copy, decide which letters
emphasize (e.g., c, m, t).

5. Record approximately twelve of each lower-case
letter in the various spaces, being careful to avoid an
obvious pattern. Print all letters so they appear
right-side up from the bottom edge of the board. (The
two players will sit side by side.)

6. Label each set to facilitate organization and
retrieval. For example, Set 1 might contain c, m, and t
while Set 2 presents b, r, and s. After eight such sets
of three, make four review sets with six letters each.
Then make two sets of twelve letters and finally one set
of twenty-four letters (omit o and x). Do the same thing
for the capital letters. Remember that the 30 sets made
thus far provide only one practice board of each type.
If you want more boards, you will need to duplicate more
forms.

7. Laminate the sheets.

8. Secure a die, two playing tokens, and five
markers to put in the bank.

Directions for playing Say and Play:

1. Pair children who are learning the three
letters.

2. Each person places a token on START before
rolling the die. The one with the higher number begins.
This means that children must be able to count dots up to
six.

MODEL 4B-1

SAY AND PLAY (enter model)

START	m	c	†	m	†	c	†
†							m
c							c
m	c	†	m	c	m	†	m

3. The first person rolls the die and moves his token from START the corresponding number of spaces if he can name the letters in each space he passes or reaches. For example, if he rolls a 3 and can name the first but not the second letter, he moves his token only to the first block. (If a child cannot identify the letter c, for example, he will be unable to move until he learns to identify it by listening to his partner's responses.)

4. The partner follows the same procedure.

5. As each youngster reaches or passes START, he takes a marker from the center of the board (the bank).

6. The first person to accumulate three markers wins.

Notes: (1) A person may not "correct" himself. His first answer is the official one. (2) This activity works well only if both children are learning the particular letters being emphasized. (3) Print each letter and record its name on a Language Master card. When children are not sure of the name of the letter or when they are using Say and Play as a self-instructional activity, they can run the card through the Language Master and receive the desired information.

B. Using the Language Master, record expressions that involve letters. Print the emphasized letters just above the sound track. Thus separate cards can be prepared for a majority of the letters of the alphabet, including the most common letters.

Letter	Record	Print
A, B, C	(Singing) A, B, C	A-B-C
B	I saw a BB gun.	B-B
E, I, O	(Singing) Old MacDonald Had a Farm E-I-E-I-O	E-I-E-I-O
J	JJ is a TV star.	J-J
K, O	It's okay with me.	O-K
B, E, I, L	(Singing) The B-i-b-l-e	B-i-b-l-e
M	May I have an M & M?	M-M
N, O	The answer is No, N-O.	N-O
B, C, N	The television station is NBC.	N-B-C
P, A	I work at the A and P	A-P
A, P, T	Mother is going to PTA.	P-T-A
A, P	We shop at the A & P.	A & P
A, S, U	I live in the USA.	U-S-A
TV	I saw the show on TV.	T-V
T	Who wore a T-shirt?	T
W	We listen to W-_____ on the radio.	W-_____
X	There's an X-mark on my paper.	X
X	They took an X-ray of my arm.	X

A, C, M, Y   We went swimming at   Y-M-C-A
                the YMCA (or YWCA).

Letters not included above are D, F, G, H, Q, R, and
Z. To use these materials, you might consider the
following strategies:

   1. After presenting lessons on letters A, B, and C
(for example), ask children to take the first Language
Master card, look at the letters, and say them. The
children can then play the card to receive feedback.

   2. An alternate procedure is to play the card (which
sings A, B, C) and show the children the letters A, B,
and C printed on the card. Later the children can try to
identify the letters and receive feedback.

   3. Wherever possible, paste clue-providing pictures
on the Language Master card. For instance, paste a
picture of a gun on the B-B card, a farmer on the E-I-O
card, etc.

C. Encourage children to teach each other the letters of
their own names. As soon as a child knows the letters of
his name, he can play teacher. For example, Ginger
Culyer has twelve letters, two of which (e, r) are
duplicates. (The G, g appears in two forms. Since
Ginger can name the letters, she can display individual
letters and tell them to a friend. The names of her
cousins, Amy and Todd Hatley, Rodney Floyd, and Jan and
Danny Blake have 5, 6, 4, 4, and 4 different letters or
letter forms, respectively. Each person is thus in a
position to share information with his partner.

D. A more systematic strategy for teaching children the
names of letters requires some special preparation. The
following steps are involved:

   1. On spirit masters print the upper- and lower-case
letters in blocks one-inch square or larger. To avoid
letter confusions (b-p, for instance), draw a heavy line
at the bottom of each block. Duplicate them on
construction paper with upper- and lower-case letters on
different colors. If possible, laminate the individual
letters. An alternative strategy is to have letters made
on more durable material by a print shop.

   2. Make a separate set of letters on a third color.
This is your set.

3. Give one copy of each set of letters (a total of 52) to each child. The materials can be stored in a cigar box, greeting card box, etc. (Alternately, distribute just the letters to be used in the lesson.)

4. Select an unknown letter in a child's name (for example, C in Culver). Begin with letters having the same upper- and lower-case forms (c, o, p, s, v, w, x, and z). Later proceed to letters that are quite similar (f, j, k, l, m, n, t, u, and y). Finally introduce letters that are somewhat different (a, b, d, e, g, h, i, q, and r). Save low-frequency letters for later (x and z, for instance).

The following instructional strategies are recommended.

PHASE ONE

1. Give each child three letter forms with diverse shapes (c, p, w, for instance).

2. Using the key shape (or a larger shape, depending on how many children are present), trace the key letter (c) with your forefinger, saying the letter name.

3. Ask each child to trace your key letter with his forefinger, saying the letter name. Be sure the child's finger comes into continuous contact with the letter.

4. Ask each child to match your key letter (c) with one of his letter forms. He should say, "This is a c, and this is a c. Note that this activity involves visual discrimination.)

PHASE TWO

1. Give each child three letter forms with similar shapes (c, G, and e, for instance).

2. Using the key shape, trace the key letter (c).

3. Ask each child to trace and say your key letter.

4. Ask each child to match your key letter with his, saying, "This is a C, and this is a c."

PHASE THREE

    1. Give each child a set of Language Master cards with <u>c</u> and the foil letters (p, w, G, and e) printed on them. The child should say either "This is a <u>c</u>." or "This is not a <u>c</u>." The child should then play the card to get feedback.

    2. (Alternate) Give each child a newspaper. Ask him to trace the <u>c's</u>, saying, "Here is a <u>c</u>."

E. Read Leonard Kessler's <u>Ghosts</u> <u>and</u> <u>Crows</u> <u>and</u> <u>Things</u> <u>with</u> <u>O's</u> (New York: Scholastic, 1976). This book portrays and identifies words that need <u>o's</u> and objects that need circles. Examples of the former include dog, frog, hog, and log; examples of the latter are baseball, ball, eye glasses, or a watch.

F. Use the Tic-Tac-Toe Board format. Either draw large boards with a pen and ruler or reproduce the model on a spirit master and laminate the copies. On a die print three letters twice each. Each child will then roll a die, and, if he can identify the letter name, place either an <u>X</u> or an <u>O</u> on the Tic-Tac-Toe board. The child who cannot name the letter forfeits his turn. His partner then rolls, and the game continues until someone completes a row of three. Many of the comments on Say and Play also apply here, for the intent is to provide another way of reinforcing the same letter-name knowledge. Additional dice can be made for other letters, both upper and lower case.

G. Use a Bingo format (called Letto) to reinforce letter-name knowledge. Construct the model with either 16 spaces (4X4) or 25 spaces (5X5). In a first set of 16 or 25 use a 1-2-3-1-2-3 pattern working from left to right and top to bottom as shown in Models 2 and 3. Do not allow "diagonals" or "corners" to win. Notice that the Bingo rules do not apply; only the format is used. There is no caller, and the object is to complete a horizontal or vertical row in a set of 16 or 25. The basic directions follow:

    The first child (as determined by a roll of a die) names a letter, and if, not challenged by his partner (notice: not his opponent), places a contruction paper taken from the color he has chosen for the activitiy over <u>one</u> space containing that letter. The partner does the children continue until someone completes a row or column.

MODEL 2   MODEL 3

(16-space Letto)   (25-space Letto)

c	g	e	m	n
e	m	n	c	g
n	c	g	e	m
g	e	m	n	c
m	n	c	g	e

c	m	t	c
m	t	c	m
t	c	m	t
c	m	t	c

Notice that Letto is the sixth type of reinforcement on exactly the same letter. Remember also that these activities can be adapted for other learnings. To be of maximum value, however, the materials should be

1. developed and sequenced to cover the range of information. Thus one set of three letters ignores the remaining 23 letters.

2. cumulated to include increasingly larger amounts of information. Thus letters may be grouped first in 3's with nine sets, then in 6's with four or five sets, then in 13's with two sets, and finally in 26's with one set.

3. labeled to facilitate housing

4. indexed on one sheet to make the selection process less cumbersome

5. laminated to keep them neat

H. Use the full letter-name value concept proposed by Donald D. Durrell (278) and incorporated into Sound Start, a program developed with Helen Murphy.
    The idea is to associate the name of a letter with a word whose sounds contain the letter name. We prefer the following words:

181

Letter	Word	Letter	Word
A, a	apron, acorn	N, n	envelope
B, b	beaver	O, o	okra, oval
C, c	ceiling	P, p	peas (arrow pointing to a pea)
D, d	deer	Q, q	
E, e	eagle	R, r	arm
F, f	Effie	S, s	Eskimo
G, g	genie	T, t	tea
H, h		U, u	uniform
I, i	icicle	V, v	veal
J, j	jail	W, w	
K, k	Kay (name the girl Kay)	X, x	X-mark
L, l	elephant	Y, y	
M, m	M and M's	Z, z	zebra

One procedure follows:

1. Prepare cards showing the pictures (or suitable alternatives). Each card should contain a picture large enough for small-group use. At the bottom of the card record the key letters to which the picture is related. Thus the picture of an acorn or apron will appear above a capital and small a.

2. Teach the children to identify the pictures. Some objects will be well known (i.e., arm, apron). Others will be unfamiliar (i.e., genie, okra).

3. Explain to the children that the letters at the bottom of the cards are in the picture shown above them. Thus, the first part of apron is /a/. Below the apron are A and a.

In the cases of f, l, m, n, s, and x the first sound is really /e/, but the letter name is the part that stands out. In elephant, for instance, the first part of

182

the word is /el/; thus the letters at the bottom are called 1's.

4. Pronounce the first word (apron, if you proceed in order) and emphasize the a. Ask, "What is this letter (and pointing to the Big A)? ...Right. And this one (pointing to the little a)? ...How do you know they're both A?" (because they're the first part of apron)

5. As children are ready, proceed to b. Then review a and b before introducing c. Review all three before going to d.

I. On a sheet of 8-1/2 x 11 inch paper, print or primary type the letters of the alphabet in random order. On the top one-half of the page, list the lower-case letters. Record the capitals on the bottom one-half of the sheet. Duplicate the sheets so every child can have one. If so, lamination is desirable.

While the child identifies the letters using your copy, use a grease pencil to record errors by circling the items on the child's copy. The child then knows the letters which he should study and, until the marks are erased, you have an individualized record of each youngster's study materials. Note that older children can be used to identify children's needs and growth in competence. For that matter any youngster who has already been checked off can teach or "test" another child. Several observations seem appropriate at this point:

1. Many children express keen interest in learning to print their own names. While this involves handwriting rather than reading, there is nevertheless a relationship. Be sure the letters which children first print (except for the first letter of a name) are the lower-case (small) letters. Many children come to school printing their names in capitals. The teacher must then reteach. Being able to print the small letters is far more important than knowing how to make the capital letters.

2. Letter-name knowledge consists of two levels: (a) recognizing the letter when someone names it and (b) naming a letter at sight. The first stage is easier than the second.

3. The fact that a child can sing the alphabet song (A through Z) does not mean he "knows" the alphabet. A

183

child does not "know" the alphabet until he can name the letters when presented randomly in print.

4. There is great variation in children's ability to learn to recognize the letters. In one study using a variety of activities and learning modalities, one child required 53 practices to master recognition of the letter b (679).

5. Some research suggests that the "critical skill in beginning reading is not knowledge of letter names but rather the ability to recognize and discriminate graphemes (494:114-115)." It may very well be that the relationship between letter-name knowledge and first-grade achievement is derived from a third factor -- family background.

Activities for developing reading readiness skills related to perception comprise the next sections of this chapter.

1. Visual Discrimination

Insofar as reading readiness is concerned, visual discrimination refers to the ability to recognize visual differences and likenesses in letters and words. It is to be distinguished from visual acuity, which merely refers to the ability to see.

Screening for visual acuity should involve a device such as Ortho-rater or Telebinocular. Unfortunately, schools and some general practioners still use the Snellen eye chart. However, that test "does not measure the clearness of vision at reading distance. Since there is little relationship between acuity at far-point and near-point, it is quite possible for children to pass the Snellen test and yet experience considerable difficulty in dealing with the printed page. A person, for example, may have good far-point acuity and poor near-point acuity. Thus the test by the Snellen tells the examiner nothing about an individual's ability to perform in school at a desk, or in industry in near-point tasks (667:368). In summary, "Continued use of the Snellen test in school vision screening tests is indefensible (667:371)." Peters (565) and Rosen (599) concur.

Visual acuity is not directly related to visual discrimination. Thus a person may have excellent acuity but poor discrimination. In such cases, visual discrimination activities should be provided.

We cannot stress too strongly the importance of using letters and words rather than geometric shapes or pictures (91, 123, 260, 351, 599, 623). Research has long indicated that visual discrimination of letters and words is more valuable than non-letter and picture shapes (41), for instruction in the latter has little effect on reading achievement (134, 599). Muehl and King (528) point out in their summary of the research that there is little or no transfer from discrimination of picture and geometric shapes to letters and words, perhaps because, as Gates (336) demonstrated, the correlations among perception of numbers, geometric symbols, and printed words average only .35.

Fortunately many youngsters develop visual discrimination abilities rather early. Paradis (556) found that 69% of 128 preschoolers and 97% of 440 middle socio-economic status kindergarten children scored 90% or higher on a measuring device featuring visual discrimination of pictures, letters, and words. Pictures and letters were rated easy; words presented moderate difficulty. With 118 lower socio-economic kindergarten children who had received no formal readiness training, Mitchell (518) found that 85% scored at least 75% on ten out of twelve pages of visual discrimination exercises. The remaining two pages dealt with picture discrimination.

A. Ask the children to select lower-case letters that correspond to a key letter. Begin with exercises using two or three choices which are considerably dissimilar in appearance.

o || m   o   t

Progress to exercises with four or five letters or numerals that are similar.

b || b   d   p   b   q   9

B. Using the procedure described above, ask pupils to work with exercises involving upper-case letters.

C. As shown next list the same five or six letters in two columns on a spirit master. Ask pupils to draw lines connecting the identical pairs. Proceed from lower-case letters to upper-case letters.

a	d
b	c
c	e
d	a
e	f
f	b

D. At a later stage, ask the children to work with upper- and lower-case letters. The easier level will involve letters with identical (C, c) or similar (Y, y) forms for both cases. The harder level will involve letters with different forms (B, b) for the two cases.

E. Develop a practice sheet for discrimination of each letter form. Forty-two exercises are needed, one for each of the keys contained in Chart 4B-1. Using a primary typewriter, type words containing at least ten of the key letters and at least five each of letters with similar visual characteristics. Chart 4B-1 suggests a possible composition for each exercise.

CHART 4B-1

RECOMMENDED COMPONENTS FOR EACH
PRACTICE EXERCISE FOR
VISUAL MEMORY AND DISCRIMINATION

Key	Ten words with	Five words each with
A	A	H, V, N
a	a	e, o, d, g
B	B	b, D, P, E, R, p, 8
b	b	d, h, p, q, B, P, 6, 9
C	C or c	G, Q, Q, U, e
D	D	B, O, P
d	d	a, b, g, p, q, 6, 9
E	E	F, M, W, 3

186

e	e	a, c, g, o
F	F	E, M, P, T
f	f	j, r, J
G	G	C, O, Q
g	g	a, b, d, e, p, q, 6, 8, 9
H	H	H, I, K, N, V, Z
h	h	b, d, k, n, y
I	I	E, F, H, J, L, T, Z
i	i	j, l
J	J	I, P, f, 7
j	j	b, d, f, i, q, r, y, P
K	K or k	E, F, H, T, Y, h, t, w, x, y
L	L	E, I, T, h, 7
l	l	i, t, 7
M	M	E, F, N, W, 3
m	m	n, u, w, 3
N	N	A, H, M, V, W, Z
n	n	h, m, re, u
O	O or o	C, D, U, a, e, o
P	P or p	B, D, E, J, b, d, g, q, 6, 9
Q	Q	C, G, O, g
q	q	a, d, g, p, 6, 8, 9
R	R	A, B, F, H, P
r	r	f, n, t, u

S	S or s	Z, g, 5
T	T	E, F, I, J, L, 7
t	t	f, k, l, r, w, y
U	U or u	C, O, m, n, r
V	V or v	A, H, N, W, X, Y, Z, y
W	W or w	E, K, M, N, V, X, Y, w, m, 3
X	X or x	K, V, Y, t, w, y, 4
Y	Y	K, T, V, X, t, 4
y	y	h, j, t, v, w, x, 4
Z	Z or z	H, I, N, V, s, 2, 5, 7

In the first set (A) the ten words with A and the five words each with H, V, N may contain those letters in any position, not just the first letter. Duplicate the material so pupils can use it after receiving instruction involving a particular letter.

F. Ask the children to identify letters identical to those you display. They should choose the letters and hold them up (stomach high). One way to provide the materials to first-graders is to duplicate the upper- and lower-case letters on construction paper, separate with a paper cutter, and distribute a complete set to each child. Each youngster can store his materials in a cigar box (greeting card box, oatmeal container, etc.).

A better (although more costly procedure) is to persuade a high school print shop to prepare sets of upper- and lower-case letters for each child. These letters, which should conform to the manuscript guide used in the school, can be printed on tagboard or some other durable material. A good size is between 1-1/2 and 2 inches square.

Begin by giving pupils two or three letters such as those identified in Activity A. After explaining directions, present one letter and ask the pupils to display an identical letter. After follow-through, present one of the other letters. This activity can be simple or complex depending upon the number of letters each child has and the extent to which they are visually similar. For very young children you will probably prefer to have someone collect the letters after each practice. Each person should collect a different letter and thus receive some additional practice.

G. Using duplicated worksheets, ask the children to identify words identical to those you display. These worksheets can be prepared by making a spirit master of selected words, producing it on construction paper, and then cutting the words apart so each child in the group has a set appropriate for his needs. Be sure to progress from gross to fine distinctions.

Discrimination	Key	Words			
Gross	run	jump	play	run	tall
Finer	run	rust	rug	run	rub
Fine	run	runs	run	ran	rung

An alternate strategy is to list the key word on the worksheet itself. The sheet then can be used as an independent activity following instruction.

H. Once again using duplicated exercises, present two columns of words which are placed in random order. Ask the children to draw lines from words in one column to the same words in a second column. Do not use more than six words in a column.

I. Ask the pupils to make cut-and-paste lists of words which begin like a key word or which contain the key letter. Words to be cut and pasted (or traced or copied, depending upon pupil proficiency) can be class-oriented items (i.e., names of pupils, class signs) or words contained in materials intended for subsequent instructional use.

2. Visual Memory

Visual memory refers to the ability to remember information presented through the visual, or seeing, channel. Children need a high degree of visual memory in order to retain the printed information they see. A study by Arthur Gates (338) of first-grade pupils found that the average number of repetitions for pupils to learn words in reading varied according to intelligence.

Thus youngsters with I.Q.'s between 120 and 129 needed an average of 20 repetitions while children with I.Q.'s between 70 and 79 needed an average of 50 repetitions per word.

Some authorities consider visual memory and discrimination activities together because the areas are so interdependent. We prefer to consider the topics separately. The following activities can be used to develop visual memory.

A. Display a letter with readily identifiable visual characteristics. An example is o. Ask pupils to study it carefully for five seconds. Then remove the visual stimulus and ask the pupils to locate and circle a similar letter in the newspaper headlines or on a spirit master.

B. Do the same with other letters, beginning with letters that are identical or almost identical in their upper- and lower-case forms. Examples include c, k, o, p, s, v, w, x, and z. Later present letters whose shapes differ depending on their case.

C. Display a letter and, after removing it, ask pupils to locate a similar letter in the newspaper, cut it out, and attach it with a clothes pin to their Every-Pupil Response (EPR) cards. They should then display their EPR cards for teacher feedback. (The card can be a 4x6 inch card or a piece of pasteboard.)

D. Display a word, preferably in the sequence presented below (with each of the stages requiring one or more sessions).

> concrete noun (one that can be
> represented pictorially)

> abstract noun (one that cannot be
> represented pictorially)

> action verb

> "glue" word (the, with, to, of, etc.)

Select words from the reading material to be used by the pupils. That is, use the locally-relevant sight-word list (158, 159). Ask pupils to study carefully the words you present for five seconds. Then remove the visual stimulus and ask the pupils to locate and circle the same word in the newspaper headlines. Be sure the word is actually in the newspaper. Note: Excellent newspapers for children include those published by Scholastic and Xerox. Otherwise-useless worksheets can be substituted for newspapers.

E. An alternate way of developing material is to type or print the word on a spirit master. If the sheets are not laminated, pupils might place Mason jar rings or lids over the appropriate words.

F. Display a word, remove it, and ask pupils to locate the same word in the newspaper or on the spirit master, cut it out, and attach it to their EPR cards. After they display their cards, provide the pupils with feedback information.

G. Place several Single Concept Cards on objects (picture side down) on the ledge of a chalkboard. Ask pupils to study the items. When they close their eyes, remove the data and ask the children to replace them, perhaps in the correct sequence.

H. Provide a spirit master with letters for pupils to trace. Provide crayons or standard size pencils for pupils to use. There is no need for the thick pencil that is so unwieldy for little hands to grasp. Nor do young children use such monstrosities at home; they learn with regular pens and pencils -- until they enter school.

I. Any activity that requires pupils to attend to letters or print is likely to facilitate the development of visual memory. Thus asking pupils to trace, copy from a model, or copy from memory can add a kinesthetic component to assist in the memory process. The latter option requires the greatest amount of visual memory. Note that tracing should involve either the finger (309) or a pencil, pen, magic marker, etc., in contact with a printing surface. Tracing in the air is of dubious value.

Illustrate on the chalkboard the direction(s) in which the letter should be printed. Thus, a b begins with a vertical stem. The circle begins at 2:00 and goes counter-clockwise. For d, the circle is produced before the stem. The pupil traces the letter three times. (While a larger number of tracing experiences is needed for manuscript practice, the purpose of this activity is simply to focus on the visual form of the letter.)

A somewhat more difficult activity involves asking the child to copy the letter from a model. This second stage should be done on lined paper since letters do not exist suspended in mid-air. They occupy positions relative to horizontal lines. At the third stage the child copies the letter without looking at the model during the copying practice.

J. Ask pupils to copy the letters you name during a finger painting session. Children can look at a model and make the letter until they are ready to do so when the model is removed. It is worth noting that retention of visual forms rather than copying per se is the crucial emphasis, for one need not be able to copy in order to learn to read (409).

3. Left-to-Right Sequence

Because the English language is written from left to right, it is important for pupils to develop eye movements which follow the desired directional path. This left-to-right progression is an important reading readiness skill (249, 712). Unfortunately, many children entering school don't know that print moves from left to right (503). Several activities can help pupils acquire this habit.

A. When pupils underline letters, words, or pictures or when they draw horizontal lines, be sure they proceed from left to right. The eyes naturally move in the same direction that the line is drawn. This comment also applies to board-work.

B. When presenting sequence pictures, begin with those whose characters face to the right. This facial posture helps move children's eyes in the same direction.

C. When teaching a child to print his name, position his hand at the left side of the paper. This leaves the child no choice but to move to the right. Spaces for a child to record his name and date on worksheets should also be provided at the left rather than the right.

D. When using dot-to-dot exercises from left to right, use several arrows to show the directional progression.

E. When pupils count objects in a row (five trains, for example) help them to count from left to right. As you demonstrate on the board, move your hand from left to right, touching or pointing to each object in turn.

F. When reading to children for the purpose of teaching left-to-right progression, move your hand in a fluid motion from left to right. Follow the same procedure when reading captions accompanying pictures, cartoon comments, statements on cereal boxes, etc.

G. When pupils name letters of the alphabet or numerals, be sure they proceed from left to right.

4. Top-to-Bottom Sequence

Likewise children must learn to read print from the top of a page to the bottom (712). Some helpful activities follow:

A. Many pupils use line markers while working with preprimers or language-experience stories on spirit masters. For young children the use of a line marker is quite acceptable if it covers print above rather than below the line being read. The reason for not covering print below that being read is that the child is obliged to stop after each line to readjust the marker. This constant interruption certainly doesn't contribute to story retention or rate of reading, especially when sentences are continued on second lines. Note that a marker placed above the top line of print can be forgotten when it is no longer needed, for the following lines are already exposed to the child.

B. When pupils are asked to count two or more rows of objects, help them to count from left to right in the first row before counting in the second (and subsequent) rows. Unless the objects are clearly grouped in columns, pupils should go across and then down.

C. Make a poster with four rows and four columns of pictures. Ask pupils to name the pictures from left to right and from top to bottom. Do the same with letters.

D. Using a spirit master, make four rows and four columns. Ask each pupil to name the pictures in left-to-right and top-to-bottom order to his partner. The partner then does the same thing.

E. Assign duties to several children and place a sentence and a picture, and a name on a sentence strip holder. For example:

Name	Sentence	Picture
Jeff	Jeff will feed the fish.	fish
Cathy	Cathy will take care of the books.	books
Lee	Lee will get the milk.	milk
Karen	Karen will take out the ball.	ball

Each morning provide practice as a guide to some of the day's activities. Jeff can try to "read" his assignment, noting that it has something to do with fish. After the first week the idea will be memorized.

Cathy should read the next line. Lee and then Karen follow. Point out the fact that the print is read from the top to the bottom. On the next morning ask if Lee is supposed to read first. Why not?

5. Word Boundaries

Research indicates kindergarten and first-grade children often do not know where one printed word stops and another word begins (125, 412, 473, 503, 584). In many cases they divide words between the tall letters rather than at the white space or at the ends of stressed words. Failure to recognize the role of space in separating words makes it difficult for children to learn to recognize sight words and to apply phonics instruction. Furthermore, children also experience difficulty in segmenting oral language (412). In a study of sixty classrooms, Durrell and Murphy found, with few exceptions, that "children could easily repeat sentences of at least six words and enjoyed doing so. It became equally obvious that few children could match words in oral sentences with words in printed sentences (281:388)." McNinch's (510) study found that the ability to discriminate boundaries of oral words was a readiness factor associated with later reading success. The following activities may help pupils distinguish visual and oral boundaries.

A. Ask pupils to select crayons of their favorite color and draw circles around each word in the headlines of a newspaper.

B. Ask pupils to take a paintbrush and paint lines between the words in newspaper headlines. Begin with headlines which have two words each on two lines. Eventually move to streamers which may have 8-10 words on a line.

C. Give pupils a copy of one page of a newspaper and ask them to cut out each word in the headlines and paste it on a sheet of paper.

D. If pupils can count, ask them to tell how many words there are in the title of a story ("The Three Little Pigs") or a sentence from a language-experience story or chart showing class responsibilities.

E. Using a nursery rhyme ("Jack Sprat") or song ("Three Blind Mice"), ask pupils to count the number of words as you and they say each line. Young children tend to either tap on their tables, chairs, or hands or touch their lips or foreheads with their fingers as they decide how many words have been said. An excellent rhyme to use at the beginning is "One, Two, Buckle My Shoe." Only two words (buckle, seven) have more than one syllable.
This activity can be handled either of two ways. One is to have pupils tap or tell the number of words. (Clapping is also helpful -- and fun. On a rainy day rabbit hopping can release tensions.) A second way is to give pairs of pupils a duplicated sheet containing the print. Use directions similar to these:

1. Ask the children to cover the page with a large marker.

2. Say the first line ("One, Two").

3. Ask pupils to hold up the number of fingers that tells how many words you said.

4. Ask pupils to slide the marker down (in this activity) and count the number of words in the same phrase. They should arrive at the same answer.

5. Ask pupils to circle the words or draw a line between them.

6. Proceed with additional lines, repeating if necessary.

F. Say a sentence. Ask pupils to say one word at a time. If necessary, say the sentence one word at a time as the pupils repeat it in the same way. Remember that young children do not necessarily know what a word is when they enter school. Also, they may not understand other relevant concepts such as beginning and ending of words. Stott (690) found that slow learners at ages 9-11 didn't necessarily know what sounds were. McDonnel and

195

Osburn (503) note that many children come to school not knowing that words and letters aren't the same.

6. Auditory Memory

This term refers to a person's ability to remember information presented through the auditory, or hearing, channel. Children need a high degree of auditory memory to retain information they hear. Research findings indicate that children vary in their rate of development of auditory memory (522). Some studies have found auditory memory and discrimination to be one of the best predictors of first-grade reading success (263, 579, 671).

Some of the following activities are closely related to the preceding topics, especially listening. This is to be expected since listening is an auditory skill.

A. Name a number of items. Ask children to name as many of them as they can. At first these items should be related to each other (all toys or games, for instance). Later they can be either unrelated or reflect two or three topics.

B. Use the "I Went to Town" technique in Chapter 4A.

C. At the end of the day, ask pupils what they have learned. Since much of their information is acquired auditorily, children should be able to mention a number of specific items. This also serves as good public relations for those parents whose first question to their returning youngsters -- "What did you learn today?" -- is sometimes sloughed off with a terse, "Nothing."

D. Ask children to retell a story told or read aloud by someone else. This activity is also related to the comprehension skill of sequencing. Example:

Barber, Martha, The Funny Old Man and the Funny Old Woman. New York: Holt, 1963.

Jack and the Beanstalk

Zemach, Margot, It Could Always Be Worse. New York: Farrar, Straus and Giroux, 1976.

F. Ask children to deliver oral rather than written messages. (Miss Fuddy says we will have twenty-four children and two adults for lunch today.) Before they leave on the errand, ask pupils to repeat the message to you. You may find some youngsters who cannot "remember" from one minute to another.

G. Read or say a short catchy poem or riddle or sing a song. Ask who can repeat it verbatim. Normally several repetitions of the item will be necessary. Also useful here are nursery rhymes, since many educationally disadvantaged youngsters have never been exposed to them.

Examples include:

"Jack and Jill"

"The Purple Cow" (Nash)

"Sequel to 'The Purple Cow'" (Nash)

H. Tape short selections on a Voxcom Card Reader (Tapecon, Inc.). Draw or paste a picture on the card to identify the content. For example, use a picture of old Bessy for "The Purple Cow." Children who need more repetitions can insert the appropriate card and talk along with your voice until they can do it.

I. When pupils are not sure what to do next, ask them rather than tell them. Example: The teacher notes that John is not at the appropriate center. Ask, "John, where should you be?" rather than say, "John, you should be in the listening center." Or when Cathy finishes her first assignment and then proceeds to do nothing, ask, "Cathy, what are you supposed to do next?" rather than, "Cathy, you're supposed to cut these four pictures apart and paste them in the right order."

J. Use a game format to develop auditory memory with the alphabet. Between two and four pupils can play at one time. The younger or slower pupil always starts first. An adult is necessary to keep score. Many young children enjoy the activity without the scoring component.

1. Using the "I'm going to town and take a format, he says the sentence and adds a word starting with a. For this he receives one point.

2. The same child then repeats the sentence with a and b. For this he receives two points.

3. When he misses, his partner has a chance to try starting at the point of the miss.

By the time the item starts with m̲, a correct series of responses is worth 13 points. The game stops at 50 points.

Jan		Danny		Notes
Score	Cum.	Score	Cum.	Danny starts the game.
		1		Danny does (a).
		2	3	Danny does (a) and (b).
		3	6	Danny does (a)-(c).
		4	10	Danny does (a)-(d).
		5	15	Danny does (a)-(e).
		6	21	Danny does (a)-(f).
				but misses (a)-(g).
7				Jan does (a)-(g).
8	15			Jan does (a)-(h).
9	24			Jan does (a)-(i).
				Etc.

7. Auditory Discrimination

Auditory discrimination (AD) refers to the ability to note differences and likenesses in sounds. As related to reading, AD relates to the ability to note differences and likenesses in speech sounds. It is not to be confused with auditory acuity, which simply refers to the ability to hear. A person with perfect auditory acuity may have very poor AD.

A number of writers and researchers have noted that auditory abilities are sometimes not fully developed until age eight or nine (522, 570, 704, 733). Wepman notes, for example:

> Some children, either innately or through very early experiences, develop their auditory abilities at an early age. They begin to speak early and progress rapidly through the acquisition of sounds...With other children, however, auditory perception develops at a

slower rate...the auditory functions develop
during the first three years of school
(733:56).

Still later he observes:

    In some instances normal development of
auditory discrimination takes place before
school age, while in other children it is not
accomplished until the eighth year. If auditory
discrimination is slow to develop, the ability
to learn to read through the sound-approach is
understandably lessened (733:58).

McGovern's survey of the literature on auditory
perception found "a direct relationship between auditory
perception ability and reading ability (505:451)."
Several research reports indicate the relationship
between poor AD and poor readers in the general
population. For instance, Poling (570) administered an
AD test to a group of first graders and obtained reading
achievement scores at the end of their first and second
years in school. She reported that pupils with poor AD
did not achieve as well in reading as did their peers
with good AD.
Morency (522) conducted a three-year study of the
development of AD and its relationship to the reading
achievement of 179 children. She noted that AD and
auditory memory were significantly correlated with
reading achievement at the end of each of the three years
of the study. Cohen (134) found that AD was essential to
reading success regardless of ethnic or socio-economic
background. However, both he and Deutsch (247) found
variations by socio-economic levels. It would seem
highly desirable, therefore, to provide specific
instruction and practice in developing AD (522,670,733).
Spache advises, "In the absence of hearing losses which
make discrimination of speech sounds impossible, poor
auditory discrimination may often be treated like any
other under-developed skill and improved by appropriate
teaching (670:305)."

Throughout this section two other key terms will be
used. Gross discrimination refers to speech sounds that
differ considerably. Hence the /b/ (read as b sound) is
grossly different from the /m/, /j/, and /k/. Gross
distinctions are easier for children to perceive than are
minimal contrasts. The minimal contrasts, or fine
distinctions, involve speech sounds that are rather close

199

in sound. Thus the /b/ is often confused with the /p/. Insofar as consonant sounds are concerned, we include the following as examples of minimal contrasts. Beside each is an example. (Diagonal lines enclose speech sounds.)

1.	/b/-/p/	bat-pat	6.	/j/-/ch/	gyp-chip
2.	/k/-/g/	cave-gave	7.	/m/-/n/	meal-kneel
3.	/ch/-/sh/	chew-shoe	8.	/s/-/z/	sue-zoo
4.	/d/-/t/	do-to	9.	/h/-/ /	heel-eel
5.	/f/-/v/	few-view			

A note of explanation is in order. The /h/ may be contrasted with no sound. The British frequently speak this way. Note that in the final position, there is no /h/. A final /f/-/th/ distinction is not shown here since it appears infrequently.

Minimal contrasts for vowels are less clearly identifiable. We include the following sounds and examples:

1.	/a/-/ou/	rat-route	9.	/ar/-/o/	cart-cot
2.	/e/-/i/	bed-bid	10.	/er/-/eer/	bird-beard
3.	/i/-/ē/	ship-sheep	11.	/or/-/ar/	porch-parch
4.	/o/-/ī/	lock-like	12.	/air/-/er/	hair-her
5.	/u/-/oo/	buck-book	13.	/aw/-/o/	yawn-yon
6.	/ā/-/e/	gate-get	14.	/oi/-/aw/	oil-awl
7.	/ō/-/or/	coat-court	15.	/ou/-/ō/	couch-coach
8.	/ū/-/ōō/	butte-boot	16.	/ü/-/ů/	suit-soot

The following pages consider activities for helping pupils develop AD:

A. Read aloud books about sounds and discuss them with children. Both teachers and parents should be aware of the advantages children receive when someone reads to them at a very early age. (The first day of a child's life is not too early to begin.) Reading to a child helps accomplish several objectives.

1. It is a highly personal one-to-one situation.

2. It provides an older model for children to imitate. Children at age one can have an interest in books, and two year-olds can "read" books which have been read to them as well as create stories while looking at books.

3. It gives a child practice in listening, an important but most overlooked learning skill.

4. It exposes children to a vocabulary that they would otherwise not readily acquire. How many adults frequently use the word nimble (Jack be nimble...) or frightened (frightened -- not scared -- Miss Muffet away)?

5. It provides a basis for discussion and opportunities for comprehension development.

6. It provides youngsters with information which they might otherwise not acquire (or not acquire until a later period of time).

7. It exposes children to two levels of sound. The lower level is non-speech AD.

Books which relate to AD include the following:

Borten, Helen, Do You Hear What I Hear? New York: Abelard-Schuman, 1960.

> Stated purpose: To introduce a young child to the world of sound.

Brown, Margaret Wise, The Quiet Noisy Book. New York: Harper, 1950.

> Stated purpose: "Designed to increase the listening skills of young children."

_____, The Indoor Noisy Book. New York: W.R. Scott, 1942.

_____, The Noisy Book. New York: W.R. Scott, 1939.

_____, The Country Noisy Book. New York: Harper.

Wolff, __Janet__, __Let's__ __Imagine__ __Sounds__. New York: Dutton, 1962.

Stated purpose: "to develop children's creative imaginations...to encourage boys and girls to explore dimensions of sounds.

The second level of sound, of course, is AD of speech sounds. The six Listen--Hear Books by Jan Slepian and Ann Seidler are designed for use in grades K-3 and include a teacher resource book. Titles include __Alfie__ __and__ __the__ __Dream__ __Machine__, __The__ __Cock__ __Who__ __Couldn't__ __Crow__, __Lester__ __and__ __the__ __Sea__ __Monster__, __Magic__ __Arthur__ __and__ __the__ __Giant__, __Mr.__ __Sipple__ __and__ __the__ __Naughty__ __Princess__, and __The__ __Roaring__ __Dragon__ __of__ __Redrose__.

For pre-school through grade two the Junior Listen--Hear books and Teacher Source Book are available for the same purpose. Titles include __The__ __Silly__ __Listening__ __Book__, __An__ __Ear__ __is__ __to__ __Hear__, __Bendemolena__, __The__ __Hungry__ __Thing__, and __Ding-Dong__, __Bing-Bong__.

The __Roaring__ __Dragon__ __of__ __Redrose__, for example, can be used to help youngsters identify the /r/, for the delightful text is liberally sprinkled with words containing that speech element. You may wish to read the text and ask children to clap their hands when they hear the /r/ or chorus the word in which the /r/ appears.

B. Use nonsense verse and tongue twisters. Children usually enjoy opportunities to play with the sounds of language. The following examples illustrate the possibilities:

/p/　Peter Piper picked
　　　A peck of pickled peppers.
　　　A peck of pickled peppers
　　　Peter Piper picked.
　　　If Peter Piper picked
　　　A peck of pickled peppers,
　　　Where's the peck of pickled peppers
　　　That Peter Piper picked?

/s/ and /sh/　She sells sea shells at the sea
　　　　　　　shore.

/s/ and /sl/　Sue saw six slick slim slender
　　　　　　　saplings.

Others you may want to consider include the
following:

/b/ Busy beavers bite bark and build big beautiful
dams.

/ch/ Chuck Chapman's children chose chocolate
covered cherries and chewing gum.

/d/ David didn't do his daily duties so Dad didn't
give him a dime.

/f/ The furry fox fixed a fine home for his family
of four.

/g/ Gertie's gray goose has got to give some good
eggs for Grandpa and Grandma.

/h/ "Howdy!" happy Harry hollered as he hopped off
his hungry horse.

/j/ Ginger James chose jam and jelly for the
judge's toast.

/k/ Karen and Carol picked cucumbers and canned
them in a corner of the kitchen.

/l/ "I love to lick lollipops," laughed Larry to
Leo.

/m/ Imagine meeting a muddy monster with many
mouths.

/n/ "I know I'll never need another new necklace,"
said Nellie to Ned.

/r/ Red Rover, Red Rover,
Send _____ right over.

/t/ The two tall tattletales told tall tales about
Tammy and Tony.

/th/ The tall thin tailor thought he saw three
thirsty thieves in the theatre on Thursday.

/v/ Virginia invited Vickie to view her valuable
vase of violets.

/w/ Where would a werewolf wear a worn watch if a
witch and a wizard warned him not to wear it?

/y/   Yes, you're young enough to yell in the young
       yeller's contest this year.

/z/   Zelda sews zippers and snaps on Zane's suits.

Many poems have one or more lines with several words
beginning with the same sound. Alliterative language is
often found in the Sounds of Language Series by Bill
Martin, Jr. (Holt). Dean Morrison's Is That a Happy
Hippopotamus? (Crowell) is another example.

C. Help pupils recognize vowel and vowel-consonant
combinations in rhyming words. Word families, or
phonograms, typically consist of one of the following
patterns:

    vowel plus vowel -- ay, ow, oy

    vowel plus consonant -- at, an, ag

    two vowels plus consonant -- eat, ate, ite

    vowel plus two consonants -- ank, ill, end

Rhyming words are important because they can often be
used to help pupils recognize vowel plus consonant
combinations. Thus, with the at family (phonogram) a
child can learn to recognize words which contain both the
short a and the final t (bat, cat, fat, hat, etc.). This
activity can be provided either of two ways. One way is
to present pictures which contain two or more rhyming
words. For example, consider the following:

    at -- a cat and a hat (Dr. Seuss) or a cat chasing
              a rat

    ack -- a person with a pack on his back

    and -- a member of a band and her hand.

    all -- a ball near a wall

    an -- a tin can and a pan in a kitchen or a man
              with a fan or van or can of something.

    en -- a hen near a pen on a farm.

    et -- a pet and a vet (picture in doctor's office)

    ill -- Jack and Jill going up the hill

<u>in</u> -- a person's skin and chin

<u>ing</u> -- a king wearing a ring

<u>ocks</u> -- a child wearing socks and playing with blocks

<u>ake</u> -- a person trying to bake (make) a cake

Another (and much easier) way of providing practice involving phonograms is through an oral procedure. Select two rhyming words (i.e., <u>ham</u> and <u>jam</u>) or two words which do not rhyme (i.e., <u>Sam</u> and <u>luck</u>). You might wish to use the practice strategy outlined below.

1. Give pupils a pair of EPR cards (278), one card with a happy face and one with a sad face.

2. Be sure pupils know the meanings of <u>same</u>, <u>not</u> <u>the</u> <u>same</u>, and <u>rhyme</u>.

3. Provide directions.

a. Pupils should place their cards on their desks, tables, or on the floor in front of them.

b. The teacher will say two words slowly.

c. If they rhyme, the children should raise their happy face cards. If they don't rhyme, the children should raise their sad face cards.

d. The children should not look at the others' cards.

e. The teacher will raise her card and tell the right answer. Discussion will follow, if necessary.

f. Pupils should lower their cards.

4. Provide ten or more of these sets of words. Even pupils who are confused should correctly respond to 50% of the items since a true-false format is used. Work toward nine correct answers out of ten sets. Note pupils who require additional assistance.

Chart 4B-2 presents many of the most common phonograms and the more frequent words which correspond to each base.

COMMON PHONOGRAMS

ack	ad	ag	ail	ain
back	bad	bag	bail	gain
hack	dad	gag	fail	lain
Jack	fad	hag	Gail	main
lack	had	lag	hail	pain
Mack	lad	rag	jail	rain
pack	mad	sag	mail	
rack	pad	tag	nail	brain
sack	sad	wag	pail	drain
tack			rail	grain
	Brad	brag	sail	Spain
black	glad	drag	tail	stain
crack		flag		train
quack		snag		sprain
slack		stag		strain
smack				
snack		shag		chain
stack				
track				
shack				

air	ake	all	am	an
fair	bake	ball	dam	ban
hair	cake	call	ham	can
pair	fake	fall	jam	Dan
	Jake	hall	Pam	fan
stair	lake	mall	ram	man
	make	tall	Sam	Nan
chair	rake	wall		pan
	sake		clam	ran
	take	small	cram	tan
	wake	stall	slam	van
			Spam	
				bran
	flake			clan
	quake			span
	snake			
	stake			
	shake			

ang	and	ane	ank	ap
bang	band	cane	bank	cap
fang	hand	Jane	rank	gap
gang	land	lane	sank	lap
hang	sand	mane	tank	map
rang		pane	yank	nap
sang	brand			rap
tang	gland	crane	blank	sap
clang	grand		clank	tap
	stand		crank	
			drank	clap
			Frank	flap
			spank	slap
				snap
				trap
				scrap
				strap
				chap

ar	are	at	ate	aw
bar	care	bat	date	jaw
far	dare	cat	gate	law
jar	fare	fat	hate	gnaw
tar	hare	hat	Kate	paw
	mare	Mat	late	raw
scar	rare	pat	mate	saw
star		rat	rate	
	blare	sat		claw
			crate	draw
	glare	brat	grate	flaw
	scare	flat	skate	slaw
	snare	scat	state	
	spare	sprat		thaw
	stare			
		that		
	share	chat		

207

ay	ear	eck	ed	eep
bay	fear	deck	bed	beep
day	gear	neck	fed	deep
Fay	hear	peck	led	jeep
gay	near	wreck	Ned	keep
hay	rear	check	red	peep
Jay	tear		Ted	
Kay	year		wed	creep
lay				sleep
may	clear		bled	steep
pay	smear		fled	sweep
ray	spear		Fred	
say			sled	sheep
way				
			shad	
clay				
gray				
stay				
sway				
tray				

ell	en	ent	et	est
bell	Ben	bent	bet	best
dell	den	dent	get	pest
fell	hen	rent	jet	rest
Nell	men	sent	let	test
sell	pen	tent	met	vest
tell	ten	vent	net	west
well		went	pet	zest
yell	Glen		set	
		Brent	vet	crest
smell	then	spent	wet	
spell			yet	chest
swell				
shell				

ick	id	ide	ig	ight
Dick	bid	hide	big	fight
kick	did	ride	dig	light
lick	hid	side	fig	might
Mick	kid	tide	pig	night
Nick	lid	wide	rig	right
pick	rid		wig	sight
Rick	rid		wig	tight
sick	Sid	bride		
tick		glide		
wick	skid	slide		bright
				flight
brick				fright
click				
quick				slight
slick				
stick				
trick				
chick				
thick				

ile	ill	im	in	ine
file	bill	dim	bin	dine
mile	dill	him	fin	fine
Nile	fill	Jim	kin	line
pile	gill	Kim	pin	mine
tile	hill	rim	sin	nine
	Jill	Tim	tin	pine
smile	kill		win	vine
	mill	skim		wine
while	pill	slim	skin	
	sill	swim	spin	spine
	till	trim	twin	swine
	will			twine
			chin	
	drill			shine
	grill			
	quill			
	spill			
	chill			
	thrill			

209

ing	ink	ip	it	ite
king	link	dip	bit	bite
ring	mink	hip	fit	kite
sing	pink	lip	hit	mite
wing	rink	nip	kit	site
zing	sink	rip	lit	
	wink	sip	pit	quite
bring		tip	sit	spite
sling	blink	zip		
sting	drink		quit	white
swing	slink	clip	spit	
	stink	drip		
		flip		
	think	grip		
		skip		
		slip		
		trip		
		chip		
		ship		
		whip		

ob	ock	od	op	ore
Bob	dock	cod	cop	bore
cob	lock	God	hop	core
job	mock	nod	mop	more
mob	rock	rod	pop	tore
rob	sock		top	
sob				score
	block		crop	snore
stob	Brock		drop	store
	clock		flop	
	crock		slop	chore
	flock		stop	shore
	frock			
	smock		chop	
	stock		shop	
	shock			

210

ot	ound	ow	ow	oy
cot	bound	bow	bow	boy
got	found	low	cow	coy
hot	hound	mow	how	Roy
lot	mound	tow	now	toy
not	pound		sow	
pot	round		vow	Troy
rot	sound	blow	wow	
tot	wound	crow		
		flow	brow	
slot	ground	glow		
spot		grow	chow	
trot		slow		
		snow		
shot				
		show		
		throw		

ub	uck	ug	um	un
cub	buck	bug	bum	bun
hub	duck	dug	gum	fun
rub	luck	hug	hum	gun
sub	suck	jug	sum	nun
tub	tuck	lug		pun
		mug	drum	run
club	cluck	rug	slum	sun
stub	stuck	tug		
	truck			spun
		drug		
	shuck	slug		
		chug		

unch			ut
bunch			but
lunch			cut
munch			hut
punch			jut
brunch			nut
			rut
crunch			shut

D. Use odd-word exercises for beginning and final consonant sounds and for vowel sounds. Paired-word practice of the type described in the preceding activity is a prerequisite for odd-word exercises. This is true for several reasons. First, odd-word exercises provide more information for youngsters to absorb and remember. Second, the guessing is decreased to one-third or one-fourth, depending on the number of items presented to children. We prefer the following strategy for using odd-word exercises:

1. Provide directions:

a. Pupils should listen as you pronounce three or four words.

b. On your second pronunciation, they should raise their thumb stomach high if they know which word does not begin (or end) with the same sound as the others (or contain the same middle sound as in the case of vowels).

c. Agree or disagree and, if necessary, discuss and repeat the items.

2. Provide sets of three words (four words can be used later). With three words, even children who are confused should correctly answer three out of ten examples (actually 33-1/3%). Thus you should work toward at least nine out of ten correct responses.

For oral practice of this type use words which cannot be pictorially represented. The concrete nouns can therefore be saved for other types of activities. Consider the six types of examples shown below:

a. Beginning /b/   -- bake   bad   tell
(gross discrimination)

b. Beginning /b/   -- bite   poor   bend
(fine discrimination)

c. Final /b/   -- rub   tied   mob
(gross discrimination)

d. Final /b/   -- hope   rob   fib
(fine discrimination)

e. Vowel /i/   -- sick   tap   grin
(gross discrimination)

f. Vowel /i/   -- his   wet   miss
   (fine discrimination)

One comment: When selecting words, be careful to
include only one repeated sound so pupils do not become
confused by the presence of additional auditory
similarities. Item g shown below is not recommended
because bake and take are rhyming words. In Item h the
two final /t/'s can cause confusion.

   g. Beginning /b/   -- bake   bad   take

   h. Vowel /i/   -- hit   sick   fat

E. Ask pupils to make up or locate rhyming words, or
words beginning or ending with the same sound. This task
is more difficult, for it requires youngsters to create
rather than recognize answers. Several strategies can be
employed here.

   1. Say a word and ask a youngster to offer a rhyme,
either a real word or a nonsense one. If you say   hat,
he may respond fat. If you say banana, he may respond
gatana.

   2. Use a variation of the "I'm Going to Town" game.
Say, "I'm going to town and take a box." The child must
repeat what you have said and add an item that begins
with the /b/. Perhaps the child will say, "I'm going to
town and take a box and a baby doll." Note: This
activity works much better for initial than for final
consonant sounds.

   3. Use the "Tell About Time." Give each child a
picture of a single object. In turn each child rises,
displays his picture, and uses it in a sentence with
another word containing the same sound. If the picture
shows a cat, a child may say

        The cat is calling her kitten.

        The cat can't catch the rat.

        The cat's name is Candy.
        (This is the easiest type.)

Next the rest of the group may offer other sentences
that contain the same sound. (This technique encourages
them to listen.) Vary the procedure by using pictures
containing many objects rather than just one.

4. Make Sounds Books. Give pupils catalogues and a key word and ask them to find some pictures which contain the same phonic element. If youngsters have not yet learned to use a scissors, just allow them to tear out the pictures. After their answers are verified, you might get older children to trim the pictures.

Let children paste the pictures on a single sheet of construction paper. The reverse side can be used on another day for another sound. After pupils have completed a number of these Sounds Pages, use a three-hole punch, reinforcements, and baby shoe laces, ribbon, or string to bind the Sounds Book. Naturally you will want a title page, and children will surely want to show their books to their friends and relatives. Later you can add words to the pictures and use the Sounds Books as a phonics guide and beginning dictionary.

F. Use Multiple Concept Pictures to help pupils learn to identify particular sounds. A Multiple Concept Picture contains a number of items rather than the one item contained in a SCC. To distinguish between the types, a Single Concept Picture may contain one apple (or even many apples), but only apples are included in the visual display. On the other hand, a Multiple Concept Picture contains several items -- perhaps an apple, orange, pear, banana, and cluster of grapes. Although a single concept -- fruit -- results from an analysis of the components of the picture, that concept depends on the multiple concepts involved in the visual display. Thus a Multiple Concept Picture is built on single concepts.

Bank Street College has developed for Macmillan a series of large pictures which can be used to provide pupils with practice in identifying certain sounds. Alternative materials can be developed simply by using readily-available pictures. For example, a picture of a farm offers several possibilities. You might mount and display the picture and ask children to identify pictures that begin with the same sound as <u>try</u>. They might notice a tree, tractor, or truck. If you provide the word <u>desk</u>, they might locate a dog, duck, or door. If you say <u>key</u>, they might find a car, can, cat, cow, or coat.

The following list provides some sample pictures which can usually be located with a minimum of difficulty. You will note that the use of adjectives (big bear) or verbs (rabbit running) can extend the opportunities for pupils to benefit from using Multiple Concept Pictures. It also fosters creative thinking.

214

/b/   boy playing ball near a building

/ch/ children at church (perhaps some chairs)

/d/   dog digging in the dirt

/f/   a farmer (with fingers and a face) near a fence
or a fisherman, fishing pole, and fish with
fins

/g/   a girl in a garden (Mary, Mary, Quite Contrary)
or playing a game

/h/   a person with a hand, head, and hat or a horse
near a house or a person wearing a helmet
riding a Honda

/j/   a general in a jeep (Beetle Bailey)

/k/   cats caring for kittens or cows caring for
calves

/l/   a lady with lips and lipstick or a lamp and a
light bulb

/m/ a mother drinking milk (with mouth) or a man
(with a mouth) and some money

/n/   a person (perhaps a nurse) with a knee, nose,
and neck

/p/   people eating a piece of pie or popcorn

/r/   person with a ring and a radio

/s/   a soldier wearing socks or a saucer and a
sandwich or soap in a sink

/sh/ a person wearing a shirt and shoes -- also has
shoulders

/t/   a teacher with teeth or a telephone and
television

/th/ a thimble and a person's thumb

/v/   vegetables near a vase of flowers

/w/ waitress or waiter wearing a watch

/y/   yellow yo-yo

/z/   zebra at a zoo

5G. Teach lessons for level 1 of AD using the model
shown in Chart 4B-3 (151:26-27).

CHART 4B-3
INITIAL CONSONANT SOUND
LEVEL 1, PART A
/b/

1. Ask the pupils to listen as you pronounce the words
in each of the following pairs. Emphasize but do not
distort the initial sounds.

       a. bull   full

       b. bull   pull

       c. bull   bull

2. Ask the pupils to pronounce the words after you, one
pair at a time.

3. Ask, "Which pair of words sounds exactly alike?
Which pairs of words do not sound alike?..." (If
necessary, repeat the words slowly, eliciting a response
after each pair.)

4. Ask, "What part of the word doesn't sound alike?..."
Elicit, "...the first part." (You may or may not want
to refer to the sound by its letter-name.)

5A. Provide practice in gross contrasts in AD. Give the
pupils three objects, two of which are identical (i.e.,
two circles and one square). Ask them to display these
EPR Cards as you pronounce the following pairs of words.
If the two words sound alike, they should raise the two
shapes that are alike. If the words do not sound alike,
they should raise two shapes that are not alike.

     Tell or show the correct answer after each pupil
response. (Use either the real or the nonsense words.)

	Real		Nonsense	
1.	boom	room	bont	ront
2.	beef	beef	berk	berk
3.	horn	born	hozz	bozz
4.	bake	bake	borve	borve
5.	bud	bud	bung	bung
6.	bite	light	boze	loaze
7.	fuzz	buzz	fodge	bodge
8.	bum	bum	boof	boof
9.	bag	tag	bult	tult
10.	boil	boil	bode	bode

5B. Provide practice in minimal contrasts in AD. Once again, ask pupils to display their EPR cards.

	Real		Nonsense	
1.	both	both	boose	boose
2.	bay	pay	buth	puth
3.	burn	burn	bots	bots
4.	bone	bone	bix	bix
5.	Pete	beat	puv	buv
6.	bark	park	borge	porge
7.	bomb	bomb	boke	boke
8.	pet	bet	pife	bife
9.	back	pack	bange	pange
10.	bars	bars	bisk	bisk

Followup: If additional practice is needed on the following day, proceed through steps 1-4. Use the following items to provide pupils with practice in AD.

5A. Provide practice in gross contrasts in AD.

	Real		Nonsense	
1.	bid	lid	bezz	lezz
2.	run	bun	rame	bame
3.	boy	boy	bince	bince
4.	burst	first	bure	fure
5.	book	book	boke	boke
6.	caught	bought	kex	bex
7.	barn	barn	bufe	bufe
8.	bench	bench	barg	barg
9.	bold	hold	bige	hige
10.	barge	barge	bool	bool

5B. Provide practice in minimal contrasts in AD.

Real		Nonsense	
1. birth	birth	bawn	bawn
2. bang	bang	bith	bith
3. path	bath	pouk	bouk
4. bend	bend	bam	bam
5. bait	bait	bink	bink
6. beg	peg	boist	poist
7. bit	pit	borf	porf
8. booth	booth	besh	besh
9. pail	bail	putch	buch
10. bike	pike	bice	pice

H. Teach lessons for level 2 of AD using the model shown in CHART 4B-4 (151:29-31):

CHART 4B-4
INITIAL CONSONANT SOUND
LEVEL 2, PART A
/b/

1. Place two key pictures (bacon and basket) on the chalkledge.

2. Ask the pupils to listen as you pronounce the words, emphasizing but not distorting the sounds.

3. Ask the pupils to pronounce the words with you, emphasizing but not distorting the sounds.

4. Ask, "How are the words alike?" Elicit, "They begin with the same sound." If necessary, ask pupils to listen as you pronounce the words again. If the pupils still can't answer correctly, supply the appropriate response.

5A. Provide practice in gross differences in AD of initial sounds. Give the pupils three objects, two of which are identical (i.e., two circles and one square). Ask them to display their EPR Cards as you pronounce the following words. If a word begins with the same sound as the key words, pupils should raise the two shapes that are alike. If the words do not begin with the same sound as the key words, the pupils should raise two shapes that are not alike.

218

Tell or show the correct answer after each pupil response. (Use either the real or the nonsense words.)

Real	Nonsense
1. bargain	bents
2. bundle	bove
3. sorrow	songe
4. business	bink
5. rusty	reen
6. careless	casp
7. bother	boft
8. family	foath
9. beautiful	borg
10. torture	targe

5B. Provide practice in minimal differences in AD of initial sounds. Once again, ask pupils to display their EPR cards.

Real	Nonsense
1. person	pank
2. better	bithe
3. punish	perf
4. bunches	bodge
5. paste	pung
6. borrow	buse
7. buster	borm
8. parents	pol
9. poison	pesh
10. balance	bives

*   *   *

Followup: If additional practice is needed on the following day, proceed through steps 1-4. Use the following items to provide pupils with practice in AD of initial sounds.

5A. Provide practice in gross differences in AD of initial sounds.

	Real	Nonsense
1.	bonfire	boke
2.	church	chup
3.	gargle	galce
4.	border	bex
5.	bouquet	bange
6.	ginger	jong
7.	booklet	bood
8.	cardboard	coost
9.	judge	joth
10.	bodyguard	borm

5B. Provide practice in minimal differences in AD of initial sounds.

	Real	Nonsense
1.	palace	pong
2.	boring	bavs
3.	bugle	buld
4.	painting	pouf
5.	pardon	pinge
6.	budget	bint
7.	possible	pum
8.	powder	pault
9.	bulletin	bool
10.	booster	barch

The following pages consider activities for helping pupils develop AD.

I. Use PAD Packs (Pictures for Auditory Discrimination) as a reinforcement activity to follow Level 2 lesson plans. A PAD Pack consists of six 3X5 inch cards with simple pictures. Four pictures should represent the key sound, one picture, the minimal contrast sound, and one picture, a grossly different sound. As an illustration for the beginning /b/, a PAD Pack might contain the following pictures:

four /b/ -- bat, ball, box, boy

one /p/ -- pot

one other -- can

For some sounds there are no minimal contrasts. In these cases, there should be four pictures containing the key sound and two pictures representing different sounds.

Chart 4B-5 contains examples of pictures to use for PAD Packs. The following criteria were used to identify recommended words:

1. If at all possible, the words should be in children's listening vocabularies.

2. The words should be capable of being represented pictorially in such a way that children could readily recognize the intended words.

3. The words for consonants could be of two or three syllables so long as the syllable which contained the key sound was accented.

4. The words for vowels should contain only one syllable.

5. The key sound should not appear twice in the same word.

6. The minimal contrast sound should not appear in the four key words.

Word counts developed by Rinsland (587) and Thorndike and Lorge (708) were especially helpful. However, other words (i.e., skateboard) were also included.

To construct PAD Packs, you might follow the procedure described below:

1. Secure pictures from catalogues, beginning dictionaries, and travel brochures. Department stores and drugstores often stock inexpensive books containing appropriate pictures. Reading readiness workbooks are another source.

2. Cut out each picture in a square and paste it near the top of the card held so that the long side is top to bottom rather than left to right. This provides plenty of room to use when placing the card in a pocket holder.

EXAMPLES OF PICTURES
FOR PAD PACKS

Initial Consonant Sounds

1. b   basket, boat, boy, barn, box, buttons, bullet
2. ch   chair, chalk, children, chicken, cheese, chalkboard, cherry, chimney
3. d   desk, door, deer, duck, dishes, devil, dime, dollar, diaper
4. f   feather, fan, farmer, fence, fish, fork, fireman, fishing pole, finger, fire, football, fort, four
5. g   garden, game, girl, gas station, golf, goose, ghost, goat, gown, guard
6. h   helicopter, hatchet, heart, hat, haystack, horn, hanger, helmet, hammer, highway, horse, hill, house, hoe, hog
7. j   jar, jacks, jack-in-the-box, jeep, jug, jumprope, jacket, jungle, gym
8. k   kangaroo, car, cows, kitten (cat), candles, coats, cows, carrots, king
9. l   lady, lipstick, lemon, lamp, lake, log, leaves, lock
10. m   mother, milk, mask, matches, motorcycle, mouth, mirror, motorboat
11. n   nuts, nail, net, nickel, nest, needle, nurse, notebook
12. p   pot, pig, pancakes, pocket, pin cushion, pillow, picnic, pirate, pear, pistol, penny, pitchfork, pie, pencil, purse, painter, pyramid, parts, parrot, peach, peanuts, pearl
13. r   rabbit, race car, radiator, rainbow, raisins, rake, rocker, rocket, radio, razor, ring, roof, rose, rowboat, rug, red, rope, rat
14. s   seven, sock, sandal, singer, soap, soldier, sink, seal, sucker
15. sh   shoes, shark, shield, shovel, shirt, shells, ship, shadow, shawl, sheep, shelves
16. t   tank, teacher, table, taxicab, tiger, teaspoon, tongue, telephone, top, television, teeth, tooth, torch, towel
17. th   thumb, thorns, thirty, thief
18. v   vest, vampire, valentine, vase, violin, vacuum, vegetable, violets, vulture
19. w   watch, wall, water, wand, waffle, watermelon, window, wagon, windmill
20. y   yarn, yellow, yard, yak, yardstick
21. z   zero, zoo, zipper, zebra

Final Consonant Sounds

22. b   taxicab, robe, crab, web, cube
23. ch watch, witch, branch, peach, match, bench, hutch, couch
24. d   bed, bird, red, lid, leopard, lizard, wood
25. f   leaf, roof, hoof, calf, loaf, knife, safe, giraffe
26. g   dog, bug, leg, pig, jug, frog, rug
27. j   cage, page, hinge, bridge
28. k   rake, chick, duck, snake, lock
29. l   owl, bowl, pole, pail, doll, circle, ball, pearl
30. m   game, ice cream, dime, gum, comb, worm, drum
31. n   telephone, sun, pen, barn
32. ng ring, king, wing, swing
33. p   cup, sheep, ship, top, lamp, mop, soup, soap
34. s   cats, ice, boots, bats, boats, coats, bus, purse, dice, mice, vase, cakes, tops, hats
35. sh bush, fish, squash, trash
36. t   goat, kite, gate, cat, suit, rat, shirt
37. th north, wreath, mouth, bath, moth, path
38. v   five, glove, dove, stove, cave, sleeve
39. z   bears, bugs, guns, cheese, boys, bags, hands, rugs, ducks, toes, girls, fuse, rose, hose, trees, pies

Initial Consonant Clusters

40. bl blocks, blanket, black, blue, blender, blinds
41. br brush, bread, brown, bride, bricks, briefcase, broom
42. dr drum, dress, dryer, drill, drapes, drawer
43. fl flag, flower, fly, flashlight
44. fr frog, frame, freezer, frying pan
45. gl glasses, gloves, glue, glider
46. gr grasshopper, grapes, grandmother, green, grill, grinder, grandfather
47. kl cloth, clown, clock, claws, closet, clothes, clippers, clock, clouds, club
48. kr crib, crayons, crab, cradle, cross
49. pl plate, plant, plane, plumber, pliers
50. pr price tag, preacher, praying hands, pretzel, prince, princess
51. qu quartet, queen, quilt, quarter
52. sk skirt, skateboard, school, scooter, scales, scarf, skillets, skunk
53. sl sliding board, slacks, sled, sleeve, slip, sliding doors, slippers
54. sm smoke, smock, smile, smear

223

Initial Consonant Clusters (cont.)

55. sn   snow, snake, snail, sneakers, snaps
56. sp   spoon, sponge, spider, spear, spool
57. st   stoplight, stork, steak, stagecoach, star, store, stairs, steps
58. sw   swing, swan, swimming pool, sweater, sweatshirt, switch
59. tr   train, tricycle, trash, tree, truck, triangle, tractor, tracks
60. tw   twins, twelve, twenty, twig

Final Consonant Clusters

61. sk   mask, desk, husk, tusk
62. st   nest, ghost, toast, vest, post, cast, fist, paste

Basic Vowel Sounds

63. a   fan, glass, ham, hand, flag, mask, clam, lamb, patch, trap, cast, tacks, cap, hat, rat, cat, lamp, stamp
64. e   sled, bell, hem, tent, well, belt, desk, ten, shelf
65. i   pig, lips, fist, six, witch, whip
66. o   fox, mop, top, clock, pot, socks, box
67. u   bus, duck, gun, gum, cup, thumb, plug, rug, sun, thumb, tongue, skunk
68. ā   jail, cape, game, skate, gate, chain, paint, vase, tape, rake, sleigh, cave, face, flame
69. ē   bee, key, seal, chief, tree, peas, three, beans, jeep, sheep, teeth, sleeve, thief
70. ī   mice, tie, tire, kite, five, ice, dice
71. ō   toast, boat, soap, goat, hoe, coat, smoke, stove, rope, toes
72. ū   tube, cube, mule, fuse

R-Controlled Sounds

73. ar   barn, jar, yarn, arm, star, car, cards, guard
74. air   hair, chair, pear, square, bear
75. er   girl, curve, shirt, nurse, purse, skirt, church
76. eer   deer, steer, tears, beard, ears, smear
77. or   door, shorts, corn, store, board, pour, horse, fork, floor, porch, four, fort, torch, stork

Diphthong	Sounds	
78.	au	lawn, yawn, saw, shawl, paw, fawn
79.	ou	mouse, gown, couch, crown, house, plow, cloud, pouch
80.	oi	boy, coin, toys, foil, point
81.	o͞o	moon, boots, tooth, spoon, stool, suit, goose, two, pool
82.	oo	cook, hook, wood, books

---

3. Make two sets of six pictures each for the 82 items shown in Chart 4B-5. One set will be for practice and one for review. The fastest sequence of grouping the pictures appears to be the following:

a. Label an envelope (in pencil) for each sound (a total of 82 envelopes).

b. Place key pictures in the envelopes first. Since there are two sets per sound, each envelope should eventually contain at least eight key words. Nevertheless, it is fine to continue placing words in the envelope because extra ones can always be removed and shifted to other envelopes.

For example, a picture of a <u>boy</u> should be placed originally in the /oi/ envelope (Set 80) rather than the initial /b/ envelope (Set 1) because the /b/ is far more common than the /oi/. However, if the word is placed in Set 1, you can eventually study all the words and move certain ones to the other sets. Hint: Final cluster sounds, R-controlled sounds, and diphthongs are the most difficult to locate. Initial consonant sounds tend to be the easiest. Save them for last.

c. After locating most of the cards for the key words in the 164 sets, use the extra cards for the minimal contrast items.

d. Finally, use the remaining cards for the foil (gross difference) items. Note: For a small number of sets it appears to be impossible to locate enough pictures to complete the category. Examples include beginning /z/, /sm/, /sn/, final /sk/, /u/, and /eer/.

4. Label the back of each card in the upper right-hand corner. We use this scheme: Pr 1 - /b/. This description translates to "Practice 1 for the /b/."

5. If desired, make the materials self-correcting. This can be done by placing four checkmarks in the left-hand corner of the back side for the four key words and two X-marks for the words which do not contain the key sound.

6. If desired, laminate the cards.

7. Store each set of six cards in some convenient manner. We prefer to use library pockets, for they are ideal in size. In this case, label the library pocket (i.e., Pr 1- /b/). Place the practice sets in one shoe box and the review sets (i.e., R 1 - /b/) in another. To keep the materials from being accidentally mixed together, locate the two boxes of PAD Packs in different areas of the room or use them on different days.

To use the PAD Packs with kindergarten, first grade, or educable mentally handicapped (EMH) children, we recommend the following strategies.

1. Use the materials after pupils receive instruction at Level 2 of AD.

2. Use one set of cards to illustrate the following procedure:

a. Shuffle the six cards.

b. Hold up each card one at a time and ask pupils to pronounce the picture word.

c. Pronounce and discuss any picture word which confuses pupils or which is unfamiliar.

d. Point to one or more large key pictures (see Activity Three) placed on a chalkboard, wall chart, sentence strip holder, etc. Ask pupils to pronounce each word with you.

e. Give each child a card with a sad face and a card with a happy face. These cards should be laminated unless you like to make them often. Even so, the children will sooner or later digest them. Be sure pupils understand the meanings of <u>same</u>, <u>not</u> <u>the</u> <u>same</u>, <u>first</u> <u>sound</u>, <u>last</u> <u>sound</u>, etc.

f. Tell pupils that you will show the PAD Pack cards one at a time. They should hold up a happy face card if the word you show begins (ends, contains) the sound of the key picture. If the key picture shows a boy, and you hold up a picture of a basket, each child should raise a happy face.

g. Display the first PAD Pack card. After pupils raise their sad or happy face cards, do the same with your card. Tell the children the correct answer and why it is right.

h. Do the same with the other cards.

3. On the following day you might use the second set of cards in the same way. As an alternative, you might use a second strategy which is especially appropriate for children in learning disability (LD) and Chapter I reading classes.

a. Follow the procedures as discussed above so pupils can acquire a concept of what is involved in the PAD Packs themselves. Use one set of materials as a demonstration set.

b. Place the appropriate set of cards in a learning center. Ask each pupil to take the six cards from the library pocket, shuffle them, and place them in two columns. The first column will have four pictures, the second column two pictures. Either you or someone you designate can check the accuracy unless you use the self-checking procedure described earlier.

c. When a pupil makes an error, he should ask for and receive help.

d. Use a Class Analysis Chart to indicate whether each pupil successfully completed the activity on the first trial or needed help. To make a Class Analysis Chart, list the names of pupils down the left side of a sheet of paper and the numbers of the PAD Pack sets across the top of the page. Record a plus for a satisfactory performance (all pictures arranged correctly) and a minus if there is an error. After additional work with other practice material, a pupil may have a minus changed to a plus. Note Chart 4B-6.

CHART 4B-6

PARTIALLY COMPLETED AUDITORY DISCRIMINATION
CLASS ANALYSIS CHART

Initial Consonant Sounds	b 1	ch 2	d 3	f 4	g 5	h 6	j 7	k 8	l 9	m 10	n etc.
Aaron	-	-	-	-							
Ben	+	-	-	+							
Chuck	+	+	+	+							
Dean	-	-	+	-							
Edgar	-	-	+	-							

A horizontal analysis of the completed portion of Chart 4B-6 indicates that Aaron is having the most difficulty with auditory discrimination and therefore needs more instruction and practice. So do Ben, Dean, and Edgar. Chuck is progressing nicely. A vertical analysis reveals that additional assistance is needed in all four phonemes (speech sounds).

J. Provide mounted pictures and ask pupils to place them into containers representing particular sounds. This can be done in any of several ways.

1. Paste four rows and four columns of library pockets to a large piece of tagboard. Label the front of each card with a picture containing a different sound. Provide a stack of mounted pictures and ask a person to place them in the appropriate holder. It is best to begin with two words (therefore using just two of the pockets) and add more sounds as further instruction is provided. We also find it helpful to allow pupils to work in pairs and eventually move to individual efforts.

2. Open the tops of pasteboard milk cartons (available from school cafeterias) so pupils can place cards in these containers. Use the strategies indicated above.

228

K. Use MAD Boxes (Materials for Auditory Discrimination) as a reinforcement activity to follow Level 2 teaching. A MAD Box contains six objects similar to those described in Activity One. Items in a MAD Box may be miniatures (i.e., small animals or tools) or real-size objects (i.e., jar, toothbrush, or pencil). Like PAD Packs, MAD Boxes may contain the same items more than once. For instance, a key may be placed in the beginning /k/ as well as the /e/ and thus appear in two MAD Boxes.

To make MAD Boxes, you can use the following procedure:

1. Use the categories identified in Chart 4B-5.

2. Gather all the "junk" that is readily available. Invite pupils to bring in odds and ends of items they don't want. Check yard sales, closets, attics, and places which have not been through spring cleaning in one or more decades. Do not use anything that must be returned.

3. Assign the materials to categories as described in PAD Packs. Obviously there will be a number of packs with fewer than the desired number of items and some packs with no materials at all. Try to make one set rather than two.

4. When a set is complete, place it in a box and label it by number. The following types of boxes are especially appropriate: cereal boxes, greeting card boxes, and 5 X 8 inch card boxes. Place the smaller boxes in large boxes by category (i.e., beginning consonant sounds in one large box, final consonant sounds in another, etc.) and label them.

To use MAD Boxes, present the materials in the same way PAD Packs are introduced to kindergarten pupils, first graders, and EMH children. An alternative strategy similar to the one used for PAD Packs can also be employed. House the materials at a learning center.

To discourage "loss" of materials, stress with pupils the importance of returning all items to the box after each practice so they can be used. Using an analogy with a children's game or puzzle, discuss how frustrating it is to begin using it and then find out some of the pieces are missing. It is difficult to make MAD Boxes materials self-correcting.

L. Make and display Sounds Charts. A Sounds Charts is a large piece of tagboard (approximately two feet square) on which are mounted two or more pictures representing a particular sound. Sounds Charts may be organized in either of two ways. One way is to attach several pictures of a sound in a particular position (except for vowels). Another way is to place beginning consonant pictures on the left side of the sheet and final consonant pictures on the right side of the sheet. You can use the words listed in Chart 4B-5 as possible items.

One further idea: After pupils acquire competence in AD, use the same Sounds Charts for introducing phonics. Simply print the corresponding word on tagboard or chartboard and attach it to the Chart either above or below the picture. Thus one chart serves two functions and may be used with pupils at two different levels within the same class.

8. Letter-Sound Associations

Although we would prefer to consider letter-sound associations (LSAs) as a series of beginning reading skills, the trend in basal readers and therefore school instruction is to view phonics as beginning at the reading readiness level. Most basal series present anywhere from about ten to thirty words at the reading readiness level.

In some texts the words are presented first and phonic generalizations (principles or "rules") are derived from the common parts. In other series the phonic elements are presented first and words which related to them follow. Since word analysis is considered in Chapter 9A, it is not discussed here.

Guidelines for Developing
Reading Readiness Skills

The final section of this chapter summarizes some key guidelines relating to the development of reading readiness.

Guideline One: "The reading readiness skills are differentiated from pre-reading skills."

As noted earlier it is important to recognize the differences between general pre-reading and reading-related skills. To illustrate, general pre-reading skills may include cutting with a scissors, identifying the major colors, and walking in a straight line. While these skills are important and while they sometimes precede the development of reading, pre-reading skills do

230

not lead to proficiency in subsequent reading achievement. Nor does the absence of their development interfere with the acquisition of reading competence. Both common sense and task analysis attest to this fact.

Guideline Two: "The cognitive component of reading readiness is considered to include at least fourteen aspects."
These components already have been identified.

Guideline Three: "Reading readiness is developed in the home, in special pre-school programs and throughout the early school years."
Even a cursory review of the reading readiness skills will result in an awareness that the home can develop some of these aspects. For instance, a parent who reads to a newborn baby is laying the groundwork for listening, speaking, oral vocabulary, oral comprehension, etc. The parent of a two-year-old who asks questions with gradually increasing complexity (insofar as the response format is concerned) develops listening, speaking and oral vocabulary, oral comprehension, etc. To illustrate, speaking skills may unfold in the following manner:

   a. Adult question: Do you love Daddy?
      Simple response: Yes

   b. Adult question: Do you love Daddy?
      Imitation response: I love(s) Daddy.

   c. Adult question: Who do you love?
      Open-ended one-word response: _____

   d. Adult question: Who do you love?
      Open-ended response (sentence): I love(s)
      _____ .

   e. Adult question: Who do you love?
      Open-ended response (multiple-part sen-
      tence): I love(s) _____ and _____ and
      _____ .

If reading readiness can be developed in the home, it can also be developed in nursery schools, Head Start, and (pre)kindergartens. Indeed, the development of reading readiness competencies should form the cognitive component of the kindergarten curriculum. Furthermore, reading readiness skills should be presented in grades one and above to pupils who are not yet ready to learn to

231

read or who are unable to profit from beginning reading instruction.

It is most unfortunate that some educators ignore or deemphasize the reading readiness skills, at the pre-first grade levels, in the first-grade for pupils who require extended reading readiness but receive only minimal (for them) assistance, in the second and subsequent grades for pupils who have not yet acquired all of the reading readiness skills that will be needed to make maximum progress in reading, or at any level when some reading readiness skills are emphasized but others treated in a perfunctory manner.

A good example of the latter problem is the over-emphasis on visual discrimination practice and the under-emphasis on AD even though the research suggests the priorities should be reversed because of pupils' needs (556). A second example is the relative deemphasis accorded to aspects such as listening, speaking, following directions, oral vocabulary, oral comprehension, and oral context as opposed to visual discrimination.

Guideline Four: "The initial development of reading readiness skills precedes the introduction of reading skills."

Many youngsters do poorly in reading because they receive reading rather than readiness instruction. For instance, Gans (335) has noted that ability to speak in complete sentences precedes the development of the ability to read complete sentences. Likewise, a pupil who experiences considerable difficulty in phonics may have an underlying problem -- deficiency in auditory discrimination. Furthermore, the pupil who cannot comprehend printed information may be unable to understand data presented orally.

The reading readiness skills are prerequisites to the reading skills. When we ignore the development of the former, we imperil pupils' acquisition of the latter. Although some children enter school possessing competence in most or all of the reading readiness skills, some children require far more assistance than they receive. These youngsters typically "fall behind" in reading and enter the secondary schools functioning at appallingly low levels of reading competence. Some pupils need more reading readiness. A delay in their reading instruction coupled with specific reading readiness instruction more than overcomes a quick start followed by frustration and failure (540).

232

Guideline Five: "The time provided for the development of reading readiness varies according to pupils' needs."

As noted above, youngsters' needs for reading readiness vary considerably. In general we can categorize the needs of pupils entering school as follows:

a. need little or no reading readiness -- may already be reading

b. need some reading readiness, particularly in certain reading readiness skills not thoroughly developed at home (particularly AD, letter-sound associations, listening and following directions in group settings, etc.)

c. need extended reading readiness, perhaps even a year or more (671) (in some cases) -- Children needing extended reading readiness often operate at oral language levels characteristic of typical two- and three-year-olds. These "bottom group" youngsters rarely have the opportunity to acquire the solid foundation of reading readiness needed to support effective reading instruction.

In recent years authorities such as Benjamin Bloom (60), John Carroll (110,112), and James Block (60) have discussed the importance of considering time a variable in learning in order that emphasis might be placed on assuring that each child achieves. Research strongly suggests that mastery teaching and learning require additional time at the outset but require less in the long run because pupils possess the essential prerequisite skills (60,63).

Guideline Six: "Instruction and practice in each aspect of reading readiness are provided each day. For non-readers and beginning readers instruction and practice form the core of the cognitive curriculum."

Research by Durrell's students indicates that the crucial variable is not the time itself but the manner in which time is used. Even though the provision of extended time does not automatically insure pupil progress, there is research evidence to indicate that, at the primary levels, increased time allocated for reading instruction is associated with higher levels of pupil performance (362).

While the Durrell-supervised studies focus on the use of EPR techniques to facilitate the maximum mental

233

involvement of youngsters, there are several other important concepts.

a. For most pupils to reach maximum progress there must be direct instruction. Furthermore, most children do not learn very well on their own (376, 378).

b. Instruction must be distinguished from practice. By itself practice is a most inefficient way of developing pupil competence because there is limited guidance, assistance, feedback, correction, and encouragement. If the old adage that "Practice makes perfect" is true, the person who practices something wrong learns to be perfectly (or consistently) wrong. How many people with an abundance of practice speak non-standard language, read words wrong, fail to read for meaning, demonstrate poor listening skills, or have almost indecipherable handwritings? Like most sayings, this one should be taken "with a grain of salt."

c. All areas of reading readiness should receive attention each day (either through instruction or planned practice). Because there are at least fourteen sub-areas, someone is likely to contend that such a guideline is impractical. However, if one notes each of the reading readiness categories, it should become readily apparent that instruction and practice in the various aspects can often be provided through the other activities being conducted. To illustrate, pupils must listen and follow directions each day. Why shouldn't a teacher provide specific instruction and practice in these two areas? Except in isolated cases, children speak every day. Why shouldn't a teacher help children improve their ability to speak? Youngsters constantly encounter new experiences, both at school and at home. Why shouldn't a teacher take advantage of these opportunities to develop new vocabulary?

It should be clear that continuous instruction and practice in the various aspects of reading readiness can provide a strong cognitive component for pupils who have not yet learned how to read.

Guideline Seven: "Diagnosis of reading readiness is based on pretests, observations, and analysis of diagnostic teaching."

234

Many aspects of reading readiness are not amenable to diagnostic testing. We do not have, for example, many diagnostic tests of oral language development components such as listening, following directions, speaking, and vocabulary. As a result we must depend on a variety of types of diagnostic devices.

a. pretests -- usually for auditory and visual discrimination and letter-sound associations

b. observations to note how well pupils function in areas such as listening, spelling, following directions, oral vocabulary, oral comprehension, oral context, auditory memory, and visual memory. Although such observations are subjective, they are based directly on the expectations made by individual teachers.

c. analysis of diagnostic teaching -- After providing instruction and practice, a teacher can analyze the effectiveness of the instructional sequence on specific pupils. To illustrate, suppose, despite repeated opportunities, certain youngsters are still unable to identify the sequence of events in a story either read or told by a teacher. This analysis of instructional effectiveness should then lead a teacher to design alternate ways of helping pupils to identify events in sequence. Indeed, the teacher might ask pupils to

1. tell the story in a group or pair
2. tell the story individually
3. draw episodes from the story
4. dictate a language-experience account of the story
5. dramatize the story
6. prepare to tell the story to another class

Thus strategies are modified to reflect the analyzed effectiveness that they exert on pupils. It is worth noting that effective instruction should not be changed unless there is reason to believe it can be improved by the intended modification(s).
Interestingly, diagnostic analysis of instruction is readily available on every occasion in which teaching occurs. Unfortunately teachers sometimes conclude that particular strategies are not working with certain youngsters (i.e., "He's just not learning those sounds," "She can't even talk in complete sentences.") without taking any action to change the learning conditions.

Analysis of diagnostic teaching assumes a "change phase" as necessary.

Guideline Eight: "The teacher diagnoses only to the extent necessary."
School beginners can tell us more about their needs during instruction than through the administration of diagnostic devices. Furthermore, if diagnosis is likely to take longer than the corresponding instruction, we are well advised to engage in diagnostic teaching (use teaching sessions to identify strengths, weaknesses, and needs). For older pupils and for youngsters who have received instruction, diagnosis can prove helpful. Even so it should be selective. That is, a child who can't make auditory discriminations of initial consonants does not need diagnosis on final consonants or on vowels.

Guideline Nine: "Activities provided for the development of reading readiness reflect the specific nature of the skills themselves."
Some reading readiness skills lend themselves to paper-and-pencil activities (visual discrimination, letter-sound associations). Others are most appropriately conducted through pictorial and/or oral means (i.e., AD, listening, oral vocabulary, oral comprehension, oral context, auditory memory). Still others can be either paper-and-pencil or oral (i.e., following directions, word boundaries, visual memory), or pupil produced (speaking). Furthermore, some of the skills lend themselves to group interaction (i.e., listening, speaking, oral vocabulary, oral comprehension, oral context) while others are highly individual in nature (i.e., auditory and visual discrimination, auditory and visual memory, following directions, LSAs).
The implications of these comments are that activities should be designed to reflect the particular nature of the skill, the instructional format, and the response format. As one illustration, let us consider following directions.

a. The instructional medium is either oral or paper-and-pencil.

b. Group size is essentially immaterial for general procedures. For new practices (i.e., test taking, some written exercises), groups should not exceed ten.

236

c. Pupil responses, whether oral or on paper, are both individual and specific. There is no room for creativity as there should be for speaking.

Guideline Ten: "Instruction occurs before assigned practice."
Like most competencies, reading readiness skills do not occur simply as a result of increased age. They require direct experiences, i.e., teaching. It is inappropriate to provide "learning activities" that make it likely certain children will flounder and fail.

Guideline Eleven: "Youngsters receive instruction in how to learn before they are expected to function independently."
Whether the activity is putting a puzzle together, counting the number of objects on a paper, or copying a sentence from a model, children need specific guidance in how to accomplish the task most effectively and efficiently.

Guideline Twelve: "Multi-sensory procedures are employed wherever possible."
The use of multi-sensory framework increases the likelihood that pupils who are weak in one learning mode will profit from exposure to the other modality. Thus, visual (pictorial), oral (auditory), vocalic (speaking), and kinesthetic (tracing or copying) strategies are often appropriate and should be used as needed.

Guideline Thirteen: "Group-based recordkeeping devices help to simplify analysis of pupil performance."
It is not at all uncommon to see either of two unsatisfactory conditions employed at the reading readiness levels. The first is the failure of some teachers to keep any records of pupil proficiency. Thus there are no indicators of growth and no data for subsequent teachers. Reading readiness skills continua are as important as skill sequences at the reading stage.
A second frequently-observed problem occurs at the opposite end of the spectrum. This problem involves the checking off of elaborate individual skills sequences. This activity is so time-consuming that it either detracts from time that more profitably could be devoted to teaching or imposes a burden on a teacher during after-school hours. It has been our experience that group profiles are quite sufficient for regular use. Individual data can be transferred periodically by paraprofessionals.

Chart 4B-7 provides one possible format to use in noting pupil performance.

CHART 4B-7

CLASS ANALYSIS CHART

FOLLOWING DIRECTIONS

Name of pupils	Does One-step	Does Two-steps	Does Three-steps	Uses Response Mode	Uses Correction Mode	Keeps Place	Completes Exercise	Works Independently

Key: Use - for no
      Use + for yes
      To change - to +, use
        a different color marker.

It is helpful to remember that a pupil can be checked off as having acquired temporary competence (i.e., in terms of present requirements) even if his answers are incorrect. Thus a child who underlines the wrong picture still receives credit for using the correct response mode.

Guideline Fourteen: "The development of reading readiness skills continues with parallel instruction even after reading instruction is begun."
There seems to be a misconception that reading readiness ends at a certain point, the same juncture at which reading instruction begins. This is most decidedly not the case. Reading readiness consists of separate skills; pupils cannot possibly possess identical degrees of competence in each area. The type of reading program provided for pupils helps determine the extent to which particular skills are necessary. For example, a heavily phonics-oriented program requires more pupil competence in AD than does a reading program using a look-say (visual) procedure in its initial stages.

Since the need for reading readiness does not end when instruction in reading begins, pupils should continue to receive appropriate instruction and practice in those aspects of reading readiness in which they still require assistance. This guidance, which should occur even after basal readers, individualized instruction, the language-experience approach, etc., are begun, should continue as long as is necessary.

Summary

Chapter 4B considers activities for developing the pre-reading skill of letter-name knowledge as well as the perceptual skills involved in reading readiness and provides both instructional and independent activities and strategies for fostering their development. It concludes with a set of guidelines for developing reading readiness.

FOR FURTHER READING

Feeley, Joan T., "Print and Reading: What Do Preschoolers Know?" Day Care and Early Education, XI, No. 3 (Spring, 1984), 26-28.

Groff, Patrick J., "Resolving the Letter-Name Controversy," Reading Teacher, XXXVII, No. 4 (January, 1984), 384-388.

CHAPTER 5

SELECTING LEARNING MATERIALS

IN READING

Introduction

The first academic decision a teacher must make at the beginning of each school year is that of ascertaining the instructional reading level of each pupil. Gone are the days (hopefully!) when every third-grader was associated with a set of third-grade materials or every seventh-grader with a set of seventh-grade books. Unless provisions are made for the manifold ways in which individuals differ, some pupils will learn very little (139, 408). The first instructional task, the selection of appropriate materials for each youngster, is much easier said than done.

Inappropriate Techniques for

Selecting Materials

Five highly unsatisfactory procedures are sometimes utilized to match books with pupils. These involve

1. The use of grade-level textbooks (54, 76, 95, 499, 588)

2. The use of one or more standardized reading or achievement test batteries (76, 95, 102, 304, 385, 405, 444, 498, 643)

3. The use of cumulative records, showing books completed during the preceding year

4. The use of teacher judgment (750)

5. The use of readability formulas (420, 495)

1. The Use of Grade-Level Textbooks. In many schools the typical practice is to assign all members of a class the grade-level books previously distributed by the principal. Unfortunately this technique creates severe psychological and learning problems for youngsters who are incapable of reading materials written at grade level.

Spend an evening in comparing reading books used two decades or so ago with those currently adopted. You will then clearly see the nature of the problem which confronts us. Today's basal readers present far more new words, far more skills, and far more sophisticated concepts than did their earlier counterparts (385, 595). Much of what we learned in high school or college is now presented at the intermediate levels.

This means, of course, that today's youngsters must learn far more than their parents did and learn it at much earlier ages. Unfortunately this expectation is completely unrealistic for many pupils. They are exposed to material for which they do not possess appropriate backgrounds. Then, because there is so much material to be covered and so little time in which to do so, many teachers march stoically on, leaving behind a mass of confused stragglers and strugglers. For these unfortunates, the use of grade-level texts is a highly effective way of unwittingly creating and extending social, emotional, and academic problems.

2. The Use of One or More Standardized Reading or Achievement Test Batteries. Just as dangerous is the practice of interpreting standardized test results on an individual basis. These data are often used for either of two purposes: (a) placement of pupils in administratively-grouped (so-called homogeneous) classes, or (b) selecting learning materials.

Regardless of which purpose is being considered, the use of standardized norm-referenced scores often leads to completely inaccurate and unacceptable results. No less an authority than Henry S. Dyer, former vice-president of Educational Testing Service, has strongly condemned the misleading use of these scores (539). Other writers have been equally concerned (98, 117, 172, 375, 444, 466, 498, 502, 552, 576, 673, 702). Goodman even declares in exasperation, "Test misuse has reached a level that would justify a five-year moratorium on such tests. Test makers won't drop the bad tests and really begin to develop tests that have some sound basis until we stop buying the bad tests (354: 631-632)."

Some of the major objections are considered next. First of all, the material used in reading tests is not necessarily typical of or even similar to that which the pupil is being taught. For example, a fourth grader who receives instruction on a second-grade level is still tested on a fourth-grade achievement test. This practice obviously denies that children are individuals with varying needs. Even if youngsters are progressing at a "normal" pace, there is no assurance that the test corresponds to the curriculum. Studies (489) show that different basal programs present material in different sequences and at different reading levels.

Second, standardized tests require pupils merely to recognize the correct answer rather than produce it themselves. Pupils will tend to score somewhat higher as a result, for by the laws of chance sheer guessing will result in correct answers for every fourth or fifth item. Edward Fry (330) refers to this as the orangoutang score. Even a monkey ought to earn this score.

Third, the time element of achievement tests arbitrarily discriminates against students who read or work slowly (117). Research among disadvantaged populations almost always discusses this point. A startling example of this type of bias occurred several years ago in one of the senior author's classes. An eighth-grade pupil named John scored 7.2 (seventh grade, second month) on the reading comprehension sub-test of a nationally-known achievement battery. Grade placement at the time of the test was 8.8, and the teacher knew from the experiences of the previous eight months that John had performed well above average in comprehension.

An examination of the test booklet indicated that John had answered the first 30 out of 60 questions. Of those 30, he had answered 28 correctly. The following afternoon, John completed the sub-test, marking his answers with a ball-point pen. Had the entire 60 questions been completed during the standard time allotment, his score would have been 10.1. A mis-interpretation of this score (caused by the time factor) would have led to the inevitable conclusion that the pupil was almost two years below grade placement and three or more years below potential in reading comprehension. In far too many cases the profiles of more methodical students are adversely affected by the time factor.

Fourth, achievement tests tend to indicate pupils' frustration levels rather than their instructional levels. Research and the literature indicate that, in general, achievement test scores measure a point at least a year beyond the level at which a pupil can be expected to function (54, 76, 95, 233, 382, 405, 516). To complicate the matter, some individuals may read as much as two or three levels below their test results while a few others may actually read at a higher level than indicated. To secure instructional materials based on achievement test scores is, therefore, little short of senseless.

Fifth, a number of extraneous factors unduly influence a pupil's measured performance on achievement tests. Illness, time of day, psychological or physical factors, confusion about the appropriate procedures to follow, or extensive guessing may invalidate the results.

242

Once again let us refer to a specific incident which occurred in the senior author's eighth-grade class. On an achievement test given in the first month of school (grade placement 8.1), one pupil scored 6.8 in reading comprehension. The teacher then asked another professional to decide what academic provisions would be appropriate. The answer: give him a book slightly below grade level. After all, the pupil's sub-score was only one month below the class median of 6.9.

The teacher chose to ignore the advice of his colleague. The reason: observation during the administration of the test showed that the pupil required less that two minutes to complete each sub-test. When timing began, he merely marked answers in a random fashion and then took a nap. At the end of each sub-test he was awakened and allowed to repeat the pattern. The pupil was, of course, a complete non-reader. A study of his test profile certainly would not have revealed such interesting and important information.

3. The Use of Cumulative Records Showing Books Completed During the Preceding Year. A third way of associating pupils with books is to select the lowest level of book that has not yet been read. While recourse to the cumulative record to determine which materials pupils have completed is useful for deciding which books are no longer appropriate from the novelty factor, there is no further value to the practice. Why? First is the summer loss of reading level and skills. For instance, Olilla (547) notes that while five-year-olds can be taught to read, the research indicates they tend to lose the skills during the summer. Perez (563) points out a study by Rude that found first graders lost significant reading ability as measured by a norm-referenced reading test as well as a significant loss of nine out of twelve reading skills measured by a criterion-referenced test. While Perez found no significant regression, we should remember that the study was conducted at a laboratory school (which usually is not a typical school) in a state (Utah) that has the highest median years of school completed in the nation. Using standardized tests on comprehension, Ross (603) found that poor readers in grade six lost an average of a full year during the summer.

Studies (230, 703) of compensatory education pupils indicate that much school year progress is lost during the summer and the shorter vacations "eliminate much of the traditional summer learning loss suffered by disadvantaged children (349: 67)." Not all children lose over the summer. For instance, above average learners often gain (603) as do intermediate summer readers (402).

243

Another problem which is often ignored when professionals refer to the cumulative record is the extent of each pupil's mastery of the material. Completing the book does not mean the child completed it successfully or understood it at all. Gans writes, "I think the worst phrase I have ever heard in education is 'We've got to cover the ground.' We cover arithmetic, we cover the social studies, and we inter the child (334:67)."

4. The Use of Teacher Judgment. While it seems logical to assume that teachers are quite accurate in determining their pupils' reading levels, this has not proved to be the case (382, 750). Furthermore, teachers are not effective in judging the difficulty of materials (511). Of course, any teacher can readily identify those pupils who read quite well or quite poorly. The difficulty lies in determining an answer to the question "How well?" or "How poorly?" At this point isolated teacher judgment is relatively ineffective. (As will be noted shortly, however, judgment does play a role in combination with another approach.)

5. The use of readability formulas. Since the classic studies of Klare (449), these formulas have become popular, especially in middle grades and above. Unfortunately, they are not very accurate (315, 420) and different formulas yield different results on the same material (289, 383, 689, 738). The formulas tend to consider only factors such as number of words per sentence, number of syllables in words, or word inclusion on a basic word list. As Nelson observes, they typically do not consider factors such as "levels of abstractions, complexity of concepts, figurative and poetic language, multiple meanings, technical and scientific vocabulary, variations in format and organization. . . . (536:621)." Thus the formulas are inappropriate for use in determining whether or not certain texts are appropriate for children (420, 495). We usually add one or more years to the published readability level to derive a more accurate score. Fitzgerald advises, "Use readability estimates with extreme caution (315:410)."

Using the Betts Criteria

How, then, shall we determine which materials are appropriate for instructional independent reading purposes? Many years ago, Emmett A. Betts (54) developed a guide which is extremely useful. Indeed, a survey (569) of reading authorities showed overwhelming acceptance of figures similar to those he proposed.

244

Betts declared that people read at three different
levels. The figures which he provided as guidelines have
been slightly modified.

CHART 5-1

BETTS CRITERIA

(MODIFIED)

Level	Word Analysis	Comprehension	Purpose
Independent	98%	90%	Homework, Recreation
Instructional	94%	70%	In-school work
Frustration	below 94%	below 70%	none

In essence, Chart 5-1 presents each of the three
levels at which youngsters (and adults!) may read,
includes an approximate percentage score for each, and
identifies the corresponding purposes.

At the independent level readers should be able,
without previous preparation or assistance, to pronounce
at least 98 words out of 100 and understand at least nine
out of ten ideas. Stated another way, they should not
miss more than two items out of a 100 word excerpt from a
story. Neither should they misunderstand or fail to
comprehend more than one point out of ten in a selection
read silently.

The independent level serves as a guideline for
homework assignments and for recreational reading
activities. For example, homework should generally be of
sufficient ease that pupils have little or no difficulty
either in pronouncing words or comprehending the message.
That homework assignments frequently violate this
principle is well-known. Indeed, the mis-assignment of
homework activities especially to low average and
below-average youngsters, often helps to create the
following problems:

1. Mama does the work.

2. Junior copies someone else's papers.

3. Junior does most of the work wrong, thus reinforcing his own mis-concepts.

245

4. Junior does a haphazard job, just enough to "get by."

5. Junior does not do the work at all.

Regardless of the course of action which Junior pursues, the final outcome remains the same. The assignment does not result in learning and therefore proves completely ineffective. Whatever its initial objective, it failed.

The second purpose of the figures presented for the independent level is to guide the location and selection of books for recreational reading. In general, recreational reading should be for pleasure; it should provide an interesting opportunity for pupils to practice the skills they are presently acquiring and to enable them to derive satisfaction from the wonderful world of books.

Recreational reading loses its pleasurable values, however, whenever the material becomes too difficult. We need to be extremely cautious in providing pupils with a specific list of required books or in encouraging them to read "challenging" books.

Poor readers who are expected to handle "challenging" books usually emerge as the victim rather than the victor. Encounters with books should not be hostile; they need not involve competition to see which one wins. Instead the challenge should be to persuade and encourage children to read and read and read -- regardless of the degree of ease of the materials.

At the instructional level readers should be able to pronounce at least 94 words out of 100 and understand at least seven out of ten ideas. In other words, they should miss no more than six words out of a 100 word passage and have comprehension difficulties with no more than three out of ten ideas in a silent reading selection.

Materials at the instructional level should be utilized by youngsters all day long in all subject areas, not just in reading class. The figures for this type of reading are somewhat lower than for the independent level because a teacher or student teacher (a pupil who teaches another pupil) is readily available to clarify any difficulties. At the end of the lesson, however, pupils should be able to handle the material at the independent level.

Insofar as classroom instruction is concerned, the figures provided in Chart 5-1 are the most important. It is a simple matter to determine whether pupils are reading material at appropriate levels of ease. Their scores on comprehension quizzes will average at least 70%, and during any oral activity they will miss no more than six words out of 100. Keep in mind, however, that the instructional level assumes the availability of a teacher to provide assistance as needed.

At the frustration level potential readers are in serious trouble. Their word analysis score falls below 94% accuracy, or their comprehension drops below 70%, or they encounter difficulty in both areas. Frequently the oral reading performance is acceptable while the silent reading is inadequate. Since the act of pronouncing words is a simpler task than comprehending, this disparity between scores is no cause for undue concern except when a teacher says, "He pronounces words so well I'll let Johnny read this book, even though he can't answer many of the questions."

This practice does pose problems for it begins with a child's weakness and proceeds to even more difficult materials. Very few youngsters recover from this obvious misplacement. The appropriate procedure is to locate material in which pupils can achieve proficiency in both word analysis and comprehension. If either score falls in the frustration range, children are frustrated even before they begin.

In Chapter 2 we considered the plight of the educationally disadvantaged, those children whose needs are not currently being met by our schools. Pupils who operate at the frustration level, pupils whose quiz grades consistently fall below 70 %, pupils whose oral performances are shattering--these are our dropouts, both psychological and physical. These youngsters are quite frequently our discipline problems, our unmotivated non-listening non-learners. We often help them establish a life pattern early, one they do learn to continue.

Frustration breeds failure, and failure breeds further frustration. Eventually both result in a reluctance or refusal to try. Indeed, youngsters may feel so threatened by the fear of failure that they become unable to achieve that which they could normally accomplish. Unfortunately, beginning in the first grade, a majority of pupils in some schools are associated with materials which are inappropriate for them because of the interest and/or readability factors. After several years of constant frustration caused by constant failure, is it any wonder pupils become excessively withdrawn, or overt discipline problems, hating school and community authority figures, education, and their more academically successful classmates?

Would we not react in the same manner in similar circumstances? Indeed, do we not every day? Those of us who are not especially competent or interested in certain areas tend to depreciate the value of these activities and avoid them whenever possible. People who do not understand or enjoy football avoid watching or attending the games and assail those who do. Poor swimmers often avoid swimming facilities and rarely take trips to the beach. People who don't enjoy cooking or who don't cook well either employ cooks or "eat out." (This does not mean that those who "eat out" can't cook well!). People who feel uncomfortable and inadequate in large social groups tend to avoid such gatherings. Some even become hermits.

This in only human nature. We would be well advised to consider the social, psychological, and educational implications of requiring or expecting youngsters to operate at their frustration levels during even part of the day. Whenever children are forced to function beyond their present capabilities, both they and their teachers fail. Indeed, pupils and educators often stay frustrated for decades at a time. Only when it is possible for youngsters to achieve success can teachers do the same.

Using the modified Betts Criteria at the beginning of school and periodically throughout the year is one essential step in preventing failure and making success possible for pupils and teachers.

Betts also listed a capacity, or listening, level which requires no reading ability of pupils. However, they must be able to comprehend seven out of ten ideas in material presented orally to establish that level. The significance of the capacity level is that youngsters who read poorly or not at all may eventually learn to read up to the point at which they can understand the material read to them. The capacity level, then, provides useful data about pupils' potentials for development.

Keep in mind, however, that the capacity level of pupils at the primary and lower intermediate levels should be interpreted with caution. Research studies indicate that pupils are more proficient in listening than in reading ability until about the seventh grade (33). This means that although younger pupils will almost invariably score higher on listening, they should not be expected to read up to this level immediately. Some first graders, for example, may function at the third-grade level in listening. These youngsters should not be expected to be able to read at a third-grade level during the year.

An Initial Reading Inventory

1. Background

An IRI is a practical device for determining the instructional and independent reading levels of all members of a class. Its use makes it possible for a teacher to select materials which every pupil can read. For primary-age children it must be given individually. Beginning with the fourth grade, it can be administered to an entire class simultaneously (171).

One can hardly read much of the practical literature without encountering what is usually referred to as an Informal Reading Inventory (33, 54, 95, 113, 498, 499, 568, 643, 657, 658, 725). You should note that the term used here is _initial_, indicating our belief that determining pupils' reading levels is a process which needs constantly to be validated. After all, as time passes, old results become inappropriate. An _Initial_ Reading Inventory, therefore, assumes that a tentative diagnosis of levels at the beginning of the school year will be followed by further checks on a frequent and systematic basis.

Since we have defined _Initial Reading Inventory_ (IRI) only in a vague fashion, let us be more specific. An IRI consists of a series of reading passages, two from the beginning of each reading level (or book) from preprimer two (traditional coding system) through grade eight. The first passage is read silently for comprehension, the second orally for word analysis purposes.

The primary teacher who uses an IRI effectively can ascertain a youngster's instructional and independent levels in approximately ten minutes. The average time required to derive the same information through the group procedure for older pupils is slightly less.

2. Purposes

Basically, there are nine possible purposes of an IRI. This device may be used to reveal

A. Independent, instructional, and frustration levels

B. Specific basic words a pupil cannot pronounce

C. Types of word analysis difficulties that present problems -- consonants, clusters, digraphs, vowels, syllabication, accents, punctuation

D. Parts of words missed -- initial, final, medial

249

E. Degree of oral reading fluency

F. Over- or under-use of contextual clues

G. Types of comprehension weaknesses -- literal, implied, or creative

H. Vocabulary strengths or weaknesses

I. Speech difficulties.

While all nine of these purposes are briefly discussed next, the major objective of this chapter is to facilitate the association of each youngster with reading materials at the appropriate levels (purpose number one).

A. Independent, instructional, and frustration levels. As just indicated, this is the major function of an IRI. Even if diagnosis beyond the determination of reading levels were not completed, the administration of this device would still have provided a very useful basis for initial instruction.

B. Specific basic words a pupil cannot pronounce. A poor reader often evinces difficulty in identifying a number of basic sight words, of which the Dolch Basic Word List (139) is the most well-known. A teacher who uses an IRI as a diagnostic device to isolate each youngster's specific needs may develop a list of basic words which present problems for each child and teach these words almost immediately. The 220 basic items in the Dolch Basic Word List comprised approximately 65% of the words in four third-grade books and 59% of the words in four sixth-grade books. A replication by Johns (431) found similar percentages. Mastery of these items obviously takes a child a long way down the road to literacy. See List A at the end of this chapter.

C. Types of word analysis errors that present problems. Some youngsters experience difficulty in identifying certain vowel and/or consonant-sound correspondences or in applying particular syllabication generalizations. Observation and identification of these problems, when used as a basis for instruction in skills, can be an effective procedure for meeting individual differences and needs.

D. Parts of words missed. Some youngsters with reading difficulties notice only the first letter or two or a

250

word. Some pay attention to the end, some attend to both the beginning and end but not the middle, and some ignore the entire word. It is quite useful to determine the elements which the reader does notice, for this provides an indication of what we must do next.

E. Degree of oral reading fluency. As a pupil reads, a teacher may derive information relative to the degree of fluency characterizing the oral reading activity. Does the child read word-by-word without any recognition of meaning? Or do the pitch, rhythm, stress, and gestures indicate comprehension even during oral reading?

F. Over- or under-use of contextual clues. While youngsters should be taught to identify new words through their use in actual sentences, it is possible to over-use this technique. Children who do this tend to create their own stories as they move along. We need to be sure of their problem just as we need to recognize the fact that the child who reads, "He rode down the street on a house," is failing to make effective use of context.

G. Types of comprehension weaknesses. Pupils often experience difficulty in comprehension. Some may evince a general pattern of weaknesses while others may have specific problems with literal or implied or creative requirements. Likewise readers of all ages often have trouble with the following comprehension skills: Main ideas, supporting details, compare and contrast, cause-effect, sequence, classification, predicting outcomes, and drawing conclusions. Analysis of (a pattern of) errors may provide clues indicating specific needs which should be met for particular students.

H. Vocabulary strengths or weaknesses. Because three questions relate to meanings of words, an IRI may also be used to provide a rough initial indication of the extent and richness of a youngster's reading, listening, and speaking vocabularies.

I. Speech difficulties. Quite frequently speech defects go unnoticed for extended periods of time through various pupil subterfuges -- failure to participate in oral discussions and mumbling or speaking softly. The use of even a brief individual oral reading selection will help to identify pupils who should be immediately referred to speech personnel.

3. Construction

Following is a sequence of steps which may be used in constructing an IRI. A school's faculty or even one or more teachers might utilize this procedure to help determine the most appropriate materials for each youngster.

Step One: "Estimate the probable range of reading ability in the class or the school."
An inventory prepared for only a first grade might well consist of materials selected from the second and third preprimers, the primer, the first reader, and the two books designated for the second grade (It is not possible to make an IRI from a first preprimer.). A fifth grade generally requires materials from primer through eight. We have already commented that the range of individual differences in reading ability becomes wider as pupils grow older.

Step Two: "Use the school's lead basal series for constructing an IRI."
As indicated in Chapter 1, it is highly desirable to utilize the same basal reading set since this provides for a continuous sequence of skill development (83, 305, 394, 568). Because some basal reading series provide materials only through grade six, it usually is necessary to locate a second series for upper-level materials. Please remember that the grade designation of a book serves only one useful function: to indicate that one text is more difficult than another in the same series (271). Materials produced by different companies often vary in their readability levels even though they bear the same grade designation (19. 386, 516, 568, 608, 738).

Step Three: "Secure single copies of the books at each level."
Either the teacher's edition or pupil's copy is satisfactory for this purpose.

Step Four: "Locate two reading selections from the beginning of each book."
The first selection should be used for silent reading: the second for oral. At the preprimer levels, the oral selections may be fifty words each. Beginning with the primer, however, the oral passages should be one hundred words. Passages for silent reading may be approximately 50 words at the preprimer levels and gradually increase to 200 words at the eighth-grade level. While story-length passages have a higher degree

of accuracy they involve too much administration time to be practical.

The paragraphs selected from each book for the second passage (oral reading) should be almost exactly 50 words (for preprimers) or 100 words (for primer through six or eight). This facilitates the use of Chart 5-1 for determining each pupil's word analysis proficiency. Obviously selections of 64 or 118 words would complicate the scoring process.

On the other hand, the silent reading passages may vary considerably. The suggestions (50 words for preprimers, 100 words for primer through six, and 200 words for grades seven and eight) are provided merely as approximate guidelines and need not be adhered to rigidly. Expressed another way: The oral reading selections must be very close to either 50 or 100 words. The silent reading passages operate under no such restriction.

When making the oral selections, do not count unusual proper nouns or foreign terms. Merely underline those words. You should count such words as a, and, and the every time they appear.

If a sentence in the oral selection does not end with the fiftieth or one hundredth word, delete words or phrases in order to obtain a paragraph which is reasonably close to the desired number of words. We suggest that selections range between 48 and 52 or 97 and 103 words in length. Examples of possible sentence changes to meet these criteria follow.

a. Early the next day, Mark rode with his father to see the damage done by the storm. (Storm is word number 106. Delete the last four words.)

b. The entire household was upset by the unexpected news, and Father was hurt most of all. (All is word number 108. End the sentence with the word news.)

c. The giant polar bear slowly lumbered toward the stream. (Stream is word number 105. Delete giant, polar and slowly.)

Step Five: "Develop questions for the first (silent) selection at each level."

For preprimer stories use four questions; for all others ten. Chart 5-2 indicates the types we use and the number of each.

CHART 5-2

QUESTIONS FOR AN IRI

Types	Preprimers	Primer through Grade Eight
Literal	No. 1	Nos. 1-3
Implied	No. 2	Nos. 4-6
Vocabulary	No. 3	Nos. 7-9
Creative	No. 4	No. 10

Reference to the chart should indicate that question two for preprimer selections is always implied, while question four is always creative. Beginning at the primer level, questions four through six are always implied, and number ten is always creative. Practice in constructing questions is provided in Chapter 11.

Step Six: "Construct a cover sheet which includes credits."
It is a standard procedure to contact publishing companies to secure written permission to duplicate excerpts from their materials. This cover sheet should also contain the words Initial Reading Inventory as well as spaces to record basic data such as the pupil's grade, name, age, data, and instructional level. A sample cover sheet is included in List B at the end of this chapter.

Step Seven: "Type the material on mimeograph stencils."
If a complete IRI is provided for each pupil, its various levels may be used periodically throughout the elementary school years. For instance, if a booklet encompassing the selections taken from all levels from the second preprimer through grade eight is used at the beginning of each school year, all teachers will be able to use the same material to determine the instructional levels for their pupils each year.
Double-space the paragraphs to make the material easier for pupils to read and allow space to note word identification errors. At the beginning levels, it is sometimes desirable to use a primary typewriter. However, this practice does tend to "mark" the material as juvenile for older pupils with reading problems. At the preprimer levels the pupils can read from the actual books. A sample format for one level is included in Lists C and D at the end of the chapter. Note the absence of any grade designation. Only the name of the book, title of the selection, and page numbers are included.

<u>Step Eight</u>: "Duplicate and collate."

One form of a complete booklet for use in grades one through eight requires two pages for each level, one for the reading selections and another for the comprehension questions. An IRI covering thirteen levels (second pre-primer through grade eight) uses 26 sheets of paper (plus one for the cover). When all the material has been collated and stapled, there should be a kit consisting of 30 booklets, one for each member of the class.

4. Administration and Interpretation:

Individual

The following steps outline a procedure for administering and interpreting an IRI. Individual diagnosis is necessary at the primary levels and at upper levels for pupils who enter school during the year.

<u>Step One</u>: "Rank pupils from low to high according to the judgment of last year's teachers."

We have already indicated that teacher opinions may vary considerably from pupils' actual instructional reading levels. Nevertheless, they are more nearly accurate than the alternatives. Check the poorest readers first, for their needs are least likely to be met if traditional grade-level materials are employed.

<u>Step Two</u>: "Begin oral reading at the lowest level (preprimer two) for the pupils assumed to be the poorest readers."

Since we can expect the pupils with the lowest rankings to read poorly or not at all, the second preprimer seems a logical place to start. (Most first preprimers do not have a sufficient number of words from which to construct a reading selection.) While progressing through the list of pupils, you may find it possible to begin at high levels.

Two points are worth keeping in mind. First, the major objective in oral reading is to determine whether or not the youngster can correctly pronounce at least 94% of the words. If he reads the first sentence or two with no difficulty whatsoever, you may reasonably conclude that the pupil's word analysis is quite proficient at that level. To save time, compliment the youngster and ask him to read aloud the next more difficult oral selection. Continue allowing the child to read aloud until he falls below the 94% mark (i.e., makes more than six errors in 100 words or more than three errors in a fifty-word selection) or until he displays obvious signs of frustration.

If the pupil's performance during the first sentence or so indicates his inability to handle the assignment, stop him to prevent continued frustration. Note the last level at which he passes the oral section without obvious frustration.

A second point to remember concerns the types of errors which are made. Certainly it is more desirable for a pupil to make the same error four times than to make four different errors. Also errors which do not significantly affect meaning (<u>play</u> for <u>played</u> or <u>these</u> for <u>those</u>) are less serious that those which severely impede comprehension (<u>horse</u> for <u>house</u> or <u>and</u> for <u>said</u>). Both of these points become crucial when a person's oral reading performance falls just below the 94% mark. Analysis of the errors themselves involves careful teacher judgment as to whether the pupil can actually handle the material.

<u>Step Three</u>: "If possible, begin silent reading two levels below the last oral selection which the child handles successfully (at least 94%)."

Let us assume the pupil scored 96% on the oral section of the primer and 91% on the first reader's oral paragraph. It is usually safe to conclude his oral level is the primer. However, we know that most people read orally at a higher level than they do silently. That is, they call words better than they comprehend. For this reason it is desirable to drop back two selections from the last oral selection which the pupil <u>passed</u> and begin the silent part of the inventory.

For instance, the child who reads the primer's oral selection with 96% accuracy should begin reading silently at the second preprimer level. Sometimes you will find the pupil's ability to understand printed material is so deficient that he cannot even pass the silent reading passage two levels below his oral level. This problem, often referred to as "word calling," is extremely common.

<u>Step Four</u>: "Proceed to easier or more difficult selections as the silent reading performance dictates."

After the youngster reads the first silent selection, there are usually three possible alternatives.

a. If the pupil correctly answers at least 70% of the questions, ask him to read the next higher silent selection. If he passes that, he may read one more selection, which is the last set he could successfully read orally. Even if he scores at least 70% on that selection, the pupil should stop. Trying to proceed further would only be a waste of time since he has already demonstrated an inability to read orally at the

next age. (If the school is using IRIs as part of a research study, allow each pupil to read until he is unable to pass the comprehension exercise.)
   b. Ask the pupil with scores less than 70% on the first set of questions to read silently the next easier level. Continue downward until he can operate at the 70% level.
   c. If the pupil cannot pass both the silent and oral selections of the lowest level (second preprimer), you may conclude he either reads little or not at all. In either case, many of the ideas mentioned in Chapter 4 should prove useful. Introduction to a first preprimer and use of the language-experience approach -- See Chapters 6, 7, 8 -- may also be considered.

Step Five: "Record the instructional level for each pupil and secure appropriate materials as an aid to grouping and teaching."
   The instructional level is the highest point at which a person is able to score at least 94% on word analysis and 70% on comprehension. If he scores very high on one and fails the other, proceed to easier passages until the correct placement is determined.
   Consider the three situations in Chart 5-3. What do you consider the appropriate instructional level for each pupil?

CHART 5-3

SOME INITIAL READING INVENTORY SCORES

Pupil	Book	Word Analysis	Comprehension
Frank	Preprimer 3	94	100
	Primer	94	90
	First Reader	95	100
	2-1	88	80
Colette	Preprimer 3	100	75
	Primer	100	75
	First Reader	100	60
	2-1	93	50
Randy	Primer	98	100
	First Reader	93	60
	2-1	93	50

   Frank's level is first reader. This is the highest point at which he achieves success on both parts of an Initial Reading Inventory.

Colette reads at the primer level but is often misplaced with a first reader simply because she pronounces words so beautifully. She probably requires a great deal of assistance on comprehension before further progress can be made.

Randy reads at the primer level but is often incorrectly misplaced with the first reader because he comes "so close" on both parts and his primer scores are so high. It is helpful to keep in mind that while his passing scores are high, Randy was reading selections secured from the first part of the book. The material is obviously going to become more difficult as time passes. To associate him with first reader material is to provide a book in which he cannot even handle the easiest materials. As soon as the instructional level is determined for each pupil, compile a master list indicating which children read at the various levels. After "grouping the groups," you are ready to organize reading level, but not skills, groups.

One further word: Diagnosis using an IRI should begin just as quickly as children become readjusted to school. In grades two and three, an IRI may be administered starting on the second or third day of school. Because each administration requires an average of ten minutes, the entire process takes about one complete school day or an hour each day for a week. (With the exception of the child who comes to school reading, kindergarten and first-grade teachers have no need to use an IRI until their pupils are assumed to be ready to use the second preprimer.)

Parent volunteers may play an extremely useful role during the first week of school. By planning activities which one or more parents can conduct, you can free yourself to determine each pupil's actual reading levels. During the first week of school parents can collect lunch, milk, and fee money, write receipts, check children's height, weight, or vision, or read stories, poems, or fables to a group, or teach a song or rhymthic activity.

5. Administration and Interpretation: Group

Beginning at the fourth grade, it is much easier to administer and interpret an IRI. This is due to the fact that the silent part of the inventory can be given to an entire class simultaneously, thus partially resolving the problem of what to do with some children while you are working with others.

The steps for utilizing an IRI include the following:

Step One: "Discuss the wide range of individual differences and the importance of recognizing and providing for them."

Using two male pupils, lead the class in understanding that different provisions must be made for people with varying characteristics. Begin the discussion by talking about the ways the two fellows differ. Common observations typically include size, color of hair or eyes, kind of clothing worn, and posture. If no one mentions the point to be considered (and the criterion used for selecting the boys), offer an additional hint by asking the fellows to sit on the desk and hold their feet side by side. Someone usually volunteers the information that one has bigger feet or wears larger shoes than the other (499).

Then ask what would happen if one boy raced the other on the playground...Which one would you expect to win?...Why?...Suppose each of them had to wear the other's shoes...What would happen to each boy?... Why?...What would it do to each one's speed?...Which shoes would be best for Danny?...Why?...for Todd?...Why?...Should all fourth graders (for instance) be required to wear the same size shoes?...Why or why not?...Eventually the class should reach the conclusion that every child needs to wear shoes that are, for him, just right. We never measure Todd's feet to buy Danny's shoes.

Next draw an analogy with reading. Assume that one fellow can read very difficult books while another boy can read books only if they aren't so hard. What would happen if we gave the fellows the wrong books? Will Danny learn very much if we give him a book that's too hard for him to read?...Why not?...Will Todd learn anything if we give him a book that's far too easy for him?...Why not?...What kind of book should each boy have?...Should all fourth graders have to read the same book?...Why not?...Having to read the wrong book is just like what?...(Wearing the wrong shoes.)

Then record the following information on the chalkboard:

Pronouncing Words - 94%

Understanding - 70%

Discuss the importance of locating for every pupil a book that is "just right." By the end of the discussion each person should know how to tell whether or not a book is appropriate. If the comprehension average falls below 70%, the book is inappropriate. If the pupil misses more than six words out of 100 on oral reading, the book is also wrong. Continuing to use that book will hurt his "feelings" just as wearing the wrong shoes will hurt his feet. (After a demonstration a little fellow once brought his book to one of the authors and asked, "Do I have to read this book? It's hurting my feelings!") A discussion of this type provides the necessary background and concept development for the next activity.

Step Two: "Distribute the booklets and explain how to use them."

Ask the class to keep the booklets closed but to fill in the blanks on the cover page. Displaying a copy of the booklet, explain the following: Pupils should read the silent selection (both columns) on page two, fold that sheet under the others, and, without referring to the story, answer the questions on the next page. Supply paper clips to hold the folded-over pages together.

To answer their queries:

a. You will not be graded on your report card.

b. We will not count off for spelling. Do the best you can and don't worry.

c. Some questions (number 2 in the preprimers and numbers 4-6 at the primer level and above) are not directly answered in the story. See if you can figure out what the answers are. You will really have to think, so use your head.

d. You are not being timed.

Since some pupils will finish before others, it is important to provide useful experiences for them while the others are still working. Before assigning the first selection, list and discuss three independent activities. (These are to be completed only after a story has been read and the questions answered.)

a. Please write and print the upper- and lower-case letters from A-Z. How many times in all should you write them?...(Four) This is ostensibly for determining their handwriting and letter formation, but it also indicates those who have not yet mastered the alphabetic sequence. Even one or two eighth graders may experience this difficulty.

b. Please write your autobiography. Discuss the meaning of the word and elicit types of information that might be included in their report. These includes answers to the following questions:

1. What is your name?

2. How old are you?

3. When is your birthday?

4. What do you look like?

5. Where do you live?

6. Who are your parents and other close relatives?

7. Who are your close friends?

8. What are your favorite games or hobbies?

9. What would you like to be when you grow up?

c. Please fill in this mimeographed form with information need for my register or cumulative file.

Since pupils rarely finish all three of these independent activities during the time their classmates are completing the first paragraphs, direct them to set their separate sheets aside and complete them only during their spare time.

Step Three: "Begin silent reading at the primer level and check the answers to the questions in class, if possible."
At the fourth-grade level, skip the preprimer selections and start with the primer paragraph. In the fifth grade start with the first reader. Move up one reading level for each grade. Even so at least one person in every class is likely to raise his hand and whisper, "I can't read this."
That's what we want to know. And we want this important information now in order to provide immediate experiences which a non-reader can handle successfully. Our favorite activity, discussed in Chapter Six, involves the use of Single Concept Cards. This provides initial success for such pupils.
It is important to circulate throughout the class and "help" pupils fold and paper clip the reading pages under

261

their booklets and answer the questions <u>without</u> referring to the story. Simply reminding the pupils to do so is not especially effective.

As soon as each person has completed the first selection, check the papers together, if possible. Ask the class to record a check mark in the left margin for the answers that are correct. Then count the checks and multiply by ten to obtain the score.

Allowing pupils to check the papers does pose some problems. First are the implied questions (numbers 4-6). Checking papers together can be a frustrating experience until pupils learn to judge whether their answers fall within the acceptable range instead of asking individually, "Is this right?"

A second problem concerns the vocabulary items (numbers 7-9). Give several examples of sentences or definitions and then ask the class to record checks if they knew what the words meant.

The third problem is related to the creative question (number 10). Since almost any answer is acceptable, ask the pupils to record a check if they answered the question.

It is always important to recheck the papers at home, especially until children have had multiple opportunities to learn how to check papers. The added advantage here is that a teacher should determine exactly what answers are acceptable and which ones are not. Someone who grades leniently may accept an answer that another teacher would reject. This is an acceptable practice, for an IRI should be checked with the same degree of strictness that will prevail in a teacher's classroom activities.

<u>Step</u> <u>Four</u>: "Assign the second (and subsequent) silent selections."

Regardless of their scores on the first story (except for pupils who obviously cannot read), every member of the class should then turn to the next silent selection and repeat the process described in Step Three. After answering ten questions, they should continue with those parts of the three independent activities which have not yet been completed.

Only two selections should be completed each day except at the seventh- and eighth-grade levels where three may be given after the first day. Beginning with the second selection, each pupil should stop reading the silent selections on an IRI whenever his comprehension score falls below 70%. The first set does not count since it is used mainly to orient pupils to the type of written procedures being utilized. It is interesting to note the fact that some pupils fail the first set and

262

pass the next (and harder) set. This typically results from their increased familiarity with the practice of answering written (implied) questions.

We sometimes find situations in which a pupil fails the first two levels given during a certain day but passes the second level. In that case, ignore the first level's low score. It might be caused by an unusually difficult passage, a hard set of questions, or lack of pupil familiarity with the topic. In some cases a youngster will score 60% on a lower level and 70% on a higher level. Both are borderline scores, for one more right or wrong answer could change the category from passing to failing. A good rule of thumb is, "When in doubt, continue to test."

Step Five: "Obtain oral evaluation scores for the ten poorest readers."

Except for very poor readers, most people score higher on oral reading than they do on silent. In a few cases pupils' comprehension performances exceed their word analysis levels. Because these particular pupils are almost invariably among the bottom one-third of a class, you can save time by checking only these youngsters for oral reading proficiency.

In most cases each of the ten pupils should read only one passage aloud, the one accompanying the silent selection read successfully. If the pupil scores at least 94% on word analysis, you need go no further. If he scores below this point, have him read aloud the next lower selection. Whichever level he passes then becomes his actual instructional level. Both the silent and oral parts must be handled successfully before the reading level can be ascertained. If IRI data are used for research purposes, all pupils should be tested on oral reading, as high as they can go.

Step Six: "Record the instructional level for each pupil and secure appropriate materials as a prelude to organizing reading-level groups."

As soon as the instruction level is recorded (on the front page) for each person, place the IRI booklets in separate stacks according to their grade indications. This process yields several useful pieces of information.

First, it tells how many levels are actually present within the class. Second, it indicates the class range, often quite a shocking revelation. Third, it indicates approximate reading levels for pupils whose performance is so far below their age levels that standard basal texts are completely inappropriate because of the interest factor.

At this point an intermediate teacher may need to locate and secure titles from series of high interest-low vocabulary series and use these materials as part of the instructional program with the poor readers involved.

Several factors seem worth mentioning. First, since grade-level designations on the spines of books indicate the sequence of difficulty of one set of material and are not equivalent from series to series, you should be cautious in concluding that a 2-1 level on an IRI is automatically a 2-1 level on Cowbody Sam (Chicago: Benefic Press) or Readers Digest Skill Builders (Pleasantville, New York: Reader's Digest Services) or Deep Sea Adventures Series (Chicago: Field Enterprises). It is not! A quick check of the pupil's ability to handle the high interest-low vocabulary material will indicate whether or not it is appropriate.

Second, high interest-low vocabulary series cannot be used effectively for instructional purposes if some copies of various titles are placed on media center shelves to be checked out by pupils. Such books must be removed from free access areas if they are to be used for instruction for poor readers. Otherwise those whose reading abilities are quite low will invariably say when we locate a high interest-low vocabulary book for their group, "Oh, I've already seen that. It's in the media center."

Third, since the number of levels will be far more than a teacher can teach, you must organize no more groups than you can teach. Unless the school has some plan for grouping, you will want to "group the groups." Chapter 12 discusses the procedure.

Only when appropriate materials--graded both by interest and reading levels--are secured should reading instruction begin. Since the entire process of administering an IRI usually requires approx imately a week, no books should be distributed until the final results are available.

Chart 5-4 outlines a schedule teachers at two different grade levels might follow in administering an IRI.

Gilmore Symbols

We suggested in Step Five that oral reading samples should be obtained for the poorest readers, that is, the first ten pupils who are unable to complete the silent IRI selections successfully.

CHART 5-4

SCHEDULE FOR ADMINISTERING
A GROUP INITIAL READING INVENTORY

Grade Four

Day 1: Discuss individual differences and the need for recognizing and providing for them. Administer and score the Primer and First Reader levels.

Day 2: Administer and score the 2-1 and 2-2 levels.

Day 3: Administer and score the 3-1 and 3-2 levels.

Day 4: Administer and score the 4 and 5 levels.

Day 5: Administer and score the 6, 7, and 8 levels.

(Some fourth-graders will score at these levels.)

Grade Seven

Day 1: Discuss individual differences and the need for recognizing and providing for them. Administer and score the 2-2 and 3-1 levels.

Day 2: Administer and score the 3-2 and 4 levels.

Day 3: Administer and score the 5 and 6 levels.

Day 4: Administer and score the 7 and 8 levels.

As each youngster reads aloud the oral selection accompanying the last silent selection he passed, you should record his performance. This task is best accomplished by providing him with a spare copy of the booklet so you can write in his.

While we prefer to use a modification of the symbols provided in the Gilmore Oral Reading Test (345), other sets of symbols may be utilized just as effectively. The suggested symbols are presented in Chart 5-5.

CHART 5-5

GILMORE SYMBOLS - MODIFIED

Type of Situation	Procedure	Example
1. Substitution	Record substitution above the correct word	brown the big black horse
2. Mispronunciation	Record mispronunciation (phonically, if necessary) above the correct word	anything to swap swap
3. Insertion	Use a caret (∧) to indicate inserted word	great the ∧ big bear
4. Omission	Circle omitted word, phrase or punctuation mark	We saw the (big) black bear in town. The next day Tom
*5. Repetition	Draw a wavy line under the word(s) or phrase repeated	The horse is in the corral.
*6. Hesitation	After two seconds place a check (✔) over the next word.	The horse is in the corral.
7. WPBT (word pronounced by teacher)	After five seconds, place a second check (✓) over the word and pronounce it.	The horse is in the corral.
*8. Pupil's correction of error	Record (C) beside the original response and do not count it as an error.	The old man lived in a sack-C shack.

*While items 5, 6, and 8 should be marked in order to indicate specific words with which the pupil is experiencing difficulty, they are not actually errors and should not be counted in the total.

Several points of clarification should be added here.

First, the difference between a mispronunciation and a substitution is that the former is not a real word and consequently will never make sense. On the other hand, a substitution is a real word which may or may not make sense. Examples of each type follow:

We rode up the street in a truck/taxi. (This type of substitution makes sense and is therefore a less severe problem (354) insofar as comprehension is concerned.)

We rode down the street on a house/horse. (This type of substitution does not make sense and is a major cause for concern.)

Tell Mark to turn on the facet/faucet. (This is a mispronunciation because facet is not a real word. This also is a cause for concern.)

Second, repetitions and hesitations are often used to give the reader more time to "figure out" the next word. If he is able to do so, neither should be consid- ered in counting the total number of errors. Techni- cally, repetitions and hesitations are not so much errors as they are indications of words which the reader needs to add to his sight vocabulary as indicated by starred items five and six. However, this point is debatable. Ekwall (296) and Silvaroli (639) count repetitions and errors. Johnson and Kress (441) do not.

Third, if a hesitation (of two seconds) eventually results in a word's being pronounced by the teacher (after five seconds), only the latter is considered. The hesitation no longer exists because it becomes a WPBT (word pronounced by teacher).

Fourth, when a pupil makes an error and corrects it spontaneously, place a capital C (for corrected) beside his original comment. No error should be recorded.

Fifth, speech difficulties should not be confused with reading problems. For example, wabbit/rabbit, wittle/little, and birfday/birthday indicate speech rather than reading problems. While you should indicate these differences, they should not be tallied as errors.

Sixth, dialectal differences should not be recorded as reading errors. For instance, dis/this, axed/asked, and screet/street are properly classified as dialect rather than reading patterns. They should be studied during the language period.

Evaluating IRIs

Schools in the process of adopting new reading books should also purchase IRIs if they are available and of good quality. Our studies of many basal IRIs convince us that they leave much to be desired. Thus we often recommend that schools or districts develop their own. In this case educators must evaluate their own product. The following statements, which form some of the criteria we use, may prove helpful (148).

A. SELECTION FACTORS

1. The selections are taken from the series of books being used for instruction. A IRI cannot be a valid indicator of a youngster's instructional level unless it is based on his or her actual or projected program (568).

2. There are two selections at each reading level from the second preprimer through the eighth or twelfth grade. One selection should be for silent reading, the other for oral reading.

3. Each passage is selected from a different story near the front of the book. The use of passages from different stories makes it possible for a teacher to individually administer the oral selections first, thereby saving administration time without providing the pupil with information which might be answers to questions on a passage being used for silent reading. The selections should be chosen from the front of the book since materials graduate in difficulty in terms of vocabulary and teachers are likely to begin instruction at the front of the text.

4. Selections are typical of the content, format, and language of the materials in the accompanying books. Thus a poem should not be used if the book is primarily prose. Nor should a dialect story or one with a number of foreign names or phrases be used unless it reflects the composition of the book.

5. The length of the oral reading selections are multiples or factors of one hundred. An oral passage of 50, 100, or 200 words facilitates the determination of the pupil's percentage of word analysis accuracy.

6. Silent reading selections gradually increase in length.

B. QUESTIONING FACTORS

1. The questions are based on the silent passages only. Since oral reading involves different skills than does silent reading, it is not desirable to follow oral reading with comprehension questions. Silent reading should always procede comprehension activities, except for diagnosis of oral reading.

2. Except at the preprimer levels, there are ten questions. The short length of the preprimer selections makes the use of four questions more practical. At all other levels, the use of ten questions (a) facilitates the determination of an accurate comprehension score, (b) provides the pupil with a fairer chance to demonstrate compentence, and (c) gives the teacher a clearer indication of the pupil's performance.

3. The questions include literal, implied, vocabulary, and creative items. We prefer a 3-3-3-1 pattern, both for IRI use and for checking on pupils' comprehension of their actual reading stories. This pattern enhances identification of the pattern of strengths and weaknesses displayed by a child. (At the preprimer levels there may be one question for each of the four types.)

4. The questions parallel the typical items used by teachers (568). Many teachers (a) offer no questions after silent reading, or (b) offer predominantly literal ones (426). Since IRIs are often made by entire faculties or system-wide committees, questioning procedures are likely to differ from the patterns used by many teachers. Comparability and therefore validity can be established if the faculty is provided instruction and guided practice in developing a set of questions for each selection in each book of the lead basal series. When housed in a central location, the questions can provide all teachers with comprehension exercises at various levels of difficulty. Cooperative development can also save teachers a tremendous amount of preparation time (174).

5. The questions are clearly worded. They avoid constructions unfamiliar to many children. Thus, "To whom did Mary give the book?" should be revised to read, "Who did Mary give the book to?"

6. The questions avoid using words which have not yet been presented in reading at that level. For example, "What relationship are Bill and Ricky?" is a poor question at the preprimer levels.

7. The questions do not answer each other. This problem can happen in two ways. First, one question may read, "What did Tom lose?" A subsequent question may ask, "What did Tom do when he lost his gloves?" If the pupil is reading and responding in a group situation (the recommended procedure in grades four and above), the second question will answer the first. A second type of overlapping question occurs when the second part of an item answers the first. Thus, "Was Tom really mad at Betsy? Why not?" is really two questions, the second of which answers the first.

8. The questions avoid the true-false format. Any question which can be answered by yes or no is true-false in nature. A less obvious but equally unacceptable pattern is found in two-option questions, such as "Did Lassie live in the city or the country?"

9. Except for vocabulary items, the questions avoid general knowledge information (17). A question should be deleted if a person can answer correctly because of his original fund of information. For example, "Where did Mark go to see the cows, horses, ducks, and chickens?" is likely to be an invalid question for comprehension purposes. One study of an achievement test revealed that low IQ boys could often score as well without the aid of the paragraphs as they could when the paragraphs were available (517).

C. CONSTRUCTION FACTORS

1. An IRI is organized in such a way that both class and individual administration are possible.

2. Two forms are developed, one for the fall and another for the spring. They make it possible for schools or teacher to determine the amount of progress during the school year by each individual. We have found it helpful to make three forms and select the two best exercises at each level to include in the two forms.

3. Answers are included for the literal and implied questions. They identify the appropriate responses for the items, assuring comparability of scoring among teachers. They also help professionals distinguish

between implied and creative questions. If the number of possible answers is fairly large, and diverse responses are acceptable, the question is probably creative. If the answers are similar and few in number, the question is probably implied.

Points to Remember

A. We have already suggested that you secure the assistance of parents or aides during the first week of school.

B. If the symbols for marking errors are unfamiliar, you may find it helpful to tape the performance of the first few children. Subsequent replay of the tape will enable you to check the accuracy of your work. Teachers are often surprised at the number of errors which originally went undetected; this is a part of the process of becoming more proficient in diagnostic analysis.

C. You may wish to record the modified Gilmore Symbols on one side of a 5 x 8 inch card and the instructional level figures of the Betts Criterial on the other, thereby providing a ready reference to refresh your memory during moments of back-to-school stress.

D. Silent reading always precedes oral reading except when a diagnostic evaluation is being conducted. The use of an IRI is such an activity. To permit silent reading beforehand would allow pupils to "cover up" some of their deficiencies and thus decrease or destroy the value of the diagnosis.

E. Two types of special situations always present themselves whenever consideration is given to providing appropriate materials for youngsters. The first concerns the specific need of a pupil who reads at a level considerably below grade placement. The second involves the extremely competent reader who operates at the opposite end of the spectrum. A consideration of each follows.

We have already suggested that a youngster in the fourth grade who reads at the first-grade level usually should not be associated with traditional materials at that level. One major problem, we said, was lack of interest.

Sixth graders may react negatively when expected to read traditional third-grade readers. For pupils of this type, an IRI may be developed using series of high

271

interest-low vocabulary materials. A simple procedure for associating these pupils with "supplementary series" would be to mark off 100 word selections near the front of each book in the series and then place the titles in order according to the level of difficulty (usually indicated opposite the title page). A quick count of oral errors may then be used to determine which book is most appropriate for a youngster. The process will be even more valuable if a check is also made of the pupil's comprehension. In this way even very poor readers may be correctly associated with interesting and appropriate materials. Some vocabulary-controlled high interest-low vocabulary series books are presented in List E at the end of the chapter.

On the other hand, a pupil who reads at a level well above grade placement may evince boredom if required to read intellectually insipid material. When these youngsters demonstrate a need for specific skills, appropriate provisions should be made. However, personalized (independent) programs should be designed for content. Much self-selection, or recreational reading, should be strongly encouraged. This type of procedure does not, of course, relieve a teacher of the responsibility for assisting these pupils in developing a variety of reading interests, of acquiring appreciation for the esthetic values of children's literature, and developing advanced reading skills. It merely adds a personalized approach to that of the basal reader.

F. Both primary and intermediate pupils may score higher than their instructional levels because only short passages are involved and long attention spans are not required. A general guideline to follow is that children should not skip books. A youngster who finished level 6 last year can enter level 7 by passing that level on the IRI, but he can not use a level 8 book by recording that IRI score. There could still be a whole book (level) of new vocabulary words, abundant practice in applying skills, and numerous skill lessons to be considered. For this child the IRI primarily tells us whether or not to provide a level 7 book.

Advantages of Using
the Modified Betts Criteria and
An Initial Reading Inventory

A. One major advantage of the proposed procedure outlined is the involvement of parents in the program of the school. All too often they are treated as the foreign component of the school community. Those parents who are (or might become) interested should be encouraged to participate directly and meaningfully in the various activities of the school. This cooperative venture should lead to their more complete awareness of what the school program includes and what the art of teaching really involves. A number of schools release faculty members for blocks of in-service time and using parent-teachers in their stead. Reports have been positive, especially from newly-involved parents.

B. A second advantage comes with the use of the tape recorder. If each pupil is taped during the administration of the oral part of an IRI, you have an accurate record to indicate initial level and subsequent progress both to youngsters and parents. Leave space on the tape for a post-test.

C. When properly used, an IRI may be highly effective initial device for determining initial grade placement in basal or supplementary materials (408, 430). No other procedure for placement comes so close to matching children with appropriate materials. This is not to deny that subsequent changes will be needed. Since youngsters learn quite rapidly when they deal with materials at their own instructional levels, re-grouping will be necessary. Flexibility merely enhances the learning process.

D. Frustration is significantly reduced when pupils can actually read the materials with which they are teamed. Teachers hold within themselves the power to make success possible or deny it. We often determine the degree of a youngster's success the day we hand him a book--whether it be a reader, a speller, a social studies, or a science book. The implications of this statement can hardly be exaggerated.
While providing information about procedures for associating pupils with appropriate books is the object of this chapter, we must once again insist strongly that similar provisions be made in every area of the curriculum. To provide appropriate materials for each pupil is to promote social-emotional development and stimulate the learning process. To distribute standard materials to all youngsters regardless of their strengths, weaknesses, and needs is to ensure the failure of many.

E. For unusually proficient readers, boredom is significantly reduced if their capabilities are recognized and met. Poor study habits and apathy or antipathy toward learning often characterize bright

273

understimulated youngsters. As a result, they frequently become under-achievers. Interestingly, the same device which enables a teacher to select appropriate learning materials for poor readers also makes it possible to provide stimulating experiences for highly academic youngsters. Strategies for teaching advanced readers are described elsewhere (196B).

F. Use of an IRI and the Betts Criteria for grouping purposes also counteracts the problem often raised by parents of highly competent students. So long as youngsters are associated with materials which are appropriate for them, no one can say that slower students are holding the faster ones back. Only when many pupils are so frustrated by the difficulty of their assignments that the teacher must go over and over and over the information is this parental complaint valid. Use of the ideas presented in this chapter can help to avoid this problem.

G. As the body of this chapter indicates, not only can you determine the probable appropriate reading material for each youngster, you can begin to discover tentative answers to a number of questions.

a. Does the pupil need assistance with implied comprehension?

b. Does he experience difficulty in pronouncing basic sight words?

c. Does he omit endings of words?

d. Does he require help in phrasing?

e. Does he ignore punctuation?

f. How extensive is his reading vocabulary?

Continued systematic observation may provide information for numerous subsequent learning activities. Under normal circumstances, months might elapse before such comparable information is available. Because an IRI reveals pupils' strengths, weaknesses, and needs in word analysis, vocabulary, and comprehension, it makes diagnostic teaching possible and practical.

H. Finally, when a poor reader spends a few minutes privately with a teacher during the first few days of school, he often becomes convinced that "things will be

274

different." First impressions make a difference. So do teachers who show that they care.

All problems, of course, don't end just because children are associated with appropriate materials. The teaching-learning process still must occur. But knowledge and attitudes are acquired and retained so much more rapidly and effectively when interesting materials are provided at the appropriate levels. Then, too, teacher morale is considerably enhanced when every pupil's learning becomes a reality. As youngsters become successful, so do we.

Summary

"Some educators believe that as many as 50 to 70 percent of students are placed in books that are too difficult (430:3)." Our observations place us in this category. At the primary level, we notice 35% of the children are currently holding inappropriate books. In grades 4-6 the figure typically approaches 50%. In grades 7 and 8 it is 65%, and in high school, where many of the poorest readers have already fallen by the wayside, the figure is 75%. Indeed, it is rare for us to find a heterogeneous class in which more than ten children can actually read grade-level books. Imagine the amount of money which is wasted on the purchase of inappropriate books!

Hillerich has observed, "If this author were asked to specify the one improvement in reading instruction that would contribute most to increased achievement in reading, the answer would be the proper placement of children in materials (408:118)."

This chapter began by contending that an Initial Reading Inventory (IRI) could provide accurate information about the appropriate reading levels of books for instructional and independent purposes. It advocated the constant use of the modified Betts Criteria and suggested specific procedures for developing an IRI and later administering it to individuals at the primary levels and the entire class at the intermediate levels.

To re-emphasize just one advantage of the use of an IRI, we would like to note again that any lesson which must be repeated several times during which more proficient pupils waste their time while some of their classmates never seem to acquire the information is a direct result of the use of inappropriate materials. Almost all children can learn to read or to read better (92). They can acquire skills and practice them in meaningful situations. But neither the proficient nor the poor readers can learn to the limits of their ability if they are allowed to move no more slowly or rapidly than their classmates.

Procrustes the robber often had unexpected visitors at night. He took them to the guest room and compared them to the size of the bed. A guest who was too tall was cut down to size. A guest who was too short was stretched to reach the length of the bed. It never seemed to occur to Procrustes that the problem lay not with the guests but with the bed.

FOR FURTHER READING

Berliner, David C., "Academic Learning Time and Reading Achievement," in Comprehension and Teaching: Research Reviews, pp. 203-226, ed. John T. Guthrie. Newark, Delaware: International Reading Association, 1981.

Coleman, Laurence J., "An Examination of Seven Techniques for Evaluating the Comprehensibility of Instructional Materials," Education and Training of the Mentally Retarded, XII, No. 4 (December, 1977), 339-344.

Culyer, Richard C., III, "Interpreting Achievement Tests: Some Areas of Concern," Clearing House, LV, No. 8 (April, 1982), 374-380.

Pikulski, John, "A Critical Review: Informal Reading Inventories," Reading Teacher, XXVIII, No. 2 (November, 1974), 141-151.

Valmont, William J., "Creating Questions for Informal Reading Inventories," Reading Teacher, XXV, No. 6 (March, 1972), 509-512.

List A

DOLCH BASIC WORD LIST

(Easier half of Dolch's Basic 220 Words)

a	did	help	no	ten
after	do	her	not	that
all	don't	here	of	the
am	down	him	old	this
an		his	on	three
and	eat		one	to
are		I	out	too
around	fast	if	over	two
as	find	in		
at	five	into	play	under
away	fly	is	put	up
	for	it		
be	from	its	ran	was
big	funny		red	we
black		jump	ride	went
blue	get		run	what
brown	give	know		who
but	go		said	will
by	going	like	saw	with
	good	little	see	
call	green	look	she	yellow
came			so	yes
can	had	make	some	you
carry	has	may	soon	your
cold	have	me	stop	
come	he	my		

(Harder half of Dolch's Basic 220 Words)

about	four	new	take	why
again	full	now	tell	wish
always			thank	work
any	gave	off	their	would
ask	goes	once	them	write
ate	got	only	then	
because	grow	open	there	
been		or	these	
before	hold	our	they	
best	hot	own	think	
better	how		those	
both	hurt	pick	today	
bring		please	together	
buy	just	pretty	try	
		pull		
clean	keep		upon	
could	kind	read	us	
cut	right	use		
	laugh	round		
does	let		very	
done	light	say		
draw	live	seven	walk	
drink	long	shall	want	
		show	warm	
eight	made	sing	wash	
every	many	sit	well	
	much	six	were	
fall	must	sleep	when	
for	myself	small	where	
first		start	which	
found	never		white	

Dolch, Edward W., <u>Teaching Primary Reading</u>. Champaign,
Illinois: The Garrard Press, 1951.

278

List B

SAMPLE COVER SHEET FOR AN IRI

PUPIL BOOKLET

INITIAL

READING

INVENTORY

C   Richard C. Culyer, III

Name of Pupil _____

Date _____

Age _____

Form _____

Instructional Level _____

Oral Reading Level _____

Comprehension Level _____

279

List C [*]

SAMPLE SELECTIONS FOR AN IRI
MAGIC WINDOWS
"Nobody Knows Me"
Page 8

Silent:

Jim didn't want to go to school. The school was new to him, for his family had just moved to the city. And it was a big school. In the little town Jim came from, everyone knew him, and he knew everyone. How was he to find friends here in this great big new school?

Jim walked very slowly to school. Cars swished past him. Horns tooted and engines roared. A policeman whistled. Tires squealed. It was all very noisy and strange to Jim who liked country sounds--birds singing, wind in the trees, a cow calling to her calf.

"Joey's Job"
Pages 18-19

Oral:

"I've got it up all right, Mom," he said, smiling proudly.

"Good boy. It wasn't too heavy for you after all," his mother said.

"No," he answered. "Now I'll start loading." His dark eyes were bright as he filled his arms with the sacks of doughnuts and put them carefully into the basket on the bike.

"Don't take too many at once," his mother said. "I don't want you to drop them in that dirty snow and ruin them."

"I'll be careful," Joey said.

His mother looked at him, "You sure you want to do this, honey?" she asked.

---

[*]Selection excerpted from pages 18-19 of William D. Sheldon and Mary C. Austin, Magic Windows. Boston: Allyn and Bacon, Inc., 1968 (Courtesy Allyn and Bacon).

SAMPLE QUESTIONS FOR AN IRI (17)

MAGIC WINDOWS

"Nobody Knows Me"

Page 8

Answer the following:

1. Why didn't Jim want to go to school?

2. Where had Jim's family just moved?

3. What sounds did Jim like?

4. How far did Jim live from school?

5. How did Jim feel?

6. Why did a policeman whistle?

7. What are <u>engines</u>?

8. What does <u>squealed</u> mean?

9. What does <u>strange</u> mean?

10. What could the boys and girls do to help make Jim feel at home?

Comprehension _____

Oral Reading _____

List E

HIGH INTEREST-LOW VOCABULARY BOOKS

A. Primary Interest

    1. Beginning-to-Read Books   Chicago: Follett

    2. Butternut Bill Series   Chicago: Benefic

    3. Button Books   Chicago: Benefic

    4. Easy Readers   New York: Grosset and Dunlap

    5. Easy-to-Read Books   Chicago: Benefic

B. Intermediate Interest

    1. American Adventure Series   New York: Harper and Row

    2. Checkered Flag Series   Chicago: Field

    3. Cowboy Sam Series   Chicago: Benefic

    4. Dan Frontier Series   Chicago: Benefic

    5. Deep-Sea Adventure Series   San Francisco: Harr Wagner

    6. First Books   New York: Franklin Watts

    7. I Want to be Books   Chicago: Children's Press

    8. Sailor Jack Books   Chicago: Benefic

    9. Treat Truck   Chicago: Benefic

    10. True Books   Chicago: Children's Press

CHAPTER 6

INITIATING BEGINNING READING INSTRUCTION

Introduction

A question frequently posed by first-grade teachers is, "How can I provide beginning instruction in reading?" The question is important because the premature and inappropriate introduction of reading instruction can lead to immediate and continuous frustration and failure, both by pupils and teachers. A child's early perceptions of school and self are influenced by the extent of his academic success (particularly in reading). Therefore, teachers who are concerned about children's self-concepts and interest in reading recognize the importance of enhancing each child's opportunities for success.

A number of factors are especially related to a child's success in beginning reading. They include the following:

1. the type of reading readiness and reading programs provided

2. the extent and quality of the child's reading readiness experiences (i.e., the degree to which he has mastered the various reading readiness skills)

3. the extent to which the child's motivation can be captured (53)

4. the amount and type of family support

5. the quality and quantity of the instruction itself (i.e., the extent to which it is mastery-based)

6. the child's physical condition (i.e., vision, hearing, general health, etc.)

7. the child's mental ability

The school has varying degrees of influence on these factors. For example, teachers can decide the type of reading readiness experiences that will be provided. The principal can decide whether the school will provide a reading program or whether each teacher will use her favorite materials and procedures in isolation from children's specific needs. On the other hand, teachers can do little about a child's mental ability other than make specific provisions for meeting his needs as they exist from day to day.

In an attempt to answer the question about how to initiate beginning reading instruction, this chapter consists of three sections: (a) strategies for initiating beginning reading instruction with words and sentences, (b) strategies for providing parallel instruction and practice, and (c) strategies for using the Language-Experience Approach.

It will be readily apparent that our preference for initiating beginning reading instruction is a visual rather than an auditory procedure. Thus we begin with whole words and present phonic generalizations after children learn to recognize several words with the same phonic element. We use this sequence for several reasons:

1. The children with whom we work, especially those outside the educational mainstream, generally learn much better this way. Others have noted the same finding (475).

2. The children are more receptive to learning when there is something they can do to show their progress. Thus they can go home and demonstrate the ability to read several words rather than announce, "I can say /puh/."

3. Many of the earliest words which children encounter are not phonically regular, and we do not wish to restrict the print to words with regular sound-symbol correspondences. However, we are strong believers in teaching phonic skills. Specific content and strategies are presented in Chapter 9. This chapter emphasizes visual procedures.

It will also be obvious that we advocate introducing words and then sentences before introducing the paragraph level at which some writers begin the language-experience approach. This corresponds to our practice of proceeding from simple to more complex.

Strategies for Initiating
Beginning Reading Instruction
With Words and Sentences

The major purpose of this section is to identify and describe some strategies which can be used to initiate beginning reading instruction. These procedures are designed to help young children bridge the gap between reading readiness and beginning reading. The entire sequence of events may be viewed as a process (160) of developing pupil competence in:

Phase 1: the appropriate reading readiness skills.

Phase 2: recognizing words presented on Single Concept Cards under short-term recall conditions.

Phase 3: recognizing words presented on Single Concept Cards under long-term recall conditions.

Phase 4: recognizing words presented in Single Concept Cards Sentences under short-term recall conditions.

Phase 5: recognizing words presented in Single Concept Card Sentences under long-term recall conditions.

The remainder of this section considers strategies for proceeding from one phase to the next.

PHASE 1: "Develop pupil competence in the appropriate reading readiness skills."

It is extremely important to determine the extent to which pupils possess competence in the reading readiness areas identified in Chapter 4A. Information regarding a pupil's competence in various aspects of reading readiness can be determined by: (a) reading readiness tests, (b) informal tests, and/or (c) analysis of general classroom performance. If these data are transferred to a class analysis chart, they provide a composite picture of individual and group performances. Chart 6-1 provides a sample format to use in recording pupil performance in various academic aspects.

It should be noted that Chart 6-1 provides a global rather than a precise indication of each pupil's performance on the various aspects of reading readiness.

CHART 6-1

READY TO READ CHECKLIST --
ACADEMIC COMPONENT

PUPIL	READING READINESS														SINGLE CONCEPT CARDS		SCC SENTENCES	
	Listening	Following directions	Speaking	Oral vocabulary	Oral context	Oral comprehension	Visual discrimination	Visual memory	Word boundaries	Left-to-right	Top-to-bottom	Auditory discrimination	Auditory memory	Letter-sound associations	Short-term recall	Long-term recall	Short-term recall	Long-term recall

Key: - = unsatisfactory
      + = satisfactory
To indicate a change in a pupil's academic
status, simply draw a vertical bar of another
color through the horizontal one.

Furthermore, it considers each aspect collectively rather than breaking each component into sub-competencies. For example, listening consists of a number of specific sub-skills. A teacher preparing to initiate beginning reading instruction does not need to assess each pupil's performance in every listening sub-skill in order to determine whether or not a pupil appears to be ready to begin receiving reading instruction. Instead the teacher should make a global judgment based on the answer to this question: Do the pupil's listening skills give him a reasonable chance to succeed in beginning reading? If the answer is "yes," the child receives a "+" for "satisfactory" regardless of his pattern of proficiency and need on the specific listening sub-skills. If the answer is "no," the child receives a "-" for "unsatisfactory," once again regardless of his pattern of performance on the corresponding sub-skills.

While finely-tuned diagnosis is very helpful for identifying pupil competencies and areas requiring additional assistance, it is of limited value in answering the question: Does Johnny appear to be ready to begin receiving reading instruction? An analogy involving early reading levels might clarify this important point.

A teacher who is presenting instruction at the primer level is very much interested in identifying each pupil's proficiency in the various aspects of reading competence. Knowledge of specific strengths, weaknesses, and needs enables her to implement a diagnostic-prescriptive instructional model. However, when the teacher considers whether or not to introduce materials at the first-reader level, she is less interested in questions such as "Can Kay make the letter-sound association for /b/?" and "Does Kay recognize the word does in context?" and more interested in the question "Is it likely that Kay will be able to achieve satisfactorily in materials at an increased level of difficulty?"

PHASE 2: "Develop pupil competence in recognizing words presented on Single Concept Cards under short-term recall conditions." (Short-term recall for SCCs is defined as recall thirty minutes after instruction and/or practice.)

Perhaps we should begin by repeating the observation that pupils do not have to possess competence in all of the designated reading readiness skills to proceed to SCCs. Nor must pupils have totally mastered any particular reading readiness skill to begin Phase 2. However, pupils need to acquire considerable competence in most or all of those skills to achieve success in beginning reading instruction. Thus, teachers should provide continuous assistance until pupils master those competencies. The key concept is that instruction in reading readiness skills does not stop the day that instruction in reading begins. Nor does consideration of the reading readiness skills end during grade one. It may be helpful to consider the following questions.

1. Do competent first-grade readers possess sufficient listening skills for their future needs?

2. Do competent first-grade readers possess sufficient following direction skills for their future needs?

3. Do competent first-grade readers possess sufficient oral vocabulary (oral comprehension, oral context, auditory memory, etc.) for their future needs?

If our answers to the above questions are no, it becomes obvious that reading readiness skills are not completely developed even among good readers at the first-grade level. Indeed, many reading readiness skills are renamed as oral language skills and are subject to continuous development throughout life.

Pupils are ready to begin using SCCs (a) when they demonstrate interest in labels present in the school and/or community and (b) when they attempt to remember (i.e., recognize by memory) the words. At this point it is appropriate to select two nouns from the materials which will one day be used for instruction. For example, if the Bookmark Reading Program, Eagle Edition (287) is the lead basal, choose two concrete nouns from the first preprimer, Sun Up. If several interlocking basal series are used for instruction, develop a locally-relevant sight word list consisting of words common to the series. Directions for doing so are included in Chapter 8. If the language-experience is used, develop a sight word list of items which pupils tend to use in their oral language. If individualized instruction involving trade books is used, use nouns common to the classroom library books and non-nouns (glue words) from a list such as the one developed by Edward Dolch (253). Additional sources of words include labels and items frequently written on the chalkboard. For example, if a class has some fish that pupils will take turns feeding, teach the word fish. If paper is labeled and stored on a particular shelf, teach the word paper.

Develop the SCCs by pasting a picture of an object on one side of a 4 X 6 or 5 X 8 inch card. Print the word, words, or phrase (car, washing machine, cluster of grapes) represented by the picture on both sides of the card. Secure pictures from catalogues, brochures, magazines, etc. One caution: Each picture should contain a single concept such as an apple or turkey rather than a complex one such as a zoo or farm.

Briefly, the instructional strategy is as follows:

FOR THE FIRST WORD

1. Using the teaching side (the side with the word and the picture) of the card, the child pronounces the name of the picture. This ensures his learning the right term (fishing rod instead of fishing pole, horse instead of pony.

2. The child studies the printed word and then looks up at you.

3. The child covers the word and names the beginning letter or prints it on a piece of paper or circles it from a list of three or four letters on a prepared sheet (Note: The implication is that the child does not have to be able to name the letters of the alphabet to use SCCs). If the word is short and conforms to phonic generalizations, you might ask the child to spell the word from memory, the purpose being to focus attention on the visual form of the word.

4. The child checks his response and studies the word a second time, looking at you when he is ready.

5. Using the testing side, the child pronounces the word (in effect, taking the test.)

6. The child turns the card over and says, "I am right." If the child is wrong, he repeats the process.

FOR THE SECOND WORD

7. The child repeats steps 1-4 using the teaching side of the card.
8. The child shuffles both cards and places them testing side up (picture side down).

9. The child pronounces each word, turning over each card and saying, "I am right." If the child is wrong, he repeats the process beginning with step 8. We can also

ask him to trace the word once or twice, saying the whole word as he does so. Kinesthetic procedures are discussed later.

APPLICATION

At first the child should study only two words in a session. Be sure these do not begin with the same letter or with letters that are easily confused. For example, one should not study boy and ball, boy and dog, or ear and car at the same time. After these are "mastered," provide extensive reinforcement in recognizing the words.

1. Present a list of three words (the two new words plus a distractor) printed in lower-case letters. Ask the child to point to and name each word he knows. This activity can be provided at varying levels of complexity.

A. Use three words, each beginning with a letter whose visual appearance differs considerably from the others and has a different visual configuration (i.e., ball, cat, mouse).

B. Use three words which are similar to each other in visual appearance (i.e., car, sun, man).

C. Use more than three words.

D. Present the same words in different sequences to inhibit memorization of the position of the word rather than the word itself.

E. Present words in different sizes and formats. For example, print the words in pencil, pen, magic marker, and crayon, varying the sizes. Use words cut from a newspaper. Pupils need to recognize words in different situations. Unfortunately, they often do not transfer from one situation to another.

When pupils are able to recognize two words easily (and, hopefully, when they ask for more instruction), prepare additional cards. On the following day, repeat the steps and, if pupils retain the information (via testing on the SCCs as well as the word lists) present two more words.

2. To provide motivated practice, print the two words on a wooden block. As an alternative, print the words on two continuous strips of paper and tape around a block. Each word will then appear three times. Invite a pair of

pupils to Roll and Read using the following directions:

A. Child 1 rolls the block (die) and reads the word, receiving one point for a correct response.

B. Child 2 rolls the die and reads the word, receiving one point for a correct response.

C. If one child challenges the other's accuracy, they refer to the SCCs. The person who is wrong loses his turn.

D. The first person to reach ten points is the winner.

E. In the next game, the person who came in second goes first.

After the third and fourth words have been presented, use different blocks. Print the first two words once each and the last two words twice each. After the fifth and sixth words are presented, print each word once on a die. When the seventh and eighth words are taught, use two dice, with each child rolling the pair and earning a possible two points at each roll. Add more dice as needed.
Roll and Read is a learning game parents can construct for their children. If used systematically and sequentially, it can gently and rapidly guide pupils into reading concrete nouns. Incidentally, the procedures described here are even more useful in working with special education pupils and other slow learners. The pupil who consistently recognizes new words (despite the format) 30 minutes after instruction meets the Phase 2 requirements.

PHASE 3: "Develop pupil competence in recognizing words presented on Single Concept Cards under long-term recall conditions." Long-term recall is defined as recall twenty-four hours or more after instruction.

Each day pupils should (a) review the words from the previous days as well as (b) study additional items. Thus a pupil might engage in the following sequence of activities:

1. Review past words.

2. Study two or more new words.

3. Teach his old or new words to a partner. The Frank Laubach "each one teach one" concept is the basic technique used here. Beginning and poor readers can work together in teaching and learning from each other. Incidentally, a complete non-reader can test another pupil just by holding a card so the picture and word side faces him.

4. Learn his partner's old or new words.

5. Use the Roll and Read dice.

6. Use Word Whiz, a game with a Bingo format that allows pupils to practice recognizing words after 16 items have been introduced. The directions are somewhat different from the traditional procedures, enabling pupils to have increased opportunities for practice. Three forms should be available so youngsters will be unable to "borrow" information from their neighbors. If basal readers are used, Word Whiz sets are available at the reading readiness and preprimer levels of a variety of series (208). A sample is provided in the next chapter.

7. Use sets of cards for Tic-Tac-Toe. Make two sets of SCCs, one for each pair of pupils. These cards need not contain pictures. Thus they can be made in large quantity by printing the words on spirit masters and duplicating them on construction paper or cardstock. Draw vertical lines at 2-13/16 inches and 5-10/16 inches and horizontal lines at 2-3/16, 4-6/16, 6-9/16, and 8-12/16. This will yield 15 spaces. Print a word in each space. Code each card with a Level-Set designation (i.e., 1A = Level 1, Set A) or use different colors of paper as the basis for the various sets.

In either case, provide a pair of pupils with two sets of cards containing words they have studied. (Separate sets may be housed in greeting card boxes and labeled 1A, 1B, 1C, etc., with the pairs of sets already cut and individually housed within the boxes in library pockets or zip-lock bags. Rubber bands and paper clips are not recommended.)

To practice, each of a pair of pupils shuffles his own set of cards (identical to his partner's set) and places the cards (word side down) on his side of the table. A Tic-Tac-Toe board, also duplicated from a spirit master, is placed at the center of the table.

Each player turns up his first card. One person begins the practice by naming the word. Unless challenged, he places his marker (a checker, for

292

instance) on any space of the Tic-Tac-Toe board and sets his card aside. If challenged successfully, he loses a turn and places the missed word in the middle of his stack. A person who unsuccessfully challenges misses his own turn. His partner names the first word in his set and, unless challenged, places a marker (a checker of another color, possibly) on an unoccupied space on the board. The game proceeds in the standard manner.

An alternate procedure can be used without the Tic-Tac-Toe board. Each pupil simply reads the first word and, unless challenged, records a point. Players pronounce their words alternately until one member wins (i.e., reaches a predetermined number of points).

8. Enter words into a Word Bank (682). A Word Bank is simply a list of words which a pupil appears to have learned. It may consist of a plastic box containing 3X5 inch cards or a greeting card or cigar box. Pupils copy the words from SCCs, from their Roll and Read dice, or from their Tic-Tac-Toe card sets.

A Word Bank may be used for a variety of purposes.

A. serve as a source of spelling words

B. provide materials for alphabetizing

C. provide words to use in teaching LSAs

D. provide words to use in teaching syllabication, compound words, contractions, and possessives

E. provide words to use in teaching prefixes, suffixes, and base words

F. provide words to use in teaching synonyms, antonyms, and homonyms

G. provide opportunities for constant review of new words

H. show beginning readers how much progress they are making

I. facilitate the writing process by serving as a reference for young writers

J. provide words to use in classifying exercises (i.e., all the foods, all the vegetables, etc.)

K. provide words to use in practicing handwriting

The actual kinesthetic practice resulting from the writing of newly-acquired words is conducive to retention. Later any word which is forgotten -- and some will be -- can be matched with the appropriate experience story to facilitate recall.

The use of a word bank by each very poor or non-reader makes it possible for him to compare his progress day by day through his gradually accumulating stock of sight words. A pupil may study his old words each day, placing a rubber band around those correctly pronounced. Word demons may be set aside for reinforcement which should be provided through a number of sentences constructed from words already known except for the demons. The reinforcement in this technique helps provide sufficient repetition of needed words without the accompanying boredom and repetition caused by use of the "same old" sentences. Pairs of pupils may also teach their words to each other, a practice which is highly motivating to some children.

One caution: The word bank idea is much less effective with youngsters who are beginning to acquire large numbers of sight words. This seems to be true for two major reasons. First, as the number of known words increases, the amount of work involved in compiling an accurate list of all items in the child's reading vocabulary becomes unbearable. Second, a child who knows a fairly large number of words cannot compare the size of his word bank with the previous day's stack in the same favorable way as can his non-reading buddy. The pupil who can recognize at least 50 concrete nouns shown on SCCs (or when presented in list form) meets the requirements of Phase 3.

PHASE 4: "Develop pupil competence in recognizing words contained in Single Concept Card Sentences under short-term recall conditions." (A Single Concept Card Sentence -- SCCS -- is a sentence dictated by a pupil about one of his Single Concept Card nouns.)

In Phases 2 and 3 pupils concentrated on learning concrete nouns, the easiest part of speech to learn. However, "noun reading" is not "real reading." The hard words ("glue" words, because they hold the sentence together) must also be learned. Sentences are more difficult than words for pupils to learn. However, there is a an available crutch, the key word. Over 80% of the words pupils use in these sentences are found on the Dolch Basic Word List or the locally-relevant sight word list.

We find the following strategy helpful for initiating sentence reading:

FOR THE FIRST SENTENCE

1. Using one of his SCCs or one of the words from his list of learned nouns, the child dictates a sentence.

2. Using a 3X5 inch card, the teacher (parent, volunteer, older pupil) prints it as dictated except when standard language errors are present. For example, if the child says, "Him and me done it," the teacher asks, "May I write 'He and I did it'?" Almost all children give their consent.

Although pupils will have received reading readiness instruction in recognizing word boundaries, it is still helpful to begin by leaving wide spaces between the words. Use cardboard or some other durable "sentence strip" material.

3. The teacher reads the printed sentence to the pupil, slowly sweeping her hand below the corresponding words.

4. The pupil reads the first sentence to the teacher.

5. The teacher uses procedures similar to those listed below to help pupils recognize individual words.

   A. Ask, "Which word is pig?" (In general, begin with the SCC, then other nouns, then action verbs, adjectives, and finally all other words.)

   B. Point to a word and ask the child to pronounce it.

   C. Use the open slot technique. Cut a rectangular slot in the middle of a 5X8 inch card. Make the slot approximately one-half inch high and 1-1/2 inches wide. Place the card over various words in a deliberate sequence as outlined above. Ask the pupil to pronounce the word exposed through the open slot. If the pupil is unable to do so, show him how to hold the bottom of the 5X8 card firmly over the sentence strip and bend the top part of the card over to reveal the entire sentence. Continue until the pupil can recognize all of the words through the open slot.

FOR THE SECOND SENTENCE

6. The teacher and the child read both SCCSs. If he misses a word, the teacher provides it and the child reads both sentences again. He must correctly pronounce each word in each sentence. When a child misses a word, ask him to:

    A. point to it
    B. look at it
    C. listen to you (or a word consultant) say it
    D. say it, and
    E. re-read the sentence.

APPLICATION

1. Ask each member of the group to teach his sentences to another pupil. This practice is a highly effective way of providing extensive reinforcement and also provides an abundance of printed materials for beginners to read. The brevity of the material facilitates frequent success and increased motivation to learn.

2. Consider only two words and sentences at a time. After these are "mastered," provide practice in extending the sentences. To illustrate, suppose the pupil dictates, "I see a big pig." Develop sentences substituting other SCCs he has learned. Record each sentence on a separate strip.

I see a big dog.	See a big tree.
I see a big man.	See a big horse.
I see a big cat.	See a big girl.
I see a big barn.	See a big apple.

To make the exercise harder, use these sentences. Notice the lower-case <u>a</u> becomes upper-case, and <u>see</u> becomes <u>sees</u>.

A dog sees a big man.	A man sees a big dog.
A dog sees a big barn.	A man sees a big cat.
A dog sees a big cat.	A man sees a big barn.

A slightly more difficult stage occurs with the change of big from one position to another.

A dog sees a big man.   A big dog sees a big man.

A big dog sees a man.

Even more difficult is the use of a greater variety of nouns in each position.

A big dog sees a man.   A cow sees a tree.

A cat sees a big apple.   A big girl sees a big horse.

If the child's second SCCS has a different descriptive adjective (i.e., "I see a little baby."), the sentence possibilities will proliferate.

A dog sees a baby cat.

A little dog sees a big cat.

A big dog sees a little baby.

Reading becomes a fun activity with the few new words thrown into all sorts of delightful combinations, on occasion even nonsense sentences. Pupils dictate "silly sentences" and put an X after them to indicate they are unrealistic. This, by the way, is a simple type of comprehension exercise (distinguishing fact from fantasy).

A big cat sees a baby barn.   X

A barn sees a baby dog.   X

I see a baby man.   X

Furthermore, pupils can sequence the ideas in terms of general size (in this case) and practice this vital comprehension skill.

baby cat, baby dog, cat, dog, man, horse, barn

The pupil who consistently recognizes new words in his classmates' sentences as well as those in the extension exercises (i.e., see, sees, big, little) thirty minutes after instruction meets the requirements of Phase 4.

297

"Develop pupil competence in recognizing words contained in Single Concept Card Sentences under long-term recall conditions."

To parallel ideas mentioned earlier in conjunction with words, a pupil might use any of the following activities:

1. Review past sentences.
2. Develop and study new sentences.
3. Teach his old or new sentences to a partner.
4. Learn his partner's old or new sentences.
5. Use the Roll and Read dice for sentence sections. Choose six words for each block. Begin with three blocks that make sentences. Use the words found in the sentence indicated by the pupils. For example:

Block 1 (Adjective)	Block 2 (Subject)	Block 3 (Action verb)
A	dog	plays
The	cat	runs
My	horse	jumps
Your	pig	walks
His	goat	eats
Her	kangaroo	sleeps

Regardless of the face of each block which appears, the child can produce a sentence. To increase the difficulty, add more blocks.

Block 4 (Preposition)	Block 5 (Pronoun)
with	me
near	you
beside	her
around	him
by	them
away from	us

Add an adjective block   or   an adverb block

big	sometimes
little	always
small	never
pretty	seldom
new	usually
old	frequently

or a color (adjective) block, which often makes silly sentences.

red	orange
green	black
blue	yellow

If three dice are used, there will be 216 possible sentences. With five dice the number of possible sentences increases to 8,776!

The following procedures can be used for providing practice with Roll and Read Sentence Sections.

A. Develop the blocks for a pair of pupils. Use the words contained in the SCCSs.

B. Each pupils rolls one die. The person whose word comes first in the alphabet begins first.

C. The first pupil rolls the dice, arranges the words into a logical order, and reads the sentence. He receives one point for reading the entire sentence. The child should tell whether or not the sentence makes sense.

D. The second pupil rolls the dice, arranges the words, and reads his sentence.

E. If the pupil misses a word, his partner (some people use the term opponent) can earn a point by reading the entire sentence. If he does so, he does not roll the dice again, for he has already earned a point.

If the second person cannot read the sentence, he then rolls the dice for his turn.

    F. The first person to read ten sentences correctly wins.

    G. In a subsequent contest, the partner goes first.

6. Ask pupils to dictate sentences from songs, jingles, or nursery rhymes. This procedure is helpful because pupils remember the content even better than they do their own words. For example, using the word <u>pig,</u> a child might dictate any of the following.

This little pig went to the market.

Once upon a time there were three little pigs.

To market, to market, to buy a fat pig
    (technically not a sentence)

7. Use sets of sentence cards for Tic-Tac-Toe. To construct the materials, simply use each person's SCCSs. Place each person's cards face down on either the left or right side of the table so the partners can sit side by side rather than across from each other. The partners will use different sentences based on their own dictation to try to complete the Tic-Tac-Toe board placed between them.
    Each person turns up one card. The one with the greater number of words in the sentence begins first by reading his sentence. Unless his partner challenges, the first person places a marker on the board. In case of a challenge, the person with the wrong answer loses his turn. A word consultant -- a pupil who recognizes many words -- serves as a reference for challenges.
    Another way of resolving a challenge is to use Language Master cards. When two pupils disagree, they simply insert the card into the Language Master, flick the switch, and listen to the right answer. This machine is ideal for providing feedback on both words and sentences. Correct sentences are set aside. Missed sentences are returned to the middle of the stack. The winner is the first person to complete three spaces in a row.
    An alternate strategy which does not involve the use of a Tic-Tac-Toe board is to award each person one point for reading a sentence with the winner being the first person to accumulate a certain number of points.
    The pupil who can read 25 or more sentences meets the requirements of Phase 5.

Strategies for Providing
Parallel Instruction and Practice

Parallel instruction is instruction using the same type of material and many (if not all) of the specifics. Several of the phases identified above can be enriched through the use of parallel instruction and/or practice. Consider the following strategies:

PHASES 2 and 3:

1. Label objects and centers in the classroom. Examples: Art Center, Mrs. Sawyer's Room, Things to Do

2. Use real-life words as motivators. Examples: Cheerios, Wheaties, Pepsi, label on milk container in the cafeteria; STOP sign or SLOW - SCHOOL, signs saying Babson Park School, BOYS and GIRLS, Perfect Attendance; names of games or toys

3. Use key words (usually titles) in newspapers. Examples: Nancy or Henry in the comics

4. Attach a child's picture (or a self-portrait) above his name. Teach pupils to recognize (a) their own names, (b) their friends' names, and (c) their classmates' names. You can facilitate this process by labeling a hook on which each child should hang his coat and hat. Also use name tags that pupils move from one board to another when they enter the class in the morning. At the beginning of the year the cards will need to be accompanied by pictures.

5. Assign classroom duties. At the beginning of the year write the names of pupils who will care for the fish on a cut-out fish. Later write the word fish followed by the names of the pupils. Still later, make the assignment in a complete sentence: "Lee and Mary will care for the fish."

6. Use the Dolch 95 common nouns as SCCs. They are available from Garrard Press, Champaign, Illinois 61820.

7. Use books which label words. Titles are often available in department stores. Examples include:

Richard Scarry books (New York: Golden Press)

McNaught, Harry, 500 Words to Grow On. New York: Random House, 1973.

301

Ogle, Lucille, and Tina Thoburn, I Spy: A Picture Book of Objects in a Child's Home Environment. New York: American Heritage, 1970.

8. Use picture dictionaries. They can be used in a variety of ways (186).

A. Oral Language. Teach children the names of pictorially-represented objects. A child who has never seen an elephant -- or perhaps has seen an elephant without having its name mentioned -- can extend his oral vocabulary by naming the objects portrayed in a picture dictionary. To achieve this purpose, pair pupils with dissimilar oral vocabularies. One child identifies the picture, receiving help only when he falters. Teach the second child (the word consultant) to use a technique similar to the following:

1. When the child misses the first word, tell him the name of the picture and some important characteristic. Example -- "That's a raisin. It's a dried grape." or "That's a scooter. You put your hands on these bars (pointing), one foot on the floorboard, and push with one foot."

2. Ask the child to repeat the word and tell you something about it.

3. When the child misses the second word, follow Steps 1 and 2.

4. Now ask the child to tell you about both words.

5. Continue with the cycle -- learn a word, review, learn another word, review, etc., until the child masters five words.

On the following day review the previous day's words before beginning another list. Either proceed through the picture dictionary page by page or according to pre-determined categories, such as vegetables.

B. Letter-Sound Association (LSA) Introduction. If the picture dictionary is organized alphabetically, use the pictures and their accompanying words as a base for presenting an LSA generalization. For example, make comments similar to the following:

1. Look at the words on page 7.

2. How are they alike? (in appearance)

302

3. Say them to yourself.

4. How else are they alike? (in initial sound)

5. What is the generalization (rule)? (The letter b represents (stands for) the first sound in **ball**.)

C. **Letter-Sound Association Practice.** If the picture dictionary is organized by topic (colors, transportation, etc.) rather than alphabetically, use it to provide pupil practice in LSAs. For example, suppose two pages display various common colors. Ask questions such as the following:

1. Which word has the same beginning sound (starts like) as **ride**? ... **put**? ... **yes**?

2. Which word has the same ending sound as **cage**? ... **would**? ... **can**?

3. Which word has the same vowel sound as **have**? ... **feet**? ... **cow**?

4. Which words begin with the same sound? (blue, black, brown and green, gray)

D. **Classification Practice.** If the dictionary is organized by topics, call attention to the natural groupings (animals, foods, toys, etc.) and ask pupils to name other objects which fit in the categories. If the picture dictionary is organized alphabetically, ask each pupil to take each word or picture or page and list other words or pictures that comprise the same group. Thus if **apple**, **ape**, **arm**, and **ax** are on one page, pupils must locate other words or pictures of foods, animals, parts of the body, and tools or weapons. They may copy these words on long strips of cardboard or on lined paper.

E. **Alphabetical Order.** After teaching alphabetization by the first letter, write five words on the board. Make each word begin with a different letter, i.e., A, B, C, D, E. Ask pupils to copy the five words and cut them out and alphabetize them. To check, they can refer to an alphabetically organized picture dictionary to see if the words are listed in the same order. The same procedure can also be used with two-letter alphabetization.

303

F. <u>Rhyming Words.</u> Ask pupils to point to a picture that rhymes with a word you specify. For example, if you say <u>fat,</u> the child may point to a <u>hat</u> or a <u>bat</u> or a <u>cat</u>. Begin by considering just one page. Later ask pupils to search for rhyming words on two or more pages. Still later ask pupils to collect and list pairs or sets of rhyming words.

G. <u>Spelling Reference.</u> If picture dictionaries are organized alphabetically, they can be used as a spelling resource. Pupils who know the first letter can zip through the appropriate pages and determine whether or not the item is included. Even if picture dictionaries are organized by topic, they can be used for this purpose. However, pupils must first identify the topic and then locate the appropriate pages.

Lead pupils to understand that some picture dictionaries include only nouns or only nouns and action verbs (with perhaps a few adjectives such as numbers and the color words). This type of activity is especially appropriate when children are engaged in creative writing activities.

H. <u>Syllabication.</u> After teaching one or more syllabication generalizations, ask pupils to turn to a specified page in their picture dictionaries and identify the number of words with two syllables. They should hold up the appropriate number of fingers (stomach high so their classmates will not see the answer).

Ask pupils to make lists of one, two, and three syllable words contained in their picture dictionaries.

Annotations of some commonly available picture or beginning dictionaries are included at the end of the chapter.

9. Help each child make his own book. Topics might include <u>My First Book of Foods</u>, <u>My Own Book of Animals</u>, <u>My Book of Colors</u>, or <u>Toys I Like</u>. You might find the following procedures helpful:

A. Everyone tries to locate catalogues, savings stamp books, magazines, etc.

B. The pupil cuts out (in block form) the picture of a favorite food (for example).

C. The pupil pastes the picture in the upper center of a sheet of paper. For smaller books, fold the sheets into halves.

D. The teacher (aide, volunteer, parent, etc.) prints the word below the picture.

E. The child studies the word.

F. The child and/or teacher repeats Steps b-e with additional pictures and words.

G. The teacher adds a title page and a sheet for pupils who read the book to sign their names and staples the pages between two sheets of construction paper.

H. The teacher prints the title and author on the cover sheet.

I. The child pastes a multiple concept card showing a variety of foods on the cover.

J. The child studies the words and eventually says them while the pictures are covered. (Hints: Skip around or present the words from the back of the book to the first. Alternately, make the last sheet a word list.)

K. The child shares his book with his friends. The book may also be displayed in the media center or in the classroom library.

PHASES 4 and 5:

1. Use the Dolch words in sentences. According to one study the overlap between words contained in lower-level basals and the Dolch words is not very large. Stated another way, some specific Dolch words would have to be taught if a systematic and sequential program involving Dolch word sentences is to be used (615).

SPARK (Systematic Practice for Achieving Reading Knowledge) is a commercial kit (198) consisting of 220 Reading Units (one for each Dolch word), with each unit of 20 sentences becoming progressively more difficult. The units use only Dolch words studied in previous units plus a small number of selected nouns.

305

2. Write simple directions on the chalkboard or in a sentence strip holder. Examples of possibilities are listed next:

Line-up:

    a. Row one may get in line (or line up).
    b. Row four may get in line (or line up).

Variations:

    a. Table one may get in line (or line up).
    b. Bob's row (or table) may get in line.
    c. The boys may get in line.
    d. The six-year-olds may get in line.

Duties:

    a. Bill may feed the fish.
    b. Tom may take up the books.
    c. Sue may answer the door.

Assignments:

    a. Lions -- please put away your books and write a story about our hamster.
    b. Tigers -- Go to the Listening Center.

Routines:

    a. It is time to go to lunch. Get out your lunch money.
    b. It is time for P.E. Please take off your shoes (or put on your gym shoes).
    c. It is time to go home. Please clean up your desk and get out your take-home reader.

Questions:

    a. Who wants to eat lunch in the cafeteria?
    b. Who wants to buy milk for recess?
    c. Who wants to take out the jump ropes today?
    d. Who has a birthday today?

At first pupils will have difficulty. However, as they acquire practice, the youngsters will learn the new words and see a very meaningful reason for learning to read.

3. Use rebus writing, an excellent way to simplify the task for beginning readers. Write a sentence and draw or paste a symbol above a key word, usually a concrete noun but sometimes an action verb. For example:

a. Row one may line up. (Put the numeral 1 above the word.)
b. The horse ate the grass. (Place pictures of a horse and grass over the corresponding words.)

The Houghton Mifflin Reading Program (277) uses rebus in its preprimers to replace the names of the speakers. Thus a picture of a bear stands for the words, "The bear said..."

4. Use written directions as a fun-time practice in following directions. Say, "Stand up if...and display a sentence strip saying such things as

a. You have on brown shoes.
b. You are six years old.
c. You are a girl.
d. You can read these words.
e. You have done your work.
f. You can read your name.

5. Help each child make his own book, this time with sentences rather than words accompanying the pictures. Use the procedure described earlier with sentences dictated and studied by the child. The child who successfully completes Phase 5 is ready for the next step -- language-experience approach (with paragraphs or stories), the basal reader, or individualized instruction using trade books. The teacher can determine the next step, confident that the child has a solid foundation on which to build.

Strategies for Using
The Language-Experience Approach
With A Class

This section assumes a teacher wishes to utilize the language-experience approach (LEA) as a follow-up to the activities described earlier in this chapter (Procedures for utilizing basals as a follow-up are presented in Chapters 7A, 7B, and 7C.). The following strategies can be used with a large group or an entire class as early as grade one (202).

1. Determine a subject that is interesting to the class. It may be some aspect of weather (snow or a hurricane), a class pet, an important current event such as a space flight, a holiday, or a person. While the topic may be selected by pupils, it is sometimes desirable for the teacher to make this decision in order to emphasize certain planned objectives.

2. Discuss the topic with the class. Ask questions designed to help pupils verbalize their feelings and share their information. Provide additional data only when their own reservoirs of experience appear inadequate. Except for unusual topics, most classes have one or more members whose wealth of information should preclude lengthy teacher comments.

3. Ask youngsters what information they would like to include in a story about the topic. Elicit discussion from as many persons as possible, but limit the written story to a reasonable length. This normally should depend on the amount of repetition, the number of new terms, sentence complexity, and the completeness of the thoughts being expressed. We prefer to use no more than four sentences.

4. Record the sentences as finally developed. Precede each with the name of the person supplying the major information. If a thought is expressed in such a way as to make it difficult to read, the group may experiment with alternate ways of saying the same thing. The final phrasing should be printed on the board or on the overhead projector. Each sentence may be similar to the following: Bobby said, "We have a pet hamster." If two youngsters collaborate on a thought, the sentence may read: Bobby and Billy said, "We have a pet hamster."
    Sometime later it may be desirable to omit the <u>Bobby</u> <u>said</u>'s. As an introductory device, however, the words identify the originator(s) of the comments, provide practice in recognizing pupil's names, and subsequently aid in teaching the use of direct comments and quotation marks.

5. Read the entire story to the class, moving your hands along the words in a slow continuous sweep. The major point to stress here is the importance of moving fluidly and fluently (although not so fast) through the story with the voice and the hands. It is not desirable to point to each word during each reading since that encourages word-by-word reading.

6. Ask pupils to come to the board (or overhead

projector) and find their names or other specific information. At this point pupils may engage in numerous activities. For example, they might

a. find their own names or the names of others

b. find the word <u>said</u> (which will occur repeatedly)

c. look for the word <u>hamster</u> (for example) and, having found it, match it with the same word elsewhere in the story (visual discrimination)

d. compare a word which appears in both capital and lower case

e. count the number of words in a sentence (to determine their ability to recognize the blank spaces as separators of words -- Many youngsters do not know where words begin and end. Is it any wonder they can hardly read?)

f. count the number of sentences (to determine their ability to recognize the function of terminal punctuation marks)

g. note different types of punctuation marks

h. note reasons for capitalizing words

i. compare words that are almost visually identical (she, she's)

j. locate all the words beginning with a certain letter or sound

k. use these words as a basis for studying letter-sound associations

l. read an entire sentence or even the selection

Pupils who find certain words may wish to underline them. Teachers just beginning to use this technique, especially with youngsters early in the first grade, should not be upset when those who insist they can find the item arrive at the board with no apparent idea of what they were asked to look for. This occurrence is a natural result of exuberance, a wish to learn to read, and a desire to please. Patience and good humor are the passwords.

7. Duplicate the story for each pupil and produce a

309

chart on tagboard for class use. On the following day, distribute copies of the experience story. Each pupil should try to read the story silently and underline the words he thinks he knows. Probably no one will recognize all the words, and many will remember only a very small portion of the material. Thoughtful study of each child's ability to recognize new words should identify the children must likely to respond to a more intensive series of experiences with print. The first youngsters to be ready may then form a group to dictate an experience story of their own or to work more intensively and extensively with the one used by the entire class. In either case, observation of the effectiveness of LEAs is far more likely to provide an accurate indication of a child's readiness to profit from formal reading activities than is a standardized reading readiness test.

8. Using a skills sequence, teach whatever skills are appropriate. Refer to the possibilities listed under Item 6. In addition, pupils might do the following:

a. underline on their sheets a word presented by the teacher (visual discrimination and matching)

b. circle words which begin with the same sound as one identified by the teacher

c. place a check in front of the sentence that answers a question posed by the teacher

d. draw arrows to rhyming words

e. cut the sentences apart and put them back together in correct sequence

f. read the sentences or story to each other.

One of the dangers of language-experience is the tendency of some teachers to ignore the systematic, sequential presentation and pupil mastery of the appropriate skills. A skills sequence is an essential guide for all teachers, regardless of the approach being used.

Any member of the group may pronounce a word which presents a problem to one of his peers. Pupils who make no mistakes should sign their names as readers of the story. Frequent practice in reading previous selections should be provided; this facilitates recall. An example may serve to illustrate the initial aspects of such a procedure.

310

Case One

At 1:30 one September afternoon, the consultant was asked to demonstrate the LEA to a class of first-year pupils. Because the demonstration was spontaneous rather than planned, there was not time to arrange an appropriate center of interest. A quick glance around the room revealed no fascinating leads -- except the teacher herself. Therefore the pupils were asked to develop a story about their teacher. The six-year-olds created the following story:

Mrs. M_____

Johnna said, "Mrs. M_____ is a pretty teacher.

Billy said, "She lets us get water when we want to."

Janice said, "She's always good to us."

Wendell said, "She lets us go to the bathroom when we have to."

We read the entire story and then discussed it.
Teacher: "Who can find the name Johnna? (Several hands, including Johnna's, shot up.)...(Pointing to Johnna) Would you come here and find your name?...Good. Now draw a line under it...(We used the same procedure for the other names.)...Now, who can find the word said? ..(Almost everyone raised his hand, but few could actually find the word and underline it.)...Who can find the word said somewhere else?...(This visual matching was somewhat easier.)...How many times did we use the word said? ..Who can find the words Mrs. M_____? ...(very easy)...What do you notice about those two words?...What kind of M? ..Why does it start with a capital letter?...Tell me, what do you notice about the way the two words sound at the beginning?...Right. Listen. Mrs. M_____. Does me sound that way at the beginning?...Does money? ..Does run? ..Good listening. (We were also developing auditory discrimination).
"Now who can find the word she? ..(very difficult -- finally someone succeeded). Who does she tell about?...Good. Who can find the word she somewhere else?... (The first response was line three, she's.). Let's look at these two words. Do they look alike at the beginning?...At the end?.... Are they the same?...Who can make up a sentence with she? ..With she's? ..What words does she's stand for?...Now who can find another

311

<u>she</u> just like the one in line two?...Right.

"Who can find two names in your story that begin with the same letter?...What is that letter?...Listen to the beginning sound. <u>Johnna</u> .. <u>Janice</u> ..What do you notice?...Right. They begin with the same sound. Does <u>Jack</u> begin that way?...Johnna. Janice. Jack?...What about Jerry?...Martha?...What do you think is the first letter in <u>jungle</u>? ...

Another day we would talk about other elements -- the comma, periods, quotation marks, the sound represented by the first letter of <u>we</u>, <u>want</u>, <u>and</u> <u>water</u>. And, of course, we would want to proceed through Steps Seven Through Ten just presented. But at least we have begun.

Strategies for Using the
Language - Experience Approach
With an Individual and a Group

1. Ask a poor or non-reader to tell you a story about something in which he is interested. It should be brief--usually fewer than 25 words for beginners. A poor reader who is older may tell a somewhat longer story depending on the extent to which he is able and willing to verbalize his experiences and the present strength of his reading vocabulary. However, it is a dangerous practice to allow most youngsters to talk at great length for dictation.

Some pupils may need prompting and guide questions to "think up" each sentence. These children often respond more satisfactorily after hearing others dictate stories. Try to secure complete sentences rather than random clauses or words. Because some children can rattle off a story in shotgun fashion, a tape recorder may prove useful. This device is also quite appropriate when you are just beginning to use the LEA.

2. Print or type the story with the necessary modifications. Make one carbon copy. Include the pupil's name and the date. Whenever possible, try to secure the "dictator's" permission to record language which facilitates the use of the story with other children. Since writing and dictation are most effective when communication is intended and expected, language modifications should attempt to keep this factor in mind.

For example, a youngster may say, "Him and me played all day." You can respond, "May I write, 'He and I played all day?'" By securing the youngster's permission, recording the modified statement, and then reading it aloud with an "Is that okay?" you present the parallel standard language pattern without rejecting the

312

idea. After recording the entire story, you may wish to read it to the child.

3. Ask the child to read his story silently, underlining each word he knows. Two points should be noted here. First, silent reading should precede oral reading. Second, emphasis should be placed on identifying words known rather that words unknown. We are stressing the positive rather than the negative.

4. Listen to the child read his story aloud. Supply all unknown words. At this point determine if the underlined items accurately reflect the reader's ability to recognize words. Some youngsters underline too many, and some too few, words. Note specific strengths, weaknesses, and needs at the bottom of your carbon copy.

5. Ask the child to read the story aloud several times, until near-perfection is achieved. Only in rare instances will one reading suffice. Most pupils will need assistance with several efforts before fluency is reached.

We have followed one especially useful procedure. First, tell a child who encounters an unknown word, "I'll tell you the word if you promise to remember it." If he misses the same word a second time, offer to tell him the word if he will trace it one or two times with the eraser of his pencil and repeat the word each time. Each time you tell a youngster a word, he must point to it and pronounce it simultaneously, close his eyes and remove his finger, and then locate and pronounce the word again. Then he starts again at the beginning of the story.

6. Use the open slot technique to determine the extent to which words are recognized by sight (i.e., in isolation). As indicated earlier, an open slot may be constructed simply by cutting a strip approximately one-half inch high and one and one-half inches long from the middle of a 4X6 inch or a 5X8 inch card. When placed over an experience story, the card should cover most or all of the selection except the word or phrase revealed by the open slot.

You can place the open slot over specific words -- those known to the reader -- to promote a feeling of success or you can expose other words to indicate additional learning which should occur. If a pupil using the open slot misses the first word, try to locate several words he knows in order to prevent frustration. Conversely, if he recognizes the first two or three, place the open slot over a difficult word.

7. Ask the child to take his story and the open slot home, study the material, and master the words via the open slot. The pupil should take the original copy home, leaving the carbon for your use. (As an alternate possibility, provide this practice during school hours as an independent activity.) It is beneficial to contact the parents to explain the procedure being used and the type of assistance which they can provide.

8. Using the carbon copy, type the story on a duplicating master and secure enough copies for each member of the group. If five persons comprise the group, prepare eight or nine copies. Place the additional sheets in folders to provide samples of work and evidence of progress. These extra copies can also be used to compile child-authored books to be catalogued and shelved in the classroom library and school media center. After all, what could be more motivating to a youngster than to see his own words in print just like the writings of other authors?

It may be appropriate to use a primary or large type typewriter. If space is available, type the story on the bottom half of the page, reserving the top half for illustrations. Provide a space for the youngster to sign his name to the story just as soon as he is able, on the second or succeeding day, to read the entire selection without error. Reserve additional space for the other members of the group to sign their names as they learn to read the selection. A sample format for an experience story is presented in Illustration 6-1.

9. On the following day, ask each child to read his story. Note his strengths, weaknesses, and needs, and make plans to provide instruction and additional practice in the use of those words with which he experiences difficulty. Certainly the just-learned words should be used in developing this additional practice with word demons.

However, we must once again emphasize: Words to be learned should be presented in context and not in isolation. While some teachers still attempt to teach pupils by using flash card words presented in isolation, it is rare to find a reading authority who recommends such a practice. Picture nouns are not presented in isolation (160, 743).

Most teachers would probably agree that child contact with words on cards (except nouns used with pictures) has little or no value. Indeed, many poor and beginning readers are forced into further frustration and failure

314

ILLUSTRATION 6-1

SAMPLE FORMAT FOR A LANGUAGE-EXPERIENCE STORY

(drawing or picture)

Frisky

Frisky is my squirrel.

Frisky has a bushy tail.

I feed Frisky some nuts.

He likes to eat them.

He lives in a tree.

Written by: _____

Read by: _____   _____

_____   _____

_____   _____

by such activities. In everyday reading, words rarely
exist in isolation, especially terms which prove
difficult to youngsters. Even those few who manage to
pronounce words in isolation often seem unable to
recognize the same terms when used in context. And this
should be expected. After all, a tree in your front yard
is easily identifiable by its position, size, shape, and
type. When transplanted in a forest, that some tree
loses its distinguishing characteristics and, except to
the very perceptive, becomes merely a part of a nebulous
mass. We recommend the use of the open slot to determine
what words have been mastered sufficiently to be
recognized without context as a replacement for the
procedure of teaching words in isolation.

10. Group children into pairs. As each person is able
to read his story without error, he should teach it to
his partners. This Paired Activity for Learning (PAL)
makes it possible for even the slower pupils to engage in
some highly appropriate teaching. After the participants
become familiar with the procedure, they often are able
to operate for ten to twenty minutes or more without
direct teacher assistance.
    After each partner learns to read a new story, he
signs his name at the bottom of the page and proceeds to
read someone else's story. He may choose a specific
selection based on his friendship with the author, and he
may read as many as his interest, ability, and time
permit. Hopefully all youngsters will teach and be
taught by others, thus freeing the teacher for additional
teaching activities.

11. Each day (or as often as practical) ask the child to
reread his previous story or stories (as well as those of
others) and to dictate a new one. The pattern is thus
repeated. This frequent exposure to high interest-low
vocabulary material is designed to stimulate active and
enthusiastic participation.

12. Help each very poor or beginning reader to organize
a word bank as described earlier (682). We find that LEA
works best with pupils who function at first or low
second-grade reading level. While the procedure does not
pay rich dividends for every disadvantaged learner, it
does provide numerous positive experiences for many.
    Perhaps we can further clarify the general approach
which has been outlined by describing several more
interesting situations in which LEA has been used.

Case Two

In a non-graded primary program with three teachers and seventy-two second-year youngsters, the average measured intelligence quotient of the group was 82. David, one of the seventeen members of his family, had a recorded I.Q. of 78, not unusual considering the educationally deprived area in which he attended school. Nevertheless, Dave was in reading group nine, reserved for those youngsters whose achievement levels were the lowest of the entire program.

The consultant was asked to suggest some way by which Dave and his peers might learn to read. First tried was an auditory procedure (phonics) which failed dismally. Nor did a kinesthetic technique (tracing) seem to pay dividends (Much time and patience are sometimes required before really observable progress is noted with this procedure.) The basal reading series had already been discarded as not adequately meeting the needs of these pupils.

The language-experience story idea was tried next. Dave mentioned his interest in squirrels and immediately dictated the story shown in Illustration 6-1.

As soon as Dave had finished dictating the story, he was invited to read the entire selection of 24 words. This he did without error. The consultant asked the teacher, who was at the front of the room, to listen to Dave read. She hurried to the back and, when Dave had successfully read his story, demonstrated her pleasure by giving him a bear hug.

Alvin, another child in group nine, was overwhelmed by the scene. He joined us and asked Dave what had happened. Perhaps the rest of the episode can best be told in dialog form.

Alvin: Dave, what'r you doin'?

Dave: I just 'rit me a story.

Alvin: Can I read it?

Dave: Sure. (He flipped the paper around, and Alvin sat down on the opposite side of the table. The consultant and the teacher stood behind Dave.)

Alvin: (After ignoring the title and pointing to the first word for several moments, he looked up at us, as youngsters often do. We gently nudged Dave's back, and he supplied the missing word.)

Dave: Frisky.

317

Alvin: Frisky...is...my...(extended pause--He looked at us; we nudged Dave.)

Dave: squirrel

Alvin: squirrel...(extended pause)

Dave: (after another gentle tap) Frisky. (Did we note a little irritation in his voice?)

Alvin: Frisky...has...a...

Dave: (immediately) bushy tail. Alvin, can't you read nothin'?

Naturally we were delighted to see the first semblance of a change in Dave's self-concept. We were pleased to have discovered a possible way for Dave to learn to read -- certainly not at grade level and obviously not even at an average pace. But the little fellow could learn to read if we would provide for individual differences in the specific approach to reading.

Case Three

Max was another youngster for whom a more traditional approach had proved unsuccessful. By age nine, Max had received hundreds of hours of individual instruction. The son of affluent parents, Max possessed high average intelligence but was a complete non-reader. He had been tutored for three months by a phonics fanatic under whom he learned not one letter-sound association. Later Max has been instructed by a flash card fiend who did somewhat better in three months -- three basic sight words were learned.

Toward the end of his third year in school, Max visited one of the authors. During the course of the conversation, the boy pointed to a window at the end of the long room and asked, "Could you shoot a beer can off that window sill?" The reply was, "No, could you?"

Max then launched into an extended monolog about his activities at the city dump -- shooting rodents and setting up beer cans as target practice when live animals failed to present themselves. He told about giving his brother judo chops and karate punches, of hitting him in the stomach, and then running off again to shoot his gun at the dump.

As fast as possible the evaluator scribbled the flow

318

of ideas, finally interrupting Max when it appeared certain he would never stop on his own volition. After the comments were transcribed into legible print, Max was asked to read his story. He looked up with expressive eyes and said, "You know I can't read. I wouldn't be here if I could."

But Max was wrong. He could read. His dictated story was just over two hundred words long, and Max read it all, missing a total of exactly twelve words. The word give was missed six times; it represented one-half of his errors.

By the end of the third reading, Max knew all but three of the words -- give in each case. And we knew what to give him -- language-experience activities. As it turned out, we subsequently discovered he profited from the use of the kinesthetic technique, and we adopted an eclectic procedure.

It would be highly gratifying to report that our ardent sportsman is now reading well, but such a rosy picture simply cannot be painted. Max returned to his classroom with traditional grade-level books in most subjects and reacted to continuous frustration and failure in the only way such denied learners can. Now, several years later, he is both a poor reader and a discipline problem.

Case Four

Le's father brought him to school one Saturday morning in the early fall and asked what could be done to help his son learn to read. The boy had just entered the third grade and had been assigned a complete set of inappropriate books.

We checked Le's reading ability and found he could not even call words at the first preprimer level on an initial reading inventory. We also determined that he had high average intelligence. Two separate language-experience activities were used during the diagnostic session, and both proved quite successful.

A German major seeking recertification at the intermediate level agreed to tutor Le after school on an irregular basis--whenever his own baseball practice and other outside activities didn't interfere. In October we checked Le again. Utilitizing LEA heavily supplemented with SCCs, the youngster was able to read at the primer level. In early May he could read at the 2-1 level. Neither the boy nor his tutor had access to the testing materials.

During the summer he had no help. That fall his teacher asked what to do about Le. It seemed he couldn't

read his fourth-grade books. We recommended
language-experience and suggested some specific
procedures. During the following years the fifth-,
sixth-, and seventh-grade teachers had similar problems.
Today Le still has grade-level textbooks. He still has
not participated in LEA during school hours. And he
still reads at a low primary level.

Case Five

Six ten-year-old boys were unable to read above the
first reader level. Because the content of the basal
materials they could read was completely devoid of
interest appeal, the boys were organized into a separate
group. A number of "different" approaches to learning
were employed, none of which initially involved basal
texts. Even supplementary books were discarded during
the first two months of the school year.

We were asked to work with each boy and subsequently
the group to determine the most effective approach(es) to
use. We started with Ricky -- a poorly dressed fellow
with a speech defect. Ricky was said to possess
below-average intelligence and came from an impoverished
family background. The first day we constructed an
experience story based on the question, "What would you
do if you were not in school today?" Ricky dictated the
following story:

Ricky's Story

I would wash the dishes and dry them.

I would clean the house and mop the floor.

I would make the beds.

Then I would put the dishes away and go
outside and play.

Ricky was asked to read his story as dictated. He
couldn't. Such a complete failure to do so is rather
unusual but not rare. A brief conversation established
the fact that he could name the letters of the alphabet
but could not make most LSAs. Auditory discrimination
was poor. The few words Ricky knew apparently had been
learned visually -- probably by a look-say procedure.

After a few practices, Rick was asked to take his
story home and to learn it well enough to recognize words
through the open slot. The following morning Rick
bounced in, presented his story, and read it with no

errors. Perhaps he had memorized it. A possibility, of course, but not so in his case. Regardless of the placement of the open slot, Rick could identify the words. He had really done his homework.

We then followed the some procedure with each of Rick's friends. Whereas Rick had acquired 24 hours to "catch on," four of his buddies were able to read their stories almost immediately (A sixth fellow with a very low measured intelligence quotient, did not respond to any procedure we used.).

The boys' reading teacher, a dedicated and talented young lady, followed the basic guidelines presented in the first part of this chapter. SCCs were also constructed by the six fellows; these materials provided effective independent learning activities. After each boy had constructed and mastered his own set, he taught the words to his peers.

Reading practice was extended by letters and messages to the boys. These notes were written on the chalkboard, and the fellows were asked to read them. The six boys helped each other with the words, and the first one able to demonstrate his reading proficiency to the teacher was then assigned to help one or more of his peers. He became Chairman of the Board. On many days one boy would teach a second, who in turn would teach a third, and so on. After the routine was established, direct teacher guidance was minimal. The boys who finished reading and teaching the material then copied the story and, using the open slot with their pals, practiced recognizing the words by sight.

Certainly they learned a great deal. The number of disciplinary actions and negative comments regarding attitudes of the six boys decreased drastically from the previous year. Indeed, one teacher insisted her main problem was the number of interruptions occasioned by the boys' trying to show her how much they had learned.

In October, the boys insisted they be given books, so we located some supplementary high interest-low vocabulary materials. The first set of books (about cowboys) was rejected by the boys; the second series, the Dan Frontier books (Chicago: Benefic), received immediate acceptance. The materials were secured and read in sequence rather than in random order. In November, the best reader of the six boys was moved from the language-experience group past a slow-moving 2-1 group into a fast-moving 2-2 group. He remained with that group for the rest of the year. In January a second child was moved, this one to the 2-1 group. Eventually another youngster was "promoted," and we found it necessary to locate more candidates for the group. Six members seem to work best.

At the end of the year, the teacher who had worked with the six boys was enthusiastic about their progress. One member of the primary team, who had previously had all six in her class and had discouraged our efforts to help them as "wasting time with people who can't learn," mumbled, "Well, it's easy to work with them. They're so motivated. You ought to see the ones I've had to work with."

Summary

This chapter addresses the question "How can I initiate beginning reading instruction?" and describes one set of procedures that can be used. Essentially the strategies proceed from words to sentences. This chapter considers LEA while the next chapters consider the basal. In support of LEA, we should note that it possesses the following advantages:

1. It is based on the specific language and experiences of the children. We should not assume that merely exposing youngsters to a variety of experiences will overcome their formal, or "standard language," deficiences. Indeed, experiences which fail to utilize the maximum value of language may lead us to assume incorrectly that language growth and development has occurred while, in actual fact, only a superficial and nebulous awareness has transpired (380).

Perhaps an example will help clarify this point. One of the authors was asked to determine the instructional reading levels of three fourth-graders who were experiencing considerable difficulty in learning to read. One little fellow whom we shall call Tommy brought his book, a 2-1 reader from Open Highways series (594). He read a page orally and another page silently. The consultant asked him to point to the picture of Pogo the elephant. This request normally would have seemed somewhat juvenile inasmuch as the bottom half of one page consisted principally of a typical second-grade elephant.

Tommy immediately pointed, however, to the clown sitting on Pogo's back. In response to the request to find another elephant, Tommy flipped several more pages and identified another clown. Obviously he was completely confused. We stopped and talked about elephants; the consultant pointed to several and asked the boy to locate some others. When asked the question, "How big is a real elephant?" Tommy separated his hands to a distance of not more than twelve inches, this despite the fact that he had seen elephants on

322

television. Tommy simply was unable to relate television elephants to book elephants, to conceptualize size, and to associate the oral and written word <u>elephant</u> with the picture. His problem, then, was one of seeing relationships and transferring learning.

One might say Tommy had been involved in an experience with elephants via television, but it certainly was not a language-experience. Probably no one had ever pointed to an elephant on television and said, "Tommy, that's an elephant."

2. LEA utilizes the actual oral language patterns of the members of the group. While these may be non-standard for everyone other than the speaker, they do exist, and with modifications necessary for communication, they must be used as the basis for instruction if maximum learning is desired. We should not presume that standard language patterns are "better" than other dialects. Dialects are not sub-standard; they are merely non-standard as compared to the patterns actually used in the vast majority of printed material. Perhaps we could learn from Bill Martin, Jr., (788) who recognizes <u>and</u> <u>accepts</u> three types of language: home rooted, formal, and literary. His objectives do not include any attempt to condemn or extinguish "unacceptable" language patterns but rather to develop proficiency with other types of usage. Hopefully we can assist youngsters in becoming more aware of the appropriate circumstances for using each type of language.

3. Child-shared language-experiences may be immensely appealing because of their emotional content and the interest factor.

4. The absence of a rigidly-controlled vocabulary tends to enhance the literary quality of the written material. Interestingly, many of the "unusual" words in experience stories are learned far more rapidly than the so-called "easy" basic sight words. These latter terms are, in actuality, the most difficult ones a youngster is called upon to learn for the following reasons: (a) They have configurations (shapes) which fail to distinguish them from other basic words; (b) they are generally phonically irregular except for their initial sounds; and (c) they are generally adjectives, verbs, and prepositions and consequently are abstract as opposed to nouns which often are concrete and therefore relatively easy to remember.

5. LEA makes it possible and educationally desirable for youngsters to teach their stories to their peers. This practice makes teachers out of beginning and poor readers. One can easily imagine the possibilities for improving youngsters' self-concepts and motivational levels.

Furthermore, an eclectic, or combination, approach to teaching is highly desirable (238). Indeed, one conclusion of the summary of the 27 United Office of Education First-Grade Studies was that the addition of a language-experience component to a basal program increased the latter's effectiveness (71).

The enumeration of these possible advantages of the Language-Experience Approach should not be construed as denying the usefulness of basals. After all, the basal's reinforcement of newly-introduced reading terms, while generally insufficient to meet the needs of slow youngsters and other disadvantaged children, is highly desirable. So too is the attention to a systematic sequential development of skills as presented in the manuals, pupils' books, and workbooks. If we really believe in the introduction, mastery, and application of word analysis, vocabulary, comprehension, and study skills, it is imperative that specific provisions be made for the presentation and practical use of skills material. Indeed, the failure of some teachers to include skills instruction as a basic component of LEA has undoubtedly contributed to its lack of success in those situations. But, then, any approach which ignores or de-emphasizes skills instruction is headed for disaster.

We believe that language-experience is a highly effective approach for some youngsters (6, 141, 380, 554, 571). Without abandoning the lead basal concepts already developed, we can utilize the strengths of each approach to meet the needs of a greater number of beginning readers than if either the basal or language-experience is used (238).

FOR FURTHER READING

Allen, Elizabeth G., and Lester L. Laminack, "Language Experience Reading -- It's a Natural!" Reading Teacher, XXXV, No. 6 (March, 1982), 708-714.

Aukerman, Robert C., Approaches to Beginning Reading, Second Edition. New York: Wiley, 1984.

Collins, Carmen, "Creating a Photo Essay," Language Arts, LVII, No. 3 (March, 1980), 268-273.

Durkin, Dolores, Getting Reading Started. Boston: Allyn, Bacon, 1982.

Harris, Mary McDonnell, "Family Forces for Early School Development of Language Fluency and Beginning Reading," in Worldwide Reading Success, pp. 55-73, ed. Harry W. Sartain. Newark, Del: IRA, 1981.

MacGinitie, Walter H., "When Should We Begin to Teach Reading?" Language Arts, LIII, No. 8 (November-December, 1976), 878-882.

Mountain, Lee, Early Reading Instruction: How to Teach Reading Before First Grade. Providence, R.I.: Jamestown, 1981.

Powers, Anne, "Sharing Language Experience Library with the Whole School," Reading Teacher, XXXIV, No. 8 (May, 1981), 892-895.

Quandt, Ivan, "Investing in Word Banks -- A Practice for Any Approach," Reading Teacher, XXVII, No. 2 (November, 1973), 171-173.

Stauffer, Russell G., "A Language Experience Approach," in First Grade Reading Programs, pp. 86-118, ed. James F. Kerfoot. Newark, Del.: IRA, 1965.

List A
SOME PICTURE OR BEGINNING DICTIONARIES

Cater, Elizabeth, ABC Words: A Coloring Dictionary. Racine, Wisc.: Western, 1971.

This coloring book dictionary presents about four words, pictures, and sentences on each page. Some of the pictures are already colored. It is appropriate for pre-kindergarten, kindergarten, and grade one.

Chambers, Selma Lola, The Little Golden Book of Words. Racine, Wisc.: Western, 1948. (Forty-first printing, 1977).

This $.49 dime-store beginning dictionary groups words and pictures by categories such as Things to Eat, Things to Play With, Things That Go, Bird, Animals, etc.

Courtis, Stuart A., and Garnette Watters, <u>Illustrated Golden Dictionary for Young Readers,</u> Revised Edition. New York: Golden Press, 1961.

The 538 pages of entries are preceded by sections entitled "Getting Acquainted With Your Dictionary," "How Your Dictionary Can Help You With Many School Subjects," and "Using Your Dictionary for Fun and Practice." Entries include accents, syllables, one to three definitions, and representative sentences. Perhaps 20% of the entries are illustrated. Some group pictures (i.e., fruit, birds, insects, railroads, etc.) are included.

Drysdale, Patrick, <u>Words to Use: A Primary Thesaurus.</u> Toronto, Canada: Gage Educational Publishing, 1971.

Words in this thesaurus are organized by ideas contained in the table of contents. Major topics include "The World We Live In," "Living Together," and "Words for Sentence Building." Under the first topic, there are six sub-areas: Space, the world, light, fire, water, and weather.
No definitions are included and there are very few pictures except for outlines of the idea for which words are grouped. As an example, over a dozen words for places to sleep are listed in an outline of a bed. This book would be useful for children in grades three and four or above.

Eastman, P. D., <u>The Cat in the Hat Beginner Book Dictionary.</u> New York: Random House, 1964.

Each of the entries in this delightful dictionary contains a picture and a sentence or phrase. Many sentences relate to others in a loosely organized series of sequenced events.

Harris, Albert J., and Mae Knight Clark, <u>My Self-Help Dictionary.</u> New York: Macmillan, 1966.

Words are listed alphabetically twice with the first letter in both upper- and lower-case. A picture either portrays the word or a sentence including the word. Projecting tabs designate the appropriate letter of the alphabet. The last page and inside cover contain suggestions for using the dictionary. It is intended for use beginning at the second preprimer reading level. The format is similar to <u>Words I Like to Read and Write.</u>

_____, My Word-Clue Dictionary. New York: Macmillan, 1967.

The format is identical to My Self-Help Dictionary. The book is intended for use by pupils reading at the second-grade level.

Jenkins, William A., and Andrew Schiller, My First Picture Dictionary. Glenview, Ill.: Scott, Foresman, 1975.

This dictionary is designed to be used after My Pictionary but before My Second Picture Dictionary. The paperback contains 865 words grouped in seven categories. Each word (listed in blue) is followed by one or more sentences. Each word is illustrated. Recommended.

McIntire, Alta, Follett Beginning to Read Picture Dictionary. Chicago: Follett, 1959.

The alphabetically arranged words and pictures are intended primarily for first grade. Two pages of sentences are included at the end.

Monroe, Marion, W. Cabell Greet, and Andrew Schiller, My Dictionary. Glenview, Ill.: Scott, Foresman, 1970.

This book contains words divided into nine categories that are color coded. An eight-page leaflet lists ideas for the teacher.

Moore, Lillian, A Child's First Picture Dictionary. New York: Grosset and Dunlap, 1948.

This brief hardback alphabetically lists words, pictures, and sentences for 302 key words common to grades one and two.

_____, The Golden Picture Dictionary. New York: Simon and Schuster, 1954.

Over 800 words for beginning readers are included in two columns. Each entry contains variant forms and one or two sentences. About 25% contain pictures. The best use would probably come with second graders.

Morgan, Joyce, and Beverly Wilbur, <u>Dent's Primary Dictionary</u>, <u>Level 1</u>.Toronto, Canada: J. M. Dent and Sons, 1959.

Designed for use with first and second graders, this dictionary has a two-track presentation. Concrete nouns are presented alphabetically with pictures. On separate pages, other words are presented alphabetically without pictures. There are no definitions or sentences.

O'Donnell, Mabel, and Willmina Townes, <u>Words I Like to Read and Write.</u> New York: Harper, 1973.

This picture dictionary is intended as a picture-story book for below average first graders and as a dictionary for average and above average children beginning in the second semester of grade one. It contains about 800 listings, of which 480 are base words.
Words as listed alphabetically with one or two sentences containing each item. When the underlined word is a noun, a picture represents it. Otherwise a picture tells about the sentence(s). The last pages contain the upper- and lower-case letters with picture words and the numerals and numbers up to 20. The format is similar to <u>My</u> <u>Self-Help</u> <u>Dictionary</u>.

_____, <u>Words to Read, Write, and Spell.</u> New York: Harper, 1973.

This dictionary of 937 main entries is intended for use in grades two, three, and four. It follows use of <u>Words I Like to Read and Write</u> and uses the same format. However, it does include syllables and accents.

Parker, Bertha Morris, <u>The New Golden Dictionary.</u> Racine, Wisc.: Western, 1972.

The first 113 pages of this dictionary contain words, sentences, and pictures. Variants (comb, combed, combing) are included. Sometimes group concepts (i.e., furniture, animals, flowers, etc.) are included with special inserts containing items in that classification. An interesting addition is the inclusion at the end of "To Parents and Teachers" and "Dictionary Games."

Reed, Mary, and Edith Oswald, <u>My First Golden Dictionary.</u> Racine, Wisc.: Western, 1976.

This tall but brief book contains two columns of words, pictures, and sentences. The material is appropriate for use in kindergarten and grades one and two.

Reid, Hale C., and Helen W. Crane, My Picture Dictionary.
    Boston: Ginn, 1963.

Words and pictures for nouns are listed in
alphabetical order. Non-noun words are listed
separately in alphabetical order. Near the end of the
book there are pictures for action words, parts of the
body, the family, toys, helpful little words, farm, city,
fruit, vegetable, weather, and number words. The last
two pages present the days of the week, color words, and
months and holidays. This book contains 177 nouns, 268
service words, and 129 words in the classification
categories.

Schulz, Charles M., The Charlie Brown Dictionary (In
    eight volumes). New York: World, 1978.

These eight volumes are identical to The Charlie
Brown Dictionary. There are 580 full-color pictures and
2400 defined words.

_____, The Charlie Brown Dictionary, New York:
    Scholastic, 1973.

This dictionary contains 2400 words for children ages
5-9. Words are defined only with words already defined,
and circular definitions (i.e., a story is a tale, a tale
is a story) are avoided.
    Each word, listed alphabetically, is followed by a
sentence or definition. About one-fourth of the words
are illustrated by pictures.

Watson, Jane Werner, Animal Dictionary. Racine, Wisc.:
    Western, 1966 (Tenth Printing, 1977).

This beginning dictionary lists words, pictures, and
sentences in alphabetical order using a two-column
format. Entries range in difficulty from cats and dogs
to centipede and chinchilla.

Willford, Robert E., and Ronald E. Reed, A Knowledge Aid
    Picture Dictionary. Niles, Illinois: Knowledge Aid
    (6633 West Howard St., 60648), 1969.

This paperback picture dictionary organizes words
into 24 categories such as colors, numbers, toys, pets,
etc.

USING BASAL READERS

PREPRIMER LEVELS

Introduction

Although there are at least 100 approaches to beginning reading instruction (27), three of these approaches are in wide use today. These include LEA, individualized instruction, and the basal reader. Because the overwhelming majority of pupils in a typical class can profit from the judicious use of the materials included in a lead basal series, this chapter considers information necessary to use the approach effectively. In any approach the needs of the class can be met only if the following provisions are made:

1. Pupils are associated with materials which they can read at their instructional levels.

2. Pupils are provided systematic and sequential instruction and practice on specific skills which they do not know but for which they possess the prerequisite competencies.

3. Pupils are given the opportunity to learn through a variety of approaches, methods, and techniques presented to accommodate learning preferences.

4. Pupils are provided with ample opportunity, in short periods, to assimilate and master the information presented.

5. Pupils are given sufficient opportunities to practice and apply the newly-acquired information. We often refer to this as extensive reinforcement.

What are a teacher's responsibilities as she initiates a program based on the use of one or more series of basal readers? We suggest she must:

1. Determine the reading level of each pupil and secure the appropriate titles from the lead basal series down to the point at which the material no longer can present an appealing atmosphere to the youngsters.

2. Use presentational techniques which stimulate thinking and reasoning skills.

3. Provide carefully-balanced and comprehensive mastery-based developmental lesson plans designed to build continuously on the pupils' strengths and to focus on their needs.

4. Organize and work with several groups.

Chapter 5 has already considered procedures for implementing the first responsibility. Item two involves skills related to word analysis, vocabulary, and comprehension; techniques are presented in each of the appropriate chapters--9, 10, and 11. This chapter focuses on item three, and Chapter 12 considers item four.

Regardless of the grade level at which it is employed, a DLP for a reading selection consists of six basic interrelated parts, all of which are intended to facilitate the development of comprehension.

1. Vocabulary development

2. Background

3. Purposes for reading

4. Silent reading

5. Evaluation, Discussion, and Oral Reading

6. Extended and related activities

You may notice the proposed sequence for the first two items is the opposite of that typically found in some basal readers. The rationale is that too often we build background and motivation for a story, whet the children's appetites, and then stop to develop vocabulary and concepts. By the time we finally get around to the story, the desire is gone. By reversing the procedure we avoid this problem and secure additional time to assure that new vocabulary is not only taught but also learned.

The six parts of a DLP are conducted somewhat differently depending upon the reading level. Thus this chapter considers basal instruction at the preprimer levels. Chapter 7B focuses on the primer through the 2-2 level (approximately), and Chapter 7C discusses the 3-1 level and above (approximately).

1. Vocabulary Development

The model for the vocabulary component of a DLP consists of five phases: (1) direct instruction, (2) in-school reinforcement, (3) at-home reinforcement, (4) test, and (5) review.

At the preprimer levels use a guide similar to the one shown in Chart 7A-1 and present the words at least one week <u>before</u> the story is to be read. The rationale for teaching new vocabulary well before children read a selection is to provide time and opportunities for youngsters to master the items. There is abundant classroom evidence that many children cannot learn new words as fast as we present them. Thus a need exists for youngsters to study and learn the new vocabulary on the days before they read the material.

CHART 7A-1
VOCABULARY INTRODUCTION
Preprimer Levels

	<u>A</u>	<u>B</u>	<u>C</u>	<u>D</u>	<u>E</u>
1.	old	old	old	old	old
2.	party	party	party	party	party
3.	cake	cake	cake	cake	cake
4.	open	open	open	open	open

_____
Parent's Signature

Print the words on first-grade paper. Give each child a duplicated sheet like the one shown in Chart 7A-1. If the group is very large, display a similar copy on the overhead projector. If the group is small, you can be close enough to the children to help them use their own sheets as they follow the procedure.

Phase 1:   Direct Instruction

1. Using Column A, ask the right-handed children to put the pointing finger of the hand they do not use in writing under the first letter of the first word (number 1-old). Ask the left-handed children to touch the first letter of the first word with their pencils.

2. Say, "I am going to say a sentence and leave a word out. You are pointing to the first letter of that word. When I say the sentence, look at the word and trace it if you know it. Then raise your thumb stomach-high to tell me you are through." Review the directions. Then say the sentence, substituting Hmm for the orally omitted word that is listed on the spirit master. Example: "Today is my birthday. I am seven years Hmm."

3. After pupils trace the word and raise their thumbs, say, "As I say the sentence again, all of you say the new word when I get to the blank. Remember: Look at the word and not at me." Then say the sentence a second time. You may instinctively wave your hands for a total group response. However, the children should look at the word rather than you when they chorus the answer. It is important for them to understand that looking at you will not help them learn to read. They should listen to you but look at print wherever it appears. Repeat the sentence: "Today is my birthday. I am seven years ____." After years, the children should chorus, "old."

4. Introduce the second word using the contextual procedure described in Steps 1-3. The children should look at the word, trace it, and raise their thumbs. Sample sentence for party: "I want you to come to my birthday Hmm."

5. After presenting the second word, review the first two words. This review may occur in several ways depending on the age and ability level of the group.

    A. Ask the children to put the pointing finger of the non-writing hand (for right-handers) or the pencil point (for lefties) on number one when you say that number. Pause. When you say, "Number one is ____," they chorus the response, being careful to look at the word rather than you. Then do the same for word two before returning to word one. Be sure to pause between the time you say the number and when you say the sentence.

B. Pair the pupils and ask them to pronounce the words to each other--number one, number two, number one for the first person and number two, number one, number two for the second person.

C. Ask an individual to respond. This procedure can be used either with a group that doesn't need the security of activities a and/or b or as a followup to those activities. As a general principle, beginners and slow groups will use activities a-c. More advanced readers will tend to use activities b and c and perhaps eventually just c.

6. Introduce the third word in the same manner described in Steps 1-3. Remember to say the sentence twice, with children looking, tracing, and raising their thumbs after the first time. Sample sentence: "I can hardly wait to blow out the candles and cut the Hmm."

7. Then review all three words in three sequences: top to bottom, bottom to top, and random order. Use activities a-c depending on the needs of the group.

8. Follow the introduction and review procedures for the fourth word. Sample sentence: "Then I'll get to Hmm all of my presents."

Several points should be discussed here. The first relates to the response when a child blurts out a wrong word. The best way to prevent the problem is to use sentences which are unambiguous, i.e., they have only one logical answer. The four sentences presented above are intended to be of that type. Suppose, however, that the child hears, "Then I'll get to Hmm all of my presents" and says Keep. Perhaps the sentence should be changed to avoid the problem. Thus, "Why don't you Hmm the door and let the dog in?"

If the child possesses some phonic skills, you have another alternative. Instead of using just context skills, help the child blend context and phonic (LSA) skills. Pointing to the first letter, ask two questions: "Does the word you said start with the same sound as this letter?...Does it make sense?"

When a child says a wrong word, ask the question that can be answered by yes. Next ask the question that can be answered no. Finally, ask the child to supply the new word (which ought to be easy since most of the children have already chorused the appropriate response).

Let's consider two opposite situations to see how the above three-part sequence is used.

SITUATION A

Sentence: "I rode down the street on a horse."

Child: "I rode down the street on a house." (a meaning error)

Teacher: "Does the word you said begin with the same sound as the first part of this word?" (pointing to the first letter of <u>horse</u> on the board)

Child: "Yes."

Teacher: "Good." (Notice the positive reinforcement for the child who may be embarrassed by the laughter of the other members of the group. Now the child has correctly answered a question and been praised.) "Does <u>house</u> make sense in our sentence?"

Child: "No."

Teacher: "Right again." (Note a second controlled response situation and a second chance to praise the child.) "What word does make sense?" (If necessary, repeat the sentence. However, this usually is not required.)

Child: "Horse."

Teacher: "Great." (Thus a blunder which might have inhibited further participation is handled gently and productively.)

Note: At this stage or reading it is highly unlikely that the child has studied either the /ou/ or the /or/. Thus it is useless to wander down that path.

SITUATION B

Sentence: "It was hard for me to pick up the big box."

Child: "It was hard for me to pick up the large box." (a letter-sound association error)

Teacher:	"Does the word you said make sense?" (Note: This is not the same question asked first in the preceding vignette. Remember that the first question should be answered by yes, for it reflects the child's strength, the second by no.)
Child:	"Yes"
Teacher:	"Good. Now tell me, does large begin with the sound this letter stands for (pointing to the first letter of big)?"
Child:	"No."
Teacher:	"Right again. Can you tell me what this word (pointing to big) is?"
Child:	"Big"
Teacher:	"Very good."

A second point relates to the number of words to introduce in a lesson. That is an individual decision which must be based on a host of factors. For example, we used only two words with our daughter Ginger when she was three years old. Despite her pleas, we refused to increase the number to three, for it is always better to leave a child begging for more than to exceed the learning limit. At age five she could handle five words at a time, but this number is not recommended for kindergarten children in general. Perhaps two words at a time is more reasonable for kindergarten children until experience provides a better number.

A third and related point concerns how often new vocabulary should be presented. That depends in considerable measure on how well children are profiting from instruction and your knowledge of how far similar children have proceeded in the past. For example, if children can easily learn four new words a day, there should be no objection to their doing so. Slower children who need more reinforcement may require fewer words at a time, be assigned fewer new sets of words, and begin later in the school year.

By noting how similar children have progressed in previous years, you can determine the number of new words in the materials the group might encounter. If a top group is likely to proceed through the first reader of a series containing 500 words in grade one (and many series have more than that), divide the number of weeks of actual reading instruction (30-32 perhaps) into the number of words to decide how many last year's group was expected to learn per week (16-18). The number of words in a list (four in this case) suggests about four lists per week. Remember that last year's group is not the one receiving instruction. It may approximate the progress of this year's group, and then again it may not. Furthermore, children are likely to learn more words later in the year and fewer words at the beginning. The best way to answer the question of how often to present a new list of new words is based on diagnostic analysis of how well children respond and how receptive they are to further learning.

Fourth, note that vocabulary is presented in context. That is, word study is developed in relationship to comprehension. One does not need to know the /o/ in order to identify old (I am seven years old.). Instead one needs to think, "What makes sense?" One does not need to know the /p/ in order to identify party (Can you come to my birthday party?). Instead one needs to think, "What makes sense?" As Farr and Rosen point out, "...using context analysis to unlock a word is the behavior most in tune with the purpose of reading...(306:188)."

Sometimes context alone provides a sufficient clue. At other times one needs to use context plus phonics (often initial sounds). For example: "I ate too many green apples. Now my stomach Hmm." Is the missing word hurts or aches? The initial sound will tell us. Context plus phonics is required. "The soldier fired the _____." Is it gun or rifle or cannon or shot? Context and phonics gives us the answer. Note that phonics by itself is not sufficient, for it does not deal with word meaning, and that is what reading is all about. A child who knows the word family (phonogram) at can say vat; the youngster who knows the ill word phonogram can say gill and sill. Pronunciation is not important, however, unless it leads to meaning, and phonics in isolation is not very helpful in this regard. A sounding-out procedure at the introductory stage of a lesson is not recommended. Phonic study comes later in the lesson plan when children can build on things they already know and thus proceed from the known to the unknown. "Context clues are most effective when they are employed along with other methods of word attack (237)."

As phonics is not recommended as the initial way of identifying new words, neither is pronunciation of the word in isolation. Thus it is not recommended that a teacher say, "This word is look. Say look." The child acquires no context skills and for that matter, no phonic

337

skills either. Edward Dolch (253), whose 220 sight words
are still the most popular word list with teachers,
presented the list along with the strong recommendation
that new words be introduced in context. We see Dolch
flash cards, but where are his ideas? Using context (and
sometimes phonics) to figure out an unknown word gives
children a skill to begin using in their own reading.
Teaching by telling denies youngster an important
learning opportunity.

Fifth, note the opportunities provided for EPR (278).
We cannot expect children to learn unless they pay
attention to instruction. We have no way of knowing from
minute to minute where children's minds are unless we use
continuous EPR techniques. Tracing and copying are EPR
strategies. So is raising one's thumb after completing a
specific assignment (in this case using context and
perhaps also phonics to identify a new word). Blurting
out answers inhibits EPR. So does calling on only one
child to answer a question. Strategies for using EPR in
a variety of subjects are discussed elsewhere (206).

Phase 2: In-School Reinforcement

After direct instruction, provide opportunities for
the child to study the new words. At first this phase
will be teacher-directed while pupils learn how to learn.
As soon as they master the self-study strategy, the
in-school reinforcement should become an independent
activity.

1. Divide the pupils into pairs in the following manner.
Using your own judgment, list the youngsters in the
approximate order of their ability to pronounce words.
In a group of ten, pair pupils 1 and 6, 2 and 7, 3 and 8,
4 and 9, and 5 and 10. Thus one member of each pair will
be in the top half of the group, and there will (may) be
a noticeable difference in the word recognition abilities
of the two members.

If a group has an odd number of children (nine, for
instance), pair numbers 1 and 6, 2 and 7, 3 and 8, and 4
and 9. Make number five your partner. Or, pair 1 and 5,
2 and 6, 3 and 7, and 4 and 8. Make number 9 your
partner. Even better, pair 2 and 6, 3 and 7, 4 and 8,
and 5 and 9. Make number 1 your partner. You can
quickly check off this person, who in turn can be a Word
Consultant (216) and help others.

2. Say, "While you study and learn your words, I'm going
to work with another group. While I'm doing something
else, I want you to work with your partner." Outline the

procedure for the children to follow.

A. Person A (the better word recognizer in the pair) should pronounce the words in Column B to the partner.

B. If Person A misses a word that Person B (the partner) cannot supply, Person A asks the Word Consultant for help and begins reading the words again, starting at the top of the list.

C. After Person A reads down the list without error, Person B reads the words from top to bottom.

D. Both children then proceed to Column C and repeat the procedures a-c, this time going from the bottom to the top.

E. Both children then return to Column B and, beginning at the top, trace each word, saying it softly at the same time. This step involves the vocalic sense and is sometimes helpful in building memory. If the word is party, the child should take the same length of time to say the word as it takes to trace it. The child should not name the individual letters of the word. Once again, anyone who needs help should ask a Word Consultant.

F. Each child then traces and says the words, from bottom to top, in Column C. (Reminder: An activity is not completed until each child can read the lists both up and down without error.)

3. After tracing and saying the words in both columns, each child goes to the Word Consultant to be checked off. The Word Consultant needs a 5 x 8 inch card containing the names of the children in the group down the left-hand side and a column for each numbered list of words across the top. When a child can say the words from top to bottom and bottom to top without error, the Word Consultant can place a check or happy face in the appropriate space.

Even better, give the Word Consultant the four words cut apart. The children must then pronounce the items in random order. A child who misses a word must wait until five other children (or the remainder of the group) have had a chance to be checked off before returning to the Word Consultant. This practice is intended to avoid two problems: (1) A child hears the right word, says it, and expects to pass. (2) A child prepares haphazardly and

339

expects to pass. We should not allow either condition to prevail.

The 5X8 inch card provides a ready record showing which pupils still need to practice their words. This record is also helpful for use with absentees and during parent conferences. One card with half-inch columns will take care of 14 lists. To keep the list from getting lost paste it to the Word Consultant's desk or on a large sheet of pasteboard.

Several factors are appropriate topics for our consideration at this point. The first is the Word Consultant. This person is a child from within the group (if possible) who provides difficult words. Use three criteria to select the Word Consultant:

a. The Word Consultant knows the words. A Word Consultant may be poor in other aspects of reading such as comprehension or phonics.

b. The Word Consultant is a self-starter. That is, this person must be able to be interrupted, provide the necessary help, and immediately return to work. (In the first grade, some groups don't have such a child.)

c. The Word Consultant uses good psychology. Thus the Word Consultant does not say, "That's a baby word," or, "You don't know that word?" or "It's so easy," or "I've told you that word a dozen times." Instead, the Word Consultant says, "That's a hard word," or "I used to have trouble with that word." Alternately the Word Consultant can supply the word, smile, and say nothing else.

Select two Word Consultants, preferably a girl and a boy at each reading level. Hopefully both will not be absent on the same day. Another reason for having a girl and a boy is that some children prefer to ask for help from a person of their own sex. If absolutely no Word Consultant can be found in a group, begin to develop the essential qualities in the children. In the meantime, use visiting Word Consultants from the next higher group.

Be sure children understand what qualifications a Word Consultant must possess. Point out examples of situations as they occur naturally in the classroom. Becoming a self-starter and using good psychology are often harder for a child to master than simply learning to recognize words.

340

Having selected the Word Consultants, point out to the group the steps to follow in seeking help. For this activity there are four parts:

a. The child who needs help goes to the Word Consultant and points to the word.

b. The child who seeks help looks at the word and asks what it is.

c. The Word Consultant pronounces the word if the other child is pointing to and looking at it. Otherwise the Word Consultant says, "I can't say it unless you point to it (look at it)." Then the Word Consultant pronounces the word.

d. The child pronounces the word while pointing to it and looking at it and then returns to work. The child should say "Thank you" and the Word Consultant respond with a smile and "You're welcome."

Please note that the Word Consultant makes only one instructional comment -- that of supplying the word. The Word Consultant never says, for example:

a. "It rhymes with _____."

b. "You know that word. It means the same thing as _____."

c. "Sound it out. What does f say?"

d. "It starts with /puh/."

It is permissible, however, for the Word Consultant to ask what the child thinks a word is. Quite frequently the insecure child makes repeated requests for assistance that are not essential from an academic point of view. In this case the dialogue might be as follows:

Child" (looking at and pointing to the word) "What's this word?"

Word Consultant: "What do you think it is?"

Child: "Old."

Word Consultant: "I thought you knew it," or "Good for you," or "You know more that you think you know."

341

If the child doesn't respond or says the wrong thing, the Word Consultant pronounces the word.

Since we can't expect Word Consultants to know when to use this technique, you may want to identify certain children who feel the need for constant assurance (It's certainly not hard to pick them out.). Then provide their names to the Word Consultant.

Role play the procedures a child and a Word Consultant should follow. At first you play the Word Consultant and let children come to you for help. Then let potential Word Consultants assume the role while you act out the various situations to which they will be expected to respond. Finally, allow the other children to ask the Word Consultant for help, for the group members must learn their part as well. Don't institute the practice until the members of the group are able to function in their roles. Otherwise the activity will be more trouble than it's worth.

To relieve the pressure on the Word Consultants, you may want to provide a mechanical assistant. Check a Language Master (or Voxcom) out of the media center, print each word to be studied by the group on a separate Language Master card, and tape record the word. Thus a child who doesn't know a word can find it by matching the Language Master card and the word on the spirit mastered sheet (visual discrimination of words). The child then inserts the card into the machine and hears the words. If a Language Master is available, the regular Word Consultant can be freed to give the tests at the end of Phase 2.

A second factor to discuss relates to tracing. The rationale for including a kinesthetic component is that different people seem to learn in different ways. Some people are visual. For them a look-say procedure seems to be highly effective. On the other hand, some people are auditory. They learn well by listening. They are sensitive to sounds, and they respond well to phonics. Still other people are vocalic. They learn by saying things aloud. They may memorize poetry this way or, at the beginning reading levels, mumble their way through a story (219) or read "silently" making as much noise as they do when reading aloud.

Some people are kinesthetic. They learn though the sense of touch, which occurs in three stages: (a) tracing, (b) copying, and (c) copying from memory. A brief discussion of each stage follows:

A. tracing. This stage was described in Phase I. Although all beginning readers should start here, older youngsters may be able to begin at Stage 2. Children who

342

are unable to trace probably are not ready to learn to read (exception: the physically handicapped).

The tracing may be done with the point of the finger in actual contact with the paper, sandpaper, or sand tray (309), or involve a writing tool -- pencil, pen, crayon, magic marker, etc. -- on the paper. In any event, tracing should not be done in the air. While the activity may be fun -- and some handwriting series even recommend it -- there appears to be little transfer from arm waving to reading.

B. copying. Children eventually proceed from the tracing to the copying stage. At this point they copy the words on the line below the print. See the format displayed in Chart 7A-1. How can you tell when children are ready to proceed from tracing to copying? Note their work, for observation will show that the transition should occur when children can (1) print neatly (that is, the letter formation is acceptable), (2) print in the space provided (that is, the letters in one column are not so large that they crowd into the next column, and (3) print rapidly enough that the act does not consume too much time.

C. copying from memory. This stage reflects the development of a child's visual memory. For young children and almost all beginners it applies only to words of five or fewer letters. Once again, observation is the best way to determine whether or not a child is ready to make the transition. Simply note children's work as they engage in this process. Can they copy from memory two-letter words? If so, can they copy three-letter words? Can they copy four-letter words? What about five-letter words? Importantly, does practice improve their ability? If frustration is present, consider reverting temporarily to Stage B (copying from a model).

A child at Stage C should study the word on the spirit master, turn the paper over and print the word in the upper left area. The child may not turn the paper over to restudy the word letter by letter but must reproduce the entire word from memory. A child who forgets -- and this certainly is understandable -- draws a single line through the partially completed word, turns the paper over for restudy, and once again prints the word on the back. By folding the right half of the paper back over the left half, the child can note the accuracy of the printed word. If the word is right, the child proceeds to the next word. Remind the child to skip all words of six or more letters. However, be prepared for

343

some children who contend they "can do it -- see?" with certain words, especially compounds (cowboy, without), or high interest words (mother, father) and affixed words (cooking, played).

Remember that certain instructional words can cause unanticipated problems. Do children know the meaning of <u>trace</u>, <u>letter</u>, <u>word</u>, <u>first</u>, <u>beginning</u>, <u>sentence</u>, <u>column</u>, etc.?

A third factor relates to correlating the language arts. If children are going to practice printing, they should use the words in the reading lesson rather than those in a handwriting book (and in grade two and above, the words in a spelling book). Thus the words on the spirit mastered sheets -- see Chart 7A-1 -- provide excellent practice, assuming the strokes represented by those letters have already been taught. The United States Office of Education's First Grade Studies found that a writing component enhanced reading growth (71, 284). Here is a natural opportunity we should not miss.

Phase 3: At-Home Reinforcement

Both research (696) and common sense suggest that retention of information is enhanced when the learning is spread over a long period of time rather than massed into a short time frame. Stated another way, what we "learn" in a hurry we also forget in a hurry. This principle is probably best illustrated by considering the major tests for which we once prepared. Many people waited until the last minute and then "crammed" until the wee hours of the morning. Although these people sometimes passed the tests, they frequently say they forgot the information almost immediately. In other words, the "learning" wasn't permanent.

In the same class there were also some people who prepared almost daily for the test they knew would be given eventually. Not only did these people usually pass (often with excellent grades), they tended to remember far more of what they studied. Their attitude was based on learning rather than on "getting by," and they prepared accordingly. These people did not cheat themselves of an education.

As applied to young children, how does spaced practice work? The first step is to recognize that the concept requires homework. There's a limit to how much spaced study can occur during the school day. As Phase 2 indicates, spaced study is utilized. However, there is need for even more such opportunities.

To begin the process, explain both to parents and children why spaced practice is necessary. Some parents oppose homework while others demand it. The key concept here is that vocabulary study at home is essential. First, it is not a busy-work identical assignment made to everyone in the class. Second, it is based directly on what has been taught and what will be expected on the following days during the reading assignment. Third, the practice material (the spirit mastered sheet) is readily available for parents to help their children. Fourth, the amount of required parent time and help is minimal.

One way to explain to parents is by a school letter, which is much better than an individual teacher's letter because it involves the entire faculty and is therefore accorded more respect. While followup can occur at the first PTA meeting or during National Education Week, both events occur too late to be the introductory medium.

The letter should include a form for parents to sign indicating their willingness to assist their children. Followup forms should also be distributed at PTA meetings. School newspapers should list the names of participating parents (and their children) by teacher to commend them and encourage others to sign. (The fact that a parent signs does not assure a commitment.)

Regardless of whether parents agree to help the children, the need for personalized followup will become obvious. Children who arrive at school with the list but without the word knowledge provide us with the information we need. Opal Johnson, a principal in Lexington, North Carolina, handles the situation by calling the parents. Although there are half a dozen variations, the basic conversation at one end of the line goes something like this.

"Hello, Mrs. _____, this is Opal Johnson, the school principal. How are you?...Fine, thank you. I'm calling about Woodrow. You know we're really working hard on vocabulary, and every teacher sends home a list of words she's been teaching. We want the parents to help their children learn the words because they are in the story the children will read the next day. Well, Woodrow just hasn't been learning his words. He only has to learn about four words each night, but he's not learning them.

"Have you seen those sheets?...You haven't? I was afraid of that. I'm afraid Woodrow has been telling his teacher some stories. He tells her every day that you won't help him, and I figured that wasn't true.

345

"Woodrow's teacher is afraid he won't pass, he's falling so far behind his group, and it's only the last of September. I told her I didn't think you would want him to be kept back next year...No, ma'am, I didn't think you would. What do you think about that?...

"I think Woodrow is too young to appreciate all you do for him. Do you think you could make him sit down and learn his words? He wouldn't have to work nearly as hard as you do. He's supposed to take five little tests. Each one takes less than a minute. (Here she explains the process.)

"I'm so glad we had this talk. You've been so helpful. I'll call you in a week or so and let you know how Woodrow is doing. By the way, Woodrow brought home a list this afternoon. His teacher made sure he had it with him. Will you see that he knows those words tomorrow morning? Maybe he should study the words before he watches TV tonight. Thanks, Mrs. _____. Goodby."

Mrs. Johnson also contacts those who don't have telephones. She reaches them at work. Lexington has a number of mills, and many parents work there. The mills supervisory personnel have been most cooperative. After a second call, parents often ask Mrs. Johnson not to call them at work. One response she sometimes gives is this: "Oh, I'm so sorry to bother you at work, Mrs. (or Mr.) _____. However, I can't reach you at home, and your child's teacher said you didn't come for the parent's conference. I don't believe you've been at any of our PTA meetings or the parent workshops, and we need to keep in touch. Don't you think that's important so your child will know you believe in education?

"Would you like to come by next week to see how well your child is doing or would you rather I call you and let you know?..." (If possible, she sets a date and time and calls if the parent does not appear.) "Thanks, Mrs. _____. I'll tell your child's teacher that I'd like to meet you when you come. Goodby."

The children should also understand what to do and why. Young people frequently fail to see the reason for doing certain things; explanations may help them understand the importance of at-home reinforcement.
The procedures for children to follow in Phase 3 (At-Home Reinforcement) are similar to those discussed in Phase 2 (In-School Reinforcement). There are, however, certain differences which are outlined next.

346

1. Instead of a classmate as a Word Consultant, there will usually be an older person. At the beginning of the year ask the parent(s) or guardian(s) to assume that responsibility or designate someone to do so. Following are some other possibilities: other family member (grandparent, aunt, uncle, older brother or sister, etc.), neighbor, or someone who rides the school bus.

2. The child studies the words and takes a series of five tests.

   A. Test one. The child reads the words down Column D. If there are any errors, the child must re-study and take the test again no sooner than five minutes later (This provides time for study, and the child should be expected to do so during this period of time.).

   B. The child traces and says the words in Column D to himself.

   C. Test two. At least 30 minutes after passing test one, the child reads the words up Column E. In a child's terms, that is the length of a regular television program. A child can look at television and be tested during the commercials.

   D. The child traces and says the words from the bottom to the top of Column E to himself.

   E. Test three. The child cuts apart each separate word in Column E (only), shuffles them, and, at least 30 minutes after test two, says the words from left to right as they appear in random order. Once again, any error requires a re-test at least five minutes later. Study hint: A child who can't seem to recognize a particular word can often do so by matching it with the corresponding word in Column D. Position of the word in a list is thus a temporary crutch used as a study aid.

   F. Test four. Thirty minutes later, the child says the words in a random order again.

   G. Test five. Thirty minutes later, the child says the words in random order again.

3. When the child successfully completes all five tests, the parent (surrogate) signs the forms to certify that the study was conducted in the proper manner. The child carries the form back to school on the following day.

Note the space provided for this purpose at the bottom of Chart 7A-1.

Several observations are pertinent. First, the entire process covers a time period of two hours. Yet the child has to study only a few minutes at a time, an advantage for someone with a short attention span. Furthermore, parents must devote less than one minute of their attention at a time to help their child (and less than five minutes in all per day for this activity).

Second, when children are through with their homework, they should stack their notebooks, spirit mastered sheets, library books, lunch money, etc., in one specific place. This practice avoids several problems: (a) the child who leaves some learning material at home; (b) the frustrated frenzy that ensues in a last-minute effort to find things; and (c) the anxiety that occurs at school and interferes with learning.

Ask parents to designate a specific place where a child's school materials can be kept safely. They should be out of reach of babies who eat them, dogs that wet on them, and siblings who draw on them or tear them up. If a specific place is designated, the papers are less likely to be thrown away or tossed into the washing machine!

Phase 4: Test

Because the story will be read one or more weeks after the words are introduced, it is important that each child proceed through Phases 1-3 on the first day. On the morning of the second and following days, these activities should occur:

1. Ask each child to pronounce the words in random order. Although this activity is simple, it is time-consuming. Consider the following alternatives:

A. Children who arrive at school early go to the cafeteria to review their words. Aides and even the principal check the children before the first bell rings. When school officially begins, the children are ready to read. Imagine how much time teachers save and how much smoother and faster lessons proceed because of this strategy. Opal Johnson, a Lexington principal, and Max Linton, principal of Polk Avenue School (Lake Wales, Florida), implemented this strategy as part of their schools' Developmental Reading Programs.

B. Children who arrive early go to the cafeteria or auditorium where aides and/or teachers check them off before school officially begins.

C. Children who arrive later go to their rooms where the teacher or aide checks off the first child, who then checks off the rest. Or, the first child checks off the second child who checks off the third, and so forth. Once again, a child who misses one or more words must wait until five other children (or the remainder of the group) have had their chance.

2. As an alternative or a followup, develop new sentences for each word. Say each sentence, omitting the key word and asking youngsters to supply it. Once again, Language Master Cards, children who have been checked off, or older children can assist.

3. Use either a 5 x 8 inch card or a Group Analysis Chart on 8-1/2 x 11 inch paper to record the data (pupils' names down the left side, the numbers of the vocabulary lists across the top). This chart (a) vividly portrays the performance of each child (no score is recorded until a proficiency of 100% is achieved), (b) provides a simple management system, (c) shows parents and children how much progress is occurring, and (d) keeps absentees from getting lost in the shuffle. They have to learn the words presented on the days they were absent. It is important to note that a beginning reader who misses school for a week -- and many young children do -- can really fall behind. When you can't read much, every day is important.

This leads to an important question: "What should we do when youngsters don't learn their words?" We know what typically happens. Since manuals suggest that stories be read shortly after new vocabulary words are presented, those pupils who are unable or unwilling to learn the words simply muddle their way through the selection. Any improvement on that situation will therefore be a decided advantage.

When the procedures described here are first implemented, some youngsters don't learn their words. Aside from the recommendations discussed elsewhere, (see Chapter 6) teachers must make a crucial instructional decision: whether to assign the story or not. To do so is to revert to the procedure which has made illiterates and underachievers of these youngsters. It seems better to do "something else" in reading that day and provide opportunities for these youngsters to learn their words.

How about teaching some skills? How about reading non-book materials (wall signs, names of children, words displayed in the school, SCCs (216), words on toys and games, etc.? If you teach skills, all who need them may be involved. If you teach more vocabulary, it will be enrichment for those who have learned their new words. Meanwhile, the other children will have time to study (or re-study) their words.

It is far better to delay the silent reading for fifteen minutes (meeting with a different group first) or even an entire day than to proceed full stream ahead -- ready or not. Notice that those who did their work the previous evening are not "held back." They do receive reading instruction although it doesn't come from the basal. One other observation: The alternative of splitting the group in half is not necessary, at least not at the present time. We must help children acquire the habit of dependability without allowing them to fall farther and farther behind in their reading materials.

There will come a time, of course, when we may decide to split a group and proceed at a much slower pace with some youngsters. By this time, however, the children will have had an opportunity to become accustomed to the procedures and to develop the appropriate study habits.

Incidentally, it helps to re-test children each day on their previous lists. Each child can be responsible for testing his groupmates on a specified list.

Phase 5: Review

The review phase is intended to be more long-term in nature than the test which follows on the day after the initial presentation of new vocabulary words. The vehicle for review, Word Whiz, is used only after the initial learning is supposed to have occurred. Thus Word Whiz is not a teaching activity but a review and long-term reinforcement strategy. Assuming that four new words are presented on each of four occasions (for a total of sixteen new words), use the Word Whiz as a fun activity for pupils who have been checked off as learning all four lists of words. The procedures are identified and described below.

1. Distribute three forms of Word Whiz to pupils in such a way that children sitting beside each other have different forms and thus cannot "use" each other's answers (The "borrowing of information" shouldn't even be necessary if pupils have learned the four sets of four words each.). Thus, if three children sit side by side,

the first person will have Form A, the second Form B, and the third Form C.

One form of Word Whiz (208), based on the 1983 Houghton Mifflin Reading Series (277), is presented in Chart 7A-2. Word Whiz materials for the preprimer levels for approximately twelve different series of basals are available.

CHART 7A-2
WORD WHIZ
HOUGHTON MIFFLIN
Boats - Form A
Pp. 1-37

with	lunch	hat	am
stop	at	out	Mr.
rabbit	live	be	turtle
win	run	race	thank

The words are placed in more or less important positions according to how difficult they are perceived to be. Thus, the hardest words are listed in positions (from left to right and top to bottom) 1, 4, 6, 7, 10, 11, 13, and 16. Words in these positions can be used to form a vertical, horizontal, or diagonal line in three different directions.

2. Explain the directions for using Word Whiz. They are quite simple. Say,

a. "When I say a word, find it on your card and cover the word with a marker."

b. "When you cover all of the words, say 'Word Whiz!'" (If all of the children know the words, they will say "Word Whiz" simultaneously.)

351

c. After the game has been played, ask each child to pronounce the words from left to right and from top to bottom on the card.

d. As an alternative to c, ask all holders of Form A to pronounce the words simultaneously. Then ask the holders of Forms B and C to follow suit.

3. Provide further instruction and practice to children who have difficulty with any of the words.

2. Background

The previous pages have considered strategies for developing vocabulary, the first step in a mastery-based DLP. After children learn the new words, develop the background of experience. At the preprimer levels there can be a serious problem if the setting of the story differs from the environment to which the child has been exposed. Thus, a selection about the country may be difficult for an urban child, and a story about the city may cause problems for a child who lives on a farm. A migrant may not have many experiences relating to a middle-class story, and a Floridian may not understand a story that involves a snowstorm.

You must know your children sufficiently well to identify the experiences that should be provided to serve as an appropriate background for reading a story. Background development can occur through the use of field trips to a farm, circus, or apartment house; pictures from a picture file coded to each story; films and filmstrips about different places; realia (real objects, such as a pinata); or visits from resource people.

If the above activities are not appropriate, ask background questions to the group. If no child possesses the information, provide the knowledge yourself. At the end of the discussion ask children to share what they have learned. (It doesn't do any good if you talk and they don't listen.) Sometimes reading selections consider topics with which all children are familiar. In this situation don't spend any time on developing background. The five or ten minutes or so can be put to much better use.

3. Purposes for Reading

The literature indicates that those who read for one or more purposes comprehend better because they approach the reading act with an attitude of inquiry (401, 404, 670, 701). Indeed, our experience has been that pupils

352

who have assigned purposes (1) are better able at the end of silent reading to answer those purposes than pupils without such assignment and (2) are better able to answer other questions as well. These findings are logical for, unless readers have a purpose, they simply plod through assigned material without comprehension or retention.

Example: Have you ever been given an assignment ("Read Chapter 7 for tomorrow.") and counted the number of pages before starting? Have you ever said to yourself at the end of a page, "Well, only 29 pages to go"? Have you ever fallen asleep -- either literally or mentally -- while reading something? Have you ever found yourself just pronouncing words rather than paying attention? If your answer to any of these questions is "yes," there must be a need for purpose setting, for you probably have not had any of the above problems while reading something for a reason more important than taking a test.

At the preprimer levels (and possibly above, depending on the type of group), children typically read one page at a time while the teacher remains with the group. The following strategies are recommended:

1. Provide one purpose prior to the silent reading of each page.

2. Choose an important question rather than an insignificant one. Thus, "What did Jane do?" is better than "Who was the girl?" Likewise, "Why was Bill going to town?" is better than "Where was Bill going?" As a general guideline, focus on questions which emphasize (a) main ideas, (b) cause-effect relationships, (c) compare-contrast, or (d) predicting outcomes.

3. Whenever possible, provide a purpose question whose answer appears in the second one-half of the assigned reading. It will keep children thinking and looking for something as long as possible.

4. Print the purpose, in the form of a question, on the board or on a chart. Examples: What idea did Bill think of? Who was not afraid? Although pupils probably will not be able to read the question at these levels, it should still be phrased as simply as possible.

5. Read the purpose question to the group. Have the children repeat it fluently as a group. The reason for asking the group to say the purpose is to assure that the question at least passes through their minds. The answer to the purpose question will be discussed after the silent reading.

353

4. Silent Reading

It is generally accepted that silent reading precedes oral reading even though young children often make as much noise in silent reading as they do in oral reading. This behavior tends to diminish or disappear as reading competence increases. At the beginning stages it should not be a cause of great concern, for some youngsters find that "mumble reading" (219) is helpful in remembering information. Remember the importance of providing materials at the instructional level. Indeed, mastery teaching is not likely to be effective if youngsters begin with materials that are inappropriate because of their difficulty. Appropriate placement is an essential prerequisite. For example, Cooper (139) found that pupils who functioned at the instructional level made the largest amount of progress. More recent research findings from the well-known Beginning Teacher Evaluation Study clearly indicate that pupils who spend large amounts of time on high success activities have higher achievement test scores, better retention over the summer, and more positive attitudes toward the school (51).

As indicated earlier, the teacher remains with the group at the preprimer levels and thus is able to provide immediate assistance to anyone who needs it. This help may include (a) pronouncing words, (b) explaining an idea, or (c) keeping on task the child who wants constant reassurance. Furthermore, the teacher may note (d) signs of frustration, (e) poor habits such as improper posture and failure to hold the book at the right distance and angle from the eyes, losing the place, moving the head rather than the eyes, etc., or (f) problems in reading rate (i.e., too fast for comprehending or too slow).

When markers must be used -- and we discourage them for all but the bottom group, first preprimer readers, and youngsters with visual problems -- they should be slender strips placed above a line of print. This placement is to avoid the interruption in reading which occurs when a child must stop at the end of the line and move the marker down to the next line. At the preprimer levels (and other levels as well), a child should read the passage more than once.

5. Evaluation, Discussion, and Oral Reading

Step 5 of a DLP includes three activities, all of which are followups of the silent reading act. At the preprimer levels, the evaluation and discussion occur simultaneously. These two activities are of great importance. Evaluation tells us how well each child is doing and the areas in which further assistance is required. Discussion provides the vehicle for clarifying any misconcepts and for extending the depth of meaning. Following are some recommendations for deriving maximum value from these activities:

1. Present questions in sequence. Although a single page may provide material for only three or four questions, these items should be presented in the order in which they occur so the story can be discussed exactly as it unfolds.

2. Ask children to hold their thumbs up when they (think they) know the answers. Provide wait-time (60S) for those who need to think, especially with more difficult questions. The research indicates that when additional thinking time was provided, the quality and quantity of responses increased, including those by slow learners. The implication is that we should discourage blurting and avoid calling on someone immediately after raising a question.

3. Allow the entire group to chorus the responses to literal questions. Anyone who blurts out an ináccurate answer or who fails to respond can usually be identified frequently enough to provide the necessary evaluative data.

4. For implied and creative questions, call on individuals. Try to avoid giving first chance to those you believe definitely know the answer or absolutely have no idea. Instead, call on someone who seems in doubt and, if necessary, ask some leading questions to encourage the development of additional thinking.

5. Include the purpose-setting question as presented earlier.

6. Record pupil performance on a Group Analysis Chart. There are two ways of doing this. Chart 7A-3 presents the simpler way, which we recommend as a beginning.

GROUP ANALYSIS CHART - COMPREHENSION
Form 1

	Preprimer 2	Story 1	Story 2	Story 3	Story 4
Alex	+++++--				
Bertha	+ -				
Celia	---				
Dacia	+				
Evander	++++ --				

A more sophisticated recordkeeping system is shown in Chart 7A-4. It should be used only after a teacher has become comfortable with Form 1 (Chart 7A-3).

CHART 7A-4
GROUP ANALYSIS CHART - COMPREHENSION
Form 2

	Preprimer 3											
	L	I	V	C	L	I	V	C	L	I	V	C
Alex	+ +	+- +	+ +									
Bertha	+ −											
Celia	− −		−									
Dacia		+										
Evander	++ ++	− −										

356

Oral reading also plays an important part in reading at these levels. It can be used for several purposes and in a variety of ways.

1. <u>Reading</u> <u>to</u> <u>prove</u> a <u>point</u>. When two people disagree on an answer or when someone is unable to supply an answer, ask the children to open their books and find the sentence that answers the question. Then call on a child who originally missed the item. Use reading to prove a point each time an implied question is asked (except when the clue is a picture rather than the print).

The following example illustrates the use of oral reading to prove a point. One of the authors taught a lesson entitled "Old Red Helps" to a group of second graders. The story is about a hound-pup with long floppy ears that made running and playing difficult. One day Hound-Pup asked Old Red, the Solomon of his species, for advice. Old Red suggested that every time Hound-Pup was fed, he should lick his bowl clean and bark three times when he could see his image in the bottom of the bowl. Hound-Pup followed his advice and, wonder of wonders, found that his ears were no longer a problem.

During the discussion we asked the question, "What happened to the size of Hound-Pup's ears during the story?" One child responded, "They was (sic) bigger." Another said they were smaller; a third child thought they had remained the same.

To save time we might have provided the correct response and hurried along. In the interest of teaching and learning, we referred the children to the story. One child read:

"Look here, Old Red!" called Hound-Pup. "The secret worked! My ears are getting smaller."
Another child countered by reading the subsequent passage.
Old Red laughed, "No," he said. "They are not smaller."
"Oh, yes," said Hound-Pup. "They are not so long now. I don't fall over them."
"I know," said Old Red. "That's because you are bigger. Your ears are bigger too. They just don't look as big (387:47)."

Reading to prove a point is a way of answering questions, a way of basing answers on text rather than opinion, and a way of conducting oral reading.

2. <u>Reading</u> <u>to</u> <u>satisfy</u> <u>pupils</u>. Young children often complain that they haven't read unless they have had some

oral reading opportunities. Dyadic (or paired) reading (278), is an appropriate vehicle for providing this experience. Pair two pupils at the same reading level. One child should be in the top one-half of the reading group and the other in the bottom one-half of the group. Both children hold the same book. The child seated on the left reads the left-hand page while the partner follows along. Then the child on the right reads the right-hand page. Either child can help the other with the words, as can the Word Consultant or the teacher. If there is a full-page picture, one child simply misses a turn. Usually five minutes of dyadic reading is sufficient. To note a child's performance, stand near the youngsters and look in another direction so you appear to be otherwise occupied. Because of the noise it is desirable to have all children engage in dyadic reading at the same time.

Skinny Books cut from discarded basals and mounted by individual story (194) are appropriate for dyadic reading at the preprimer levels, for the vocabulary must be carefully controlled and the children should operate independently (at least 98% word accuracy and at least 90% comprehension). Other appropriate materials are supplementary reading books or the basal selections they have read previously.

3. <u>Reading for teaching</u>. A variant of dyadic reading can be used by pairs of pupils with similar reading levels who read to and teach each other. Each child selects a piece of material, either of the kinds just mentioned or self-authored and typed.

The first child reads the material to the partner who follows along and, at the end of a sentence, paragraph, or page, reads it in the same manner. The procedure is as follows:

A. The first reader chooses material to read, and the teacher decides how much the child shall teach at any one session. The amount depends on the second child's reading status and the difficulty of the first child's material.

B. The first reader and the partner sit side by side so both can see the printed information.

C. The first reader reads sentence one, and the second reader repeats it (i.e., provides a xerox version), being careful to look at the words.

D. The first reader reads sentence two, and the second reader repeats it.

E. The first reader then asks the second child to read both sentences and provides help only as necessary. The second child must read both sentences without help to complete this step.

F. Additional sentences and reviews of everything covered so far are provided until the designated material is learned.

G. The children then exchange roles with the "learner" playing the "teacher" on the same material.

4. Reading for diagnosis. Round robin oral reading is probably the most abused aspect of primary grade reading. When asked why they have children read aloud, most teachers reply, "So I can find out what words they don't know." The need is valid. It is the procedures that are questionable. The following problems are frequently observed.

A. One child reads while the others do nothing, even though the teacher has directed them to "follow along" and "pay attention."

B. The fast reader moves at such a rapid pace that the slow readers are unable to keep up, sometimes falling a page behind. Having lost their place, the slow readers are unable to find it.

C. The slow reader proceeds so slowly that the fast reader must abandon a natural reading rate and practice plodding along.

D. Some children count ahead to see which page or paragraph is theirs. Naturally they are not paying attention, and, if a child reads the wrong amount of material, the ones who carefully planned ahead in order to provide a polished performance may be chastised.

E. The child who misses many words is humiliated during every oral reading session (This problem would not occur, of course, if appropriate materials were provided.).

F. The activity consumes considerable time with no evidence that youngsters necessarily improve their oral reading. Instead many children seem to miss the same words day after day.

G. The teacher sometimes is not even involved in the lesson. She may be writing assignments on the board, checking papers, gathering or distributing materials, etc.

H. The teacher rarely records the words the children miss and provides no followup instruction and/or practice so children will improve their oral reading performance. If children read orally for diagnosis, we must note their problems and provide appropriate assistance. Otherwise the oral reading becomes an end in itself rather than a means to an end.

The round robin oral reading activity can be improved by using it as a listening activity for the other children. That is, all children should keep their books closed except for the oral reader. One child will then receive oral reading practice while others receive listening practice. The following procedures may be helpful:

A. Give the children a supplementary reading book and assign certain sentences, paragraphs, or pages to various youngsters. Each child then reads his part silently in preparation for the sharing time.

B. While the child reads to the group, note any errors. The procedures for doing so are described in Chapter 5.

C. After the first child reads a part, ask questions to the other members of the group. They keep their books closed with either their hands or their bookmarks at the appropriate page. They use the thumbs-up procedure to express an interest in responding. The books are opened when children disagree on an answer and must read to prove a point.

D. Repeat the procedures with the other children in the group.

The obvious advantage of this procedure is that it meets two objectives simultaneously. First, it provides opportunities for children to receive practice in listening, a much-needed experience. Second, it gives a child an opportunity to read orally while the teacher notes the performance.

An alternative to the round robin procedure is to meet with one child at a time to provide oral reading practice and identify the most important needs. The following procedures may be helpful:

A. In a quiet area of the room place two pupil chairs or desks at least ten feet apart. For a right-handed teacher, place a chair or desk slightly behind and to the right of the pupil seat that is on the right. For a left-handed teacher, place a chair or desk slightly behind and to the left of the pupil seat that is on the left. The intent is to create a setting in which the teacher sits slightly behind a child who is reading orally and at least ten feet away from the child who is waiting for a turn. The teacher's chair or desk is arranged so that her writing hand is the greatest distance from both children. Thus any note taking can be done with minimal pupil distraction.

B. Explain the seating pattern to the children. One child will be with you while a second youngster sits in the waiting area. When the oral reader is finished, the second child joins the teacher while the child who read orally tells another child to go to the waiting area. A child at the waiting area practices the page or pages that have been assigned. If you want youngsters to read without prior presentation (in order to see how pupils solve possible problems), provide the materials without specifying the pages to practice.

C. Secure a spiral notebook and make a table of contents listing the names of the children in alphabetical order by reading group. Record the name of each child on a separate page.

D. Place a sheet of carbon paper and a plain piece of paper on the child's notebook page so both of you can have a record of the missed words. Record the child's name and the date on the two copies.

E. As the child reads, list each difficult word (i.e., one that is not attempted, is missed, or causes a long pause before correct identification) and the page number on which it appears in the book. The child will therefore be able to refer to the word in context. After removing the carbon, note on your copy any additional problems (i.e., fluency, speech, finger pointing).

361

F. Assign a Word Consultant to help the child learn the words.

G. Teach all children the following study strategy.

1. The child begins at the top of the list, pronounces the words, and places a check to the right side. This process continues until the youngster misses a word. The Word Consultant should point out any overlooked error.

2. On missing a word, the child looks it up in his book and tries to identify it by context. The youngster who can do so says the word and returns to the top of the list, once again recording checks for correct responses.

3. If the child cannot identify the item in context, the Word Consultant pronounces the word, the child repeats it, reads the sentence, and returns to the top of the list.

4. After reading all the way down the list without any help, the child reads up the list.

5. Then the child reads the previously-read oral passage to the Word Consultant.

6. A child who has difficulty (i.e., misses two or more words) repeats 1-4 and either traces or copies and says the words after reading down (and up) the list.

7. The child who successfully reads the oral passage to the Word Consultant re-reads it to a tape recorder or the teacher.

An important note of caution: One does not count dialect as a reading error (357, 429, 559, 656). Thus a black child who says "He jump up and down" may evince a need for oral language help with he jumps (and probably talks, writes, sings, rides, etc.) but not reading, for the child simply is reading print the way he "knows" (believes) is correct. Teachers must be sensitive to the language of their children so they do not confuse oral language differences with reading errors.

Oral readers may have difficulty besides missing words. More sophisticated problems such as fluency are better left for teaching instruction with participants coming from several groups.

6. Extended and Related Activities

The final step of a mastery-based DLP involves extended and related activities. Possibilities include the following:

1. Have pupils read the same level of book in an earlier edition. For example, the vocabulary in the Bookmark Reading Program's Sunup in 1979 and 1983 is almost identical, yet the stories are almost completely different.

2. Provide the Skinny Books (216) mentioned earlier. A child who completes his assigned work reads the stories in order. If necessary, a specific block of time is provided for Skinny Book reading. These materials are provided at children's independent levels. As an approximation the following comparisons may be helpful.

Instructional Level	Independent Level
PP3	PP1
Primer	PP2
First Reader	PP3
2-1	Primer
2-2	First Reader
3-1	2-1
3-2	2-2
4	3-1

These figures assume that the lead basal series and the recreational reading series are of similar difficulty and have a considerable overlapping of vocabulary. Some series are much more difficult than others, and the vocabulary at various levels of some series differs considerably from the words at similar levels in other series. Thus, these factors must be carefully considered when providing sets of Skinny Books.

Southwest Elementary School (Lexington, North Carolina) catalogued over 5,600 Skinny Books from five different non-instructional basal reading series. Teachers can check out one or more sets for each reading group. With five series represented, there is abundant opportunity for horizontal practice.

3. When skills are to be used in a specific selection, teach the ones that accompany the next lesson so children will have time to master them before reading the selection. Thus, if children are supposed to apply the

/a/ (as in cat) to some new words in a lesson, teach the skill at least one day earlier.

4. When skills are to be derived from a certain lesson, teach them immediately following the selection. You can determine from the manual which of these two procedures is appropriate. Strategies for teaching specific skills are described in the appropriate chapters.

5. Encourage children to practice reading so they can read to the kindergarten children and their own pre-school siblings and friends.

Summary

This chapter has described strategies for teaching mastery-based Developmental Lesson Plans at the preprimer levels (and primer level for the educable mentally retarded). Emphasis was placed on direct instruction, follow through both at school and at home, and pupil accountability during the testing and review phases.

FOR FURTHER READING

Anderson, Betty, "The Missing Ingredient: Fluent Oral Reading," Elementary School Journal, LXXXI, No. 3 (January, 1981), 173-177.

Fernald, Grace, Remedial Techniques in Basic School Subjects. New York: McGraw-Hill, 1943.

Harman, Susan, "Are Reversals a Symptom of Dyslexia?" Reading Teacher, XXXV, No. 7 (January, 1982), 427-428.

Heckelman, R. G., "Using the Neurological Impress Remedial-Reading Technique," Academic Therapy Quarterly, I (Summer, 1966), 235-239.

Hoskisson, Kenneth, "Reading Readiness: Three Viewpoints," Elementary School Journal, LXXVIII (September, 1977), 45-52.

_____, Thomas M. Sherman, and Linda L. Smith, "Assisted Reading and Parent Involvement," Reading Teacher, XXVII, No. 7 (April, 1974), 710-714.

Manning, John, and A. Brown, A Classroom Teacher's Digest
of Reading Instruction. Minneapolis, Minn.: North
and South Central Pyramid's Reading Program of the
Minneapolis Public Schools, 1972.

Rhodes, Lynn K., "I Can Read! Predictable Books on
Resources for Reading and Writing Instruction,"
Reading Teacher, XXXIV, No. 5 (February, 1981),
511-518.

Samuels, S. Jay, "The Method of Repeated Readings,"
Reading Teacher, XXXII, No. 4 (January, 1979),
403-408.

Sheldon, William D., "Basal Reader Approaches," in First
Grade Reading Programs, pp. 28-44, ed. James F.
Kerfoot. Newark, Del.: IRA, 1965.

Spiegel, Dixie Lee, "Six Alternatives to the Directed
Reading Activity," Reading Teacher, XXXIV, No. 8
(May, 1981), 914-920.

Vite, Irene, "A Primary Teacher's Experience," in
Individualizing Reading Practices, pp. 18-43, ed.
Alice Miel. New York: Bureau of Publications,
Columbia University, 1958.

USING BASAL READERS

PRIMER THROUGH 2-2 LEVEL

Introduction

We read much these days of procedures for teaching. Russell Stauffer (680) has described the Directed Reading-Thinking Activity, and the authors of basal series have devised procedures to accompany the reading selections. Unfortunately, however, most strategies and recommendations focus on teaching rather than on learning. Thus a teacher may follow a prescribed lesson plan and still have large numbers of youngsters who fail to acquire reading competencies.

One reason seems to be the difference between the amount a teacher teaches and a learner learns. If a teacher teaches ten new words but a child learns only three, we have a problem. If a teacher teaches the use of certain comprehension skills but children don't learn them, we have another problem. If a teacher fails to use wait-time or EPR, youngsters are inadvertently discouraged from thinking. Models for teaching need built-in strategies for encouraging and expecting youngsters to master the material. The amount of learning should approximate the amount of teaching.

Two suggestions seem appropriate. First, a (prospective) teacher of grade two or above may decide to skip chapter 7A. That is not wise, for it contains a number of principles that are referred to here but not discussed in any depth. If you have omitted the previous chapter, we recommend that you read it before proceeding with the present chapter.

Second, remember that the model described earlier may need to be extended upward for some youngsters, especially slow learners and the educable mentally handicapped. Continue to use Model 1 until you think the group is ready for Model 2. Then try the new adaptation, allowing time for both you and the youngsters to become accustomed to it. Next evaluate the success of Model 2. Are children doing better with it now than they were ten days ago? If not, revert to Model 1 or consider some adaption of Model 2 to make it more useful. On the other hand, if children do become increasingly able to use Model 2, your diagnostic analysis of the teaching act itself provides the assurance that it is an appropriate set of strategies.

1. Vocabulary

Let's look, now, at vocabulary development as it relates to Model 2. In general, Model 2 is used from the primer level through the 2-2 level. Model 2 applies to reading levels at which the new vocabulary words tend to be in the children's listening vocabulary but not in their reading vocabulary. Thus, the emphasis is on using context and phonic skills to identify words already known in their spoken forms. A more difficult aspect, identifying words that are unknown in their oral form and (usually) their printed form as well, is the focus of Model 3, which is considered in the next chapter.

At the primer, first reader, 2-1 and 2-2 levels, print the words in two columns on a chalkboard. Better still, record them on a lined wall or floor chart or on a transparency. They will then be available for use on the following days and next year as well. See Chart 7B-1 for an example.

CHART 7B-1
VOCABULARY INTRODUCTION
Primer through 2-2 Level

1.	went	6.	day
2.	want	7.	old
3.	was	8.	her
4.	there	9.	lunchroom
5.	one	10.	works

Signature

Each child should have a vocabulary notebook. This can be either the spiral-bound version or a sheaf of lined papers stapled together and covered with construction paper (Some children either don't have the money to purchase the notebooks, their parents don't approve of the expense, or they never seem to secure the materials.). For teacher-made notebooks the recommended size is 4-1/4 X 11 inches, or two notebooks cut from one stack of 8-1/2 X 11 inch paper. Staple the material at the top slightly to the left of center. Ask children to number from one to ten, skipping a line each time. They should not copy the words before the lesson starts. At this point children should be ready for the five-phase vocabulary development program.

Phase 1: Direct Instruction

1. Ask the children to label the list with a number you provide -- list 7, for example -- and, if right-handed, put the pointing finger of their left hand on number 1 in their notebooks. Left-handed children should use their pens or pencils to point to the appropriate place.

2. Say, "As I say a sentence with a word left out, copy this word (point to it) in your notebook if you know it. Then raise your thumb stomach-high to tell me that you know the word and have copied it." Say the sentence, substituting Hmm for the orally omitted word or phrase and simultaneously pointing to it on the board, transparency, or floor (wall) chart. Example for went: We got into our car and Hmm to town."

3. After pupils print the words and raise their thumbs stomach-high, say, "As I say the sentence this time, I'm going to leave out the word (or phrase). When I get to the missing word, all of you should pronounce it together. Remember to look at the word and not at me." Then say the sentence a second time: "We got into our car and _____ to town."
    As mentioned in Chapter 7A, you may instinctively wave your hands for a total group response. However, the children should look at the word rather than you when they chorus went. They should respond to the context of the sentence rather than to your gesture.

4. Introduce the second word using the contextual procedure outlined in Steps 1-3. Sample sentence for want: "Yes, Jason, what do you Hmm now?"

5. After presenting the second word, review the first two. Depending on the needs of the children, you might do the review (a) with the entire group, (b) with pairs, or (c) with individuals. In general, the slower the group, the more likely you should use all three responses. With more rapid learners use just paired and/or individual response. In any case, be certain that specific children who need this review receive it. There is little advantage to giving every child in the group the same opportunity when three pupils seem to need additional review practice. Incidentally, with some groups you may prefer to review after every third or fourth word rather than after every word. That's a matter of teacher judgment.

6. Introduce the third word as described above.

7. Then review all three words in three sequences: top to bottom, bottom to top, and random order. Use group, paired activities, and individual responses as needed.

8. Follow the same introductory and review procedures for the remainder of the words. When pupils mis-identify a word that you point to on the board, use the procedures described on pages ___ - ___.

At least three important observations should be made at this point. First, there is nothing magic about the number of words in a list. Although ten words are shown in Chart 7B-1, you might prefer to use two lists of five rather than one list of ten. Once again, that is a matter of teacher judgment. Whatever is most effective is most preferred.

Second, list the words on the board in the same order that the context exercises are presented. This procedure approximates the reading act in which children see the actual unknown word. Do not use a sentence and then ask a child to decide which of the listed words completes the blank. There are several reasons:

A. If pupils must decide which word on a list is the one that completes the blank, they are engaged in a testing rather than a teaching exercise.

B. If the pupils already recognize the words on the board, they don't need the instructional lesson that is being provided.

C. If the pupils can't find the words on the board, the lesson will be time-consuming and frustrating.

D. The activity of asking children to identify which words fills in the blank is a spelling rather than a reading experience. Children think the right word (through context) and then search for a word that spells the sounds they're thinking. Not only do spelling authorities suggest that the reading of specific words be well developed before those items are spelled (253,632), the focus of the activity is changed from word recognition (part of reading) to spelling.

Third, you may prefer to have one or more groups join the one receiving the vocabulary instruction. The strategy works this way. The teacher calls Kelvin's group and the next group(s) below it. Both groups will receive instruction, but the objectives for each will differ. Kelvin's group will have two objectives: (a)

369

apply the skill of context (and sometimes phonics) to identify the words that belong in the sentences you provide, and (b) study and learn the assigned words. Any lower group will have only one objective: Apply the skill of context (and perhaps phonics) to identify the new words. In other words, the lower group has an extra measure of practice in thinking. These are children who, without thinking, will read <u>was</u> for <u>saw</u> or <u>and</u> for <u>said</u>. Poor readers need all the instruction and practice we can provide in thinking about what makes sense; providing one or two additional context lessons decreases the instructional burden. It also resolves the problem of securing independent activities for that group during this period of time.

Although the youngsters in the lower group(s) are not expected to engage in the second objective (learning the new words), teachers using these procedures have observed some incidental learning. There seem to be two reasons: (a) the words for the upper group are considered "important" because the better readers study them, and (b) youngsters interested in advancing to the next group find that learning the words is certainly one way of preparing to do so.

If you utilize this procedure, call on and be sure to commend youngsters in the lower group(s) who "figure out" the words. This attention is certain to stimulate their interest in learning. Merging two or more groups within Model 2 for the vocabulary introduction (i.e., context lesson) is one way of meeting youngsters' needs.

Phase 2: In-School Reinforcement

Many of the procedures that are appropriate here are similar or identical to those described in Phase 2 of Model 1. See Chapter 7A.

1. Divide the pupils into pairs.

2. Teach them how to study and say the words from top to bottom and bottom to top.

3. After both pupils complete their pronunciation assignments, they copy and softly say each word three times, once beside the item and twice on the blank line between the two numbers. Show the children exactly where they should print so they can cut off the right column for subsequent use in random-word study.

370

4. Each child then goes to the Word Consultant to be checked off, and the data are recorded on a chart. As indicated earlier, any child who misses a word must wait until five others have been tested or until all of the remaining members of the group have had their opportunity.

Phase 3: At-Home Reinforcement

Each child is expected to take the vocabulary notebook home. To ensure that this does happen, stand at the door, check to be sure each child has the vocabulary notebook, any other books with assignments, a trade (library) book, any notes, papers to be signed, etc., and say goodby individually. If children don't take their books home, it is unlikely that they will secure the information from someone else and complete the assignments. The at-home reinforcement can be handled in the following manner:

1. Explain to parents and pupils why the at-home study is important. This may not be easy, for every set of basal materials with which we are familiar presents the new vocabulary the same day the children read the story. Could this be one reason youngsters don't learn the words and then have difficulty comprehending?

Ask parents if they have ever been to a talk at which they took notes. If they say no, ask if they ever took notes in school. Then ask why. Their answer ("Because I couldn't remember everything that was said.") is the reason children must take words home for study. They can't learn the words during the time that is provided in school. They need more study time.

Identify someone as the homework helper (parent, guardian, older brother or sister, other relative, neighbor, friend, etc.). Ask each child to take the following five tests from this person:

A. Test one. Say the words from top to bottom in the notebook list. If there is an error, go back to the beginning, say the words, and wait five minutes before taking test one again.

B. Test two. Wait 30 minutes and then say the words from the bottom to the top of the notebook list. Once again, if there is an error, go back to the ending, say the words, and wait five minutes before going over the list again.

C. Test three. Cut the notebook page down the center in such a way that two copies of each word (the one printed originally as well as the word copied below it) remain in the notebook and two copies are cut off. Cut each word apart so there are twice as many strips as there are different words (that is, two copies of each word). Shuffle them and practice saying the words. If you forget a word, match it to one in the notebook. Often the placement of a word in a list facilitates memory. Thirty minutes after test two (activity b), say the 20 words (if there are ten words in a list) in random order. If there are any mistakes, return to the top and go through the list, wait five minutes, and try again. Keep trying until you succeed.

D. Test four. Thirty minutes later shuffle and say the words again, repeating at five-minute intervals if there is an error.

E. Test five. Thirty minutes later shuffle and say the word again, repeating at five-minute intervals if there is an error. The homework helper then signs the notebook page indicating the child has satisfactorily completed the assignment.

Several comments seem appropriate here. First, teach the parents who attend PTA, open house, parent workshops, etc., how to be at-home helpers. Use the ideas discussed in conjunction with the Word Consultant. Because many parents may not be available for such instruction, teach the children what to do. Use role-playing sessions where you represent the parent. Give children an opportunity to try to explain what you should do. Let the other children critique the session. Prepare at least two demonstrations for use at a PTA meeting.

Second, the question has been raised about whether the five tests outlined above might be frustrating to a child. While anything is possible, of course, considerable frustration in this activity is unlikely for two reasons: (1) assuming the child is provided learning materials at the appropriate level, acquiring the new vocabulary should not pose a major problem. Most children have far more difficulty with comprehension than with vocabulary at their reading level, (2) if the words were pre-taught in context and Phase 2 (In-School Reinforcement) was provided, the child will have demonstrated initial mastery even before leaving school.

<u>Phase 4</u>:   <u>Test</u>:

On the following day, give the vocabulary test the
first thing in the morning. Whenever possible, give it
before school to save valuable in-class time. If
necessary, give it during school while lunch and milk
money are being collected. An adult volunteer could be
of tremendous value during a ten-minute period. Some
possibilities: (a) Can a parent who brings his or her
children stay for a few minutes and administer the
vocabulary tests? (Remember: there will be several
groups.) (b) Can specialized personnel involved in
pull-out programs provide assistance? Chapter I, EMH,
and LD teachers, for example, may not begin their classes
when the bell rings. They might be available to check
the youngsters in their programs. This service would
also help coordinate the activities of the classroom and
special teachers. (c) Can some older pupils start their
school day by spending five to ten minutes testing the
younger children? (Older children can take their own
written vocabulary tests before school starts. For that
matter, they can test younger children before school
starts and proceed to their own classes on time.).
Several alternatives for testing are listed below.

1. One testing procedure is simply to ask each child to
pronounce the words when presented in random order. This
procedure is the first one described in Model 1 and is
not recommended unless no other alternatives are
feasible. A pronunciation test represents a very low
level of performance because it does not focus on
context.

2. For children who have difficulty printing, provide a
spirit mastered sheet with the words and lines in a
column. Five or more consecutive quizzes can be typed on
a spirit master because very little space is required.
After duplicating the quizzes, cut them apart. Chart
7B-2 shows a quiz at the primer level.

Each child listens to the first sentence you read and
places a <u>1</u> before the correct word. For example: "At
11:00 we go to eat in the <u>Hmm</u>." The second and
successive sentences are handled in the same manner.
There is one problem. A child who records the wrong
number for item three, for example, will then want
certain ones repeated. That irritates some teachers.
You might tape record the sentences as you go and, if
anyone want to have certain ones repeated, simply rewind
and replay the entire test.

Name _____

_____ one		_____ want	
_____ was		_____ works	
_____ old		_____ went	
_____ lunchroom		_____ her	
_____ day		_____ there	

An alternative to the above procedure, especially for a small group, is to use a Language Master with each sentence labeled by number. Children then go to a learning station, play the cards, and record the numbers on their spirit mastered sheets. If they need to replay a card, there's no problem.

Hint: It is not necessary to print the sentence on the Language Master card. If you do, however, some children will "pick up" some of the vocabulary in the sentence, thus acquiring some incidental learning. Don't forget to leave a blank for the omitted word. For maximum value, label and file the cards for future use.

To check the papers, pronounce the word and give the number which should appear before it. Thus, "went - 5" or "5 - went." A child records a check mark in the left margin for a correct answer or circles an incorrect one. An alternate way of checking is to read or say the original sentences in the order used before. The children then chorus the answer and you identify the number. Thus you say, "At 11:00 we go to eat in the _____ ." When the children say "lunchroom," you say, "Put a check mark in front of lunchroom if you have a 1 there. If you don't have a 1, circle the number you put there (or circle the word itself)." One potential problem: A child who doesn't know the words won't know whether an answer is right or wrong. However, that child shouldn't be allowed to get this far without learning the words. Because it is difficult for some young children at the primer and first reader levels to check their papers, you will want to double-check their work.

3. A third alternative for testing is to ask each child to number from one to ten on a strip of paper (remember that a whole sheet is a waste as well as an inconvenience). Then read sentences, providing time for children to print the appropriate word. Once again, this activity can be provided by a variety of adults, older children, the tape recorder, or a Language Master.

4. Beginning at the 2-1 reading level (and even before, according to some teachers at schools with which we have worked), it is possible to conduct the testing exercises in an even better way. Chart 7B-3 shows an actual context reading exercise (195) based on the second grade level of the <u>South Carolina Word List</u> (665). The words are printed at the top of a spirit master, and children fill in the blanks. Note that this activity is most appropriate under certain circumstances.

A. A lead basal series is used rather than a variety of texts from different series used randomly by a variety of teachers. Thus vocabulary introduction is systematic and sequential from one reading level to the next because of a school-wide reading adoption.

B. Children are provided materials at their instructional level. Thus it is reasonable to assume that they have encountered and learned the other words in the sentences and are ready and able to learn the words listed at the top of the testing exercises.

C. All other words in the sentences have been presented in previous levels of the series. Thus, in contrast to workbooks, which often seem to have been constructed without regard for vocabulary control, these sentences are based on previous reading content.

D. Mastery teaching of the words in the series is provided. Thus not only have children encountered the words, they have learned them.

When written vocabulary tests are possible, the following practices might be employed.:

1. Duplicate the answers.

2. Place them in a designated area of the class convenient to the members of the group.

VOCABULARY TEST
Second-Grade Level

dad	maybe	cannot	been
today	want	please	its
say	anyone		

Directions: Please fill in the blanks with the words listed above.

1. We will go to a farm _____.

2. I _____ bat a ball far.

3. May I _____ have some money?

4. Do not ride home with _____ but me.

5. My _____ is Mr. Brown.

6. I do not _____ to eat fish.

7. The turtle is on _____ back.

8. _____ I will, and _____ I will not.

9. Where did the King _____ we had to go?

10. We have _____ to the zoo.

3. Tell the children that as they arrive at class, they should take a spirit mastered copy and immediately complete the exercise. Normally three or four minutes will be enough time. Dawdlers, doodlers, and those who haven't studied will take longer. Set a time limit that is comfortable and reasonable. Children who don't complete the exercise will have an opportunity to take it over. Those who get to class early will have additional time since you won't start the timing until the bell rings.

Note several advantages. First, children are "encouraged" to complete an assignment in a reasonable length of time. Second, school begins when the bell rings, even if lunch and milk money must be collected. There is little or no wasted time. Third, children receive some extra reading practice. Fourth, discipline problems are decreased because the day begins with structure. Of course, children should have specific independent activities to complete as soon as the test is completed, or chaos and wasted time can still ensue.

4. Teach the children how to take the test. The following steps may be helpful:

A. The pupils should read the ten words at the top of the exercise.

B. The pupils should read the first sentence, filling in the word if they are sure which word belongs (You may direct pupils to write the answers on a separate sheet of paper to save the copies. If so, cut notebook paper into five columns and keep the strips in a box. Have someone distribute them at the appropriate time.)

C. Pupils who are not sure proceed to the next sentence(s), completing those about which they are certain.

D. The pupils place a small check mark beside each word that is used.

E. The pupils read through the sentences a second time (and perhaps a third time) to identify the rest of the answers. At this point all words at the top of the page should be checked.

F. The pupils may ask for help in reading the sentences but not in pronouncing any of the ten words. Be sure to designate Word Consultants.

5. Check the papers. This simple act may be conducted in a variety of ways, depending on whether we consider the checking perspective, the pupil perspective, or the teacher perspective. From the checking perspective, the following comments to children seem appropriate:

A. Record a check mark in the left margin if the filled-in word is correct.

B. Circle the number of an item that is wrong. X marks reflect the negative, and it seems more sound, especially for young children, to emphasize the positive. At upper grade levels, particularly where only a small percentage of examples is missed, X marks may be more reasonable.

C. If ten items are used, count the number of check marks, record that figure in the upper right-hand corner, add a zero (to multiply by ten and get the score), and circle it. Note: If the number of check marks is not acceptable, don't score the paper at all, for the child

377

will be required to take the quiz over. If five items are used, each answer will count twenty, of course.

D. Do not count off for spelling. These are new reading words, and children should not be expected to learn to spell them for some time.

From the pupil perspective, the following comments are germane:

1. Preferably children should check their own papers so that they can receive immediate feedback concerning the accuracy of their work.

2. If one or two children tend to cheat while checking their papers, have them exchange papers with their groupmates. Do not punish the rest of the group for the habits of a few. These pupils will simply have to look to their right or left during the checking process to obtain feedback. If other pupils ask why you're having some youngsters exchange papers, reply, "Because I want to," or "It's a secret." Obviously you should talk to the specific children involved. Sometimes a "word to the wise is sufficient," sometimes not. You will then want to talk to the parent(s) or guardian(s). Placing those who cheat at the front of the group is not really a solution, for the desired outcomes are children who don't cheat, not youngsters who don't cheat when being directly observed. Nor is the use of a special checking crayon, magic marker, or pen the solution. However, these ideas may give you some temporary relief as you implement the procedure.

Another way of dealing with cheaters is to collect their papers and check them yourself. This procedure is less desirable than alternative two because your time and attention should be focused on the group rather than the papers of the pupils involved. Then, too, those children do not receive immediate feedback.

3. Do not allow pupils to exchange with people in front or behind them. That complicates the immediate feedback process and lengthens the checking time by requiring it twice.

4. Do not take the papers home for checking. These testing exercises are sufficiently simple to score that pupils can do so. All you need to do is to note quickly how well children perform in checking the vocabulary papers. To this end you should spot-check the papers for

378

accuracy. Pupils who check someone else's papers should record at the top, "checked by _____." Remember that there are children who seem unable to check anyone's paper. Pair these children with pupils who are very good at checking papers.

Insofar as the teacher perspective is concerned, the following alternatives should be noted:

1. If pupils tend to do quite well on vocabulary -- and this applies to any group -- simply pronounce the answers quickly (Number 1 is "her," number 2 is "day," etc.) There is nothing to be gained by extending the checking process. The group's past performance will indicate whether or not this strategy should be employed.

2. If many pupils tend to miss several words, read the sentence and the answer, proceeding at a slower pace for the words that present problems. Alternately read the sentence and have the group chorus the answer.

3. If pupils need oral reading practice (usually a bottom group), have a different child read each sentence and provide the correct response. Note any errors for subsequent study.

4. Record the acceptable scores on a Group Analysis Chart. If you must record the unacceptable scores, do so lightly in pencil.

5. Make provisions for pupils who did not pass the test to take it over after lunch. The easiest practice is to use the same testing sheet, for it avoids the necessity of constructing another exercise. If you are concerned about children's memorizing the sequence of answers, cut off the numbers, cut apart the sentences, shuffle them, and have the pupils arrange them in the order in which the words appear at the top. Assign a test consultant (someone who made one hundred on the test) to supervise this activity. There's rarely a cheating problem in this situation.

Several observations relate to the information presented in the testing section. First, you must decide whether to use the word "test" or something more euphemistic, perhaps "game." Our preference is to call a test a test since children who recognize it as such may question our credibility. Furthermore, some people grow up to fear tests. If tests are here to stay -- and they seem to be -- we may as well try to create conditions under which children perceive tests positively. "A test is a way of finding out if you have learned the things I taught..." (later) "Yes, you have learned. Aren't you proud of yourself?"...(or) "I think you need to study some more, Archie; you haven't learned this yet, have you?"...(or) "What does this score mean, John?...What can you do about it?"

Second, the question often arises, "How many times do you give a re-test?" The answer: "As often as necessary." Children who don't know the basic words are certainly not going to progress in reading. Missing five words today, five tomorrow, and five two days later will produce only one result: illiteracy. A more appropriate question might be asked: "Why isn't Cathy passing the test?" (a) Is she at the wrong reading level? (b) Does she have a physical problem (vision, colds, headaches, asthma, malnutrition, etc.)? (c) Does she have a home problem (parental disinterest, trauma such as divorce, death of a family member, friend, pet)? (d) Is she disinterested, discouraged, or lonely?

While we are not psychologists or guidance counselors, observation, contacts with parents, the child's friends or former teachers, a review of school records, or referral may provide keen insight. In the meantime, all children are expected to try to learn the words. Given the appropriate reading level and direct instruction, there is no educational reason why a child needs to take a test more than twice. Perhaps an illustration will show what can occur.

A boy whom we shall call Billy was not a very good learner. He read well below grade level and had the reputation for being lazy. Although he could do the work assigned, he often declined to do so. The teacher decided Billy would stay after school on each day he didn't do his homework. He then spent that time preparing Billy (and others) for the next day. When Billy made 100 on vocabulary, that was no surprise, for any child, even someone in a bottom group, can do that. When Billy made three 100's in a row, the teacher publicly complimented him. By the fifth or sixth test, people were asking Billy about his score. By the tenth test, the teacher announced that Billy had tied the record for consecutive 100's. Billy made 26 consecutive 100's on vocabulary, a record of which he was very proud. Billy didn't need multiple opportunities to re-take the vocabulary quizzes, for a string of perfect scores became his incentive. Unfortunately a series of bad

380

grades can kill incentive. Therefore, one allows pupils to take quizzes over for a psychological reason. Furthermore, we should avoid evaluating a pupil's performance on a day-to-day basis until the youngster achieves the specific objectives. Of what value is it to note that Cecil is 40% competent today, like the Dow Jones average, up ten points from yesterday? It is far better to wait until Cecil knows the words and then evaluate this progress. Like General Electric, "Progress is our most important product."

A third point for consideration is the minimal satisfactory score for these vocabulary tests. While teachers and/or schools should make the final decisions based on their preferences, some recommendations may be helpful.

Reading Level	Minimum Score
Preprimers	100%
Primer, First Reader	100%
2-1, 2-2	90%
3-1, 3-2	80%
4 and above	70%

The rationale for progressively decreasing the minimum score relates to the frequency of the words. Practically all of the words at the first-grade level are basic. Therefore, children should master them. By the time one reaches the fourth-grade reading level, the words are not as important as the earlier ones, and a smaller percentage of accuracy can be reasonably justified. Remember that the figures identified above are reading levels and not grade levels. Where 100% is the only acceptable score, happy faces can be substituted for 100% in a Group Analysis Chart.

Finally, discuss ways to prevent cheating during the test-taking activity.

A. Put away all vocabulary notebooks.

B. Use your non-writing hand to shield the answers.

C. For tests on which you simply record the missing word, use a cover sheet. "If I can see your answer, so can someone else."

D. A person who deliberately lets someone copy his or her paper is guilty of cheating.

E. Changing an answer after the checking process begins is cheating.

F. Deliberately marking a wrong answer right is cheating.

G. Sit as far away from other test takers as you can (Taking a test at a group table is not recommended.).

Phase 5: Review

After each ten lists of words (regardless of whether the lists are five or ten words long), provide a review. The purpose, of course, is to encourage long-term retention. The following procedures can be used to provide this review at the primer and first reader levels.

1. List the words on one spirit master in ten groups. If there are five words per group, the spirit master will contain fifty words; if ten words per group, a total of one hundred words. There should be a line before each word. The words should be grouped in such a way that the items from each original list are scattered throughout all ten lists. Thus the words are associated with a different set from that provided by the testing exercise. Label each section from A to J and draw a box around it.

2. Tell the children a review test will be provided on the following day. Show them which word lists to study (i.e., 5-1 through 5-10 if level 5 represents the primer or first reader). Be sure they take their vocabulary notebooks home for study. Better still, give each child a copy of the spirit master containing the words. If you take that option, include a place at the bottom for the parent to sign when the child has read the words. Be sure to tell the parents and children that the test is not just reading the words but fitting them into sentences.

3. On the following day, read or say sentences for one section at a time and ask the children to place the number before the appropriate word. Begin each new section of sentences with number one. You might want to take a break, even if only fifty words are used.

382

4. Check the papers using the procedures that seem most appropriate.

5. Multiply the checkmarks by two if there are 50 items or by one if there are 100 words.

6. Record the scores on a specially designated area on the Group Analysis Chart.

Two other procedures can be used. The children can simply be asked to pronounce all of the words on the spirit mastered sheet. As indicated earlier, this is not especially desirable because of the lack of contextual application. Another way of providing review is to show children the words in groups, read a sentence, and ask them to write the word. If this strategy is used, the review activity must definitely be administered in parts, for the amount of copying involved will prove tiring to children.

For pupils at the 2-1 and 2-2 reading levels, a different set of procedures can be used for review purposes. These procedures are described next.

1. Tell the members of the group that they will have a review test on the next day. They can prepare for it by studying the ten most recent lists of words.

2. Provide the review after every 100 words (usually ten lists of ten words each). The 100 words can be on five pages in a multiple-choice format. Chart 7B-4 presents an actual review exercise, (205) based on level 2-1 of HBJ's Bookmark Reading Program (287). Each exercise is labeled A, B, C, D or E, and includes approximately two words from each of the ten lists. Thus, once again, the review words are mixed with words different from those presented in the testing exercises. Note also that contextual application is involved just as in testing procedures.

3. Teach the children how to take the review. Let us use Chart 7B-4 as an example.

A. The pupil should first read the 20 words in the left column.

B. The pupil should read the first sentence (Sentence A) in the second column and decide what word would make sense in the blank.

Lists 1-10, Sheet A

Directions: Please write the correct letter to the left
of the number.

1. Let's   A. One of my _____ came out.

2. him   B. What is the ___ animal you know?

3. elephant   C. I don't _____ what you do.

4. own   D. Be _____ so I can go to sleep.

5. firefighter   E. I did not ride the _____.

6. ball   F. What birds live by the _____?

7. quiet   G. We saw a _____ at the zoo.

8. long   H. A fox is a _____ animal.

9. try   I. It is time to play _____.

10. wild   J. School is out. _____ go.

11. teeth   K. That book is _____.

12. boots   L. I will _____ to come over today.

13. monkey   M. This is my _____ junk.

14. care   N. The tomato made my _____ soft.

15. fiction   O. I pulled the sheet over my ____.

16. peel   P. I put on my __ and went outside.

17. fastest   Q. Did Dad thank the _____?

18. head   R. I gave _____ my funny book.

19. sea   S. That is a very _____ feather.

20. bread   T. Will you ___ this potato for me?

C. The pupil who "knows" the missing word should locate it in the left-hand column, place the letter A before that number, and place a small check mark before Sentence A to indicate that it has been used.

D. The pupil who does not know the missing word should proceed to Sentences B, C, etc., answering, locating, recording letters, and checking off sentences through T.

E. The pupil should then return to the first sentence still unmatched and scan the word list. This strategy should be used to make all matches with which the pupil feels comfortable.

F. Finally the pupil should go through a third time, working with the sentences and words that have not yet been paired. Hopefully, there will be very few of these, for the study that has occurred before should have made the youngsters familiar with the words. Almost all of the words at the 2-1 and 2-2 reading levels will have been in children's listening vocabularies even before instruction. Thus major emphasis should be on recognizing the words. Since the sentences themselves contain only words presented at previous reading levels, there should be no serious problem in this regard.

4. Administer the review exercises one page at a time. Since this will become an independent activity after the first time it is done, you can work with other groups. You may want to select one or two Word Consultants from a group with which you are not working (unless the top group is taking the review -- and it should not need much assistance) to provide help in reading the sentences (but not the words in the left column).

Each child completes Sheet A, places it face down in the appropriate area -- five labeled spirit master or file folder boxes are useful here -- and secures the next sheet. Pupils should not keep the spirit mastered sheets together for several reasons: (a) With five sheets, it's easy to misplace one. (b) It takes a long time for children to complete all five sheets, and cheating can occur during these intervals. If the review is given over a two- or three-day period, assign one or two sheets per day. (c) Any sheets that are "lost" may compromise the integrity of the review.

5. Check the papers with the group. Distribute the papers (one set at a time) and give the children directions for scoring them.

A. If the answer is right, put a check in the left margin.

B. If the answer is wrong, circle the wrong letter and record the correct letter in the extreme left margin.

C. Count the number of checks and place that number underlined at the top of the page on the left. It is not the grade.

D. Repeat steps a-c with each of the other sheets.

E. Add the five numbers to get the grade. Record it in a circle at the top right of Sheet A.

6. Give the children an opportunity to study their errors. They may sit together in pairs for this activity, for once again you may be working with another group. Any child who doesn't understand something after consulting with one or more groupmates should write you a note (on a separate sheet of paper) asking about one or more specific items. The note not only provides a realistic opportunity to use a variety of written language skills, it avoids the stress and strain of isolated problems that consume group time. Questions, whether legitimate or not, can be dealt with later after you have an opportunity to recheck the paper.

7. Collect the papers, spot-check the corrections, double-check the addition, and record the scores in a special column on a Group Analysis Chart. Review exercises cannot be taken over. They represent the longest recall period except for the end-of-book mastery tests.

2. Background

Research with second graders suggests that children who have more knowledge of the subject of a selection have better comprehension of the passage than their peers who have little specific information (358). The following suggestions may prove helpful:

1. Read the selection to identify information children should possess in order to understand the story. The need for background may relate to

a. a different part of the country or world

b. a particular genre (play, fairy tale, poem, etc.)

c. a different period of time (past or future)

d. a particular type of subject matter (science or social studies, for instance)

2. Secure resources that will help provide background. These materials include any of the following:

a. maps and globes. Show where the story occurred.

b. realia (real objects). Display an ant colony. Set up any display before school starts so you don't have to spend instructional time on this activity.

c. pictures from a picture file. Show pictures of an Indian village.

d. films or filmstrips about the ocean or desert

e. guest speaker - veterinarian or engineer

f. field trip to a museum or nature center

3. Ask background questions to the group. If no child possesses the information, provide the knowledge yourself.

Example: Where is the ocean on the map (globe)?...Where do we live?...How far away would that be?...How do you know?...

4. Some stories have settings similar to those in which children live. Other stories have backgrounds that are similar to each other (as in fairy tales). Instead of taking 5 or 10 minutes or more to develop background, proceed to the next step of a Developmental Lesson Plan.

3. Purposes for Reading

The following pages identify recommendations for use at the primer through 2-2 reading level (approximately).

1. At the primer and first reader level, provide one purpose question. At the 2-1 and 2-2 levels, provide one or two purpose questions.

2. Print the purpose question on the chalkboard or the floor or wall chart. If the questions are listed on charts, they can be recorded below the corresponding word lists. An alternate possibility is to use spiral-bound charts 12 to 18 inches high just for purpose questions.

3. Ask a good reader to read the questions aloud while the other children follow along. Then ask the entire group to read the questions in unison and then try to say them without looking at the chart. The questions should be in their minds rather than just on the board.

4. As soon as children are able to write well enough, ask them to write the answer(s) to the purpose question(s) after reading silently. As in Model 1, children will eventually consider the purpose question(s) as part of the post-reading discussion.

5. If more than one purpose question is provided, it may be appropriate to include one at the implied (inferential) level. This practice should stimulate some higher-level thinking.

Whenever purpose-setting questions are being developed (or secured from a manual), it is helpful to remember a study (45) of two well-known basal series that found (a) some purposes were too narrow, (b) some purposes proved misleading, and (c) some purposes revealed too much of the story content.

Perhaps one other point ought to be considered here. The end result of reading instruction in terms of purpose-setting should be independent readers who can establish their own worthwhile purpose questions. That is what we do: We read to find out (a) what policy a leader has enunciated, (b) how to prepare a new dish, (c) how to complete a particular legal form, (d) what problem has overwhelmed Charlie Brown or (e) what additives are contained in a particular brand of food. We have a purpose; thus we read for meaning, and we read with comprehension. As Stauffer (680) observes, "Possession of the ability to declare purposes makes the difference between an able reader -- alert, flexible, and curious -- and an intellectual bungler." From an instructional point of view, there are three stages of development of purpose-setting questions.

Stage 1: The teacher establishes one or more purposes for reading, thus serving as a model for the subsequent development of pupil competence in this area.

388

Stage 2: The teacher and the children jointly establish purposes for reading. The children can thus assume more responsibility as they are able, under teacher guidance, to develop important purpose questions. At this stage the teacher asks children to offer a purpose question. If they do well, she asks for a second one. If it also is appropriate, she may stop. If it is inappropriate, she may add a third purpose. At some point it may be helpful to discuss the quality of the purpose-setting questions.

Stage 3: The children establish their own purposes for reading. This is the most mature behavior; it requires careful nurturing by a succession of teachers who recognize the importance of developing this skill.

4. Silent Reading

Beginning at the primer level, teachers should try to leave the group while it does silent reading and check on the progress of the other children. This "weaning away" process is possible for several reasons. First, children at the primer level and above should read several pages (sometimes a full story, at other times part of a selection) rather than just a page or two at a time. Thus there is time for the teacher to move elsewhere. Second, these children are familiar with the procedures and thus are able to function more efficiently and effectively than they could several months earlier. Third, they know much more vocabulary (usually around 100 words from the preprimers). Fourth, some of the children read well enough to qualify as word consultants when their groupmates need assistance. Indeed, a Babson Park (Florida) second grader showed her concern when a visitor helped a child in her group by announcing, "You're not supposed to help. I'm the word insultant."

When a child does not know a word, the Word Consultant should use a five-step procedure, the first four steps being identical to those discussed earlier.

Step 1: The asker points to the word.

Step 2: The asker looks at the word and asks for help.

Step 3: The Word Consultant says the word.

Step 4: The asker repeats the word.

Step 5: The asker reads the sentence to the Word Consultant, says "thank you," and returns to his seat.

While children read the selections to themselves (once or twice), the teacher can (a) convene another group or (b) check on the progress of individual children. Because the separation bothers some children, it may be accomplished in steps.

1. Stand rather than sit while the group reads.

2. Stand nearby but look at the group.

3. Stand farther away but look at the group.

4. Stand nearby but don't look at the group.

5. Stand farther away and don't look at the group.

6. Stand but work with another group.

At various points is is helpful to compliment the children on how well they were able to work independently. They should also be complimented for engaging in post-reading independent activities. These include educationally defensible followup activities, recreational reading, or enrichment activities. Two samples follow:

1. After reading a story about animals, children may look at some animal books and make a list of five animals each that are air, land, and water creatures.

2. After reading a story about a visit to a farm, children list the letters of the alphabet from A to Z and write a farm word beginning with each letter. They may use resource books from the library.

In each activity children should be encouraged to print neatly (relate to handwriting) and read each other's lists (thereby learning some new words as each person plays teacher with his or her words).
Independent activities should not be viewed as busy-work activities. Too many children spend too much time coloring objects they don't recognize, copying board material they can't read, completing workbook exercises they don't understand, playing games with little or no value, or doing assignments they long ago mastered. Busy-work assignments are neither pedagogically nor psychologically sound.

5. Evaluation, Discussion, and Oral Reading

At the primer and first reader levels these procedures are identical to those used at the preprimer levels. See Chapter 7A.

At the 2-1 level and above, the procedures for evaluation, discussion, and oral reading include several considerable variations. The first major difference is that written comprehension questions follow the full-length selection. These questions are important for a variety of reasons. First, they provide the best opportunity for every child to become mentally involved in a selection. While it is easy for pupils to hide their problems in an oral discussion, the EPR nature of a written quiz assures that a teacher will become aware of the specific nature of any child's comprehension problem. Second, "Tests are probably the most effective form of motivation available to the teacher. Research evidence is quite consistent: Students in classrooms where there are frequent achievement tests on course content learn more and learn better than students who are not frequently tested (509:4)." Third, the presence of comprehension scores encourages teachers to provide either easier or more difficult materials as needed. Fourth, the availability of comprehension scores assures that this component of reading will not be overlooked or deemphasized. Fifth, the information can be shared with parents to justify grades, explain the need for assigning more appropriate materials, or encourage pupil placement in a special program. Specific strategies for evaluation, discussion, and oral reading are presented on the following pages.

1. Develop or secure written questions for the full-length selections. Use a combination of literal, implied, vocabulary, and creative items. We prefer a 3-3-3-1 pattern after Marksheffel (487) for several reasons. First, it gives equal weight to literal, implied, and vocabulary questions. Second, since almost any answer is acceptable for a creative question, the one "free" item does not distort the results of the comprehension exercise. Third, if 70% is considered passing, a complete deficiency in one aspect will not result in a failing score. Fourth, the pattern matches the IRI format we prefer. Betts (55) recommends that children's understanding be checked in IRI testing situations, and Cunningham notes, "For example, if literal, implied, critical (creative), and vocabulary questions are included in an IRI, they should be included

391

on comprehension quizzes following the silent reading of stories (218:52)."

Research dating back half a century makes it clear that the ability to answer literal questions does not assure the ability to make inferences (46, 248, 722). Unfortunately, a fifty-year summary of research by Gall (331) found that about 75% of teachers' questions were literal. The problem is more clearly understoood when we read Smith's observation, "Teachers ask questions at the same level as those found in the instructional materials prepared for their use in reading (646:97)."

Constructing quality questions is not easy to do. Guidelines for doing so have already been discussed. They have been used in the development of comprehension exercises based on a number of reading series (209-213). A sample exercise based on the Houghton Mifflin Reading Series (277) is shown in Chart 7B-5 (211). These materials should be duplicated for use throughout an entire school.

CHART 7B-5
SPINNERS
"The Duck in the Gun"
Pages 157-169

Directions: Please answer the following questions.

1. Why was the duck in the gun?

2. How did the soldiers make money while the war was called off?

3. What did the general do when the war was called off for good?

4. How were the general and his men alike?

5. The general "coughed and looked at the floor" when he asked the Prime Minister for a gun. Why?

6. How was the Prime Minister very clever?

7. What is a white flag?

8. Use waddling in a sentence.

9. What does shabby mean?

10. What do you think caused the war in the first place?

2. Ask pupils to secure either a comprehension booklet (containing exercises for an entire level) or copy of an individual exercise from a designated place (top of a bookcase, a table, a chair, etc.). The sequence of pupil activities is (a) read the selection one or more times, (b) put the book away, (c) secure the materials, and (d) complete the assignment.

A number of specific procedures for completing the exercises are listed below (155).

A. Read each sentence twice.

B. If you don't know a word or don't understand the question, ask a Word Consultant.

C. Skip questions you're not sure about and answer those you know first. Then go back and answer all of the other questions.

D. Write each answer in a complete sentence.

E. Answer each question based on the story and not just on your general knowledge. For example, if the story tells what tricks a bear can do and there is a question about that, list the tricks the books says a bear can do and not the ones you may have seen one do.

F. When answering implied questions (numbers 4-6 in the model recommended here), write the answer and then tell what information "gives away" the answer.

G. If a question asks for several answers, write as many as you can.

H. Use the vocabulary word the same way it is used in the reading selection. For example, if the story tells about the West Coast, don't write a sentence that tells how to coast down a hill.

I. Note the question word. For instance, if it is why, your answer should have because in the mid- dle of it (i.e., Tom kicked the cat because he was angry.).

Where usually means you must give a place.
When usually means you must give a time.
Who usually means you must give a person.
How many or how much usually means you must give either a number or words like many, few, a lot, or most.

393

J. Check to see if a question has two or more parts. Be sure to answer all parts.

K. Answer all questions, especially numbers 4-6 (implied) and 10 (creative). Many times you really know the answer but aren't sure (for implieds). Almost any reasonable answer will be accepted for a creative response.

L. Proofread your paper to be sure you don't make a careless error (e.g., leave out an important word, substitute one word for another -- <u>before</u> or <u>after</u> -- or omit or insert <u>not</u>).

3. Identify specific independent activities for children to pursue when they complete the comprehension exercise. These may be long-term (read a trade book, listen to a taped story, use the SRA Multi-Level kits, etc.) or short-term (study or take spelling words, rework missed problems, write something, etc.) The intents, of course, are to help children avoid the tendency to waste time and to provide productive learning experiences.

4. On returning to the group, lead a discussion of the story. This discussion should be thorough and sequential. Include two broad categories of questions. The first questions are the Stage Questions. They include items of the types listed below.

a. Who are the characters (people or animals)?

b. Who are the main characters?

c. Where did the story take place?

d. When did the story take place?

e. What kind of story is it?

The Stage Questions are intended to do just what the name suggests -- set the stage for the story.
The bulk of the questions are the Story Questions. These questions are intended to provide a deeper understanding of the passage, its general content, implied meanings, more subtle nuances, and picture interpretation. Brown, <u>et al</u>. (84) found that young readers rarely drew inferences except during probing discussions. This finding is perhaps the best justification for a thorough discussion of a story.

For all implied questions ask pupils to answer the additional question, "How do you know?" In this case as well as when pupils seem unsure of themselves, ask the members to locate the sentence(s) or paragraph(s) providing specific answers or important clues. If necessary provide the page number. Note that children will be using oral reading to prove a point.

As appropriate, include questions which focus on main ideas, major supporting details, classifying, sequencing, compare-contrast, cause-effect, and predicting outcomes. Picture, listening, and reading activities for building pupil competence in these areas as well as making inferences are discussed in Chapter 11. Be sure to include a discussion of the purpose-setting questions. Remind the children that certain ones were designated as purpose questions.

Use EPR and wait-time (as needed) for all questions. Either allow all children to chorus an answer (as in the case of a literal question) or call on several individuals to provide vocabulary, implied, and creative answers. At the upper grade levels you may want to have pupils respond individually rather than collectively.

5. After the discussion, help children check their papers. The general guidelines provided for vocabulary tests on pages 377-378 are appropriate here. Several additional comments may prove helpful.

A. It should not take long for children to check the papers, for all of the quiz questions should have been included in the discussion.

B. Children should record a check for a correct answer, draw a line through the words for an incorrect answer, and place a question mark for an answer about which they are not certain (i.e., they can't read the words or the response has borderline accuracy). A question with two parts may have a "+5" recorded in the margin. For three parts, use "+3," "+7," or a check mark.

C. The children should count each mark as ten points and add the score, recording it at the top of the paper (Pupils who check others' papers should also record "checked by ____."). No score is recorded for a paper with a question mark in the left-hand column.

D. Spot-check the papers, record the correct score on a Group Analysis Chart, and return the papers to the group.

E. Each child takes another sheet of paper (or writes on the bottom or back of the exercise) and corrects the wrong answers. This aspect has two parts: (1) list the right answer and (2) identify the page(s) and paragraph(s) or picture which specifies the appropriate response or provides relevant clues.

F. Correct reworked papers and record on the Group Analysis Chart a final score (which should always be 100). Thus a pupil's score for a comprehension exercise may be 70/100 (70 original and 100 final) or 85/100 or 100 if a perfect score was earned the first time.

G. After three or more comprehension exercises, a child whose average (before rework) falls below 70% is considered for lower placement. Conversely, a child with an average of 90% or above is considered for higher placement or enrichment activities.

H. The children record their own scores in a notebook or, more diagnostically, on a chart that identifies pupil performance on each type of question. Chart 7B-6 provides a simple, yet graphic, means of showing pupil progress. Youngsters place a dot in the center of each block to indicate the number of correct responses for each category of question (literal, implied, vocabulary, creative). After each story they can use straight lines to connect the dots. An alternate procedure is to color the columns as if they were bar graphs. Thus all four blocks would be colored if a pupil answered the three literal questions correctly.

Later use the children's answer sheets as the basis for English lessons. Remember also that the written exercises provide valuable information about children's specific comprehension needs. For example, provide specific group instruction for children who have difficulty with implied meanings. Children from different groups may come together for this instruction so long as the practice material is within their reading ability.

A variety of oral reading procedures has already been presented. There are, however, several other possibilities.

1. <u>Oral reading for entertaining others</u>. Some reading selections lend themselves to oral reading before an audience. Plays are especially appropriate for this purpose. The following suggestions can enhance the quality of the presentation.

CHART 7B-6
PUPIL PROGRESS - COMPREHENSION

Story Number

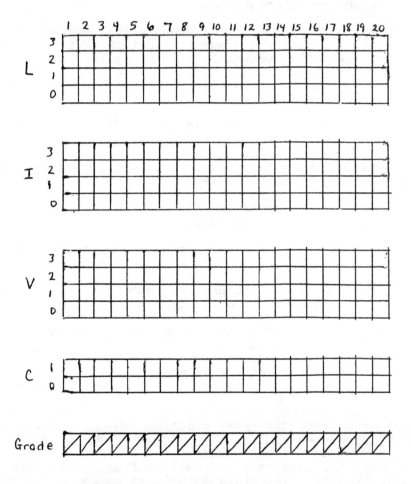

A. Select an oral reading selection with enough characters so that each person in the group can have a role. Remember to include a narrator.

B. Appoint an assistant director to help you manage the first presentation and to direct the next presentation and train another assistant.

C. Let each person in the group sign up for a reading with a limit of three persons to try for each part. For example, the first person chooses one part, the second person chooses a part, etc., until all members of the group have chosen once.

D. Hold try-outs for the parts with three applicants. Either the group or the teacher can choose the person who will eventually read the part.

E. Allow those who haven't received parts to make a second choice. Hold more try-outs.

F. Be sure pupils can read their parts fluently (or can learn to do so).

G. Have pupils mark in pencil a dot beside each place they should begin to read.

H. Schedule teaching sessions as the developmental reading instruction for the day.

I. Schedule the practices as an independent activity rather than the reading instruction.

J. Provide sufficient help so that pupils can handle the names of people and places without stumbling.

K. Provide enough practice so that pupils need not keep their eyes glued to the text.

L. Have groups of pupils meet to work on selected parts, saving the beginning-to-end practice until later.

M. Tape record the sessions and ask pupils to analyze the tapes of their practice and performance to suggest improvements.

N. Provide audience situations from other class-rooms. In-class presentations help in correcting tech-nical problems, but they are optional since members of other groups are already familiar with the selection.

2. <u>Choral reading</u>. Poetry and prose can be used for choral reading. The following recommendations may help.

A. Select a poem with a rhythm that is easy to produce and a message that is appealing. Examples: "The Three Billy Goat Gruff," "There Was An Old Lady Who Swallowed a Fly."

B. Group pupils for the parts. Examples: Boys may represent the low voices and girls the high. Pairs or triplets may be assigned certain parts. Assign the slowest children the refrain ("And the goblins will get you if you don't watch out.") or the most well-known part ("Listen my children and you shall hear...").

C. Try to include at least one good reader in each sub-group.

D. Have each group practice separately before you put it all together.

E. Be sure pupils can pronounce the words, know what they mean, and can interpret the poem or story. We have heard too many examples like "while angels washed their flocks by night."

F. If necessary, distribute copies of the reading with slanted lines to show where children should pause in their breathing. Later help children decide where to mark the pauses.

6. Extended and Related Activities

The final step of a mastery-based DLP involves extended and related activities. The major activities are of two types: (a) followup reading and (b) skills instruction and practice. Comments about each of these aspects are listed below.

<u>Followup Reading</u>

Provide pupils with opportunities that take advantage of their instructional reading interests or that provide abundant practice in reading. Consider the following possibilities:

1. Provide the Skinny Books mentioned in Chapter 7A. The procedures for constructing and using them are outlined in Chapter 8.

2. Provide full-length books from which individual chapters or sections were abstracted in the basal series. For example, if an excerpt from Charlotte's Web (White) appears in the pupil text, secure the full-length book from the media center and have it readily available to check out to a pupil who says, "Gee, I really liked that story." This procedure is better than sending the child to the media center to get the book, for it may not be a part of the collection or it may be checked out. In either case the delay or disappointment may discourage future attempts to locate material.

If a school media center has a policy of securing books with excerpts in basal materials, the director can develop a list, by reading level, of the trade books and their titles.

3. Provide other books by the same author as the basal reading selection. A child who likes an excerpt from Little House on the Prairie (Wilder) may wish to read any one of a dozen books by that author. These books should also be secured and listed by the media director.

4. Provide other books on the same topic. If a child likes an excerpt from Misty of Chincoteague (Henry), secure other horse stories, being careful that they are no more difficult than Misty and, hopefully, somewhat easier. Topical lists classified by general reading level are a boon for the child who has clearly-defined interests and for the reluctant reader.

5. Encourage children to write stories or poems of their own. House these peer-produced books in classroom libraries and the school media center and publicize their availability. This activity relates reading and language arts and also requires an illustrator.

6. Encourage children to read stories to other children, either in the class or in another grade. Some good readers could provide valuable assistance in before- or after-school "story-time" and could read to small groups of youngsters whose parents are attending PTA.

7. Recognize children who read. Give ribbons, patches, badges, buttons, etc. for reading. Each recognition may be related to a certain number of books or even a specified number of papers read. Give T-shirts (secure second and third quality items from manufacturers) saying, "I have read 100 books." The senior author was the first person to develop and

implement this strategy. Give light-weight jackets with the school name (Yoder School, Mebane, North Carolina). Secure financial assistance from business leaders who might see the public relations values.

Make arrangements for pupils who read to receive free hamburgers and soft drinks from fast-food services. Publicize the arrangements in the local newspaper. Take pictures of children who read a great deal (especially those who are changing their reading habits) and submit them along with an article to the local newspaper. A lengthy discussion of reading incentives is beyond the scope of this publication.

Skills Introduction and Practice

With the exception of the specific skills needed to develop vocabulary (context plus letter-sound association), establish purposes (a study skill), and foster comprehension of the selection, the entire aspect of skill development occurs as part of Step 6 of a DLP.

A skill development program should focus on the skills that follow a particular story and those needed by the children to cope with the next selection. The pertinent skills comprise six categories as outlined below.

1. Reading Readiness (including pre-reading skills, those aspects that occur before reading but do not necessarily contribute to it) -- at upper levels extended to include all language skills. The fourteen reading readiness skills were discussed in Chapters 4A and 4B.

2. Word Analysis and Recognition

    A. Context (for pronunciation)
    B. Letter-Sound Associations
    C. Structure
        (1) affixes and base words
        (2) root words
        (3) syllabication
        (4) primary and secondary accents
    D. Dictionary Usage
    E. Sight Words

3. Vocabulary Skills -- examples such as
    A. Context (for word meaning)
    B. Synonyms, antonyms, homonyms
    C. Multiple meaning words
    D. Affixes and root words (for meaning)
    E. Figurative expressions

4. Comprehension Skills -- literal, implied, and creative or critical levels -- components such as
   A. Main ideas
   B. Major supporting details
   C. Classification
   D. Sequence
   E. Compare-contrast
   F. Cause-effect
   G. Predicting outcomes

5. Study Skills -- examples such as
   A. Locational Skills
      (1) parts of books
      (2) reference sources
      (3) card catalog
   B. Organizational Skills
      (1) note taking
      (2) summarizing
      (3) outlining
      (4) reporting
   C. Evaluative Skills
      (1) author's competence
      (2) author's purpose
      (3) propaganda techniques
      (4) accuracy and completeness of information
      (5) relevance of information

6. Literary Skills -- examples such as
   A. Theme and plot
   B. Mood
   C. Setting
   D. Characterization
   E. Genre

Summary

This chapter has considered strategies for teaching Developmental Lesson Plans at the primer through 2-2 level. Once again, emphasis was placed on pupil accountability. It should be noted that a strong comprehension strand permeates the lesson, for each of the steps of a DLP emphasizes comprehension:

1. Vocabulary development enhances comprehension.

2. Background knowledge enhances comprehension.

3. Purpose questions enhance comprehension.

4. Silent reading focuses on comprehension.

5. Evaluation and discussion focus on comprehension. They are most valuable if they are structured rather than random (428).

6. Extended and related activities often focus on comprehension.

FOR FURTHER READING

Duffelmeyer, Frederick A., "Introducing Words in Context," Wisconsin State Reading Journal, XXVI, No. 3 (Spring, 1982), 4-6.

Ekwall, Eldon E., Locating and Correcting Reading Difficulties, Fourth Edition. Columbus, Ohio: Merrill, 1985.

Johnson, Kenneth R., "Black Dialect Shift in Oral Reading," Journal of Reading, XVIII, No. 7 (April, 1975), 535-540.

Lewis, Marston B., and Yvonne B. Morrow, "Parent Involvement - It Works," Florida Reading Quarterly, XXI, No. 4 (June, 1985), 18-20.

Sartain, Harry W., "Administrative Responsibilities for In-Service Training in Combining Sequential and Individualized Reading," in Sequential Development of Reading Abilities, pp. 187-190, ed. Helen M. Robinson. Chicago: University of Chicago Press, 1960.

USING BASAL READERS

3-1 LEVEL AND ABOVE

Introduction

Chapter 7B described Model 2 for vocabulary development, a series of procedures generally intended for use at the primer through the 2-2 reading level. You will remember that Model 2 is appropriate when pupils normally recognize the new words in their listening but not their reading vocabularies. This chapter considers Model 3, which is appropriate when many of the new words in basal materials are unknown in children's oral language. Remember that many comments which appeared in Chapters 7A and 7B are also appropriate here.

1. Vocabulary

As one proceeds through a reading series, the levels increasingly use words whose oral forms are unknown. This change from orally known to orally unknown words tends to be gradual although not necessarily smooth. Thus a 3-2 level will tend to have more words outside a child's oral language than will a 3-1 level. Within a book, particularly at the upper primary levels, the first one-half of the stories will tend to have fewer such words than will the second one-half of the selections. However, there will be variations by story even at the primary reading levels and sometimes dramatically so at the intermediate reading levels and above. For example, the number of new words in the stories in one fifth-grade book ranges from fewer than ten to eighty! Many other basal series at the same levels have the same wide disparity within levels.

Teachers often observe that one level of a series appears to be more difficult than the preceding level or, more frequently, that a huge gap seems to exist between two consecutive levels with the second title being extremely difficult as compared to the immediately-lower level. The absence of a gradual progression in difficulty contributes to reading difficulty in terms of vocabulary and conceptual load -- the lack of children's experience in terms of specific selections. The problem is complicated by the fact that by the 3-1 reading level

404

some manuals no longer list all of the new vocabulary words. Although some words are listed, large numbers of items presented in the selections are not. The rationale for listing only a part of the new words often includes the following statements:

1. Children should use their phonic and structural skills to decode the words with previously-presented grapheme-phoneme correspondences. The problem: their knowledge of skills tends to be at a lower level than their general reading ability. Note how many youngsters in a 3-2 book, for example, lack skills presented at lower levels and assumed to be mastered by the 3-2 level. Note the workbook and duplicating master exercises about which teachers can often say, "There's no way they'll ever be able to do this. They don't know the prerequisites."
We cannot assume that children possess phonic and structural analysis skills simply because they have been presented in manuals at lower reading levels. Even if these skills were in fact taught -- and a teacher who is considering skipping certain skills should remember that previous teachers may have done the same thing -- we have no assurance that the skills were mastered and retained. Words listed as decodable, assumed, word family, etc., may be known to the children. On the other hand, they may not be. In any given group some children will know these items while others won't. We should not assume the words are known.

2. Children should use their contextual skills to figure out the meanings (and at lower reading levels, especially, the pronunciations) of new words. However, research indicates many children in elementary grades are not particularly effective in using context skills. McKee (507) found that children could use context clues effectively in only one-third of the situations. Bradbury's study (reported by Burns - 100) produced the same figure for fourth graders. Furthermore, a number of studies at Boston University indicate that "children in the intermediate grades vary greatly in their ability to identify words and to derive meanings from context (100:82)." Tinker and McCullough observe, "A surprising number of children make little or no use of context in trying to discover the meanings of strange words (710:140)." Strang, et al. (693) found that even high school and college students had only a "vague notion" of how to use the various types of context clues with unfamiliar words.

Ineffective use of context is especially true of poor readers (26, 355). The problem may be caused in part by a reading series that stresses reading as word pronunciation) particularly in the primary grades), or it may result from the failure of teachers to provide children with systematic instruction and practice using a wide variety of types of context clues (672). Depending on whose classification is used, there are from seven to thirteen different types, and the categories are not identical from author to author. Furthermore, competence in one type of context clue does not assure proficiency in other types. In any event, the use of context has been a standard recommendation in the literature (72, 146, 221, 306, 392, 507, 670). Research conducted by Gipe (346) with over 200 third and fifth graders found that of four methods of vocabulary development, context was the most effective and dictionary use was least helpful.

3. Children don't need to know the meaning of every new word in the story. While this may be true, the statement ignores several important points. (a) Our failure to present the new words denies youngsters of increased opportunities for learning to use a variety of types of context clues. (b) The abundance of new vocabulary in some stories complicates the learning process for a child. Imagine how confused you are when reading something with many new words (i.e., a car manual, an insurance policy, government regulations, crocheting directions, or "simple" legal documents). Do you need to understand the vocabulary in these materials? Do children need to know the vocabulary in their reading? Is their failure to do so one of the problems in the content areas?

One objective of a basal series (reading or otherwise) ought to be to help youngsters become conversant with the vocabulary. Leaving them "on their own" is not necessarily the best way, for the research once again suggests that direct instructional procedures for developing vocabulary are more effective than simply letting youngsters "read-read-read" (567) or rely on incidental teaching (78, 227). The New York City Board of Education (537) reports that poor readers do profit from instruction in context clues. We have noted in a research study (187) of the use of a contextual approach to vocabulary development that the median gain in vocabulary for an entire school increased from two months during the baseline year to at least 1.0 year annually for the next three years. Approximately 40% of the children were minorities, and all youngsters were tested.

406

In his summary of research, Spache notes that growth in context usage "does not improve spontaneously with age or maturity (670: 382)." It must be taught. More recently, he notes that the use of context clues is not very well taught (672).

Context does not always provide a clear meaning -- not just a general idea -- of the term. What do we often do when encountering a large number of words we do not know? Although a few people read with a dictionary at their side, the majority of adults do not consult a dictionary very frequently. Needless to say, neither do children. What do they -- and we -- do when encountering an unknown word? Use as much context as possible and, if that's not enough, skip it. The question then arises, "Is this the response we want our youngsters to make in an instructional or recreational setting?" Surely not.

We contend that teachers should present all new vocabulary words except proper nouns in context prior to the silent reading. Children will thus benefit in four ways: (a) They will learn more words. (b) They will have additional guided practice and discussion of a variety of context skills. (c) They can avoid the habit -- at least instructionally -- of skipping words they don't know. (d) They will have a much better chance of comprehending the reading passage. After all, vocabulary has been identified as one of two major factors enhancing comprehension (231). Indeed, vocabulary knowledge and general reading comprehension are highly correlated (16). We have seen only one child who was poor in vocabulary and excellent in comprehension. Understanding words is one base for understanding passages. The greater our vocabularies, the better are our chances for being good comprehenders.

The comment is sometimes made that children whose teachers present the vocabulary prior to the lesson deny the youngsters an opportunity to learn the words on their own. The proper place for learning "on one's own" is independent-level reading (that is, library reading). Youngsters will surely have abundant opportunities to encounter new vocabulary terms during their recreational or home-reading assignments. The more competence we can provide youngsters instructionally, the better they will function independently.

If we agree that the new vocabulary should be taught, we can then provide strategies for assuring that youngsters acquire both the skills of context and the word knowledge itself. Once again, remember that Model 3 is appropriate when the words tend not to be in children's oral vocabularies. These words include three types: (a) words outside a child's listening and reading

407

vocabularies (i.e., brisk, defy), (b) words in a child's listening but not reading vocabulary (i.e., ricochet, pharoah, ocean), or (c) words in a child's reading (decoding) but not listening vocabulary (i.e., vat, wick, vane). Model 3 is also appropriate when known words with unknown meanings are presented (i.e., wake of a boat, sober meaning "serious," pipe a tune).

Print the words in two columns on the chalkboard, wall or floor chart, or transparency (see Chart 7C-1). Be sure to include the number of the list and the level unless grade levels are recorded on the book (Examples: G-2 is Book G, list 2; 9-4 is Level 9, list 4, but not 3-1, List 2 because that material might be used by fifth graders). Printing is usually preferred because many teachers print more neatly than they write, and the youngsters are less likely to copy printed information incorrectly. Also, particularly for bottom groups in grades three and four, the transition from manuscript to cursive is not mastered. Vocabulary introduction is not the way to correlate handwriting and reading.

See that each child has a vocabulary notebook. Schoolmade ones should use 8-1/2 X 11 inch lined paper with 20-30 sheets covered with construction paper and stapled at the left side or top. A steno pad is not wide enough and should not be used. Children should label the notebooks "Vocabulary" and record their names on the outside to facilitate the return of "lost, strayed, or stolen" booklets.

CHART 7C-1
VOCABULARY INTRODUCTION
Grade 4

1. brisk	6. simulated
2. defy	7. sketched
3. valve	8. debut
4. tether	9. vast
5. punctured	10. blob

Ask children to draw a vertical line on each page dividing it into a one-third section on the left and a two-thirds section on the right. Each morning when the children see a list of vocabulary words designated for their group, they should either print or write the words in the left column, numbering and skipping a line between each. An expression of three or four words (i.e., foot of the tree, shift for yourself) may be recorded on two lines. No print should cross the vertical dividing line. Having copied the words or phrases, the pupils are ready for the five-phase vocabulary development procedure. Chart 7C-2 provides ten sentences to be used in the teaching exercise.

CHART 7C-2
TEACHING EXERCISE
Grade 4

1. Hurry up and close that door before all of my papers blow off the desk. It is really <u>brisk</u> today.

2. You can't make me shut up. I <u>defy</u> you to try.

3. Turn off the cold water <u>valve</u>.

4. Most cowboys <u>tether</u> their horses to the hitching post.

5. A nail <u>punctured</u> the front tire of my bicycle.

6. Our class <u>simulated</u> the debates between the two candidates for president.

7. The artist quickly <u>sketched</u> the outline of the desert scene.

8. The actress made her stage <u>debut</u> at age five.

9. A <u>vast</u> ocean separates North America and Europe.

10. I dropped a <u>blob</u> of grease on my coat.

Remember that the italicized words are the new items. Some of the new words are phonically regular, others are not; some are in children's oral languages but not their written language; some are not in any of the children's vocabularies.

Phase 1: Direct Instruction

1. Tell the pupils you will read or say a sentence with a <u>Hmm</u> standing for an omitted word or phrase. When you point to that phrase, they should write the definition in the right-hand area beside number one. They should then raise their thumbs stomach-high to let you know they have finished. Provide sentence one. Example for <u>brisk</u>: "Hurry up and close that door before all of my papers

blow off the desk. It is really <u>hmm</u> today."

2. After pupils record their definitions and raise their thumbs stomach-high, say, "I'm going to repeat the sentence. This time I want you to say the word together when I get to the blank. Look at the word and not at me." Then repeat the sentence, allowing the group to chorus the word.

Some words will be fairly simple to pronounce because of the regularity of their letter-sound associations. Thus <u>brisk</u> is phonically predictable, and some children will automatically be able to decode it. Other words will be more difficult to pronounce as you will see in Step 5.

Two further observations: First, some teachers prefer to have an individual rather than the group pronounce each word. Our preference for the group chorus mode is the opportunity it provides for EPR (278), a technique that encourages more active mental participation by each pupil. Second, notice that you should not pronounce the words for the children. This gives them an opportunity to try to figure out the words, a practice that parallels the reading act. Even when we assume that youngsters will be unable to figure out the words, it helps to know how they try to pronounce the items. For example, do they misrepresent the <u>au</u> in <u>faucet</u>, making it a long <u>a</u>? If so, we know something to teach at a later point. Do they say <u>kuh-nife</u> for <u>knife</u>? If so, we know something to teach. Telling the children the words ahead of time precludes a wealth of diagnostically-important data.

3. Now ask the group to provide definitions. The thumbs-up procedure is not necessary here, for youngsters have already had an opportunity to think. Once again they can chorus their response. The most common answers are <u>windy</u>, <u>breezy</u>, and <u>cold</u>. Since the latter definition is incorrect, you may want to repeat the sentence and ask the individual the following questions:

    a. "What's happening in the sentence?" (The papers are about to blow off my desk.)

    b. "Why is it happening?" (The door is open.) With this response ask, "Why else?" (It's windy.)

    c. "Good. What does <u>brisk</u> mean?" (Windy.)

An alternate response:_____

a. "Does <u>cold</u> make the papers blow off the desk?" (No.)

b. "What does?" (The wind.)

c. "Right."

In each case the focus is on clarifying the meaning of the sentence through the relationship of the words. This is more instructive than simply saying, "Yes, <u>windy</u> is right."

Ask each pupil to change an incorrect or incomplete definition. Thus the child who said <u>cold</u> should strike through the original definition and record the revised one (Erasing is time consuming for some pupils.).

Incidentally, some pupils prefer to draw pictures of some concrete words in lieu of written definitions. For example, they may draw a picture of a sword, hatchet, or hammock. Part of the reason seems to be time-related (It's faster to draw a picture.), part relates to difficulty in writing (Sometimes it's hard to find words one can spell to define the word.), and part is motivation (Drawing definitions is more fun than writing them.). Boys seem to use the drawing mode far more frequently than do girls.

4. When the word is outside the oral language of the children, provide opportunities for using it in oral sentences. You may need to provide one or more sentences to prime the pump: "In brisk weather a lot of leaves blow off the trees...One brisk day the man's hat went flying down the street." Then encourage some youngsters to provide examples. It is not essential that every child contribute a sentence. The important thing is that the group begin to become familiar with the spoken term.

You may want to ask what happens when the weather is brisk or in what seasons the weather is brisk. Children typically reply in a phrase that doesn't include the word. Ask them to use the word in a complete sentence. "I wear my coat when it's brisk outside...It's brisk in the springtime." You may need to provide a word or two to help to get the child started. Example: "It (pause) is (pause) brisk (pause) when?"

5. Using the procedure described in steps 2-4, present the second sentence. Example for <u>defy</u>: "You can't make me shut up. I <u>Hmm</u> you to try." If someone happens to know the pronunciation, that's fine. It is of little use

411

to spend several minutes with pupils shouting out a variety of mispronunciations, in effect sharing their ignorance. Later you may want to teach a lesson in which words are accented on the second syllable with the y representing the long i sound (defy, deny, reply, comply, rely, supply, etc.). There is no reason to "mention" (269) that generalization at this time. Save if for later.

If nobody knows the pronunciation, provide it yourself. The children are not prepared to use discovery learning in this instance. Now proceed to the definition and sentence development as before. When you present words whose meanings are known to the group as soon as pronunciation is determined (i.e., ocean, chorus), simply skip the oral sentences, for they serve no useful function.

When you use a word with a variety of meanings which children either know or should know, restrict the discussion to (a) the meaning as used in the sentence, (b) an observation that words have meaning only in context (in the sentences in which they appear), and (c) a statement that the group will consider other meanings later. Once again, this is not the time to "mention" topics that deserve a fuller treatment.

6. Depending on the needs of the group, review the pronunciations after three to five words. Use any of three modes: (a) whole group, (b) pairs, each saying the words to the other, or (c) individual. Bottom groups tend to profit from all three, top groups from any of the three.

7. After presenting all ten words, make two assignments. First, ask each child to write a sentence with each word or phrase underlined and be prepared to turn it in on the morning of the following day. Like all written work, the paper should be labeled properly. The major points of emphasis should be on correct use of the vocabulary term, simple spelling (concern for the spelling of the basic words but not sophisticated ones), capitalization, punctuation, neatness, variety (not "I saw a mongoose...I saw a picket fence...I saw a escalator."), and completeness (not "It was brisk...I am morose."). This strategy is an excellent way to interrelate the language arts. Ask the children to write their sentences in such a way that there will be a space between each one to rewrite each sentence if necessary. One way to explain this is to tell children to leave four empty lines between each sentence.

412

The second assignment is two-fold. Ask each pupil to study the pronunciations and meanings both in class and at home in preparation for the test on the following day. After the first few sessions, the in-class study will become an independent activity.

8. Teach the group a four-part procedure for studying the words. Each part is described below.

A. Cover the definitions column with a folded sheet of paper (so you can't see through it). Look at the first word or phrase. Say what it means (Undependable and very slow children should move their lips when they do this. Other children can just think the definition.). Slide the cover sheet down two spaces to check your response. If you were correct, look at the second word or phrase. Define it and slide the cover sheet down. When you miss a word, that's okay. After all, you're not supposed to know them yet. Just study the definition and slide the cover paper back to number one. Start again. Each time you miss, study and return to the top. Continue until you can provide all ten definitions without error. This technique is study step one.

B. Use the same procedure but begin with number ten and work up.

C. Now cover the words column. Begin with the first definition. Say or think the word. Slide the cover down. Continue as described in part A.

D. Finally use the same procedure described in part A but begin with number ten and work up to number one. This is study step four and concludes the process.

A study procedure of this type provides a great deal of review. In part A, for example, the definitions at the top of the page receive much review. Indeed, if none of the words were originally known to the child, the first definition would be studied once and reviewed nine times. In part B, the bottom definitions are reviewed most frequently. In parts C and D, the words themselves are reviewed with the top and bottom ones, respectively, receiving the most attention. Thus children are never given a list and expected to deal with them in a haphazard way. They study only one word at a time, and they have abundant opportunities for review.

It should be readily obvious that (a) a child has a specific way of studying the new vocabulary, (b) this study technique takes longer than the cursory procedure

413

used by many children, (c) it is practically guaranteed to be effective, for long-term retention is almost certain to improve, and (d) it makes the teacher responsible for something reasonable -- teaching -- and places the responsibility for learning on the child.

It should also be noted that study of both words and definitions is intended to provide assistance in entering the word into both the children's reading and writing vocabularies.

Phase 2: In-School Reinforcement

At this point the pupils are ready to study their new vocabulary. The following procedures should be considered:

1. Associate each child with a partner. Children may select their own if they demonstrate the ability to work together productively and quietly. Otherwise you will assign the pairs.

2. One member of the pair will pronounce the ten words from top to bottom while the other looks and listens. If the first member makes any mistakes, the partner will provide assistance. If neither person knows, the first person should use the services of a Word Consultant or the Language Master. In case of error, the pronouncer always returns to the top of the list. When the first person successfully accomplishes the task, the second person follows the same procedure. Both youngsters then take turns pronouncing the words from bottom to top.

Incidentally, if pronounciation is a real problem, that indicates a need for more careful review as outlined in Step 6 of Phase 1. If pronunciation is no problem at all, deemphasize the review step.

3. After both children have pronounced the words both ways, they begin individual study of the vocabulary meanings in their notebooks using the four-part study procedure. If the new vocabulary words are presented in the afternoon -- and that is our recommendation -- the pupils may have time to do the pronunciation part at school but will have to continue the definitions part at home.

The rationale for introducing new vocabulary in the afternoon is that it is an activity in which children can become actively engaged mentally because of the constant EPR. Many other activities, especially formal ones such as lectures, tend to be more effective earlier in the day. In departmentalized and block schedules, it may be

414

impossible for the vocabulary presentation to occur in the afternoon for each group. For these situations the recommendation is that the vocabulary presentation occur near the end of the block.

Phase 3: At-Home Reinforcement

1. At indicated above, the pupils should continue studying the notebook information at home until it is mastered.

2. A parent (or someone else who agrees to assume the responsibility) pronounces the words in random order, and the child provides the definition. Then the parent supplies the definitions (or shows the sketch), and the pupil identifies the terms. The parent circles any information that is missed so the child knows where to re-study.

3. If necessary the pupil studies and takes the test again.

4. Whenever a child misses no more than one out of ten on each side (at the 3-1 and 3-2 reading levels) or two on each side (at the fourth-grade reading level or above), the parent signs his or her name at the bottom of the notebook page. These scores are ten points higher than will be expected at school, thus allowing for a small amount of forgetting. As in previous situations, a teacher can then note whether the parents are cooperating. Note: Expect some forged signatures. If you send home letters on the first day of school outlining expectations, you may wish to have parents sign and return them. These signatures are usually genuine. If the letter to be returned has specific information to which the parent may need to refer, send two copies. Otherwise the parent won't be able to follow through on your comments.

5. The child then writes ten sentences, one with each word. This step is the first point at which a youngster should be able to so without referring to the notebook. The biggest problem to be faced in this regard is the use of the new term as the wrong part of speech ("I was morosely when we lost the game.") or in an incorrect sense ("We extinguish -- put out or turn out -- the cat at night."). Incidentally, research indicates that youngsters who are required to write sentences make more progress than pupils who do not engage in this activity (346).

Phase 4: Test

1. There is little difference between the testing format used in Model 3 and that used in 2-1 and 2-2 reading levels of Model 2. See pages 376-378 for a consideration of the recommended procedures.

2. When pupils fail to achieve the established proficiency level, direct them to study during their "spare time" and take another test after lunch (or on the following day in classrooms that are not self-contained). Note: The "spare time" comes after they complete other independent activities you assign. Children should remember that the study of vocabulary is essentially an at-home assignment. Class time can be used only if they finish the in-school assignments which are first priority. To allow otherwise is to encourage children not to study vocabulary at home. It also precludes spaced study. It is worth noting that pupils provided materials via the IRI rarely have difficulty learning the vocabulary. A person who fails the vocabulary test normally does so for some other reason.

3. Identify several pupils whose ten sentences are usually well developed. Select one of those sets, check to be sure the work is acceptable, number the terms in random order, and ask a pupil who scored 100% initially to administer the test orally to those who need to take it over.

4. After the test, pair the pupils and ask them to revise their sentences if necessary. The pairs should consider the points of emphasis identified in Part 7 of Phase 1 (page 412). If no changes need to be made, the space below the sentence is left blank. If any change is required -- even an omitted period -- the person recopies the sentence. Changes in the original sentences may not be made during the paired study procedure, for proofreading should have occurred previously. Many opportunities for new learning should occur here. and the sentences assignment should be used as one basis for instruction in written language.
   Please note that slow groups may have considerable difficulty in getting their thoughts onto paper. Teacher judgment concerning what is reasonable and realistic is important in this regard. The expectation of one group in a class may differ from that of another group.

<u>Phase 5</u>: <u>Review</u>

The review for Model 3 is handled in the same way as the review of reading levels 2-1 and 2-2. Refer to the comments on pages 382-386.

2. Background

The previous pages have considered strategies for developing vocabulary, the first step in a mastery-based DLP. After children learn the vocabulary, it is time to develop the background of experience. It is important to remember that as the reading level increases, so does the likelihood that the content will be outside the knowledge of the children (687). The following suggestions may prove helpful:

1. Read the selection to identify information children should possess in order to understand the story. The need for background information may relate to

a. a different part of the country or world

b. a different period of time (past or future)

c. a particular genre (biography, fairy tale, myth, etc.)

d. a particular style of writing (dialect, mountain language)

e. a particular mood (humor, satire)

f. a particular type of subject matter (a subject such as science or social studies or a subtopic such as archaeology or astronomy)

2. Secure materials that will help provide background. These materials may include any of the following:

a. maps and globes. Show where the story occurred.

b. realia (real objects). Example: Display a loom. Set up any displays before school starts so you don't have to spend instructional time on this activity.

c. pictures from a picture file. Show pictures of the general setting.

d. field trip. Visit a farm or attend a circus.

3. Ask background questions to the group. If no member of the group possesses the information, provide the knowledge yourself. Examples: Where on this map was Paul Bunyan supposed to have lived?...How was life different in 1492?...Why do cities have such tall buildings?

4. When stories have backgrounds which are unlikely to present difficulties, minimize this aspect of the Developmental Lesson Plan. Normally it should not be necessary to spend more than 5-10 minutes on the development of background.

3. Purposes for Reading

The story is told of a minister who dropped a new quarter into the collection plate. At the conclusion of the service, he was surprised and disappointed to observe the shiny silver coin was the only occupant of the collection plate. When he commented on the fact, his young son replied, "Well, Dad, if you had put more into it, you would have gotten more out of it."

The same observation applies to comprehension. Pupils get out of their reading what they take or put into it. Our attempts to focus on vocabulary and concept development and background and motivation are intended to provide young learners with something to take into the act of reading. In addition, however, they must also put something into the effort. This something is purpose for reading. Almost everyone has a purpose in his reading behavior. Some read to please a teacher or parent, "to get it over with," or to avoid punishment or failure. Others are motivated by the handwriting on the walls, a love letter or note, selected excerpts from a juicy novel, directions for putting a model car together, or a driver's education manual. While most everyday reading is not this stimulating, much of it can be made more pleasant and more productive if the learner is actively looking for something (133, 404, 740, 753).

4. Silent Reading

As children grow older and, hopefully, acquire increased competence in reading, they should be able to read silently with only occasional help from a word consultant and only rare help from a teacher. There are several problems that sometimes occur. First, some children, especially boys, try to see who can finish first. This problem can be avoided by pointing out that no awards are given for speed reading and written comprehension exercises follow each story. Second, some stories are sufficiently difficult (for any of a variety of reasons) that children should be encouraged to read each selection twice. Third, if children have acquired the habit of holding either their books or their heads at odd angles while reading, this problem should be corrected. The book should be held by both hands 12-18 inches from the eyes. It should not lie on the desk or table, for the angle of vision varies considerably from the top to the bottom of the page.

5. Evaluation, Discussion, and Oral Reading

The procedures used at the 3-1 level and above are identical to those employed at the 2-1 and 2-2 levels. Thus you should refer to pages 391-399 for specific practices and recommendations.

6. Extended and Related Activities

Pages 399-402 describe activities in which pupils can engage. Additional suggestions are listed below.

1. Encourage children to develop creative reports on their reading. Examples of reports which we received from our elementary pupils include the following:

    a. an apron made from a pattern in a book
    b. an experiment described in a trade book
    c. an oil painting of a horse
    d. a trumpet solo using music that appeared in a library book
    e. Spanish games taught to our class during the physical educational period
    f. a diary Columbus might have kept

Indeed, the creative book reports were so numerous that the principal scheduled a two-day display and invited the parents to attend.

2. Encourage children to write a different ending to the story. This activity is most timely when someone comments that the story didn't end the way he thought or wished it would. Then make the suggestion. The assignment may be for extra credit.

3. Help youngsters write to favorite authors and request information about their lives, their childhood days, how they became interested in writing, how they got started,

what trials and tribulations confront would-be authors, and what advice they would offer. Be sure pupils first consult reference books such as Junior Book of Authors before they ask questions that are readily answered by common sources.

4. Encourage children to write stories. In the second grade Ginger read several plays and decided to create one for the neighborhood children. One weekend she did a rough draft, complete with odd names of characters, reworked it so it was legible, and had a friend help her do a radio theater reading.

5. Encourage children to write selections in different forms. For example, they might change a poem into prose or a short story into a play. Alternately, they might like to write a newspaper account based on the story. Be sure they include headlines.

6. Ask children to write a selected story as it might occur in another country or in another time period. There are many versions of fairy tales (Cinderella, for instance). Nail Soup is a variant of Stone Soup.

Summary

This chapter has considered specific strategies for creating and using DLPs beginning at the third-grade reading levels. You should "pick and choose" aspects that seem most likely to address the particular needs of your pupils. When certain aspects of your lessons work well (i.e., they result in pupil progress), continue to use them. Hopefully you will be able to adopt or adapt some ideas presented here to increase the quality and quantity of children's learning.

FOR FURTHER READING

Fitzgerald, Gisela G., "Why Kids Can Read the Book But Not the Workbook." Reading Teacher, XXXII, No. 8 (May, 1979), 930-932.

Heinrich, June S., "Elementary Oral Reading: Methods and Materials," Reading Teacher, XXX, No. 1 (October, 1976), 10-15.

Jevitz, Lucille, and Donald W. Meints, "Be A Better Book Buyer: Guidelines for Textbook Evaluation," Journal of Reading, XXII, No. 8 (May, 1979), 734-738.

CHAPTER 8

PROVIDING EXTENSIVE REINFORCEMENT

Introduction

<u>Extensive</u> <u>reinforcement</u> refers to the provision of additional teaching and learning experiences for those pupils who require repeated instruction and practice with specific skills, concepts, and attitudes. It recognizes the fact that educationally disadvantaged youngsters often require much more meaningful repetitive contact with material to be learned than is provided in most basal reading programs (329). The literature clearly recognizes the need for special provisions for our educationally disadvantaged children (87, 329, 710).

Too often the common responses to this need are inadequate or insufficient. The three procedures most frequently used with educationally disadvantaged learners appear to be the following:

1. Teaching the lesson without providing additional reinforcement.

2. Providing additional practice by repeating the instructional activity with the same material. That is, reading the story aloud twice or completing the same worksheet twice.

3. Providing additional parallel instruction, material, and practice.

Whether they are intended to or not, most basal readers present a systematic, sequential series of learning experiences appropriate primarily for pupils in the high average and above range of intelligence and socio-economic status. It has long been assumed -- and incorrectly so -- that educationally disadvantaged youngsters can make effective use of these materials merely by reducing the <u>rate</u> at which the information is covered. While the idea of providing for individual differences by adjusting the pace of instruction certainly <u>sounds</u> <u>like</u> an academically respectable suggestion, it alone is completely ineffective in meeting the needs of our disadvantaged. Far too much attention has been focused on providing for one type of individual difference--rate of learning--and far too little (if any)

421

consideration given to the many additional ways in which learners differ. This misplaced emphasis has contributed directly to the failure of some schools to meet the real needs of many pupils. It is long past time to abandon a bandwagon built solely on the chassis called rate.

Nor is isolated drill necessarily the solution to the problem. While we certainly do not oppose all types of activities involving drill, it is impossible to accept some of the unfortunate procedures currently utilized in some classrooms. Let us consider three examples:

It is a typical practice in many rooms for a teacher to require pupils to study and master a number of basic sight words presented on flash cards. Except when concrete nouns are being considered -- and these are rarely the terms which present difficulty to pupils -- the practice is an unproductive use of instructional time and effort (113, 461). Regardless of the intensive and extensive nature of isolated practice, satisfactory results are rarely obtained (743), except with some bright youngsters. For them, of course, almost anything works.

With these thoughts in mind, let us consider some procedures designed to meet the reading needs of these potential learners. The following paragraphs discuss ways of providing extensive reinforcement for pupils who currently are not profiting from instruction.

Suggested Classroom Practices

Practice One: Use the Cumulative Teaching/Cumulative Testing Technique (152).

While everyone agrees that learning is cumulative, few people discuss the obvious fact that failure is also cumulative. For example, the teacher who presents a reading story with six new words often equates the lesson with the children's learning. Unfortunately, the learning disabled, slow learners, unmotivated youngsters, and poor readers frequently master only one or two new words (missing the other four or five) and thus begin the next lesson with a word "deficit" that increases with each lesson. This tendency is pronounced at the first- and second-grade reading levels, regardless of pupils' ages. It is also common when the instructional materials have little or no vocabulary control, which is typical of many reading series and other textbooks. The preventative measure, of course, is to be certain that a child acquires one competency before proceeding to another of the same type. We call this cumulative teaching.

The concept of cumulative teaching and testing is built on the assumptions that (1) learning tasks can be sequenced, (2) mastery of each learning task should be required, and (3) a review should occur after each new learning task is added. Let us consider each of these aspects briefly.

Learning tasks can be sequenced so as to maximize the likelihood that pupils will proceed from one lower-level task to a more advanced lesson. Skills scope and sequence outlines are constructed largely on intuitive sequences, for there is little research evidence about the most productive specific sequence.

Mastery of each learning task should be required before a new skill is introduced. The work of John Carroll (112) and Benjamin Bloom (62) confirms the importance of teaching for mastery. Research summaries by James Block (60) indicate that, when mastery teaching strategies are used, the top 80% of a class can acquire information typically learned by only the top 20% of a class. These techniques usually require no more that 10 to 20% additional teaching time at the beginning. Because pupils master the "basics," the amount of learning time decreases as more complex information is presented.

A review should occur after each new learning component is added. We often see children who seem to "learn" each skill as it is presented but who are nevertheless unable to apply the skill in context with other skills. For example, a pupil may know the sounds of letters in isolation and still not be able to combine them to read unfamiliar words.

Cumulative teaching/testing is designed to help each child apply a skill in gradually increasing units of difficulty. At first the youngster focuses on the skill itself. Next he studies a second skill. Then he reviews both skills before proceeding to a third one. The cumulative teaching model is as follows:

1. Item A
2. Item B
3. Review of Items A and B
4. Item C
5. Review of Items A-C
6. Item D
7. Review of Items A-D, etc.

Subsequent instruction continues the sequence above, gradually dropping the early items when they are well learned. It is important to remember, however, that not all children need review after each new piece of information is taught. For some, a review after every two, three, or even four new items is appropriate.

Let us now apply the cumulative teaching/testing procedure to some sample learning activities for comprehension, word analysis, and sight vocabulary.

<u>Main Ideas</u>. One of the most difficult reading skills for pupils to acquire is the ability to identify the main idea. To teach this skill, first sequence the tasks to be presented. The activities will focus on four aspects: (1) main idea in the initial sentence, (2) main idea in the final sentence, (3) main idea implied rather than specifically stated, and (4) main idea in the middle.

To initiate instruction, present a series of paragraphs which contain main ideas expressed in the first sentence (introductory statement). Next, provide guided practice in underlining main ideas found in this position. When pupils begin to acquire facility in this activity, present paragraphs which have main ideas in the final sentence (summary statement).

After pupils have successfully practiced underlining these main ideas (perhaps with colored crayons or pencils), provide instruction and practice using paragraphs which contain main ideas in one of the two positions. This step is more difficult, for youngsters cannot depend on following the repetitive pattern that characterizes the study of a single skill.

Next, help pupils identify implied main ideas. After they demonstrate initial facility in this aspect, provide paragraphs containing main ideas of all these types. Finally, introduce embedded main ideas and then review all four types. In each case pupils should not advance to the next stage until they demonstrate initial mastery of the preceding skill.

The pattern for cumulative teaching/testing of the four types of paragraph organization is as follows:

1. Type A (main idea at the beginning of a paragraph)
2. Type B (main idea at the end)
3. Types A and B (main idea at the beginning or end)
4. Type C (main idea implied)
5. Types A-C (main idea at the beginning, end, or implied)
6. Type D (main idea in the middle)
7. Types A-D (main idea in any of the above positions)

Word Analysis: Phonics. As a second example of the cumulative teaching/testing technique, let us consider the presentation of letter-sound associations to a group of youngsters. After teaching the pupils that b=/b/, for example, check to be certain the children have recognized the relationship. Almost invariably it will be necessary to present several more lessons on the same topic and to provide additional follow up practice materials.

Later present a lesson on f = /f/. Once again, check for initial mastery and present additional instruction and practice materials. Then review both letter-sound associations before introducing a third set of relationships. The instructional/reinforcement pattern follows:

1. Teach b
2. Teach f
3. Review b and f
4. Teach m
5. Review b,f,and m
6. Teach d
7. Review b, f, m, and d etc.

It is important to remember that phonic practice should always include contextual application. Unfortunately, most commercial phonic materials omit this very important step.

Sight Vocabulary. One of the first learning tasks for beginning readers of any age is the mastery of the basic sight vocabulary, and many youngsters need more instruction and practice in sight vocabulary than is provided by the classroom curriculum. A sight word deficit may occur in two ways: a pupil may master only part of a list of four or five words (for instance) and fall behind for the day, or a pupil may master only a few lists of words and fall behind for the year (and potentially forever). Development of a group analysis chart from the cumulative teaching/testing pattern shown below will help prevent students from developing such deficits.

1. Vocabulary List 1
2. Vocabulary List 2
3. Review of Vocabulary Lists 1-2
4. Vocabulary List 3
5. Review of Vocabulary Lists 1-3
6. Vocabulary List 4
7. Review of Vocabulary Lists 1-4, etc.

425

Make a chart with the names of pupils down the left side and record the vocabulary list and review sequence across the top. Pupils can progress at their own rate, receiving additional help as needed.

Since the cumulative teaching/testing technique can be applied to any subject at any grade level, it would be easy to list hundreds of other applications: teaching the names of the letters of the alphabet, number facts, spelling patterns, map-reading skills, the mechanics of handwriting, and so. It also can be used for behavior development.

The technique also has much to say to those who develop instructional materials and those who select school-wide reading programs. Committees which evaluate instructional materials should always pay attention to the nature and quality of the reinforcement program built into the materials. A manual may suggest 16 different skills lessons to accompany a story, but there is probably very little opportunity for the teacher or school to organize the curriculum in a way that will ensure mastery teaching.

Cumulative teaching/testing is not new except for its name. Review has long been used by parents and teachers to maximize learning. Yet despite its simplicity, the concept is frequently overlooked. New materials with less vocabulary control and more natural language patterns often mean less reinforcement of new learning. Workbooks usually provide far more practice exercises on single skills than they provide for systematic reviews of previously introduced items. Parental and school pressures to finish books often result in cursory attention to cumulative teaching and mastery.

Curriculum development need not begin with a new curriculum. Instead we can restructure our resources and use them in more efficient and effective ways. One way to increase learning is to study our current curricula and add cumulative teaching/cumulative testing procedures where they are needed.

Practice Two: For the educationally disadvantaged, provide many reading books at the same approximate level before moving upward.

Stated another way, this suggestion might read: Develop reading proficiency through horizontal rather than vertical instruction (124, 403, 650). At the first-grade level, a basal series typically consists of several readiness books, three or four preprimers, a primer, and a first reader. Grade levels two and three usually have two books each. Beginning with the fourth grade, there is usually only one book per level, with the

426

last title representing either a sixth- or eighth-grade level of difficulty.

Realizing the importance of a sequential development of language, word analysis, vocabulary, comprehension, literature, and study skills, we recognize that developmental materials should be presented in the order in which they appear. That is to say, we do not skip around within a book or among books just because a particular selection is appealing or timely.

We have suggested that most basal reading books prove most effective with high average and above average pupils. Because the educationally disadvantaged require additional contact with low level materials before they can achieve mastery, it is necessary to modify traditional approaches. On a broad and rather superficial basis, we might classify readers' instructional needs as indicated in Chart 8-1.

CHART 8-1

SUGGESTED INSTRUCTIONAL PROGRAMS
FOR THREE TYPES OF LEARNERS

Group	Needs
1. Above average readers	One book at each primary level for instruction in basic skills
2. Low average readers	Two or three books at each primary level for instruction in basic skills
3. Below average readers	Four or five books at each primary level for instruction in basic skills

Chart 8-1 suggests that at least three kinds of basal reader sequences should be provided, with each type being determined by the responses pupils make to their instruction.

In general, the more educationally disadvantaged the pupil, the more need he has for horizontal reinforcement (i.e., teaching based on additional materials at the same approximate level usually from other series) rather than vertical instruction (i.e., teaching based on another book at a higher level in the same series). What happens as a result of horizontal reinforcement? (1) Fewer new

427

words are introduced, (2) the words are repeated more frequently, (3) there are fewer skills because only the skills included at that level in the lead basal series are studied, and (4) the skills are repeated more frequently. To apply the information contained in Chart 8-1, contrast the programs which might then be provided for readers with two different types of needs. Charts 8-2 and 8-3 illustrate a vertical progression for a more accomplished reader and a horizontal growth pattern for an educationally disadvantaged child.

CHART 8-2

POSSIBLE SEQUENCE FOR A RAPID LEARNER *

Materials (Series A)	New Words	Cumulative Reading Words
Readiness Review		
	minimal	minimal
Preprimer 1	33	33
Preprimer 2	31	64 (excluding enrichment words)
Preprimer 3	26	90 (excluding enrichment words)
Primer	106	196 (excluding enrichment words)
First Reader	210	406 (excluding enrichment words)

* Based on an analysis and comparison of the vocabulary of one basal reading series.

Several observations should be made about the information presented in Charts 8-2 and 8-3. First, some pupils requiring the extended readiness efforts discussed in Chapter 4 may not begin the formal reading program until their third year in school. When pupils come to the school functioning two or three or four years below the typical language and experience levels necessary for success in beginning reading, we cannot ignore these needs and proceed to more sophisticated tasks.

428

CHART 8-3

POSSIBLE SEQUENCE FOR AN
EDUCATIONALLY DISADVANTAGED LEARNER *

Materials	Words	New Words If Used In This Sequence	Cumulative Reading Words
First year:			
Extended readiness up to one year if necessary	Minimal	Minimal	Minimal
Second year (?)			
Preprimer 1 (Series 1)	12	12	12
Preprimer 1 (Series 2)	20	15	27
Preprimer 2 (Series 1)	20	13	40
Preprimer 1 (Series 3)	28	21	61
Preprimer 1 (Series 4)	33	16	77
Preprimer 2 (Series 3)	22	14	91
Preprimer 3 (Series 1)	22	10	101
Preprimer 2 (Series 4)	31	22	123
Total thus far	188	123	123

* Based on an analysis and comparison of the vocabulary of four basal reading series.

Instead we must abandon the traditional concept which delegates particular books to a certain grade level and instead provide instruction and practice at the lowest levels at which gaps in the learner's body of knowledge first occur. A six-year-old who operates at a three-year-old level in language and experience is not going to learn to read in September or in January. Hopefully he will not even be pressured to do so. Extended readiness would be far more appropriate (582).

A second point demonstrated by Charts 8-2 and 8-3 is that an above-average learner using Series A is expected to master 90 words presented in the three preprimers. In contrast, an educationally disadvantaged learner is expected to learn only 40 words in his first three preprimers (Preprimer 1 in Series 1, Preprimer 1 in Series 2, and Preprimer 2 in Series 1). Not until he has successfully completed six preprimers will the pupil be expected to read 91 words.

Third, notice the typical first-grade program for above average learners includes over 400 words while the eight preprimers used for less proficient readers present only 123 words. Although the pace or rate of introduction of new words is obviously much slower in the latter case, the major element involved is the opportunity teachers have for providing extensive reinforcement of the material that has already been presented. Merely to present information at a decelerated pace does not significantly enhance the likelihood of learning. Extensive reinforcement in additional lower-level material does.

While a critic might correctly declare that youngsters involved in this process are introduced to a much smaller number of words, the rejoinder is that these pupils are much more likely to master a stock of basic sight words. We much prefer to see a youngster attempt less and achieve more rather than try more and learn less. Perhaps the implementation of this philosophy would result in dramatic decreases in the vast numbers of poor readers at the primary, intermediate, and high school levels. Indeed, in their classic study, Arthur I. Gates and David H. Russell (340) found that average and low reading readiness first-grade groups taught a restricted vocabulary program scored higher on four standardized tests than did groups taught more extensive vocabulary programs. A number of writers recognize the value of a horizontal progression for extensive reinforcement (124, 403, 446, 650, 710).

At the intermediate and high school levels, the feeling is often expressed, "If he hasn't learned to read in all these years, he's not likely to learn now." This unfortunate philosophy completely ignores the fact that many of these youngsters have never been taught at their own instructional levels. In grade one they were given material for which they were not ready. At the end of the year they were either sent to a second-grade classs which often began with 2-1 books or were retained in grade one to repeat the whole series of books. In either case, however, far too little attention was directed toward providing appropriate learning experiences. Under such circumstances, effective learning is next to impossible.

Fourth, a teacher proceeds horizontally until her children are ready to return to the lead basal and move vertically. This determination can be made in several ways: (a) use the IRI passage from the beginning of the next level, (b) readminister the end-of-book mastery tests for two topics: vocabulary and comprehension, both of which should be passed, (c) try the children out on one or two selections from the next vertical book.

Fifth, contrary to what one might expect, a preprimer three in one series might be easier than a preprimer two in another. One cannot simply proceed through five first preprimers, five second preprimers, etc. Specific procedures for a school or district to use in sequencing two or more series are provided elsewhere (201) and are not produced here.

Practice Three: Develop a classroom (or locally) relevant sight word list (158, 159).

Some states (e.g., South Carolina, Florida) have mandated sight word lists for various grade levels. In other states it is assumed that the vocabulary of the instructional materials comprises the sight vocabulary list (i.e., the words children are expected to recognize at sight). A problem arises, however, if one uses several materials (as in practice two).

There is an abundance of research evidence to demonstrate that there is very little overlapping of the vocabulary of any two basal reading series (59, 436, 548, 583, 595, 615). In general the comparability of vocabulary in any two series usually falls between 35% and 50%. The fact that series present large numbers of different words assumes tremendous significance when the faculty of a school uses a wide variety of materials or when the materials being used possess little or no effective vocabulary control, as is true in the content areas and in materials designated grade two or three and above.

In the first situation, the use of multiple materials can present an insurmountable barrier for a young learner or a poor reader. This is true because the use of a book in one series assumes the pupil's mastery of the vocabulary at the previous levels in that series. The random use of instructional materials by an individual teacher or by consecutive teachers may retard the educational progress of some children. In the second situation, removal of vocabulary restrictions simultaneously "enriches" the language and overwhelms the youngster who is unable to maintain the learning pace required by the materials. Exposed to more information, many children simply learn less.

431

We have said that research indicates the uniqueness of much of the vocabulary in various stages of materials. This fact has led a large number of investigators to study the efficacy of various word lists and to either accept them or offer alternative listings (120, 253, 389, 411, 432, 454, 471, 553). There are over 100 word lists in the literature (435).

Indeed, the Delaware study (615) found that the popular Dolch Word List did not have a strong correspondence to the word corpus derived from their study of ten basal series. Perhaps a new concept is needed, one that can prove more helpful in identifying the most important sight words for beginning readers.

We propose that these most important sight words be the ones which will occur in most of the materials being used with children in a particular school or school system. Thus the words to be included on a Basic Sight Word List will depend on their inclusion in the materials most frequently used in the local schools.

For example, if a "linguistic" series presents "Dan can fan a fat cat." and "A pig can jig." one type of word list should be developed to correspond to the mastery learning expectations inherent in this material. Conversely, if the basals emphasize more natural language patterns, _here_, _me_, _play_, _said_, _who_, and _you_ will be basic words.

If we agree that the items on the basic sight word list should correspond to the expectations of the instructional series, we can immediately note the implications. First, the Dolch Word List and its alternatives are _general_ lists reflecting the vocabulary of a large range of material, much of which may be unavailable to pupils beginning to read. A teacher's use of the books' word lists and a general word list such as the Dolch require that pupils learn two vocabularies instead of one. This fact is especially ironic when Chapter I children are involved, for disadvantaged learners are least likely to be able to cope with a basal list in the homeroom and a general list in the reading lab. The greater the divergence between the two lists, the greater the actual problem.

A second implication is related to the first. A specific, locally-relevant, list must correspond to the instructional materials being utilized. For example, if a single series is utilized for all pupils, the list accompanying the basal readers may be used. Some schools and systems use co-basals, tri-basals, or as many as five series so competent readers can move vertically throughout a lead basal while less capable pupils move horizontally through several series at gradually

432

increasing levels before progressing vertically. Interested readers can refer to one of the readings at the end of this chapter for specific procedures on how to develop a locally - relevant basic word list.

Practice Four: Once preprimers or other books are introduced, teach the material no faster than the youngsters learn it. Provide reinforcement by developing additional sentences using the new words.

It is almost impossible to overstate the case for matching the teaching-learning rates. Teaching and learning should not be confused; they are not the same. Teaching is viewed here as the act of presenting information related to specific facts, concepts, skills, and attitudes and of facilitating pupils' insight through questions asked or experiences provided. On the other hand, learning is considered as the pupils' act of actively acquiring and utilizing the facts, skills, and concepts, which have been presented or experienced.

As a result, teaching may occur without consequent learning. For example, a teacher working with ten pupils on a specific skill may be successful in teaching one-half of the group. The other five may fail to benefit from the activity because they

1. already possess the skill

2. lack appropriate prerequisite skills

3. require a different presentational medium

4. need additional instruction and practice

Of course, there are numerous other possibilities, but the point to be clarified here is this: Most teaching results in some learning and some non-learning. Our acceptance of this fact makes it possible for us to consider two broader questions:

1. Which youngsters have acquired the information that was presented?

2. For the others, why has the teaching failed to result in learning?

(Incidentally, the suggested relationship between teaching and learning does not necessarily apply in one-to-one situations. Here it may be quite possible to say a teacher has not taught if a youngster fails to learn.)

433

Whenever some members of a group learn, something obviously has been taught to someone. One of our tasks is to increase the percentage of planned learning in our classes. To do so, of course, we must sometimes change what we teach as well as the way we present it.

Having made this point, let us consider the problems involved in assuring ourselves that we teach no faster than pupils learn. We have already considered the importance of locating appropriate materials for each pupil and through avoiding the temptation of moving our educationally disadvantaged youngsters through the information too rapidly. Unfortunately, even teachers who are careful to delay formal reading instruction until children have acquired the necessary oral language skills frequently make this mistake. We often see the results in classroom with learners at primary reading levels. Ask the members of a "low group" to read aloud, and what do you normally find? A large proportion operating at the frustration level in word recognition. When they read silently, many also operate at the frustration level in comprehension.

If these children initially were associated with the appropriate material, we can draw only one conclusion: For some reason the instructional pace has proceeded without regard for pupil mastery. If a pupil can initially pronounce 94 out of 100 running words in a reading selection and comprehend at least 70% of the material read silently, he may be said to read at the instructional level. The material is appropriate, at least from the standpoint of reading difficulty.

Perhaps a few weeks later a teacher will discover through oral reading activities that the child's word recognition is now at the frustration rather than the instructional level. From silent reading she may find that comprehension has shown a similar decline. The occurrence of either problem is a clear indication of an overdue need for extensive reinforcement with the most recently-introduced words, concepts, or skills. As a general practice, teachers should resist the impulse to present additional material until the old information has been acquired. Translated into practical terms, the suggestion reads as follows: Be sure a child can recognize and read fairly easily the four new words presented in one story before advancing to the next lesson. Be sure the child does not progress to additional instructional units until he has initially mastered the present one.

After all, a youngster who does not learn these four items will then have a double assignment (perhaps eight words) in the next lesson. It is naive to assume that a

434

pupil who experiences difficulty with Lesson 12 will succeed in Lesson 13. As pupils at low reading levels move through the increasingly-difficult pages of a book, they often fall farther and farther "behind." The answer is not to sigh and move on. Instead, at least part of the solution lies in providing reinforcement instruction and practice with these four new words (as well as skills). When reasonable competence is achieved, the teacher and pupils may move on -- together.

To provide additional meaningful contacts with difficult new words, locate or develop supplementary exercises with these items. The other words in the sentences should already have become part of the pupils' reading vocabularies. The word list at the end of the preceding basal text is the quickest and most effective way of locating words to use in sentences. It should be pointed out, however, that unless sentence-level reinforcement is provided each day, the practice simply will not be effective.

Perhaps an example will clarify the problems which arise when extensive reinforcement is not provided on a consistent basis. The senior author was asked to determine, individually, the instructional reading levels of 140 second and third graders. The process required almost three school days. At the end of that time we secured for almost every pupil an appropriate book.

One week later seven youngsters who were suspected by their teachers of having received inappropriate materials were rechecked. New books were provided for all seven.

Two of the 140 pupils required extended readiness. Nine more initially used the Language-Experience Approach almost exclusively. Seven others could read from the beginning of the first preprimer, and three more from a second preprimer. All ten youngsters associated with preprimers were below average in measured intelligence.

A little over one month after pupils had been associated with what the teachers considered to be appropriate materials, the consultant was asked to teach a demonstration lesson from a story toward the end of the second preprimer. According to the regular teacher, the members of that group simply were not learning anything; they just couldn't read the stories.

The consultant studied the material, referred to the complete word list at the end of the first preprimer and to the first part of the second preprimer's list, and used these "known" words to construct sentences providing additional contact with the new items. These sentences were duplicated and distributed to the group. Before reading the story we discussed the new words in context and worked with the supplementary sentences.

435

Nevertheless, the lesson was a complete failure. Only one of the ten pupils could read the duplicated material. The other nine could not even pronounce 75% of the "known" words. These were youngsters who only a month before were quite able to pronounce at least 94% of the words in their assigned books. None scored as high as 70% on comprehension during the lesson.

Despite careful initial placement based on 94% word analysis and 70% comprehension, the pupils had been provided so little reinforcement that they were quite unable to cope with the printed page. The teacher had merely been covering pages, wasting time, and inadvertently preventing pupil progress. To make matters worse, she had combined the original first preprimer group with the second preprimer group and given the children the latter rather than the former text. The teacher was not aware that pupils may be quite capable of reading material at the beginning of the book but not in the middle or at the end.

Initial placement is the first step in good teaching, not the last. Anything worth teaching is worth learning, and anything worth learning should be mastered before more complex tasks are assigned.

Practice Five: Use workbook materials accompanying the basal readers and those from other series only when they are appropriate.

Because they do form part of a Developmental Reading Program, workbooks should be used with their basal readers. Without belaboring the controversy over questionable uses of these materials (319, 462, 705, 723), we contend that those who misuse workbooks also tend to misuse basal readers. Competent teachers and educationally disadvantaged youngsters should not be deprived of such practice material merely because others fail to use the exercises correctly. As mentioned earlier, two wrongs simply do not equal one right. Practical program development followed by class-to-class assistance would seem to be a much more desirable alternative.

However, several cautions should be noted in the use of workbook materials. As studies (314, 686) indicate and as many teachers have observed, these activity sheets are often written at higher reading levels than the basals they accompany. This fact effectively eliminates their use in many situations. The same problem is even more severe when reinforcement materials are selected from alternate basal series or trade books.

Because of these potential pitfalls, we recommend that any extensive reinforcement material be previewed carefully to determine its appropriateness insofar as sight words and word analysis, vocabulary, and comprehension skills are concerned. Switching from one series of material to another without adequate correlating skills provisions only produces problems (710).

In general one can say that extensive reinforcement provided through independent workbook activities is educationally acceptable only when certain basic practices are followed. These include the following:

1. The material has previously been discussed and studied.

2. Motivation, or purpose for performing the activity, has been captured.

3. Youngsters know their work will be checked and discussed as soon as possible.

4. Youngsters know they will be encouraged, expected, and assisted to correct their errors and learn from their mistakes.

5. The assignment is made after pupils have indicated some initial proficiency in coping with the content involved. (A person who does not understand the information during its presentation is not asked to complete the assignment independently.)

6. Youngsters are capable of reading the material, not just the basal reader it accompanies.

7. Youngsters possess the prerequisite skills assumed by the assignment.

If these guidelines are followed, many concerns about the misuses of workbooks will be resolved. They include: (1) lack of pre-examination by the teacher, (2) using workbook assignments as busywork, (3) using workbook assignments for disciplinary purposes, (4) inadequate teacher preparation of assignments, (5) careless distribution of the books, (6) using workbook assignments as art lessons, (7) overuse of workbooks resulting in reduction of valuable free time, and (8) inadequate study by the teacher of the pupils' completed assignments (261:77).

Practice Six: Wherever realistic and whenever possible, use basic sight words in the classroom.

There are daily opportunities for systematically exposing pupils to meaningful words in print. Certainly

437

children should learn to recognize the printed forms of their names, and they may wish to learn the names of several close friends. The posting of daily or weekly duty rosters may provide additional opportunities. For examples, print information of the following type on a bulletin board.

Bill may feed the fish.

Karen may pass out the books.

Joe may get the milk.

Paulette may greet the visitors.

Pupils should be encouraged to stop and read the assignments as often as they are changed. Even if only one person can read the material, many of the others will soon be able to recognize the sentences and words by listening to their classmates read aloud. To facilitate children's initial identification and recognition of words, you may wish to place pictures of drawings above the key words. In this case visual representations for fish, books, and milk would be needed. Later discontinue this rebus writing. Recognition of the printed names of children can also be enhanced by placing a photograph of each person beside or above his name.

Other words can also be learned functionally. The boys' bathroom should be appropriately labeled. Shelves should be labeled so children can return objects to designated areas. Most teachers prefer to keep paints, paste, clay, paper, crayons, and rulers in specified locations. Pupils should have the opportunity of becoming aware of these words as well as the experience of classifying sets of objects and of keeping supplies in order. (A list of basic sight words is included in Chapter 5.)

One should not over-interpret the suggestion to present words to beginning readers. We are not recommending that a teacher label all the items in a classroom. Unfortunately there is a tendency on the part of a few parents to put 5 x 8 inch cards with printed words "all over the place." With few exceptions we cannot teach our babies to read -- regardless of how clever we are (257). Indeed, studies of children who could read when they entered school found many of them learned to do so without any type of formal instruction (266).

438

Practice Seven: Provide reading materials which use sequential patterns of repetition.

Gates (338) found that the average number of contacts a first grader with an I.Q. of 70-80 needed to acquire certain sight words was approximately 45. His friend with an I.Q. of 120-129 might require only 20 contacts. Recognition of this finding should encourage us to provide additional reinforcement as needed.

One way to provide additional contact with basic sight words is to use reading selections with repetitive patterns. These may be of several varieties. One type (cumulative) is that exemplified by "The House That Jack Built" and "The Twelve Days of Christmas." Here each stanza incorporates the preceding comments and extends the story. Youngsters thus receive a delightful experience plus extensive reinforcement.

A second type of repetitive pattern uses the base phrase but constructs a new ending for each stanza. Books using this format include the following:

Domjan, Joseph, I Went to the Market. New York: Holt, Rinehart and Winston, 1970.

Martin, Bill, Jr., Brown Bear, Brown Bear, What Do You See?; A Ghost Story; King of the Mountain; Monday, Monday, I Like Monday; When It Rains, It Rains; Whistle, Mary, Whistle. All published by Holt in 1970.

Tolstoy, Alexei, The Great Big Enormous Turnip. Glenview, Illinois: Scott, Foresman, 1976.

Practice Eight: Record the words to songs, jingles, poems, riddles, and other easily remembered information for pupils to practice reading.

Data of this type, which are already part of youngsters' oral language, can be recorded on wall charts and read to children (324) or used in read-along material with a tape recorder (121). This factor makes it possible for them to practice reading material which has meaning and includes a self-correcting component. To be certain they have really learned the printed form of the work, children should use the open slot technique described in Chapter 6.

Examples of types of information which pupils can use for practicing their reading include the following:

Nursery rhymes

Songs children sing, both inside and outside of class

Riddles, especially of the Little Moron variety (because of the simplified vocabulary level)

Simple poems such as "Purple Cow" and "London Bridge"

Slogans such as "I can't believe I ate the whole thing."

Sports cheers (Give me an A...)

Practice Nine: Take positive steps to ensure that youngsters normally select recreational reading books written at their independent levels.

One of the best ways to practice and improve reading skill is to read widely and wisely (333, 435). However, one cannot practice and improve that which one does not have. For this reason it is extremely important to teach the language, word analysis, vocabulary, literature, comprehension, and study skills and then provide an abundance of suitable material for the extensive reinforcement of this instruction.

All too often our educationally disadvantaged youngsters select books which are unlikely to affect any growth of any type. One study (523) found that 40% of the children were unable to select appropriate books. Thus it is typical to observe poor readers carrying home thick books and later returning these ponderous volumes without having acquired any information or literary appreciation or skill. We would do well to keep five general principles in mind when our pupils select books.

1. Recreational reading should be at the independent level. With few exceptions, youngsters should be allowed to select only those books which they can read at the independent level. We have previously suggested the figures of 98% accuracy for word analysis and 90% for comprehension. Even here we should keep one point in mind. The pupil who encounters two new words out of 100 may have 20 new words, unless they are repeated, in a 1000-word selection. For many youngsters, the burden is impossibly heavy.

Youngsters seem to learn best when learning is easy (333) and not too lengthy (635). It is not difficult to accept the fact that educationally disadvantaged pupils can increase their reading rates and acquire a few new words if the material, in general, is well within their present capabilities. Except when interest is quite high, very few poor readers are willing to muddle through a book at their instructional levels, and none at all

440

will work long at the frustration level. Especially because youngsters engaged in recreational reading do not normally have an adult present, the material must be sufficiently easy to allow understanding and enjoyment without stress and strain.

How can we determine quickly if a youngster can read a library book at the independent level? Quite simply. Merely ask the pupil to read orally fifty words from a randomly-selected portion of the book. More than one error, especially if it involves potential meaning difficulties, is a cause for concern. Surely three errors would indicate the book is unsatisfactory. (Several exceptions will soon be noted.)

Some people advocate a practice of asking pupils to check the readability of their own books by holding up one finger for each word they do not know. If they need more than one hand to record the number of unknown words on a page, the book is judged too difficult. This procedure is unacceptable for several reasons. First, no reference is made to the number of words on a page. Five errors on a page of 300 words might be acceptable, but suppose only 70 words are on the page. A designated number of errors without regard for the total number of words does not seem defensible.

Second, many children, especially poor readers, are notoriously ineffective in detemining which words they do not know. As a result, most poor readers are incapable of assuming this responsibility. Selecting a book for recreational reading is not an activity we should take lightly. Anytime a child reads recreationally, he should select a book somewhat below the level he reads with teacher guidance and assistance.

Since we cannot reasonably expect pupils to assess their own competency, teachers and media specialists should combine their efforts to see that the youngsters who check out books can actually hope to be able to read them.

2. Interest should play a major role in book selection. One should expect those who use the media center to select books which appeal to their interests. For educationally disadvantaged pupils this problem is complicated by the fact that very few available books really meet these needs. Media centers should stock a number of appropriate books and publicize these materials. Books at the lowest reading levels are so few and so scattered throughout the "Easy Section" that one can hardly find the titles without an exhaustive and exhausting search. For this reason it seems highly desirable to shelve the Easy Books by assumed interest

441

and reading levels rather than by general classification. After all, for poor readers most "easy" books are hard.

Except for the topic demanded by the ardent enthusiast or for books with predominant pictures, illustrations, charts, models, or similar graphic presentations, we should attempt to match both reading levels and interests. In this way we can help make it possible for readers to read about material in which they are interested. Keep in mind that because picture books and those filled with graphics may be selected for purposes other than reading, the readability factor is of less significance here.

The selection of materials to purchase for the media center as well as the identification and location of books presently available on specific topics at various levels of reading difficulty should depend partially on the administration and interpretation of an interest inventory. Normally this should be conducted at the first of the year and perhaps later if interests appear to have changed or broadened. For poor readers and writers, it may be necessary to obtain information individually or in small groups, perhaps during the time they are in a reading or readiness group. Two sample Interest Inventories are presented at the end of this chapter.

3. A pupil who discovers he does not enjoy a book should return it immediately. An illustration comes from a recent experience. A number of pupils not directly supervised by the teacher were reading at their desks or were otherwise engaged in some endeavor. Once the authors observed a fellow idling away his time. Our conversation is summarized below.

Consultant: Why aren't you reading?

Boy: I don't like my book.

Consultant: Well, why don't you get another one?

Boy: I can't. We can't get new books until we finish the one we're reading now.

Consultant: How does your teacher know when you read a book?

Boy: We have to write a report, and we can't get a new book 'til we do that.

Consultant: Why don't you like your book?

Boy: It's too hard...I don't know a lot of the words.

Consultant: Well, that seems like a good reason for getting a new book...if you can't read all the hard words.

Boy: Yeah, but library period don't come 'til Thursday nohow.

Some schools with full-time media specialists have provisions for pupils to come at any time to exchange books. One person from each class is given a large plywood key which entitles him to return and secure books at any convenient moments during the day. Obviously the teacher's shared responsibility to match interests and reading levels passes to the media specialist in this type of situation.

Another implication here is that media centers should be open both before and after school. Similarly, the policy of allowing pupils to have only one book at a time needs to be abandoned since it assures children of having no other book to read as soon as one title is completed.

4. Teachers should accompany their classes to the library. This practice is important for several reasons. First, only the teacher knows the instructional and independent levels of the children. Therefore, only the teacher is adequately prepared to help youngsters locate appropriate books. Second, even if a media specialist possessed this information, she would not have time to help twenty-five or thirty children select books. Except in small schools, she may not even know the children's names. Third, even if the media specialist knew the children by name, knew their instructional and independent reading levels, and had time to help them consider and select books, the absence of the teacher would set a poor example. The situation is analogous to the take your child to church versus send your child to church. Teachers should be at the media center to (a) help their children select books, (b) provide coordination with the media center's skill development program, (c) select professional books or children's books to read, and (d) be caught in the act of reading a book or journal or newspapers.

Practice Ten: Institute a Reading Encouragement and Development (READ) plan (188).

443

A Developmental Reading Program includes both attention to specific skills and provisions for planned practice (753). Evidence suggests that direct instruction plus planned practice yield superior results to either component by itself.

The literature also suggests that the development of the reading habit and positive attitude toward reading should begin early (580). Thus kindergarten and first-grade classrooms provide the first opportunities for school children to blend information about reading with reading itself. In the kindergarten particularly, and for many first graders, the "reading" may be in the form of wordless books.

From a psychological perspective, children need long-term goals and short-term milestones (check points) as means of recognizing and rewarding their progress. You might set a goal of having each child read at least 100 books during the school year. Based on 180 school days, that is approximately one book every other day. Based on a nine-month school year, this is almost exactly three books per seven-day period.

The number 100 is not magic. It is reachable, however, if materials are available to meet children's needs. For example, poor readers may use Skinny Books (194).

To develop a project, (1) brainstorm a number of recognition strategies that involve school personnel and are likely to encourage children and parents to support the effort. (2) determine the feasibility of each strategy in terms of time, cost, personnel support, and effectiveness. (3) assign each reward to a short-term milestone (in this case, every fifth book read).

One possible sequence of events is listed below. The numeral on the left refers to the number of books read by a child.

5 The teacher sends a note to the parents.

10 The class applauds the child.

15 The teacher sends a second note to the parents.

20 The teacher gives a certificate indicating the child has read twenty books.

25 The media specialist visits the class and commends the child. She leads the class in quiet applause, with hands stopping before they come into contact with each other.

30   The media specialist sends a note to the parents.

35 The teacher (school) gives the child a free book.

40   The teacher gives a certificate indicating the child has read forty books.

45   The teacher telephones the parents.

50   The physical education teacher visits the class, commends the children, and leads them in applause, with each clapping hands with another child.

55   The teacher posts the child's picture and brief comments on the Teacher's Honor Board (The principal may do the same for A Principal's Honor Board.). The board should be located in the hall so many children can see the information.

60   The principal sends a note to the parents.

65   The child reads a book to his class.

70   The teacher (school) gives the child a second free book.

75   The principal visits the class and commends the child.

80   The teacher gives a certificate indicating the child has read eighty books.

85   The teacher sends a third note to the parents.

90   The child is captain for a week (or receives some other special privilege). The teacher leads applause by clapping behind her back.

95   The child reads a book to another class.

100 In front of the class, the principal gives the child a "100 book" certificate and a T-shirt saying "I have read 100 books." Someone takes the child's picture (in a group with others who meet the goal) and writes an accompanying newspaper article. The principal sends a note to the parents and recognizes the child at the school's Awards Day Program.

445

Several comments seem appropriate.

1. Although Project READ can be conducted on a classroom basis, it is preferable to involve the entire school.

2. The recognitions are for purposes of illustration. Teachers may prefer to create their own. For example, at one school one of the recognitions for the first-grade children to read 100 books was an opportunity to visit the president of the local college.

Other types of recognitions are possible. These include a free hamburger and soft drink at a fast-food service, recognition at PTA, video taping, "name calling" on a local Information Exchange radio program, a wide range of charting devices (gold stars, segmented bookworms, clowns to be dressed as additional books are read, etc.).

3. The certificates may be designed by an artist, teacher, parent, or pupil. Duplicate certificates on four different colors of paper.

4. Reading is Fun-damental (RIF) grants allow 10% of the books to be used for individual purposes. Classes with book clubs (Scholastic, Xerox, etc.) receive free books. Publishers may be willing to contribute paperbacks in exchange for some publicity. If necessary, a PTA might allocate money for purchasing the gift books.

5. The kindergarten child who "reads" a wordless book to a class will be telling the story.

6. The senior author, who claims credit for originating the "Talking T-shirt" reward, has found that poorer readers want the T-shirts because they proclaim the youngsters aren't "dumb."

7. Classroom libraries would be helpful, as would special displays in the media center of books beginners can read.

8. An introductory letter should explain Project READ to parents. It should be followed by periodic notes to parents that either can be mimeographed forms with spaces for names of persons and numbers of books to be inserted or standard forms individually typed or written. A secretary or aide can type the notes ahead of time since, for example, the parents of every child are likely to receive the first notes.

August 26, 198_

Dear Parents:

For several years I have been concerned that our children do not read very much outside of school. This habit makes it hard for them to use the information that I teach; therefore they don't learn as much in reading as they could and should.

The things you and I remember from our school days are the things we used. We have long ago forgotten the things we didn't use (algebra, foreign language, etc.). This year I am asking you to help me in Project READ (Reading Encouragement and Development). I hope your child will read 100 books. I do not care how easy the books are. My main concern is in developing the _habit_ of reading and an _interest_ in reading.

I have developed a recognition plan -- see the enclosed sheet -- and have discussed it with the children. Each year the PTA gives each teacher $50.00 to buy school materials. I shall use that money to help pay for the project.

As you can imagine, it would be impossible for me to check to be certain each child actually has read each book. If the child received the recognitions without reading the books, he/she wouldn't develop the habit of reading, acquire a positive attitude toward reading, or progress in reading. Furthermore, the child would not learn the value of honesty.

Therefore I am asking you to fill out a Book Report Form for every book your child reads. You may send in a form if (a) the child reads the book to you or someone else or (b) the child reads the book silently and tells you about it. The Book Report Contest is another way of being sure a child reads the book. Even if you have never read the book, ask your child to ask you questions. If you can answer a question, you get a point. The first person to reach five points wins. Either way you know the child has read the book. In the space on the Book Report Form, please list some words the child missed and needs to study.

Thank you for your help. You will note from the enclosed schedule that I will send my first note when your child reads his/her fifth book. I'm looking forward to a READing year.

Sincerely,

Ginger Culyer
Teacher

BOOK REPORT FORM

Book Number _____

_____ has read _____, by

_____. He/She missed the following words:

_____

_____. He/She thought the book

was _____.

_____
Parent

_____
Date

_____

September 10, 198_

Dear Mr. and Mrs. Walton:

I am pleased that John-Boy has already read five
books this year. Thank you for helping him get into the
reading habit. When John-Boy finishes his tenth book, I
will recognize him in front of the class, and when he
completes his fifteenth book, I'll send you a note. I
hope he'll read 100 books this year.
Thank you again for your help.

Sincerely,

Ginger Culyer
Teacher

448

October 1, 198_

Dear Mr. and Mrs. Walton:

As John-Boy may have told you, he has now read 15 books. I'm pleased with his recreational reading and your support of our READ project. When John-Boy finishes his twentieth book, he will receive a certificate, and when he reads his twenty-fifth book, our school media specialist will publicly recognize him.
Thanks so much for your support.

Sincerely,

Ginger Culyer
Teacher

November 1, 198_

Dear Mr. and Mrs. Walton:

Last week I visited John-Boy's class to recognize him for his recreational reading. As of today he has read 30 books, and I'm delighted he's developing the habit of reading. I wish all children would read 30 minutes a day, 365 days a year. It would certainly help improve their reading.
When John-Boy reads his thirty-fifth book, he will receive a free book, and he will receive another certificate after reading his fortieth book. His teacher will call you when John-Boy reads his forty-fifth book.
Thanks again for encouraging and helping John-Boy.

Sincerely,

Terry Ford
Media Specialist

449

February 1, 198_

Dear Mr. and Mrs. Walton:

I am pleased that John-Boy has read sixty books so far this school year. We believe children become good readers by receiving good teaching at school and a lot of practice at home. John-Boy's teacher has been pleased with your support of our READ project. It is so good to have parents who are willing to work with the school.

John-Boy will get to read a book to his class when he finishes number 65. He will receive another free book after reading number 70. I will visit John-Boy in class when he reads number 75.

Thank you for your continued support.

Sincerely,

(Mrs.) Opal Johnson
Principal

March 15, 198_

Dear Mr. and Mrs. Walton:

John-Boy now has read 85 books and is getting very close to his goal. He will receive special privileges on completion of 90 books, and he will have a chance to read a book to another class when he finishes number 95. A lot of wonderful things will happen when John-Boy reads his one hundredth book.

I hope John-Boy knows how lucky he is to have your help and support in Project READ. We certainly appreciate you.

Sincerely,

Ginger Culyer
Teacher

450

May 12, 198_

Dear Mr. and Mrs. Walton:

Congratulations to you and John-Boy! He has finished his one hundredth book. If you will let us know when you can be at school for ten minutes, we will award the T-shirt at that time. We will also recognize John-Boy at our Awards Day Program. We are planning a newspaper article and pictures of children who read 100 books, and of course, John-Boy will receive a special certificate.

Please continue to encourage John-Boy to read during the rest of the school year and throughout the summer. During the last week of school I will send home a summer reading list. This list can help keep John-Boy from losing his reading ability during the vacation months. Unfortunately our school has had a real problem in this regard.

Many thanks for your help.

Sincerely,

(Mrs.) Opal Johnson
Principal

Practice Eleven: Encourage beginning and poor readers to read at least one hundred Skinny Books each year.

A Skinny Book (194) is really short, preferably not more than 20-30 pages for intermediate and high school students and 5-10 pages for lower primary-age pupils. It may be a full-length book or one cut into segments. Listed below are the steps for stimulating pupils to read by using Skinny Books and some sound psychology. The idea reflects Roma Gans' statement: "The best drill in reading is to read many easy books (333:35)."

1. Secure from the media specialist a list of titles that fall into the Skinny Book category. While the compilation of such a list obviously requires time, it is essential. A shelf or so completed each day will get the project started. Even more progress can be made if, instead of several faculty meetings, teachers gather in the media center and share the fun.

2. Separate non-instructional primary-level books

451

into their individual stories so each one becomes a Skinny Book. For first- and second-grade use, secure a number of preprimers and primers, separating each one into individual stories. Since preprimer stories usually begin on the right-hand side of the page, only one copy is needed for each title. Two copies of each book will be needed starting at the primer level.

Try to secure as many titles as possible from series other than those being used for instructional purposes. Try also to ensure continuous progress by using consecutive books with a series. For example, if you use preprimer one and preprimer three from a certain series, try to locate or order preprimer two.

Follow the same procedure with whatever primary-level materials have the greatest amount of interest appeal. High interest-low vocabulary materials not being used for instructional purposes may become Skinny Books. For example, secure consecutive titles from the Cowboy Sam series and separate each book into its individual stories.

Two companies that sell new and used basals are Adams Book Company (50 Washington Street, Brooklyn, New York 11210) and Wilcox and Follett (1000 West Washington Boulevard, Chicago, Illinois 60607).

3. Mount and label each story as a Skinny Book. After trimming off the top and bottom white space, staple or sew each Skinny Book into a manila or wallpaper sample folder. Legal-size folders are best for preprimers because two Skinny Book covers can be cut from one folder. For taller books the 8-1/2 x 11 inch folder is better.

If a story begins on the left side of the page or ends on the right side, you will need to staple, sew, or paste that page to the manila folder. On the outside record the name of the book and the number of the story to make it possible for children to read stories sequentially and facilitates refiling. Recording the title of the story is optional except when content-area stories are being used. Even then the topic is often more useful than the title.

4. Identify each set of Skinny Books by approximate reading level. This designation may be indicated by a magic marker dot, each color representing a different reading level. For example, a first- or second-grade classroom might use the following pattern:

Green   - Preprimer One

Red   - Preprimer Two

Orange   - Preprimer Three

White   - Primer (Use india ink.)

The fact that the first letters spell a word (GROW) facilitates quick indentification of the level. The next two levels may be represented by Blue and Yellow (BY) before the entire pattern is repeated.

5. House each set of Skinny Books in a convenient location. Basal reader stories may be filled by series and books with each set of Skinny Books placed in a separate location to prevent crowds of people. Large detergent boxes can be cut down into excellent containers. To provide stability, place a 2 x 4 inch board in the bottom of the box.

6. Develop a Group Analysis Chart to facilitate the assignment of suggested readings and to note each pupil's progress. On a spirit master mark off 1-1/2 inches at the left and 1-1/2 inches at the top. Divide the rest of the space into half-inch squares. The result will be a checkerboard with space down the side for 19 names and room across the top for 14 books. Record the names of the children and duplicate a large number of Group Analysis Charts. Two spirit masters are required per class.

As primary pupils complete each Skinny Book, you, an aide, a volunteer, or even an upper-grade student may record a check under the appropriate numbered selection (The 1-1/2 inch square in the upper left-hand corner of the chart can be used to indicate the title of the set of Skinny Books.). Separate charts can be used to represent different sets of Skinny Books.

To facilitate the selection of Skinny Books at pupils' independent reading levels, you should be certain that the materials use one or more levels below their instructional reading level as determined by an Initial Reading Inventory. Chart 8-4 contains a Skinny Book Checkoff Chart.

7. Discuss with the class the purpose and use of Skinny Books. At the primary and intermediate levels, discussion should focus on the following points:

A. Learning to read has two components -- studying skills and practicing them.

B. The more a person reads, the more he improves his reading.

453

CHART 8-4

SKINNY BOOK CHECKOFF CHART *

<u>AT</u> <u>HOME</u>
(Allyn, Bacon)

Story Number

Name	1	2	3	4	5	6	7	8	9	10	11	12
Barbara	✓	✓	✓	✓	✓	✓						
Brenda												
Candy	✓	✓	✓									
Denise	✓	✓	✓	✓								
Elaine	✓	✓	✓	✓	✓							
Freida												

* A check (✓) is placed beside the name of a pupil reading Skinny Books at that level. Other children are reading Skinny Books at another level and require a similar chart.

C. A person who wishes to improve his reading should try to read as many as one a day. By reading one book every other day, a person will read 100 during the year.

D. Whenever a new word appears, pupils should ask the Word Consultant for help. To foster retention of the word, they should write it in their notebooks for subsequent study. Knowledge of these new words is proof that they have improved their reading by using that book.

8. Develop a procedure for assuring that Skinny Books are actually read. Obviously no teacher can read

454

all of the selections a class of pupils might encounter. While a host of traditional practices are readily available, we have found one procedure especially effective.

Each child who completes a Skinny Book is asked to develop ten questions. As time permits, pupils challenge the teacher to a Book Report Contest. Each person asks his questions, and the teacher receives one point for responding correctly. When she is wrong, the pupil answers his own question and receives the point. Not only is the procedure highly motivating because it allows youngsters to fox the "old folks," it assures us that books have been read. After all, how else can one develop and answer questions?

It is interesting to note the progressive improvement in the quality of questions. Almost invariably the first Book Report Contest consists of questions such as (1) Was the boy's name John? (2) Did he live on a farm? (3) Did he like to go to the rodeo? Naturally you will have little difficulty in answering such questions correctly and winning the contest even though you haven't read the book.

After one or two such encounters, however, pupils suddenly change their interrogation pattern: (1) What was the boy's name? (2) Where did he live? (3) What did he like to do? Of course, you can no longer win. Nevertheless, your objective is accomplished.

One further advantage of this procedure lies in its use to help children improve their questioning practices. For example, when you help pupils improve their abilities to comprehend main ideas and major supporting details, sequence events, predict outcomes, draw conclusions, or note compare-contrast or cause-effect relationships, they can practice these skills and develop new kinds of questions. The game-like format facilitates a tremendous amount of learning.

Several variations of the Book Report Contest are possible. For example, pupils may challenge others who have already read their book. Or they may challenge visitors such as the principal, volunteers, or aides.

9. Assign homework requiring all pupils to read Skinny Books to their younger brothers and sisters or neighborhood children. This procedure serves several useful functions. First, it provides a "cover" for poor readers who are usually reluctant to use Skinny Books. When all members of a class or school are expected to read to young children, poor readers are not stigmatized by possessing lower-level materials nor penalized for reading them. After all, they must prepare their

homework assignments, and __all__ children are doing the same thing!

Second, young children, especially those who normally do not receive the benefits of extensive literary and listening experiences, can be assured of contact with at least 180 books during the school year. Research indicates that youngsters who are frequently "read to" subsequently make significant gains in achievement (129-131).

Third, effective use of media center facilities and increased contact with good books can be fostered by the media specialist's efforts to assist youngsters in locating books appropriate to the age and interest levels of their siblings. Besides assisting school-age youngsters, we are attempting to prevent reading failure among the pre-school population.

Fourth, the entire activity can serve as a highly effective springboard for working with intonation and non-verbal expression, for developing questioning procedures for interpreting pictures and print, and for considering such factors as careful and correct handling of books and left-to-right and top-to-bottom sequences.

Fifth, by asking parents to complete a form indicating their children's "teacher aide" activities, the school demonstrates its interest in communicating positively with the home. Parents can help children with their homework. See Chart 8-5 for a sample format of a reporting form.

CHART 8-5

TEACHER AIDE'S REPORT

On _____ January 7 _____ , 19__86__, I read

_____ The Big Orange Thing _____ to

_____ Rodney Floyd and Amy Hatley _____ .

I thought the story was (too easy, too hard)

for____them____. _____They_____ disliked it.

Signed _____ Todd Hatley _____

Witness _____ Mrs. Brice Smith _____

__Practice__ __Twelve__: Provide daily opportunities for children to read in school.

456

Lyman Hunt (421) is generally credited with instituting sustained silent reading procedures. Sometimes referred to as USSR (Uninterrupted Sustained Silent Reading <421, 616) or SSR (Sustained Silent Reading <332, 500, 520), or Book Time (416) for first grades, the procedure often provides time for all children and sometimes teachers and other school personnel to read at the same time.

An alternate way of providing planned reading time is to schedule it as an independent activity for children to do while you work with another group of youngsters. We recommend that each child read independently at least 30 minutes daily at school and another 30 minutes at home.

<u>Practice Thirteen</u>: Provide frequent opportunities for pupils who have acquired initial competence in a skill to teach it to others. Many youngsters who are in the process of acquiring mastery of a particular skill need an abundance of practice to internalize the information. Because it is difficult to convince children who have just performed admirably on an immediate recall test that they still need assistance, we must utilize motivating ways of providing further practice. Perhaps the most effective technique is being a teacher's aide. Thus the child who is learning reinforces his newly-acquired knowledge by teaching it to someone else, either a peer or a younger pupil.

Confucius is said to have noted that "a thousand mile's journey begins with the first step." Extensive reinforcement activities can be highly effective in ensuring that the first steps toward literacy are strong and confident.

Summary

This chapter contends that many instructional practices currently utilized in our schools are quite inappropriate for the educationally disadvantaged child. We suggested a number of specific classroom practices which can be used to provide extensive reinforcement experiences. During the course of our discussion we propose seven criteria to be used when providing independent workbook activities.

Underlying this chapter is the philosophy that if we do nothing else, we must be certain that our instruction results in pupils' mastery of the basic sight vocabulary and word analysis, vocabulary, and comprehension skills. Until these are developed, no significant academic growth is likely to occur. As Schiffman observes, "If the newly acquired reading skills are not augmented by substantial reinforcement and practice..., there is little reason to anticipate significant long run benefit. No one would expect a good diet at the age of eight to protect against malnutrition at ten (629:136)."

FOR FURTHER READING

Bridge, Connie, Peter N. Winograd, and Darliene Haley, "Using Predictable Materials Vs. Preprimers to Teach Beginning Sight Words," Reading Teacher, XXXVI, No. 9 (May, 1983), 884-891.

Canney, George F., "Making Games More Relevant for Reading," Reading Teacher, XXXII, No. 1 (October, 1978), 10-14.

"Children's Books About Special Children: A Selected Bibliography," Childhood Education, LVII, No. 4 (March-April, 1981), 205-208.

Culyer, Richard, "How to Develop a Locally-Relevant Basic Sight Word List," Vineyard Newsletter, II, No. 2 (1976), 11-19.

Gambrell, Linda B., "Getting Started with Sustained Silent Reading and Keeping It Going," Reading Teacher, XXXII, No. 3 (December, 1978), 328-331.

Ganz, Paul, and Mary B. Theofield, "Suggestions for Starting SSR," Journal of Reading, XVII, No. 8 (May, 1974), 614-616.

Gilles, Joanne, "Preferred Picks: Materials for Classroom Teachers with Special Students," The Pointer, XXIV, No. 3 (Spring, 1980), 82-87.

Greenbaum, Judith, Marilyn Varas, and Geraldine Markel, "Using Books about Handicapped Children," Reading Teacher, XXXIII, No. 4 (January, 1980), 416-419.

Hong, Laraine K., "Modifying Sustained Silent Reading for Beginning Readers," Reading Teacher XXXIV, No. 8 (May, 1981), 888-891.

Jett-Simpson, Mary, "21 Ways to Build Positive Experiences with Books and Reading," Wisconsin State Reading Association Journal, XVI, No. 2 (Winter, 1982) 6-7.

Madden, Peter, "Magazines and Newspapers for Children," Childhood Education, LIII, No. 6 (April-May, 1977) 328-330, 332, 334-336.

McCracken, Robert A., and Marlene J. McCracken, "Modeling is the Key to Sustained Silent Reading," Reading Teacher, XXXI, No. 4 (January, 1978), 406-408.

McNamara, Margaret, "Reading is Fun-damental," in Reading Rx: Better Teachers, Better Supervisors, Better Programs, pp. 123-128, ed. Joseph S. Nemeth. Newark, Del.: IRA, 1975.

Moe, Alden J., and Carol Hopkins, "Jingles, Jokes, Limericks, Poems, Proverbs, Puns, Puzzles and Riddles: Fast Reading for Reluctant Readers," Language Arts, LV, No. 8 (November-December, 1978), 957-965, 1003.

_____, Carol Hopkins, and Joan Halajko, "Published Games for Reading Instruction," Indiana Reading Quarterly, VII, No. 2 (Winter, 1975), 13-15, 24.

Monson, Dianne, and Cynthia Shurtleff, "Altering Attitudes Toward the Physically Handicapped Through Print and Non-Print Media," Language Arts, LVI, No. 2 (February, 1979), 163-170.

Moore, Jesse, Clarence J. Jones, and Douglas C. Miller, "What We Know After a Decade of Sustained Silent Reading," Reading Teacher, XXXIII, No. 4 (January, 1980), 445-449.

Polloway, Edward A., and Carolyn H. Polloway, "Survival Words for Disabled Readers," Academic Therapy, XVI, No. 4 (March, 1981), 443-448.

Roeder, Harold H., and Nancy Lee, "25 Teacher-Tested Ways to Encourage Voluntary Reading," Reading Teacher, XXVII, No. 1 (October, 1973), 48-50.

Sadoski, Mark C., "Ten Years of Uninterrupted Sustained Silent Reading," Reading Improvement, XVII, No. 2 (Summer, 1980), 153-156.

Wagoner, Shirley A., "The Portrayal of the Cognitively Disabled in Children's Literature," Reading Teacher, XXXVII, No. 6 (February, 1984), 502-508.

459

List A

INTEREST INVENTORY ONE

Name _____ Date _____

Grade _____ Age _____

1. How many brothers do you have? _____

   What are their ages? _____

2. How many sisters do you have? _____

   What are their ages? _____

3. What kind of work does your father do? _____

   _____

   Your mother? _____

4. List three things you usually do after school.

   _____

5. List three things you usually do on the weekends

   or in the summer. _____

   _____

6. How much time each day do you usually watch TV?

   _____

   List your favorite programs. _____

   _____

7. How often do you go to the movies? _____

   List your favorite kinds of movies (animal

   stories, fairy tale, war, mystery, etc.)

   _____

8. Have you ever been to a zoo? _____ Circus?

    _____ Fair? _____ Museum? _____

    Summer camp? _____

9. Have you ever ridden in a plane? _____ Ship?

    _____ Small boat? _____ Train? _____

10. Do you like to play games? _____ If so,

    what are your favorites? _____

11. Do you play or watch sports? _____ If so, what

    are your favorites? _____

12. Are you a member of any clubs? _____ If so,

    name them. _____

13. Do you have any hobbies? _____ If so, name

    them. _____

14. Do you like to read? _____ Why or why not?

    _____

15. If you like to read, tell what kinds of books you

    like. _____

    _____

16. List some really good books you have read. _____

    _____

17. List some books (or kinds of books) you do not

    like. _____

    _____

18. Do you like school? _____

461

19. What is your favorite subject? _____

    Why?_____

20. Which subject do you like least? _____

    Why?_____

21. What would you like to do when you grow up? _____

    _____

22. Name three people you want to be like. _____

    _____

23. Why do you want to be like them? _____

    _____

24. Do you like to read to other people? _____

    Do you like other people to read to you? _____

25. How many hours a week do you read just for fun?

    _____

26. How many books do you own? _____

    How did you get them? _____

27. Who are your best friends? _____

    _____

    What do you like about them? _____

    _____

28. If you could have three wishes, what would they

    be?_____

INTEREST INVENTORY TWO

TYPES OF TRADE BOOKS

Name: _____   Date: _____.

Age: _____   Teacher: _____.

Grade:_____   Independent Level: _____.

Directions: We are interested in helping you find books
that you want to read. Different kinds of books are
listed below. Circle the 1 if you would REALLY LIKE to
read that kind of book. Circle the 2 if you would LIKE
to read that kind. Circle the 3 if you would NOT LIKE to
read that kind.   If this list does not mention your
favorite kind of book, write it in.

Animals	1 2 3	Fiction 1 2 3
Dinosaurs	1 2 3	History 1 2 3
Horses	1 2 3	Hunting, Fishing 1 2 3
Pets	1 2 3	Jobs 1 2 3
Talking Animals	1 2 3	Jokes-riddles 1 2 3
Wild Animals	1 2 3	Mysteries 1 2 3
_____	1 2 3	Science 1 2 3
Bible Stories	1 2 3	Science fiction 1 2 3
Biographies	1 2 3	Short stories 1 2 3
About men	1 2 3	Space 1 2 3
About women	1 2 3	Sports 1 2 3
About Blacks	1 2 3	Baseball 1 2 3
About Indians	1 2 3	Basketball 1 2 3
About _____	1 2 3	Football 1 2 3
Cars, trucks, Motorcycles	1 2 3	_____ 1 2 3
Fairy Tales	1 2 3	_____ 1 2 3

Section III. PROVIDING GROWTH IN BASIC SKILLS
DEVELOPMENT

464

TEACHING SELECTED WORD ANALYSIS SKILLS

Introduction

At various intervals throughout this book we have referred to the basic word analysis, vocabulary, comprehension, and study skills. This chapter pursues the first of these topics. Previously we accepted William Gray's definition of reading (365) as a "meaning-getting" process involving the use of word analysis skills such as context, phonics, structure, and the dictionary as the supporting cast.

With this thought in mind, let us briefly explore six important related questions.

A. What are the various kinds of word analysis skills, and what are their advantages and disadvantages?

B. What is the typical general sequence for presenting phonic and structural skills?

C. How can each pupil's phonic knowledge be determined as a basis for grouping and teaching?

D. What guidelines can be used in developing word analysis skills?

E. How can phonic and structural skills be taught in context to associate meaning and pronunciation?

F. What kinds of activities can be used to reinforce phonic skills?

Discussion of each of these is considered in a separate section in this chapter.

Questions

A. <u>What are the various kinds of word analysis skills, and what are their advantages and disadvantages?</u>

Regardless of his age, a reader has approximately eight options when he encounters an unknown word in print. He may

1. Do nothing and skip it.

2. Ask someone.

3. Use configuration clues.

4. Use picture clues.

5. Employ phonic anaylsis.

6. Employ structural analysis.

7. Employ contextual analysis.

8. Use a dictionary.

Numbers one and two -- that is, skipping the word or asking someone -- are ineffective techniques. The practice of skipping the words is of negative value because it usually leads to difficulty in comprehending the meaning of a sentence or passage. While it does serve to meet an immediate need, the practice of asking someone for assistance is of little long-term value because it results in the pronunciation of a specified word rather than in the development of skill in analyzing words.

Numbers three and four -- that is, using configuration and picture clues -- are initial and temporary aids in word analysis. They provide initial assistance for beginning readers but are of little value for pupils above the second-grade reading level.

Numbers five through eight -- the use of phonic, structural, and contextual analysis, and the dictionary -- are the permanent aids in word analysis. While initial instruction in the use of these techniques occurs in the first grade, any necessary reintroduction and extensive reinforcement should be provided throughout the school years. With minor exceptions, these four techniques provide the most efficient and effective ways of analyzing unknown words.

Having mentioned eight possible options a reader might consider when encountering new words, let us discuss the last six, some in greater detail than others. We shall ignore the first practice as ineffective and the second as inefficient.

3. Configuration refers to the shape of words. As an initial aid, we have said, the discrimination of shapes has its advantages. There are two basic types of configuration. The first type is external. Consider the

466

word <u>father</u>. Its configuration is ⬚. The configuration of monkey is ⬚. A youngster just learning to read sometimes finds the overall shape, or gestalt, of a word helpful in pronouncing it. But what happens when he begins to encounter a host of new words, many with the same external pattern? For instance, note this pattern: ⬚. <u>Book</u>, <u>bark</u>, <u>bank</u>, <u>hand</u>, <u>head</u>, and many more simple words introduced in the first and second grades conform to this pattern. At this point the use of configuration becomes not an aid but a handicap.

The second type of configuration is internal. Notice the word <u>look</u>. Some teachers encourage youngsters to remember the word by its two eyes "looking" at us. But what about <u>moon</u>, <u>book</u>, <u>boot</u>, <u>took</u>, etc., which also have "two eyes"? Here again, configuration eventually becomes a handicap rather than an aid. As a useful analysis technique, it must limit itself to the early part of the first grade.

4. Picture clues are used most frequently at the primary reading levels. Certainly in the very early grades they have a temporary value. Most basal readers employ picture clues. The picture may show a boy and a girl playing with a bright red ball. Sally, or Mike, or Ricky will then say, "I want to play _____ too." The unknown word, of course, is <u>ball</u>. A quick look at the picture provides the necessary cue. A similar picture found on one of the succeeding pages of the basal reader may cue the proper response until the young reader is able to pronounce the word without a picture clue.

Beyond the early primary years, however, picture clues contribute little toward word analysis development. First, they do not teach any permanent skills. Second, they may distract attention from the graphic text. The reader's tendency to abandon the printed message in search of a pictoral clue inhibits the development of left-to-right eye movements and causes the young reader to lose his place and often his train of thought. Third, many words cannot be pictorially represented. Examples include <u>honor</u>, <u>truth</u>, <u>better</u>, and <u>nice</u>. More crucially, the most difficult words a child is asked to learn, i.e., those included on the Dolch Basic Word List, are rarely capable of being pictorially represented. We cannot use pictures to represent <u>how</u>, <u>who</u>, <u>why</u>, <u>when</u>, <u>then</u>, <u>they</u>, <u>them</u>, <u>where</u>, <u>said</u>, <u>and</u>, <u>was</u>, <u>saw</u>, <u>these</u>, and <u>those</u>. Fourth, the number of pictures in books decreases as printed material increases, in effect forcing older readers to rely on techniques other than picture clues. So picture clues are a useful but temporary aid in developing effective word-analysis skills.

5. <u>Phonic analysis</u> is the first of the permanent identification skills. Simply stated, this skill involves the pronunciation of a printed wordform by associating letters with corresponding speech sounds and then blending the information into meaningful wholes. Phonic analysis is sometimes referred to as the use of letter-sound associations, sound-symbol relationships, or phoneme-grapheme correspondences.

The primary advantage of phonics lies in the fact that it does, in a large number of cases, result in the pronunciation of an unknown word. Some disadvantages, however, should be mentioned. First, the fact that a youngster can pronounce words does not mean that he understands their meanings. Far too many children call words but cannot read. This fact is true both at the primary and intermediate levels.

Many primary teachers hear parents say, "But I know Calvin can read. I heard him just last night." Even teachers often succumb to this pitfall when they use oral reading ability as a substitute for comprehension checks based on silent reading. Second, youngsters taught to read primarily or exclusively by an isolated phonic procedure often become word-by-word readers. They spend a great deal of time analyzing and reanalyzing words they should already know at sight. This tends to retard development of an appropriate rate of reading.

Third, typical teaching practices used in presenting the phonic skills often present consonants and consonant blends (or clusters) in isolation and distort the sounds they represent. The letter <u>b</u> often becomes /buh/; <u>c</u> /kuh/; <u>d</u> /duh/. For many pupils this practice inhibits the development of the ability to blend consonant sounds as well as consonant and vowel sounds into recognizable wholes. Fourth, many words or parts of words are phonically irregular. These include a large number of the basic sight words already mentioned as the most difficult for children to master. Examples of basic words with irregular elements include <u>who</u>, <u>woman</u>, <u>give</u>, <u>get</u>, <u>come</u>, <u>sure</u>, <u>was</u>, and <u>their</u>. Therefore this technique is of little or no value insofar as they are concerned.

6. <u>Structural analysis</u> involves the breaking down of words into syllables, base words, root words, and affixes (prefixes and suffixes). The major advantage of the use of structural analysis is that it does assist a reader in breaking down longer words into their more manageable components. This process naturally facilitates the pronunciation of many terms.

One disadvantage of structural analysis is its dependence on its sister skill, phonic analysis. A youngster who can break a word down into syllables but cannot pronounce the syllables still has a problem. Second, many of the structural generalizations regarding syllabication include a number of exceptions. Third, the syllabication aspect of structural analysis does not produce meaning, although the affixes and root words may.

7. Contextual analysis involves the determination of the pronunciation of a word by its use in a sentence of paragraph. Examples include the following:

> John fell down on the sidewalk, and his nose began to _____.

> Then John began to _____.

Even without seeing the first word, you know it is bleed. The word fits and completes the sentence thought. The second sentence leads you to expect the word cry. Many times a word can be pronounced by its context alone.

To develop a pupil's ability to use context effectively, present sentences or paragraphs similar to the one above and omit the words. The youngster could mention several logical choices to complete the blanks. For example, a number of answers might be given in the following setting.

> Mother said, "Tom, how did you get so wet?"

> "I fell into a _____," Tom said.

Was it a pool, puddle, pond, stream, river, branch, creek, lake, or ditch? Who knows? Of course, if the words starts with a d, the answer is obvious. Context plus the initial consonant sound provides the answer. If the word begins with a p, there are at least three possibilities. If that word ends with a d, however, we know it is pond. Here the final consonant sound is also needed (508).

The primary advantage of context is that attention is focused on the written word as it relates to meaning. Word analysis and comprehension occur simultaneously. When a youngster pays attention to the context, he does not make many of the ridiculous "guesses" we sometimes hear.

Of course, context has its disadvantages. It may be ineffective in certain situations without the concurrent use of phonics. Furthermore, some words cannot be identified by the context in which they appear. Consider these sentences.

I see a _____.

Mr. _____ came to see me.

Here context does not provide sufficient clues. A "creative reader" who over-uses context may experience severe comprehension difficulties.

8. While the dictionary is a permanent aid in word analysis, it usually should not be employed initially or extensively. Certainly words with fine shades of meaning should be checked in the dictionary, but over-use of this reference is a time-consuming and inefficient process, especially for poor readers.

Proper use of the dictionary is a high-level skill involving a number of specific sub-skills. For instance, a reader must understand and be able to alphabetize and to use guide words and the phonetic key. He must understand the meanings of the terms synonym, antonym, homonym, and a wide range of additional dictionary vocabulary. He must be able to determine which definition is appropriate for his use. Unless these skills have been acquired, there is little value in expecting a youngster to refer to the dictionary for his word analysis needs.

The major advantage of the use of a dictionary, then, is access to a wide variety of information on practically every aspect of pronunciation and meaning. The major disadvantages are three in number. First, pupils must possess numerous phonic, structural, and contextual skills plus other dictionary-related proficiencies in order to use the material. Second, a dictionary is not always available for immediate use. Third, frequent recourse to this reference interferes with the train of thought and interest. It simply is too time consuming.

This discussion completes our review of the ineffective, inefficient, temporary, and permanent aids on word identification. We have listed and briefly considered the major advantages and disadvantages of each. Keeping these points in mind, let us now consider the broad spectrum of skills involved in word analysis.

No one of these skills exists in isolation from the others. Phonic analysis is useful, but it depends on context for meaning. Structural analysis is also helpful, but phonic analysis is needed to pronounce each syllable, and contextual skills are needed for meaning.

Context is useful, but phonic and structural analysis or the dictionary may be necessary to decide which of several definitions is the appropriate response. Then, too, the dictionary is useful, but its effectiveness depends on the reader's ability to (1) understand phonic and structural analysis to use the key words, and (2) select the meaning appropriate to the context of the story.

So it is that the permanent aids to word identification are interdependent. They do not -- they cannot -- exist in isolation. A teacher who presents or over-emphasizes only one or two of these aids does not give youngsters the necessary variety of techniques they need to cope with every reading situation.

A second comment is derived from the first. Each of these techniques is appropriate at certain times. Children should be encouraged to try a second technique or combination of techniques if the first does not work. A knowledge of and proficiency in a variety of techniques coupled with the ability to shift from one to another as the occasion demands helps to ensure that reading competence will develop. Once again we need to encourage and enable children to be eclectic (673).

Let us expand on this idea. Each of the sentences below includes an underlined term which might be identified by one or more of the permanent word analysis skills. Check yourself to see how well you can determine the appropriate techniques. Consider both pronunciation and meaning.

1. We saw a <u>snipe</u> fly to the top of the barn.

2. Billy saw a <u>locomotive</u> in town.

3. Tom got out the old <u>lawn</u> <u>mower</u> and started to cut the grass.

4. Mother <u>put</u> <u>up</u> soup all day long.

Number one may be pronounced by phonics and defined by context. The reader who recognizes the influence of a final <u>e</u> on a preceding vowel of an accented syllable if only one consonant or consonant digraph intervenes can pronounce the word with little difficulty.

Number two depends mainly on structure with support from phonics. The reader who knows that a consonant between two vowels often begins a new syllable can syllabicate the word (lo-co-mo-tive), keeping the <u>tive</u> intact. Although meaning might not create any problems,

471

a child will need to consult a dictionary if the word is not in his oral vocabulary.

Number three depends on context. The reader who experiences difficulty in identifying the words should be encouraged to read through the sentence and then decide what makes sense. We suggest that you not ask the pupil to sound out the first word as /luh/+/aw/+/nuh/.

The last example contains a regional expression which normally creates difficulty for readers from other geographical areas. Pupils who think Mother stacked jars or cans of soup on shelves all day long should be encouraged to refer to a dictionary for a more appropriate meaning.

A third comment regarding an eclectic teaching procedure is this: Before introducing a skill to a group of youngsters, determine which pupils already possess the information by the use of a series of diagnostic pretests. We shall return to this point later in the chapter.

Many pupils are bored because they already understand and apply the skills being presented. A quick check prior to teaching a skill or lesson would help prevent this. Unfortunately, some teachers rationalize, "The review will be good for them." Those who already possess the skill about to be taught could more effectively use their time reading.

Fourth, a great deal of controversy has centered around the question, "Which is better -- phonics or sight vocabulary?" There need not be a problem here. When the youngster begins to read, the first words he learns are the basic sight words. Sometime later, after he has mastered some sight words, he begins to acquire phonic generalizations. Common elements in his sight vocabulary are used for this purpose. Three or four sight words beginning with the sound represented by b, for instance, can be used to develop the appropriate sound-symbol relationship. The Single Concept Cards are especially useful for developing sight vocabulary words containing a specific sound.

The teaching of phonic skills, then, is derived from sight vocabulary words. As far as pronouncing words is concerned, the objective of reading instruction is to make every word a sight word, that is, one recognizable immediately. So an extensive sight vocabulary comes from words originally developed by phonic analysis. Each reinforces the other and provides a background for the development of further competence. Our overall goal of reading instruction is to develop readers who understand, readers who think critically, readers who react to and act on what they read. And they must be able to identify and recognize words in order to do all of this.

The fifth and last point is this: The word analysis skills do not develop naturally. Like other skills they must be taught and reviewed -- systematically and sequentially (89, 363, 747) -- at all grade levels, including middle school (372) and high school (29, 95, 406, 701). This job is the responsibility of each teacher, and a portion of our salaries comes to us with the expectation that we can -- and do -- teach the basic reading skills.

B. What is a typical general sequence for presenting phonic and structural skills?

We have long contended that all learning has an over-arching sequence that can rarely be ignored without causing severe damage to the learning process. The purpose of this section is to present a typical general skills sequence for phonic and structural analysis and to comment briefly on definitions of various components as well as their significance. Please note: The following sequence is general, not specific. There is no such thing as a specific sequence of phonic and structural skills (673) except as it relates to a particular source of material. Refer to Chart 9A-1.

CHART 9A-1

GENERAL SEQUENCE OF PHONIC AND STRUCTURAL SKILLS

I. Reading Readiness skills

    A. Visual discrimination and memory

    B. Auditory discrimination and memory

II. Reading skills (Letter-sound associations, sound-symbol correspondences, phonics, or phoneme-grapheme relationships)

    A. Consonants -- initial, final, medial

    B. Consonant clusters and digraphs -- initial, final, medial

    C. Vowels -- Short, long, digraphs, r-controlled, diphthongs, special cases

    D. Structure -- Base words, root words, affixes (prefixes and suffixes), syllabication

E. Accents -- Primary, secondary.

You should remember Chart 9A-1 includes information on phonics and structure only. Dictionary use is involved only incidentally, and contextual application not at all. Also note that consideration is focused here only on several aspects of word analysis. Vocabulary and comprehension are not involved.

Now let us review some terms as they are used in this chapter and discuss the relative placement of various items. In Chapter 4B we observed that <u>visual discrimination</u> refers to a person's ability to note differences and likenesses in shapes. As applied to reading, the ability refers specifically to visually distinguishing individual letters and words from each other. A pupil with good visual discrimination should be able to note that <u>b</u> looks different from <u>d</u>, <u>p</u> from <u>q</u>, <u>e</u> from <u>a</u>, <u>c</u> from <u>e</u>, <u>m</u> from <u>n</u>. He should also recognize the visual differences in words such as <u>diary</u> and <u>dairy</u>, <u>form</u> and <u>from</u>, <u>want</u> and <u>went</u>, and <u>through</u>, <u>though</u>, and <u>thorough</u>.

Visual discrimination is not the same as <u>visual acuity</u>, which refers to a person's ability to see either at near-point or far-point. People with almost perfect visual acuity may have very poor visual discrimination. The former deals with the ability to see, the latter with the images the mind records.

Remember that <u>auditory discrimination</u> (AD) refers to a person's ability to note differences and likenesses in sounds. As applied to reading, the ability refers to distinguishing between the sounds which are represented by the alphabetic symbols. A person with good AD should be able to note that the sound represented by <u>b</u> is different from the sound represented by <u>p</u>, <u>k</u> from <u>g</u>, and <u>f</u> from <u>th</u>. He should also recognize the auditory differences in words such as <u>pin</u> and <u>pen</u>, <u>build</u> and <u>built</u>, and <u>picture</u> and <u>pitcher</u>.

AD is not the same as <u>auditory acuity</u>, which refers to a person's ability to hear. People with almost perfect auditory acuity may have very poor AD. The former refers to the ability to hear, the latter to the ability to differentiate between sounds.

Before a youngster can learn to read via a phonics procedure, he normally must possess a certain degree of facility in one or both of these discrimination areas. A marked inability to function effectively in one of the reading readiness skills may result in total reading failure if a teacher neglects to provide instruction and practice in the stronger area while attempting to

474

remediate the weaknesses in the deficient aspect.

For example, research indicates that disadvantaged youngsters tend to be more visual that auditory (667). Indeed, Wepman (735) contends that for some children normal development of AD can be delayed until age eight. The educational implications are clear. A youngster with poor AD cannot be expected to learn effectively by an auditory modality, i.e., phonics. Nor can many slow or disadvantaged children (246, 512b, 522, 735). Yet the common technique (and sometimes the only one) used by many primary teachers involves a phonic procedure. Many children who cannot discriminate between sounds are expected to omit that step and advance to phonic instruction. This tendency to overlook the value of the preceding proficiency in order to present the more sophisticated reading material is one of the major causes of school difficulties in learning.

A second cause of reading difficulty is closely allied to the first - the failure of some teachers to recognize that some pupils learn significantly better by one sensory modality than by the others. The three major sensory modalities are visual, auditory, and kinesthetic (sense of touch and movement). (We consider tactile as being interrelated with kinesthetic.)

A third cause of reading difficulty is the tendency of some teachers to teach according to their own strengths rather than those of their pupils. In practice, many teachers seem to identify themselves with one of two opposing viewpoints: (1) Teach to a child's strengths since this is the area in which he is best able to learn (744). (2) Teach to a child's weaknesses since he obviously requires assistance in this area.

We have already advocated a middle-ground approach, an eclectic procedure. That is, we believe a teacher should begin her instruction by building on the child's diagnosed strengths. After he has accumulated a background of successful experiences, the child should be provided instruction and practice in the areas known to be deficient. At no time should the strength-based teaching activities be eliminated. They should continue to be used for two purposes: (1) to insure continuous progress in at least one medium of learning, and (2) to provide frequent successful experiences to offset initial difficulties with the weak channel of acquiring information.

To be more specific: Suppose Francisco has poor AD but learns well through a visual approach. For some time to come, Francisco may be perfectly capable of continuing to learn rapidly and effectively only through a look-say procedure. The time may come, however, when Francisco will no longer be able to cope with the number of words being presented. Nor will he be able to identify new words after the security of a controlled vocabulary is past. By this time far too many words will engulf him almost simultaneously, making his learning procedure of mastering one word at a time almost useless.

Francisco needs to acquire facility in AD, a prerequisite to mastery of the phonic skills. An intensive program in phonics will certainly not yield beneficial results because he does not possess the essential background competency. Unless we make adequate provisions for taking advantage of pupil strengths and teaching prerequisite skills, many youngsters will never develop to their fullest reading potential. Success in reading requires successful experiences in the reading readiness skills

Now let us consider the reading skills. The use of letter-sound associations requires a person to relate the arbitrary set of alphabetic symbols to the speech sounds they represent. A person with good auditory-visual discrimination should be able to note that boy, bat, ball, box, and Bill all begin with the same sound and the same letter.

Consonants are generally presented before vowels for several reasons. First, most consonants consistently represent the same sound. A few represents two major sounds: C (/s/, /k/); G (/g/, /j/); and S (/s/, /z/). On the other hand, a vowel may represent many sounds. A may be used to indicate at least nine different sounds.

A second reason for beginning with consonants is the frequency with which they initiate words. The vast majority of words begin with consonants, and English-speaking youngsters are expected to learn to read from left to right, identifying words in that sequence.

Most teaching materials present beginning consonant sounds first since items in this position are easiest to learn. Later the same sounds are presented at the ends of words, and finally in the medial position. Examples of words with a b in each position would include bat, rob, and robot. We do not consider it very important or productive to emphasize medial consonant sounds since most of these become initial or final sounds when syllabication is applied. For example, the b's in robot, tumbler, cabin, and timber are only medial until the words are syllabicated. Then robot and timber have initial b's in their second syllables, cabin has a final b in its first syllable, and tumbler has an initial cluster in the second syllable.

There are 21 fairly consistent consonant letters, all letters except a, e, i, o, and u. Two consonant letters, w and y, are vowels except when they initiate a word or syllable. Two vowel letters, i and u, often function as consonants.

After the most frequently used consonants have been learned, we present the common consonant clusters and consonant digraphs. A consonant cluster represents two or more joined, or blended, consonant sounds. Most often the consonant clusters include either an l, r, or s. A youngster who does not make associations relating to consonant sounds cannot learn the clusters without first mastering the prerequisite skill. For example, if Amy does not associate b with the initial sound of boy or l with the initial sound of lamb, she cannot be expected to associate bl with the initial sound of blue.

A consonant digraph consists of two or more letters which represent a sound different from the ones they normally represent when used individually. All of the consonant digraphs we recognize contain the letter h. Both consonant clusters and consonant digraphs are normally presented in the initial position and later the final and medial positions. Once again, we contend that the study of medial position clusters and digraphs is not especially productive.

As mentioned earlier, the vowel letters may represent many different sounds. Most materials consider short sounds before long sounds. The major reason for presenting the more difficult items first is one of functional utility. The most frequently-used vowel sounds in beginning reading materials are short, hence the desirability of providing instruction with maximal application opportunities.

Short vowel sounds are presented both in initial and medial positions (and, cat). The long vowel sounds usually follow the pattern long vowel-consonant-silent e, which is acceptable for accented syllables.

Vowel digraphs are presented next. These are two vowels letters which represent one speech sound. That sound may be either long or short. Many basal readers and phonics workbooks teach a rule expressed in one of the two following ways:

1. If two vowels go walking, the first one does the talking.

2. If two vowels come together, the first one is long, and the second one is silent.

Research studies have indicated these two different ways of expressing the same idea are incorrectly stated (37, 128, 300). A generalization or a rule or a principle must be true in a majority of cases or it becomes an exception rather than a guideline. In a majority of the primary-level words, the principle stated above is not applicable. The educational implication is that teachers who present this rule teach their youngsters to be wrong more than they are right. To be really effective, a generalization should apply to at least three-fourths of the possible situations (128). We can hardly afford to consume our time teaching "principles" which are exceptions.

Consider the following words and their vowels.

1.	boat	4.	tough	7.	their
2.	chief	5.	hair	8.	broad
3.	bread	6.	eight		

Boat conforms to the generalization. The oa represents the long sound with which we associate /ō/. Chief is an exception. The ie represents the long sound /ē/. Bread is an exception. The ea represents the short sound of /e/. Tough is an exception. The ou represents the short sound of /u/. Hair is an exception. The ai plus r represents an R-controlled sound. Eight is an exception. The ei before g represents the long sound /ā/. Their is an exception. The eir represents an R-controlled sound. Broad is an exception. The oa represents the /au/ sound.

These few examples should indicate rather clearly the danger of teaching children to look for two vowels and to consider the first as representing a long vowel sound. The generalization applies only to vowel pairs ai, ay, oa, and ee.

R-controlled vowels represent modified sounds. The visual pattern consists of one or two vowels plus an r. In the case of two vowels plus r, one vowel may be a terminal e, or both vowels may precede the r. The most frequent R-controlled combinations are ar; err, air, and are; or; and er, ir, and ur.

Diphthongs are vowel pairs which represent a sound different from the ones they often represent. The most frequent diphthongs are same-sounding pairs: oi and oy, au and aw, ou and ow. Two other sets have different sounds: oo and oo, ew, ui, and ue. All of the sounds represented by diphthongs are exceptions to the rule regarding "two vowels go walking."

Special cases include the sound represented by the schwa and the L-controlled pattern. While dictionaries differ in the diacritical marks they use to represent the sound of /uh/, some now use the schwa symbol (**ə**) to represent any /uh/ sound, whether or not it occurs in an accented syllable.

After the major vowel patterns have been presented, most materials introduce structural analysis. Base and root words, affixes (prefixes and suffixes), and syllabication principles are presented. Thus <u>farm</u> becomes <u>farms</u>, <u>farmed</u>, <u>farmer</u>, <u>farming</u>, <u>farmers</u>. <u>Tie</u> becomes <u>tied</u>, <u>ties</u>, <u>untied</u>, <u>unties</u>, <u>untie</u>. Roots, affixes, and syllabication are so interrelated as to be almost indistinguishable. The most frequent affixes are suffixes rather than prefixes. Common suffixes include <u>s</u>, <u>es</u>, <u>ed</u>, <u>ing</u>, <u>er</u>, <u>est</u>, <u>ly</u>, <u>ful</u>, and '<u>s</u>.

Finally, principles relating to word accenting are presented. The primary accent is considered first, and, as multi-syllable words appear, the secondary accent is introduced.

Some good books which focus on the phonic skills have been written by Durkin (268), Heilman (399), Schell (627), and Wilson and Hall (744).

C. <u>How can each pupil's phonic knowledge be determined as a basis for grouping and teaching?</u>

Since it is inappropriate to attempt to teach the letter-sound associations, or phonic skills, before determining each child's specific strengths and weaknesses (744), let us consider some simple diagnostic procedures arranged in categories. While they require very little time to administer, these diagnostic pretests (DPTs) reveal a wealth of material on which grouping and instruction can be based.

You might begin by administering the Wepman Auditory Discrimination Test (734) or the Culyer AUDIT (15) to identify the children who will require extensive experience at this level before becoming able to derive maximum benefit from the introduction of letter-sound associations.

Chart 9A-2 presents one form of the Wepman.

While Wepman suggests that each child receive an individual administration of the test, we have found it possible to obtain similar results by using the following group procedure:

1. Ask the children to number their papers from 1-40 (or provide mimeographed sheets containing the numbers).

479

CHART 9A-2
WEPMAN AUDITORY DISCRIMINATION TEST *
FORM II

#	Word pair	X	Y		#	Word pair	X	Y
1.	gear – beer		■		21.	bar – bar	■	
2.	cad – cab		■		22.	bum – bun		■
3.	led – lad		■		23.	lave – lathe		■
4.	thief – sheaf		■		24.	shot – shop		■
5.	sake – shake		■		25.	wedge – wedge	■	
6.	jail – jail	■			26.	suck – sock		■
7.	ball – ball	■			27.	vie – thy		■
8.	lake – lake	■			28.	rich – rich	■	
9.	bead – deed		■		29.	pit – kit		■
10.	rub – rug		■		30.	guile – dial		■
11.	wing – wing	■			31.	rash – wrath		■
12.	gall – goal		■		32.	chew – chew	■	
13.	pet – pit		■		33.	gag – sag		■
14.	lit – lick		■		34.	phase – phase	■	
15.	bug – bud		■		35.	sick – thick		■
16.	lass – lath		■		36.	wreath – reef		■
17.	cope – coke		■		37.	map – nap		■
18.	pool – tool		■		38.	muss – mush		■
19.	zone – zone	■			39.	cart – tart		■
20.	fret – threat		■		40.	cuff – cuss		■

2. Teach the children the meaning of _same_ and _different_. A sample procedure for doing so is contained in Chapter Ten.

3. Record a capital S and D on the chalkboard. Be sure children can copy the two letters. (Variation: Use a happy face and a sad face.)

4. Explain the procedure to be followed. The children will listen to you pronounce the words. Sometimes they will be the same, and sometimes they will be different. If the two words sound the same, the children should place an S (or happy face) on their papers. If the two words are different, the children should record a D (or sad face).

Provide sufficient practice to familiarize the children with the procedure. Pairs for "different" may be _bat_, _but_; _show_, _shoe_; _game_, _gain_ . Pairs for "same" may be _run_, _run_; _cheese_, _cheese_; _word_, _word_.

6. Pronounce each set of words clearly. Do not distort any sounds, (i.e., do not say _bug-guh_ for _bug_).

Stand behind the group so the children cannot see your lips move.

Since there are only two possible answers for each of the forty pairs of words, a child can receive an inflated score just by guessing.

The Wepman Auditory Discrimination Test, which measures gross rather than fine AD capabilities, identifies youngsters with severe AD difficulties and emphasizes the need for concentrated instruction in this area as well as the desirability of employing additional or alternative modes of learning.

Knowledge of this information makes it possible to select and use techniques presented in Chapter 4B. One caution: Like all other tests of this type, discrimination tests are dialectally biased. Therefore, extremely erratic patterns should be interpreted with care. After youngsters have been tested to determine the extent of their AD ability, you can administer the first category of tests covering letter-sound associations.

According to the general skills sequence presented earlier in this chapter, the consonant sound associations are taught first. Thus, you might administer Form A of the Diagnostic Tests in Chart 9A-3.

DIAGNOSTIC TESTS FOR INITIAL CONSONANT SOUNDS

Directions: Present one form of the following words and ask each pupil to try to pronounce each word. Note on a Class Analysis Chart whether or not he correctly identifies each initial sounds.

Examples:	Printed words	Sounds
	daffin	d
	porty	p

	Form A	Form B	Sounds
1.	sorple	sagle	s
2.	norpie	nofis	n
3.	gacker	guspy	g
4.	zurfel	zopple	z
5.	bim	bilp	b
6.	rister	roggin	r
7.	collup	canbra	k
8.	dist	dast	d
9.	verk	vorp	v
10.	limple	lobbis	l
11.	yonce	yast	y
12.	jast	jollum	j
13.	terba	tiffle	t
14.	wagle	wubs	w
15.	fosh	fube	f
16.	morge	merse	m
17.	piffle	porfy	p

18.	hurp	hickle	h
19.	kibe	keft	k
20.	cib	cild	s
21.	gend	gike	j

To avoid gathering information which will not be used, administer subsequent tests only to children who miss very few items. For example, a pupil who misses only one of 21 initial consonant items needs further diagnostic evaluation. His classmate who misses eleven items does not now evince that need. Further diagnosis for the latter pupil should occur only after he has achieved competence in his present areas of deficiency.

Tests for the next category of diagnosis, the Initial Consonant Blend and Digraph Sounds, are presented in Chart 9A-4.

CHART 9A-4

DIAGNOSTIC TESTS FOR INITIAL CONSONANT BLENDS

AND DIGRAPH SOUNDS

A. Initial Consonant Blend Sounds

Directions: Present one form of the following words and ask each pupil individually to try to pronounce each word. Note on a Class Analysis Chart whether or not he correctly identifies the two or three sounds represented by each initial consonant blend (cluster).

Examples: Printed Words   Sounds

                trooze   tr
                plurs   pl

Form A	Form B	Answers (Sounds)
1. grom	griz	gr
2. snull	snaff	sn
3. prot	prif	pr

483

4.	blit	blat	bl
5.	frud	frang	fr
6.	spoog	spef	sp
7.	gliz	glep	gl
8.	swez	swood	sw
9.	brep	brom	br
10.	skibe	skend	sk
11.	drupper	dron	dr
12.	stip	stug	st
13.	trosket	triddle	tr
14.	crung	crit	kr
15.	smil	smud	sm
16.	pline	plass	pl
17.	quam	quan	kw
19.	slud	slef	sl
20.	floop	flut	fl
21.	clat	clond	kl
22.	scug	scom	sk
23.	dwick	dwap	dw
24.	scros	scrang	skr
25.	splef	splom	spl
26.	squim	squit	skw
27.	sprom	sprim	spr
28.	strill	stref	str

B. Initial Consonant Digraph Sound

Directions: Present one form of the following words and ask each pupil to try to pronounce each word. Note on a Class Analysis Chart whether or not he correctly identifies the sounds represented by each initial consonant digraph.

1.	thopper	theddle	th
2.	phessy	phimmet	f
3.	choffle	chuppy	ch
4.	whull	whit	hw or w
5.	shomper	shuggle	sh

The last three diagnostic tests consider vowel patterns. Chart 9A-5 presents tests on the long and short vowels, Chart 9A-6 the diphthongs, and Chart 9A-7 the R-controlled sounds.

CHART 9A-5

DIAGNOSTIC TESTS FOR LONG AND SHORT VOWELS

Directions: Present one form of the following words and ask each pupil to try to pronounce each word. Note on a Class Analysis Chart whether or not he correctly identifies the sound represented by each vowel pattern.

	Form A	Form B	Answers (Sounds)
1.	jope	yope	ō
2.	gled	letch	e
3.	gabe	lafe	ā
4.	shug	thunk	u
5.	fap	tath	a
6.	mipe	sipe	ī
7.	lods	fod	o

485

8.	feen	neep	$\bar{e}$
9.	fube	pume	$\widehat{u}$
10.	nid	zilt	i
11.	tay	zay	$\bar{a}$
12.	preed	sleen	$\bar{e}$
13.	naid	baim	$\bar{a}$
14.	roaf	loab	$\bar{o}$

CHART 9A-6

DIAGNOSTIC TESTS FOR DIPHTHONG SOUNDS

Directions: Present one form of the following words and   ask each pupil to try to pronounce each word.   Note on   a   Class Analysis Chart whether or not   he   correctly identifies   the sounds represented by each vowel pattern.

	Form A	Form B	Answers (Sounds)
1.	troin	gloid	oy
2.	joom	gloop	$\overline{oo}$
3.	mouch	roush	ou
4.	cawn	stawn	aw
5.	groy	thoy	oy
6.	spown	glown	ou
7.	laut	raud	aw
8.	prue	slue	$\overline{oo}$
9.	juit	tuid	$\overline{oo}$

DIAGNOSTIC TESTS FOR R-CONTROLLED VOWEL SOUNDS

Directions: Present one form of the following words and ask each pupil to try to pronounce each word.   Note on   a   Class   Analysis Chart whether or not   he   correctly identifies   the   sound represented by   each   R-controlled vowel pattern.

Form A	Form B	Answers (Sounds)
1. smort	zorp	or
2. snarp	slart	ar
3. slear	flear	ear
4. murd	blurk	er
5. plair	zair	air
6. twer	sher	er
7. nare	slare	air
8. fleer	sweer	ear
9. glir	mir	er

After   each diagnostic test has been administered and scored,   you   can   chart the results   to   facilitate   the identification   of   specific   skills   which   should   be presented and the skills groups that should be organized. Except   for   pupils operating at the first-grade   reading level,   the   simplest   procedure is to complete   a   Class Analysis   Chart, listing the names of the pupils down the left side of the sheet and the number of each item across the   top.   Chart 9A-8 shows a Class Analysis Chart   (CAC) for the diagnostic pretest on initial consonants.

To   complete   the chart, simply record an   X   in   the appropriate   column   to   indicate   an   error.   After instruction and practice have been provided in all areas, administer the second form of the test and circle the X's to indicate proficiency.

CLASS ANALYSIS CHART

Initial Consonant Sounds	1 s (s)	2 n	3 g (g)	4 2	5 b	6 r	7 x (c)	8 d	9 v	10 l	11 y	12 j	13 t	14 w
Mona			x	x		x	x		x			x		
Nora							x		x					x
Opal	x			x		x					x	x		
Patsy			x	x			x				x			x
Rachel				x					x			x		
Sandy	x					x	x		x		x			x
Theresa			x									x		
Vera	x	x	x	x			x			x	x	x		x
Wandra							x							
Zora			x			x						x		

Grouping for skills instruction then becomes quite simple. When preparing to teach the letter-sound association for s, use the Class Analysis Chart to identify the pupils who should receive such guidance. All pupils with an X in that column receive instruction.

Because such groups are organized for a specific purpose, they will be disbanded as soon as the instructional objective has been met. In actual practice this may mean a skills group will meet for ten or fifteen minutes on two consecutive days and, if every pupil masters the item--which is quite unlikely--the group will simply fade into oblivion. A more realistic result is that the size of the group will change after a session or two, with those who experience difficulty in achieving initial mastery of the skill remaining until learning occurs or you decide the task was improperly assigned.

The end result of this procedure is that the diagnostic pretest on initial consonant sounds might identify 21 different specific needs, with two, or three being considered each week. That is, the 21 skills groups will not operate simultaneously; instead, the organizational plan for providing instruction in letter-sound associations skills groups might be prepared for the next several months.

Two skill groups may meet daily--one for children needing assistance at the lower levels and another for their more advanced classmates. The development of Class Analysis Charts is required to parallel the pretests presented in Charts 9A-2 through 9A-7.

One further reminder: many teachers regard such pretesting as a waste of time. They prefer to teach everyone in a certain group the same thing, whether or not he is ready for it, and whether or not he needs it. Although frequently justified as "reinforcement," the practice of teaching the entire group the same skill is an unfair procedure for children and a wasteful one insofar as the utilization of teaching and learning time is concerned. Except for most first-grade level readers, we do not believe that the page by page teaching of word analysis skills from a manual or workbook is sufficient to meet the needs of children. The assumption that pupils' reading levels and their skill needs correspond is incorrect.

D. **What guidelines can be used in developing word analysis skills?**

Despite the fact that the market is glutted with programs on one or more aspects of word identification, classroom procedures sometimes leave much to be desired. Hopefully the comments contained here will clarify key points and summarize pathways to more effective practices. The guidelines (157) are grouped into the following categories: (a) general, (b) letter-sound associations and syllabication, (c) context, (d) oral reading, (e) the dictionary, and (f) word recognition.

GENERAL

Guideline One: "Plan a comprehensive word analysis program in the classroom."

Readers who encounter unknown words have a variety of options. They can (a) ignore the word, (b) ask for help, (c) use the configuration, or shape, of the word, (d) use picture clues, (e) use phonics, (f) use context, (g) use syllabication, or (h) use a dictionary. As noted earlier, the first two options are of little or no value, for no skill development occurs. The next two options are temporary aids, and the last four options are the permanent aids to word analysis. Classroom reading instruction should focus on the last four areas.

Guideline Two: "Provide activities for teaching,

practice (testing), and reviewing."

Each of these types of activities is important, and each can make its own contribution to pupil competence in phonic knowledge. However, balance is important. To illustrate, if children receive mostly practice and reinforcement, they may constantly record wrong answers because of the lack of instruction. Although practice makes perfect, practice doing things wrong results in incompetence (a _perfectly_ horrible performance).

Instruction is therefore important. Direct instruction consistently has been identified as a key component of effective regular (50, 322) and compensatory (662, 677, 731) programs, as well as with urban disadvantaged black children (391). This direct instruction usually involves teacher-children dialogue (explanation, illustration, guided practice, immediate feedback, correction, and more explanation, etc.). Direct instruction can also occur with teacher substitutes (aides, volunteers, older children) or, on occasion, with selected machines such as the Language Master or tape recorder. Please note that many "teaching machines" do not teach at all. They test and/or provide review, making them more appropriate for those functions.

Practice is a typical way in which testing occurs. Thus a child receives a duplicated exercise and is instructed to complete it. A pupil who satisfactorily does so either (a) already possessed the information or (b) benefited from the preparatory instruction. In the former case, the instruction and practice were wasted, since no additional learning occurred. In the latter case, instruction plus practice (the test) proved effective.

On the other hand, a child may receive an assignment without preparatory instruction. The most common result is that the youngster completes the assignment unsatisfactorily. Further practice (testing) is unlikely to be helpful unless instruction first occurs. Thus, as important as practice is, the activity alone is of limited value without instruction.

Review activities are defined here as exercises that include at least two different skills. Thus an activity may review four different vowel sounds. Review exercises should not be provided until instruction and practice have occurred for each component included in the activity.

Guideline Three: "Develop reading readiness skills that serve as a basis for pupil competence in word analysis."

Four reading readiness skills are of paramount importance in this respect. They are visual discrimination, visual memory, auditory discrimination, and auditory memory. Activities for developing these skills are presented in Chapter 4B. Research indicates that AD is a rather severe deficiency among some young learners (735). When phonic procedures are to be used in instruction, it is especially important that pupils possess a sufficient amount of AD to cope with subsequent instruction. Furthermore, pupils should receive assistance in making ADs of a variety of types, progressing from gross to fine distinctions of sounds.

Guideline Four: "Conduct diagnosis to identify pupil and skill group needs."

We have already mentioned AD as an area of concern. Likewise we have presented pretests on various phonic skills. One caution: Diagnostic pretests need not be administered to pupils who have not been exposed to the content. Thus a DPT on initial consonant sounds should not be given to beginning first graders since it is assumed they have not had much instruction in that area. An exception would occur if letter-sound associations were taught systematically at the kindergarten level.

Guideline Five: "Use a Class Analysis Chart to identify pupils who should receive instruction."

The purpose of a Class Analysis Chart is to gather data for grouping and teaching purposes. Therefore, the data from each DPT should be recorded on Class Analysis Charts with the skills items listed across the top and the names of pupils down the side. When it is time to teach, simply group the pupils who have X's (or some other identifying symbol) in the particular skills column.

Guideline Six: "Teach to a child's strengths while remediating the weakness."

As one example, a child who is deficient in AD should receive instruction in visual procedures while the teacher attempts to build the background for subsequent instruction in phonics.

Guideline Seven: "Relate the various word analysis clues to each other."

Only on rare occasions does a child use one type of word identification clue to the exclusion of the others.

491

By far the more common occurrence is the use of several strategies to decode a new word. A combined procedure is likely to enhance one's competence in word analysis.

Guideline Eight: "Teach skills without exclusive dependence on the basal program's presentation."
Most teachers will probably agree that children tend to read at higher levels than they skill. This observation implies that the skills accompanying basal readers are sometimes too difficult for children, especially poor readers. The problem is exacerbated when skills presented in basal readers assume pupil competence in lower-level skills. Thus, a 2-1 manual may ask youngsters who have not yet learned the letter-sound association for s (though it has been presented) to learn sp, st, sl, sm, etc. The prevalence of this problem suggests that teachers should present the lower-level word analysis skills that children need rather than rely exclusively on the ones contained at a particular reading level.

Guideline Nine: "Use a multi-sensory approach to word identification."
If it is true that youngsters learn best in varied ways -- visual, auditory, kinesthetic, or eclectic (combined) -- teachers can facilitate learning by including elements of each sensory channel in day-to-day instruction. Thus, a word analysis lesson might include auditory and visual discrimination components. We might also expect children to write or trace the letter-sound association being presented. There is evidence to indicate that an auditory strategy is not very effective with first and second graders with low mental ages (256).

Guideline Ten: "Use the cumulative teaching/ cumulative testing technique (152)."
Word analysis skills are quickly lost when they are not renewed frequently. This observation suggests the desirability of providing frequent reviews. Each review should contain slightly more information than the previous such exercise.
For pupils who do not require as much cumulative testing, the procedure can be modified by teaching several letter-sound associations before adding the review phase. Old items included on the review may be deleted after pupils appear to have mastered them.

Guideline Eleven: "Include an application phase in which pupils must demonstrate the ability to use the skills."

492

Far too often we see pupils who can identify a letter-sound association but who cannot use the information to decode new words encountered in their reading. The materials and methods used to present phonic generalizations are often at fault here, for they rarely go beyond the sound-symbol correspondence (673). If we don't teach children to transfer information, it is unreasonable to expect them to do so.

Instruction in letter-sound associations should include an application phase in which pupils must demonstrate their ability to apply the knowledge. Additional follow up lessons may well be required to provide the necessary instruction and practice in transfer. A set of materials with a strong application phase is available for use with primary, elementary, learning disabled, and EMH children (214).

<u>Guideline Twelve</u>: "Distinguish between reading phonics and spelling phonics."

Very few writers have drawn the critical distinction between these two aspects (145, 564, 606). In essence reading phonics refers to seeing the word and thinking of the appropriate sounds while spelling phonics refers to thinking the word and identifying the corresponding letters. To illustrate, in <u>back</u> the reader sees the final <u>k</u> and thinks the /k/ sound. To spell the word, however, a person thinks the final /k/ and spells it <u>ck</u> because it followed a short vowel sound. After a long vowel sound, the speller would use only <u>k</u> and include a final <u>e</u> to accompany the long /ā/ (bake).

Unfortunately many educators, including writers of commercial materials for teachers and children (for example, spelling series) seem to confuse the two types of phonics. As Personke notes, "There is a great tendency among the writers and users of spelling textbooks to use the generalizations from the phonics program in reading. Spelling and reading, while obviously very closely related, are opposite processes. One is a recognition task, the other a recall task (564:154)." The net result may well be children who "know" phonics but spell words wrong because they use reading phonics rather than spelling phonics.

It appears that the junior author was the first person to identify the spelling phonics generalizations (145). Furthermore, she has identified the level at which each generalization first appears and has provided lists of common words containing the various phonic elements.

493

LETTER-SOUND ASSOCIATIONS AND SYLLABICATION

Guideline One: "Provide instruction in letter-sound associations and syllabication according to some skills sequence."

We use the outline presented in Chart 9A-1. Several points should be remembered. First, common letter-sound associations (LSAs) should be presented in the sequence shown in the chart. Uncommon ones need not be. For example, LSAs for b, f, l, r, s, t, etc., should be presented according to the outline, for they are required for higher-level learning (bl, br, fl, fr, etc.). Less common elements (j, v, y, z) need not be presented at the same time as the other LSAs associations, for they are less likely to be needed by children and are less likely to interfere with subsequent learning.

Second, the introduction of vowels does not need to be delayed until all of the consonant clusters and consonant digraphs have been presented. Vowels should follow consonants, however, since most consonant sounds are rather stable and most words begin with consonants.

Guideline Two: "Teach the consonants, consonant clusters, and consonant digraphs in the initial, final, and then medial positions."

Because we learn to read left to right and because it is easier to teach consonant sounds in the initial position, we present these first. Next we present final sounds. Medial sounds are the last and most difficult to teach. Actually it is possible to avoid teaching medial consonants, clusters, and digraphs by presenting them as the first or last sounds of a syllable. Thus the br in cobra and vibrate may be taught as beginning a syllable rather than coming in the middle of a word.

Guideline Three: "Teach generalizations that possess a high degree of accuracy."

Theodore Clymer (128) suggests a 75% criterion, and most subsequent writers have employed the same figure. Some phonic generalizations are inaccurately stated and thus do not possess a high degree of accuracy. One caution: Some generalizations are accurate at the lower-grade levels (when the words reflect a limited range of phonic possibilities). At the upper-grade levels, the generalizations may need to be revised. This is no problem. Old generalizations can continue to be useful with a little face-lifting. Bailey (37), Burmeister (96, 97), Emans (300), and Mazurkiewicz (494) present information about the per cent of accuracy of phonic generalizations.

Guideline Four: "Teach the common phonic options that apply to particular letters or letter pairs."

Sometimes certain letters or letter pairs possess two or more options insofar as sounds are concerned. These optional sounds should be presented at the same time so pupils will have alternative courses of action during the decoding process. For instance, ow may represent the /ō/ or the /ou/. The letters ea may represent /e/ or /e/.

Guideline Five: "Use analytic rather than synthetic procedures."

Analytic procedures proceed from the whole to the part. Thus the b represents the first sound in words such as boy, box, bat, and ball. On the other hand, synthetic procedures proceed from the part to the whole. Thus one learns the /b/ sound, the /a/ sound and the /t/ sound and blends them to produce the word bat. While most reading authorities recommend analytic procedures, most teachers seem to use synthetic strategies.

Guideline Six: "Avoid distorting the sounds of consonants, clusters, and consonant digraphs."

Distortion of sound occurs when a person attempts to produce an isolated consonant sound and, in the process, inserts an /uh/ at the end. Thus the word blend may be distorted as /buh/ plus /luh/ plus /e/ plus /nuh/ plus /duh/, hardly a reasonable equivalent. While it is possible for some sounds to be pronounced in isolation, it is difficult to teach children which ones can be and even more difficult to teach them to identify the distorted sounds. Note: Vowels can be pronounced without regard to distortion because no /uh/ sound is included at the end of each.

Guideline Seven: "Teach phonograms (word families)."

Phonograms are worth teaching for several reasons. First, it is easier for first graders to learn them than short vowels (751). Second, they decrease the amount of blending that is required. If the word bat is taught as /b/ plus /at/ rather than /b/ plus /a/ plus /t/, there is only one blending of word parts rather than two. Third, phonograms are useful as bases for working with initial consonant substitution (b plus at or c plus at, etc.).

Guideline Eight: "Avoid the use of consonant clusters when presenting consonant sounds."

For example, when teaching the /f/ sound, a teacher might use farm, face, funny or fence but not frog or fruit. The latter words should be saved until consonant clusters are being taught.

Guideline Nine: "Use words that highlight the sound(s) being presented."

When presenting initial consonant sounds, use single syllable words or words accented on the first syllable. When presenting final consonant sounds, use single syllable words or words accented on the final syllable. The same advice applies for consonant clusters and consonant digraphs. When presenting vowels, use single syllable words or words with the accented syllable containing the vowel.

Guideline Ten: "Use nonsense words or difficult real words to test pupils' initial mastery of LSAs and auditory discrimination."

We recommend the use of real words with kindergartners and first graders. With older pupils the use of real words may not provide an accurate indication of performance if youngsters remember the visual aspects of the words. Thus these children should be presented nonsense words or difficult real words (i.e., items which they are unlikely to have seen in reading) as their practice material. It is only fair to note that some authors oppose the use of nonsense words.

Guideline Eleven: "When selecting practice materials, choose exercises that accurately identify the type of practice they provide."

Consider, for example, several pages of exercises from material published by one company.

1. Exercise Focus: Short vowel a

    Contents: Picture of a man and three words:
    man, mad, map

    Directions: Draw a ring around the word that tells the name of the picture.

    Observation: This exercise tests the final consonant sound, not the vowel a.

2. Exercise Focus: Short vowel a

    Contents: Picture of a pan and the sentence "I can see the ____." Three words are listed below: pan, ran, tan

    Directions: Look at the picture. Read the sentence. Draw a ring around the word that belongs in the sentence and print it on line.

Observation: This exercise tests the initial consonant sound, not the vowel a.

3. Exercise Focus: Short vowel a

    Contents: Three letters -- s, c, f -- and the word bat

    Directions: Make new words by changing the beginning consonant in each word below. Print the new words on the lines.

    Observation: This exercise tests initial consonant substitution, not the vowel a.

As another illustration, read the following sentences. Which one can be used to test children's ability to apply a short vowel generalization?

A. I like to eat chocolate pie.

B. A long fence runs around our pasture.

The answer is Sentence A, for children cannot decode the word simply by looking at the ch. The word could also be cherry, chess, or cheese. Only when the child reaches the short o does he know the word in print. Sentences for vowel sounds must either contain new words beginning with the vowel sound (sometimes an impossibility, always very difficult) or have two or more meaningful words which begin with the same consonant, cluster, or digraph. Sentence B can be used to test a pupil's ability to apply the LSA for /p/.

Guideline Twelve: "Use accurate and well-constructed teaching, practice (testing) and review materials."
Many phonics materials contain a large number of errors. Types of common problems include the following:

a. incorrectly identifying the vowel or consonant sound. For example, one set of materials identifies fruit and ruler as long /u/.

b. using words accented on the second syllable when the initial consonant sound in being taught. Children have difficulty hearing the unstressed initial consonant. Examples: balloon and banana for the /b/.

497

c. using consonant clusters when only consonants are taught. Examples: _frog_ for /f/, _train_ for /t/.

d. using words outside children's oral vocabularies. Examples: _vat_ for /v/, _yak_ for /y/.

e. using words children cannot read to introduce phonic generalizations. We recommend that a phonic skill not be introduced until children can read at least four or five words containing that element.

f. using words with the same sound repeated, making it possible for children to get the right answer for the wrong reason. Example: _baby_ for /b/, _cake_ for /k/.

g. using words containing the minimal contrast sound, thus making the activity more difficult than it has to be. Examples: _moon_ for /m/, _five_ for /f/.

h. using two-syllable words when vowels are being taught. Thus children must contend with two vowels sounds rather than one.

Guideline Thirteen: "Avoid drill work that does not facilitate the development of reading competence."
An excellent example of a commercial program that permits pupils to "do something without doing anything" is a set of programmed readers. Pupils can fill in a succession of blanks with the letter _a_, for example, and still be unable to pronounce the words. Likewise, pupils are sometimes asked to syllabicate words without being expected to pronounce the terms. Syllabication that does not lead to pronunciation is relatively useless.

CONTEXT

Guideline One: "Use examples which reflect the category of skill being presented."
Sometimes we confuse one skill category with another with the result being fuzzy teaching and fuzzy learning. Note the following examples:

A. I ate too many green apples. Now I have a stomach _____ .

B. Granny is old, but I am _____ .

Both of these examples involve the use of context. A reader paying attention to the print would not need to see any of the letters in the blanks in order to pronounce them. These sentences are useful for teaching pupils the skill of context usage, either orally or in print.

Now look at the next two sentences. How do they differ from the first two examples?

C. I ate too many green apples. Now my stomach _____.

D. I drank a _____ of milk for lunch.

Several words could logically fit into each of these blanks. Thus a reader needs to use context plus initial consonant sound to determine the new word. If, in Example C, the word begins with h, the word will be hurts. It it begins with a, the word will be aches.

Depending on the initial letter, the answer to Example D might be glass, cup, pint, or lot. Examples C and D are appropriate for use in developing context plus initial consonant or vowel sound.

Guideline Two: "Use examples which reflect a variety of types of context clues."

Although authorities do not agree on the number and categories of context clues, they do agree that context clues should be taught in a systematic manner. As a minimum we should probably provide instruction and practice in the following:

A. Indirect experience (When I broke my leg, the doctor put it in a cast.)

B. Direct experience (Today is my birthday. I am seven years old.)

C. Definition (A canine is a dog.)

ORAL READING

Guideline One: "Do not use the read-along technique for groups of poor readers."

Whether read-along involves a taped program or a group of youngsters in a reading group, the result is often the same. Few pupils follow along; most are looking at the pictures or the wrong words or, even worse, are on a different page. A read-along procedure for a pupil receiving individual help is acceptable.

499

Most good readers don't need the read-along procedure, just a person to help them with a few unknown words.

Guideline Two: "Use oral reading for listening development."
If pupils are to practice oral reading, their groupmates should close their books and listen. At the end of the paragraph(s), the teacher can direct questions to the listeners, never to the oral reader.

Guideline Three: "Provide materials that oral readers can use with at least 94% accuracy."
A pupil operating at the instructional level will not typically miss more than six words out of 100. Pupils who miss large numbers of words will not only have far too many words to learn but derive little satisfaction and self-worth from the experience.

Guideline Four: "Deemphasize or eliminate oral reading for diagnosis for good readers."
This guideline applies to the top group as early as grade one. While children at that age perceive oral reading as fun, it nevertheless is a waste of diagnostic time for good readers. They should spend that time reading silently. An abundance of oral reading is likely to inhibit the development of a rapid rate of silent reading. There are, however, valid reasons for providing oral reading. See Chapters 7A and 7B.

Guideline Five: "Provide silent reading before oral reading except for diagnostic purposes."
Since oral reading is normally used to convey information, it seems only fair to provide pupils with opportunities to prepare for their "sharing" experience. Preparation is not necessary if oral reading is conducted for diagnosis, for then we want to know what a child's problems are so we can provide assistance.

Guideline Six: "Use pupils' oral errors as the basis for subsequent instruction and practice activities."
Recording a pupil's oral reading performance makes it possible to use the experience as a diagnostic teaching session. Several comments are related to this guideline. First, you should utilize some systematic procedure for noting pupil performance. We prefer the modified Gilmore symbols although others are probably just as good. Second, specific strategies must be used to ensure that pupils do in fact learn and retain the words with which they experience difficulty. See Chapters 7A and 7B.

500

Guideline Seven: "Do not consider dialect patterns and speech errors as reading errors."

While it is helpful to mark speech and dialect patterns, they should not be included in the oral reading error count because neither one is reading. Thus, "I see a wittle wabbit" does not have any oral reading errors even though it may indicate a need for screening by a speech therapist. Likewise, "We done our work" reflects a language pattern and is not classified as a reading error. Language assistance is far more likely to help the child than is drill on did. Adults who sound the t in often, pronounce harass with an accent on the second syllable, or say goin', and runnin' should understand the importance of distinguishing between reading and speaking ability.

Guideline Eight: "Respond appropriately to oral reading errors."

Both the context of the sentence or paragraph and the pupil's word analysis skills competence dictate the response a teacher should make to a child's oral reading performance. The following situations illustrate the most common possibilities:

A. If the missed word is known to the child, say, "Reread the sentence (or paragraph)." Or say, "Skip that word and come back to it after you finish reading the sentence (or paragraph)."

B. If the error can be corrected by the use of phonics, say, "Sound it out." Or say, "I believe you can figure it out by the sounds."

C. If the error can be corrected by the use of syllabication, say, "Try dividing it into syllables the way we did last week."

D. If the child does not have the requisite skills or if the unknown word is not amenable to any of these strategies, use the following sequence:

1. The child points to the word.

2. The child looks at the word.

3. The teacher says the word.

4. The child repeats the word.

5. The child rereads the sentence.

Guideline Nine: "Note the frequency of each type of word analysis error in oral reading."

Some youngsters lack self-confidence. They may simply refuse to try words they can actually pronounce. Other youngsters may say non-meaningful words indicating a lack of attention to the context. Still others may substitute meaningful words, a problem of far less concern. Yet others may read word by word and require assistance in reading orally fluently.

DICTIONARY

Guideline One: "Use a variety of dictionaries, including picture dictionaries."

In considering ways of meeting youngsters' needs, we often think about textbooks and workbooks rather than dictionaries. At the same point many pupils have extreme difficulty using the standard dictionaries provided for their use. We recommend that dictionaries be provided according to pupils' reading levels. An annotated list of some beginning and picture dictionaries is contained in Chapter 6.

Guideline Two: "Teach pupils to use the pronunciation keys accompanying the glossary and the dictionary."

Use of a pronunciation key assumes that pupils have already learned the various common consonant and vowel LSAs and can handle topics such as diacritical marks, phonic respellings, guide words, and alphabetical order. These topics are best presented in conjunction with the study of a glossary.

As a general rule, the dictionary is the last of the word analysis skills to be developed because it builds on competence in phonics, structure, and context.

WORD RECOGNITION

Guideline One: "Teach new words in context rather than in isolation."

It is recommended that words be presented in a meaningful context. For concrete nouns and action verbs, use SCCs. Here the picture provides the context. Either a phrase or a sentence should be used to introduce other words (the Dolch 220, for example).

Guideline Two: "After testing new words in context, test them in isolation, either on word cards or lists."

502

As noted earlier, the result of instruction in word analysis should be the development of a pupil's supply of words recognized by sight. Using either cards or a list of words, a pupil should be able, after instruction, to name the words at sight. If new words are presented in the context of a story, they can be tested through the use of the open slot, a card or piece of paper with a rectangular opening wide enough to expose a word. Because a pupil who can recognize a word in context will not necessarily be able to recognize it in another context, a teacher is wise to use an isolated list of words for final testing.

E. How can phonic and structural skills be taught in context, thereby associating meaning and pronunciation?

In section two of this chapter we discussed the general sequence of phonic and structural skills and noted that context was not considered in the model. Each teacher has the opportunity of deciding whether she wishes to teach the LSAs without regard to meaning or whether she wishes to interweave pronunciation with comprehension.

We have suggested that decoding without understanding is nothing more than pseudo-reading, that reading is comprehension rather than a prerequisite to meaning. Thus, an exponent of the Gray definition does not say, "He reads well, but he doesn't understand a thing." Rather he comments, "Tom's oral reading is excellent, but he has severe difficulties in comprehension. He can pronounce words at 3-1, but he reads at 2-1."

Chart 9A-9 contains information on how to teach an LSA, using initial v = /v/ as an example. The material is taken from Practice Exercises in Phonics (214).

Several points relative to this eight-step outline seem appropriate. Words included in Step One should meet as many of the following criteria as possible.

1. They should be a part of the child's reading vocabulary (268).

2. They should be accented on the first syllable or be one-syllable words. (The letter beginning the accented syllable receives the most stress. Using a word with an unaccented first syllable requires a pupil to note a secondary rather than a primary stressed sound.

503

OUTLINE FOR TEACHING A LETTER-SOUND ASSOCIATION

Initial <u>V</u>

1. List the following words on the board.

> Vance (name of a boy in class)
> vine
> vest
> Valentine

2. Ask, "How are all of these words alike?" Elicit, "They all begin with the same letter. That letter is <u>V</u>," Underline the letter.

3. Pronounce the words slowly, emphasizing but not distorting the sounds.

4. Ask the pupils to pronounce the words with you.

5. Ask, "How else are these words alike?" Elicit, "They all begin with the same sound." If the pupils have difficulty, say, "You have already told me these words begin with the same letter. Listen to me say the words again. Then tell me how else they are alike." Then pronounce the words a second time. If necessary, say, "They all begin with the same letter. They also begin with the same _____."

6. Ask pupils to use their EPR cards as you pronounce the following nonsense words (or words whose spelling they would not be expected to identify.). Provide feedback after each response.

> vorgle   vapid
> vanquish   fickle
> regent   vinyl
> futile

7. Ask pupils to name other words (or raise pictures) which begin with the sound being studied. Their peers should react to these words by presenting their EPR cards. Provide feedback after each response.

8A. Pronounce the following sentences and ask pupils to supply words which make sense <u>and</u> begin with the same sound.

Have you ever bought any _____ ? (Vegetables, vehicles, vitamins, vases, vacuum cleaners)

The doctor gave me some _____ . (Vitamins, vaccinations).

Here come the _____ . (Visitors, vehicles)

8B. Ask pupils to read each of the following sentences and supply one or more words which make sense and begin with the same sound.

Bill has a new _____ . (Volleyball, vehicle).

Is this _____ yours? (Volleyball, vehicle, vest).

We live in a _____ . (Valley, village).

8C. Ask pupils to read the following sentences to see if they can pronounce the underlined words.

I cannot talk today. I have lost my voice.

Bill and I are going to visit Bob.

We like to eat vegetables.

Who are you going to vote for?

Her hat is made of velvet.

Mother said her ring was valuable.

I like to put vinegar on some of my food.

A lion and a tiger are very big.

An apple has a lot of vitamins.

Can you sing one verse for me?

(As an alternate procedure, you may record each underlined word on the chalkboard or a transparency. Read each sentence twice. On the first reading, omit the word recorded on the board or transparency (and underlined above). Ask pupils to raise their YES cards if they know the new word. Then read the sentence a second time, inviting the group to respond together when you reach the new word.).

505

3. Words used for teaching initial consonant sounds should not begin with consonant clusters.

4. Whenever possible, the words should be nouns or action verbs. SCCs can be used to teach the words about to be presented in a lesson on LSAs.

5. At least one of the words should begin with a capital letter so that children can note the two printed forms of each letter.

Step Two of the teaching procedure provides the learner with an opportunity to discriminate visually the initial consonant letter. Step Five is quite difficult, especially when the eight-step procedure is being presented for the first time. After three sessions, most youngsters begin to "catch on" to the auditory similarities of the key words.

For Step Six, EPR cards may be constructed from 3x5 inch cards, one containing a large YES and one with a NO. Each child needs a set of two so he can react to the words pronounced by the teacher and later his classmates. If the new word begins with the same sound (not necessarily the same letter) as the key word, the child holds the YES card. If not, he raises the NO card. EPR allows the teacher to observe which pupils are experiencing unusual difficulties in making auditory discriminations at the recognition level in listening.

Step Seven provides the same type of practice except for the fact that auditory discrimination practice for those who volunteer is at the reproduction rather than the recognition level.

By far the most important aspect of the entire procedure, however, is Step Eight. It is here that meaning and pronunciation merge (673), and real reading and thinking result. Pupils first respond orally, naming several words which might fit into a spoken context. Next they read sentences themselves and supply one or more appropriate words. Finally, pupils are asked to read sentences which contain unknown words (268) and to use context plus initial consonant sounds to determine the underlined items.

At the lower-primary levels it will usually be necessary for you to read the sentences presented in Steps 8B and 8C, allowing the children to fill in orally the missing words in the first case and to identify the new underlined word in the second case.

This eight-step procedure can be used to teach the sounds represented by the other consonants, clusters, and consonant digraphs, both in initial and final positions.

It can also be utilized for introducing the sounds represented by single vowels and the various vowel combinations. Please note: At no point does the lesson consider the /v/ in isolation. The /v/ is not /vuh/. It is the first sound in <u>valentine</u>, for example. Letter sounds should be studied in words rather than in isolation (365, 371, 392).

Vowel situations are handled in a slightly different way, for they usually occur in the middle of the word. Since the initial consonant must not "give away" the answer, there must be at least two words which make sense and begin with the same letter. The child cannot be certain of the word until he uses his knowledge of vowel sounds. See Chart 9A-10 for an exercise involving the letters <u>or</u>.

CHART 9A-10

OUTLINE FOR TEACHING A LETTER-SOUND ASSOCIATION (214)

Initial or Medial <u>or</u>

1. Print the following words on the chalkboard: or, for, horse, store.

2. Ask, "How are these words alike?" Elicit, "They all have <u>or</u>." Underline these letters.

3. Ask the pupils to listen to you pronounce the words. Do so slowly, emphasizing but not distorting the sound.

4. Ask the pupils to pronounce the words with you.

5A. Ask, "How else are all of these words alike?" Elicit, "They all have the same vowel sound." If the pupils have difficulty, say, "Listen as I pronounce them again." Then do so. If they still have difficulty, say, "You have already told me these words contain the same vowel plus <u>R</u> pattern. They also have the same _____." (sound)

5B. Lead the pupils to note that the <u>or</u> pattern usually represents the special sound as in (any of the words in Step 1). The R-controlled sound is /or/.

6. Ask pupils to display their EPR cards as you pronounce the following nonsense words (or words whose spelling they would not be expected to identify). Provide feedback after each response.

507

	Real	Nonsense
1.	fort	corb
2.	groan	troze
3.	clothes	flome
4.	Lord	torf
5.	form	shors
6.	broke	smone
7.	chose	tose
8.	horn	norg
9.	stork	plord
10.	both	hogue

7. Ask pupils to name other words (or display pictures) which might contain the sound being studied. Their peers should react to these words by presenting their EPR cards. Provide feedback after each response.

8A. Pronounce the following sentence and ask pupils to supply words which make sense and contain the key sound.

1. The man was trapped in the _____. (storm, fort, etc.)

8B. If possible, ask pupils to read the following sentences to see if they can pronounce the underlined words. If necessary, ask pupils to read just the underlined word (printed on the board) after you have read the rest of the sentence aloud.

1. My jacket is torn.

2. Mother made my brother sit in the corner.

3. My sister was born on a Monday.

4. I need to take the cord off the box.

508

5. I like to play the <u>organ</u> at church.

6. Put the chairs out on the <u>porch</u>.

7. Will you help me <u>organize</u> the books into two stacks?

8. The boy does not have a mother or father. He is an <u>orphan</u>.

9. We saw the <u>porpoise</u> jump out of the water.

10. The man had a lot of <u>corn</u> on his farm.

Note that in Step 8B there are at least two possible answers for each underlined word except when the <u>or</u> comes at the beginning. For example, in sentence one (My jacket is <u>torn</u>.), the unknown word might be <u>tan</u> or <u>tight</u>. The child cannot tell by looking at the <u>t</u> and must instead proceed to the element being taught (<u>or</u>).

Chart 9A-11 presents an outline of the procedure for teaching a syllabication generalization relating to a consonant plus <u>le</u> as a final syllable.

Notice Step Eight expects youngsters to use phonic and structural skills to pronounce the new words and contextual clues to identify the meanings of the underlined terms. Emphasis on this type of procedure seems most likely to yield tangible results insofar as comprehension is concerned. And the procedures presented above may be modified to fit the teaching of almost any skill in almost any subject area.

F. <u>What kinds of activities can be used to reinforce phonic skills?</u>

This section identifies sample activities that can be used to teach, test (provide practice), or review phonic skills. Many of the activities have multiple applications with a variety of phonic elements. Although some activities overlap two of the categories, the ideas are classified as essentially (a) teaching, (b) practice (testing), or (c) review (several items presented in the same activity).

Chart 9A-11 presents an outline of the procedure for teaching a syllabication generalization relating to a consonant plus <u>le</u> as a final syllable.

CHART 9A-11

OUTLINE FOR TEACHING A SYLLABICATION GENERALIZATION

Consonant plus <u>le</u>

1. List the following words on the board.

    Myrtle (Name of a girl in class)
    table
    apple
    candle
    Bible

2. Ask, "How are they all alike?" Elicit the desired visual information. They all end in a consonant plus <u>le</u>.

3. Pronounce the words slowly, emphasizing but not distorting the sounds.

4. Ask the pupils to pronounce the words with you.

5A. Ask, "How else are all of these words alike?" Elicit information relative to the number of syllables and the auditory syllabic division. Syllabicate the words on the board. They all have two syllables.

                Myr - tle   ap - ple
                ta - ble   can - dle
                Bi - ble

5B. Ask, "What generalization, or rule, can you give for syllabicating these words?" Elicit the general principle. One consonant plus <u>le</u> forms the last syllable of some words. If the preceding syllable ends in a vowel, that vowel usually represents the long sound (as in <u>table</u> and <u>Bible</u>).

6. Ask pupils to use their EPR cards as you syllabicate on the board the following nonsense words (or words whose pronunciation they would not be expected to recognize). Provide feedback after each response.

                cradle   staple   tweedle

                stifle   stable   doodle

510

7. Ask pupils to syllabicate the words presented in the following list. Provide feedback.

feeble	bugle	Scrabble
maple	sable	noodle
rifle	purple	fable

8. Ask pupils to read the following sentences to see if they can pronounce and define the underline words:

We put the bridle on the horse.

Mother dipped soup out of the pot with a long ladle.

The doctor told me to gargle with salt and warm water.

The steeple of the church is on fire.

Did you see the football player fumble the ball?

Mother told me not to shuffle my feet.

Put the horse in the stable.

"What kind of dog is that?" "A poodle."

Come right home after school, Bill. Don't stand around and dawdle.

It didn't cost much. I just paid a trifle for it.

TEACHING

1. Use Phonics Charts. These are large tagboard sheets with five pictures and words representing a sound (examples: bat, ball, box, boy, bus). Use the following strategies:

a. Ask the children to pronounce the words.

b. Ask the children to tell two ways in which the words are alike (visually and auditorily)

c. Place some printed words on a wall chart. Ask the children to tell whether or not the word begins with (ends, contains) the letter being studied.

e. Ask the children to clip from a newspaper headline words that contain the <u>letter</u> <u>and</u> <u>sound</u> being studied.

f. Pronounce selected words, asking the children to respond individually.

Use the EPR by providing every child with Yes-No cares or some alternate -- Happy and Sad Faces, slate boards, etc. Without manipulatives children may use: thumbs up - thumbs down, two fingers crossed or separated, etc. In each case provide immediate feedback by supplying the correct response after children have had adequate time to respond. Note the children who have serious difficulties. Remember that the exercise uses a true-false format. Thus 50% accuracy tells us nothing, for that is random guessing. Expect 90% accuracy, which means the child who guesses right on five items must <u>know</u> four out of the other five answers.

2. For older children, use an abbreviated discovery technique, keeping in mind the fact that it does not work well with some children.

a. List words representing two different sounds of a letter on the board. Examples: cat, cent, city, come, cub, icy.

b. Ask children to tell how they know when the key letter (c -- the chimney on the roof) stands for each sound (/k/ and /s/).

c. Lead them to record the generalization or the rule (if they can write) or say it. "A <u>c</u> before an <u>a</u>, <u>o</u>, or <u>u</u> stands for the /k/. A <u>c</u> before an <u>e</u>, <u>i</u> or <u>y</u> stands for the /s/."

d. Ask children to mark words (either /k/ or /s/) and <u>pronounce</u> <u>them</u>. The words should either be nonsense words or words not in the pupils' reading vocabularies. Examples: cag, ceg, cig, cog, cug, or cab, cell, cinders, cot ,cuff, Cyrus. Be concerned only with the correct pronunciation of the element (first part of the word) being presented.

e. Ask children to place the words in two parts of a house, put each sound in the attic, and put the letter in the chimney. Example:

Letter		c
Sound	k	s
	cat	cent
Associations	come	city
	cub	icy

3. Use the "Look and Hook" procedure. Make a Phonic Board consisting of three rows and three columns of screw-in hooks (with curved ends to prevent accidents). Make a number of "Look and Hook" cards by punching a hole in the top of the short side of each 3x5 inch card. If necessary glue on a reinforcement. The easier level should consist of pictures and words. The harder level should contain just pictures.

On the middle hook (row 2, column 2) place a card with the letter-sound picture pattern (i.e., b = ball, d = dog). These symbols stand for the following: "The /b/ sound stands for the first sound of ball; the /d/ sound stands for the first sound of dog."

In a 6x9 inch brown manila envelope, place a number of Level 1 (picture and word) or Level 2 (picture only) items. Level 1 is mainly visual discrimination; Level 2 is really letter-sound associations. Ask one child at a time to place the appropriate cards on the hooks. (More than one card may be placed on a hook.) Ask the child to place the extra foil items in the envelope.

Make the material self-correcting by identifying on the back side of each card the beginning sound at the left, the vowel sound in the center, and the final sound at the right. Thus the cards can be used for three different phonic activities.

"Look and Hook" can be constructed in a different way. Instead of using hooks, mount sign out pockets for library cards on the tagboard. In either case you will need hundreds of cards. PAD Packs (see Chapter 4B) can

513

be used for Level 2. The Phonic Board can be used for practically all phonic activities and thus is a valuable part of the classroom.

4. Use the Language Master to tape question-and-answer activities for instructional purposes. The Language Master has two tracks, one for "the teacher" and one for "the child." However, the tracks can be used for "the question" and "the answer" with the child or pair of children responding orally between the two taped segments. It can also be used to present two pieces of information.

Segments might be recorded with the following patterns:

a. Positive: The vowel sound in ask, man, and tack is /a/.
Negative: The vowel sound in rain and take is not /a/.

b. Positive: The vowel sound in glad, fast, and ran is /a/.
Negative: The vowel sound in like, write, and type is not /a/.

c. Question: What is the vowel sound in ax, cat, and fan? (Child to respond orally)
Answer: The vowel sound in ax, cat, and fan is /a/.

d. Question: What is the sound of the short a? (Child to respond orally)
Answer: The sound of the short a is /a/ as in ax.

e. Question: Do tack and made have the same /a/ sound? (Child to respond orally)
Answer: Tack has the /a/ sound. Made does not have the /a/ sound.

A careful study of the five sets of recordings shown above will reveal that a and b identify words that represent the key vowel sound and alternate sounds. C asks for the sound as it appears in word s, and D requires identification of the sound from memory. E presents two words and asks whether they represent the key sound. Neither word, one word, or both words may contain the key element.

514

To make sets of Language Master cards, identify the key sound and sounds which are somewhat similar. Follow the patterns shown above to develop instructional sequences. There should be a number of cards with the pattern shown in Item e. Label each card and house the set in a numbered and labeled envelope.

5. Use STEP (Self-Teaching Exercises in Phonics) as a way of helping children do independent study of LSAs for vowels. STEP is intended to be both a teaching and a testing (practice) step following initial instruction. The first type of STEP card is designed for teaching. Each 3x5 inch card contains two levels.

Level A: Word and sound on the same side (Example: break + /ā/)

Level B. Picture and sound on the same side (Example: Picture of a tray + /ā/)

In level A the association is a letter-sound proceeding as does reading. In Level B the association is picture-sound, with elements of reading and spelling.

Whenever possible, use words that cannot be pictorially represented in Level A, saving pictorial words for Level B. It is also desirable to present different written patterns that children will need to read as specific vowel sounds. For example, children will often see ai, ay and a-consonant-silent-e (e.g., make) and need to respond with the /ā/.

For each vowel sound (short and long vowels, vowel digraphs, R-controlled vowels, diphthongs, and special cases not including the schwa) make at least two sets of teaching cards. There should be at least five sets of practice cards (and preferably more). The physical format for the second type of STEP card is shown below:

Level A: Word on one side -- Word and sound on the other side
(Example: tough -- tough + /u/)

Level B: Picture on one side -- Picture and sound on the other side
(Example: Picture of a bug -- picture of a bug + /u/)

Please note that the practice cards contain the question on one side and answer on the other. Thus the practice cards are self-correcting. Instructional and self-study procedures are identified below.

a. The child receives initial and follow up instruction on a particular vowel LSA.

b. The child receives a set of Level A <u>Teaching</u> cards. The set contains six cards, four of which present words with the key sound and two of which present words with another sound.

c. The child says the word and the vowel sound, usually aloud at the beginning stages and later silently.

d. When the child thinks he can distinguish between the key sound represented by the four cards and the foil sound(s), he proceeds to the Level A <u>Practice</u> cards.

e. Using the question side (word only for Level A, picture only for Level B), the child places in a column the four cards that contain the key sound. He places the two foil cards in a second column.

f. The child turns the cards over to correct his work.

g. The child receives additional instruction as needed until he can complete the consecutive activities without error.

Then the child proceeds to Level B and follows Steps <u>b-d</u> with Teaching cards and Steps <u>e-g</u> with Practice cards. The sequence thus proceeds as shown below:

1. Level A: Teach

2. Level A: Practice

3. Level B: Teach

4. Level B: Practice

PRACTICE

There are many possible practice activities for reinforcing LSAs. The following paragraphs describe some of the more productive strategies.

1. Provide catalogues and ask children to locate items that contain the sound being studied. For instance, if the beginning /b/ is being considered, children may cut

out pictures of bicycles, babies, balls, beds, belts, etc. Overlook any items which do not conform to the guidelines presented earlier. For instance, accept without negative comment <u>baby</u>, even though it contains two /b/ sounds.

2. Help children make a phonics dictionary. They might use the following procedure:

a. Find five pictures (preferably not representing the words on the Phonics Charts mentioned earlier).

b. Show the pictures to the Phonics Consultant. If they are approved as actually containing the sound being studied, paste them on one sheet of paper.

c. Either label each word or have someone print the words below the pictures. Also label the top left of the reverse side with the letter and sound (<u>b</u> = /b/ or <u>c</u> = /k/). Add more pages as each LSA is introduced. One added advantage of a Phonics Dictionary is that is can also serve as a source of new words for readers and as a spelling guide for writers. Use construction paper with reinforced holes and brads. Place several of the booklets in a learning center.

3. Make Sound Sleds by attaching straws for runners to the bottoms of greeting card boxes. Label each box with a sound (/k/ or /o/) on the sides. A pipe cleaner inserted in holes punched in the front and back of each box can attach the sleds. Children should then bring small toys (of little or no value) to place in the appropriate sled.
A seasonal or holiday motif can accompany the lead sled (reindeer and Santa Claus for Christmas, Pilgrims coming home from a hunt or going to church, a bunny rabbit with a basket of Easter eggs leading the sleds, etc.).

4. Use the "name as many as" technique. After teaching an LSA, ask each child to look around and count on his fingers each word that contains the key sound. Provide this activity in a variety of settings so you will elicit different words (in the room, in the cafeteria, on the playground, in the media center). As a variation ask children to do "name as many" in pairs. This paired activity for learning (PAL) not only makes learning more fun, it also gives each child feedback from his peer, provides a temporary crutch (a friend), and results in a

517

high level of individual mental activity. You may prefer
to limit the activity to one minute of thinking time just
before lunch, at the end of school, or in other "tiny"
moments.

5. Use newspaper headlines. Pronounce a word containing
the key sound and ask the children to circle every word
in the newspaper headlines that has the sound being
studied. For instance, if the sound is /k/, say calf
(for example). Children should then circle words such as
Canada, Cuba, King, and coming. Notice that both c and
k can represent the /k/. Two newspapers are enough for
an entire class if each child uses just one page.

6. For vowel sounds ask children to read a paragraph and
identify the words which contain the key sound. To make
the activity even easier, tell how many key words are
found in the paragraph. Written materials can come from
basals, library books, or language-experience stories.

7. Use silly sentences. Ask children to make up
sentences, reasonable or silly, that contain many of the
key sounds, either consonants or vowels. Examples
include:

Billy Burns bought a big blue bike. (Accept the
    consonant blend in blue.)

Maud saw slaw on the lawn in August.

This activity is great fun, and it has the advantage
of promoting other skills such as sentence expansion and
auditory memory. Furthermore, other children can then
try to name all of the key words.

8. Play Phonics Seesaw. This activity derives its name
from the fact that some children will be "up" while
others are "down." Give each child a number of cards,
each of which contains a printed word in his reading
vocabulary. Each child squats and, at your request,
looks at his first word. If it contains the sound you
name, the child stands and holds his word so you can see
it. If his word does not contain the sound you name, the
child continues to squat. You can also (a) display a
picture representing a beginning, ending, or vowel sound,
(b) say a word, or (c) present a written word. Each
child should have ten cards, about half of which contain
the key sound.
    The alternate activity is for each child to hold a
card containing a letter-sound and respond to your

518

pictures. Regardless of which technique is used, be sure to provide immediate feedback so children will know whether or not their responses are accurate.

REVIEW

The purpose of a review exercise is to provide children with opportunities to recognize LSAs when several different elements are present. Obviously a review should include only the phonic elements that have been studied thus far. For this reason such practice exercises must be constructed or purchased to coincide with a specific sequence of phonic skill development. They should never be assigned at random.

The following activities represent appropriate strategies for helping pupils bridge the gap between the study of individual letter-sounds and the use of a wide variety of phonic skills.

1. Use Phonics Bingo. Construct sets of cards for the LSAs in one category, such as initial consonants, short and long vowels, etc. The basic steps for constructing Phonics Bingo are listed below:

a. Identify the number of initial letter sounds to teach (There are 21.).

b. Choose the first sixteen items for Part 1 of Set 1. The remaining items plus the hardest 11 out of the first 16 will become Part 2 of Set 1.

c. Divide the 16 sounds into four groups of four sounds each. For purposes of illustration, let us consider b, m, j, t as the first four letter-sounds.

d. Divide three spirit masters into 16 boxes each (four rows and four columns). Leave space at the top of each spirit master to write the category (i.e., initial consonants, long and short vowels, etc.), the Form letter (A, B, or C), and Part 1 or Part 2. For example, the heading might be:

PHONICS BINGO

Initial Consonant Sounds - Form A

Part 1

e. On each spirit master record the first four sounds four times each. Use a different pattern for each card. Thus children will have difficulty looking on someone else's paper because the positions of the letters will be different. Be sure to print neatly and in large (but lower-case) letters.

f. Duplicate each form on construction paper, making at least four copies of each form (providing enough material for 12 children to use simultaneously). You might wish to use one color of construction paper to represent each set of Phonics Bingo games.

g. Laminate the cards.

h. Mount 16 pictures, four beginning with each of the four sounds. On the back, label each picture to facilitate replacing the materials in the right container (for instance, Initial Consonant Sounds: Part 1).

i. Secure small strips of tagboard, checkers, etc., for markers. Try to locate 16 per card.

j. House Part 1 of the set in a box or manila envelope and label it.

Several comments are important. First, repeat the procedure three times (for the second, third, and fourth groups of four sounds and words). Second, repeat the procedure to review eight sounds (instead of four), printing each word twice (instead of four times). Third, list each of the 16 sounds one time each for a large-scale review. Thus children will have review experiences in the following sequence:

a. first set of 4 letter-sounds

b. second set of 4 letter-sounds

c. first set of 8 letter-sounds

d. third set of 4 letter-sounds

e. fourth set of 4 letter sounds

f. second set of 8 letter-sounds

g. first set of 16 letter-sounds

520

After completing the large-scale review of sixteen letter-sounds, teach the remaining letter-sounds while constructing Part 2 of Initial Consonant Sounds. Similar Phonics Bingo exercises can be developed as needed for the other phonic elements.

The procedures for playing Phonics Bingo are quite simple. A leader (an aide, volunteer, older child, etc.) displays a picture, and each child covers <u>one</u> letter-sound (in this case). Note that the child <u>has</u> four options in this exercise and should choose the option which is most likely to result in a straight line of covered letter-sounds.

The child who covers four items in a row and calls Bingo must pronounce a word with each letter-sound as he uncovers it. He then replaces the covers (if correct) and continues to participate, working toward a second Bingo. Thus there is a succession of winners. The exercise continues until someone has a completely-covered sheet. (That will occur at the same time if everyone "knows his phonics.")

2. On a hopscotch outline on the schoolground, tape ten pieces of masking tape, labeling each piece with a letter-sound. Children can play hopscotch the usual way, except they must name a word beginning with each letter-sound.

An alternate procedure can be used if simple drawings replace the ten letter-sounds. In this variation each player must name the sound (beginning, ending, or vowel) represented by the picture. The masking tape lasts only one period unless it is placed in a corner of each shape.

3. Play Spin and Win. Make a simple "spinning wheel" from a piece of pasteboard and a large brad inserted in such a way that the head is on the back. Draw a circle around the board and divide it into four parts (for example). Label each with a letter-sound.

Next take a discarded checkerboard and tape pictures on 27 of the outside squares all the way around. If four sounds are being reviewed, approximately seven spaces will contain pictures representing each sound. Designate one space as GO, and secure several tokens to represent the players.

Each of the two players holds the pasteboard frame and spins the arrow. The person whose spin ends on a pre-arranged letter-sound becomes the first player. He spins and moves his token to the first position on the checkerboard that contains a picture with that sound <u>if</u> he can name the sounds shown by each picture he must pass to reach that point. The player who is unable to do so does not advance and loses his turn. His partner -- not his opponent -- then spins and moves. The winner is the first person to circle the board.

A variation of this activity is to use a spinning wheel with pictures and a checkerboard with letters representing sounds. In order to move, a child must name a word containing the sound.

4. Use a Phonics Bee. Organize two groups of about five children each and place them in two lines. Say a word and ask the first child to identify the key sound. If he misses, ask the first member of the other team. Do not repeat the question. Continue until a certain number of points is reached. No one sits down. Thus listening and participation by all members are encouraged.

For a variant form of this activity, give a vowel sound, and ask children to name an example. As an alternative, show a word or picture and ask children to identify the sound.

5. Organize a scavenger hunt. Give each child a duplicated sheet containing a picture illustrating each sound that has been presented. Ask each child to bring to school a bag containing an item representing each sound. The bag may also contain real objects (soap), toy objects (toy car), object parts (wheel on a car), or pictures (picture of a quilt).

6. Play Old Maid. For each picture card make a corresponding letter-sound card as shown in the examples below for a long and short vowel (including vowel digraph) activity. (I and y represent the same /i/).

Picture Card	Sound Card
cat	/a/
cake	/ā/
peas	/ē/
bread	/e/

A set of Old Maid cards for long and short vowels will consist of ten picture cards and ten sound cards, or ten word cards and ten sound cards, or ten picture cards and ten word cards. In the latter case a picture card (calf) might be matched with a word card (glad). Place all cards in a stack. Each of two players draws three cards from the deck. One person then draws a card and, if he can make a match, places a pair of cards on the table and explains the match: "Cat has the /a/ sound" or Calf and glad have the /a/ sound." The players continue their alternate drawings until all cards have been drawn. The person with the largest number of matched pairs wins.

7. Use a die. On a wooden block (cube) print four letter-sounds (two of them twice). A pair of children can alternately roll the die and name a word than contains the letter-sound that shows on top. Words may not be repeated during the activity. Each child receives one point for each correct response. The game ends when one person reaches 25 points (having named approximately six words with each letter-sound). Label a die for each group of four letter-sounds. Dice may also be used in place of the spinner described in activity three above.

Summary

We began this chapter by outlining six questions for which answers would be sought.

1. What are the various kinds of word analysis skills, and what are their advantages and disadvantages?

2. What is a typical general sequence for presenting phonic and structural skills?

3. How can each pupil's phonic knowledge be determined as a basis for grouping and teaching?

4. What guidelines can be used in developing word analysis skills?

5. How can phonic and structural skills be taught in context to associate meaning and pronunciation?

6. What kinds of activities can be used to reinforce phonic skills?

While the information presented in this chapter is necessarily brief, it is intended to focus on general procedures and specific practices which must be followed if an adequate program of word analysis is to be provided for every pupil.

FOR FURTHER READING

Cheek, Earl H., "A Hierarchy for Teaching Phoneme-Grapheme Correspondences in Beginning Reading," Reading Improvement, XVII, No. 3 (Fall, 1980), 200-207.

Durkin, Dolores, Strategies for Identifying Words: A Workbook for Teachers and Those Preparing to Teach, Second Edition. Boston: Allyn, Bacon, 1981.

Harman, Susan, "Are Reversals A Symptom of Dyslexia?" Reading Teacher, XXXV, No. 4 (January, 1982), 424-428.

Heilman, Arthur, Phonics in Proper Perspective, Fifth Edition. Columbus, Ohio: Merrill, 1985.

Rogers, Norma, "Teaching Tips," Indiana Reading Quarterly, IX, No. 1 (Fall, 1976), 4-8.

_____, "Teaching Tips," Indiana Reading Quarterly, IX, No. 2 (Winter, 1977) 6-9, 31.

Spiegel, Dixie Lee, and Carol Rogers, "Teacher Responses to Miscues During Oral Reading by Second-Grade Students," Journal of Educational Research, LXXIV, No. 1 (September-October, 1980), 8-12.

Stotsky, Sandra L., "Teaching Prefixes: Facts and Fallacies," Language Arts", LIV, No. 8 (November-December, 1977), 887-890.

LEARNING SELECTED WORD ANALYSIS SKILLS
Introduction

When we invite workshop participants to propose
topics for consideration, one aspect of reading --
phonics -- invariably receives strong support. Because
of the need indicated by the interest in the topic, we
have chosen to present in an easily accessible manner
some of the phonic skills. The topic merits more
attention than the space provided here. The references
at the end of Chapter 9A contain excellent sources which
are more comprehensive.

The remainder of this chapter presents selected
generalizations about (a) LSAs organized in the general
sequence of consonants, clusters and digraphs, short and
long vowels, R-controlled vowels, and diphthongs, (b)
diacritical marks, (c) syllabication, and (d) accents.
Some of the generalizations are quite common and can be
presented in kindergarten (depending on the philosophy of
the school and teacher) or grade one. Others are more
appropriate for presentation at the junior high school
level. Each teacher must decide what to teach to which
pupils. This overview presents the information without
attempting to code it by grade level or key it to a
specific basal series.

A type of programmed instruction using the discovery
technique is used here to present the information. Study
the following material by using a 5x8 inch card to mask
the answer(s) and writing the correct responses in the
appropriate boxes or blanks. Then remove the card and
check the answer(s). After studying the first two
examples, you should find the subsequent exercises
somewhat easier. However, a few items almost invariably
"stump" most teachers. Perfectly obvious LSAs (i.e., the
letter b represents the /b/) are not included. Now,

let's see how much you know.

Generalizations: Letter-Sound Associations

Consonants

1. Sometimes the letter b does not represent a sound. List the following words in two columns and then write the two circumstances under which the b is "silent" (i.e., does not represent a sound). The b in the top box (penthouse) represents the letter being considered. The uncircled letters in the second row of boxes (top floor of an apartment building) represent the sound while the circled letters represent the "silent" letters. The empty spaces in the larger boxes (the other floors of the apartment) are to be filled in with words possessing the appropriate LSA.

climb   lamb

debt   doubt

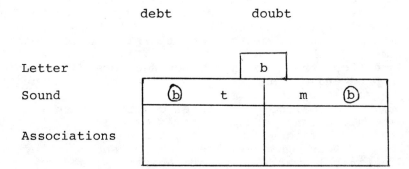

Generalization 1: A b is "silent" when _____ or _____.

Answers:

Letter   b

Sound   ⓑ t   m ⓑ

Associations   debt   climb
               doubt   lamb

A b is "silent" when it comes before a t or after an m. An alternate way of saying this is that bt represents the + sound (shown as /+/) and mb represents the /m/.

Question: If b is "silent" after m, how do you   explain timber, lumber, and umbrella?

Answer: The generalization does not apply if the m and the b are in different syllables. Add the words "in the same syllable" to Generalization 1.

You will   note that mb will be taught far earlier   than bt, which may never receive instruction because of its infrequent usage.

2. The letter c usually represents one of two sounds. Use the following words to complete the chart and then write the two related generalizations. Fill in the appropriate sound at the top of each column. Note the c in the penthouse indicates the letter which is being studied.

cat	come
cent	cup
city	cyclone

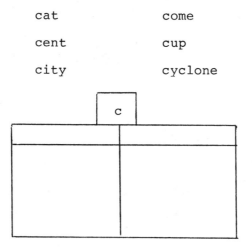

Generalization 2: A c usually represents the _____ sound when _____.

Generalization 3: A c usually represents the _____ sound when _____.

Answers:

	c	
k		**s**
cat		cent
come		city
cups		cyclone*

*The second c in <u>cyclone</u> qualifies for inclusion in the first column.

A c usually represents the /k/ when it comes before a, o, or u. Note: there is no such thing as a /c/. The letter c usually represents either the /k/ or the /s/.

A c usually represents the /s/ when it comes before e, i, or y. The /k/ is sometimes referred to as the "hard" sound and the /s/ as the "soft" sound.

Question: Sometimes a c comes before an l or r as in <u>clear</u>, <u>clock</u>, <u>cream</u>, and <u>cry</u>. What sound does it represent then?

Generalization 4: A c followed by an l or r represents the _____ sound.

Answer: A c followed by an l or r represents the /k/.

3. The letter c often comes before a k as in the following words. Write a generalization for the consonants and a generalization for the vowel.

tack	sick
wreck	lock
	duck

Generalization 5: A c before a k _____.

Generalization 6: A vowel before a ck _____.

Answers: A c before a k is "silent". Stated otherwise, a ck represents the /k/. The single vowel which typically precedes a ck is usually short.

4. Group the following words into the chart below and

then write two related generalizations. Be sure to fill in the penthouse with the common letters and the two columns on the top floor with the sounds those common letters represent.

```
        scat          scout
        scent         scum
        science       scythe
```

Generalization 7: The letters _____ represent the _____ sounds when they _____.

Generalization 8: The letters _____ represent the _____ sound when they _____.

Answers:

sc	
sk	s ©
scat	scent
scout	science
scum	scythe

The letters sc represents the /sk/ when they come before a, o, and u. The letters sc represent the /s/ when they come before e, i, or y. Note the relationship of these words to Generalizations 2 and 3.

5. Group the following words into the next chart and write the two appropriate generalizations.

```
        moccasin      accurate
        accent        accommodate
        accident
```

529

Generalization 9: The letters _____ represent the
_____ sound when they _____.

Generalization 10: The letters _____ represent the
_____ sounds when they _____.

Answers:

cc	
k	ks
moccasin	accent
accommodate	accident
accurate	

The letters cc represent the /k/ when they are followed
by a, o, or u. The letters cc represent the /ks/ when
they are followed by e or i. Once again, note the
relationship to Generalizations 2 and 3.

6. Organize the following words into the chart and write
an appropriate generalization.

adjective   adjoin

edge   judge

ridge

Generalization 11: A _____ is "silent" when
_____ or when _____.

530

Answers:

dg	dj
ⓓ j	ⓓ j
edge	adjective
ridge	adjoin
judge	

A d is "silent" when it comes before a g or when it comes before a j.

7. The letters ed represent three special sounds. Use the words shown below to identify the possibilities.

handed	chased
cooked	started
panted	stopped
bragged	oiled
fanned	nodded

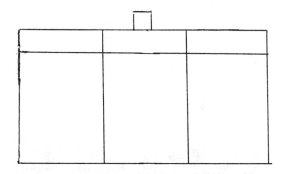

Generalization 12: The letters ed at the end of an action word may represent the _____ or the _____ or the _____ sounds.

531

Answers:

	ed	
d	t	id
bragged	cooked	handed
fanned	chased	panted
oiled	stopped	started
		nodded

The letters ed at the end of a an action word may represent either the /d/ or the /t/ or the /id/. Children usually identify the correct sound from their oral language rather than through reading instruction.

8. The letter g usually represents one or two sounds. Use the following words to complete the chart and then write the two related generalizations.

game	go
gentle	gum
gaint	gym

Generalization 13: A g usually represents the _____ sound when it _____.

Generalization 14: A g usually represents the _____ sound when it _____.

Answers:

	g	j
	game	gentle
	go	giant
	gum	gym

A g usually represents the /g/ when it comes before an a, o, or u. A g usually represents the /j/ when it comes before e, i, or y. The /g/ is often referred to as the "hard" sound and the /j/ as the "soft" sound. Note the relationship between the generalizations for c and g.

9. What can you say about the following words?

gnat   gnu
sign   reign

Generalization 15: A g usually _____ when _____.

Answer: A g usually is "silent" when it comes before an n. Stated otherwise, a gn usually represents the /n/ (in the same syllable).

10. What do you note about the following words?

sight   thought
weight   caught

Generalization 16: The letters _____ usually _____ when _____.

Answer: The letters gh usually are "silent" when they come before a t. Stated otherwise, the letters ght usually represent the /t/.

11. The next list of words illustrates three rather uncommon LSAs. Complete the chart and identify the generalizations.

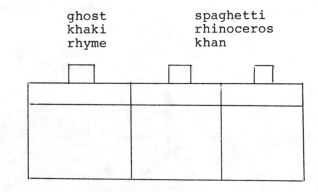

```
        ghost            spaghetti
        khaki            rhinoceros
        rhyme            khan
```

Generalization 17: The   letter   _____   usually
_____ when _____.

Answers:

gh	kh	rh
g (h)	k (h)	r (h)
ghost	khaki	rhyme
spaghetti	khan	rhinoceros

The letter h usually is "silent" when it comes after a
g, k, or r.

Question: State the information in another way.   Hint:
Refer to the answers to some of the earlier questions.

Answers: The letters gh usually represent the /g/, the
letters kh usually represent the /k/, and the letters rh
usually represent the /r/.

12. Using   the   words   listed   below,   state   a
generalization.

    knight   knife   know   knew

Generalization 18: The   letter   _____   usually
_____ when _____.

Answer: The letter k usually is "silent" when it comes
before n.

534

Question: How else can it be stated?

Answer: The letters kn usually represent the /n/.

13. Study the next group of words and develop a generalization.

    palm   almonds   salmon   calm

Generalization 19: The letter _____ usually _____ when _____ .

Answer: The letter l usually is "silent" when it comes in the alm combination. Stated otherwise, an l is "silent" when it comes between an a and an m. Note that an a must come before the l. In elm and film, for example, the l's are not "silent".

14. Complete the chart and state three generalizations based on the next list of words.

         pneumonia   pneumatic drill
         psychology   ptolemy
         ptomaine poisoning   psalms

Generalization 20: A _____ usually _____ when _____ .

Answers:

pn	ps	pt
(p) n	(p) s	(p) t
pneumonia	psychology	ptomaine poisoning
pneumatic drill	psalms	ptolemy

A p usually is "silent" when it comes before an n, s, or t. You will note that this set of generalizations will not likely be taught prior to the junior high school years.

15. The letter s may represent four different sounds. Classify the words into the four groups. You do not need to decide when s represents each sound.

see	sugar
sure	saw
has	hands
vision	fusion

Generalization 21: The letter _____ may represent any of the following sounds: _____, _____, _____, or _____.

Answers:

s			
s	sh	z	zh
see	sure	has	vision
saw	sugar	hands	fusion

The letter s may represent any of the following sounds: /s/, /z/, /sh/, or /zh/. Usually an initial s represents the /s/, and an s in the sion combination represents the /zh/. An s at the end of a word may represent either an /s/ or /z/. Pupils' oral language will provide the most helpful clue when the word is plural. There are very few times when s represents the /sh/. Teaching it is therefore of dubious value. Sample words should be taught by sight.

16. In three instances the letter t does not represent a speech sound. Use the information below to identify these situations.

watch   pitch
fasten   wrestle
castle   moisten

Generalization 22: A _____ when _____, it _____, or it _____.

t		
(t) ch	s (t) en	s (t) le
watch	fasten	castle
pitch	moisten	wrestle

A t usually is "silent" when it comes before ch, or when it comes in the sten combination at the end of a word, or when it comes in the stle combination.

17. What generalization can you draw from the words listed below?

write   wrench   wrong   wrestle

Generalization 23: The letter _____ usually _____.

Answer: The letter w usually is "silent" when it comes before an r.

18. The letter x may represent three sounds.   Identify
them and write the generalization.

       xylophone   exam
       box   exaggerate
       xerox   ax

Generalization 24:   The _____ when
_____ _____. It may also represent the
_____ or the _____ sounds.

Answers:

	x	
z	ks	gz
xylophone	box	exaggerate
xerox*	ax	exam

    *Xerox may also be listed in the ks category.

The letter x usually represents the /z/ when it comes at
the beginning of a word. It may also represent the /ks/
(which is the most common option) or the /gz/. X has no
sound of its own.

CONSONANT CLUSTERS

    Consonant clusters are two or three joined consonant
sounds.   They normally consist of consonant letters but
may on occasion be represented by letters commonly
thought to be vowels. For example, qu is a consonant
cluster because the letters qu represent /kw/. Q has no
sound of its own.

    Please circle the consonant clusters in the following
words. Some words contain two consonant clusters.   There
are fifteen in all.

538

bridge	sleepy	blast	cross
request	cleats	risk	program
wasp	friends	twenty	flowers

Answers: Reading down the lists, br, qu, st, sp, sl, cl, fr, bl, st, sk, tw, cr, pr, gr, and fl.

Most, but not all, consonant clusters contain one of three particular letters. Look back at the list of words and name the three letters. They are _____, _____, and _____.

Answers: The three letters are l, r, and s. In a few cases a letter representing the /w/ (either a w or a u) is also part of a consonant cluster.

Consonant clusters with l or r normally are not syllabicated. That is, they form a part of only one syllable.

CONSONANT DIGRAPHS

A consonant digraph is a sound which is represented by two (and sometimes three) letters. These letters, however, do not represent the sound normally associated with them. A consonant digraph usually includes a particular letter. Circle the consonant digraphs in the list below and then identify the key letter.

church	shovel	thick
whisper	tough	photograph

Question: The key letter is _____.

Answers: The consonant digraph letters are ch, ch, wh, sh, gh, th, ph, and ph. The key letter is h.

Several consonant digraph letters are worth noting.

1. The letters ch may represent three different common speech sounds. Organize the following words and identify the generalization. There is no way of identifying when ch represents each of the sounds.

check	watch
chorus	ache
machine	mustache

539

Generalization 25: The letters ch usually represent either the _____, _____, or _____ sound.

Answers:

ch		
ch	sh	k
check	machine	chorus
watch	mustache	ache

The letters ch usually represent either the /ch/, /sh/, or /k/, in that order.

2. Look at the words in the next list and identify the generalization for the letters ph.

photograph   elephant   phonics   telephone

Generalization 26: The letters ph usually _____.

Answer: The letters ph usually represent the /f/.

3. One of the most difficult auditory distinctions involves the two different sounds which the letters th represent. Group the following words into two lists according to the different sounds of th.

thick   thought
there   thunder
these   that

Generalization 27: The letters th may represent the sound as contained in the word _____ or the sound as contained in the word _____.

540

	th	th
	thick	there
	thought	these
	thunder	that

The letters th may represent the sound as contained in the word thick or the sound as contained in the word there. The distinction between the unvoiced or voiceless th (the apartments on the left) and the voiced th (the apartments on the right) is not very important for teaching purposes because most pupils acquire the ability to use the appropriate sound through their oral language.

4. The letters wh represent the last consonant digraph to be considered here. Note the following words and complete the generalization.

   while   where   when   why

Generalization 28: The letters wh usually _____.

Answer: The letters wh usually represent the /hw/. In practice this sound is very difficult to teach. First of all, some teachers and children do not say /hw/. Second, it is far easier to teach the wh letters as a "silent" h following a w or as wh represents the /w/. Oral language usually resolves the problem with instruction having little effect on pronunciation.

SHORT AND LONG VOWELS

1. Divide the following words into two groups according to their vowels sounds. Then state two generalizations.

age	add	lake	match
as	ate	back	gate

a	ā

541

Generalization 1: The single vowel a usually represents the _____ sound when it comes _____ or _____ of a word.

Generalization 2: The letter a followed by a _____ and a _____ usually is _____.

Answers:

a	
a	ā
as	age
add	ate
back	lake
match	gate

The single vowel a usually represents the short sound when it comes in the beginning or middle of a word. The letter a followed by a consonant and a final e usually is long. Note the absence in the chart of a diacritical mark over the short a. This absence automatically signals a short vowel sound.

After syllabication and accenting principles have been introduced, the generalization for short vowel sounds can be extended from single-syllable to polysyllabic words. Thus the first syllables in such words as fancy, candle, and gallon will be included since the syllable being considered is accented.

2. Note the words in the list below. Place them in the appropriate category and state a generalization for each vowel sound.

bed	eve	Pete	scene
neck	end	Ed	cede

542

Generalization 3: The single vowel e usually represents the _____ sound when it comes _____ or _____ of a word.

Generalization 4: The letter e followed by a _____ and a _____ usually _____ .

Answers:

e	
e	ē
bed	eve
neck	scene
end	Pete
Ed	cede

The single vowel e usually represents the short sound when it comes in the beginning or middle or a word. The letter e followed by a single consonant and a final e usually is long.

3. Study the words in the next list and group them by auditory and visual similarities. Then state two generalizations.

hit	wide	in	big
mile	is	Ike	ice

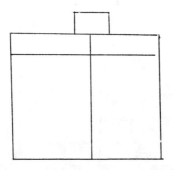

Generalization 5: The single vowel i usually _____
when it _____ .

Generalization 6: The letter i usually _____ when it
is followed by _____ .

Answers:

i	
i	ī
hit	mile
is	wide
in	Ike
big	ice

The single vowel i usually is short when it comes in the
beginning or middle of a word. The letter i usually is
long when it is followed by a single consonant and a
final e.

4. Look at the following words and use them to complete
the chart. Then state two generalizations.

rode	got	rope	bone
ox	broke	hop	odd

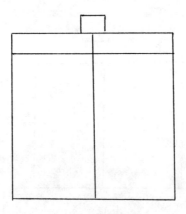

544

Generalization 7: The single vowel o usually _____ when it _____.

Generalization 8: The letter o usually _____ when it is followed by _____.

Answers:

o	
ŏ	ō
ox	rode
got	broke
hop	rope
odd	bone

The single vowel o usually is short when it comes in the beginning or middle of a word. The letter o usually is long when it is followed by a single consonant and a final e.

5. Study the words in the list below. After completing the chart, develop two generalizations.

huge   cut   mule   bug

up   cube   us   fuse

Generalization 9: The single vowel u usually _____ when it _____.

Generalization 10: The letter u sometimes _____ when it is followed by _____.

545

Answers:

u	
u	u
up	huge
cut	cube
us	mule
bug	fuse

The single vowel <u>u</u> usually is short when it comes in the beginning or middle of a word. The letter <u>u</u> sometimes is long when it is followed by a single consonant and a final <u>e</u>.

It is worth noting that the letter <u>u</u> followed by a single consonant and a final <u>e</u> may represent the two-dot <u>u</u> (or o͞o) sound as in <u>Luke</u>. Pupils should consider both options.

VOWEL DIGRAPHS

A vowel digraph consists of two vowels which represent a speech sound typically associated with one of its members. The speech sound may be long or short and may be associated with either the first or the second letter of the digraph. While a number of vowel pairs are digraphs, very few possess 75% functional utility. In several situations, therefore, it is necessary for a reader to consider options rather than rely on a single generalization.

6. Study the words in the following list. Then develop a generalization which reflects the visual and auditory similarities of the words.

            aim   aid
            may   stay

Generalization 11: The letters _____ and _____ usually represent the _____ sound. The letters _____ usually come _____ while the letters _____ usually come _____.

546

Answer: The letters <u>ai</u> and <u>ay</u> usually represent the /ā/. The letters <u>ai</u> usually come in the beginning or middle of a word or syllable while the letters <u>ay</u> usually come at the end of a word or syllable.

7. Use these words to develop a generalization.

see	babies
hurried	trees

Generalization 12: The letters _____ and _____ usually represent the _____ sound.

Answer: The letters <u>ee</u> and <u>ie</u> usually represent the /ē/. Most of the exceptions to the <u>ie</u> generalization relate to one-syllable words such as <u>lie</u>, <u>die</u>, <u>tie</u>, and <u>pie</u>.

8. Study the words shown below and identify the generalization.

coat	oats
oak	road

Generalization 13: The letters _____ usually _____.

Answer: The letters <u>oa</u> usually represent the /ō/.

9. Group the following words into two lists and develop some generalizations.

ceiling	reign
either	receive
weigh	eight

Generalization 14: The letters _____ represent the _____ sound when _____.

Generalization 15: The letters _____ usually represent the _____ sound.

Answers:

	ei	
ā		ē
weigh		ceiling
reign		either
eight		receive

The letters ei represent the /ā/ when they are followed by the letter g. The letters ei usually represent the /ē/ especially when they follow the letter c.

10. Study the words listed below and write a generalization with two parts.

deaf   bread
sea   reach
leap   breath

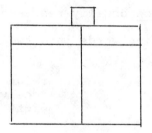

Generalization 16: The letters _____ may represent either _____.

Answers:

	ea	
ē		e
sea		deaf
leap		bread
reach		breath

The letters ea may represent either the /ē/ or the /e/.

11. Note the following words and develop a similar generalization with two parts.

grow	know
cow	towel
now	show

Generalization 17: The letters _____ may represent either _____ or _____.

Answers:

ōw	
ō	ou
grow	cow
know	now
slow	towel

The letters ow may represent either the /ō/ or the /ou/. In the latter case, the ow is a diphthong rather than a vowel digraph.

R-CONTROLLED VOWELS

An R-controlled situation occurs when the sound represented by one or more vowels is influenced by an r, usually following the vowel(s) but sometimes occurring between two vowels. The vowel sound is neither long nor short but modified, i.e., R-controlled.

12. Note the visual and auditory similarities of the following words and develop a generalization.

car	mark
arm	stars

Generalization 18: A single vowel a̱ followed by _____ usually represents the _____ sound.

Answer: A single vowel a̱ followed by an ṟ usually represents the /ar/.

13. Study the words shown below. Then complete the chart and write a generalization.

air	stairs	error	perish
care	share	fair	dare
merit	ferry	terrible	very

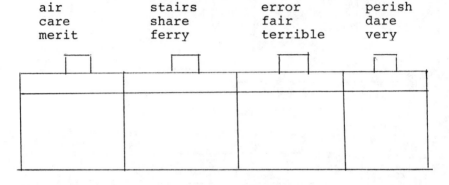

Generalization 19: The letters _____, _____, and _____ usually represent the _____ sound.

Answers:

air	are	err	er*
âr	âr	âr	âr
air	care	ferry	merit
stairs	share	error	perish
fair	dare	terrible	very

*plus a following vowel

The letters air, are, err, and er plus a following vowel usually represent the /air/.

14. Look at the next group of words. Then complete the chart and develop a generalization.

| her | fur | bird | fern |
| dirt | | burn | |

Generalization 20: A single vowel _____, _____, or _____ followed by a _____ usually represents the _____ sound.

Answers:

er	ir	ur
er	er	er
her	dirt	fur
fern	bird	burn

A single vowel e, i, or u followed by r usually represents the /er/ (or ər). Stated another way, er, ir, and ur usually represent the /er/.

15. Study the next words, complete the chart, and state a generalization.

| ear | cheer | deer | clear |
| dear | | steer | |

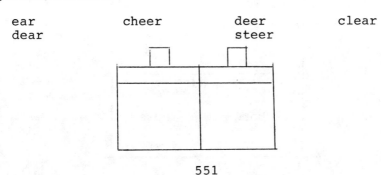

Generalization 21: The letters _____ usually represent the _____ sound.

Answers:

ear	eer
eer	eer
ear	deer
dear	cheer
clear	steer

The letters <u>ear</u> and <u>eer</u> usually represent the /eer/. Stated another way, the letters <u>ea</u> and <u>ee</u> plus <u>r</u> usually represent the /eer/.

16. Note the following words, complete the chart, and develop a generalization.

         more   born
         cord   fork
         shore   store

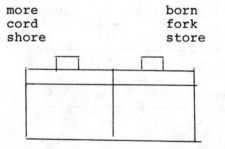

Generalization 22: The letters _____ and _____ usually _____.

Answers:

or	ore
or	or
cord	more
born	shore
fork	store

552

The letters or and ore usually represent the /or/.

DIPHTHONGS

A diphthong is two vowels which represent a sound different from that typically represented by either of the letters. Thus the sound is neither short nor long. Most diphthongs are clustered into pairs of spellings representing the same sound.

17. Look at the words listed below and develop a generalization.

        saw   law
        audience   caught

Generalization 23: The letters _____ usually _____ .

Answer: The letters aw and au usually represent the same sound, the /aw/.

18. Study the following words and develop an appropriate generalization.

        out   sound
        plow   vowel

Generalization 24: _____ .

Answer: The letter ou and ow usually represent the /ou/. It is worth remembering that ow will be a diphthong only when it represents the /ou/. If it represents the /o/, it is a vowel digraph.

19. From the words listed below write an appropriate generalization.

        boy   toys
        oil   coins

Generalization 25: _____ The letters _____ usually come _____ while the letters ____ usually come ____ .

Answer: The letters oi and oy usually represent the /oi/. The letters oy usually come at the end of a word or syllable while the letters oi usually come in the beginning or middle or a word or syllable.

553

20. Note the words listed below and complete the chart. Then write a two-part generalization.

        book   wood   boot
        moon   food   shook

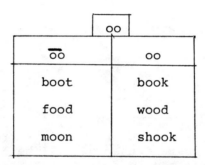

Generalization 26: The letters _____ usually represent either the ____ as in ____ or the ____ sound as in ____.

Answers:

	oo
ō̄o	oo
boot	book
food	wood
moon	shook

The letters oo usually represent the /ō̄o/ as in boot or the /oo/ as in book.

21. Look at the following words, complete the chart, and write a two-part generalization.

    true   crew   blue   fruit   bruise
    suit   grew   clues   blew

554

Generalization 27: The letters _____.

Answers:

ue	ui	ew
ü	ü	ü
true	fruit	grew
blue	suit	blew
clues	bruise	crew

The letters ue and ui usually represent the /ü/ or the /ōō/. Some speakers pronounce some words as /ū/ rather than as /ü/. Examples are Tuesday and due.

SPECIAL CASES

22. Sometimes a consonant affects the sound of the following vowel. Note the visual and auditory similarities in the following words and state a generalization.

    waddle   wasp   swan   squash
    squad   squander

Generalization 28: The sound of _____ changes the short vowel sound of the following _____ to _____.

Answer:
The /w/ changes the short vowel sound of the following a to /o/ (or /ä/). We might consider this as a W-controlled situation.

23. The /w/ also influences other following letters. Develop a generalization based on the following words.

    work   word   war   worst
    dwarf   quartz

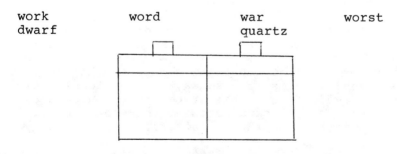

Generalization 29: The sound of _____ changes the following _____ sound to _____ and the _____ sound to ____.

Answers:

wor	war
er	or
work	war
word	dwarf
worst	quartz

The /w/ changes the following /or/ to /er/ and the /ar/ to /or/.

24. What generalization can you develop by noting the following words?

gracious   social   ancient

Generalization 30: The letters _____ often represent the _____ sound when they _____.

Answer:

The letters ci often represent the /sh/ when they come before a vowel suffix. The letters commonly appearing in such situations are ous, al, and ent.

25. Develop a generalization from the words shown below.

donkey   lovely   baby   monkey
funny   turkey

Generalization 31: The letters _____ and _____ represent the _____ when _____.

Answer: The letters y and ey represent the /ē/ when they come at the end of a word in an unaccented syllable.

26. Perhaps the last important phonic element that needs to be mentioned is the schwa, which looks like an inverted reversed e. This symbol represents the /u/. Many vowel letters can represent the schwa sound. For example, note the underlined letters.

above   pencil   common   fasten   uncle

Letters representing the /er/ are often shown with the schwa. Thus

> her can become hər
> bird can become bərd
> fur can become fər

Only one generalization related to the schwa is especially helpful. Carefully study the following words and try to write an appropriate generalization.

upon   connect   mayor   beggar   teacher

Generalization 32: A vowel that would normally be short or R-controlled will usually represent a _____ sound when _____.

Answer:

A vowel that would normally be short or R-controlled will usually represent a schwa (or /u/) when it comes in a unaccented syllable.

Diacritical Marks

In the course of this overview we have identified several symbols for marking vowels. Chart 9B-1 identifies the names and functions of these symbols.

CHART 9B-1
DIACRITICAL MARKS

Symbol*	Name and Function
‾	Macron (long sound)
˘	Breve (short sound, usually not marked)
ᷰ	Breve circumflex (over o̲)
∧	Circumflex (over o̲r̲; sometimes over i̲r̲ and u̲r̲)
˙˙	Two-dot Italian (over a̲r̲ and a̲; over u̲)
˙	One-dot Italian (over a̲ and e̲r̲)
ə	Schwa (to represent short u̲)

*Not all symbols are included here. A dictionary key will display several others.

557

Some sounds are represented in different ways. Chart 9B-2 presents some common vowel equivalents and sample words.

CHART 9B-2

ạ̈	swap	=	o	shop			
ȧ	aroma	=	u	up			
ẹr	her	=	ir	fir	=	ur	fur
ọ	soft	=	au	cause			
u̇	put	=	oo	foot			
ü	Ruth	=	o͞o	booth			

Syllabication Generalizations

The following pages provide information about a number of important syllabication generalizations. The sequence is somewhat similar to that proposed by McFeely (504).

1. Study the words shown below. How are they alike? What generalization can you draw?

    cowboy   someone   baseball   outside

2. How are the next words alike? What is the generalization?

    farmer   foolish   jumping   handed

Generalization 2: Divide words so the suffix is a separate syllable.

3. Syllabicate and develop a generalization.

    rewrite   unwrap   preheat   misspell

Generalization 3: Divide words so the prefix is a separate syllable.

4. Divide the following words into two groups. What generalization can you develop? When does it apply?

    handed   chased   hunted   started
    cooked   faded   tried   teased

Generalization 4: When a word ends in ed, the suffix forms a separate syllable if it is preceded by t or d (handed, hunted, started, faded). If the letter before the ed is not t or d, the ed does not form a separate syllable.

5A. How are the next words alike? State a generalization.

funny   daddy   rabbit   bully

Generalization 5A: Words with two identical consonants usually are divided between the two consonants.

Note that words such as spelled, looked, and stopped are not divided. Refer to generalization four.

5B. Study the following words and develop a generalization.

carton   window   after   elbow

Generalization 5B: Words with two different consonants usually are divided between the two consonants.

Note: Words with consonant clusters involving r or l (e.g., cobra, secret) or consonant digraphs (e.g., father, mother) usually are not divided between the two consonants.

6. Arrange the following words into two groups according to their vowel sounds and syllabic division. Then state a two-part generalization telling when each part applies.

finish   baby   final   habit

Generalization 6: When one consonant comes between two vowels, the consonant either ends one syllable or starts the other.

If the syllable ends in a consonant, we call it a closed syllable, and the preceding single vowel usually is short. If the syllable ends in a vowel, we call it an open syllable, and the vowel usually is long if the syllable is accented. Otherwise the vowel will probably represent the schwa sound. Approximately 50% of the elementary words with the vowel-consonant-vowel pattern end in the consonant, and the other one-half end in a vowel. Therefore, children must learn to consider both options.

7. How are the following words alike? State a generalization.

rifle   sample

Generalization 7: If a words ends in a consonant plus le, those three letters form the final syllable. However, the generalization does not apply in words such as tickle, chuckle, tackle, and buckle. In each of these cases the ck represents one sound (/k/) and is not divided. Thus, one divides a ckle word in such a way that ck ends the syllable, and le is the final syllable (tack-le).

8. Syllabicate the following words and develop a generalization.

oyster   forest   stapler
burglar   vowel

Generalization 8: Diphthongs, R-controlled letters, and consonant clusters (except for those with s) usually are not divided.

9. What do you notice about each of the following? Syllabicate and draw a generalization.

Leo   lion
dial   dual

Generalization 9: In each case there is an odd vowel combination. In such situations, divide between the vowels. Usually the first vowel (in the open syllable) will be long, and the second vowel will represent the schwa sound.

In the course of completing these exercises, you have probably noted that every syllable has a vowel sound. It may or may not have a consonant sound. One further point: The purpose of syllabication is to enable a child to come close enough to a pronunciation to recognize the word. Thus it is inappropriate to distribute a list of words for pupils to syllabicate and then fail to ask them to pronounce the items.

Below is information about a number of generalizations on accents. The generalizations are somewhat similar to those proposed by Winkley (745).

560

Accent Generalizations

1. Study the words below. What accent generalization can you draw?

baby   curtain   register   verify
handle   funny   manual   formula

Generalization 1: A two- or three-syllable word typically is accented on the first syllable.

2. What do the words listed next have in common? State a generalization.

reread   depress   unfair
insecure   preheat   illegal

Generalization 2: Each word has a prefix. Usually we don't accent prefixes. Accent a root (usually Latin or Greek) or a base word (such as <u>fair</u> or <u>legal</u>) rather than a prefix.

3. How are the following words alike? What accent generalization can you develop?

government   action   teacher
foolish   climbing

Generalization 3: Each word has a suffix. Usually we don't accent suffixes. Accent a root or a base word (such as <u>fool</u> or <u>climb</u>) rather than a suffix.

4. Note how the following words are alike and develop a generalization.

parade   device   divine   complete

Generalization 4: If a word ends in a long vowel sound, the final syllable usually is accented.

5. How are the following words alike? Develop a generalization.

composition   constitution   locomotion   generation

Generalization 5: Long words ending in <u>tion</u> often have two accented syllables. The primary (heavy) accent usually falls on the syllable before <u>tion</u>, and the secondary (light) accent is two syllables before the primary accent.

As we noted in the section on syllabication, the purpose of accenting is to come close enough to a word we recognize orally to pronounce it. Pupils should acquire a "set for diversity," trying an alternate strategy if the first one fails to pay dividends.

Summary

The preceding pages are intended to provide only an overview of selected phonic and structural knowledge. Much more comprehensive treatment is contained in the suggestions for further study in this chapter and in Chapter 9A.

Most generalizations have exceptions. When the generalizations are appropriate for pupils' present needs, they can be justified, until pupils are ready for more sophisticated concepts. For example, a vowel followed by a consonant and a final e has been described here as typically long. (Exceptions include come, some, give, and have.) Later pupils will encounter polysyllabic words in which the unaccented final syllable contains a vowel-consonant-final e pattern that requires a more elaborately-stated generalization. (Examples include manage, exquisite, and menace.) Finally, only phonic and structural generalizations have been presented. Information on other word analysis skills is included in other chapters.

FOR FURTHER READING

Burmeister, Lou E., "Content of a Phonics Program Based on Particularly Useful Generalizations," in Reading Methods and Teacher Improvement, pp. 27-39, ed. Nila Banton Smith. Newark, Del.: IRA, 1971.

Dechant, Emerald V., Improving the Teaching of Reading, Third Edition. Englewood Cliffs, N.J.: Prentice-Hall, 1982.

Wilson, Robert M., and MaryAnne Hall, Programmed Word Attack for Teachers, Fourth Edition. Columbus, Ohio: Merrill, 1984.

CHAPTER 10

IDEAS FOR DEVELOPING VOCABULARY

Introduction

There are four obvious vocabularies -- reading, writing, listening, and speaking -- plus one lesser-known but important aspect, the thinking vocabulary. The latter consists of elements common to the preceding four. Chart 10-1 explains the interrelationships of each.

CHART 10-1

THE VOCABULARIES

Oral

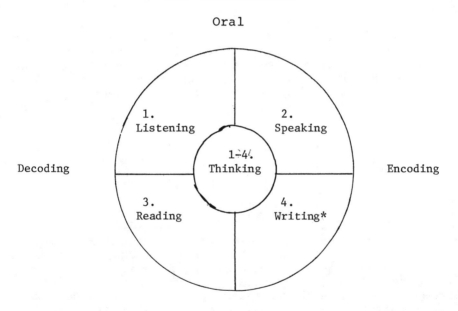

Graphic or Written

*includes composition, grammar, handwriting, and spelling

Thoughtful study of Chart 10-1 should reveal several worthwhile points. First, listening and reading involve decoding. They require a learner to recognize the symbols through which information is communicated.

Speaking and writing involve encoding. That is, they require a person to produce the oral or written symbols necessary to transmit information. Because it is a simpler task to <u>recognize</u> symbols than to produce them (64, 317, 564), a youngster's listening vocabulary is generally larger than his speaking, and his reading is usually greater than his writing. Keeping these factors in mind helps us avoid asking pupils to spell words which are just being introduced at the listening and/or reading levels (73). Further comments are made later.

Third, listening and speaking involve oral language development. No direct "on paper" assignments are necessary or even appropriate for expanding vocabulary strength in these areas. Reading and writing involve graphic skills. In these areas, specific planned practice with printed material seems highly desirable.

Fourth, the thinking vocabulary may be considered as that element which binds the four areas of listening, speaking, reading, and writing. Indeed, without a thinking vocabulary we could neither acquire, manipulate, nor disseminate ideas. Fifth, overall development of the four "basic" vocabularies normally proceeds along a continuum of four overlapping levels. Competence in the spoken language is a prerequisite for progress at the graphic, or print, stage (470). See Chart 10-2.

CHART 10-2

Sequence of Vocabulary Development

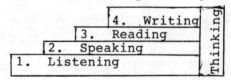

Infants listen (i.e., become aware of aural stimuli), even before the time of birth. Near the end of the first year they produce sequences of sounds which we identify as words. These vocal efforts represent children's attempts to imitate the speech patterns common to their environments. Those whose parents speak French do likewise; those whose parents speak with Southern accents do likewise. The fact that we normally imitate prevailing speech patterns helps to explain both the standard and non-standard language dialects of different societies.

About the sixth year, a youngster learns to read. This accomplishment is shortly followed (or immediately preceded, depending upon one's point of view) by the ability to produce sentences and paragraphs on paper (unless one of the preceding vocabularies has not been adequately developed. When this occurs, growth at the higher levels is either inhibited or prevented.)

More specifically, a child whose listening vocabulary is impoverished is simply incapable at the present time of acquiring and utilizing an extensive speaking vocabulary. A youngster whose speaking vocabulary is underdeveloped cannot presently learn to read well. He may learn to decode well but not to comprehend. Finally, the person whose reading ability is poorly developed normally cannot become proficient in writing (composition, grammar, and spelling).

Research makes it clear that vocabulary competence is one of the major components of comprehension (232, 415, 675, 707). The size of a child's vocabulary is a good predictor of his reading achievement (137).

This chapter addresses the following topics: (a) questionable classroom practices, (b) suggested classroom practices (general, listening, speaking, reading, and writing), and (c) guidelines for developing vocabulary.

Questionable Classroom Practices

Because vocabulary development is crucial to subsequent competence in comprehension, it is especially unfortunate when classroom procedures inhabit or prevent its facile growth. Examples of classroom procedures with dubious value are presented below.

Questionable Practice One: "Expecting pupils to engage in formal spelling activities before they have developed the ability to read at approximately the early second-grade level."

We have already suggested that recognizing a word in print is a considerably easier task than producing (spelling) it from memory. Therefore, it does not seem desirable to expect youngsters to spell words which they are just learning to recognize. This is the reason spelling is not normally included (except incidentally) in the first-grade curriculum.

While average and above average second-grade children may possess backgrounds sufficient to enable them to begin "book" spelling (assuming this is even desirable!), those who read at or below the primer or first reader level would derive much more benefit from planned informal activities of an immediately practical nature. For instance, you might consider relating phonic analysis to spelling rather than to reading, especially for those words which have systematic letter-sound associations. Functional informal spelling might also be used in conjunction with experience stories and with letter-writing activities. Indeed, Bloomer (66) found that vocabulary knowledge facilitated pupils' correct spelling and reading of words. Certainly there are few benefits to be gained in trying to teach very poor readers to spell (482). This fact is equally true of second graders and eighth graders. Priority, time, and energy should be focused on teaching those pupils to read (better).

Questionable Practice Two: "Expecting pupils to learn to spell new content-related words being developed at the listening and reading levels."

Terms whose meanings are unknown are new words, and, if correct spelling is expected, a youngster must master decoding and encoding simultaneously--even though one builds on the other. In general, a pupil should be able to recognize a word quickly and accurately before he is expected to produce (spell) it. At the primary levels, the process may require six months or a year for some youngsters. Even at the intermediate levels an extended period of time may well elapse before children are sufficiently familiar with the visual forms and meaning to spell the word correctly (694). Indeed, the repeated visual contact and recognition may well lead to subsequent efficient spelling.

It seems inappropriate, therefore, for teachers to "count off" for misspelled new and technical words in content areas such as science and social studies. While proponents of such a practice often stress the importance of correlating instruction in the various areas of the curriculum, we consider this procedure self-defeating, especially for poor readers.

Probably no one would question the desirability of helping readers become aware of their misspelling of common words. Certainly no one would question the wisdom of helping and assisting readers to master these functional terms. Hopefully, few would object to making notations of incorrectly spelled common words only, without reducing scores in the content subject. This practice should not, of course, preclude our using spelling (and grammatical) errors as bases for subsequent instruction, practice, and mastery. Misspelled words in social studies represent spelling problems, not history problems. They should be treated as such.

Questionable Practice Three: "Expecting pupils to determine meanings of words presented in isolation." (195)

566

Several types of questionable activities readily fall into this category: (a) assigning spelling words to be defined, (b) listing isolated reading, social studies, and science terms to be learned, and (c) distributing mimeographed sheets of words to be studied by advanced pupils and college-preparatory students. All three types of activities involve an unsatisfactory procedure: studying words without regard for their contextual settings.

Most words have ambiguous meanings when presented in isolation. Sentences and paragraphs are needed to delineate meaning. Extinguish may mean to put out, but do we extinguish the cat at night? And what is a cat -- a domesticated furry creature, a circus or zoo animal, or a hippy?

> At lunch time the worker climbed down from
> the cat and ate his lunch in the shade.

Only by using context can we recognize that cat is a shortened form for the heavy machine called a caterpillar. If we wish to help pupils avoid or overcome the habit of merely memorizing and disgorging random odds and ends of information, we must avoid the practice of asking them to "look up" lists of words.

How many teachers, one wonders, have been asked, "Which definition should I copy down?" And how many have received papers containing the first or shortest definition copied from a dictionary or glossary without understanding or learning? This response is to be expected when such assignments are made. And, to complicate the matter, why should a pupil be asked to spell words whose meanings he does not even know?

Questionable Practice Four: "Presenting new words by telling pupils their meanings."

A closely-related questionable practice involves placing new words on a chalkboard or a mimeographed sheet and then telling pupils the meanings of the words. While this technique avoids the problem expressed in Questionable Practice Three, it creates another: Not only does it present the new words in isolation, it prevents the youngsters from determining the meanings through context, thereby excluding the development of vocabulary skill. Alternative procedures are included on subsequent pages.

Questionable Practice Five: "Teaching the meanings of new terms after the lesson has been read or studied."

The placement of isolated word lists at the ends of

chapters in some content-area textbooks tends to inhibit the introduction of vocabulary before the reading assignment. As an instructional practice, it seem highly desirable to present new terms before the reading act occurs. Learning new vocabulary after the story has been read and the immediate need for the information is past does not seem likely to positively influence the level of motivation. At best, such teaching is non-sequential. At worst it is useless.

Questionable Practice Six: "Presenting vocabulary terms in their written forms before introducing their oral symbols."

We have said previously that vocabulary develops sequentially--first listening, then speaking, then reading, and finally sentence and paragraph writing. This being the case, we should find it quite useful to present new vocabulary through listening activities and provide extended experience through reading. Likewise we first should provide practice in speaking and later progress to written activities.

Observations of the language development of youngsters indicate they acquire the ability to pronounce and define new terms much more rapidly and efficiently if these words have first been presented through functional oral experiences. Therefore, we should discuss new words orally before introducing their printed forms.

A further application extends to educationally disadvantaged children. At all grade levels there are numbers of youngsters whose listening and speaking vocabularies are extremely limited. At the primary levels, these youngsters are often pushed into formal reading activities before their oral development is sufficiently extensive to allow them to take advantage of these experiences. If our objective is to produce youngsters who can read efficiently and effectively, we might begin by developing a strong background of listening and speaking experiences. To do otherwise is to invite--even to cause--permanent failure as early as age six.

Suggested Classroom Practices

With these thoughts in mind, let us consider some practices designed to enhance the development of the four basic vocabularies. The ideas presented here are intended to serve mainly as stimuli. Hopefully they will foster creative thought and action based on varying classroom situations. Numerous ideas are contained in excellent books by Edgar Dale and Joseph O'Rourke (227) and Johnson and Pearson (435b). We have used the ideas discussed here and found them to be successful.

The following practices are discussed under five major topics: (a) general, (b) listening, (c) speaking, (d) reading, and (e) writing. Some activities relate to several areas.

GENERAL

Practice One: "Teach the use of contextual analysis as the primary technique for determining the meanings of unknown words."

To understand and appreciate the influence which context has on our daily reading, please take the test presented in Chart 10-3.

CHART 10-3

TEST--WORDS IN ISOLATION

Directions: Write the definitions of the following words:

1.	ibex	6.	lexicographers
2.	apogee	7.	imminent
3.	perigee	8.	inchoate
4.	incarcerated	9.	lethargic
5.	recalcitrant	10.	incessantly

Are you through? Did you write the definition of each word? How did you do? Now take the test presented in Chart 10-4.

CHART 10-4

VOCABULARY TEST - WORDS IN CONTEXT

Directions: Write the definitions of the underlined words.

1. The ibex, a wild mountain goat, lived on rocky ledges.

2, 3. The new satellite is now orbiting the earth. Its apogee is 123, and its perigee 92, miles.

569

4. The policemen captured the bank robber and
    immediately incarcerated him.

5. Such recalcitrant behavior as disobedience and
    stubbornness simply must be overcome.

6. A staff of lexicographers worked ten years to
    write the new dictionary.

7. Hurry and close the shutters. Take the clothes
    off the lines and put them in the house. A storm
    appears imminent.

8. Could I call you back later and let you know?
    Right now my plans are inchoate.

9. Because I knew Ray was so energetic and active, I
    was surprised to find his brother Hal so very
    lethargic.

10. What a big mouth. I've never seen anyone talk so
    incessantly. I thought she would never shut up.

Are you through? Did you write the definition of
each underlined word? Now check your answers with some
sample possibilities listed next.

1. A wild mountain goat

2. Highest or furthest point in a satellite's orbit.

3. Lowest or nearest point in a satellite's orbit

4. Imprisoned

5. Rebellious; stubborn

6. Dictionary writers

7. About to happen

8. Incomplete

9. Inactive; not energetic

10. Without stopping; unceasingly

How well did you do? Now compare your two test
scores. Did you score higher on the second test? If
so, you can easily recognize the reason: Contextual

usage is extremely important in determining meanings of unfamiliar words (or of words used with different meanings).

Since context is by far the quickest and most effective procedure for determining and retaining the meanings of unknown words, it seems highly desirable to provide abundant specific instruction and practice in this skill (298). A number of writers have identified types of context clues (244, 264, 298).

A brief look at the ten examples presented in Chart 10-4 should reveal several types of contextual clues with which youngsters should become familiar.

1. Appositive. Except at the end of a sentence, this re-statement of the unfamiliar term is distinguished by a pair of punctuation marks, commas, brackets, parentheses, or dashes. Regardless of the mark, the reader should learn to anticipate and recognize the accompanying definition. Refer to example one.

2. Summary. A series of items preceded or followed by a general all-inclusive statement is a key to a summary statement or term. In example seven, the sentences preceding the underlined term contain information which helps a perceptive reader to define the unknown word.

3. Contrast. Sometimes one (part of a) sentence makes a statement in contrast to the other. Frequently we recognize such contrasts by the use of key words such as though, although, while, but, yet, nevertheless, and even though. Sentence nine is an example of contrast even though it does not contain one of the frequently-used clues just mentioned.

4. Direct or vicarious experience. Sometimes the experiences we have had or have witnessed primarily through reading, watching television or movies, or listening to the radio or to others help us to determine the meanings of unfamiliar words. For instance, while many of us have had little experience in robbing banks, we recognize in example four the police officer's first responsibility: to arrest the accused and take the person to jail.

5. Direct statement of description, function, or classification. In sentence six, the definition is stated by identifying the type of word undertaken by a lexicographer. Another example: We hired six fruit pickers to harvest our crop of avocadoes and mangoes.

6. Example. Sometimes sentences include examples of the new term. Key words to recognize include as, such as, like, i.e., e.g., for example, for instance, especially, including, and among these. Example five demonstrates this type of context clue.

Hopefully this brief discussion will help make you aware of the importance of teaching the various types of context clues. It is helpful to remember that the use of context may be taught orally through listening activities just as well as it may be taught graphically through reading. Certainly pre-schoolers should learn to employ context; non-readers and poor readers should also learn to use this procedure orally as a prelude and accompaniment to reading instruction.

The material presented in Chart 10-5 delineates a procedure for teaching one type of context clue. Other writers have presented helpful information (227, 244, 264, 298).

Practice Two: "Present new words in any lesson prior to the pupil's contact with the reading assignment."
With the exception of several points which require elaboration, we are omitting a number of appropriate items already discussed under Vocabulary and Concept Development in Chapter 4A. We recommended there that unknown words be presented in a different context embracing the same meaning. For example, a story may mention the fact that Ben Franklin's mother told him to go fly his kite since the day was so brisk. The teaching sentence might be read orally except for the unknown word.

The trees sway back and forth on brisk spring days.

Point to the word brisk and invite pupils both to pronounce and define it. Use the same pattern for all other words which pupils cannot define by the story's context. See Chapters 7A, 7B, and 7C for specific procedures.

Practice Three: "Provide sufficient opportunities for reinforcing new terms."
Ask your pupils to keep vocabulary notebooks to record the isolated terms followed by the orally-presented sentences and, whenever, desirable, definitions derived from the context. This practice facilitates further study of the words either at the same time selections are read or subsequently for a review. Groups of five or ten words are labeled as V1, V2, V3 (Vocabulary Lists 1, 2, 3). See Chapter 7B.

CHART 10-5

TEACHING A CONTEXT CLUE

1. Say, "Many sentences contain phrases which help us learn the meanings of new words. If you have a sharp eye, you will begin to notice these phrases and learn many new words. I have written several sentences on the board. Each contains an unknown word which is underlined. The meaning of that unknown word is given in the sentence. See if you can draw an arrow from the new word to its meaning. Then circle the phrase, usually two or three words, which gives away the idea." Be sure the pupils can read the material; otherwise the practice will be useless.

2. (On the board) A. In Japan the law-making body is known as <u>the Diet</u>. B. A <u>misdemeanor</u> is a small crime.

3. Explain to the pupils the fact that the Diet is the Japanese law-making group, and the key phrase is <u>is known as</u>. For Sentence B, a misdemeanor is a small crime, and the key word is <u>is</u>. If more instruction and practice is needed, provide them. If not, assign a practice sheet containing the following items.

   We speak of lions and tigers as big cats.
   Socrates, Plato, and Aristotle are regarded as three of the greatest Greek philosophers.
   The senior with the highest grades was designated class valedictorian.
   An amiable fellow is considered friendly.
   A left-handed pitcher is often called a southpaw.
   Iran was once known as Persia.
   The father of all gods was named Zeus.
   The term <u>impoverished</u> refers to being poor.
   A dove is sometimes used to represent peace.
   The czar was recognized as the leader of the Russian people.

4. Check and teach from the practice sheet. Then ask pupils to notice examples of this type of context clue in their reading and to call them to the attention of the class. If necessary, provide another exercise of the same type on a subsequent day.

On the day following the introduction of new words, check the extent of mastery by the following procedure. First, re-number the five or ten words and develop sentences with the terms omitted. (For convenience, the sentences may be presented orally; however, there is nothing to preclude your using the overhead projector or mimeographed sheets to present the sentences in their written forms.)

For younger and slower children it may be desirable to list the ten words on the board for the review to facilitate recall and/or spelling. However, you should move gradually toward total unassisted recall. Certainly spelling errors should not be used to reduce scores. (More proficient spellers tend to study and learn the new words in anticipation of producing them while inefficient spellers often need to concentrate on acquiring a stock of meanings and learn to spell less difficult terms.)

Second, pronounce each sentence (if oral presentation is being used) and allow the group to write the correct response. Whenever possible, children should check their own papers; this enables them to recognize and learn from their own mistakes. Should an exchange of papers be necessary, youngsters sitting side-by-side should swap papers so each can see his own responses. Careful seating arrangements may preclude mutual agreements to "overlook" errors.

Third, allow and encourage people who are dissatisfied with their scores (10, 20, 30, etc.) to re-study the terms in their spare time. The vocabulary notebook comes in handy here, as well as for those youngsters who have been absent. Any child who originally achieved proficiency (90%) may then act as a student teacher and administer the review. Fourth, substitute the "new" score for the "old." Anyone who is still dissatisfied with his efforts may try again on the following day. This delay discourages too hasty re-study efforts.

Fifth, allow individuals or pairs to develop new sentences with the same contextual definitions. Five different lists of these might well be combined into one large set of fifty sentences with the key words omitted. Such a sheet might be duplicated by pupils, many of whom can be taught to prepare a spirit master. If the sheet includes words discussed during a period of several days or a week, it is useful to list all of the possible answers at the top of the page.

A question is often raised about the policy of giving youngsters a second or third chance to improve their scores. Will it not encourage sloppy efforts on the original review? The answer is clearly no. Using the technique in the classroom has convinced us that the characteristics of most children prevent or minimize this problem: (a) Because youngsters like to get out of doing things over, they study and learn in order to avoid subsequent assignments. (b) Some youngsters le``` more slowly than others because they need additional contact and repetitions.

Perhaps a philosophical observation is appropriate here. Our major cognitive concern is to assist youngsters to learn. If an evaluation is the terminal activity the result of which cannot be altered, children have little motivation to study and master whatever remains unlearned. If the vocabulary items presented for study are really worth knowing, we should be anxious to allow youngsters the additional time and practice required for retentive learning. Then when they achieve the specific instructional objective, fairness seems to insist that the recorded score reflect their final efforts.

Two further points seem worth mentioning. First, you may find youngsters able to serve as student teachers even during the initial evaluation. If one or more children can actively observe you for a few weeks in preparation for handling this assignment, a great deal of instructional time may be saved while youngsters begin to assume responsibility for their own progress.

Second, in an era when we are emphasizing the development of responsibility toward others and independence in individual action, it is important to recognize the preparation of such practice material not as busy-work or teacher relief but as cooperative development of learning activities. A number of other activities which might be considered as reinforcement are discussed on subsequent pages.

Practice Four: "Develop an interest in and appreciation for new and unusual words."

Several activities might be considered here. First, make a habit of calling attention to new words as they normally occur in daily conversations. Second, plan to introduce several interesting new words each day, especially terms which children can easily assimilate into their daily language. Some teachers emphasize one new word on the board each day and encourage youngsters to use it at every possible opportunity. This practice should certainly prove worthwhile. Third discuss origins and uses of interesting words and secure from the media center such books as the following:

575

Asimov, Isaac, <u>Words from the Myths</u>. Boston: Houghton, 1961.

Epstein, Sam, and Beryl Epstein, <u>First Book of Words</u>. New York: Watts, 1954.

Krauss, Ruth, <u>A Hole is to Dig</u>. New York: Harper, 1952.

Merriam, Eve, <u>A Gaggle of Geese</u>. New York: Knopf, 1960.

_____, <u>Small Fry</u>. New York: Knopf, 1965.

Nurnberg, Maxwell, <u>Wonders in Words</u>. Englewood Cliffs, N.J.: Prentice-Hall, 1968.

Pitt, Valerie, <u>Let's Find Out About Names</u>. New York: Watts, 1971.

Radlauer, Ruth Shaw, <u>Good Times with Words</u>. Chicago: Melmont, 1963.

Rand, Ann, and Paul Rand, <u>Sparkle and Spin: A Book About Words</u>. New York: Harcourt, 1957.

Reid, Alastair, <u>Ounce, Dice, Trice</u>. Boston: Little, Brown, 1958.

Taylor, Margaret, <u>Whts Yr Nm?</u> New York: Harcourt, 1971.

van Gelden, Rosalind, <u>Monkeys Have Tales</u>. New York: McKay, 1966.

White, Mary Sue, <u>Word Twins</u>. Nashville, Tenn.: Abingdon, 1961.

Fourth, demonstrate (or have pupils do so) words which lend themselves to this appealing technique. While adjectives and verbs are often quite appropriate for use, even prepositions can be demonstrated. Chart 10-6 presents a few words whose meanings can be clarified through demonstration.

We use words from reading selections as the base for this type of active involvement. These items may be listed on the chalkboard to facilitate recall as each term is demonstrated. Actually this technique can be used for teaching or testing.

CHART 10-6

WORDS TO DEMONSTRATE

Adjectives	Action Verbs	Prepositions (primary levels)
haughty	stride	below
despondent	demolish	above
sultry	harass	near
fidgety	meander	far
morose	eradicate	over
exultant	denounce	under
sarcastic	glare	beside
gregarious	compel	beneath
sullen	shuffle	between
fastidious	waddle	through

For teaching purposes, list the words on the board and provide context through your actions. For example, glare at some pupil and ask, "Why do you think I glared at Selma?. . . Glare at the person next to you. . . Now write a sentence with the word (or one of its inflections--glared, glares, glaring)." Help pupils avoid insipid sentences such as "I glared at the boy." or "He glared at me." Instead encourage them to use a special word (because or when in this case) to give the sentence more meaning. (Lydia glared at Austin because he wanted homework on the weekends.)

For testing purposes, ask each pupil to demonstrate a particular word while his classmates respond either orally or on paper. For more formal testing, do the demonstrating yourself and ask the class to record their responses.

Practice Five: "Recognize pupils when they use new or interesting words."

All too often we tend to notice errors and emphasize weaknesses when we might, by drawing attention to the positive, reinforce children's tentative experiments in the use of novel terms. Indeed, too many red slashes and too few positive comments tend to inhibit or destroy the desire to write. Oral communication interrupted by constant corrections and requests for rephrasing also languishes.

While specific procedures for oral and written development may vary according to the personality and preference of diverse types of youngsters as well as the activity, you may wish to consider the following possibilities: (a) a positive comment to the child in

577

front of the class or group, (b) a positive comment made privately, (c) a note or telephone call to the parents or child to acknowledge his tendency toward extended language usage, or (d) a notation on paper referring to a felicitous use of words (with an arrow designating examples).

Practice Six: "Teach children when and how to use their dictionaries efficiently and effectively."
While the dictionary is usually the last resort for a reader with a problem, it is, nevertheless, a useful tool, certainly one with which he should be familiar. Most of the information provided with each word entry is somehow related to vocabulary growth and development. Even the phonic respelling may provide the key to a meaning, especially when the word is a part of the listening vocabulary, but the visual form is unknown.
For intermediate-level pupils an open-book diagnostic pretest on dictionary usage will help indicate some topics which should be presented. Chart 10-7 contains a sample pretest.

CHART 10-7

DIAGNOSTIC PRETEST ON

DICTIONARY USAGE

Directions: Locate in your dictionary the following data:

Guide Words

1. What are the guide words on the pages on which your first and last names would be found?

Spelling

2. What are the preferred spellings of each?
   a. catalogue or catalog
   b. defense or defence
   c. sulfur or sulphur

Hyphenation

3. Which of the following should be hyphenated?
   a. throwaway   c. cooperate
   b. doublepark   d. grassroots

CHART 10-7
(Cont.)

Syllabication

4. Where should each of the following be syllabicated?
 a. emphasis   d. story
 b. event   e. played
 c. multimillionaire f. your name

Misspellings

5. Which of the following are misspelled? Spell them correctly.
 a. accomodation   f. gauge
 b. similiar   g. morgage
 c. disatisfied   h. recieve
 d. sacreligious   i. mispell
 e. diptheria   j. government

Accenting

6. Accent the following:
 a. prevention   c. hypothesis
 b. consideration   d. your name

Usage

7. What do the following words have in common?
 a. convert   c. object
 b. refuse   d. minute

Pronunciation

8. What is the preferred pronunciation?
 a. ration   c. data
 b. advertisement   d. diphthong

Abbreviations

9. What term does each of the following represent?
 a. As   e. ff.
 b. IE   f. i.e.
 c. e.g.   g. obs.
 d. etym.   h. v.t.

CHART 10-7
(Cont.)

Part of Speech

10. How many parts of speech are shown for each of the following?
    a. bell   c. trick
    b. most   d. well

Plurals

11. What are the plurals for the following?
    a. cherub   c. index
    b. curriculum   d. mother-in-law

Singulars

12. What are the singulars for the following?
    a. data   c. vertices
    b. pants   d. measles

Past Tense

13. What is the past tense of each?
    a. bid   c. hit
    b. abide   d. strive

Past Participle

14. What is the past participle of each?
    a. bid   c. swim
    b. write   d. come

Comparative and Superlative

15. What are the comparative and superlative forms of each?
    a. simple   c. good
    b. furious   d. dry

Definitions

16. How many definitions are there for the following?

    a. bat   c. black
    b. run   d. fable

CHART 10-7
(Cont.)

Foreign Expressions

   17. What does each mean?
      a. laissez-faire   d. esse quam videri
      b. raison d'etre   e. e pluribus unum
      c. sine qua non

Synonyms

   18. List all synonyms given for the following.
      a. check   c. steal
      b. big   d. lie

Antonyms

   19. List all antonyms given for the following.
      a. minute   c. friendly
      b. old   d. considerate

Etymology

   20. From what language did each of the following come?
      a. Madras   d. pasteurized
      b. calico   e. bolo
      c. coffee   f. adobe

Word Associations

   21. What word do you associate with each of the following? And will join each pair. Examples: fine and dandy; bright and early
      a. Damon and   e. Guelphs and
      b. Punch and   f. block and
      c. Lancelot and   g. Jack and
      d. lares and   h. rave and

At all grade levels specific instruction and practice should be provided in such areas as the following:

   1. Usage labels -- colloquial, dialect, slang

   2. Examples of usage -- sentences or phrases

   3. Multiple meanings of words

4. Figurative expressions -- similes, metaphors, hyperboles

5. Synonyms, antonyms, homonyms

6. Affixes and roots

Suggested practices related to teaching the last four items are discussed next.

Practice Seven: "Help youngsters learn to recognize and interpret figurative language and expressions (492)."
One study of four third-grade reading books revealed a total of 424 figurative expressions. Two fourth-grade books contained 845 figurative expressions (370). The greater the number of idioms, the greater is the likelihood that pupils will experience comprehension difficulty (293.) Many implied meanings are overlooked simply because youngsters interpret figurative expressions literally. This fact is especially true of the educationally disadvantaged, whose backgrounds are often devoid of such phrases. Even more distressing are the cases in which children verbalize expressions without understanding their meanings. Consider the confusion and misconceptions caused when people misinterpret the following figurative expressions.

1. Little pitchers have big ears.
2. He really hit the ceiling.
3. She's a real gold digger.
4. Marcia knows on which side her bread is buttered.
5. That Alicia really burns me up.
6. I gave Mark a taste of his own medicine.
7. Someone needs to light a fire under that fellow.
8. I really shot the bull on that last test.
9. He's a fence sitter.
10. Gerard has put his foot into his mouth again.
11. She really knows how to wind him around her finger.
12. The collection was just a drop in the bucket.
13. I paid her a compliment.
14. His eyes were as big as saucers.
15. You know Smith doesn't have a chance. He's a dark horse.
16. The old cowboy kicked the bucket.
17. Sidney jumped out of the frying pan into the fire.
18. Okay, kid, I'll let you go this time, but you had better keep your nose clean.

An excellent related book to read to pupils at the upper intermediate levels is Norton Juster's Phantom Tollbooth (New York: Epstein and Carroll, 1961). It is a veritable gold mine of figurative language.

Because practically every basal reading selection, even at the primary level, contains at least several figurative expressions, be ready to discuss these and prevent or clarify possible misconceptions. You might also encourage the members of your class to listen and read to collect figurative expressions along with their likely meanings. Once again, pairs of children might want to work together before large-group sharing occurs.

Practice Eight: "Teach multiple meanings of words and provide abundant practice."

The research suggests that a child who knows or derives one meaning of a word often becomes confused when encountering the same word in a setting that suggests a different meaning (736). This situation is probably true for at least two reasons. First, a second meaning is usually less common than a first meaning, making the learning task more difficult. Second, a person who knows one meaning of a word often develops a "mind-set" which predisposes him to assume that the word will continue to represent the meaning with which he is familiar, even when the context suggests otherwise.

Large numbers of words, especially the shorter ones, represent numerous meanings, with some words having over one hundred different definitions. For example, how many definitions can you quickly provide for run, top, horse, stop, white, hide, leaf, and bat?

Chart 10-8 presents a type of practice which might be useful.

CHART 10-8

EXERCISE FOR SELECTING APPROPRIATE DEFINITION

Directions: Write the letter of the definition which explains the meaning of each underlined word.

    a. to move rapidly (verb)

    b. a rip or tear (noun)

    c. small stream (noun)

    d. to try for election to office (verb)

    e. a score in baseball or softball (noun)

CHART 10-8
(Cont.)

_____ 1. Mrs. Brown developed a <u>run</u> in her hose.

_____ 2. The heavy mill wheel was set in the south <u>run</u>.

_____ 3. One <u>run</u> is in, and two are out in the ninth.

_____ 4. I should like to <u>run</u> for mayor soon.

_____ 5. Would you <u>run</u> to the store and get some candy?

Not only do exercises of this type provide practice in selecting appropriate definitions, they may also introduce youngsters to new meanings of old words (definition <u>c</u>, for example). Discussion should reveal any confused concepts such as two mentioned in a third-grade class. While considering various meanings of the word <u>fair</u>, Dennie voiced his meaning, "You know, when two people get together and have a fair."

While studying the word <u>stag</u> in a reading story, a little girl asked, "What is a stag party?" A bright little boy promptly responded, "You know, it's when a lot of men get together and shoot deer."

To foster understanding of multiple meanings, you might wish to read Clifford Eth's <u>A Bear Before Breakfast</u> (New York: G. P. Putnam's Sons) or Eudora Welty's <u>The Shoe Bird</u> (New York: Harcourt). With older pupils you might read and discuss the following anonymous poem:

Remember When

Remember when hippie meant big in the hips,
And a trip involved travel in cars, planes and ships?
When pot was a vessel for cooking things in,
And hooked was what grandmother's rugs may have been?
When fix was a verb that meant mend or repair?
And be-in meant merely existing somewhere?
When neat meant well-organized, tidy and clean,
And grass was a ground cover, normally green?
When groovy meant furrowed with channels and hollows.
And birds were winged creatures, like robins and swallows?
When fuzz was a substance, real fluffy, like lint,
And bread came from bakeries and not from the mint?
When roll meant a bun, and rock was a stone.
And hang-up was something you did with a phone?
It's groovy, man, groovy, but English it's not.
Methinks that our language is going to pot.

Practice Nine: "Teach pupils to recognize, recall, and learn to use synonyms, antonyms, homonyms, and other words with related meanings. Provide practice in doing so."

One principle of psychology is that information is readily acquired when related data are organized and grouped into some meaningful array. Several implications for curriculum development and classroom instruction can be drawn from this observation.

1. Synonyms. Help children recognize words which represent similar or identical meanings. As children become more mature, help them distinguish among shades of difference in meanings. For example, stout, fat, and obese all refer to the concept of heavy (people), but each conveys a different connotation.

At the elementary levels most words have at least one synonym (faucet and spigot, shovel and spade, mean and bad). Even general words at the secondary levels typically have synonyms (euthanasia and mercy killing, ottoman and foot stool, chronometer and ship's clock.

2. Antonyms. Help children identify antonyms for words they already know. Sometimes this involves the use of prefixes.

spell	misspell
tied	untied
possible	impossible
regular	irregular
legal	illegal
finite	infinite

and sometimes the study of new words.

masculine	feminine
optimist	pessimist
wealthy	penniless
torrid	frigid

585

3. <u>Part-whole</u> relationships. Take advantage of opportunities to develop words related in terms of the part-whole aspect. For example, consider the following:

<u>Whole</u>	<u>Part</u>
ladder, chair	rungs
door	knob, hinges
window	ledge, sill, pane
human body	shin, nape, wrist, heel
book	spine

4. <u>Thematic</u> terms. Develop vocabulary related to a particular topic (i.e., seasons, holidays, community helpers, geographical region, period of time, etc.). For example, a study of weather words might include some of the following:

brisk	torrid	mild
sultry	frigid	precipitation
squall	tornado	hurricane
overcast	cyclone	travelers' advisory
alert	watch	parched
high pressure	barometer	heat wave

Give one or more pairs of children several words for which they are expected to list all the general synonyms they know or can find. Partners may do this as soon as they have completed their regular assignments. While dictionaries and other references may be used, each of the pair are expected to be able to pronounce, define or use in sentences the words they record as synonyms.

After everyone has had opportunities to pair off and study, the entire group or class can then volunteer terms to be listed on the chalkboard or overhead projector and discussed. Although youngsters of differing abilities may engage in the same activity, individual differences are provided for by the various possible benefits learners derive. For example, some children may learn (a) to recognize the printed forms of some words, (b) to spell some words, (c) to pronounce some words, (d) to

586

recognize new words through listening, or (e) to use new words in their speaking.

In addition, pupils will acquire various amounts of these competencies. Chart 10-9 presents several synonyms for introductory use with just a few responses we have received from classes.

CHART 10-9

EXAMPLES OF SYNONYM CHAINS

Stimulus	Synonyms
Friend	Pal, buddy, colleague, companion, comrade, partner, chum, "brother"
Big	Large, great, tall, huge, tremendous, gigantic, fat, enormous, gargantuan
Hello	Hi, Hey, Good morning, greetings, Howdy, salutations, bonjour
Small	Tiny, minute, teeny, little, mini, wee, mite, minuscule, infinitesimal
Road	Street, path, highway, byway, boulevard, lane, turnpike, avenue, route, thoroughfare, railroad track, interstate, trail
House	Home, mobile home, hotel, motel, shack, hut, mansion, palace, castle, apartment, tenement, penthouse, flat, igloo, tent, longhouse, wigwam, tepee, hacienda, cottage, (animal homes) web, cave, nest, hive, cage

Here is the technique. Ask youngsters to take a sheet of paper and quarter it. Usually most children exhibit perturbed looks until someone decides what to do. Then they follow suit. After the children have folded their papers, supply four key words (friend, big, road, and house, for example) and announce that only one will be discussed each day. Each pair of pupils should list as many as possible, but both must know the meanings of the word they record. (An igloo is a dome-shaped Eskimo home, for example).

During their free time, children may gather words. Later, ask each group to suggest and define a word they think no one else listed. Record it on the board and ask how many others also listed it. This practice helps avoid the proliferation of terms everyone knows and concentrates on items likely to be unknown to some members of the class. As words are listed on the chalkboard, encourage children to record in their notebooks any new words they learn along with sentences or definitions.

For practice with antonyms, distribute sentences which contain word opposites. Pupils should circle or under- line the contrasting terms. See Chart 10-10.

CHART 10-10

EXERCISE FOR SELECTING ANTONYMS

Directions: In each example there are two antonyms. Circle them.

1. Would you like a large or a small piece of cake?

2. Michael cried when he stumped his toe, but his big brother just laughed.

3. The heathen chief was rather surprised to see Christian explorers headed toward him.

4. Mary is the affable type; her brother Bill is rather reserved around strangers.

5. Before you begin your dessert, I want you to finish your salad.

Provide or solicit words for which pairs of pupils are asked to list antonyms and synonyms for the use of other members of their groups. Similar procedures can be used for homonyms and near-homonyms (words which sound almost alike). Two good books by Fred Gwynne are A Chocolate Moose for Dinner and The King Who Rained (New York: Windmill, 1976 and 1970, respectively). Lists A and B at the end of the chapter contain words and activities involving antonyms. List C includes over 200 homonyms and near-homonyms.

Practice Ten: "Teach affixes (prefixes and suffixes) and root words."

We often begin an introduction of affixes and roots by writing the word biped on the board and asking pupils who are bipeds to raise their hands. Very few will un- til they are told that a biped is one who has two legs.

We then proceed to discuss bi (two) and ped (foot). Members of the class name familiar examples containing one or the other element (bifocals, bicycle, biannual, biennial, binoculars, pedestrian, pedal, piedmont, pied piper, peddler, pedestal, centipede, millipede). These words are written on the board to familiarize youngsters with their printed forms.

Using elements of any of the terms already listed, we continue. From the cent in centipede we have 100 (century, centurion, centennial, per cent). From the milli in millipede we have 1000 (million, millennium, milligram). From the ann in biannual and the enn in biennial we have year (annual, anniversary, perennial). And on and on.

A reinforcement technique that pays dividends is team testing. After a group has studied the words resulting from any vocabulary discussion, pairs of youngsters construct a matching or fill-in-the-blank test to administer to some other pair. The people who construct the test develop the answer key, in effect taking their own test. The other pair take the test separately, each correct individual response contributing to a single PAL score. Chart 10-11 includes a guide pupils might use for constructing tests.

CHART 10-11

USING AFFIXES AND ROOT WORDS

Directions: Write the letter to the left of the number it matches.

1. centipede

A. A _____ used to walk from place to place to sell goods.

2. peddler

B. In North Carolina the legislature has _____ sessions. It meets every other year.

3. centurion

C. We watch car races by looking through _____.

4. piedmont

D. A _____ is a worm which supposedly has 1000 legs.

5. biennial

E. The lion sat on the _____ before jumping down to do some tricks.

6. pedestal

F. A worm which supposedly has 100 legs is called a _____.

7. millipede

G. A driver is supposed to give the right-of-way to every _____.

589

CHART 10-11
(Cont.)

8. centennial   H. We live in the ____, the flat land between the mountains and the coast.

9. binoculars   I. Boone, North Carolina, has celebrated its ____, or one hundredth birthday.

10. pedestrian   J. In ancient Rome a ____ was the leader of one hundred soldiers.

A second way of helping youngsters become aware of the importance and meanings of affixes and roots is to use another version of the discovery technique. Present a list of words containing a common element. Ask pupils to identify the similarity and develop a common definition. Chart 10-12 includes samples of several possible lists for presentation.

CHART 10-12

ROOTS WORDS AND AFFIXES
FOR USE WITH THE DISCOVERY TECHNIQUE

porter	tricycle	hopeless
export	triangle	useless
import	tripod	penniless
portable	triple	careless

A five-step procedure can be used for teaching purposes.

1. Present four or five words whose meanings are generally known to the class or group.

2. Ask how the words are alike in form. (In the first list, for example, all words contain the element port.)

3. Ask how the words are like each other in meaning. (They all involve the meaning to carry.)

CHART 10-12
(Cont.)

4. Ask for a generalization. (<u>Port</u> often means to <u>carry</u>.)

5. Provide practice with new words. The exercise generally should include samples in which context and affixes and/or roots play a part in determining meaning. Sentences similar to the following might be used:

a. The businessman left his <u>portfolio</u> on the table.

b. The two explorers <u>portaged</u> their canoes overland from one river to the other.

c. The criminal was finally <u>deported</u> from the United States to his own country.

This type of procedure also adapts well to the paired activity for learning mentioned earlier. Pairs work together in locating new items. The subsequent group discussion allows them to pool and share their knowledge. Once again, youngsters should be able to use any new terms in correct sentences. Too, they may wish to develop exercises for each other. Since this activity invariably helps them to learn, it should by all means be encouraged.

<u>Practice Eleven</u>: "Provide opportunities for the class to see you reading for a few minutes each day."
All too often teachers read only outside of class. Many pupils, especially the disadvantaged, never see an adult read silently. They need a model, someone who not only teaches reading, but teaches by reading. And it is worth remembering that children tend to prefer the same books as their teachers (142).
At brief intervals during the day, children should see you reading: children's literature (to keep up-to-date), an article from a newspaper or magazine, the jokes from <u>Today's Education</u>, or some other printed matter. Whenever possible, share this information with the class. As a protective measure, inform the principal of the purpose of such reading.
Note: Encourage parents to read to their children. Connor (137) advises, "If adults in the family have set an example of reading, reading becomes a symbol of growing up, and the child wants to do what his parents do -- read."

LISTENING

Practice One: "Read to the class at least thirty
minutes each day."
     The materials used for this type of oral reading
should be carefully selected to provide opportunities to
develop concepts, moral and ethical values, and an
appreciation for good literature.
     Some of the best examples of materials to use for
vocabulary and concept development are the True Books
(Chicago: Children's Press) and the more difficult First
Books (Watts). Both series contain many dozens of titles
on almost every topic of interest to youngsters.
Teachers at the primary levels should consider reading
great numbers of these books to their classes, for the
concepts and vocabulary they develop are important but
unknown to many pupils. Many of the First Books should
also be used at the intermediate levels. Sample titles
from both series are included in Lists D and E at the end
of this chapter.
     In addition, guidance counselors are increasingly
advocating that we familiarize our pupils with the world
of work. Too many young people know only the names of
their parents' occupations. Their concepts of the actual
work involved are often inaccurate and inadequate (373,
544, 733). The I Want to Be Books (Chicago: Children's
Press) for primary and What It's Like Series (Chicago:
Reilly and Lee Books) for intermediate levels should
prove quite useful.
     To enhance the development of moral and ethical
values of intermediate pupils, read articles from
Guideposts (Mt. Carmel, N.Y.), an excellent collection of
appealing stories. Wee Wisdom (Unity Village, Mo.:
University School of Christianity) is recommended for the
primary levels.
     Bible stories are also especially important. It is
even possible to relate them to the curriculum because so
much literature refers to Biblical material. Two good
books for primary use are Mary Crockett Norfleet's With
Happy Voices (Richmond, Va.: John Knox Press, 1969) and
Anne deVries' The Children's Bible (St. Louis: Concordia
Publishing House).
     Titles of outstanding literature to read to your
classes are included in some of the references at the end
of this chapter (115, 347, 512). Especially useful is
the material used by Cohen (129-132) in an experiment
with socially disadvantaged second graders to determine
if reading literature selections daily was superior to
the use of literature as a spare-time treat. Results of
the study indicated pupils to whom literary selections

were read daily gained in both quantity and quality of vocabulary and in reading comprehension.

Many children, particularly poor readers, will never have an opportunity to marvel at the sounds of the language except through oral involvement. For example, many of the Newbery winners are too difficult for most elementary youngsters to read (234). We need a carefully-planned oral literature program, and we need it daily. (Additional books not already mentioned are presented in List F at the end of the chapter.)

Reading to a class can take several forms. Headphones can be used for small groups, although facial expressions and gestures will be missing. Pupils at higher grade levels may be invited to share their talents in oral reading by presenting selected materials of high literary content. Adults (aides, parents, other interested citizens) may volunteer to read. So long as the material is read with enthusiasm, we may be satisfied.

One caution: Children should not "follow along" in their own books if the purpose is to help them recognize the words. Observations indicate that those who can read the words do not profit from the experience. Indeed, their silent reading may even become slower because they are "keeping down" with the oral presentation. At the same time those who do not read well tend to lose their places and muddle through the selection. While one word is being pronounced orally, they are looking at other words. We have been completely unsuccessful in determining from observations of children using headphones for read-along practice just which sentences were being read. In a number of cases pupils using headphones had different pages of their books open. Therefore, we suggest that either the records or tapes be turned off or that the books be closed (except to look at the pictures). Of course, the same comment applies to the use of oral reading as it is currently conducted with basal readers.

A second caution: It will be necessary at times to pause, call attention to, and discuss especially harmonious words and expressions. While such meanderings need not lead us far afield, they may yet invest these terms with greater depths of meaning.

Scott's teacher habitually paused during her reading to the class and asked, "Do you know what _____ means in this sentence?" After checking to be sure, she continued with the story. Because of this practice, the teacher was not at all surprised when one of the members of her class presented an oral report including the word nationalities and then stopped. "Nationalities comes from nation. It means different countries. Our nationality is American," he commented. Having clarified the meaning, Scott continued with his presentation. Numerous examples of vocabulary techniques used in her class are presented by Gail Culyer in Translating Theory Into Practice (146).

Practice Two: "Use new words in your oral conversation."
Repeated exposure helps us incorporate the terms we hear into our own language patterns. Even as adults we are constantly adding numerous terms to our own vocabularies. Through the mass media and our conversations with others, we come into contact with hippies, speed, multi-media, pot, schema, cyclamates, dyslexia, individualized instruction, metacognition, empty sets, multiple adoptions, instructional objectives, linguistics, and many more. So it is with youngsters.

Practice Three: "Teach specific concepts which frequently present difficulty."
One good example involves same and different. Because this concept is really quite complex, you may need to present several lessons on this topic. Chart 10-13 outlines one possible procedure.

Practice Four: "Call attention to new vocabulary in films, computer programs, filmstrips, records, tape recordings, radio, movies, and television."
The entire aspect of listening has, in general, remained virtually unexplored. Part of the reason teachers should preview films and filmstrips and pre-aud tapes and records is to discover specific items needing additional clarification. A useful reference is A Treasury of Audio-Visual Aids (Plainville, Conn.: Kalart Company, 1966). We are concerned by the failure of some teachers to regard a film, for instance, as a lesson plan requiring the same introductory and follow-through activities as a directed reading assignment.
Instead, the pattern sometimes found in schools involves a teacher's showing a film or filmstrip with no preparation and little apparent concern for its immediate correlation with the course of study. Under such circumstances, the audio-visual material would seem to have no more educational value than the weekly ten-cent movies we used to see at school. When used properly, however, these media can be quite beneficial.

CHART 10-13

SAME AND DIFFERENT

1. Display several sample objects. Say, "These are the same. They are alike. Can anyone tell me how they are the same or alike?" Use objects which allow children to recognize obvious likenesses in color, size, shape, name, texture, or taste.
2. Say, "I am going to show you some objects. I want you to tell me how these things are the same. How are they alike?" Then display the objects.
3. Say, "Name some things and tell me how they are alike, how they are the same." Ask the pupils to respond.
4. Display objects that are not alike. Ask, "Are these the same? Are they alike?" Use objects which allow pupils to recognize obvious differences in color, size, shape, name, texture, or taste. Ask, "How are they not alike?" Invite the pupils to respond.
5. Say, "When things are not alike, not the same, we say they are different. This _____ is different from this _____ because it _____." Say, "Tell me how these things are different." Display objects or pictures. Youngsters should respond, "This _____ is different from _____ because it _____."
6. Say, "Tell me some things that are different and how they are different." Invite the pupils to respond.
7. Give pupils three items or three pictures, two of which are alike. Ask each to raise two of the objects and say, "These two are alike because _____." Then they should raise another group of two and say, "These two are different because _____."

Let us consider one example for relating vocabulary and concept development to audio-visual materials. One episode of the Beverly Hillbillies focused on the grunion run in Southern California. Jethro, who had never heard of a grunion, thought an invasion was about to occur and with patriotic fervor set about to warn his unsuspecting friends. The show was quite hilarious for those who grasped Jethro's problem. Seven-year-old Todd throughly enjoyed the program because he had just read the first twenty pages of Ann Stepp's Grunion Out of Water (Irving-on-Hudson, N.Y.: Harvey House, 1971).

Practice Five: "Use field trips to develop and extend vocabulary."

Sometimes teachers load the class into a bus or several station wagons or march them around the block without planning ways of using the immediate environment to enhance vocabulary development. Like films and filmstrips, field trips should follow the basic lesson plan outline found in most reading textbooks. They are, or ought to be, directed learning activities designed to achieve specific outcomes. Used carefully, they can provide really enlightening experiences.

SPEAKING

Practice One: "Use the show and tell technique at the primary levels and the presentation and explanation of results at the immediate levels."

Perhaps primary teachers do the most effective job of encouraging children to listen to each other in a planned fashion. We should encourage pupils at all levels to bring to class interesting items, assist them in developing explanations of the materials, and provide daily opportunities for displaying and discussing these centers of interest. Indeed, this material is one possible source for the experience stories. Almost any object provides opportunities for vocabulary development if we but consider the possibilities. A door has a set of hinges and knobs, windows have panes and sills, books have spines and indexes. At the intermediate levels, some teachers refer to this as Bring and Brag. The basic idea is the same, but the format is more sophisticated.

Practice Two: "Provide frequent opportunities for pupils to use new words."

These may well be informal occasions scattered throughout the day. One effective technique is to allow and encourage youngsters to discuss events, films, or other "happenings." If you provide sufficient introduction and reinforcement of new terms at the listening and reading levels, and if the class climate is conducive to the trial-and-error practice needed for vocabulary expression, pupils will begin to develop more elaborate modes of communication. This development takes time, of course, but it should be done.

READING

Practice One: "Encourage wide reading and provide class time for this activity."

At least thirty minutes of free time should be allocated each day for free reading. During these intervals, youngsters should begin, complete, and perhaps discuss in small groups books of their own choosing. One of the most difficult tasks for some pupils is that of beginning a new book. Continuing an interesting one is not especially difficult.

As adults we often experience this problem. Perhaps you can think of some book you have been planning to read for several months or longer. Possibly you have proscrastinated until memory of the original intention has faded into peaceful oblivion.

Certainly youngsters are this way. If we help them find time to begin a book, it is much more likely that they will continue it on their own. Indeed, it is quite paradoxical that our schools often spend so much time in teaching youngsters how to read that they never have time to read.

Several writers (397, 566) have suggested that periods be scheduled when both teachers and pupils read simultaneously. Alternately, provide for recreational reading at different times for different members of the class. It may well be an independent activity to be pursued by one group, while another works directly with the teacher. Or it may follow any experience in which some youngsters complete their work before others.

Those who read widely and wisely usually read well. Practice makes perfect if and when practice involves the use of appropriate materials. With the exception of direct instruction, there is no better single way of developing an extensive reading vocabulary than letting youngsters read. And read some more. And more. And more.

Both Arkley (18) and Godfrey (35) have produced recommended lists of books for primary readers.

<u>Practice Two</u>: "Present the written forms of spontaneously-used new words on the chalkboard or overhead projector."

Typically our discussions of new words go no further than the development of oral vocabulary. As a direct consequence, children often fail to recognize the same terms in their printed materials. This point was vividly illustrated when we engaged in some demonstration diagnosis and teaching of mathematics to third-graders. Almost three-fourths of the two classes needed assistance in pronouncing the words <u>circle</u>, <u>square</u>, and <u>rectangle</u>. Yet 90% could draw the figures when they were told the words.

At every practical opportunity we should convert many of our oral words into their written counterparts to provide an additional type of learning activity for those who are ready and able to profit from this experience. Likewise, whenever pupils have occasion to use new words in their oral communication, we should record the written forms on the board.

Practice Three: "Use pictures and real objects to develop and extend concepts and vocabulary."
Ask pupils to locate pictures which illustrate specific vocabulary being developed. Not only can this be fun, it serves as a highly effective visual means of teaching and reinforcing word meanings. When introducing nouns, show the actual object (if possible) or a picture, and then discuss the qualities of the word. A picture file and SCCs can be helpful here.

WRITING

Practice One: "Encourage and assist children to engage in a great deal of writing of many different types."
Provide pupils with daily opportunities for writing and sharing their creations--narrative, descriptive, persuasive, expository--with others. Explore with the media specialist the possibility of binding a child's collection of his own writing, cataloguing it, and placing it on one of the display shelves. Few potential writers can resist the temptation to see themselves in print.
Or use pictures to suggest possible themes. Use the Story Boards (Boston: Houghton Mifflin). Use Unfinished Stories for Use in the Classroom (Washington, D.C.: National Education Association, 1968). Begin fanciful tales by saying, "Once upon a time...," stopping, and pointing to a person who must continue until you designate his successor. It is best to stop each contributor in the middle of a sentence, thereby suspending the plot and action and paving the way for a possible new train of thought by a different story-teller. For writing purposes, allow children to begin stories and then pass them to their peers for continuation, each one signing his name as co-author. This activity, of course, is independent.
Encourage pupils to write descriptive or creative sentences or stories with new vocabulary terms. Some positively hilarious compositions can result. It helps, of course, to select a topic based on the type of words being used. For instance, if haughty, despondent,

598

harass, demolish, and denounce are included on a list, suggest the topic "My Brother Got Married." Other possibilities include "My Teacher" (always a favorite--the topic, not the person), "Susie and Her Baseball Team," and "How to Cook a Dinosaur."

Use music; encourage pupils to write their impressions. What images are conjured up, what stories does the music tell? The following compositions are quite useful for this purpose.

> "Peer Gynt Suite--In the Hall of the Mountain King"--Grieg
> "Ride of the Valkyries"--Wagner
> "Hansel and Gretel Overture"--Humperdinck
> "Sorceror's Apprentice"--Dukas
> "The Moldau"--Smetana
> "Surprise Symphony"--Haydn
> "Toreador Song"--Bizet
> "Flight of the Bumblebee"--Rimsky-Korsakov
> "Turkish March"--Mozart
> "Fountains"--Ravel
> "Carnival of the Animals"--Saint Saens
> "Little Fugue"--Bach
> "Sixth Symphony"--Tchaikovsky

Assign specific topics or allow youngsters to develop their own. Several may wish to pool their efforts and co-author a play, poem, short story, or novel.

The September 5, 1970, edition of the Charlotte Observer printed an article about a five-year-old English girl who had signed a contract to publish the novel she was currently writing. Perhaps our classes are teeming with unrecognized literary giants merely waiting for the opportunity to expand and reveal themselves.

Guidelines for Developing Vocabulary

The following guidelines summarize some of the previous recommended activities and identify other points to remember (156).

Guideline One: "Begin developing children's vocabulary in kindergarten. Advise parents to being developing vocabulary during their children's first year."

Research indicates that the quality and quantity of a six-year-old's vocabulary may differ considerably from his peer's. These differences cannot be attributed to the school program; they are a product of family and community characteristics and experiences. Since it is clear that a significant correlation exists between pre-schoolers' oral language (which includes vocabulary) and subsequent reading achievement, we cannot over-emphasize the need for encouraging parents and kindergarten teachers to help children develop their vocabularies. Studies of children at age one (425), two (323), and three (103) demonstrate the positive effect that (for instance) reading to children has on their language and vocabulary development. Research with disadvantaged second graders indicates that reading to them daily results in significant gains in both comprehension and vocabulary (129-132).

Guideline Two: "Develop listening, speaking, reading, and writing vocabularies."
Because of the interrelatedness of the vocabularies, one might assume falsely that transfer occurs from one aspect to another (86). The size and quality of each type of vocabulary varies within each person. For example, children tend to learn more effectively through listening than through reading until approximately grade six or seven (47, 101, 258, 614, 666). Likewise a person's listening vocabulary exceeds his speaking vocabulary and his reading exceeds his writing vocabulary. In order to possess real vocabulary competence, a person must be able to use a wide range of vocabulary in the listening, speaking, reading, writing, and, of course, in the thinking areas.
The implications of the sequence aspect of this guideline are seen in their application to classroom practice. For example, children should recognize (read) new words without difficulty before they are expected to write (spell) them. Schonell (632) suggests that an interval of approximately six months to one year often exists between the time children encounter words in reading and the time they learn to spell the items. Many bright children, of course, tend to acquire a writing vocabulary incidentally. Furthermore, written vocabulary is best developed when pupils possess the meanings in their oral language (469). Thus a teacher who wishes to develop her pupils' ability to read and write new vocabulary is well advised to present the items in their oral aspects first.

Guideline Three: "Provide specific direct instruction in vocabulary development."
Numerous studies demonstrate the superiority of direct over incidental instruction in increasing pupil competence in vocabulary (295, 365, 414). While incidental learning can and does occur, a planned program

600

is almost always superior to incidental means for developing any type of skill. Vocabulary acquisition is no exception. Dale and O'Rourke note, "Vocabulary development in school must be a planned program. The research in the field indicates that this is a sound principle. Incidental teaching, alone, tends to become accidental teaching (227:5)." Petty, Herald, and Stoll observe that "...it is possible to note accumulating evidence to dispel the widely held notion that having students 'read, read, read' is a satisfactory method for teaching vocabulary (567:84)."

Guideline Four: "Present vocabulary in context rather than in isolation."
The three most common types of context are pictorial, concrete, and abstract. To illustrate, let us consider the following examples:

1. (pictorial) - Ask the pupils to point out the person in a picture who is turning on the faucet. The child who is accustomed to hearing an expression such as "Turn on the water" can thus extend his vocabulary through pictorial context.

2. (concrete) - Ask a pupil to turn off the faucet so the water won't drip. A child does so, thus illustrating the term.

3. (abstract) - Print the word faucet on the chalkboard or floor chart and say or read a sentence: "Turn off the Hmm so the water won't drip." Ask pupils to pronounce and define the word. The following possibilities exist:

a. Some pupils may be able to pronounce and define the word.

b. Some pupils may be able to define the word by context but be unable to pronounce the word (because it is not in their oral vocabularies and they lack the appropriate phonic knowledge).

c. Some pupils may be able to pronounce the word (by using phonic and structural clues) but be unable to define the word (either because of lack of facility in context or lack of experiential background or both).

601

d. Some pupils may be unable either to pronounce or define the word.

The preceding comments suggest that presentation of new words in context is important, with the medium (pictorial, concrete, abstract) dependent upon the specific situation. Two implications may be drawn. First, SCCs (pictures and words on one side and words on the other side) involve items in context. They meet the guideline. Second, flash cards with words other than concrete nouns and action verbs involve an isolated presentation and are therefore to be used for testing rather than teaching purposes.

Guideline Five: "Provide instruction in a variety of types of context clues."
As noted earlier, numerous authorities stress the importance of context (365, 508). Unfortunately very few authors provide any really practical advice regarding the various types of context clues and procedures for teaching them. Some writers (13, 227, 244, 501) offer taxonomies, and others (21, 24, 244, 264, 298), especially Dale and O'Rourke (227) offer practical suggestions for developing vocabulary through context.

Guideline Six: "To develop reading vocabulary, use materials at pupils' instructional levels."
It is unreasonable to expect people to increase their vocabularies when the level of difficulty of the material causes a frustrating experience. When instructional-level books, newspapers, magazines, etc., are provided, pupils are able, both psychologically and academically, to acquire the new items.

Guideline Seven: "When teaching, proceed from large-group instruction to paired activities for learning to individual practice."
As a general principle, instruction begins with the group. It then proceeds to pairs of pupils so each member can have increased opportunities for practicing the information but still retain the support of a partner in case of difficulty. After sufficient practice, each pupil should be expected to function separately. Thus teaching is a group and later a paired activity. Tests and reviews are individual activities.

Guideline Eight: "Expect pupils to demonstrate initial mastery of new vocabulary items before they read selections containing those words."

602

Some authors (685) suggest that the pre-teaching of vocabulary is either unimportant or undesirable. They reason that children need independent opportunities to unlock meanings of new words. While this observation may very well be true, it would appear to be more applicable to the recreational phase of reading rather than to the instructional phase. Then, too, there are other problems with the laissez-faire attitude. The first is the assumption that pupils possess the various types of context skills needed to identify new vocabulary. The second is the frequency with which words appear in contextual settings that do not elucidate their meanings. Unfortunately, the net result for all readers but especially average and below average learners is a reduction in the amount of vocabulary growth.

Except when pupils possess competence in a wide array of context skills and when the new words themselves are embedded in rich contexts, it seems crucial to expect them to study new vocabulary and to demonstrate initial proficiency prior to reading the selection.

Guideline Nine: "Administer vocabulary tests in a written format."

While it is relatively simple for a teacher to check pupil knowledge of word pronunciation, it is difficult to identify the extent to which youngsters recognize the meanings of new words. There are several ways of testing vocabulary knowledge of new words: (a) The teacher pronounces a word, and the children write the appropriate definition (i.e., the one being studied) or a sentence using the word. (b) The teacher provides an oral definition, and the children write the word. (c) The teacher pronounces sentences different from those used in the teaching exercise, and the children write the appropriate words. (d) The teacher produces different sentences on a spirit master (as in C), and the children write the appropriate words.

Alternatives A and B are not very productive, for they are time consuming, requiring the presence of the teacher, and rely on rote memory of a small number of items. Alternative C is a better strategy, for children must apply the information they have been stud- ying. The major disadvantage of C is that a teacher must be present. Alternative D is recommended, for it involves application of knowledge in an independent setting.

We have found that written vocabulary tests can be provided as early as the 2-1 reading level. See Chapters 7B and 7C. Vocabulary programs using teaching, testing, and review exercises for grades 1-12 are available (195, 215).

Guideline <u>Ten</u>:   "Provide   regularly-spaced vocabulary reviews."
    The   research on retention has amply documented the
importance of spaced reviews. As indicated above, we
recommend that after ten sets of vocabulary items (a
total of 100 words) have been presented and studied,
there should be a comprehensive review test. Like other
information, vocabulary is best retained when it is
referred to periodically, in children's daily activities
as well as through the guaranteed systematic contact
provided by vocabulary review tests. See Chapters 7A and
7B.

    Guideline <u>Eleven</u>: "Encourage children to use the new
vocabulary that is being developed. Recognize those who
do so.
    The vocabulary development of pupils occurs both as a
result of teaching and the attitude of the teacher.
Children who apply throughout the day what they are
studying are likely to remember the information.   This
application is especially crucial in speaking and
writing.   Of course, the recognition of pupils who use
the new vocabulary illustrates the importance a teacher
attaches to the application of information and
simultaneously encourages youngsters to continue to grow.

    Guideline <u>Twelve</u>:   "Develop new vocabulary in all
areas of the curriculum."
    The recommendation that vocabulary be developed in
all subject areas is important for several reasons.
First, each subject area has its own specific vocabulary.
Thus in mathematics one studies <u>radius</u>, <u>pi</u>, <u>cummutative
property</u>, <u>rectangle</u>, and <u>cyclinder</u>. In social studies
one encounters <u>federalism</u>, <u>amnesty</u>, <u>proclamation</u>,
<u>primogeniture</u>, and <u>the Allies</u>. In language one meets
<u>salutation</u>, <u>predicate</u>, <u>narrator</u>, and <u>homonym</u>.   At the
same time, a <u>general</u> rather than <u>specific</u> vocabulary
characterizes much of the basal-reading type of material.
The only teacher who can develop specific vocabulary is
the content teacher.
    Second, many words represent different meanings when
they are found in various subject areas. For instance,
consider the different meanings of the following words.

<u>Word</u>	<u>Subject</u>
chord	music and mathematics
feet	health, mathematics, and literature

proper	mathematics and language
correspondence	mathematics and language
league	physical education, mathematics, and social studies

Guideline Thirteen: "Monitor pupil progress throughout the year to assure that youngsters are constantly acquiring the necessary vocabulary."

In demonstration projects, we use Group Analysis Charts. Names of pupils are listed down the left side, and the numbers or titles of the vocabulary lists are recorded across the top. Pupils who score less than a certain score are required to study and take the quiz over again. Scores are recorded and averages noted. It has been our experience that, almost without exception, pupils who average at least 70% on comprehension maintain a much higher average on vocabulary.

Guideline Fourteen: "Teach pupils to associate the vocabulary meanings of symbols."

It is often easier for writers to use symbols rather than actual words. Pupils should learn to recognize symbols as one form of vocabulary. Samples include the following:

Non-verbal: x (multiply, by as in 2x4 feet, unknown element)

Abbreviations: lb., etc., M, Jr.

Acronyms: VISTA, PAL, UNESCO, PUSH

Guideline Fifteen: "Avoid the use of strategies which interfere with vocabulary development."

In our zest to develop pupil proficiency in vocabulary, we sometimes use procedures which inadvertently interfere with the learning process. Sample practices which are not recommended include the following:

1. Use baby talk. Children must relearn horsie as horse, doggie as dog, and "I wuv oo" as "I love you".

2. As an instructional exercise, ask pupils to look up new words in a dictionary. Pupils often try to locate words when they are unable to use the dictionary efficiently or effectively. Upon locating the words,

605

they don't know which definition is appropriate and frequently copy the shortest entry. Finally, pupils cannot study and learn the meanings, a factor which destroys the value of the activity itself.

3. Use new vocabulary when introducing new concepts. Vocabulary can interfere with pupil learning. For example, a primary teacher who uses only the term synonym when first talking about words which mean about the same thing will actually inhibit pupil learning, for the new term will cloud children's concepts of what is being taught. In like manner, a first-grade teacher who uses the term associative property when introducing the mathematical principle involved will interfere with pupils' acquiring the proficiency toward which instruction is being provided. It is generally wise to proceed from the known to the unknown. In the first example, a teacher should use the term means about the same thing as. In the second example, a teacher can use the term associative property after pupils have learned how to apply the skill involved and when they need to know the term to cope with information presented in their textbooks.

Guideline Sixteen: "Teach pupils how to study their vocabulary assignments."
Far too often children receive assignments with the admonition, "Now take this home (or back to your seat) and study it." A missing link which enables pupils to do so efficiently and effectively is the inclusion of a study procedure. We find it helpful to use a four-part plan. If words are listed on the left side of a page of notebook paper and definitions or illustrations are shown on the right side, a youngster can cover the right side with a 3x5 inch card or a heavy sheet of paper. The study procedure is outlined in Chapter 7B.

Summary

In its original form vocabulary is a part of oral language. Only in the past few millennia have we added the graphic reproduction of language to our list of accomplishments. We believe vocabulary should be fun and functional. Contrary to the few who contend otherwise, vocabulary can be developed.
After discussing six questionable practices, we suggested various types of activities in which specific guidance could enhance the development of vocabulary. These areas were classified are general, listening, speaking, reading, and writing to signify the diverse

606

aspects by which vocabulary and language should be developed. Finally we offered some guidelines for use in developing vocabulary.

FOR FURTHER READING

Brown, Jennifer, "Reading Aloud," Elementary English, L, No. 4 (April, 1973), 635-636.

Brown, Rexel E., "Figurative Language: A Gordian's Knot for Young Readers," Indiana Reading Quarterly, IX, No. 3 (Spring, 1977), 23-26, 31.

Dale, Edgar, and Joseph O'Rourke, Techniques for Teaching Vocabulary, Palo Alto, Cal.: Field, 1971.

Duffelmeyer, Frederick A., "Introducing Words in Context," Wisconsin State Reading Association Journal, XXVI, No. 3 (Spring, 1982), 4-6.

Dulin, Kenneth L., "Using Context Clues in Word Recognition and Comprehension," Reading Teacher, XXIII, No. 5 (February, 1970), 440-445, 469.

Emans, Robert, "Context Clues," in Elementary Reading Instruction, Selected Materials, pp. 197-207, eds. Althea Beery, Thomas C. Barrett, and William R. Powell. Boston: Allyn, Bacon, 1969.

Fillmer, H. Thompson, "A Generative Vocabulary Program for Grades 4-6," Elementary School Journal, LXXVIII, No. 1 (September, 1977), 53-58.

Geraets, Gertrude, "Developing Word Consciousness," Indiana Reading Quarterly, IX, No. 1 (Fall, 1976), 28-31.

Groff, Patrick, "The Controversy over Reading Vocabulary," Wisconsin State Reading Association Journal, XXV, No. 2 (January, 1981), 6-8.

Johnson, Dale, and P. David Pearson, Teaching Reading Vocabulary, Second Edition. New York: Holt, 1984.

List A

ANTONYMS

Directions: Write the words which are the opposites of the following.

add	front	morning	rich	sweet
afraid	give	near	right	throw
all	good	neat	rough	top
always	happy	new	rude	true
begin	high	night	short	up
best	hungry	old	sick	wet
black	large	open	single	whisper
buy	leave	over	sit	wild
clear	light	plus	skinny	winner
come	love	pretty	slow	winter
early	man	quiet	soft	work
easy	many	real	spring	your

List B

Directions: List each of the following words in the correct column.

New	Old	Large	Small
	ancient		dwarf
	antique		gigantic
	fresh		great
	modern		huge
	obsolete		little
	original		midget
	out-dated		miniature
			minute
			tiny
			tremendous

Good	Bad	Many	Few
	brave		all
	dependable		couple
	friendly		everyone
	greedy		least
	kind		million
	loyal		more
	mean		most
	naughty		numerous
	rude		several
	truthful		some

Rough	Smooth	Wet	Dry
	bristles		damp
	feathers		desert
	fur		dew
	glass		dust
	gravel		ice
	sandpaper		powder
	silk		soup
	straw		stream
			water

Over	Under	Man	Woman
	above		aunt
	below		brother

609

beneath	daughter
high	father
low	mother
on	nephew
top	niece
upon	sister
	son
	uncle

Quiet	Noisy	Rich	Poor
	fight		abundant
	loud		Cadillac
	lullaby		charge
	pacifier		credit
	peaceful		money
	scream		penniless
	silent		wealthy
	sleep		valuable
	thunder		
	whisper		

Foods that grow

above the ground	below the ground	Wild Animals	Tame Animals
	beets		bear
	cabbage		crocodile
	corn		dog
	cucumbers		fox
	okra		gorilla
	peanuts		hamster
	peas		horse
	potatoes		lion
	squash		rabbit
	turnips		panther

Sweet	Sour
	bitter
	dessert
	honey
	molasses
	salty
	stale
	sugar
	vinegar

List C

HOMONYMS AND NEAR - HOMONYMS

ail	ale		done	dun	
air	heir		faint	feint	
all	awl		fair	fare	
allowed	aloud		faker	fakir	
alter	altar		feat	feet	
ate	eight		ferry	fairy	
an	Ann		flee	flea	
base	bass		flow	floe	
bear	bare		fir	fur	
beat	beet		flew	flue	flu
beau	bow		flocks	phlox	
beaut	butte		flow	flo	
beech	beach		four	fore	for
beer	bier		fourth	forth	
berry	bury		fowl	foul	
berth	birth		freeze	frieze	
bite	bight	byte	gale	Gail	Gayle
blew	blue		gamble	gambol	
board	bored		gate	gait	
bolder	boulder		gild	guild	
born	borne		gneiss	nice	
bow	bough		great	grate	
bowl	boll		groan	grown	
break	brake		hail	hale	
bridal	bridle		hair	hare	
brows	browse		hall	haul	
but	butt		handsome	hansom	
by	bye	buy	hanger	hangar	
cane	Cain		hear	here	
cannon	canon		heard	herd	
capital	Capitol		hew	hue	
cash	cache		hi	high	
cell	sell		him	hymn	
cellar	seller		hoes	hose	
cent	sent	scent	hole	whole	
cereal	serial		I	eye	aye
choose	chews		idol	idle	idyll
chic	sheik		in	inn	
claws	clause	Claus	it's	its	
click	clique		knave	nave	
coarse	course		knew	new	gnu
colonel	kernel		knight	night	
compliment	complement		knot	not	
creak	creek		know	no	
daze	days		lacks	lax	

611

deer	dear		lain	lane	
dessert	desert		lesson	lessen	
dew	due		lie	lye	
die	dye		load	lode	
dine	dyne		maid	made	
doe	dough		mail	male	
main	mane		sea	see	
mall	maul		seed	cede	
mantle	mantel		seem	seam	
marshall	martial		sew	so	
maze	maize		shoe	shoo	
meat	meet	mete	shown	shone	
medal	meddle		sight	site	cite
miner	minor		signet	cygnet	
missile	missal		slay	sleigh	
mite	might		sole	soul	
morn	mourn		staid	stayed	
nay	neigh		stair	stare	
need	kneed		stake	steak	
nix	nicks		steel	steal	
none	nun		straight	strait	
oh	owe		style	stile	
one	won		sum	some	
or	ore		sun	son	
our	hour		surf	serf	
pail	pale		tacks	tax	
pain	pane		tail	tale	
peak	peek		taut	taught	
pear	pair	pare	tee	tea	
peat	Pete		tern	turn	
peel	peal		threw	through	
peer	pier		tide	tied	
pi	pie		tier	tear	
piece	peace		to	two	too
plain	plane		tow	toe	
prays	preys	praise	troop	troupe	
pride	pried		vail	veil	vale
principal	principle		vein	vain	vane
profit	prophet		very	vary	
quay	key		waist	waste	
queue	cue		wait	weight	
raise	raze	rays	war	wore	
rap	wrap		ware	wear	
red	read		warn	worn	
reed	read		wave	waive	
reign	rain		way	weigh	
right	write		we	wee	

List C
(Cont.)

ring	wring	weather	whether
road	rode	week	weak
role	roll	we'll	wheel
rote	wrote	which	witch
rout	route	whine	wine
row	roe	wood	would
sac	sack	yoke	yolk
sale	sail		
scene	seen		

List D

SAMPLE LIST OF TRUE BOOKS

(Chicago: Children's Press)

Ballard, ...True Book of Reptiles

Carlisle, ...Bridges

Carona, ...Chemistry, ...Numbers

Carter, ...Oceans, ...Ships and Seaports, ...Houses

Clark, ...Dinosaurs

Elkin, ...Money

Frahm, ...Bacteria

Friskey, ...Birds We Know

Leavitt, ...Tools for Building

Lewellen, ...Farm Animals, ...Knights

Miner, ...Our Post Office and Its Helpers, ...Policemen and Firemen, ...Plants

Nighbert, ...Cloth

Podendorf, ...Spiders, ...Insects, ...Pebbles and Shells

Posell, ...Dogs

Purcell, ...Holidays and Special Days

List E

SAMPLE LIST OF FIRST BOOKS

(New York: Watts)

Bendick, ...First Book of Airplanes; First Book of Space
Travel

Bothwell, ...Roads

Brewster, ...Eskimos; ...Cowboys

Campbell, ...Trains

Cormack, ...Trees

Epstein, ...Glass; ...Mexico

Heal, ...American

Rogers, ...Cotton

Smith, ...Conservation

Stoddard, ...Television

Strealfield, ...England

Williamson, ...Bugs

LIST F

SOME CLASSICS TOO GOOD TO MISS

Primary

Alexander, Martha, Blackboard Bear. New York: Dial,
1969.

Aruego, Jose, Look What I Can Do. New York: Scribner,
1971.

Brown, Marcia. Stone Soup. New York: Scribner, 1947.

Ciardi, John, The Monster Den. Philadelphia:
Lippincott, 1963.

Credle, Ellis, <u>Down</u> <u>Down</u> <u>the</u> <u>Mountain</u>. Camden, N.J.: Thomas Nelson and Sons, 1961.

Fisher, Aileen. <u>Clean</u> <u>As</u> <u>a</u> <u>Whistle</u>. New York: Crowell, 1969.

_____, <u>Sing</u>, <u>Little</u> <u>Mouse</u>. New York: Crowell, 1969.

Francoise, <u>The</u> <u>Thank-You</u> <u>Book</u>. New York: Scribner, 1947.

Graham, Kenneth, <u>The</u> <u>Reluctant</u> <u>Dragon</u>. New York: Holiday, 1953.

Hill, Elizabeth, <u>Evan's</u> <u>Corner</u>. New York: Holt, 1967.

Lombardo, Kathleen, <u>Macaroni</u>. New York: Random, 1968.

Matsuno, Masako, <u>Taro</u> <u>and</u> <u>the</u> <u>Tofu</u>. Cleveland, 1962.

Piper, Watty, <u>The</u> <u>Little</u> <u>Engine</u> <u>That</u> <u>Could</u>. New York: Platt and Munk, 1954.

Potter, Beatrix, <u>Tale</u> <u>of</u> <u>Peter</u> <u>Rabbit</u>. New York: Warne, 1904.

Sendak, Maurice, <u>Chicken</u> <u>Soup</u> <u>With</u> <u>Rice</u>. New York: Scholastic, 1962.

Seuss, Dr., <u>And</u> <u>To</u> <u>Think</u> <u>That</u> <u>I</u> <u>Saw</u> <u>It</u> <u>On</u> <u>Mulberry</u> <u>Street</u>. New York: Vanguard Press, 1937.

_____, <u>The</u> <u>Five</u> <u>Hundred</u> <u>Hats</u> <u>of</u> <u>Bartholomew</u> <u>Cubbins</u>. New York: Vanguard, 1938.

Sloboldkina, Esphyr, <u>Caps</u> <u>For</u> <u>Sale</u>. New York: Scott, 1947.

Steptoe, John, <u>Stevie</u>. New York: Harper and Row, 1969.

Tworkov, Jack, <u>The</u> <u>Camel</u> <u>Who</u> <u>Took</u> <u>a</u> <u>Walk</u>. New York: Dutton, 1951.

White, E.B., <u>Charlotte's</u> <u>Web</u>. New York: Harper, 1952.

Yashima, Taro, <u>Crow</u> <u>Boy</u>. New York: Viking, 1955.

Intermediate

Alexander, Lloyd, The Black Cauldron. New York: Holt, 1965.

_____, The Book of Three. New York: Holt, 1964.

_____, The Castle of Blyr. New York: Holt, 1966.

_____, The High King. New York: Holt, 1968.

_____, Taran Wanderer. New York: Holt, 1967.

Armstrong, William H., Sounder. New York: Harper, 1970.

Behn, Harry, Faraway Lurs. Cleveland: World, 1963.

Butterworth, Oliver, The Enormous Egg. Boston: Little, Brown, 1956.

Caudill, Rebecca, A Certain Small Shepherd. New York: Holt, 1965.

DeJong, Meindert, Along Came a Dog. New York: Harper, 1958.

_____, The House of Sixty Fathers. New York: Harper, 1956.

_____, Hurry Home, Candy. New York: Harper, 1953.

_____, Shadrach. New York: Harper and Brothers, 1953.

_____, The Tower by the Sea. New York: Harper, 1950.

Glasgow, Aline, The Pair of Shoes. New York: Dial, 1971.

Hamilton, Virginia, The House of Dies Drear. Toronto, Canada: Macmillan, 1968.

Houston, James, Wolf Run. New York: Harcourt, 1971.

Hunt, Irene, Up a Road Slowly. Chicago: Follett, 1966.

Jackson, Jesse, Call Me Charlie. New York: Harper, 1945.

_____, Tessie. New York: Dell, 1968.

Konigsburg, E.L., From the Mixed-Up Files of Mrs. Basil E. Frankweiler. New York: Atheneum, 1970.

_____, Jennifer, Hecate, MacBeth, William McKinley, and Me, Elizabeth. New York: Atheneum, 1968.

Krumgold, Joseph, Onion John. New York: Crowell, 1959.

Lenski, Lois, Strawberry Girl. Philadelphia: Lippincott, 1945.

O'Brien, Robert C., Mrs. Frisby and the Rats of NIMH. New York: Atheneum, 1971.

O'Dell, Scott, The Black Pearl. Boston: Houghton, 1967.

_____, Sing Down the Moon. Boston: Houghton, 1970.

Selden, George, The Cricket in Times Square. New York: Farrar, Straus and Giroux, 1960.

Taylor, Theodore, The Cay. New York: Doubleday, 1969.

Warner, Gertrude, The Boxcar Children. Chicago: Scott, Foresman, 1950.

White, E.B. The Trumpet of the Swan. New York: Harper, 1970.

Wilder, Laura Ingalls, Little House on the Prairie books. New York: Harper.

Wojciechowska, Maia, Shadow of a Bull. New York: Atheneum, 1965.

CHAPTER 11

IDEAS FOR DEVELOPING COMPREHENSION

Introduction

By far the least emphasized of all the basic skills is the cluster referred to as comprehension. In many schools it is possible to find some teachers who are unable even to name several types of comprehension, much less recommend procedures for developing proficiency in the various components.

This chapter therefore consists of four primary aspects: (1) developing an awareness of and proficiency in creating questions representing literal, implied (or inferential), and creative comprehension, (2) presenting selected comprehension skills and suggesting activities and materials through which instruction might be enhanced at the picture, listening, and reading stages, (3) offering guidelines for use in developing comprehension, and (4) discussing sample techniques for teaching comprehension skills.

A systematic and sequential program emphasizing proficiency in the various types of comprehension will go far toward preventing the problems which so often confront our would-be readers. We hear their complaints each day.

"I have to read everything at least twice to understand it."

"I can pronounce all the words, but you had better not ask me any questions."

"I got a lot of ideas out of the book, but none of them seem to fit together."

One thing these people lack is the ability to organize concepts and relate them to each other. The overall structure of information is referred to as schemata (singular is schema). What implication does this problem have for teachers?

"Basically, teachers should realize that schemata are simply ways of organizing information in memory, that schemata create expectations about what appears in print, and perhaps most important, teachers need to vary both questioning techniques and instructional content so that students can develop all reading skills they will need to increase their comprehension of the world in print and the world in general (303:29)."

This chapter addresses both techniques and content. Pupils--indeed, all literate persons--read different pieces of material with varying degrees of understanding. While a variety of comprehension taxonomies exist (42,64, 401,610,624), we focus here on a model with three facets: literal, inferential or implied, and creative (109).

1. Literal comprehension involves merely the parroting of specific information gained by reading the lines. Consider the following sentence:

Tom put on his hat, coat, and gloves and then went outside.

What would be a literal question? Any of the following would be possible.

A. What was the boy's name? (Tom)
B. What did he put on? (His hat, coat, and gloves)
C. Where did he go? (Outside)

In each case you observe the answer is specifically stated in the text. That is, it may be underlined, circled, or copied onto a sheet of paper.

2. Inferential or implied comprehension goes a step further. At this point a reader must read not only the lines but read and think between the lines. In the same sentence, what would be an inferential or implied question?
Any of the following would be possible:

A. What sort of weather was there? (Cold)

B. What season of the year is it? (Most likely winter)

C. How do you know Tom was not two or three years old? (Children at those ages usually require assistance in donning their clothes.)

Inferential or implied comprehension, then, requires the reader or listener to infer meanings based on his own experiences and from information given in a selection. He may be asked to predict outcomes, recognize cause-effect relationships, or sense the mood, tone, or point of view. All the above--and more--relate to inferential comprehension. The answers are not stated;they are implied. The competent reader recognizes these implications and makes inferences. Remember that writers and speakers imply. Readers and listeners infer.

It is interesting to note that youngsters asked to supply answers often respond, "But it don't say." While the material does not specifically say, it does offer hints at the appropriate response for the reader who has acquired the habit of reading between the lines.

3. _Creative_ _interpretation_ is the third level of comprehension. To operate creatively, a reader must be able to relate specific ideas and learnings to new or different situations. In other words, he must read beyond the lines. Returning to the original example, what creative questions might you ask? Either of the following would be possible:

A. Why did Tom go outside? (To run an errand, play with his pet, visit someone, go ice skating, go to school, perform a chore, and so forth)

B. How did Tom feel about going outside? (Perhaps angry at having to run an errand, anxious to play with his pet, happy to see a friend, reluctant to go to school, or relieved to get away from his family)

When creative questions are utilized, many different answers are acceptable. Different people interpret situations in various ways, and so long as their perceptions are not inconsistent with the printed context, we have the responsibility to value their responses. (One answer which obviously should be counted wrong is, "Tom went outside to go swimming in the pond." This answer is completely inconsistent with Tom's wearing his hat, coat, and gloves.)

A problem which often confronts teachers is that of determining which types of questions are being asked. There is a fairly simple way of doing so. If the answer is specifically stated in the text, the question is literal. If several answers within a narrow range are acceptable but none are specifically stated (or the connection between several ideas is not specified), the question is implied or inferential. If almost any answer is acceptable, and many contrasting responses are recognized, the question is creative.

Now let us study some sample sentences and practice developing questions at the three levels of comprehension. The following material will be most helpful if you think through it.

> Wearing his new football uniform, John Smith rode home on his bicycle.

What literal questions might you ask? Any of the following would be possible:

A. Who rode home on his bicycle? (John Smith)

B. What was John wearing? (A new football uniform)

C. How did John get home? (He rode his bicycle.)

D. Who wore a new football uniform? (John Smith)

We have said the answers to any questions of this type can be obtained merely by underlining, circling, or copying the appropriate words in the selection.

Based on the same sentence, what inferential or implied questions can you suggest? Any of the following would be possible:

A. What season of the year is it? How do you know? (It is autumn; that is the season when football is most often played.)

B. In what month(s) did this story most likely take place? How do you know? (Football is often played in September, October, November, December, and January. However, since John probably would be issued a new uniform at the beginning of the season, the months of August and September are the most likely answers.)

C. What time of day is it? How do you know? (Unless the team is practicing on Saturday, it is probably around 5:00 or 6:00 in the evening. Football practice would probably begin right after school and continue for several hours until dinnertime.)

D. How old is John? How do you know? (He is

probably between eight and fifteen years old. Very little organized football is played by children younger than eight. Most students sixteen and older would drive or ride home in cars. Also, the older boys most likely would shower and change back to street clothes before returning home.)

E. How far from home has John been practicing? (Not far, probably not more than a mile)

Now let's consider some imagery questions. These include four parallel kinds: (a) visual, (b) auditory, (c) olfactory, and (d) kinesthetic. A fifth kind refers to mood. All five types can be literal, implied or inferential, or creative, depending on the circumstances. Let us explore each of these briefly by asking the following questions:

A. What does John Smith <u>see</u> on his way home? (Since it is early in the fall, he may see brightly colored leaves on the trees and on the ground. If the wind is blowing, John may see whirlwinds of leaves. If the wind is still, people may be raking and burning the leaves. Children may be outside--tossing footballs, playing hopscotch, or jumping in the leaves. Smoke may be rising from some chimneys.
(Since it is late in the evening, some parents may be driving home from work, making traffic heavier than usual. Someone may be delivering the evening paper. If John is riding home with several of his friends, he may see other boys in new uniforms and a number of bicycles with various accessories and in many different physical conditions.) Seeing brightly-colored leaves and a lot of traffic is implied. We expect that. Seeing children play hopscotch or ride bicycles with certain attachments is creative.

B. What does John Smith <u>hear</u> on his way home? (Because of the mass traffic, John should hear car horns and the squeal of wheels. While riding over leaves, he should hear them crumble, and if leaves are burning, he may hear the crackling. John's bicycle may even have an attachment that clatters against the spokes and creates a staccato sound as he rides. Because children usually play "out loud," John will hear them as well as any neighborhood pets. If John lives in the country, he may hear cows mooing and a swift stream swirling.) Hearing car horns and wheel noises is implied. We expect them at that time of day. Hearing the crackle of burning leaves is creative.

C. What does John Smith smell on his way home? (Perhaps he will smell the smoke of burning leaves and the exhaust fumes from passing cars. Food aromas should be present, both those from homes and from businesses, such as fish camps and bakeries. A variety of industries such as tobacco processors, fertilizers, and paper mills may indicate their presence. New-mown hay and apple orchards have distinctive fragrances too. And then there is John himself, although this smell may go unnoticed by him.) Smelling exhaust fumes and food aromas is implied. They're logical at that time of day. Smelling the smoke of burning leaves is creative. That doesn't have to happen.

D. What things does John Smith feel on his way home? (He probably feels the shifting of the shoulder and hip pads and the weight of his helmet. His hands may be on the plastic handle grips or, if they come loose, on the steel bars. Bumps in the road and the interaction of his cleats with the pedals should be noticeable. Drops of perspiration may be trickling down his face or body, and hunger pangs should be present. If he played throughout the game, John should be exhausted.) The perspiration and the pads are implied. The exhaustion is creative. John may not have played.

E. What comments can be made about John's mood? (He could be happy because he received a new uniform, the symbol of "making the team." If he played in the game or scrimmage, any conversation which transpired between him and the buddies riding his way will focus on the various highlights of the afternoon--the time he ran over "Fats" Donohugh for a touchdown. Conveniently he may forget the three times "Fats" ran over him to score. Alternately, he may be unhappy because he performed poorly or his team lost or he didn't get to play.) All possibilities are creative.

F. What do you think will happen as John rides into his driveway? (We can imagine several things. For instance, John may drop the bicycle in the driveway and run to the house, taking any steps two at a time. On the other hand, he might trudge down the walk to the house. A "what do you think" refers to a creative question.)

G. What do you think might be John's first comments?

1. Guess what! I made the team!

2. Hey, Mom, look at this neat uniform!

623

3. What are we having for supper? I'm starved!

H. It is quite possible that his mother will respond to his first comment with one of the following remarks:

1. Did you make the team?

2. How did you do in the game?

3. There's an apple in the refrigerator. We'll have supper in about an hour.

4. Don't slam the door.

5. Don't walk on my clean floor with those dirty shoes.

The guided practice presented above should facilitate your developing questions at each of the three levels for the following sentence:

John Roberts flies his Piper Cub on the weekends that he does not work.

Spend a few minutes developing some questions and classifying them by type. Some possible items follow:

1. Literal

A. What is the man's name? (John Roberts)

B. What does he do? (Fly a Piper Cub)

C. When does he do this? (On the weekends that he does not work)

2. Implied or Inferential

A. What is a Piper Cub? (Apparently a plane of some type)

B. What is its size? (Small; Cub refers to something little.)

C. How does John Roberts feel about flying? (He likes it; otherwise he wouldn't fly when he was off from work.)

624

D. How old is he? (At least 16--a Federal Aviation Agency requirement for flying; since the plane is his, he must have a job with a good salary. Therefore John is likely to be at least in his mid-twenties.)

E. How can you tell whether John Roberts flies his Piper Cub every weekend? (He can't fly every weekend, because he is only off from work on some weekends.)

F. What type of job is he likely to have? How do you know? (Business, professional, or managerial as opposed to unskilled or semi-skilled labor; These types of occupations are more likely to have employers who work on some but not all weekends.)

G. How do you know he is not a teacher? (First, teachers are not off any weekends. Second, teachers usually cannot afford to own planes.)

3. Creative (A host of possible answers)

A. What specific job does John Roberts have?

B. Why does John Roberts fly a Piper Cub?

C. What does he think about while flying?

D. Where does he fly?

E. Who flies with him?

F. What does he see (hear, smell, feel) as he flies?

You should notice that each question is stated in a manner designed to avoid a true-false response. After all, people should be able to score 50% without even having read the selection if the following items were used:

A. Did John Roberts fly a Piper Cub?

B. Does he fly every weekend?

C. Is a Piper Cub a small plane?

D. Does John Roberts make a lot of money?

625

D. Does he live in the city or the country?

Try to avoid asking questions which have only two options. Check your questions and revise those which begin with these words: Is, are, was, were, do, does, did, can, could, will, have, would, and should.

One final sentence may serve to reinforce the practice of developing questions at the various levels of comprehension.

The harvest moon shone brightly on the sand
as the tide came in.

See how easily you can develop some good questions for each type. Then check the following for additional possibilities:

1. Literal

A. How did the moon shine? (Brightly)

B. What kind of moon was it? (Harvest)

C. What else was happening? (The tide was coming in.)

2. Implied or Inferential

A. About what time was it? (Late evening or night)

B. What season of the year was it? (Probably fall)

C. Where in the United States could this scene take place? (At or near the coast; possibly inland along a major river.)

D. Describe the weather. (Probably clear and calm)

3. Creative

A. Who do you think is on the beach?

B. What sounds could you hear? (Note: "What sounds will you hear?" is an implied question. Will and should refer to implied questions while could and might refer to creative.

C. What could you see?

D. What smells might you smell?

E. How do you feel?

Several points are worth emphasizing. First, so far we have considered only the sentence level of comprehending literal, inferential or implied, and creative meanings. Because of the sequential nature of learning, it seems essential to help children master the sentence before progressing to the paragraph and story levels. After all, how can someone possibly understand a story when he doesn't even comprehend the sentences themselves? While comprehension quizzes following silent reading practices are obviously desirable, it behooves each of us to begin at the beginning and proceed from there.

Second, readers tend to function at the level at which questions are asked (114, 375, 426, 748). For example, if only literal items are posed, children may become very proficient at parroting answers. If, on the other hand, they are asked to read for and think at deeper and broader levels of understanding, and if they are given instruction and guided practice in doing so, they will refine their powers of comprehension.

This statement is not to say that teachers should ignore the literal level, for it is essential. But we can provide a balanced approach by asking appropriate questions and developing those deeper, more analytical levels of comprehension (375). Children and adults should learn to read the lines, read between the lines, and read beyond the lines (226).

A third point to remember is that children need specific instruction in developing facility in comprehension. Merely telling them to "try harder" or "pay more attention" is not very helpful. Whole-class, small group, paired, and individual discussion of sample items such as the three sentences already provided can facilitate comprehension development.

Fourth, concentrated practice with written comprehension exercises seems especially essential. Some teachers just discuss a story orally, a procedure which means that each member of the group is unlikely to be asked more than one question. Under such circumstances it is practically impossible to clarify misconcepts because they hardly even know which difficulties confront various pupils.

Sentences and paragraphs to use in helping children acquire facility in literal, implied or inferential, and creative understanding are included in Practice Exercises

627

Specific Comprehension Skills

While authorities have identified numerous comprehension (or thinking) skills or processes, we shall concern ourselves here with only the following six items:

1. Main ideas or topics
2. Major supporting details
3. Classification
4. Sequence
5. Predicting outcomes
6. Compare-contrast
7. Cause-effect

All of these topics can be presented at the picture, listening, and reading stages. Indeed, half a century ago Miller (513) found that primary children often failed to note the most important parts of a picture. "Thus the ability to interpret pictures is not natural; it must be learned (107:12)." Research indicates that listening comprehension lessons followed by reading comprehension instruction is superior to reading comprehension assignments alone (104). Furthermore, developing certain listening skills in reading results in the improvement of the corresponding reading skills (413, 607, 670, 700).

Each of the skills mentioned above can be presented to non-readers at early ages, including pre-schoolers. Indeed, if the works of Jerome Bruner (88) and Benjamin S. Bloom (63) have any implication for teachers, it is that comprehension proficiencies can and should be developed early and systematically. For our purposes, this means that two-year-olds and seventh-grade non-readers should use pictorial material and listening experiences for initial contact with the comprehension skills. Only those who can read should utilize the third stage of instruction and practice.

1. Main Ideas or Topics

A. Picture Stage

1. Display a Single Concept Card and ask what object is represented.

2. Display a picture and ask (for example) what state or section of the country it represents. Travel

folders, brochures, and post cards are also useful. For younger children, you might use the following:

    a. Picture of a boy (The topic is the boy, not his height, age, or clothing.)

    b. Picture of three children playing in a sandpile. (The main idea is the children are playing. The number of children and the area of their play are supporting details).

    c. Picture of trees bending, rain pelting down, and water running in the street (The main idea is that the storm is serious.)

3. Display a picture or art print and ask pupils to provide a title. The title usually is a topic.

4. Display a picture and ask pupils what emotion is represented.

B. Listening Stage

1. Dictate sentences and ask pupils to tell you the main idea in a few (usually three or four) words. Begin with simple sentences and progress to complex ones. People familiar with diagramming patterns should recognize the main idea as being the data contained across the top line.

    a. Simple sentence:
The little girl in the corner was crying. (The main idea is the girl was crying. The facts that she was little and standing in a corner are supporting details.)

    b. Compound sentence:
The brown and white hound dog chased the frightened little rabbit, but it got away by running under the fence. (The main idea is the dog chased the rabbit, but it escaped. The dog's color, the bunny's fear, and the method of avoiding capture are supporting details.)

    c. Complex sentence:
While Mother was in town buying some groceries for our party this weekend, we had a telephone call from my brother who is stationed in Lebanon. (The main idea is the brother called. The facts that he is in Lebanon, Mother was buying

629

groceries, and we are planning a party are
supporting details.

2. Dictate paragraphs and ask pupils to tell which
sentence represents the main idea. There are four basic
patterns: first sentence, last sentence, a medial
sentence, and implied rather than specifically stated.
An example of each type follows:

a. Mother said my room was a mess. The bed had
not been made, and my pajamas were on the floor.
Even though I had shoved some games under the
bed, several pieces of one puzzle had become
stained by some spilled orange juice. (The main
idea is stated in the first sentence.)

b. First I wrote each spelling word fifteen
times. Next I read the history chapter--all 27
pages--pretty quickly. The questions at the end
had to be answered because my teacher always
checks those in class first thing. Then I wrote
a two-page paper on "Why I like school." Miss
Gooly likes that topic. Finally, I threw down my
pen. I had finished my homework! (The main idea
is stated in the last sentence.)

c. All morning long I dug potatoes and fought
the heat and little black bugs. Finally Dad
hollered, "How about stopping a while and helping
me lift these beams in place?" "Gosh," I
groaned, "Life on a farm is just one blamed job
after another!" But off I trotted. After we got
the roof supports braced, Dad "suggested" that I
might want to clear the trash out of the branch
and hustle some water to Mom so she could start
putting up soup. Suggested! Ha! That was no
suggestion. That was a nice way of telling me
what to do next. (The main idea is found in this
medial sentence: "Life on a farm is just one
blamed job after another!")

d. Now where else in the world can people
criticize the government when they disagree with
its policies? Where else can people worship as
they please if they are so inclined? Where else
can free citizens meet and form organizations
based on common interests? And where else are
people granted protection under a government of
laws instead of men? (The main idea is implied.
It is that our form of government grants certain

630

freedoms which others don't.)

Instruction and practice in recognizing main ideas of four types of paragraphs should follow a particular seven-step sequence.

1. Type 1 (Main idea at first)

2. Type 2 (Main idea at end)

3. Combinations of Types 1 and 2

4. Type 3 (Main idea inferred)

5. Combinations of Types 1, 2, and 3

6. Type 4 (Main idea in the middle)

7. Combination of Types 1, 2, 3, and 4

One or more practice exercises, complete with instruction, should focus on Type 1, Main idea in the first sentence of a paragraph. When children seem to recognize this location of main idea, proceed to instruction and practice in Type 2, Main idea in the last sentence of a paragraph. After this skill appears to have been mastered, move to the next step in the sequence, that is, paragraphs in which pupils must identify main ideas found either in the first or last sentences. Continue this progression through all seven steps.

Obviously the latter steps are far more difficult than the first items in the sequence. Logically, therefore, an increased emphasis and amount of time, practice, and material must be allocated to this study. As a consequence, weeks or even months may be necessary to secure satisfactory results in one of the latter areas.

3. Play or sing songs and ask pupils to tell the main ideas or topics or develop titles. Some examples include the following:

"This Land Is Your Land"

"I'm Going To Leave Old Texas Now"

"Mulberry Bush"

"All Through the Night"

4. Read poems and ask pupils to tell the main ideas or develop titles. (Titles are not necessarily the same as main ideas.) Some examples include the following:

"Trees," by Joyce Kilmer

"Fog," by Carl Sandburg

"Twas the Night Before Christmas," by Moore.

5. Read fables and ask pupils to tell the morals or lessons to be gained. These morals are the main idea at the implied level. Some examples include the following:

"The Fox and the Grapes"

"Belling the Cat"

"Chanticleer and the Fox"

"The Hare and the Tortoise"

"The Country Mouse and the City Mouse"

"The Bundle of Sticks"

6. Read short stories and ask pupils to tell the main ideas or develop titles. Some examples include the following:

Brown, Marcia, Stone Soup. New York: Scribner, 1947.

Fenner, Phyllis R. (comp.), Princesses and Peasant Boys. New York: Knopf, 1944.

Kipling, Rudyard, The Jungle Book. New York: Doubleday, 1946.

Slobodkina, Esphyr, Caps for Sale. New York: Scott, 1947.

Uchida, Yoshiko, The Magic Listening Cap. New York: Harcourt, 1955.

C. Reading Stage

Any activity included in the Listening Stage can be

632

utilized here. The only difference is the mode of communication. Therefore the following information includes only ideas not previously presented.

1. Mount the body of a newspaper article on construction paper and paste the headline on the reverse side. Ask pupil to read the article and determine appropriate titles. Before checking the reverse side to read one possible answer, pupils should write their suggestion(s). They should understand that a number of alternatives are possible, not just the headlines listed on the reverse side of the paper.

Materials published by children's magazines, Scholastic Book Services, and Xerox Publications (My Weekly Reader) are especially useful for securing simple material to use with younger children.

2. Using ten pieces of construction paper, mount five headlines and five articles on separate strips. Ask pupils to read the information and match each with the appropriate headline. This exercise may range from simple to complex depending upon the material that is used. For instance, if each article deals with a different subject (space, baseball, animals, toys, and family or drugs, pollution, foreign affairs, elections, and poverty), the task may be fairly simple. On the other hand, matching five articles and headlines with the same general topic may be a far more complex task.

To make these materials self-scoring, record parallel answers on backs (i.e., 1-A, 2-B, 3-C, 4-D, 5-E). Practice exercises should be housed in envelopes, preferably the sturdy manila type. Complete sets may also be numerically labeled by assumed level of difficulty. That is, easy sets may be numbered from 1-50, harder ones from 51-100 and the most difficult 101-150.

3. Mount cartoons and their captions on construction paper as described above and ask pupils to match them.

4. Compile a list of books that pupils can skim through to get the main idea. Then ask them to match the book titles with five main ideas. Note the following example:

BOOKS/STATEMENTS SETS
Set 1

Directions: Skim through the following books. When you are through, read the statements listed below. Match

633

them to the book titles by placing the appropriate letter to the left of each number.

1.	Little House on the Prairie	A.	Fern saves a pig that is about to be killed.
2.	Charlotte's Web	B.	People in the city have a lot of interesting experiences.
3.	The People Downstairs	C.	Ma and Pa have some exciting adventures.
4.	The Courage of Sarah Noble	D.	A race car driver speeds down the highway at midnight.
5.	Miss Esta Maude's Secret	E.	Tall John and the Indians are real friends.

5. Mount advertisements and captions about jobs and personnel wanted and objects for sale or wanted. Use the procedure described in number two and ask pupils to match the items.

6. After pupils have dictated a language-experience story, ask them to suggest a title. What title would you give the following story?

> My teacher is Miss Gumbo.
> She has red hair.
> She wears high heels.
> She has a big white ring.
> Miss Gumbo likes to sing.
> Sometimes she reads us a story.
> She sure can read.

7. When pupils write paragraphs or stories, ask them to suggest titles. What title (topic) would you give to the following story?

> We used to have a chicken. She was so stupid we called her Dumb Cluck. She would follow us around everywhere we went. One day Mother was making a cake, and Dumb Cluck tried to roost in the oven. Do you know what happened? We had baked chicken for lunch.

8. Provide a paragraph of basic information and ask pupils to construct a Western Union telegram consisting of no more than fifteen words. As one example, the following information might be presented to children.

Information to be sent to Grandma Blake: Your two grandchildren, Danny and Jan, are coming to see you on Thursday, April 1, 1987. They will arrive at the Trailways Bus Station in San Diego, California, at 11:11 a.m. They will be bringing two jars of your favorite jelly. Please meet them.

9. Ask pupils to write a paragraph in twenty-five words or less. Topics might include "Why I Like (or Dislike) School," "Why _____ Is My Best Friend," or "Why I Like To _____."

2. Major Supporting Details

Proficiency in this skill may be developed concurrently with instruction on main ideas. In general, the materials used to develop an awareness of major supporting details are the same as those utilized for main ideas. The essential difference is in the key question asked, "How do you know _____ is the main idea?" A few sample activities related to those already suggested under Main Ideas are included simply to provide ideas.

A. Picture Stage

1. Display a picture portraying a state or section of the country and ask to be reminded of the topic. Then ask, "How do you know this picture represents Florida? What parts of the picture tell you that?"

2. Display a picture and ask pupils to tell you why they selected a certain title.

3. Display a picture and ask children how they knew a certain emotion was represented.

B. Listening Stage

1. After pupils have identified the main idea of a dictated sentence, ask what words tell about the main idea. These of course, are supporting details.

2. After pupils have identified the main idea of a dictated paragraph, ask what sentences tell more about the main idea.

C. Reading Stage

1. Ask pupils to read the headlines of a newspaper or children's magazine article and then read the body to answer the following questions:

    a. Who did or said it?

    b. What was done or said?

    c. Where did it occur?

    d. When did it occur?

    e. How was it done?

    f. Why is it important?

In general the answers to most, but not all, of these questions can be derived by reading the first one or two paragraphs of an article. The use of this procedure is an excellent way of providing purpose for reading. Six questions are provided, and the pupil is asked to locate their answers. Several (usually items a and b) can be determined from study of the headline itself while any of the remaining items typically come from the body of the materials.

2. Ask pupils to read captions of want ads and write descriptions of the personnel whom they are seeking.

3. Classification

Often referred to as categorization, this skill requires youngsters to recognize both similarities and differences in objects, pictures, words, ideas, and in increasingly complex abstractions. It has been called "one of the most fundamental human cognitive abilities (344:538)."

A. Picture Stage

1. Mount pictures of three diverse categories of simple objects. These might include a number of different breeds of dogs (hound, chihuahua, terrier, poodle); types of chairs (stool, ottoman, high chair);

and kinds of clothing pantsuit, slacks, pants). For young children, mount one picture for each of the three categories--dogs, chair, clothing--on a large sheet of paper. Ask the pupils to place each of the smaller pictures under the appropriate category.

2. Select pictures to represent three similar or parallel categories. Mount approximately five pictures representing each category for a total of about fifteen items. Take one picture from each category and place it on a table. Ask pupils to place the remaining pictures in one of the three groups. Later give them pictures either without revealing the number of groups or without presenting a pictured sample of each group. Incidentally, real objects may also be used for this practice. One caution: Be sure pupils can identify the objects before attempting to categorize them.

As a practice activity, suppose you had pictures of each of the following. Into what categories would they be grouped?

a. clipper ship   f. submarine   k. helicopter

b. rowboat   g. prairie schooner l. automobile

c. conestoga   h. blimp   m. trailer

d. barge   l. train   n. horse

e. jet   j. dirigible   o. balloon

They are all means of transportation: land, air, and water. Consequently three groups of pictures should emerge. Similar sets of pictures might be developed for meats, vegetables, or fruits; furniture found in the kitchen, living room, or bathroom; woodwind, percussion, string, or brass instruments; and fish, birds, reptiles, or mammals.

Provide answers on the reverse side by labeling all of one type A, a second type B, and so forth. As an alternative, make an answer key and keep it at your desk.

3. Ask pupils to note how objects within the class or at home are grouped. For instance, all books with the red spine are together on the shelf. All the encyclopedias are side by side. Certain drawers or closet space is allocated for specific items. The poster paper goes in one place, the rulers in another.

B. Listening Stage

1. Pronounce words which fall into one of three categories. Ask pupils to identify the groups and, working as PALs, to classify each. The items may be those used above or be similar to the following sets.

    a. Names of persons--names of places--names of things

    b. Work--recreation--both

    c. Countries--continents--states

    d. American--French--Greek

    e. Words which express fear--love--hatred

    f. Gases--liquids--solids

    g. Bones--organs--muscles

    h. Trees--bushes--plants

2. After reading some stories to the class, ask pupils to classify them by poetry, fairy tale, or tall tale; fiction, biography, or autobiography; fable, myth, or talking animal.

3. Ask pupils to classify their television watching or radio listening by types of programs (comedy, mystery, science, sports, etc.)

C. Reading Stage

Once again it is possible to use the material contained in the picture and listening stages. Only the medium of presentation needs to change. The following are additional ideas:

1. Divide a spirit master in half and print eight words in each column. The sixteen words should represent three or four categories of objects such as those already mentioned or the following:

    a. Islands--peninsulas--straits
    b. Artists--musicians--writers
    c. Explorers--pioneers--patriots

Run the spirit master off onto construction paper and

make ten copies, which is enough for twenty pupils working together. Either leave the sheets whole or have the children cut the paper into individual segments and then classify. If the construction paper is left whole, pupils copy their answers onto another sheet of paper. This alternative is preferred for young children.

Material based on this idea is available commercially. The Vocabulary Improvement Practice (283) contains lists of words which must be classified under one of three headings. They are self-scoring.

2. For literature, give pupils a list of short selections to read and ask them to classify the stories.

3. For social studies, give pupils a list of terms and ask them to classify the items. Note the following:

CHART 11-1

TERMS NOT CATEGORIZED

Legislative	Executive	Judicial
senator	governor	umpire
justice	representative	sheriff
judge	arbitrator	whip
mayor	burgess	referee
president	Secretary of State	councilman

TERMS CATEGORIZED

Legislative	Executive	Judicial
senator	president	justice
representative	mayor	judge
burgess	Secretary of State	arbitrator
councilman	governor	umpire
whip	sheriff	referee

4. In math, ask pupils to classify problems by the process through which they can be solved (add, subtract, multiply, divide, combination).

639

5. Ask pupils to classify fractions (rational numbers) by type: proper, improper, wholes. Or group them into their completely reduced bases. For instance, 3/6, 8/16 and 14/28 all belong in the 1/2 group while 18/27, 4/6, and 6/9 all belong in the 2/3 group.

6. Ask primary pupils to classify objects by shape (square, rectangle, circle, triangle) or color.

7. Put the titles of library books either on small cards or on a spirit master. Ask pupils to classify the books according to the Dewey Decimal System.

4. Sequence

This skill is sometimes referred to as chronological order. Social studies teachers often promote an understanding of sequencing through the use of time lines. Information may be sequenced according to date, size, number, age, time, or intensity.

A. Picture Stage

1. Locate picture sequences in reading readiness workbooks and ask the pupils to arrange them. These generally have only three or four frames, a factor which facilitates initial mastery.

2. Cut out the pictures and mount them on construction paper. Ask the pupils to arrange the items in correct order. For example, use pictures of cars produced in 1900, 1930, 1950, and 1980. (Models of 1955, 1965, 1975, and 1985 would be even harder for most people.) Another set might include pictures of a house in various stages of construction: cleared land, the foundation, erection of external supports, the roof, completed house. On the back of the construction paper, indicate correct answers. To separate one set from another, use numbers to indicate sets and letters to indicate sequence. For example, set seven might consist of five frames labeled 7A, 7B, 7C, 7D, and 7E.

3. After pupils have begun to acquire initial proficiency in sequencing, encourage them to draw and mount their own frames and see if their partners can arrange the items correctly.

4. Use segmented advertisements typical of those found in women's magazines. For example, one series of five pictures considers pizza. Frame one shows the box

of pizza mix; frame two depicts the dough. In frame three the other ingredients are added, and in frame four the concoction is placed in the oven. In the final frame two happy people share the joys of their labors.

5. Cut out comic strips from the daily newspaper and paste each frame on construction paper slightly larger than the strip itself. Use comics without words ("Henry," "Life with Lucky.") for poorer or beginning readers. The use of comic strips is desirable both at the picture and reading stages. Those with words cannot be used at the low first-grade level.

Several suggestions are worth remembering. First, avoid any strips which include foreign dialects, murder, sadism, or difficult vocabulary level. Second, after pupils have demonstrated ability to cope with the three or four frames typical of daily comics, advance to the Sunday selections which are considerably longer. Third, when printed materials are used, try to locate low reading levels. Examples include "The Ryatts," "The Dripples," "Donald Duck," and "Nancy."

Fourth, when selecting material, read through the story twice, noting whether the frames actually form a logically sequential story which can be reconstructed by the pupils. On occasion it may be necessary to delete an ambiguous frame.

Fifth, allow pupils using comic strips to work together, each one exchanging information with the other about the suggested sequence and the reasoning behind the proposed choice. Pupils should be encouraged to proof check their work by orally telling to each other the story portrayed by the comics. Quite frequently the activity uncovers a previously unnoticed error. Finally they may check the correct sequence recorded on the back.

B. Listening Stage

1. Read complex sentences and ask pupils to tell which part really happened first, regardless of its placement in the sentence. Examples may include the following:

a. Before the rain fell, the temperature was much warmer.

b. We stopped playing after Jack got hit by the ball.

c. Since May has finished her homework, she may go outside.

641

d. When you are through chopping wood, please bring
in an armload.

Children need to become aware of the fact that
certain words often indicate time sequence. Typical
items are <u>before</u>, <u>after</u>, <u>since</u>, <u>although</u>, <u>because</u>, <u>when</u>,
and <u>if</u>.

2. Read a story to the class or a group and ask them
to repeat it in sequence. Examples may include such
primary selections as <u>Caps for Sale</u>, "Little Red Riding
Hood," "The Three Bears," or "The Three Little Pigs."
Upper-level selections may include "Pigs Is Pigs," and
Marcia Brown's <u>Stone Soup</u> (New York: Scribner, 1947).
In each case ask pupils to listen for a specific purpose.
For instance, "Listen to find out what happened each time
one of the three Billy Goats Gruff met the troll at the
bridge."

C. <u>Reading Stage</u>

1. Print the words for numbers on cards and ask
pupils to sequence them. The same may be done for
letters of the alphabet, days of the week, and months of
the year.

2. Print the name of some people in the class and
ask pupils to sequence them. Begin by using only one
name beginning with each letter (Annette, Indy, Jake,
Geraldine). Later include names which begin with the
same letter (Brenda, Bill, and Bob) or letters (Mark,
Mary, Maria, Marvin, Marty.)

3. Print single words which may be sequenced.

a. hut, cabin, house, mansion, palace (splendor)

b. baby, toddler, child, youth, teenager, adult
(age)

c. freezing, cold, cool, warm, hot, boiling (heat)

4. Print or type single sentences from a paragraph
or very short story on construction paper. Ask pupils to
sequence them. Provide this activity at two different
levels of difficulty. The easier type involves sentences
which interlock like the pieces of a puzzle. The fact
that one sentence ends in the middle of a line and the

642

next begins at that point helps the pupil initially.
Later provide sentences all of which start at the left
margin.

5. Cut articles into paragraphs and paste them on
separate sheets of construction paper. Then ask pupils
to sequence these. Once again children's magazines may
be utilized for primary-level needs. Older pupils may
use newspapers. Try to secure interesting materials;
sports, science, space, and women's sections articles can
be especially enjoyable to otherwise reluctant learners.

6. In social studies, list a series of events and
ask pupils to sequence them. Sometimes the section of a
book may also be "pulled out" for sequencing.

Once again, allow youngsters to work together on this
type of exercise. When they disagree, pupils should
attempt to justify their reasons and resolve their
problems. In itself this interaction can produce highly
desirable educational outcomes. Of course pupils will
eventually refer to the backs of the strips to determine
their accuracy.

While sequence strips add a motivating factor to the
development of proficiency in skills, they should not be
allowed to become a meaningless busy-work type of
activity. Like any other learning experience, these
activities should provide young learners with an
opportunity to make errors which then become the basis
for specific teaching.

7. In social studies, ask pupils to list the steps
in selecting a president, of making a law, or sewing a
colonial dress.

8. In mathematics and science, ask pupils to list
the sequence of steps required to solve a particular
problem or experiment. The steps involved in the
formation of coal or oil may be used with upper-grade
pupils. They may also name the major bones of the body
from head to feet.

9. Put call numbers of books on cards or spirit
masters. Ask pupils to sequence the order in which the
books would be found on the shelves of the library.

10. For comic strips whose stories continue from one
day to the next, cut out the entire segment for several
consecutive days or weeks and ask pupils to sequence
them. ("Jackson Twins", "Mark Trail"). Use the same
procedure for news articles.

For pupils who experience considerable difficulty in acquiring this skill, there are several practices you may wish to utilize. First, be sure to progress slowly from three of four frames to longer ones. Many people are simply overwhelmed if long selections are presented too quickly. Second, if a duplicated worksheet includes statements to be sequenced, ask pupils to cut the items apart first. Suggest they decide, without looking at the printed items, which event occurred first. Pupils should then locate that item and decide what came next, locate the item, and so on. Third, give a pupil an entire article in sequence. After reading it, he may be directed to scramble the parts and place them back in sequence.

5. Predicting Outcomes

A. Picture Stage

1. Use pictures and ask pupils to tell what they think will happen next. Examples might include a forester chopping down a tree, a baby about to touch a hot pan, or a person about to step on a banana peel.

2. Using a carefully-selected series of pictures or an illustrated story, ask pupils to look at the first illustration and decide the type of story to be read. Next they should look at the second picture and, if necessary, modify their thinking. While showing additional illustrations, change the questions. Ask, "Who do you think are the main characters?" "What are they like?" and "Where does the story take place?" This approach is often advocated by Stauffer (683).

B. Listening Stage

1. Pronounce special words or phrases and ask pupils to tell what is supposed to happen next. Examples may include the following: "Timber," "Fore," "On your mark," or "4-3-2-1." Or use sounds: Three bells or a sneeze.

2. Dictate sentences and ask pupils to complete the unfinished portion. Examples might include the following:

a. I have told you a ...

b. She saw him out of the corner of ...

c. My aching feet are ... (or My tooth is ...)

644

d. It is raining ...

Of course, an easier type of activity here is one in which couplets are read and pupils are asked to identify the missing rhyming word. Examples include the following:

a. Red Rover, Red Rover
   Send Billy right _____ .

b. Mary had a little lamb
   Little lamb, Little lamb,
   Mary had a little lamb,
   Its fleece was white as _____ .

Books by Dr. Seuss (New York: Random House) and Bill Martin, Jr. (New York: Holt) are especially useful for this type of activity.

3. Ask pupils to predict during a commercial how a program will end. Remind them to do this orally to someone and to tell why they think a certain event will occur.

4. Read paragraphs and incomplete stories and ask pupils to develop endings.

5. Ask pupils to compose group stories. Begin the process by starting, "Once upon a time there was ..." and pointing to one child. Let him supply one or two sentences, stopping him in the middle of a sentence (and hence the middle of an idea) and asking another person to continue. The stories often turn out to be hilarious, and listening and speaking skills are promoted simultaneously.

C. Reading Stage

1. Use a set of daily comic strips from a continuing series and ask pupils to tell what they think will happen next (or eventually).

2. Give pupils the ingredients of a recipe and ask them to predict the finished product. Or give them a series of directions and ask them to predict the eventual destination.

3. Ask pupils to read stories or books and provide possible endings. Perhaps the classic example is the story of "The Lady and the Tiger." We used this

successfully in encouraging pupils to predict outcomes. Interestingly, there seems to be a relationship between the sex of the writer and the ending. Girls almost always wrote that when the princess discovered which door restrained the tiger, she told her love, and he was able to choose the door with the beautiful commoner destined to become his bride.

But the boys didn't tell it this way. Some of them wrote that the princess discovered the secret but, rather than relinquish her lover to another woman, she lied to him, and the poor man was destroyed as a result of the betrayal. Other boys said, "She lied to him, but she was a girl and he knew she would lie. So when she told him which gate to open, he ignored her advice and opened the other, riding off with the beautiful commoner and leaving the princess in a very angry mood. A sequel written in the same vein is "The Discourager of Hesitancy" (in Level 14 of Young America Reading Series. Chicago: Rand McNally, 1974).

"The Little Knight" by Ann Rowe (Glenview, Ill: Scott, Foresman) is an example at the primary level. The king and queen live in a cold castle, and a lonely dragon lives in a cave. The knight sent to "do something" becomes warm by the fire from the friendly dragon's nose. At this point, ask the children, "How do you think the knight can solve the problem and make everyone happy?" Or, while a child is reading Meindert DeJong's Shadrach (New York: Harper, 1953), ask him to predict, from something he read earlier, just where the rabbit disappeared.

4. In social studies, ask pupils to predict how the present might be somewhat different if certain events had not occurred.

a. John Wilkes Booth had not killed Abraham Lincoln.

b. The colonies had not defeated England in the Revolutionary War.

c. The North had not won the Civil War.

d. Pearl Harbor had not been bombed.

6. Compare and Contrast

One of the most basic comprehension skills involves the ability to note ways in which two ideas or subjects are either alike or different (or perhaps both). For example, ability to distinguish main ideas and major supporting details in an outgrowth of competence in noting ways in which language units are similar or different. In each of the practice activities below, the term compare is intended to include the term contrast. Thus, a request to compare two objects or ideas directs the pupil to note ways in which they are both alike and different.

A. Picture Stage

1. Present buttons or other objects of various shapes, sizes, colors, and texture. Ask children, "How are they alike? How are they different?"

2. Using pictures from Sunday comic pages, ask pupils to tell how the two differ. A number of objects will be missing in the second picture. "Hocus Focus" is commonly found in a number of Sunday papers.

3. Present two or more members of a class of objects. Ask, "How are a _____ and a _____ alike?" Present, for example, a piece of chalk, a crayon, a pen, a pencil, and a magic marker. Or, use items such as a book and newspaper, flashlight and candle, clock and calendar, house trailer and nest, box and pocket, harmonica and trumpet, cocoon and banana peel, church bell and siren, yardstick and odometer.

4. As a more difficult activity, ask children how certain objects are different. Some of the writing implements listed above are liquid, some solid; also the situations in which they are used are different. A pen is appropriate for writing a letter, a piece of chalk for writing on the board, etc. Differences might also be noted in color, shape, and size.

5. Ask pupils to compare pictures of homes, people, automobiles, animals, tools, clothing, musical instruments, etc.

6. For art, ask pupils to compare illustrations in children's books. They might consider examples by Symeon Shimin, Garth Williams, Wesley Dennis, Maurice Sendak, Ezra Jack Keats, and Brian Wildsmith.

7. Also for art, ask children to compare architectural features such as columns (doric, ionic, corinthian) or schools of art (Dutch school, Flemish school, etc.).

647

8. Ask youngsters to compare two objects advertised in a catalog, newspaper, or magazine. For example, they might compare two models of minibikes, blenders, tents, watches, etc.

9. Ask how two members of the class are alike and different. Consider physical differences as well as interests.

10. Ask children to compare two television programs or movies (i.e., westerns, news programs, "soapies", comedies, mysteries, science fiction, etc.).

B. Listening Stage

1. Read two paragraphs aloud. Use a monotone in one presentation and a voice filled with intonation in the other. Ask the class to compare the two presentations.

2. Read stories from Guideposts and Wee Wisdom. Ask youngsters to compare them.

3. Read a story and poem (or play) on the same subject. Ask pupils to compare them. For example, read "The Midnight Ride of Paul Revere" and the corresponding chapter from a biography of Revere.

4. Make two presentations on a topic, each one from a different point of view. For example, make two presentations on communism versus democracy, the morality of the Revolutionary War, Northern versus Southern viewpoints of the Civil War, etc.

5. Ask the class to compare two versions of the same song by different singers or musicians.

6. Read stories to the class. Ask how they are alike and different. For example, use fables and biography, later adding animal stories, poetry, myths, legends, tall tales, fiction, autobiography, etc.

7. Read a description of two people, two places, two games, two countries, etc. Ask pupils to notice the comparisons.

8. Using the tape recorder at the beginning of the year, ask children to read a prepared selection and tell a story. Then play the material and ask each child to compare his presentation with a desirable model. Later in the year, record the oral reading a second time and

ask them to compare their two presentations.

C. Reading Stage

1. Ask pupils to compare the special meanings of words. For example, use plump, fat, and obese (the first is positive, the second is negative, and the last refers to a medical problem). Other examples include thrifty and stingy, slim and skinny, poor and impoverished, tall and statuesque.

2. Ask pupils to compare the coverage of a certain event by two different newspapers. The event may be a political speech, account of an accident, or a description of a condition that is said to exist.

3. Ask youngsters to read two books on the same subject and note the comparisons. For example, use books on John Henry, Paul Bunyan, Abraham Lincoln, or Miss Baker, the Space Monkey. At the upper grade levels, pupils might read two accounts of the life of George Washington or Franklin Roosevelt or Mary McLeod Bethune.

4. Ask pupils to compare the editorial policies of Newsweek and the New York Times, Reader's Digest and the Washington Post, or a state or national paper and the local one.

5. Locate a book and a tape recording of the material. Ask youngsters to compare the two. Even better, provide these two media presentations after children have seen the movie based on the book. For example, many of the Newbery award winners have been made into movies, and several companies, including Miller-Brody and Weston Woods, have produced audio tapes of these books.

6. Ask members of the class to compare two books (articles, poems, songs) by the same author. For example, use material by Lois Lenski, Dr. Seuss, Laura Ingalls Wilder, Lloyd Alexander, E. B. White, and Stephen Foster. With older pupils, use the Bible, Dickens, Shakespeare, Hawthorne, and Poe.

7. Ask pupils to read and compare two or more editorials on the same subject. Encourage them to observe which commmentators have somewhat comparable philosophies.

8. After they have finished a book, ask youngsters to compare themselves with one of the characters. They may also compare the setting, time, etc.

9. Ask children to compare the information contained in two or more reference sources or textbooks. The data do not always agree.

10. After pupils have written accounts of how to make something or how to go from one place to another, ask them to work in pairs and compare their directions. If necessary, they may rewrite the information.

7. Cause-Effect

A. Picture Stage

1. Present two pictures. Ask people to decide which one caused the other.

2. On a field trip, ask the group to note examples of soil erosion and decide what causes contributed to the present problem.

3. Ask children to notice situations which are likely to create safety or health hazards. (For example, poor wiring, blockaded doors, unsanitary conditions, glass on the playground, etc.).

B. Listening Stage

1. Ask someone to tell something he did and why he did it. The classmates should then attempt to identify both the cause and the effect.

2. Discuss cause-effect situations in real life. For example, suppose people are too noisy in the cafeteria. Then the principal or the teacher requires that everyone must eat in silence for a designated period of time. Ask, "What is the cause? What is the effect?" You may prefer to go even further and discuss the question, "How can you avoid the effect?"

3. When two people get into a fight or have some other type of disagreement, ask them or the class to identify the cause-effect relationships. For example, Tom was lying in his seat with his feet in the aisle. Bob tripped over them. When Tom laughed, Bob tried to kick his feet out of the aisle. This action made Tom mad, and he called Bob a name. Bob in turn pushed Tom.

Tom then punched Bob in the chin. People should note that each cause led to an effect which in turn became a cause for the next effect.

4. Read sentences aloud. Ask the pupils to identify the part of each that is the cause and the part which is the effect.

5. Read a story to the class. Ask, "Why did _____ happen?" as a way of identifying the cause. Or, working in the reverse fashion, say, "The story says _____ happened. What do you think caused that?" An excellent book to use at the primary levels is Charlotte's Zolotow's Quarreling Book.

6. Ask pupils who watch television programs to list cause-effect situations they observe.

C. Reading Stage

1. Teach key words often used to indicate the presenting of a cause-effect relationship. Some of the more frequently used key words are since, because, therefore, as a result, when, if, the result (outcome was...), and for (meaning because).

2. Ask pupils to read sentences which contain cause-effect relationships and key identifying words. Ask them to underline the cause and so label it and underline and label the effect. They should circle the key word.

3. For social studies and science, construct a chart which identifies cause-effect relationships. For example, the class may chart some of the major events of the American Revolution or Civil War, the passage of key laws, or the impact of certain inventions or discoveries. They may do the same for science experiments.

4. Ask people who read mystery books to tell why a person committed his crime.

Guidelines for Developing Comprehension (155)

We hear much these days about skills. Professional books identify skills and arrange them in taxonomies. Accreditation agencies require the development of skills continua, and federal and state education agencies lend their support to the movement. Publishers provide diagnostic materials and services and sometimes

651

prescriptive references for various categories of skills. The popular press and the public demand that teachers stress the basic skills.

As a result of the emphasis on skills development, it seems ironic that very few sources provide practical guidelines for enhancing pupil proficiency in these skills. After all, the effective use of materials and the productive employment of ideas require adherence to certain operational principles. The purpose of this section is to summarize guidelines for developing comprehension skills.

Guideline One: "Begin developing children's comprehension in kindergarten. Advise parents to begin prior to their children's first birthday."

It is important to recognize that comprehension is understanding, comprehension is thinking (612). Children begin thinking and understanding during their first year. The quality of their understanding depends in large measure on the experiences which they encounter, the language which they hear and use, and the explanations which they receive. The child who asks "Why?" invites a cause-effect answer. The question "When?" opens the door to a sequence response. The opportunities are manifold.

Parents should begin the process of developing the children's comprehension abilities at home. This, of course, implies a school responsibility for providing parents with specific training. Beginning in the kindergarten, teachers should systematically enrich children's capabilities in comprehension. Beginning in grade one they should develop written comprehension (400).

Guideline Two: "Develop specific comprehension rather than rely only on general comprehension (2, 274)."

Exercises at the ends of reading selections often include a potpourri of questions with insufficient material and emphasis to teach or practice particular comprehension skills. Specific exercises should be provided for levels (literal, implied, and creative) and skills (main ideas, major supporting details, sequencing, classification, predicting outcomes, cause-effect, compare-contrast, etc.)

Far too often teachers pose a few cursory questions to ascertain the extent to which pupils understand a reading passage but fail to use a reading or listening selection to develop additional competence in specific skills. Research indicates, for example, that the kinds of questions raised by teachers affect the quality of pupils' comprehension (419, 699). Thus teachers who fail to move beyond the literal level limit opportunities for their pupils to develop this skill. One study found that 97% of the questions developed by teachers focused on literal responses (426). Another study reported that only 10% of the teachers asked implied questions (558). Other studies find that a majority of all questions posed during reading lessons are literal (43, 249B, 375, 529, 609). Possibly this results from the fact that basal manuals emphasize literal questions more than the other types (138, 395). Fortunately, the skill of effective questioning can be developed (29). Specific inservice activities should be planned to assist teachers in improving their questioning techniques.

Because different selections lend themselves to different types of questions (29), it is important for the teacher to analyze reading passages to determine which types of comprehension skills can be developed or practiced. For example, Goldilocks and the Three Bears lends itself to sequencing, Little Red Riding Hood to predicting outcomes, and Cheese, Peas, and Chocolate Pudding and Bread and Jam for Frances to compare and contrast.

Questions raised after silent reading might include literal, implied, vocabulary, and creative replies. We prefer a 3-3-3-1 pattern (after Marksheffel, 487). Of course, there are other possibilities. For instance, Ransom (580) prefers to use four literal, four implied or inferred, and two creative questions. Within this framework a teacher can then develop questions which require pupils to utilize a variety of specific comprehension skills. One study found that pupils who had inference quizzes for eight weeks were better than the control group in drawing other inferences (326). Another study (419) found essentially the same thing.

Guideline Three: "Proceed from words to sentences to paragraphs to pages to selections."

It seems reasonable to progress from shorter units to longer ones rather than to begin with an entire selection (392). Failure to adhere to this sequence often results in pupils' misunderstanding a longer selection because they didn't comprehend individual sentences and paragraphs.

Guideline Four: "Proceed from the picture stage to the listening stage to the reading stage (162)."

We have already noted that attention to the development of comprehension should begin during the first year of a child's life. Both pictures and listening are appropriate media for fostering

653

comprehension development among young children as well as among school-age pupils, both developmentally and remedially. For example, one can introduce a comprehension skill by presenting and discussing pictures or real objects. The next stage is to relate the skill orally through discussion (listening and speaking) before finally applying it to reading (stage three). As Hansen has noted, "Sentence speaking is a prerequisite for sentence reading (381)."

Numerous writers have noted the importance of developing listening comprehension as a prerequisite to reading comprehension (110, 220, 267, 439, 649, 726). Moffett (519) suggests that both reading and listening comprehension are aspects of a general factor called comprehension.

Guideline Five: "When teaching, proceed from large-group instruction to paired activities for learning (PALs) to individual practice."

Large-group instruction provides the initial basis for developing a comprehension skill. As pupils begin to practice the skill, they need multiple guided opportunities to do so. Large-group practice does not assure that pupils will acquire the needed competence. Furthermore, individual study makes it difficult for children to bridge the gap between teacher instruction and independent application. PAL tactics require more involvement for individuals without removing the security of a partner to offer assistance and encouragement. Thus an appropriate sequence is group presentation, paired study within the group, and finally individual practice. Spache notes, "Of all the organizational changes that are supposed to be helpful, only those advocating using pupil teams or pupil tutors seem currently to be achieving an impact upon pupil growth in reading (666:291)."

Guideline Six: "Use the EPR technique. Ask pupils to use EPR cards or strategies to respond silently so others will have additional time to think."

There is a general agreement about the need to involve pupils mentally during the teaching-learning process. Unfortunately, classroom procedures often allow one youngster to "blurt out" the answer, causing others in the class or group to parrot the response whether or not it makes sense. The need therefore exists for a procedure which minimizes initial pupil response while simultaneously providing other youngsters with thinking time. Children who have increased time to think (wait-time) produce more elaborate answers with increased quality (605).

Guideline Seven: "Provide direct instruction (explanation, demonstration, guided practice, feedback, and correction) before assigning independent activities."

Even good readers should be taught directly in order to develop proficiency in comprehension skills (28, 660, 748). Management systems are inappropriate for developing comprehension (36) or checking it off (434). After all, "Assigning is not synonymous with teaching (541:7)." There simply does not appear to be an effective alternative to teacher-pupil dialogue. Unfortunately, it appears that teachers spend less than 1% of their time teaching comprehension (272), and basal series provide "little instruction" in comprehension (269). Direct instruction materials and related practice exercises are available (213B).

It is desirable to require pupils to demonstrate initial competence instructionally before beginning independent tasks. Teach a lesson, demonstrating and explaining the procedure. After providing sufficient elaboration, ask pairs of pupils to demonstrate the behavior. Next, ask individuals to perform without assistance. When youngsters seem to "catch on," administer a quiz of four items. Provide independent practice opportunities for the pupils who demonstrate initial competence (i.e., answer at least three of the four items correctly following instruction). Provide additional instruction for those who still need it.

Guideline Eight: "Use materials at the pupils' independent reading levels if possible (29). If not, use materials at their instructional levels."

The Betts Criteria (56) suggest that word analysis competence for the independent level should be approximately 99%. Comprehension based on silent reading should equal or exceed 90%. Thus the reading material is sufficiently simple that pupils can concentrate on developing the skill being presented. If material cannot be provided at pupils' independent levels, an alternative strategy is to use information at their instructional levels (i.e., at least 95% word accuracy and 70% comprehension). Research suggests that children can develop the higher-level comprehension skills when they have appropriate materials (140, 481).

Guideline Nine: "Provide pupils with a purpose for reading (541, 670) until they are able to develop their own purposes (485). Motivation and comprehension are enhanced when pupils know what they are seeking (592)."

With young readers it is helpful to record one or more purpose questions on the chalkboard or chart so they can refer to the purposes. Beginning readers can be asked to chorus the purpose question raised by the teacher or by one or more of their peers. This response mode requires that they listen to the purpose questions.

Guideline Ten: "Base comprehension questions on silent rather than on oral reading."
There is considerable evidence that silent and oral reading are not identical processes. One typically reads orally to communicate information (i.e., "Listen to this article in the newspaper.") and silently to acquire information. Comprehension exercises should thus be based on previous silent reading with the pupils anticipating some followup activity (709).

Guideline Eleven: "Use the cumulative teaching/ cumulative testing procedure."
As noted elsewhere, this technique requires that a review step follow the introduction and initial mastery of each new skill. Use of the procedure provides assurance that pupils have learned the present information before they are exposed to more knowledge.

Guideline Twelve: "To the extent that is possible, develop comprehension in a sequential manner."
While there are no clear-cut sequences of comprehension (649) because the content and difficulty of the material often determine the skills which can be developed, there are some general recommendations. We know, for instance, that main ideas and major supporting details can be taught simultaneously. We also know that instruction in the study skill of outlining depends on those two skills plus classification and sequencing. Cause-effect must precede predicting outcomes, and compare - contrast must come before classification.

Guideline Thirteen: "Provide written comprehension questions beginning at the 2-1 reading level."
Pupils who function at any of the first-grade reading levels (preprimers, primer, first reader) are usually unable to write answers to comprehension questions. Discussion of the story and development of comprehension must therefore occur almost exclusively through oral activities. By the 2-1 reading level, however, most pupils should be able to answer written questions following their silent reading and preceding the group discussion. This procedure makes it possible for every pupil to receive abundant individual practice in comprehending. We currently are exploring the possibility that written questions can be used at the

656

primer and first reader levels for older pupils(527).

Guideline Fourteen: "Provide explicit directions to children answering written questions."
We have found it helpful to provide the following suggestions listed on pages 398-399.

Guideline Fifteen: "Monitor pupil progress throughout the year to assure that youngsters are constantly able to comprehend their materials."
"Evaluation is an ongoing process. It should be a continuous process occurring throughout the program (706:387)." Pupils should understand that the use of comprehension questions provides a teacher with clues about their instructional needs (655).
We have found it helpful to explain to pupils and parents the following criteria based on a series of comprehension exercises following the silent reading.

Average Score	Significance
91 or higher	Consider for higher placement and/or enrichment
70-90	Appropriate placement
69 or lower	Consider for lower placement

One low score is not a cause for concern; a pattern of low scores is. Analysis of pupil performance on written comprehension exercises can provide useful clues to continuing skill needs.
For pupils who read below the 2-1 level, use a Group Analysis Chart showing the name of the pupil down the left side and the reading selection across the top. Use +'s and -'s to indicate pupil performance on the questions. Focus on two or three pre-selected pupils each day. See Chapter 7A.

Guideline Sixteen: "Develop comprehension in all appropriate subject areas (401, 541)."
There is little transfer of comprehension when different types of activities are involved (23, 69, 70, 663). The research and literature suggest that comprehension demands differ when narrative and expository materials are utilized. A pupil's ability to comprehend a basal reading selection does not assure his success with social studies or science content. Furthermore, the ability to comprehend a novel does not guarantee proficiency in interpreting a fable, a poem, or

a satirical article. Each separate type of writing requires specific instruction.

A corollary is that each teacher, regardless of discipline, must develop the comprehension skills related to that subject. No reading teacher can teach pupils to comprehend science and social studies materials, for she does not use those types of books.

Guideline Seventeen: "Use passage-dependent questions. Avoid questions that can be answered by common knowledge or by the content of the questions themselves (17, 577)."

It is a common practice for publishers of practice and testing materials to use questions that can be answered either through a reader's background of experience or through reading other questions. For example, Tuinman (719) administered five standardized comprehension tests to 6,000 middle-grade pupils and concluded that none of the tests satisfactorily met the desired criteria. Other researchers have also documented the extent of the problem (11, 307, 573, 577). Unfortunately, passage-dependent questions do not indicate the extent to which pupils comprehend printed information. Questions must be so selected that pupils will typically score zero if they do not read the text. (The only exception is for vocabulary questions. Here it is impossible to know whether pupils understand a given word before encountering it in a reading passage.) Fortunately, there are materials that avoid the use of passage-dependent questions and that encompass a variety of comprehension skills.

Guideline Eighteen: "Require pupils to produce answers rather than to select answers from a list."

A fill-in test is better than a multiple-choice, both in terms of the cognitive aspect and for eliminating the guessing factor. It is worth remembering that a four-item multiple-choice test gives the typical pupil a score of 25% even if he does not read the selection and the test. Then, too, if reading is to be used for a purpose, pupils must have information in their production capabilities rather than just in their recognition abilities. Finally, the production of answers permits pupils to use the language skills of handwriting, composition, and spelling, a factor reflecting the interrelatedness of the language aids. As Johnson notes, "Rarely do readers meet a situation comparable to a multiple-choice test question...In fact, the hallmark of their becoming self-directing readers is that they are able to produce their own answers...(440:155)."

Guideline Nineteen: "Use discussion to foster the development of comprehension."

"Oral discussion is vital to the development of basic understanding (229)." There is widespread recognition in the literature of the importance of a thorough discussion of pupils' silent reading (393, 592), and the research base is equally convincing (12, 699, 748). The discussion should assist pupils in classifying fuzzy or missed concepts, in developing (further) appreciation of well-turned phrases, puns, onomatopoeia, similes, metaphors, etc., and in engaging in critical and creative thinking. And isn't that what comprehension is all about?

Developing Comprehension: Some Techniques

Earlier in this chapter we suggested procedures for enhancing children's ability to comprehend literal, implied, and creative meanings. The following exercises and comments are designed to serve as possible techniques for teaching some of the comprehension skills.

Example 1 is a full-scale outline of the key elements in a lesson plan on making inferences at the paragraph level. Each of the subsequent examples merely provides a skeletal outline of the instructional phase.

Example 1:   Inferences in Reading

Objective: To develop pupils' ability to make inferences using paragraphs at the reading stage

Prerequisite Skills: Ability to make inferences at the picture (or visual) stage; ability to make inferences at the sentence level at the listening and reading stages; ability to make inferences at the paragraph level at the listening stage

Diagnostic Strategies

Step One: (Diagnostic pretest) At the beginning of the year in grade three and above, administer DPTs for pictures as well as for the listening and reading stages for sentences and paragraphs. Various pupils may exempt certain instructional sessions and the related independent activities, for they may have demonstrated competence during the preceding year(s). The series of DPTs is used for placement purposes (i.e., deciding where to begin for various groups of pupils). If you begin instruction below the paragraph level in reading, check to be certain that pupils have demonstrated competence in the immediately preceding prerequisite skill (making inferences at the paragraph level of the listening stage). Only those pupils who have met this requirement as shown on a Class or Group Analysis Chart should participate in the instruction.

Please note that a pupil enters instruction via the results of the DPTs or by responding successfully to instruction on the preceding competency.

In either case, select an exercise that represents the difficulty level you will expect your pupils to master. Do not choose the easiest exercise, for pupils who pass it will exempt direct instruction and the related practice and probably will not acquire further competence. Then circulate throughout the class, encouraging pupils to record two responses for each question -- the answer and the clue(s) that gave away the answer.

Step Two: (Determination of criterion score) Decide what score exempts a person from direct instruction and practice. The score applies either to the DPTs or to the final IAs of the preceding skill activity.

Step Three: (Correction of papers) Either check the DPTs yourself or, if pupils have been engaged in activities similar in format, allow them to exchange papers and check them. Check IAs in the regular manner. Separate DPTs into two stacks: those that meet the criterion score and those that do not.

Step Four: (Recording of pupil performance data) Record the data on the Group or Class Analysis Chart.

Step Five: (Differential diagnosis and/or assignments) If pupils have never been exposed to instruction involving paragraph-level inferential reading, it may not be necessary to administer the DPT. In that case, provide opportunites for pupils who met the criterion score at the paragraph level to read recreationally.

Instructional Strategies

Step One: (Initiatory Activity) On the day before the lesson, read to the class a selection from Encyclopedia Brown. This activity serves two purposes. First, it provides a practical application of the listening lessons that were taught previously. Without any discussion, ask the pupils to write a paragraph identifying the guilty party and the clue that provided

660

the answer. Collect the papers and save them for the next day. Second, reading the story serves as the initiating activity for the skills lesson.

Step Two: (Review of previous learning) Working with the pupils who have demonstrated competence in listening comprehension at the paragraph level, remind them that just as they listened to figure out clues, so must they be able to figure out clues when reading. Be sure pupils understand that the picture interpretation, the inferential reading of sentences, and the making of inferences in orally-presented sentences and paragraphs all relate to the current lesson. Pupils will use those skills to help them develop competence in comprehending written paragraphs. This strategy facilitates the use of prior knowledge and enhances transfer. Depending on the group, you may want to review listening at the paragraph level and/or reading at the sentence level.

Step Three: (Explanation) Unless the following questions have been asked at the listening stage for paragraphs, ask them here.

a. How are paragraphs different from sentences?... (They are longer.)

b. Why is it harder to read a paragraph than it is to read a sentence?...(You have to comprehend each sentence. You must relate each sentence to the other sentences. You have to remember more information).

Point out that when you read a paragraph you must put the ideas together somewhat like you do with the pieces of a puzzle. One sentence may have an idea that makes you think of one thing, while another sentence might have a clue that makes you change your mind. This situation is true in reading just as it is in working a puzzle. Two pieces may seem to fit together, but if the colors don't match, one clue (the shape) will confuse you if you don't pay attention to the other clue (the colors). You can't be sure of an answer until you put all of the ideas together, just as it takes all of the pieces of a puzzle to show the big picture.

Tell the group that comprehension is (a) reading the lines and (b) reading between the lines (226). Simple questions involve reading the lines. The answers are there, and you can underline them. Thinking questions, however, make you read between the lines. They make you figure out answers; they make you decide the reasons certain answers are right. Good detectives <u>make</u>

661

inferences. They put separate ideas together and come up with answers, just as readers put separate sentences together to figure things out. Remind the pupils that it is essential for them to use their own prior knowledge. Sometimes their background of information can help in figuring out some hidden meanings. Sometimes their background of information is their very best clue.

Print on the board: "Purpose: to figure out hidden meanings in paragraphs as Encyclopedia Brown does."

Remind the group that good readers and listeners must think just as detectives do. Let someone tell about a key paragraph from the mystery story you read yesterday. If nobody can provide the clue, read it yourself. Ask if anyone who gave the wrong solution yesterday can do it right today. Then ask someone to tell the right answer and how they figured out the solution to the problem.

Step Four: (Demonstration) Distribute a handout containing a paragraph and a series of questions (See Chart 11-2). Ask pupils to read the paragraphs silently. Then ask them to follow along as one pupil reads the paragraph orally. The example follows.

Used here as a teaching exercise, it has the same format as the pages found in Practice Exercises in Reading Comprehension (PERC), IB: Making Inferences (Paragraphs) (213B).

Model the thinking behavior that you want pupils to use. This thinking is at the heart of the teaching process. Thinking out loud might decide the answers to each question. For instance, using the first question in Chart 11-2, you might say something like this:

1. What game does Joey play?...He plays ball. He pitched a no-hitter, hit two home runs, and runs the bases. The game must be baseball or softball. My answer is, "He plays baseball or softball." My next line starts with "I know" and tells the give-away clues. My answer is, "You hit home runs, throw a no-hitter, and run the bases in softball or baseball."

Print those answers under question 1 and ask the pupils to do likewise on their sheets. It may be helpful to print the answers on the board or on the overhead projector as a model. Remind the group that the first line should have the answer, and the second line should start with "I know" and tell what clues the person used.

Do the second sentence in the same manner, asking pupils to read it silently and then follow along as one pupil reads it orally. Think aloud how pupils should decide the answers.

662

CHART 11-2
TEACHING EXERCISE FOR
MAKING INFERENCES AT THE
PARAGRAPH LEVEL (READING STAGE)

Directions: Please read the following paragraph and
    answer every question. Then tell how you figure out
    the answer.

        That Joey surely can play ball. Last night he
        threw another no-hitter. Last week he hit two
        home runs against the best team in town. And
        everyone knows he really can run the bases.

1. What game does Joey play? _____

2. What position does he play? _____

3. How big is the place where he lives? _____

4. How old is Joey? _____

5. In what place is Joey's team? (How good is his

team?) _____

6. In what other sport should Joey be good? _____

7. What did Joey have to do to become the way he is?

_____

8. What probably is Joey's best class in school? ____

9. What does Joey probably want to do some day? _____

10. How does the writer feel about Joey? _____

        2. What position does he play?... That's easy. He
        threw a no-hitter. He must be a pitcher. My answers
        are, "He is a pitcher. I know he threw a no-hitter."

        Then print the answers under question 2 and ask the
pupils to do likewise. Proceed to question 3 in the same
manner. The thinking process might be like this:

        3. How big is the place where he lives?... Let's
        see. He must live in a town, and that's not nearly
        as big as a city, but it's a bigger place than the
        country. There must be several teams in town. One

663

of them is the best team, so there must be at least three teams in the town. Therefore the town is not very small. My answers are, "He lives in a place that is not very large and not very small. I know the town has several teams and is not big enough to be called a city." (It is unreasonable to expect young pupils to know the population of a town).

Encourage the pupils to write their answers before you put an appropriate wording on the board or overhead projector.

Model the response to the fourth question, perhaps in the following way:

4. How old is Joey?...If he plays ball for a team, he must be at least eight or nine. He doesn't play in the big leagues because those teams are in cities and not towns. Besides, you won't find several big league teams in one town. Also I don't think you call a man Joey. Probably it would be Joe or Mr. _____. Joey could be in high school, I guess, so he might be 17 or 18. My answers are, "He is between 8 or 9 and 17 or 18. I know he has to be old enough to be on a team but probably not older than high school age because of his name and because he doesn't play major league ball.

Once again, encourage pupils to record their responses before you show them how you wrote the information.

Step Five: (Guided practice, feedback, and correction) If the demonstration is going well, proceed to the guided practice, feedback, and correction phase. If not, continue the demonstrations.

Divide the children into pairs, with each one expected to whisper to the partner the correct answer and the reasoning behind that decision. This Paired Activity for Learning helps bridge the gap between teacher-directed instruction and individual pupil responses.

Ask the group to read the fifth paragraph to themselves and then follow along as one pupil reads it. Then ask the pairs to answer the question and give their reasoning.

Monitor pupil performance by circulating among the children and offering assistance, encouraging, questioning a response, complimenting, etc. For instance, ask a person with a wrong answer to explain the thinking process. Help the person discover the presence

664

of other clues and/or use prior knowledge. After the people are through, ask one or two pupils to explain their reasoning and then read their answers. The process for question five might be something like this:

5. In what place is Joey's team? (How good is his team?)...If they played the best team in town, they're not number one. If Joey has thrown another no-hitter, the team must be doing well, because usually you don't score any runs if someone throws a no-hitter against you. Joey probably has pitched some other good games. My answers are, "The team is not in first place, but it probably is in second or third place. (Any position other than first is possible, of course.) I know Joey has thrown at least two no-hitters, and his team probably has won those games. It may have won other games he pitched.

With the group, clarify any misconceptions and identify any overlooked clues. Be sure pupils record the answer in their first sentence or phrase (if they are not yet able to write complete sentences) and the reasoning in the second sentence. If any pair of pupils recorded the answers correctly, allow them to work separately on the next question while the other pupils work in pairs.

Proceed in the same manner through the sixth paragraph, monitoring the pupils' efforts. One or more pupils should then explain their reasoning and read their answers. The process might be similar to this:

6. In what other sport should Joey be good?...If he threw a no-hitter, he must have a strong arm. That might make him good as a football quarterback, but he might be too small to play football...Let's see if there is a better clue. Hitting home runs won't help him play another sport. If he can run the bases well, he must be fast. I bet he would be good in racing (like track). My answers are, "He should be good in track. I know he can run fast."

Check the responses individually (or in pairs), providing assistance as needed. Ask each person to respond to question seven individually. At this point pupils should read the question to themselves, decide on the answer and the reasoning, and record the information. During that time you should monitor their work and provide assistance as needed. Then ask one or two pupils to explain their answer and their reasoning, after which the other pupils can review their responses if necessary. The thinking process might be something like this:

7. What did Joey have to do to become the way he is?... How is he? He is a good ball player. How did he get to be that way?... I don't see any clues in the paragraph, so I should look for clues in my background of knowledge. You have to practice a lot to become good in anything. My answers are, "He had to practice a lot for a long time. I know that's how you become good at something."

Monitor while pupils read and answer the questions. As each child successfully responds, record one (or two, depending on your scoring preference) check marks per question. If there is a problem, stop and assist the child, remembering to circle the item (or the beginning of the first or second answer space). If the responses are correct, tell the pupils to proceed to the next question.

Possible thoughts for the remaining questions are listed next.

8. What probably is Joey's best class in school?... That one is easy. It seems clear that P.E. would be his best subject. I'll say, "P.E. I know because he's good in a lot of things that you do in P.E."

9. What does Joey probably want to do some day?... He probably would like to be a ball player. People who are good at things when they're young usually want to keep doing them when they're older. My answers are, "He would like to be a ball player. I know because he's good at what he does and must like it."

10. How does the writer feel about Joey?... He says only good things about Joey, so he must like him. Those are my answers.

Assuming the pupils are making satisfactory progress, proceed to the four-item quiz. If pupils are having difficulty, continue in the above manner with another exercise. This continued activity occurs on another day.

Evaluative Strategies

Step One: (Diagnostic posttest) Administer a four-item quiz (See Chart 11-3), asking each pupil to read the paragraph and questions silently and then follow along as somone reads the items aloud. During the quiz monitor the performance, but do not provide assistance in identifying specific answers.

CHART 11-3
FOUR-ITEM QUIZ FOR
MAKING INFERENCES AT THE
PARAGRAPH LEVEL (READING STAGE)

Directions: Please read the following paragraph and answer every question. Then tell how you figured out the answer.

> Ann swam quickly over to her friend and
> grabbed her arm. The other girl screamed
> and swung her arms wildly back and forth.
> Finally someone blew a whistle and came
> to help.

1. Where did the story take place?

_____

2. What was the problem?

_____

3. Who blew the whistle?

_____

4. How did the person who blew the whistle help?

_____

Answers:

1. It took place at a swimming pool, lake, pond, ocean, etc.
    I know Ann swam to her.

2. Ann's friend was drowning.
    I know the girl screamed and swung her arms wildly back and forth. Someone came to help.

3. The lifeguard blew the whistle.
    I know that's the only person who would have a whistle.

4. The person jumped into the water to save the girl.
    I know that's what a person would do if someone was screaming and swinging her arms in the water.

You may refer pupils to suggestions posted on a board. For instance:

1. Read each selection twice.

2. Think about what you knew before you read the story.

3. Decide what answer makes the most sense and is most likely to be true.

4. Answer each question as completely as possible.

5. Tell how you figured out the answer.

As an alternative to the four-item quiz, use the last four questions on the teaching exercise. Of course, if pupils do not do very well on those items, they may require further guided practice, feedback, and correction before beginning a four-item quiz.

Step Two: (Correction of papers) Check the answers to the four-item quiz, preferably as they are being recorded. For example, circulate throughout the group, recording a check mark beside each correct item, a circle around the number of an item (or the space) with a wrong answer, and a 1/2 if part of the answer is right and part is wrong or incomplete. Using this procedure, you should be able to complete the checking of the papers almost as quickly as the pupils finish their work. The answers for the four-item quiz are listed below the last question on the chart.

Especially as pupils begin the four-item quiz, you will have an opportunity to monitor the performance of pupils in other groups.

Step Three: (The recording of pupil scores) Record the scores on the Class or Group Analysis Chart similar to the one shown in Chart 11-4. The information can be shown as the items right rather than numerical scores. Remember: You must decide whether to consider the questions as four items and thus have some scores like 1 1/2, 2 1/2, etc., or consider the questions as having eight answers and thus avoid the fractions.

Step Four: (Differential assignments) Assign the first Independent Activity (IA) to each pupil who performs satisfactorily on the four-item quiz.

CHART 11-4
CLASS OR GROUP ANALYSIS CHART

INFERENTIAL
COMPREHENSION: Four-
READING   Item IA IA IA IA IA IA IA IA IA
     DPT   Quiz 1   2   3   4   5   6   7   8   9

	Item Quiz	IA 1	IA 2	IA 3	IA 4	IA 5	IA 6	IA 7	IA 8	IA 9
Audrey										
Bynum										
Carol										
Della										
Eddie										

A pupil should earn at least three checks out of four possibilities or six checks out of eight. Use the exercises in Practice Exercises in Reading Comprehension (PERC), Book 1B (213B). There are thirty exercises, each containing one paragraph followed by a series of questions. You may either use the first exercise in the booklet as Independent Activity (IA) 1, or "skip around" and use some other exercise for this purpose.

Provide additional instruction and guided practice to pupils who do not reach the criterion figure. Remember the importance of asking pupils to explain how they figured out their answers. Their responses can provide insight into their thought processes. Note that this meta-cognitive strategy permeates the entire Developmental Lesson Plan on a comprehension skill, for it in- cludes an explanation of how to reason out answers as well as the pupils' explanations of their thinking processes.

In the case of the inferential meanings, the reteaching can occur using the four-item quiz. For instance, you can lead pupils who miss question one to review their thinking, using their prior knowledge and the clues in the text. They should then rewrite their responses on the reverse side of the sheet. Use the same reteaching procedure for questions two through four.

Note that the individual checking procedure tells a child the answer is wrong but does not provide the correct answer. Thus a four-item quiz in this case is especially useful for reteaching purposes. Whenever it seems reasonable, assign the first IA on the same day to these "second-chance" youngsters. It simplifies checking and reteaching if you can keep the pupils together.

Step Five: (Followup on Independent Activity 1) On the following day, check IA 1 and discuss it as thoroughly as necessary. Remember that any discussion on the thinking processes used in determining the correct answer is teaching comprehension while simply identifying an answer as right or wrong is assessing (or testing) comprehension. Although both are necessary, the teaching strategy pays richer dividends.

Ask pupils to record their scores (unless you plan to assume that responsibility) and to correct their errors. Then record the pupil performance data on the Class Analysis Chart. Use fractions (if that is what you did on the four-item quiz) or use the numerals 0-8. Since you will expect pupils to correct their errors, you need a way of being certain they have done so. One way is to make diagonal slashes under each IA, recording the original score in the upper left-hand corner and listing the final score (either 7 or 14) in the lower right-hand corner. The alternate procedure is to write the original score in the block and underline it when the corrections are made.

Step Six: (Followup for mastery) Assign IA 2 for the following day. Once again, choose any exercise you feel is appropriate. At this point you must decide how to use additional exercises in PERC 1B. You might provide one exercise per day, exempting pupils who achieve the criterion score (perhaps 6, 6 1/2, or 7 correct) on two or three consecutive days. Remember that paragraph interpretation is a prerequisite for interpreting longer passages. Thus the basics (paragraphs in this case) should have a high criterion score.

It is not essential that you use every exercise. The important thing is that you provide appropriate direct instruction and sufficient IAs and reteaching sessions for pupils to demonstrate mastery at this level.

Step Seven: (Application) Provide frequent opportunities for pupils to apply their tentatively-acquired skill. For example, you might ask inferential questions such as the following:

a. From the first paragraph of the story, what can you figure out about (the character, setting, problem)?

b. How did (the character) change during the story?

c. What quality(ies) made (the character) successful or unsuccessful?

d. What does the writer want you to think about the topic?

e. Which character was especially (clever, resourceful, thoughtful)?

Example 2: Main Idea in Reading

The first example, shown in Chart 11-5, corresponds to Type I listed under the reading section of Main Ideas. Comprehensive lesson plan models and practice materials for main ideas are provided elsewhere (213B).

You might use the following teaching procedures:

Step One: Secure materials well below the children's instructional reading levels: Distribute one copy to each member of the group. The reason for selecting simple materials is to free the pupils from having to concentrate on pronouncing words and learning new vocabulary. Their attention and energy may be focused on the specific skill being presented. If some of the children are likely to be unable to read the material, you may wish to pair them with youngsters who can. In this fashion one member of the pair will operate at the listening stage, the other at the reading stage.

Step Two: Provide each pupil with one yellow and one blue pencil or crayon. While the specific colors themselves are unimportant, both should be fairly light, and they should contrast with each other.

Step Three: Explain the fact that a main idea in a paragraph is the one sentence that summarizes everything else. Pupils should expect to find main ideas anywhere in a paragraph. To determine whether or not they have correctly selected a main idea, youngsters may try this check. If every other sentence tells something about the one they chose, their answer is correct. If not, they should look again.

Step Four: Provide instruction and practice on the items listed in Chart 11-5. The dialogue and procedure might go something like this:
"How many sentences are there in the first paragraph?... How can you tell?... Good. Would you listen carefully as Bill reads the paragraph? Then I'm going to ask you to note the sentence that is the main idea." (Some pupils will listen while others will follow along silently. The latter is preferable.)

671

CHART 11-5
PARAGRAPH COMPREHENSION
MAIN IDEAS

1. (1) Mother was really mad! (2) Her face was as red as a beet, and she was yelling at the top of her lungs. (3) She pointed her finger at the two boys and dared them to make another sound. (4) We could tell that her hand was really shaking.

2. (1) My brother is very good to other people. (2) When it snows, he shovels the sidewalk for old Mr. Lane. (3) In the summer he helps Mrs. Lee pick vegetables from her garden. (4) Even at home he helps Tom and me with our schoolwork.

3. (1) The circus has come to town. (2) The elephants are pulling the red wagons into place. (3) The strong men are putting up the big tent. (4) Some of the performers are practicing their acts. (5) A few of the workers are feeding the hungry animals.

4A. (1) Bill can really play ball. (2) Yesterday he hit two home runs in one game. (3) Just last week he pitched a no-hitter against the best team in town. (4) And everyone knows that he can really run the bases.

4B. (1) I have a really playful puppy. (2) Spotty always runs to meet me when I come home from school. (3) He also stays at my feet and tries to untie my shoes. (4) Spotty likes to sit in my lap, but he never stays quiet, not even for one minute.

5A. (1) Mother put the cake in the center of the table and began to light the candles. (2) Meanwhile Dad was taping balloons to the ceiling. (3) Even little Ricky helped by putting candy and cookies on each paper plate. (4) Finally they were ready for the birthday party.

5B. (1) Mark and his friends were outside playing football. (2) Jim and Joe were busy chasing each other. (3) Some of the girls were playing jacks or jump rope. (4) Even the teachers had smiles on their faces as they talked to one another. (5) It seemed that everyone was having a lot of fun.

"Please read the paragraph to yourself or your partner. Then decide which numbered sentence is the main idea. When you think you know, hold up the EPR card with that number. If I nod "yes", color the entire sentence yellow. If not, go back and read again."

Allow children time to decide. As they hold up their EPR cards -- they need five for this exercise -- provide the appropriate response and help those who require assistance. When they are ready, discuss paragraph one. Each child should have colored the first sentence yellow.

Rhetorically, "How do you know sentence one is the main idea?... Okay, look at each of the sentences. Why was Mother's face as red as a beet?... Why was Mother yelling at the top of her lungs?... Why did Mother point her finger and dare the boys to make a sound?... Why was Mother's hand shaking?... Because all sentences refer to sentence one, it is the main idea. Because all the other sentences tell something about the main idea, they are called supporting details. Please color them blue.

"Look at paragraph two. Janet, please read it for us... Now reread the paragraph. When you think you know the main idea, hold up the EPR card, and color your sentence if you are right."

Once again circulate among the pupils, assisting those who require help. When everyone is through, discuss the correct answer and the reasons for selecting it. Explain, "Sentence one is the right answer because all of the other sentences tell how good my brother is. Sentence two tells how he helps Mr. Lane, sentence three tells how he helps Mrs. Lee, and sentence four tells how he helps Tom and me."

If someone suggests a different response, perhaps sentence four, ask, "Do all of the sentences tell about helping Tom and me with our homework?... Does sentence one?... Sentence two?... Sentence three?..." Be sure the pupils have colored the main idea sentence in one color and the major supporting detail sentences in another color.

Proceed in the same manner to paragraph three, which also contains a first-sentence main idea. That's what we're teaching, according to the seven-step pattern presented under Main Ideas: "Reading" paragraphs. Notice number four has two examples. Tell the class that one of the two may have a main idea somewhere besides the first sentence. This should preclude their automatically assuming the identical format will be followed. (Both still conform to the first sentence pattern. For number five, issue another warning. This time both of the paragraphs have the main idea at the end.)

Pupils who have evinced little difficulty with the teacher-directed, individual, or paired activity should then be provided with a similar set of materials for independent practice. Others may require some practice, perhaps conducted by their newly-proficient peers. The purpose of the colors is to enhance the difference between main ideas and supporting details for those who find the visual contrast helpful in clarifying ideas.

Example 3: Cause-Effect in Reading

The following material assumes similar information has previously been presented at the picture and listening stages and will subsequently be provided at the paragraph and story levels.

Step One: Say, "Many times a writer will tell you that one event leads up to another. Sometimes he or she does not tell you directly that certain results were caused by certain events. But if you read carefully and note a few special words which are clues, you will see that one event does cause another. We call these situations cause-effect relationships.
"I have written several sentences on the board. Each contains a cause and an effect. Watch me draw a straight line down between the two and circle the key word that doesn't fit in either part. Then, write the word cause (or the letter c) above one part and effect (or e) above the other."

Step Two: Have someone read the sentences on the board:

A. Tom stayed home because he had a cold.

B. Since you have helped me all day long, I am going to take you to the movies.

Step Three: Explain to the pupils thatin the first sentence Tom stayed home is the effect, and because he had a cold is the cause. In the second sentence you have helped me all day long is the cause, and I am going to take you to the movies is the effect. Lines should be drawn before because and I. The pupils should recognize because and since as the key words. If more instruction and practice are needed, provide them. If not, assign the practice sheet displayed in Chart 11-6.

674

CHART 11-6

CAUSE-EFFECT RELATIONSHIPS

Directions: Please draw a line between the cause and the effect and label each.

1. We did not plow the garden because it was too wet.

2. I really studied hard for my last social studies test. As a result I made a 95.

3. (Note to mother) "Bill never does his work. Therefore I have decided to keep him after school."

4. Dad really seems unhappy. His football team must have lost again.

5. When Marshall saw the water bill, he really hit the ceiling.

6. Did you hear about the party at Sandy's house? Someone broke a lamp, and Sandy is going to have to pay for it.

7. I gave my Dad a special gift for his birthday because he is always so good to me.

8. "Our turkey died." "Why?" "It drank too much water."

9. Since I always seem to get a cold afterward, I have quit playing in the snow.

10. I'm going to read that new book. Everyone says it's great.

Step Four: Check and teach from the practice sheet. Then ask pupils to notice examples of this type of relationship in their reading and to call them to the attention of the class. If necessary, provide another exercise of the same type on a subsequent day.

Example 4: Sequencing in Reading

Step One: Discuss a procedure pupils can use to note time sequence. Say, "Most writers provide clues to tell you that certain events happened before or after other events. Careful readers note these clues and understand the sequence of events in a story.

675

"I have written several sentences on the board. Each contains two events, one of which occurred before the other. I will draw a circle around the word that indicates time. Then I will place a <u>1</u> over the sentence part which occurred first and a <u>2</u> over the part which occurred second."

<u>Step Two</u>: Record sample sentences on the chalkboard (or present them on an overhead projector and have someone read them.

A. Tomorrow we will go to the movies, but today we must clean up the yard.

B. Dad lit some candles after the lights went out.

<u>Step Three</u>: Discuss the responses. In the first sentence, circle <u>tomorrow</u> and <u>today</u>. Place a <u>1</u> over "we must clean up the yard" and a <u>2</u> over "we will go to the movies." In the second sentence, circle the word <u>after</u>. A <u>1</u> should be placed over "the lights went out" and a <u>2</u> over "Dad lit some candles."

<u>Step Four</u>: When pupils appear to have acquired initial competence in noting time sequence, provide a practice exercise. See Chart 11-7.

CHART 11-7

TIME SEQUENCE: SENTENCE LEVEL

Directions: Please draw a circle around the word or words which indicate time. Then place a <u>1</u> over the sentence part which happened first and a <u>2</u> over the part which happened second.

1. Bob decided to study after he made an F on the test.

2. Now we watch television in the evenings, but I remember when we sit around the radio after supper.

3. I have not seen Sue since we were in the Girl Scouts.

4. If you practice your lessons, you will learn to play the piano well.

5. Everyone had ignored the new boy until Tom decided to be friendly.

676

6. You may go out to play when you have finished your homework.

7. Although he had never driven a tractor before, Mark climbed into the driver's seat.

8. Before you go to bed, you had better brush your teeth.

9. Let's play softball now. Later we can mow the lawn.

10. The movie was really good, but I had seen it before.

Step Five: Check and teach from the practice sheet. After using the practice sheet as a study exercise, ask pupils to note examples of the type of relationship in their reading and to call them to the attention of the class. If necessary, provide another exercise of the same type on a subsequent day.

Example 5: Sequencing Pictures (180):

Step One: Display a set of four pictures labeled A, B, C, and D. These pictures should approximate the maturity levels of the pupils. Thus a first- or second-grade class might use frames taken form a reading readiness workbook. Junior high materials might be cut from magazines. Pictures (as illustrations) can also relate to content areas. Large pictures are better than small pictures for group work. For preservation purposes, the pictures should be mounted, laminated, and filed under some topic such as "Sequencing-Picture Stage."

Step Two: Develop four statements, one sentence describing each picture. The sentences describing the four pictures might be similar to the following:

A. The boy is walking down the street.

B. He sees a baby bird that fell out of the tree.

C. He is getting a ladder.

D. He is putting the baby bird back into the nest.

Step Three: Shuffle the four pictures and replace them on the chalkledge in random order. If pupils are unable to see the accompanying letters, print them just above the pictures on the chalkboard.

Step Four: Ask the children to number their slates (or papers) from 1-4 and to fill in an A, B, C, or D to show the order in which the events occurred.

Step Five: Discuss the study procedure. Youngsters should decide what happened first, locate that picture, and record its letter beside number 1. Next they should decide the second thing that happened, locate that picture, and write its letter beside number 2.

Step Six: Check the papers with the children. Tell which picture came first and put that letter beside number 1 on the paper. Each of the other three sentences should be handled in the same manner. Pupils who answer all four items correctly should record a large check mark in the left margin. If any item is incorrectly sequenced, they should draw a neat circle around the entire set of four responses. There should be no X marks. Later the four pictures should be re-shuffled, and the children should do the exercise again. If additional instruction and practice is necessary (and with younger and slower pupils it certainly will be), provide further activities of the same type.

Example 6: Sequencing in Listening: A Followup

Step One: Read to the group four sentences in the right order. This material should be within their listening levels but not necessarily within their reading levels. Tell the members of the group, "Listen to the sentences I am going to read to you. Let me show you how I decide. Then explain how you know if they are in the right order." You might use the following sentences:

A. One day a farmer learned that his prize cow was gone.

B. He set out down the road to try to find her.

C. Late in the evening the farmer found his cow in a nearby village.

D. He led her home with a happy heart.

678

<u>Step Two</u>: Read a set of four sentences in the wrong order. Rhetorically, "Are the sentences in the right or wrong order?... How do you know?" Use the following sentences:

A. The battery was dead.

B. Carl put on his coat and gloves and went outside into the frosty night.

C. He turned on the ignition, but nothing happened.

D. He unlocked the car door and slipped behind the steering wheel.

<u>Step Three</u>: Discuss the concept of "key words" -- words that summarize the sentence (in this case) and facilitate memory of the information. The use of key words also makes it possible for students to use the Every-Pupil Response without writing out the entire information. Say, "Key words are something like main ideas or topics. Do you remember when we first began to talk about main ideas of sentences?... In Sentence A, the key word is <u>battery</u>. If you can remember <u>battery</u>, you will probably remember the whole sentence. Let me reread Sentence A. When I'm through, I'd like for you to write the letter <u>A</u> and the key word <u>battery</u> beside it on your slate (or piece of paper). Okay?... 'A. The battery was dead.'

"Now let's see what you can do with the next sentence. It has two key words... 'B. Carl put on his coat and gloves and went outside into the frosty night.'... On your slates (or papers) put a <u>B</u> and the words that will help you remember the sentence ... Did you put <u>went outside</u>? That would be my choice of key words. Or maybe you put <u>coat</u> and <u>gloves</u>. That's all right too if it helps you remember the entire sentence. Tell me, why isn't <u>Carl</u> a good key word? ... (It could refer to three different sentences.) ... Why isn't <u>frosty night</u> a good answer? ... (All four sentences tell about a frosty night.) ... Key words usually include action verbs or nouns that tell about just one sentence.

"Let me read the next sentence; write the letter and the key word or words... 'He turned on the ignition, but nothing happened.' ... What is the key word? (ignition) ... Now let's do the last sentence ... 'He unlocked the car door and slipped behind the steering wheel.' ... Did you put <u>unlocked car</u>? ... (<u>Steering wheel</u> might also be acceptable.) ... "

Step Four: Ask the students to sequence the four sentences. Say, "In the left margin -- Where is that? -- draw a line beside each letter. In a minute I'm going to ask you to number the sentences in the correct order from 1-4. Listen as I read the four sentences. Each time check your key word or words. (Re-read all four sentences, including the letter preceding each.) .. Now decide what happened first in the paragraph. Put a 1 in front of that letter. Put a 2 in front of the second thing that happened, and so on ... " Check the responses (4A, 1B, 3C, 2D). Say, "If your letters match your numbers, you get one big checkmark in the left margin. If the letters and numbers don't match, draw a neat circle around the set of four examples." Note: You're also teaching listening and auditory memory skills.

Summary

More than any other one comment, teachers complain, "He just doesn't seem to understand the material even though he can read (call) every word." We agree with the magnitude and prevalence of the problem and submit that specific instruction combined with subsequent related practice are essential if growth in reading and thinking are to occur.

How readers process print is a matter of great debate. Some theorists (355, 647) believe a reader uses a top-down model, a point of view that emphasizes a person's expectation of getting meaning as the key to reading. Other scholars (360, 455) prefer a bottom-up model, which stresses that reading begins with letters and sounds and progresses toward meaning. We agree with those (327, 364, 608, 611) who favor an interactive model that contends both the expectation of meaning and the decoding aspects are interrelated and are of paramount importance.

This chapter focused on four significant topics relating to developing proficiency in comprehension. First we attempted to develop an understanding of three levels at which materials can often be interpreted. Next we presented selected specific skills which a competent reader possesses and utilizes during the comprehension process. Then we offered guidelines for use in developing comprehension. Finally we outlined some sample techniques for developing comprehension skills with a group or a class.

FOR FURTHER READING

Baumann, James F., and Garibeth Cassidy Schmitt, "The What, Why, How, and When of Comprehension Instruction," Reading Teacher, XXXIX, No. 7 (March, 1986), 640-646.

Clary, Linda Mixon, "How Well Do You Teach Critical Reading?" Reading Teacher, XXXI, No. 2 (November, 1977), 142-146.

Durkin, Dolores, "Reading Comprehension Instruction in Five Basal Reading Series," Reading Research Quarterly, XVI, No. 4 (Summer, 1981), 515-544.

———, "What Classroom Observations Reveal about Reading Comprehension Instruction," Reading Research Quarterly, XIV, No. 4 (1978-1979), 481-533.

Flamond, Ruth, "Critical Reading," in New Perspectives in Reading Instruction," pp. 256-261, ed. Albert J. Mazurkiewicz. New York: Pitman, 1964.

Glass, Patricia, A., "Comprehension - A Vital Skill," in Education for Tomorrow -- Reading, pp. 47-55, ed. Arthur W. Heilman. University Park: Pennsylvania State University, 1965.

Gray, William S., "The Major Aspects of Reading," in Sequential Development of Reading Abilities, pp. 8-24, ed. Helen M. Robinson. Chicago: University of Chicago Press, 1960.

Herber, Harold L., and Joan B. Nelson, "Questioning Is Not the Answer," Journal of Reading, XVIII, No. 7 (April, 1975), 512-517.

Ladd, Eleanor M., "The Expansion Model for Teaching the Main Idea," The Tar Heel Reading Journal, III, No. 2 (Summer, 1983), 3-10.

Pearson, P. David, and Dale D. Johnson, Teaching Reading Comprehension, New York: Holt, 1978.

Smith, Helen K., "Sequence in Comprehension," in Sequential Development of Reading Abilities, pp. 51-56, ed. Helen M. Robinson. Chicago: University of Chicago Press, 1960.

Section IV. PROVIDING A FRAMEWORK FOR
INSTRUCTION AND INDEPENDENT ACTIVITIES

Chapter 12 Organizing for Instruction

CHAPTER 12

ORGANIZING FOR INSTRUCTION

Introduction

One short chapter cannot claim to provide sufficient information on how to organize for instruction, for situational differences are manifold. They include (a) the grade level being considered, (b) the general level of achievement in the class, (c) the amount of time for each subject, (d) the school's organizational structure (self-contained, block, departmentalized), and (e) the teacher's ability to manage various groups successfully. This chapter thus provides only selected possibilities; individual teachers will need to adapt them to fit their specific classes.

The components of this chapter include the following: (a) guidelines for using learning centers and independent activities, (b) sample independent activities (both short- and long-term), (c) sample learning center outlines, (d) grouping and organization procedures, (e) principles and practices for effective classroom management, and (f) first weeks' activities.

Guidelines for Using Learning Centers
and Independent Activities

As we consider the effective uses of learning centers and their accompanying independent activities, a number of significant points should be clarified. These are stated as guidelines (177).

Guideline One: "Use learning centers and independent activities for educationally valid purposes and not for busy-work."

It is not educationally defensible to assign activities merely to keep children busy. All activities should be assigned for specific educational purposes.

683

Guideline Two: "Use learning centers and independent activities to reinforce skills, concepts, facts, and attitudes which have already been presented, either by the teacher or a student teacher."

In general, therefore, do not expect pupils to teach themselves information, especially that which involves reading skills.

Guideline Three: "Whenever possible, coordinate materials presented in learning centers with other skills, concepts, or reading materials rather than present them in haphazard fashion."

It would be quite inappropriate for a teacher to conceive of a wide variety of materials as the solution to the multiple needs of her pupils. Uncoordinated material and information is quite unlikely to result in any meaningful motivation or academic growth. The use of SRA Multi-Level kits on Monday, Barnell Loft materials on Tuesday, Spectrum on Wednesday, McCall-Crabbs on Thursday, and Steck-Vaughan workbooks on Friday is a poor imitation of the individualized instruction idea.

Guideline Four: "Remember that children using learning centers and independent activities should not necessarily have the same assignments."

While there certainly is a common body of knowledge which most pupils should possess, the majority of all activities definitely should not be identical. If providing identical assignments is the objective, textbooks can be used with far less trouble. Learning centers should not be considered merely as collections of materials through which pupils work their way activity by activity with the only noticeable difference being the rate of acquisition.

Guideline Five: "Base the use of a variety of learning centers and independent activities on a diagnostic analysis of the specific strengths, weaknesses, and needs of individuals."

For example, if Marva needs practice in visual discrimination of letters, she may be referred to a center which contains two sets each of the upper- and lower-case letters of the alphabet. Taking an envelope which contains two sets of four lower-case letters, she may practice matching the letters and be checked off by a student teacher before moving to another related task. Her friend Anjana may need practice in auditory discrimination and therefore be referred to a more appropriate area and different set of materials. The pre-determination of needs should lead to selection and

684

use of a variety of appropriate materials.

Guideline Six: "In general, assign pupils to specific learning centers and activities rather than expect them to possess the ability to select activities most appropriate for their development."

The strong implication here is that most children require a structured and guided learning environment rather than one based upon their own provincial perceptions of important needs. Our concepts differ drastically from those used in some classrooms. This philosophical dichotomy is well worth recognizing and resolving, for a teacher's perception of her role determines in large part the organizational patterns and procedures she utilizes. This perception also influences the amount of systematic instruction and guidance she offers.

Guideline Seven: "Use learning centers and independent activities during those times certain pupils are not working under the direct supervision of the master teacher."

This practice allows the teacher to work with a group and then assign the members specific followup activities to pursue while she convenes another group. Materials with which pupils work should be reviewed by the teacher with the intention of determining subsequent instruction and practice efforts.

Guideline Eight: "At the end of a lesson, ask children to express, either in written or oral form, what they have learned during the session."

Unless pupils recognize their own growth, the level of motivation can never be of sufficient degree to sustain learning efforts.

Guideline Nine: "Involve children in the development of learning centers and independent activities."

Those who understand why something is being done and have an active role in organizing information are far more likely to be receptive to its use and to handle the material more carefully. Even kindergartners can lend their services.

Sample Independent Activities

In terms of the nature and amount of time pupils require to complete assignments, we can classify them into long- or short-term activities. We might consider a short-term activity one which can be completed in a few minutes and/or which typically can be interrupted without destroying the child's thought. Conversely, a long-term activity is one that requires more time to complete and should not be interrupted. To illustrate, taking a spelling quiz is a short-term independent activity while reading a library book would be a long-term activity. In both cases the activities are conducted without the direct supervision of the teacher. Examples of short-term independent activities include:

1. dictate sentences or stories on a tape recorder

2. complete worksheets, workbooks, puzzles

3. study SCCs (for vocabulary development or for word recognition) and be tested.

4. do selected activities from a reading readiness kit

5. look at and study wordless books

6. work with auditory discrimination materials such as MAD Bags and PAD Packs

7. make a sounds book

8. copy sentences or a short paragraph from a spirit master (for kindergarten and first graders) or from the board (in grade two and above)

9. do selected activities from a vocabulary kit of ideas

10. study vocabulary words

11. take a vocabulary test or retest

12. write sentences with new vocabulary words

13. study teaching bulletin boards and charts and take the corresponding tests

14. use short skill development material (e.g., McCall-Crabbs, Durrell and Murphy's Vocabulary Improvement Practice)

15. be checked off by some child on a specific skill.

16. do rework (correct errors on previous exercises)

17. do selected activities from a comprehension kit

18. read to someone else (practicing one's oral reading while entertaining someone)

19. study spelling words and take a test

20. make a spelling dictionary.

21. engage in short activities at a learning center

22. complete a graph showing performance or progress

23. take a diagnostic pretest

24. keep a diary or journal

Examples of long-term independent activities include:

1. listen to a story via headphones

2. do a skill exercise correlated to a listening tape

3. use a long skill practice material (e.g., SRA Multi-Level kit)

4. read a library book

5. answer written comprehension questions based on a reading passage

6. work on a written report

7. write a story or passage (descriptive, narrative, expository, persuasive)

8. revise the paper or passage

9. develop a special project

10. engage in long activities at a learning center

One way to organize independent activities is to develop and distribute daily or weekly charts outlining activities for pupils to complete. The use of activity charts has several advantages. First, the charts explicitly identify the expectations made of the child. At conference time, parents can also note that activities are clearly indicated. Second, the chart can be filled in as the pupil satisfactorily completes assignments.

Checkoff can be handled either by a teacher or by a child. Spaces can be filled with happy faces, letter, or numerical grades, or colored in with magic markers.

A third advantage is that the teacher has a simple way of noting whether or not pupils have completed specific tasks. This advantage is quite important, for the Educational Testing Service found that in the second grade one of the effective teaching strategies was that pupils who were not receiving direct instruction continued to work on their assignments (322).

An activities chart helps keep pupils on task and therefore increases the rate of learning. Chart 12-1, (206) presents a wide array of activities which might be appropriate for various individuals within a primary class. A teacher using an adaptation of this chart should identify the activities to be used by the different groups in the classroom. Chart 12-2 (206) presents a much simpler chart designed for use by the pupils in one group. Note that both of these charts are designed for weekly use.

Sample Learning Center Outlines

This section presents ideas for developing fifteen different learning centers and their accompanying independent activities (177). The following assumptions underline the activities:

1. Learning centers and independent activities can be provided for any subject area or topic at any grade level from kindergarten through college. The ones included here are not intended to be exhaustive.

2. Only a few learning centers should be provided at a time. The availability of too many lead to clutter and confusion.

3. The equipment listed in each category is not essential. Cassettes and record players are desirable luxuries but not essentials. So are commercial printed materials.

4. The information presented here should be read at the implied level and adapted to fit the situation.

Each topic listed below includes (a) a suggested physical location, if necessary, (b) a statement of useful material and equipment, and (c) sample independent activities to be found at the learning center.

Chart 12-1

INDEPENDENT ACTIVITIES
MASTER CHECK-OFF CHART

Name: _____   Dates: _____

	M	Tu	W	Th	F
Do PAD Packs.					
Learn Single Concept Cards (SCCs).					
Learn SCC Sentences.					
Learn Dolch Word Sentences (SPARK).					
Dictate story.					
Read dictated stories.					
Read classmates' stories.					
Read Floor Chart Notes.					
Do planned vocabulary.					
Learn reading vocabulary.					
Learn oral vocabulary.					
Do daily writing.					
Do worksheets.					
Reviews SCCs.					
Review SCC Sentences.					
Review SPARK Sentences.					
Use Listening Center.					
Review your stories.					
Review classmates' stories.					
Review Floor Chart Notes.					

689

CHART 12-1
(Cont.)

Take Daily Spelling.					
Rework spelling exercises.					
Do Rework Reading.					
Do Rework Daily Writing.					

Chart 12-2

INDEPENDENT ACTIVITIES
CHECK-OFF CHART

Name: _____   Dates: _____

	M	Tu	W	Th	F
Learn Single Concept Cards (SCCs).					
Learn SCC Sentences.					
Learn Word Sentences (SPARK).					
Use Listening Center.					
Dictate story.					
Read dictated story.					
Learn reading vocabulary.					
Do worksheets.					

1. Alphabet and Word Center. This area might be located at the front of a class away from the door and the reading circle. While the chart of sequenced letters is usually found above the chalkboard, it should be placed in several rows on a bulletin board if the former space is too high for children to see easily. The floor charts of words should be located in a free area which does not inhibit access to a couple of individual tables and chairs where children can study the alphabet.

690

The Alphabet and Word Center may include several durable sets of the letter forms of the alphabet, both upper and lower cases. These letters can be constructed of plywood, perhaps by a high school printshop or vocational class. Less permanent ones can be cut from sandpaper and used with youngsters who need the kinesthetic experience. Use tin shears rather than scissors.

In addition, letters made on tagboard or plywood should also be available. The first type allows children to associate the letter forms with the sense of touch. The second is useful for more advanced activities involving visual discrimination.

If the above are not practical, print both upper- and lower-case letters on spirit masters and run these off on colored construction paper. All primary children and poor readers (even at the intermediate levels) should keep complete sets of letters in the cigar or shoe boxes located at their desks.

A chart showing the alphabet may be available as well as a series of large floor charts with common words grouped into easily-located categories (Food, Nature, Animals, Action Words, Little Words). Pictionaries and/or dictionaries should be provided. Specific activities and materials include the following:

A. Envelopes, each containing two sets of four or five upper-case letters for the child to match. Later he does the same with lower-case letters, and later with upper- and lower-case letters.

B. Envelopes, each containing two sets of eight or nine upper-case letters for the child to match. Later he does the same with lower-case letters, and later with upper- and lower-case letters.

C. Envelope containing two sets of upper-case letters for the child to match. Later he does the same with lower-case letters, and later with upper- and lower-case letters.

D. Envelopes, each containing four or five sequential letters of the alphabet. The child sequences them and checks himself one of three ways: (1) by referring to the alphabet charts on the board, (2) by referring to a 3x5 inch answer card placed in the envelope, or (3) by looking on the reverse sides of the letters and reading the numerals 1, 2, 3, 4, 5.

E. Envelopes, each containing eight or nine sequential letters of the alphabet. The child sequences them and checks himself.

F. Envelopes containing all 26 letters. The child sequences them and checks himself. Activities D-F should involve both upper- and lower-case letters. In addition, develop a sheet listing the contents of each envelope so you can more efficiently and effectively select the appropriate items for study.

G. Envelopes containing SCCs in groups of five or ten. Envelopes can be labeled by number with higher numbers representing more difficult words. Even high school foreign language and other subject-matter teachers can use this type of material for both advanced and slower pupils.

H. Floor charts of words classified by types. Examples include pages entitled People in Our Class (with names printed beside their photographs), Seasons and seasonal words, Holiday words, Days of the week, Months of the year, Colors, and Numbers. Many of these may be accompanied by pasted-on pictures, making the charts gigantic SCCs. While most of the above categories refer to nouns, other parts of speech can also be utilized. Charts can include words for <u>said</u>, <u>big</u>, <u>pretty</u>, <u>little</u>, <u>nice</u>, and <u>good</u>.

I. Charts on 8-1/2 x 11 pasteboard presenting synonyms, antonyms, or homonyms in sentences. These may be loose-leafed into one or more notebooks, especially for intermediate-level pupils. Information of this type should be developed and extended continuously by various pupils. Reinforcements will prevent the pages from being accidentally torn from the notebook. The charts mentioned in H-I serve several purposes. They can be used in conjunction with vocabulary development, the Spelling Center, and the Writing Center for aspiring authors.

2. <u>Sounds and Syllables Center</u>. Because many of the activities require careful hearing and AD, the Sounds and Syllables Center should be constructed in the quietest possible area. It also needs to be located near an electrical outlet. The area can include a large number of SCCs with pictures only (no words). A sufficient number of these should be available to allow pupils to locate pictures with the various beginning and ending sounds and the different numbers of syllables. Real objects representing these sounds and headphones and

records or cassette tapes might also be provided. While workbooks and workboxes can also be located here, they are discussed in a separate section. Specific materials and activities include the following:

A. Envelopes, each containing pictures beginning with two or three different sounds. The child classifies the pictures according to initial sound and proof-checks his responses by whispering the words in each category to hear if they sound right. If pictures are mounted on cardboard or construction paper, answers may be recorded on the back. For example, if a set of pictures represents the initial sounds of K, G, and H, the K pictures may be labeled 1, G pictures 2, and H pictures 3. Real items contained in a small box can also be classified by sound. The answers can be written on the bottom of the items. Packs of pictures can be developed for all consonant sounds, whether initial or final, the consonant blends and digraphs, vowels (short, long, diphthongs), "r"-controlled combinations, one, two, and three syllable words, and words accented on various syllables.

B. Envelopes, each containing pictures representing five or six sounds. The child classifies all of these as indicated above.

C. Envelopes, each containing pictures representing eight or nine (or more) sounds. The child classifies these.

D. Magazines from which the child is asked to select, cut, classify, and mount pictures representing the various sounds and numbers of syllables. An individual Sounds Book can be modeled after the one developed by a class. Later the printed words may be added beside the pictures. Paste one picture on each page to represent each sound and serve as a guide.

E. Tapes or records presenting practice in auditory discrimination. The Listen and Do records (Boston: Houghton Mifflin) are quite useful for this purpose. They are accompanied by worksheets to be completed by the child and are extremely-well constructed. Their major disadvantage is the failure to provide sufficient response time for some children. Another very good set of materials constructed with a sensible philosophy is the Talking Alphabet (Glenview, Illinois: Scott, Foresman). Both materials include records. Teach children in small groups how to operate a record player and include actual practice by each person. Usually the Sounds and Syllables Center will have several pupils working simultaneously on a specified exercise. One member of the group may then be designated to operate the record player. Children should understand this machine is not a toy.

Members assigned certain practices are those who require additional reinforcement and practice related to the skills being presented in the group instruction. Therefore, children do not work their way through a set of records or other materials. Except for a few advanced youngsters, children utilize the Sounds and Syllables Center activities as followups rather than as preludes to or substitutes for instruction.

3. Listening and Looking Center. Like the preceding area, this center must be located near an electrical outlet and preferably in a quiet space. The listening and Looking Center can include headphones, a tape recorder or cassette and tapes, filmstrips, and an individual viewer. The following materials and activities may be provided:

A. Listening Tapes (Chicago: SRA) with workbooks. Pupils who require additional practice in the ability to listen can utilize these materials.

B. The Listening Skill Builders accompanying the SRA Primary Multi-Level kits. The short stories designed to be read by the teacher are also available on tape and can be used with headphones for a group of pupils. In either case, a large group should practice using the Listening Skill Builders under direct teacher guidance before proceeding on their own.

C. Filmstrips related to topics being studied. A class considering World Regions may wish to secure the appropriate filmstrips to supplement other materials. Several cautions should be noted in this regard. First, preview possible selections to determine their readability and potential contribution to the topic. Many filmstrips are simply too sophisticated for young readers. There is little value in frustrating a poor reader, regardless of the medium used. Second, don't use filmstrips to occupy a person's time or to include another medium for the sake of "show." Third, attach a list of new words presented in context and ask pupils to note the meanings of these words (or phrases). This practice should extend the vocabulary of the viewer and encourage him to note unknown terms rather than simply

694

skip them. Fourth, attach a list of two or three questions to provide purpose for viewing. Expect pupils to observe several major ideas; initial questions will help direct their thinking. Fifth, wherever possible, teach some pupils how to locate and select useful filmstrips housed in the media center.

D. Pictures related to some topic being studied. Because visuals have the capacity to elucidate much that would otherwise remain nebulous, use pictorial representation in conjunction with practically every aspect of teaching and learning. Collect pictures daily -- from newspapers, magazines, posters, advertisements, travel folders, discarded library books, display materials in stores, and post cards. Ask pupils to do likewise. These materials may be classified, dated, mounted, and filed. Since pictures will be considered under several subsequent centers, they will not receive further elaboration here.

4. Realia Center. This center is a fancy name for a Show and Tell or Bring and Brag Center. It may be located along the window sill or on top of several book-cases. Pupils and teachers who bring interesting objects from home should display and label these attractions and perhaps discuss them in print. (At the primary levels, oral discussion is more effective.) Contents of the explanatory sentences or paragraphs may include the name, purpose, construction, and use as well as other interesting data. A purely arbitrary decision may place realia in this center or one of the subject areas.

(If pupils are encouraged to print information relative to their contributions, you should provide several sessions on manuscript printing. These lessons are especially necessary at the intermediate levels when youngsters seem to forget how to make capital and small letters and when to use each. Observers in intermediate and high school classrooms invariably see walls covered with mis-printed manuscript.)

Encourage observers at a realia center to study the item, read the accompanying data (if any), and perhaps even use the reference materials to learn more about the topic. Change displays each week or as often as pupils seem to acquire the information presented (or reject it). The use of a few well-chosen and -displayed objects is preferable to a conglomerated mass.

Possible objects to include in a Realia Center are driftwood, Mexican jumping beans, Panama hat, lariat, bridle, halter, bonnet, tongue of a shoe, kaleidoscope, visors, colander, magnet, letter opener, hornet's nest, zucchini, loom, flatiron, vial of medicine, cornucopeia, strip of suede cloth, linoleum, dwarf tree, level, guppies, ball of cotton, cactus plant, and vest. For maximum effectiveness, correlate information presented in a Realia Center with material discussed in the content areas. Objects can also stimulate creative writing.

5. <u>Picture Center</u>. In actuality, a Picture Center is an area for the development of vocabulary which can be visually presented. A number of mounted pictures can be located in any area where a draft is unlikely. A box containing pictures separated into manila folders is one possibility, a filing cabinet a second, and a bulletin board a third (for display purposes.) The following materials and activities can be utilized:

A. SCCs for both good and poor readers. Learners of all ages from pre-kindergarten through adult can encounter new vocabulary through the use of these cards. Use five or ten 3x5, 4x6 or 5x8 inch cards containing no print but merely pictures to introduce new concepts. Primary youngsters may encounter <u>broccoli</u>, <u>priest</u>, <u>cottage</u>, <u>elevator</u>, <u>skyscraper</u>, and <u>hourglass</u> for the first time. Older pupils may become acquainted with <u>archipelago</u>, <u>hansom</u>, <u>gable</u>, <u>mastodon</u>, <u>parfait</u>, <u>cumberbund</u>, <u>tetrahedron</u>, <u>gondola</u>, and <u>silhouette</u>.
Pupils can study one group of cards, be checked for mastery, and move on to another if they are successful. More sophisticated words can be grouped into separate sets and labeled with higher numbers. For example, the easiest items may be put in sets 1-99, the harder ones in sets 100-199, and the most difficult in sets 200 and up.
It is useful to reiterate that at this stage the SCCs contain only pictures. After pupils have become familiar with the pictorial representations, they might use the same or similar cards with the words printed on both sides. The word side can then be used to determine the pupils' ability to pronounce the word, the word and picture side by side to study the meaning, and the word side used a second time for testing purposes.

B. Cards to teach basic concepts. Paste a number of simple objects or their pictures on an 8 1/2 x 11 piece of tagboard or construction paper and ask pupils to tell what object is <u>above</u>, <u>below, to, the, right or left</u>, or <u>beside</u> a specified item. Or ask what objects are <u>near</u> or <u>far away from</u> or <u>between</u> others. Ask which object is in <u>the middle or center</u>, which two are <u>the same</u>, which one <u>is between</u> two others.

696

C. Multiple Concept Cards, or a Picture File. Aside from the fact that a variety of nouns can be introduced via pictures of all sizes, a teacher who carefully composes her questions can present numerous possibilities for vocabulary growth. Consider adjectives, for example. Pupils working with a file of pictures can be asked to find the picture that shows (1) a boy with grimy hands, (2) a bedraggled coat, (3) a despondent boy, (4) an elated team, (5) a serene evening, (6) a vacant house, (7) an irate parent. Or verbs can be studied by using questions that ask pupils to find a picture that shows (1) a mother chastising her son, (2) a boy compelling his brother to do something, (3) a machine demolishing a building, (4) one person mimicking another, (5) an athlete sprinting, or (6) a man shearing a sheep.

Providing the types of experiences indicated above involves more than making assignments. Follow-through is essential. Youngsters need feedback regarding the accuracy of their responses, and the teacher needs to be certain the material presented has been learned. A check-off sheet for each set of questions should be developed and kept current either by the teacher or the children.

6. Context Center. Since only a table is needed to display the materials, a bookcase or closet shelf can be labeled and used for this purpose. The area might include materials and activities similar to the following:

A. A number of sentences or paragraphs which introduce new words. Such practice exercises can be secured from workbooks accompanying the lead or supplementary readers or constructed to meet a special need for which other materials are not available. Because context usage is a universal skill, numerous exercises should be provided to reflect each type of context clue. In cases where development of the skills of using context to determine meaning is being emphasized, all children who can read the material may utilize the exercises. Only pupils quite intent on extending their vocabularies should be expected to learn the actual meanings involved.

B. Commercial material designed to provide practice in context. One published item which may be useful is Using the Context Books A-F (Barnell Loft). Pupils using these materials should operate at various levels based on their own proficiencies rather than working through the materials with the rate of covering material being the only individual difference under consideration. Children who miss certain items should be expected to learn from their mistakes. Individual assistance from either a teacher or a student teacher usually will be necessary.

C. Pupil-provided exercises. Encourage pupils to submit sentences with new words so their peers may have additional interesting materials with which to practice. Those who serve as developers of materials may also serve as checkers-off of their classmates' proficiency.

D. Exercises involving new words presented in supplementary books being utilized for free reading opportunities. Type the words used in these stories on construction paper. Direct pupils to underline the items as they read a specified selection. Pupils use the story context rather than the dictionary to define the words.

After having read the story and studied the words in context, the pupil can then check his ability to acquire vocabulary through context by completing a sheet using different sentences with the new words. Children fill in the blanks by selecting items listed at the bottom of the page. A sample exercise taken from the files of the junior author is included in Charts 12-3 and 12-4.

CHART 12-3

CONTEXT PRACTICE SHEET*

WORDS FOR V-9

(Note: The following information can be typed on a sheet of construction paper. An asterisk means the word has several meanings, but the use in the story may be a different one from that known by the child.)

Direction: As you meet the words typed below while reading the story on pages 34-42 of Finding the Way, draw a light circle around them.

After finishing the story, check these words to be certain you know their meanings. Then secure the V-9 sentences to see how clever you are.

1.	panic	6.	tangle
*2.	guide	7.	fell
*3.	cape	8.	fertile
4.	vineyard	9.	legend
5.	earnest	*10.	vision

*Material to be read is found in Sheldon, William, et al., Finding the Way, Centennial Edition, Boston: Allyn, Bacon, 1968.

CHART 12-4

CONTEXT PRACTICE SHEET

SENTENCES FOR V-9

(Note: There are items, three of which involve com-
monly-known definitions of words used with different
meanings in the story. Each correct response is worth
eight points. A perfect score is 104.)

Directions: Using the words below, some of them
twice, complete the sentences. Then come to my desk,
write in the correct answers of any you miss, and learn
those words. How clever are you?

panic	vineyard	tangle	fertile
guide*	earnest	fell	legend
cape*			vision*

1. That land jutting out into the sea is called a(n)
   _____.

2. Let's _____ a large tree for Christmas.

3. May I _____ you to the right highway?

4. My _____ is 20/20.

5. I'm not sure this story is true. It may be a(n)
   _____.

6. Stay calm and cool. Don't _____.

7. The forest is a _____ of overgrown vines.

8. Batman borrowed Robin's _____.

9. All day long the farmer worked in his _____.

10. Last night I had a(n) _____ that three of us found
    the lost gold mine.

11. The _____ showed me how to find the best fishing
    places.

12. Farmers often moved westward to find _____ soil.

13. Are you teasing me, or are you really _____?

7. <u>Comprehension</u> <u>Center</u>. This center normally requires a table and at least two chairs plus a number of envelopes of material. Various comprehension skills can be presented in three different ways -- through listening, pictures, and reading. The construction of these materials is detailed in Chapter 11. Only one additional point needs to be made. As indicated earlier in this chapter, pupils should be provided experiences which reflect their own patterns of strengths and weaknesses rather than be turned loose to "have a good time."

8. <u>Language-Experience</u> <u>Center</u>. This area needs a cassette tape recorder, a table, and a chair, thus making it one of the simplest spaces to provide. The major activity is the taping of sentences and stories dictated by pupils operating at low reading levels. This information is subsequently typed or printed and used as the basis for reading instruction and practice, both for the pupil himself and for others with similar needs. The language-experience activity may be used to teach reading to people who read no higher than second-grade level, regardless of their ages. At the upper levels, pupil secretaries can replace the tape recorder.

9. <u>Reading</u> <u>Center</u>. This area might consist of a table or rotating book rack placed beneath a bulletin board. Satellite reading centers should be located at each person's desk or preferably in a quiet area covered with a rug and furnished with a rocking chair, sofa or cushions, padded chairs, and foot stools. Most of these items can be secured second-hand if announcements are issued through the school. Cushions and pads might be homemade, and filled boxes covered with dyed burlap can serve as footstools. Children using such an area should be allowed to assume any posture they wish so long as it does not affect the movement of their peers. Most children and adults find it quite difficult to relax and enjoy reading when they must sit with hands in lap and feet flat on the floor.

The central area should consist of a small number of books on a table or, even better, a number of paperbacks placed in a rotating rack. Book jackets, published book reviews, and pupil-developed creative book reports can be attached to the bulletin boards or placed in a display area. Numerous creative ways to tell about books are suggested by Englebright (302) and Decker (240).

10. <u>Literature</u> <u>Center</u>. The Literature Center requires the same basic materials as does the Reading Center. In

700

addition, a cassette player and headphones are useful. Activities include the following:

A. Listening to the recordings of the Newbery Award books. Many pupils will never possess sufficient reading ability to enjoy these literary gems. Listening provides a medium by which these juvenile classics can enrich the lives of poor readers. Even for the proficient readers, listening provides a magnificent opportunity to allow the finest of universal themes to permeate the receptive soul. (You may prefer to include this activity in the Listening and Looking Center.)

B. Securing and reading books clearly identifiable as classics. These items should include the Caldecott Award winners and runners-up as well as the hundreds of books which have earned for their writers, translators, and illustrators one or more of the fifty major book awards presented annually. Consult the latest edition of Margaret Colbert's <u>Children</u>'s <u>Books</u>: <u>Awards</u> <u>and</u> <u>Prizes</u> (135). All types of selections should be represented (poetry, folk tales, animal stories, plays, mythology, history, problem-solving situations, etc.).

11. <u>Workbox</u> <u>Center</u>. As mentioned earlier, much of the information here can be placed in the various subject areas represented by learning centers rather than occupy one central space. This decision is up to the teacher. For purposes of our consideration, however, the ideas are presented together. The desirable materials include several sturdy boxes, an abundance of 8 1/2 x 11 inch construction paper of various colors (or manila folders), and two pupil workbooks and one teacher's copy at every level from the lowest through one level above the grade placement of the class. The workboxes can be placed on several tables or on the tops of low bookcases. A teacher fortunate enough to have one will find a filing cabinet quite desirable.

Workboxes are nothing more than two workbooks torn apart and mounted separately on colored paper according to grade level. Thus an initial set of reading materials for grade four will consist of workboxes developed from practice materials from grades one through five for the lead basal and later for supplementary series. Each grade level can be represented by construction paper of different colors. One classification scheme is shown below.

701

Grade 1 - <u>G</u>reen	Grade 5 - <u>G</u>reen
Grade 2 - <u>R</u>ed	Grade 6 - <u>R</u>ed
Grade 3 - <u>O</u>range	Grade 7 - <u>O</u>range
Grade 4 - <u>W</u>hite	Grade 8 - <u>W</u>hite

Key: GROW

Workboxes are subject to the same types of uses and mis-uses as their parent workbooks. Judicious use requires, therefore, that certain basic principles and practices be followed.

A. Workbox material should be provided only after instruction has occurred.

B. Students should work selected pages based on the identification of specific needs rather than work their way through a box.

C. Assignments prescribed should not only focus on specific skill needs but reflect the learner's general reading level. Many workbooks are written at a higher reading level than the books they accompany. As a result, pupils who can read the books sometimes have extreme difficulty reading and completing the independent assignments. The problem is complicated when the materials are selected from "other" series.

D. Pupils should have their papers checked promptly and be expected to rework incorrect items.

E. Workbox material should be considered a supplementary reinforcing agent rather than a program for learning.

F. When using these and all other materials, pupils should expect to receive scores of approximately 70-80% at least. Frequent scores below this point are a clear sign of improper material. Consistent scores of 90-100% before rework indicate the material probably is too simple.

Workboxes can be developed in reading, spelling, mathematics, language, social studies, and science. While their construction requires time (three hours per box), the material when selected and utilized carefully

702

helps make it possible for teachers to provide for the wide range of individual differences in their classes.

The teacher's copy of the workbook accompanying the workbox contains both an answer guide and a table of contents or an index. Referring to various levels of the guides, you can determine the lowest points at which certain skills are presented and then teach and assign the appropriate pages, moving upward from level to level for those who are able to read the information and cope with the specific information being presented.

12. Writing Center. Like the Reading Center, this area consists of a central space plus satellite centers. The major "furnishings" are pictures, a 3x5 or 5x8 inch file box of story starters, class-composed articles, and school or class newspapers. Materials and activities may include the following:

A. Story Starters (Ginn) to stimulate creative writing. Present several of these pictures to provide ideas for composition.

B. Teacher- and pupil-selected pictures for the same purpose. The final pages of Life Magazines are especially useful for this purpose.

C. Story Boards (Boston: Houghton Mifflin) for the same purpose. The major difference in the two materials is the latter's mass of two or three solid colors and somewhat abstract designs. They have proved quite useful for encouraging both written and oral expression.

D. The Unfinished Stories for Use in the Classroom for ascertaining children's reactions to problems.

E. A series of file box cards, each containing a part of a sentence or even the beginning of a plot. A pupil selects a card and develops a story. All of these materials can encourage children to write. Their compositions should then be made available for the class to read. After all, what is more stimulating to a writer than the hope or expectation that his brain-child will be enjoyed by someone else? Very few authors compose solely for their own satisfaction; yet many schools provide their authors-in-residence with only one reader -- the teacher. This practice should be abandoned.

F. Business and friendly letters and notes. Requests for information, invitations to attend "open house," sharing "What we've been learning in school" with parents, sending cards to sick classmates, and corresponding with pen pals offer pupils practical opportunities to develop and apply letter- and note-writing skills.

G. Class or school newspaper articles. One of the keys in which writing can be stimulated is through the publication of a periodic newspaper or newsletter. Study of the form and content of such information may require facilities of a News Center.

13. <u>Records Center</u>. This area provides both pupils and teachers with information relative to their achievement of specific objectives. Provide class or group charts with the names of boys and girls listed down the left margin and ten to fifteen columns across the top. Indicate home assignments completed and reworked with check marks in the appropriate columns. Record in-class evaluations by numerical score and then update the chart when a pupil subsequently scores higher on the same information. You will need a number of record sheets, for different group of pupils use different materials at different levels. So long as pupils are associated with appropriate materials (by level and skill need), it may be acceptable for them to see their records and those of their classmates. All should be capable of achieving, and evaluative marks result from pupil performance based on reasonable expectations. Slower pupils do not tend to score lower grades under such a plan of organization.

Seeing positive scores beside the names of slow learners encourages all pupils to commit themselves to study efforts, and seeing evidence of their own progress further stimulates the willingness to pursue academic pathways. The location of a Records Center can be on the teacher's desk or a small one nearby. Children should also be encouraged to keep their own records.

One other piece of information should be contained in a Records Center. That is a notebook with loose-leaf pages designated for each pupil. During the day each person should place a sheet containing his independent activities, results, and reactions in the notebook. This procedure provides day-by-day information on the amount and quality of work being done, opinions of the pupils, and background data for further guidance. Study of each pupil's progress should enable you to suggest on the daily record or during group or individual conferences other activities to pursue independently.

Produce standard forms on spirit masters and distribute as necessary so all information will be presented in a readily useable format. Designate spaces at the top for name and date. Include column headings for Subject, Specific Activity, Results and Reactions. Excerpts from Nelson's record of independent activities are presented below as Chart 12-5.

CHART 12-5

INDEPENDENT ACTIVITIES--NELSON

Subject	Specific Activity	Results and Reactions
Math	Studied the measures of time, weight, and distance.	Made 90 - Corrected my paper - (5,280 ft. = 1 mile) Made 100 the second time.
Pictures	Studied Sets 9 and 10. Studied Set 100.	Made 100 and 90 (veil). They were easy! On last set made 80, but it took a real long time. (ottoman, andirons)
Writing	Wrote a story - "Complaints of a Pencil"	Bill says it's keen. It's in the box.
News	Read about the war in Lebanon.	It didn't make sense.

14. Diagnostic Center. Quality education begins with a careful diagnostic analysis of each learner's specific strengths, weaknesses, and needs. Inventories are needed in reading, spelling, language, mathematics, science, and social studies to determine areas of proficiency and topics for which initial or further instruction is needed. Diagnostic pretests are also needed to determine knowledge of phonic, structural, contextual, and dictionary skills, mastery of specific major facts (names of the alphabet letters, colors, days of the week, months of the year, basic words), and ability to cope with literal, implied, and creative meanings. Dozens of additional items might be mentioned here, but a few should indicate the fact that sound classroom instruction depends upon initial diagnosis in August and frequent supplementary checks throughout the year.

Pupils who are ready to begin studying a topic should be given DPTs to determine their degree of familiarity with the various sub-items comprising that topic. In general these DPTs should be similar to the posttests currently used to conclude most units of study. If two forms are available, one can be given prior to instruction, the other afterwards. This center can be housed in a filing cabinet or in manila folders carefully catalogued in a wooden crate. Two dependable pupils might be trained to secure and refile information. Because specific diagnostic pretests are included elsewhere, they are not reproduced here.

15. <u>Make-up Center</u>. During the course of a typical year, members of a class miss hundreds of days due to illness or other causes. Many of these pupils are slow learners who cannot afford to miss even one day of instruction. For primary youngsters, an extended absence is even more of a cause for concern. To alleviate this type of situation, you should file copies of any materials you use and assign one or more pupil assistants to help the absentee on his return to school. The Make-up Center requires only the previous days' materials and two desks pushed together.

At the intermediate levels, you might tape a presentation and make it available to the absentees as well as to those who can profit from a second contact with the data. If the presentation is a lecture, it can be used later to teach outlining and note taking.

Grouping and Organization Procedures

Consideration of the topic of reading-level (as opposed to skills) grouping requires that we identify answers to some crucial questions.

1. How many reading-level groups should I have in my class?

2. How can I organize my class to have the most appropriate number of reading levels?

3. How can I provide flexibility so pupils who need to move from one level to another have the opportunity of doing so?

4. How can I work with several groups at the same timme?

While none of these questions has a simple answer, all must be resolved satisfactorily if maximum progress is to occur.

1. How many reading-level groups should I have in my class? Several guiding principles are involved here. First, no teacher should organize more groups that she can handle effectively. For many teachers, the number is three. Zintz and Maggart (753) have observed that a three-group plan may well be the best way to initiate instruction at the beginning of the school year.

The second guiding principle is that there should be enough groups to permit the teacher to be instructionally involved on a continuous basis. In practice, this means that at least two groups are necessary. Thus a teacher can provide instruction to one group and, while it works on independent activities (reading the selection, for instance), teach another group. The use of whole-class instruction leaves the teacher with no instructional possibilities while the children read their selections, answer comprehension questions, etc. The research relative to teacher time on task makes it clear that achievement is correlated with high levels of teacher time on task (752).

A third principle is that there should be adequate opportunity for each child to receive appropriate instruction. Thus a completely individualized program is not recommended, for each of thirty pupils receives an average of only two minutes of instruction per hour. This amount is hardly sufficient to justify school attendance. From a practical point of view the use of five or more groups is undesirable, for each additional group decreases the amount of instructional time available for each reading-level group.

A fourth principle is that the group's size should be such that pupils have frequent opportunities to be intimately involved in the interaction of the lesson. Too large a group will diminish the participation opportunities while a group that is too small will decrease the chances of benefiting from the interactions with others.

In general it seems reasonable to conclude that the traditional three-group organization is preferable. Such an organization can have several advantages: (a) One group is always available for instruction, (b) each group can receive instruction daily, (c) the size of each group is, on the average, ten or less, facilitating increased opportunities for involvement of all pupils, and (d) most teachers can (learn to) handle three groups. As a matter of fact, first-grade teachers sometimes begin with two or three groups and, because of differential rates of pupil progress, end up with as many as four or five groups! The fact that primary teachers can handle three or more groups suggests that upper-grade teachers can (learn to) do the same thing.

707

There are situations in which two groups may be necessary or appropriate. These include circumstances in which there are (a) very short and unalterable lengths of time allocated for reading and overall low performance and (b) very small class sizes (i.e., 16 or 18).

2. How can I organize my class to have the most appropriate number of reading levels? There are several ways of grouping pupils to minimize teacher planning and maximize pupil progress. The first strategy -- and our preference -- is stratified homogeneous grouping. Under this plan data about all pupils in grade two or higher are used to assign each teacher three distinct reading levels. To illustrate, suppose the 90 pupils in grade three are administered an Initial Reading Inventory. The principal or the three second-grade teachers record the appropriate pupil data(i.e., race, sex, silent reading level, oral reading level, total instructional level, last book read, vocabulary and comprehension scores from the last end-of-book mastery test and/or average scores on the vocabulary and comprehension quizzes for that book), and personal reminders (i.e., "Don't put Joey and Marcus in the same class.")

Assign groups in such a way that each teacher has a high group, an average group, and a bottom group. Thus, one teacher might have a 2-1, a primer, and a beginning reader group. The second teacher might have a 2-1, primer, and preprimer three group. The third teacher might have a 2-1, first reader, and preprimer two group. Note that some levels (i.e., 2-1 and primer) might have enough pupils to justify their being split into several sections. One such group might consist of pupils believed to be faster learners (i.e., they might have higher percentages at the same reading levels or their individual scores are consistently high or they have high vocabulary but low oral reading scores).

Administrative homogeneous grouping is desirable, for it practically assures that every child will be provided appropriate materials. The assignment of pupils requires less than two hours. Accuracy is considerably enhanced if fall rather than spring IRI scores are used.

A second strategy for organizing the class involves the use of what we call "grouping the groups." If an IRI indicates the need for instruction encompassing materials at six different levels, a teacher might be able to pair adjacent levels to form a group. Thus the primer and first reader levels might be paired to form a primer group. Always use the lower of the two levels so all children will have material they can read. Grouping the groups represents a compromise between what is desirable

708

(all children's having appropriate materials) and what is realistic (teachers can't have an inordinate number of levels).

This type of grouping is the traditional strategy teachers have used to telescope (for example) six levels into one. It differs primarily in the combining of levels into the lower rather than the higher of the two levels. Because grouping the groups does result in the underplacement of some pupils, it requires that teachers pay special attention to providing enrichment experiences.

Because the range of reading levels in a class increases with the grade level, it is quite possible to have six or more levels as early as the second grade, even if no child reads above grade level. One strategy for avoiding a proliferation of levels is to arrange with another teacher to allow pupils to visit each other's reading groups. Thus, for instruction, the only two children at the preprimer three level in Mrs. Simpson's room might have reading with the six preprimer three children in Mrs. Blanton's room. At the same time, all three of Mrs. Blanton's primer-level readers might join Mrs. Simpson's five primer-level readers. Each teacher thus loses a level, and each group receives additional instructional time.

We recommend that teachers provide "visiting pupil" status for their children with teachers in the following order of preference: (a) a teacher at the same grade level, (b) a teacher at a higher level, and (c) a teacher at a lower level.

3. How can I provide flexibility so pupils who need to move from one group to another have the opportunity of doing so? We should remember that reading-level and skills grouping are not the same thing. An IRI identifies a pupil's instructional and independent reading levels while skill diagnostic pretests measure a pupil's performance in a range of skill competences. Except for the convenience of basal placement, skills do not possess levels. Thus, for example, the /a/ is assigned to a level according to a specific series. One series might present it at the preprimer one level while another series introduces it at the primer level. Research indicates that the placement of word analysis skills is not consistent from series to series (619, 620, 688). Furthermore, some categories of skills repeat themselves at almost all levels. Examples include vocabulary and comprehension, where specific skills are never mastered (in contrast to many word analysis skills).

709

Most children tend to read (i.e., comprehend) at a higher "level" than they skill. Thus, a child who has an appropriate reading-level text may lack some skills presented at lower levels. It would not make sense to give the child instructional material based on his skill level. Instead, one provides skills instruction based on a pupil's skill needs and instructional reading materials based on a child's reading level. (Incidentally, some children skill at a higher level than they read. These situations exist when youngsters spend inordinate amounts of time working on isolated skills (and their companion checkoff exercises) and relatively smaller amounts of times engaging in reading practice.)

Specific instruction directed toward diagnosed skill tends to result in higher "levels" of skill performance. This change in "level" can occur quite rapidly, especially when few skills are needed and when a diagnostic-prescriptive model is used. Skill groups often exist for less than a week. The short a group, for instance, is disbanded as soon as the pupils who need it (regardless of their instructional level) master the information. At the 2-1 level and above, effective skills instruction is characterized by the constantly changing membership in the skills groups. On the other hand, reading levels tend to remain stationary. Appropriate placement and mastery-based instruction typically result in a stable group. Reinforcement assistance is provided to those who need it, and enrichment experiences are offered to those at the other end of the spectrum.

There are circumstances, however, when individual children proceed at a much faster pace than do their groupmates. These children usually are somewhat brighter, and often engage in much more recreational reading than do their peers. As a result they appear to be under-challenged by their present placement. At the same time they may not be ready to advance to the next higher group, for the vocabulary between the book the child is presently using and the point at which the higher group presently reads may be considerable. If a teacher proceeds in a traditional way through the skills development program, there will also be some "gaps" caused by transition from one book to another. Then, too, there is the possibility that a child will not be able to maintain the pace of the higher group.

Perhaps the most practical solution to the flexible movement problem is "open grouping," a procedure advocated by Robert M. Wilson (742), in which pupils are allowed to participate in reading lessons in groups other than their own. Thus a child reading at a 2-2 level may wish to attend a lesson being read and discussed by a 3-2 group. Not only does this participation have the potential for expanding the youngster's competence, it can be used to determine the need for regrouping. When a child complains that the work is too easy, open grouping provides an opportunity to prove he is capable of operating at a higher level. If a reassignment seems in order, a special consultant should help the youngster bridge the gap between the two levels. This bridge is especially important for the vocabulary aspects of the series.

Open grouping can also benefit the pupil who needs the additional instruction and practice in comprehension that is provided through reading and discussing a second selection at a lower level of difficulty (assuming the child has not already read the book). One further comment: Pupils who participate in two reading-level groups are expected to complete the appropriate activities assigned to both groups.

4. How can I work with several groups at the same time? Although organizing groups is almost as difficult to do on paper as it is in a real setting, we will attempt to outline one possible procedure at two grade levels. The first hypothetical situation involves a second grade with four levels of approximately five pupils each and several more pupils operating at both lower and upper points. Chart 12-6 shows the distribution of children by reading levels.

CHART 12-6

READING LEVELS IN A SECOND-GRADE CLASS

Level	Pupils	Level	Pupils
Non-reading	2	First Reader	5
Second Preprimer	5	2-1	5
Third Preprimer	2	Above 2-1	3
Primer	5		

Even a casual observer will readily note that this class has one non-reading level and at least six levels. The three pupils who read above the 2-1 level should present few problems. For them, basal reading plus individualized instruction is likely to prove effective. They should be given abundant opportunities to read.

711

Conversely, the six children at the bottom of the class can probably benefit from intensive specific readiness experiences which, except for the bottom two cases, may accompany actual reading instruction.

Several of the groups should be grouped. One possibility is to group the first reader and primer levels and the second and third preprimer levels. The 2-1 level would be the third group. The non-readers and third preprimer readers should be visiting pupils as are the advanced readers. If administrative heterogeneous grouping is used, it may not be necessary to group the groups or have visiting pupils.

The second hypothetical illustration of how several groups might be organized involves a sixth-grade class. Four levels consist of five pupils each; several other pupils operate either at higher or lower levels. Chart 12-7 shows the distribution of pupils by reading level.

CHART 12-7

READING LEVELS IN A SIXTH-GRADE CLASS

Level	Pupils	Level	Pupils
Non-reading	1	5	5
1	3	6	5
3	5	Above 6	3
4	5		

Once again it is easy to note that a profileration of reading abilities is present -- one non-reading and at least seven reading levels. Actually, if we define reading level by the titles of the books in each basal series, we would have more than this, for grade levels two and three really consist of two books each. And grade level one actually has five books! For the sake of convenience we have combined some of these levels. For instance, pupils capable of reading at the 3-1 and 3-2 levels are using a 3-1 book and are designated as level three on the chart. As noted earlier, whenever groups are combined, they take the lower book as their initial instructional device.

Pupils functioning below grade level three probably should use the language-experience approach and/or high interest-low vocabulary series books. The three who read above the sixth-grade level should have abundant opportunities to read trade books related to their basal.

712

Strategies are described elsewhere (196B).

The higher the reading level, the greater the need for stratified heterogeneous grouping. If this happens, each of three sixth-grade teachers likely will have no more than three groups. The levels for one teacher might be six, four, and two. If stratified heterogeneous grouping is not possible, grouping the groups can be used once more in combining level 5 into level 4. Although this combination is not desirable for it reflects a range of almost two grades of reading levels into one, it seems essential from a pragmatic point of view.

At this level the use of visiting pupils is crucial. The non-readers, as well as those who operate at the first-grade, second-grade, and above-grade levels, should become visiting pupils.

Our discussion of the range of levels in either a second-grade or a sixth-grade class and the alternative strategies for minimizing the number of reading level groups leads naturally to our consideration of the original question of how to teach the groups. Chart 12-8 presents a possible outline of a day's activities in grade two.

Several comments may be helpful in interpreting Chart 12-8. First, it is intended as a hypothetical model that must be adapted to the real-life situation. For example, schools may not start or stop at the assumed hours. Second, it takes more time on Monday to discharge clerical responsibilities. However, these and other mundane but necessary activities can be conducted in less time when specific plans are made to use time as effectively as possible. Third, the time frames meet the generally recognized state requirements. Fourth, the time frames refer to average rather than a specified daily number of minutes. One should not stop a lesson just because the long hand of a clock moves six degrees. (This problem happens, by the way, especially in a departmentalized structure.) Fifth, the bracketed information indicates the presence of the teacher.

Sixth, at 9:30 on alternate days, a teacher might teach a higher-level skill to another group of pupils. Seventh, pupils at the primer and first reader levels (and certainly the preprimer two level) should be exempted from formal spelling instruction. Eighth, at 10:25 on alternate days there might be a higher level of handwriting instruction—cursive, for instance.

Ninth, a morning break can occur by groups while others remain on task. Thus children go individually to the restrooms and quietly eat their snacks and talk. This activity certainly is less distracting than the

713

CHART 12-8

ORGANIZATION FOR INSTRUCTION--GRADE 2

TIME	2-1	PRIMER/FIRST READER	PREPRIMER 2
8:20-8:35	School starts. Greet children. Collect lunch and milk money. Say the Pledge of Allegiance. Sing a song. Go over what each group should no independently.		
	Take written vocabulary quiz while money is being collected. Restudy and retake as necessary.	Take vocabulary quiz with Word Consultants or the written quiz while money is being collected. Restudy and retake as necessary.	Take vocabulary test with Word Consultants while money is collected. Restudy and retake if necessary.
8:35-9:00	Do long-term Independent Activity (IA) such as SRA Kit, listening tape, or planned reading.	Do long-term Independent Activity such as SRA Kit. In any remaining time, do short-term IA such as 10-minute report.	⎰Background ⎱Purpose Silent Reading Discussion, Evaluation, Oral Reading
9:00-9:10	(continued above). Do short-term such as 10-minute report or daily spelling.	⎰(Possibly check vocabulary quiz.) ⎱Background. Purpose	Study SCCs. Be checked off by Word Consultant. Dictate SCCs. Study them.
9:10-9:20	⎰(Possibly check vocabulary quiz.) ⎱Background Purpose	Do silent reading	
9:20-9:35	Do silent reading. Answer written comprehension questions.	Teach low-level skill to some pupils. Others do IA's.	Teach low-level skill to some pupils. Others do IA's.

714

CHART 12-8
(continued)

Time			
9:35–9:50	(continued above)	Discussion, evaluation, oral reading	Do skills follow-up or other IA's.
9:50–10:15	Discussion / Check questions / Story-based Extended and Related Activities	Do skills follow-up. Read Skinny Books. Study SCCs. Be checked off by Word Consultant. Dictate SCCs. Study them.	Work at Listening Station and/or read Skinny Books.
10:15–10:25	Spelling Instruction	(continued above)	(continued above)
10:25–10:35	Do skills follow-up from previous day.	Handwriting instruction. → Handwriting instruction.	
10:35–11:05	LANGUAGE		
11:05–11:30	Do math practice. Do math rework.	First-grade math (some pupils from two reading groups.)	
11:30–11:50	Second-grade math (some pupils from two reading groups)	Do math rework. Do rework.	
11:50–12:20	LUNCH		
12:20–12:50	Social Studies		
12:50–1:20	Music or Art		
1:20–1:50	Physical Education		
1:50–2:20	Science/Health		

715

CHART 12-8
(continued)

2:20-2:50*	Vocabulary presentation	Listen to vocabulary presentation.	Listen to vocabulary presentation.
2 days read to class	Study vocabulary	Vocabulary presentation.	Listen to vocabulary presentation.
2 days read to class	Do handwriting practice.	Study vocabulary.	
1 day library	Do rework.	Read Skinny Books.	Vocabulary presentation.
	Do math practice.	Do rework.	

What Did You Learn Today?—Cleanup—Gather Books

2:50-3:00	
3:00	School ends. Say good-bye to children. Put work on board for next day.

*Go to the library one day a week.
Read to class perhaps at end of library period and 15 minutes each of other four days.
Teach new vocabulary to appropriate groups approximately 15 minutes daily.

block play in kindergarten. The same caution applies to
the use of a rest period after lunch. Not all pupils
need the rest; nor are all willing to take it. Use this
time to record stories dictated by the poorest readers,
to teach a skill to several pupils, or teach a brief
lesson in some other area. Don't walk around the room
saying, "I see someone who's not taking his nap." Tenth,
in reading the Developmental Lesson Plan sequence
continues from day to day. A good place to break--if you
have a choice--is after the answering of written
questions for the 2-1 level or after the discussion at
any level. If you stop after silent reading, we
recommend that another silent reading be an Independent
Activity for the following day.

Chart 12-9 presents a possible outline of a day's
activities in grade six.

In addition to the comments following Chart 12-8, the
following items might be helpful. First, there is no opportunity for the second-grade reading group to have
thirty minutes to read recreationally. As the schedule
continues on the following day, that time will occur.
One of the victims of the decreased amount of time for
reading instruction is planned practice. Another victim,
according to National Assessments of Education Progress
(NAEP) data is achievement. Although nine-year-olds
continued to progress in reading, the performance of
13-year-olds has remained relatively stable, in 1981
(533). In the most recent (1985) summaries, all three
age groups have made little or no progress.

Second, teachers should note the extent to which
activities consume time that could be used for
instruction. To illustrate, teachers often administer
tests to the entire class at the same time. This
practice is a questionable use of time, for as much as an
hour might be consumed during which the teacher provides
no instruction. Class tests often can be given to
one-half of the pupils while the others receive
instruction. Stated another way: Class tests should be
considered independent activities rather than
instructional activities. As another example, when a
large portion of a class is absent because of band,
chorus, or the latest virus, a teacher has an excellent
opportunity to conduct small group and individual
instruction. Unfortunately, such occasions are often
set aside for homework study because "so many people are
absent." The theory seems to be that if we can't teach
the whole group, we won't teach anyone.

CHART 12-9

ORGANIZATION FOR INSTRUCTION -- GRADE 6

TIME	6	4	2
8:20-8:30	School starts. Greet children. Say the Pledge of Allegiance. Go over what each group should do independently. While the children take their vocabulary quizzes, collect lunch and milk money. Pupils who don't achieve satisfactorily restudy and retake as soon as possible.		
8:30-8:40	Do long-term IA such as SRA Kit, listening tape, or planned reading.	Do short-term IA such as worksheet exercises.	Background Purpose
8:40-8:55	Background Purpose	Background Purpose	Do silent reading Answer written comprehension questions.
8:55-9:05	Story-based Extended and Related Activities from previous lesson.	Do silent reading. Answer written comprehension questions.	(continued above)
9:05-9:15	Background Purpose	(continued above)	Discussion Check questions. Story-based Extended and Related Activities.
9:15-9:45	Do silent reading. Answer written comprehension questions.	Do long-term IA such as planned reading.	
9:45-10:00	Higher-level spelling with handwriting instruction.	Do lower-level spelling and handwriting practice.	
10:00-10:45	LANGUAGE		

718

CHART 12-9
(continued)

Time			
10:45–11:05	Sixth-grade math (some pupils from two reading groups.)	Do math practice. Do math rework.	
11:05–11:30	Do math practice	Lower-level math (some pupils from two reading groups.)	
11:30–12:00	LUNCH		
12:00–12:45	Social Studies		
12:45–1:30	Science/Health		
1:30–2:00	Music or Art		
2:00–2:30	Physical Education		
2:30–3:00*	Vocabulary presentation. Study vocabulary. Do handwriting practice. Study vocabulary. Do rework. Do math practice.	Listen to vocabulary presentation. Vocabulary presentation. Study vocabulary. Do rework.	Listen to vocabulary presentation or do IA. Listen to vocabulary presentation. Vocabulary presentation.
3:00–3:10	What Did You Learn Today? — Cleanup — Gather Books		
3:10	School ends. Say good-bye to children. Put work on board for next day.		

*Go to the library one day a week.
Read to the class fifteen minutes each of the other four days.
Teach new vocabulary to appropriate groups approximately 15 minutes daily.

719

Another excellent opportunity is lost if pupils are not allowed to enter the classroom before the classes start. Pupils who reach school early should not be herded into long crowded halls and auditoriums. What better time could there be to provide individual or small-group instruction than at an early hour when young minds are still fresh and the number of pupils is small?

Third, the curriculum tends to be correlated and coordinated rather than segmented and compartmentalized under the outline presented on the previous pages. As a consequence, youngsters may read, write, listen, and spell during the same block of time (For that matter, we see nothing wrong with allowing math, social studies, and science learnings to occur at this time, especially for pupils who are already quite proficient in the broad language arts area.). Going a step further, instruction in spelling may be provided as an integral part of the Developmental Lesson Plan. The only adaptation needed is to summon those who are engaged in independent activities.

Fourth, a procedure of this type requires careful pre-planning. It does not lend itself to on-the-spot preparation. A teacher who uses this pattern of organization cannot read her story while the children read theirs. Instead she must conceive of her major outside-of-school responsibility as planning sufficient valid learning experiences for all members of the class, realizing that most pupils who meander throughout the class when they should be otherwise occupied either have activities too simple for their use or are incapable of completing their designated assignments.

Principles and Practices for
Effective Classroom Management

In recent years researchers (82, 83, 303B, 353, 600, 601) have noted that teacher competence in classroom management is associated with pupil progress and Evertson, et al (303b) have written an excellent book of recommendations based on their research. Brophy has observed that the major part of effective classroom management involves preparation and planning for an appropriate physical environment, modeling and role playing desired behavior, establishing and maintaining routines, and providing an appropriate curriculum. Efforts seemed directed to prevention of problems and immediate resolution of difficulties that did arise. Indeed studies by Kounin and others (452) found the effective classroom managers demonstrated certain behaviors. These are listed below with some of our suggestions.

720

1. <u>With-it-ness</u> (being aware of potential problems and nipping them in the bud)

   A. Identify potential problem causers by contacting previous teachers. Enlist these pupils in assisting you during the first days of school.

   B. Surround problem causers with dependable pupils rather than seating them near other problem causers.

   C. When teaching, sit or stand in such a way that you can see all other groups and individuals.

2. <u>Overlapping-ness</u> (being able to do more than one thing at a time)

   A. While talking to one child, occasionally glance at the rest of the class.

   B. While preprimer level pupils read two pages silently, for example, check a set of their exercises or record the grades.

   C. While pronouncing spelling words or giving dictation, check attendance or distribute papers.

   D. While one primary child reads the silent passage of an IRI, move to the other side of the room and ask another child to do the same.

   E. While the intermediate class reads the silent passage of an IRI, administer the oral part to a child who has already "topped out" on the silent reading.

   F. At the second-grade level or above, consider presenting vocabulary words to two groups at the same time. This technique gives the pupils in the first group time to record the definitions while you pronounce the context sentence for the second group.

3. <u>Signal continuity and momentum</u> (proceeding at a brisk pace with few interruptions)

   A. Be prepared, both in terms of the lesson and the organizational structure of the class.

   B. Have all materials handy (manuals, charts, workbooks, texts, etc.)

C. Teach pupils how to come quickly to the reading group with all of their materials or -- as some writers have suggested -- go to the reading group.

D. Have material printed on the board before school starts so class time is not used for that purpose.

E. Have duplicated materials organized and ready to distribute.

F. Have independent activities listed on the board in the sequence pupils should complete them.

G. Use quiet reprimands by going to a (potentially) disruptive or offtask pupil to get the child back on task.

H. Use frequent eye contact with pupils who are inattentive to their work.

I. When interruptions occur (intercom, fire drill, unexpected parent visit), remind the pupils to return to work.

J. Have audio-visual equipment ready to use (i.e, records handy, equipment plugged in, films and filmstrips threaded).

K. Announce several minutes before a transition that it is about to occur. This provides time for pupils to get ready for the activity change.

4. Group alerting and accountability in lessons

A. Use the EPR technique (278).

B. Use delayed EPR. That is, ask a question and tell pupils not to display the answer until you ask for it.

C. Use wait-time (605). That is, provide time for pupils to think and respond.

D. Avoid activities that have few people engaged in on-task behavior. Examples include Go Fish, spelling bees, individuals solving problems at the board, and the traditional round robin oral reading.

E. Call pupils' names only after you have asked a question and paused.

F. Call on pupils in random rather than a clearly perceived order.

G. Tell pupils when you're about to pose a difficult question.

H. Issue a challenge by telling selected pupils they won't be able to solve a certain problem.

5. Variety and challenge is seatwork

A. Provide seatwork which is neither so easy that it's boring or so difficult that it's frustrating.

B. Provide varied practice activities designed to accomplish the same objective. For instance, pupils might practice a skill using a tachistoscope, dice, tic tac toe, card games, etc.

C. For slow learners and insecure or poorly motivated pupils, divide exercises into smaller segments. For example, cut worksheets into two sections.

D. Provide incentives for seatwork. Examples: Practice this story so you can read it to the kindergarten. Write a letter to send to the sick coach. Revise this story so it can be submitted to the school newspaper.

First Weeks' Activities

The first week of school sets the stage for the remaining 35 weeks. The nature and quality of the activities conducted during the first five to ten days determined in large part the effectiveness of instruction during the remainder of the year. The emphasis of the first few weeks should be on (a) diagnosis, (b) teaching pupils how to study and learn, (c) establishing rules, routines, and procedures, and (d) reviewing basic information pupils have managed to lose during the summer.

While adaptations are necessary, both by grade levels and by time frames, the following information should provide some suggestions for consideration:

DIAGNOSIS

Grade 1. Week 1: Teach instructional language and testing procedures and establish rapport. Week 2: For pupils who are ready, administer diagnostic pretests on reading skills. For pupils who recognize words,

723

administer any appropriate levels of the IRI. For pupils who possess auditory discrimination, administer phonics diagnostic pretests.

Grades 2 and 3. Weeks 1 and 2: Establish rapport and review instructional language and testing procedures. On the third day begin administering an IRI to individuals. Do five or six daily (taking one hour to 90 minutes per day) for about five days. Use an aide to work with the rest of the class. Ask a Chapter I, LD, or EMH teacher to administer IRIs to her (possible) pupils.

Administer (DPTs) in reading skills. Administer reading readiness DPTs to pupils who are unable to read.

Grades 4-8. Week 1: Establish rapport and on the second full day of school begin administering group IRIs for the silent reading. Do two reading levels daily, taking less than an hour per day for four days. Begin at a very low level so pupils will have the first levels as practice for the harder ones to come and so even the poorest readers will have a chance to pass. In grade four begin with primer and first reader on day one, 2-1 and 2-2 on day two, 3-1 and 3-2 on day three, and the grade 4 book on day four. In grade five begin with the first reader and 2-1 level; in grade six start with the 2-1 and 2-2 levels. In grade seven administer the 2-2 and 3-1 levels, and give the 3-1 and 3-2 levels in grade eight. For the poorest readers (or for everyone if you want to give an end-of-year IRI to measure progress), give the oral reading part. It should take no more than five minutes per person.

Begin giving skills DPTs during the first full day of school (unless it is also the very first day). Continue as time permits throughout the first week and if necessary into the second week. Administer an interest inventory.

TEACHING PUPILS HOW TO STUDY AND LEARN

Grade 1. Week 1: Teach pupils how to use self-learning cumulative teaching/cumulative testing material such as SCCs. These can be either for word recognition or vocabulary development. Teach pupils to develop and dictate SCCs. Begin teaching pupils how to use the appropriate procedures for studying vocabulary presented in the spirit mastered Model 1 format (See Chapter 7A). Begin teaching pupils how to use learning centers as well as audio-visual materials such as tape recorders and language masters. Role play the activities whenever possible.

Grades 2-8. Week 1: Teach pupils how to use self-study cumulative teaching/cumulative testing materials such as SCCs and vocabulary (and, at some reading levels) definitions recorded in their notebooks. Begin teaching (or review) pupils how to use Learning Centers as well as tape recorders, record players, computers, and language masters.
Week 2: Teach pupils how to locate books in the library and how to determine whether the book is appropriate. Use role playing activities.

ESTABLISHING RULES, ROUTINES, AND PROCEDURES

Grades 1-8. Weeks 1-2: Establish with the help of the pupils the class rules. Keep them short and clear. Discuss and post them as well as any school rules that apply. Post and discuss a schedule of coursework similar to those shown in Charts 12-1 and 12-2. At the first-grade level use pictures (rebus) to illustrate the words. Establish a location for each group's independent activities and the order in which they are to be done by the sequence in which they appear on the board.

Discuss and role play common practices such as where, how, and when to secure materials (papers, textbooks, workbooks, etc.), how to complete them, and where and when to return them. Discuss and practice rework procedures. Develop, discuss, and display procedures for recording progress (both individual for pupil use and collective for group use). Teach and role play the use of word consultants. Discuss the importance of pupil time on task (getting started and staying on task). Use the clock to teach pupils to monitor their time. For instance, "You should finish this page by the time the long hand is on seven" (grade one) "or by 9:35". Provide simple independent assignments for the child to complete under your direct supervision. Then provide some hard activities which require pupils to seek help and skip certain items.

Provide or require bookbags and help pupils learn to pack the appropriate materials (library book, letter to parents, homework assignments) at the end of the day. Discuss the importance of homework and role play the necessary procedures.

REVIEWING BASIC INFORMATION

Grade 1. Weeks 1-2: Provide instruction and guided practice in using levels of listening comprehension for sentences (two per day for 30-45 minutes). Provide pictures for the study of other comprehension skills

725

(i.e., main ideas, predicting outcomes). Provide instruction and practice at Level 1 or 2 of auditory discrimination. In later weeks use paragraphs for developing levels of listening comprehension.

Grades 2-8. Week 1: Provide instruction and guided practice in using levels of comprehension, first at the listening stage for sentences and then at the reading stage. Do two sentences daily for 30-45 minutes. Week 2: Provide similar instruction and practice at both the listening and the reading levels for paragraphs.

During both weeks provide very easy Skinny Books from which pupils select titles to read. In grade two, for instance, a child might read Story 1 of the first preprimer and answer four questions listed at the end. By making a perfect score, the child can go to the next level (preprimer two) and read Story 1. A child who misses a question returns to the previous level and reads through each story in sequence. The practice helps identify an independent reading level at about the same time an IRI is being administered.

Summary

A speaker once advised a group of teachers, "Hard work done well looks easy." She may have had in mind the polished presentations of public performers. Indeed, these performances seem so effortless that one could assume falsely that little effort is involved. Not so. Except in fantasy-land, there are no shortcuts to competent performance. In education there is no royal road to learning; neither is there a royal road to teaching. Competence in teaching requires content knowledge, diagnostic, instructional and evaluative strategies, planning and organizational skills, a caring attitude, and a commitment to do whatever is necessary to create an environment in which every child achieves success every day.

Rome was not built in a day, we are told. Neither does competence develop overnight. The poet Goethe remarked during his eightieth year that he had not yet learned all he needed to know about reading. His observation reminds us that learning is not the exclusive province of the very young.

Several years ago an article in the Reading Teacher (38) suggested that the difference between a good teacher and a mediocre teacher was that the former performed "slightly" better each day. Over the period of a year the 180 "slightly" better days produced a significant difference in the quality of teaching and of learning.

An anonymous poet once penned these words of commitment.

I am only one
But I am one
I cannot do everything,
But I can do something.
When I can do,
I ought to do,
And, by the grace of God,
I will do.

We hope this book will encourage and help you to do "slightly better" each day as you help shape the future of your children.

FOR FURTHER READING

Bliesmer, Emery P., "Classroom Management and Teaching Reading," in Improving Reading Through Classroom Practices," pp. 22-29, ed. Arthur Heilman. University Park: Pennsylvania State University, 1966.

Brophy, Jere E., "Classroom Organization and Management," Elementary School Journal, LXXXIII, No. 4 (March, 1983), 265-285.

Cruickshank, Donald R., and Richard Callahan, "The Other Side of the Desk: Stages and Problems of Teacher Development," Elementary School Journal, LXXXIII, No. 3 (January, 1983), 251-258.

Evertson, Carolyn M., et al., Classroom Management for Elementary Teachers. Englewood Cliffs, N.J.: Prentice-Hall, 1984.

REFERENCES

1. Adams, Henry, The Education of Henry Adams. New York: Modern Library, 1931.

2. Alano, Angeles C., "Collect, Adapt, and Use Varied Reading Materials," Reading Teacher, XXX, No. 8 (May, 1977), 875-879.

3. Allen, Charles M., Combating the Dropout Problem. Chicago: SRA, 1956.

4. Allen, James E., Jr. "The Right to Read - Target for the 70's," Address to the National Association of State Boards of Education, Los Angeles, California, September 23, 1969.

5. Allen, Roach Van, Attitudes and the Art of Teaching. Washington, D. C.: National Education Association, 1965.

6. _____, "The Language Experience Approach," in Teaching Young Children to Read, pp. 59-67, ed. Warren G. Cutts. Washington, D. C.: United States Office of Education, 1964.

7. _____, Language Experience Activities, Second Edition. Boston: Houghton Mifflin, 1982.

9. Allington, Richard L., "Improving Content Area Instruction in the Middle School," Journal of Reading, XVIII, No. 6 (March, 1975), 455-461. (a)

10. _____, "Sticks and Stones ... but, Will Names Never Hurt Them?" Reading Teacher, XXVIII, No. 4 (January, 1975), 364-369. (b)

11. _____, Laura Chodos, Jane Donarachi, and Sharon Truex, "Passage Dependency: Four Diagnostic Oral Reading Tests," Reading Teacher, XXX, No. 7 (January, 1977), 369-375.

12. Almy, Millie, Young Children's Thinking. New York: Teachers College Press, Columbia University, 1966.

13. Ames, Wilbur S., "The Development of a Classification Scheme of Contextual Aids," Reading Research Quarterly, II, No. 1 (Fall, 1966), 56-82.

14. Ammon, Richard, "Generating Expectancies to Enhance Comprehension," Reading Teacher, XXIX, No. 3 (December, 1975), 245-249.

15. Anderson, Richard B., et al., Evaluation of the Effectiveness of 17 Follow-Through Models (for Abt Associates). Washington, D.C.: U.S.O.E., April, 1977.

16. Anderson, R.C., and P. Freebody, Vocabulary Knowledge. Technical Report No. 136. Champaign: University of Illinois at Urbana- Champaign, 1979.

17. Applebee, Arthur R., "Silent Reading Tests - What Do They Measure?" School Review, LXXX (November, 1971), 86-93.

18. Arkley, Rose, "Independent Reading for First Grades: A Listing," Elementary English, XLVI, No. 4 (April, 1969), 444-465.

19. Arnold, Richard D., "Retention in Reading of Disadvantaged Mexican-Children During the Summer Months," Address to the International Reading Association, Boston, April, 1968.

20. Artley, A. Sterl, "Are Secondary Developmental Reading Programs Feasible?" in Quest for Competency in Teaching Reading, pp. 74-83, ed. Howard A. Klein. Newark, Del: International Reading Association. 1972.

21. _____, "Developing the Use of Context," in Developing Vocabulary and Word Attack Skills, pp. 91-93, eds. Donald L. Cleland and Josephine T. Benson. Pittsburgh: University of Pittsburgh, 1962.

22. _____, "The Development of Reading Maturity in High School: Implication of the Gray-Rogers Study," Educational Administration and Supervision, LXIII (October, 1957), 321-328.

23. _____ "A Study of Certain Relationships Existing Between General Reading Comprehension and Reading Comprehension in Specific Subject-Matter Areas," Journal of Educational Research, XXXVII (1944), 464-473.

24. _____, "Teaching Word Meaning Through Context," Elementary English Review. XX, No. 1 (January, 1943), 68-74.

25. Ashton-Warner, Sylvia, Teacher. New York: Bantam, 1963.

26. Au, Kathryn Hu-Pei, "Analyzing Oral Reading Errors to Improve Instruction," Reading Teacher, XXXI, No. 1 (October, 1977), 46-49.

27. Aukerman, Robert C. Approaches to Beginning Reading, Second Edition. New York: Wiley, 1984.

28. Aulls, Mark W., The Content-Referenced Reading Survey Instrument. Moundsview, Minn.: Moundsview Public Schools, 1975.

29. _____, Developmental and Remedial Reading in the Middle Grades. Boston: Allyn, Bacon, 1978.

30. Austin, Mary C., "Problem Readers," in Reading: Seventy-Five Years of Progress, pp. 152-153, ed. H. Alan Robinson. Chicago: University of Chicago Press, 1966.

31. _____, "Strategies for Evaluating Reading Pro-grams: Elememtary Level," in Diagnostic View-points in Reading, pp. 8-18, ed. Robert E. Liebert. Newark, Del.: IRA, 1971.

32. _____, and Coleman Morrison, The First R: The Harvard Report on Reading in Elementary Schools. New York: Macmillan, 1963.

33. _____, et al., Reading Evaluation: Appraisal Techniques for School and Classroom. New York: Ronald Press, 1961.

34. _____, et al., The Torch Lighters: Tomorrow's Teachers of Reading. Cambridge, Mass.: Harvard University Press, 1961.

35. Axelrod, Jerome, "Some Flaws in Commercial Reading Comprehension Materials," Journal of Reading, XVII, No. 6 (March, 1974), 474-479.

36. Bagford, Jack, "Management Systems and Comprehension: Do Not Mix," Language Arts, LIV, No. 5 (May, 1977), 517-520.

37. Bailey, Mildred Hart, "The Utility of Phonic Generalizations in Grades Ones Through Six," Reading Teacher, XX, No. 5 (February, 1967), 413-418.

38. Baker, Marie, "A Little Better," Reading Teacher, XXVI, No. 8 (May, 1973), 829-830.

39. Baratz, Joan C., and Roger Shuy (editors), Teaching Black Children to Read. Washington, D.C.: Center for Applied Linguistics, 1969.

40. Barrett, Thomas, "Goals of the Reading Program: The Basis for Evaluation," in The Evaluation of Children's Reading Achievement, ed. Thomas C. Barrett. Newark, Del.: IRA, 1967.

731

41. ____, "The Relationship Between Measures of Pre-reading Visual Discrimination and First Grade Reading Achievement: A Review of the Literature," Reading Research Quarterly, I (Fall, 1965), 51-76.

42. ____, Taxonomy of Reading Comprehension. Lexington, Mass.: Ginn, 1972.

43. Bartolome, Paz I., "Teachers' Objectives and Questions in Primary Reading," Reading Teacher, XXIII, No. 1 (October, 1969), 27-33.

44. Batinch, Mary Ellen, "Language-Experience Activities," Reading Teacher, XXIII, No. 6 (March, 1970), 539-546, 564.

45. Beck, Isabel L., Ellen S. McCaslin, and Margaret G. McKeown, "Basal Readers' Purpose for Story Reading: Smoothly Paving the Road or Setting up a Detour?" Elementary School Journal, LXXXI, No. 3 (January, 1981), 156-161.

46. Bedell, R. C., Relationship Between the Ability to Recall and the Ability to Infer in Specific Learning Situations. Bulletin 34, No. 9. Kirksville: Northeast Missouri State Teachers College, 1934.

47. Beery, Althea, "Experiences in Listening," Elementary English", XXVIII, No. 2 (February, 1951), 130-132.

48. ____, "Interrelationships Between Listening and Other Language Arts Areas," Elementary English, XXXI, No. 3 (March, 1954), 164-172.

49. Bell, Terrel H., "A More Viable Home-School Partnership," Address to the American Association of School Administrators, Austin, Texas, February 23, 1975.

50. Bennett, Neville, Teaching Styles and Pupil Progress. Cambridge, Mass.: Harvard University Press, 1976.

51. Berliner, David C., "Academic Learning Time and Reading Achievement," in Comprehension and Teaching: Research Reviews, pp. 203-226, ed. John T. Guthrie. Newark, Del.: IRA, 1981.

52. Berretta, Shirley, "Self-Concept Development in the Reading Program," Reading Teacher, XXIV, No. 3 (December, 1970), 232-238.

53. Betts, Emmett, "Capturing Reading Motivation," in Motivating Children and Young Adults to Read, pp. 63-70, eds. James L.

Thomas and Ruth M. Loring. Phoenix, Arizona: Oryx Press, 1979.

54. _____, Foundations of Reading Instruction. New York: American Book, 1946.

55. _____, Foundations of Reading Instruction. New York: Americal Book, 1950.

56. _____, Foundations of Reading Instruction with an Emphasis on Differentiated Guidance. New York: American Book, 1957.

57. _____, Handbook on Corrective Reading. Chicago: Wheeler Publishing, 1956.

58. Bianchi, Evelyn S., High School Dropouts. Washington, D.C.: NEA, 1959.

59. Bliesmer, Emery P., "Sequence of Reading Skills in Reading: Is There Really One?" in Current Issues in Reading, pp. 125-133, ed. Nila Banton Smith. Newark, Del.: IRA, 1969.

60. Block, James H. Mastery Learning: Theory and Practice. New York: Holt, 1971.

61. _____, Schools, Society, and Mastery Learning. New York: Holt, 1974.

62. Bloom, Benjamin, Human Characteristics and School Learning. New York: McGraw-Hill, 1976.

63. _____, Stability and Change in Human Characteristics. New York: Wiley, 1964.

64. _____, (editor), Taxonomy of Educational Objectives: Cognitive Domain. New York: McKay, 1956.

65. _____, J. Thomas Hastings, and George Madaus, Handbook on Formative and Summative Evaluation of Student Learning. New York: McGraw-Hill, 1971.

66. Bloomer, R. H., "Concepts of Meaning and the Reading and Spelling Difficulties of Words," Journal of Educational Research, LIV (January, 1961), 178-182.

67. Board of Education of the City of New York, "Basic Teaching Strategies," in Reading Disabilities: Selections on Identification and Treatment, pp. 579-597, ed. Harold Newman. New York: Odyssey, 1969.

733

68. ____, "Developing a Meaning Vocabulary," in Reading Disabilities: Selections on Identification and Treatment, pp. 265-283, ed. Harold Newman. New York: Odyssey, 1969.

69. Bond, Eldon A., Tenth-Grade Abilities and Achievements. New York: Bureau of Publications, Teachers College, Columbia University, 1940.

70. Bond, Eva, Reading and Ninth-Grade Achievement. New York: Bureau of Publications, Teachers College, Columbia University, 1938.

71. Bond, Guy L., and Robert Dykstra, "The Cooperative Program in First Grade Instruction," Reading Research Quarterly, II, No. 4 (Summer, 1967), 5-142.

72. Bond, Guy L., and Miles A. Tinker, Reading Difficulties: Their Diagnosis and Correction, Third Edition. New York: Appleton-Century-Crofts, 1973.

73. ____, Miles A. Tinker, Barbara B. Wasson, and John Wasson, Reading Difficulties: Their Diagnosis and Correction, Fifth Edition. New York: Appleton-Century-Crofts, 1984.

74. ____, and Eva Bond Wagner, Teaching the Child to Read, Fourth Edition. New York: Macmillan, 1966.

75. Botel, Morton, "Evaluating Progress in Reading," in New Perspectives in Reading Instruction: A Book of Readings, pp. 366-374, ed. Albert J. Mazurkiewicz. New York: Pitman, 1964.

76. ____, How to Teach Reading. Chicago: Follett, 1963.

77. Bottom, Raymond, The Education of Disadvantaged Children. West Nyack, New York: Parker, 1970.

78. Bougere, Marguerite, "Vocabulary Development in the Primary Grades," in Forging Ahead in Reading, pp. 75-78, ed. J. Allen Figurel. Newark, Del.: IRA, 1968.

79. Bowren, F. F., "The Status of Reading Services in New Mexico Secondary Schools," Journal of Reading, XIII, No. 7 (April, 1970), 513-518.

80. Bracken, Dorothy Kendall, Listening Skills Program. Chicago: SRA, 1970.

81. Bronfenbrenner, Urie, "Is Early Intervention Effective?" Day Care and Early Education, II (November, 1974), 15-18, 44.

82. Brophy, Jere, "Classroom Organization and Management," *Elementary School Journal*, LXXXIII, No. 4 (March, 1983), 265-285.

83. ____, "Teacher Behavior and Its Effects," *Journal of Educational Psychology*, LXXI (1979), 733-750.

84. Brown, Ann L., et al., *Intrusion of a Thematic Idea in Children's Comprehension and Retention of Stories*. Technical Report No. 18. Urbana: University of Illinois Center for the Study of Reading, February, 1977.

85. Brown, Don A., "Measuring the Reading Ability and Potential of Illiterates," in *Measurement and Evaluation of Reading*, pp. 154-165, ed. Roger Farr. New York: Harcourt, 1970.

86. Brown, Rexel E., "A Three-Dimensional Approach for Teaching Vocabulary," *Indiana Reading Quarterly*, VII, No. 2 (Winter, 1975), 5-8, 31.

87. Brueckner, Leo J., and Guy L. Bond, *Diagnosis and Treatment of Learning Difficulties*. New York: Appleton-Century-Crofts, 1955.

88. Bruner, Jerome S., *The Process of Education*. Cambridge, Mass.: Harvard University Press, 1960.

89. ____, *Toward a Theory of Instruction*. Cambridge, Mass.: Belknap Press of Harvard University Press, 1966.

90. Brzeinski, Joseph E., "Beginning Reading in Denver," *Reading Teacher*, XVIII, No. 1 (October, 1964), 16-21.

91. Buehler, Carl J. (ed.) *Directory of Learning Resources for Reading*. Gales Ferry, Conn.: Education Systems, 1978.

92. Bullock, Harrison, "The Non-Reading Pupil in Person," in *Reading Disabilities: Selections on Identification and Treatment*, pp. 1-17, ed. Harold Newman. New York: Odyssey, 1969.

93. Burgett, Russ, "The Need for Developmental Reading Programs at the High School Level: A Letter to Parents," *Wisconsin State Reading Association Journal*, XXV, No. 3 (March, 1981), 32.

94. Burmeister, Lou E., "Content of a Phonics Program Based on Particularly Useful Generalizations," in *Reading Methods and Teacher Improvement*, pp. 27-39, ed. Nila Banton Smith. Newark, Del.: IRA, 1971.

95. _____, Reading Strategies for Middle and Secondary School Teachers. Reading, Mass.: Addison-Wesley, 1978.

96. _____, "Usefulness of Phonic Generalizations," Reading Teacher, XXI, No. 4 (January, 1968), 349-356, 360.

97. "Vowel Pairs," Reading Teacher, XXI (February, 1968), 445-452.

98. Burnett, Richard W., "Assessing Reading Progress," in Reading in the Middle School, pp. 57-64, ed. Gerald G. Duffy. Newark, Del.: IRA, 1975.

99. _____, "Helping the Disabled Reader," in Reading in the Middle Schools, pp. 103-111, ed. Gerald G. Duffy. Newark: Del.: IRA, 1974.

100. Burns, Paul C., "Vocabulary Growth Through the Use of Context in Elementary Grades," in Forging Ahead in Reading, pp. 79-85, ed. J. Allen Figurel. Newark, Del.: IRA, 1968.

101. Burns, Paul, Betty Broman, and Alberta Wantling, The Language Arts in Childhood Education, Second Edition. Chicago: Rand McNally, 1971.

102. Burron, Arnold, and Amos L. Claybaugh, Using Reading to Teach Subject Matter: Fundamentals for Content Teachers. Columbus, Ohio: Merrill, 1974.

103. Burroughs M., The Stimulation of Verbal Behavior in Culturally Disadvantaged Three-Year-Olds. Unpublished doctoral dissertation, Michigan State University, 1972.

104. Bursuk, Laura Z., "Evaluation of Correlated Listening-Reading Comprehension Lessons," in Quest for Competency in Teaching Reading, pp. 262-268, ed. Howard A. Klein. Newark, Del.: IRA, 1972.

105. Burt, Velma, "A Daily Story Approach to Beginning Reading," Reading Teacher, XXIII, No. 6 (March, 1970), 507-510, 515.

106. Calhoun, John A., and Raymond C. Cullins, "A Positive View of Programs for Early Childhood Intervention," Theory into Practice, XX (Spring, 1981), 135-140.

107. Campbell, Patricia F., "What Do Children See in Mathematics Textbook Pictures?" Arithmetic Teacher, XXVIII, No. 5 (January, 1981), 12-16.

736

108. Carillo, Lawrence W., "Fonyx," Reading Teacher, XXX, No. 3 (December, 1976), 280-282.

109. Carner, Richard, "Levels of Questioning," Education", LXXXIII (May, 1963), 546-550.

110. Carroll, John B., "Developmental Parameters of Reading Comprehension, " in Cognition, Curriculum, and Comprehension, pp. 1-15, ed. John T. Guthrie. Newark, Del.: IRA, 1977.

111. _____, Language and Thought. Englewood Cliffs, N.J.: Prentice-Hall, 1964.

112. _____, "A Model of School Learning," Teachers College Record, XLIV (1963), 723-733.

113. Carter, Homer L.J., and Dorothy J. McGinnis, Teaching Individuals to Read. Boston: Heath, 1962.

114. Caskey, Helen J., "Guidelines for Teaching Comprehension," in Readings on Teaching Reading, pp. 192-201, eds. Sam L. Sebesta and Carl J. Wallen. Chicago: SRA, 1972.

115. Catterson, Jane (editor), Children and Literature. Newark, Del.: IRA, 1970.

116. Chall, Jeanne S., "Ask Him to Try on the Book for Fit," Reading Teacher, VII, No. 3 (December, 1953), 83-88.

117. _____, "Interpreting the Results of Standardized Achievement Tests," in Measurement and Evaluation of Reading, pp. 51-59, ed. Roger Farr. New York: Harcourt, 1970.

118. _____, Learning to Read: The Great Debate. New York: McGraw-Hill, 1967.

119. _____, Readability: An Appraisal of Research and Application. Columbus: Ohio State University, 1958.

120. Chester, Robert, and Wayne Otto, "Children's Sight Words -- Printed Material or Oral Presentation," Journal of Educational Research, LXVII, No. 6 (February, 1974), 247-252.

121. Chomsky, Carol, "After Decoding: What?" Language Arts, LIII, No. 3 (March, 1976), 288-296.

122. Chow, Stanley, Pat Elmore, and Vicki Ertle, _Early Childhood Education_, PREP Report 37. Washington, D. C.: U.S. Department of Health, Education, and Welfare, 1972.

123. Church, M., "Does Visual Perception Training Help Beginning Readers?" _Reading Teacher_, XXVII, No. 4 (January, 1974), pp. 361-364.

124. Clay, Marie M., "Early Childhood and Cultural Diversity in New Zealand," _Reading Teacher_, XXIX, No. 4 (January, 1976), 333-341.

125. Clay, M., _Emergent Reading Behavior_. Unpublished doctoral dissertation. University of Auckland, Auckland, New Zealand, 1966.

126. Cleland, Donald L., "The McCracken Procedures in Teaching Reading," in _New Perspectives in Reading Instruction: A Book of Readings_, pp. 491-505, ed. Albert J. Mazurkiewicz. New York: Pitman, 1964.

127. Clements, Zacharie J., "Taking All Students From Where They Really Are," _NAASP Bulletin_, LX (April, 1976), 104-108.

128. Clymer, Theodore, "The Utility of Phonic Generalizations in the Primary Grades," _Reading Teacher_, XVI, No. 4 (January, 1963), 252,258.

129. Cohen, Dorothy, The Effect of a Special Program in Literature on the Vocabulary and Reading Achievement of Second Grade Children in Special Service Schools. Unpublished doctoral dissertation, New York University, 1966.

130. _____, "Effect of a Special Program in Literature on Vocabulary and Reading Achievement," in _Reading and Realism_, pp. 754-757, ed. J. Allen Figurel. Newark, Del.: IRA, 1969.

131. _____, "The Effect of Literature on Vocabulary and Reading Achievement," _Elementary English_, XXXV, No. 2 (February, 1968), 209-213.

132. _____, "Word Meaning and the Literary Experience in Early Childhood," _Elementary English_", XLVI, No. 7 (November, 1969), 914-925.

133. Cohen, Lorraine S., "Begin Critical Reading in Elementary School," in _Aspects of Reading_, pp. 25-27, ed. Eldonna L. Evertts. Champaign, Illinois: National Council of Teachers of English, 1970.

134. Cohen, S. Alan, "Some Conclusions about Teaching Reading to Disadvantaged Children," <u>Reading Teacher</u> XX, No. 5 (February, 1967), 433-435.

135. Colbert, Margaret (compiler), <u>Children's Books: Awards and Prizes</u>. New York: Children's Book Council.

136. Condit, Martha Olson, "If Only the Teacher Had Stayed With the Class," <u>Elementary English</u>, LII, No. 5 (May, 1975), 664-666.

137. Connor, Marjorie, "Elementary Reading Teachers and the School Psychologist," <u>Reading Teacher</u>, XXIII, No. 2 (November, 1969), 151-155.

138. Cooke, D. A., An Analysis of Reading Comprehension Questions in Basal Series According to the Barrett Taxonomy. Unpublished doctoral dissertation, Cornell University, 1970.

139. Cooper, J. Louis, The Effect of Adjustment of Basal Reading Materials on Reading Achievement. Unpublished doctoral dissertation, Boston University, 1952.

140. Covington, M. V., "Some Experimental Evidence on Teaching for Creative Understanding," <u>Reading Teacher</u>, XX (1967), 390-396.

141. Cramer, Ronald L., "Dialectology – A Case for Language Experience," <u>Reading Teacher</u>, XXV, No. 1 (October, 1971, 33-39.

142. Cullinan, Bernice E., <u>Literature for Children: Its Discipline and Content</u>. Dubuque, Iowa: William C. Brown, 1971.

143. _____, H. Jagger, and Dorothy Strickland, "Language Expansion for Black Children in the Primary Grades: A Research Report," <u>Young Children</u>, XXIX (January, 1974), 163-172.

144. Culyer, Gail B., "Exercises for Teaching English as a Second Language," <u>Vineyard Newsletter</u>, V, Nos. 1-2 (1979), 1-9.

145. _____, <u>A New Approach to Selecting Spelling Words</u>. Mt. Gilead, N.C.: Vineyard Press, 1974.

146. _____, "Techniques for Developing Reading Vocabulary," in <u>Translating Theory into Practice</u>, pp. 76-85, ed. Richard C. Culyer, III. Mt. Gilead: North Carolina Council of International Reading Association, 1972.

147. Culyer, Richard C., III, <u>Activities</u> <u>for</u> <u>Teaching</u> <u>Letter-Sound</u> <u>Associations</u>. Mt. Gilead, N.C.: Vineyard Press, 1980.

148. _____, "Criteria for Evaluating Initial Reading Inventories," <u>Vineyard</u> <u>Newsletter</u>, I, No. 3 (1975), 21-26.

149. _____, <u>Criteria</u> <u>for</u> <u>Observing</u> <u>in</u> <u>the</u> <u>Schools</u>: <u>A</u>. Mt. Gilead, N.C.: Vineyard Press, 1978.

150. _____ <u>Culyer</u> <u>Auditory</u> <u>Discrimination</u> <u>Exercises</u> <u>and</u> <u>Test</u> (<u>CADET</u>). Mt. Gilead, N.C.: Vineyard Press, 1978.

151. _____, <u>Culyer</u> <u>Auditory</u> <u>Discrimination</u> <u>Exercises</u> <u>and</u> <u>Test</u> <u>Manual</u>. Mt. Gilead, N.C.: Vineyard Press, 1977.

152. _____, "Cumulative Teaching, Better Learning," <u>Academic</u> <u>Therapy</u>, XVII, No. 5 (May, 1982), 537-542.

153. _____, <u>Diagnostic-Prescriptive</u> <u>Techniques</u>. Mt. Gilead, N.C.: Vineyard Press, 1977.

154. _____, <u>Extensive</u> <u>Reinforcement</u>: <u>Hope</u> <u>for</u> <u>the</u> <u>Disadvantaged</u>. Mt. Gilead, N.C.: Vineyard Press, 1971.

155. _____, "Guidelines for Skill Development: Comprehension," <u>Clearing</u> <u>House</u>, LV, No. 3 (November, 1981), 121-126.

156. _____, "Guidelines for Skill Development: Vocabulary," <u>Reading</u> <u>Teacher</u>, XXXII, No. 3 (December, 1978), 316-322.

157. _____, "Guidelines for Skill Development: Word Attack," <u>Reading</u> <u>Teacher</u>, XXXII, No. 4 (January, 1979), 425-433.

157B. _____, <u>Handbook</u> <u>for</u> <u>Making</u> <u>Inferences</u>. Mt. Gilead, N. C.: Vineyard Press, 1986.

158. _____, "How to Develop a Locally-Relevant Basic Sight Word List," <u>Vineyard</u> <u>Newsletter</u>, II, No. 2 (1976), 11-19.

159. _____, "How to Develop a Locally Relevant Sight Word List," <u>Reading</u> <u>Teacher</u>, XXXV, No. 5 (February, 1982), 596-597.

160. _____, <u>How</u> <u>to</u> <u>Initiate</u> <u>Beginning</u> <u>Reading</u> <u>Instruction</u>. Mt. Gilead, N.C.: Vineyard Press, 1969.

161. _____, <u>How</u> <u>to</u> <u>Teach</u> <u>Mastery-Based</u> <u>Developmental</u> <u>Lesson</u> <u>Plans</u>. Mt. Gilead, N.C.: Vineyard Press, 1983.

162. _____, <u>Ideas</u> <u>for</u> <u>Developing</u> <u>Comprehension</u>. Mt. Gilead, N.C.: Vineyard Press, 1968.

163. _____, Ideas for Developing Comprehension: A. Mt. Gilead, N.C.: Vineyard Press, 1974.

164. _____, Ideas for Developing Comprehension: B. Mt. Gilead, N.C.: Vineyard Press, 1974.

165. _____, Ideas for Developing Comprehension: C. Mt. Gilead, N.C.: Vineyard Press, 1974.

166. _____, Ideas for Developing Reading Readiness: A. Mt. Gilead, N.C.: Vineyard Press, 1979.

167. _____, Ideas for Developing Reading Readiness: B. Mt. Gilead, N.C.: Vineyard Press, 1979.

168. _____, Ideas for Developing Reading Readiness: C. Mt. Gilead, N.C.: Vineyard Press, 1979.

169. Culyer, Ideas for Teaching Reading. Mt. Gilead, N.C.: Vineyard Press, 1972.

170. _____, Ideas for Teaching Vocabulary. Mt. Gilead, N.C.: Vineyard Press, 1971.

171. _____, An Initial Reading Inventory: Forms A and B. Mt. Gilead, N.C.: Vineyard Press, 1970.

172. _____, Ideas for Teaching Study Skills. Mt. Gilead, N.C.: Vineyard Press, n.d.

173. _____, Initiating a Developmental Reading Program: A. Mt. Gilead, N.C.: Vineyard Press, 1975.

174. _____, Initiating a Developmental Reading Program: B. Mt. Gilead, N.C.: Vineyard Press, 1975.

175. _____, Initiating a Developmental Reading Program: C. Mt. Gilead, N.C.: Vineyard Press, 1982.

176. _____, "Interpreting Achievement Tests: Some Areas of Concern," Clearing House, LV, No. 8 (April, 1982), 374-380.

177. _____, Learning Centers and Independent Activities. Mt. Gilead, N.C.: Vineyard Press, 1972.

178. _____, Mastery Teaching. Mt. Gilead, N.C.: Vineyard Press, 1978.

179. _____, Models for Lesson Plans: A. Mt. Gilead, N.C.: Vineyard Press, 1976.

180. ____, _Models for Lesson Plans_: B. Mt. Gilead, N.C.: Vineyard Press, 1976.

181. ____, _Models for Lesson Plans_: C. Mt. Gilead, N.C.: Vineyard Press, 1976.

182. ____, _Models for Lesson Plans_: D. Mt. Gilead, N.C.: Vineyard Press, 1976.

183. ____, "A New Procedure for Anticipating Student Progress," _Vineyard Newsletter_, I, No. 2 (1975), 16-20.

184. ____, _Organizing and Providing for Individual Differences in the Content Areas_ (in preparation)

185. ____, _Organizing for Individual Differences in the Language Arts_. Mt. Gilead, N.C.: Vineyard Press, 1969.

186. ____, "Picture and Beginning Dictionaries and How to Use Them," _Tar Heel Reading Journal_, II, No. 2 (Spring, 1981), 21-27.

187. ____, "Project IRIS: A Program that Works with ALL Children," _NCCIRA Newsletter_, XI, No. 3 (March, 1980), 2-4.

188. ____, "Project READ (Reading Encouragement and Development)," _Early Years_, XV, No. 9 (May, 1985), 24,32.

189. ____, _Reading Handbook for Principals: How to Organize and Administer a Developmental Reading Program_ (in preparation)

190. ____, _Roles and Responsibilities for a Developmental Reading Program_.

191. ____, _Selecting and Using Materials_: A. Mt. Gilead, N.C.: Vineyard Press, 1974.

192. ____, _Selecting and Using Materials_: B. Mt. Gilead, N.C.: Vineyard Press, 1974.

193. ____, _Selecting and Using Materials_: C. Mt. Gilead, N.C.: Vineyard Press, 1974.

194. ____, "Skinny Books and Reading," _Language Arts_, LIII, No. 6 (September, 1975), 793-796.

195. ____, _South Carolina Vocabulary Development Program_. Mt. Gilead, N.C.: Vineyard Press, 1982.

196.   ____, *Strategies for Implementing a Developmental Reading Program*. Mt. Gilead, N.C.: Vineyard Press, 1974.

196B.   ____, *Strategies for Teaching Advanced Readers* (STAR). Mt. Gilead, N. C.: Vineyard Press, 1984.

197.   ____, "A Study of the Characteristics of Elementary School Students Designated by School Personnel as Probable Dropouts," Unpublished paper, Appalachian State University, 1970.

198.   ____, *Systematic Practice for Achieving Reading Knowledge* (SPARK). Mt. Gilead, N.C.: Vineyard Press, 1979.

199.   ____, *Teaching Work Attack Skills*. Mt. Gilead, N.C.: Vineyard Press, 1971.

200.   ____, "Using a Group Informal Reading Inventory," in *Translating Theory into Practice*, pp. 65-75, ed. Richard C. Culyer, III. Mt. Gilead, N.C.: NCCIRA, 1972.

201.   ____, "Using Multiple Adoptions Systematically and Sequentially," *Vineyard Newsletter*, I, Nos. 9-10 (1975), 79-95, 97.

202.   ____, *Using the Language Experience Approach*. Mt. Gilead, N.C.: Vineyard Press, 1971.

203.   ____, "Using Wordless Books to Foster Reading, Part I," *Vineyard Newsletter*, II, No. 1 (1977), 1-11.

204.   ____, "Using Wordless Books to Foster Reading, Part II," *Vineyard Newsletter*, V, No. 4 (1979), 42-48.

205.   ____, *Vocabulary Exercises based on Harcourt Brace Jovanovich's Bookmark Reading Program, Eagle Edition*. Mt. Gilead, N.C.: Vineyard Press, 1985.

206.   ____, *Ways of Increasing the Learning Rate*. Mt. Gilead, N.C.: Vineyard Press, 1980.

207.   ____, *Ways to Use Time Wisely*. Mt. Gilead, N.C.: Vineyard Press, 1977.

208.   ____, *Word Whiz*. Mt. Gilead, N.C.: Vineyard Press, 1983.

209.   ____, and Gail B. Culyer, *Comprehension Questions based on Ginn 720 Rainbow Edition*. Mt. Gilead, N.C.: Vineyard Press, 1981.

210. _____, and Gail B. Culyer, Comprehension Questions based on Harcourt Brace Jovanovich's Bookmark Reading Program, Eagle Edition. Mt. Gilead, N.C.: Vineyard Press, 1985.

211. _____, and Gail B. Culyer, Comprehension Questions based on the Houghton Mifflin Reading Series (1980-1983). Mt. Gilead, N.C.: Vineyard Press, 1984.

212. _____, and Gail B. Culyer, Comprehension Questions based on the Macmillan Series. Mt. Gilead, N.C.: Vineyard Press, 1984.

213. _____, and Gail B. Culyer, Comprehension Questions based on the Rand McNally's Young America Series. Mt. Gilead, N.C.: Vineyard Press, 1981.

213B. _____, and Gail B. Culyer, Practice Exercises in Reading Comprehension (PERC). Mt. Gilead, N.C.: Vineyard Press, 1986.

214. _____, and Gail B. Culyer, Practice Exercises in Phonics (PEP). Mt. Gilead, N.C.: Vineyard Press, 1977.

215. _____, and Gail B. Culyer, Vocabulary Exercises for Young America. Mt. Gilead, N.C.: Vineyard Press, 1976.

216. _____, and Gail B. Culyer, Ways to Make Learning Fun. Mt. Gilead, N.C.: Vineyard Press, 1974.

217. Cunningham, Patricia M., "Book Boards to Encourage Reading," Reading Teacher, XXXV, No. 6 (March, 1982), 730.

218. _____, "Match Informal Evaluation to Your Teaching Practices," Reading Teacher, XXXI, No. 1 (October, 1977), 51-56.

219. _____, "'Mumble Reading' for Beginning Readers," Reading Teacher, XXXI, No. 4 (January, 1978), 409-411.

220. _____, "Transferring Comprehension from Listening to Reading," Reading Teacher, XXIX, No. 2 (November, 1975), 169-172.

221. _____ et al., Reading in Elementary Classrooms: Strategies and Observations. New York: Longman, 1983.

222. Curry, Robert L., "Teaching the Decoding Skills," in Improving Reading in Secondary Schools, pp. 84-93, ed. Lawrence E. Hafner. New York: Macmillan, 1967.

223. Cutts, Warren G., "Does the Teacher Really Matter?" Reading Teacher, XXVIII, No. 5 (February, 1975), 449-452.

744

224.   , Modern Reading Instruction. New York: Center   for
     Applied Research in Education, 1964.

225. Dale, Edgar, "The Art of Reading," The News Letter, XI
     (February, 1946), 1.

226.   , "The Critical Reader," The Newsletter, XXX, No. 4
     (1965), 1-4.

227.   , and Joseph O'Rourke, Techniques of Teaching
     Vocabulary. Palo Alto, Calif.: Field, 1971.

228. Dallmann, Martha, Roger L. Rouch, Lynette Y. C. Char, and John
     J. DeBoer, The Teaching of Reading, Sixth Edition.   New
     York: Holt, 1982.

229. Daniels, Paul R., and George E. Mason, "Comprehension," in
     Perspectives in Reading -- Corrective Reading in the
     Elementary Classroom, pp. 109-128, eds. Marjorie Seddon
     Johnson and Roy A. Kress. Newark, Del.: IRA, 1967.

230. David, Jane L., and Sol H. Pelavin, Research on the
     Effectiveness of Compensatory Education Programs; A
     Reanalyses of Data. Menlo Park, Calif.: Stanford Research
     Institute, 1977.

231. David, S. B., Identification and Measurement of Reading Skills
     of High School Students, Cooperative Research Project, pp.
     73-75, No. 3029, U.S.O.E., 1965.

232. Davis, Fredrick, "Research in Comprehension in Reading,"
     Reading Research Quarterly, III, No. 4 (Summer, 1968),
     499-545.

233. Davis, Sister Mary C., The Relative Effectiveness of Certain
     Evaluative Criteria for Determining Reading Levels. Unpub-
     lished doctoral dissertation, Temple University, 1964.

234. Dawson, Mildred A. (Compiler), Developing Comprehension
     Including Critical Reading. Newark, Del.: IRA, 1968.

235.   , "Developing Interest in Books," in Quest for Competency
     in Teaching Reading, pp. 36-41, ed. Howard A. Klein.
     Newark, Del.: IRA, 1972.

236. Day, W.P., and B.R. Beach, A Survey of the Research Comparing
     the Visual and Auditory Presentation of Information,
     Technical Report, No. 5921. Dayton, Ohio: U.S. Air Force
     Base, 1950.

237. DeBoer, John J., and Martha Dallman, The Teaching of Reading. Second Edition. New York: Holt, 1964.

238. Dechant, Emerald V., Improving the Teaching of Reading, Third Edition. Englewood Cliffs, N.J.: Prentice-Hall, 1982.

239. _____, "Why An Eclectic Approach in Reading Instruction?" in Vistas in Reading, pp. 28-32, ed. J. Allen Figurel. Newark, Del.: IRA, 1966.

240. Decker, Isabel M., 100 Novel Ways With Book Reports. New York: Citation Press, 1969.

241. Degler, Lois Sauer, "Putting Words into Wordless Books," Reading Teacher, XXXII, No. 4 (January, 1979), 399-402.

242. DeHirsch, Katrina, "Psychological Correlates of the Reading Process," in Challenge and Experiment in Reading, pp. 218-226, ed. J. Allen Figurel. New York: IRA, 1962.

243. _____, Jeannette J. Jansky, and William S. Langford, Predicting Reading Failure: A Preliminary Study. New York: Harper, 1966.

244. Deighton, Lee C., Vocabulary Development in the Classroom. New York: Teachers College, Columbia University, 1966.

245. Dentler, Robert A., and Mary Ellen Warshauer, Big City Dropouts. New York: Center for Urban Education, 1965.

246. Deutsch, Cynthia P., "Auditory Discrimination and Learning: Social Factors," Merrill-Palmer Quarterly of Behavior and Development, X (July, 1964), 277-296.

247. Deutsch, Martin, "The Disadvantaged Child and the Learning Process," in Education in Depressed Areas, ed. Harry Passow. New York: Teachers College Press, 1963.

248. Dewey, J.C., "The Acquisition of Facts as a Measure of Reading Comprehension," Elementary School Journal, XXXV, No. 3 (January, 1935), 346-348.

249. Dieffenderfer, Carol, "Reading Concepts of Special Interest to Parents," Reading Teacher, XXX, No. 8 (May, 1977), 916-921.

249B. Dietz, Jeanne G., Use of Teachers' Questions in Promoting Critical Reading Comprehension in the Primary Grades. Research Report, University of Central Florida, June, 1981.

250. Dillar, Camille, "Let's Talk About It, Or Reading Related Conversation," Oklahoma Reader, XVI, No. 3 (1981), 4-5.

251. di Lorenzo, L.J., and R. Salter, "An Evaluative Study of Prekindergarten Programs for Educationally Disadvantaged Children: A Follow-up and Replication," Exceptional Children, XXXV (October, 1968), 111-119.

252. Dinkmeyer, Don, and Rudolf Dreikurs, Encouraging Children to Learn: The Encouragement Process. Englewood Cliffs, N.J.: Prentice-Hall, 1963.

253. Dolch, Edward W., "A Basic Sight Vocabulary," Elementary School Journal, XXXVI, No. 5 (February, 1936), 456-460.

254. _____, Psychology and the Teaching of Reading, Second Edition. Champaign, Ill.: Garrard, 1951.

255. _____, Teaching Primary Reading. Champaign, Ill.: Garrard, 1951.

256. _____, and Maurine Bloomster, "Phonic Readiness," Elementary School Journal, XXXVIII, (November, 1937), 201-205.

257. Doman, Glenn, How to Teach Your Baby to Read: The Gentle Revolution. New York: Random House, 1963.

258. Donoghue, Mildred R., The Child and the English Language Arts. Dubuque, Iowa: William C. Brown, 1971.

259. Donovan, David L., "Schools Do Make a Difference," Michigan School Board Journal, XXIX (July-August, 1982), 8-11.

260. Downing, John, and Sara Lundsteen, "Understanding New Perspectives of Early Childhood: What Does Research Tell Us About Children?" in Handbook for Administrators and Teachers: Reading in the Kindergarten. Newark, Del.: IRA, 1980.

261. Dresden, Dorothy, "Use and Misuse of Workbooks and Teachers' Guides in Kindergarten Through Grade Three," in Materials for Reading, pp. 75-78, ed. Helen M. Robinson. Chicago: University of Chicago Press, 1957.

262. Duke, Daniel, "Leadership Functions and Instructional Effectiveness," Education Digest, XLVIII, No. 7 (March, 1983), 20-23.

263. Duker, Sam, "Basics in Critical Listening," English Journal, LXI, No. 8 (November, 1962), 565-567.

264. Dulin, Kenneth L., "Using Context Clues in Word Recognition and Comprehension," Reading Teacher, XXIII, No. 5 (February, 1970), 440-445, 469.

265. Durkin, Dolores, "The Achievement of Pre-school Readers: Two Longitudinal Studies," Reading Research Quarterly, I, No. 4 (Summer, 1966), 5-34.

266. _____, Children Who Read Early. Boston: Allyn, Bacon, 1970.

267. _____, "Identifying Significant Reading Skills in Kindergarten Through Grade Three," in Reading: Seventy-Five Years of Progress, pp. 33-36, ed. H. Alan Robinson. Chicago: University of Chicago Press, 1966.

268. _____, Phonics, Linguistics, and the Teaching of Reading, Second Edition. New York: Teachers College Press, 1974.

269. _____, "Reading Comprehension Instruction in Five Basal Reading Series," Reading Research Quarterly, XVI, No. 4 (Summer, 1981), 515-544.

270. _____, "Some Questions about Questionable Instructional Materials," Reading Teacher XXVIII, No. 1 (October, 1974), 13-17.

271. _____, Teaching Children to Read, Third Edition. Boston: Allyn, Bacon, 1980.

272. _____, "What Classroom Observations Reveal about Reading Comprehension Instruction," Reading Research Quarterly, XIV, No. 4 (1978-79), 481-533.

273. _____, Richard C. Anderson, and Marilyn Jager Adams, "Beginning Reading: Theory and Practice," Language Arts, LV, No. 1 (January, 1978), 19-25.

274. Durr, William K., "Comprehension Abilities -- Some Ways to Improve Them," Magazine for Elementary Teachers, I, No. 1 (1979), 8-9, 21.

275. _____, Teaching Critical Reading in the Intermediate Grades. Boston: Houghton Mifflin, 1967.

276. _____, (editor), Reading Instruction: Dimensions and Issues. Boston: Houghton Mifflin, 1967.

277. _____, et al., Houghton Mifflin Reading Series. Boston: Houghton Mifflin, 1983.

278. Durrell, Donald D., Address at Gardner Webb College, Boiling Springs, N.C., 1970.

279. _____, Improving Reading Instruction. Yonkers-on-Hudson, New York: World Book, 1956.

280. _____, and Jane Catterson, Manual of Directions: Durrell Analysis of Reading Difficulty, Revised Edition. New York: Psychological Corporation, 1980.

281. _____, and Helen A. Murphy, "A Prereading Phonics Inventory," Reading Teacher, XXXI, No. 4 (January, 1978), 385-390.

282. _____, et al., "Success in First Grade Reading," Journal of Education, CXL (February, 1958), 1-48.

283. _____, et al., Vocabulary Improvement Practice. New York: Harcourt, 1975.

284. Dykstra, Robert, "Summary of the Second-Grade Phase of the Cooperative Research Program in Primary Reading Instruction," Reading Research Quarterly, IV, No. 1 (Fall, 1968), pp. 49-70.

285. Early, Margaret, "The Four-Wheel Drive," Elementary English, LI, No. 5 (May, 1974), 707-712.

286. _____, "What Does Research Reveal About Successful Reading Programs?" English Journal, LVIII, No. 4 (April, 1969), 534-547.

287. Early, Margaret, et al., Bookmark Reading Program, Eagle Edition. New York: Harcourt, 1983.

288. Eastland, Patricia, "'Read-aloud' Stories in the Primary Literature Program," Reading Teacher XXII, No. 3 (December, 1968), 216-222.

289. Eberwein, Lowell D., "The Variability of Readability of Basal Reader Textbook and How Much Teachers Know About It," Reading World, XVIII (March, 1979), 259-272.

290. Education Briefs," Education Digest, XLII, No. 2 (November, 1976), 66-67.

291. "Education Plan Sound - Report," in Charlotte Observer, April 23, 1972.

292. Educational Testing Service, Focus: Learning to Read. Princeton, N. J.: Educational Testing Service, 1978.

293. Edwards, Peter, "The Effect of Idioms on Children's Reading and Understanding of Prose," in Teachers, Tangibles and Techniques: Comprehension of Content in Reading, pp. 37-46, ed. Bonnie Smith Schulwitz. Newark, Del.: IRA, 1975.

294. Edwards, Thomas J., "Teaching Reading: A Critique," in The Disabled Reader: Education of the Dyslexic Child, pp. 349-362, ed. John Money. Baltimore, Md.: Johns Hopkins Press, 1966.

295. Eicholz, G., and R. Barbe, "An Experiment in Vocabulary Development," Educational Research Bulletin, XL (1961), 1-7.

296. Ekwall, Eldon E., "Should Repetitions Be Counted as Errors?" Reading Teacher, XXVII, No. 4 (January, 1974), 365-367.

297. Ellinger, Beatrice D., "Literature for Head Start Classes," Elementary English, XLIII, No. 5 (May, 1966), 453-459.

298. Emans, Robert, "Context Clues," in Elementary Reading Instruction: Selected Materials, pp. 197-207, eds. Althea Beery, Thomas C. Barrett, and William R. Powell. Boston: Allyn, Bacon, 1969.

299. ____, "Phonics: A Look Ahead," in Readings on Teaching Reading, pp. 180-191, eds. Sam L. Sebesta and Carl J. Wallen. Chicago: SRA, 1972.

300. ____, "When Two Vowels Go Walking and Other Such Things," Reading Teacher, XXI, No. 3 (December, 1967), 262-269.

301. ____, "The Usefulness of Phonic Generalizations Above the Primary Grades," Reading Teacher, XX, No. 5 (February, 1967), 419-425.

302. Englebright, Curtis L., "Sixty-one Ways to Tell About Books," Instructor, LXXIX, No. 3 (November, 1969), 70-71.

303. ERIC Clearinghouse on Reading and Communication Skills, "Fact Sheet: Schemata," Wisconsin State Reading Association Journal, XXVI, No. 3 (Spring, 1982), 27-29.

303B. Evertson, Carolyn M., et al., Classroom Management for Elementary Teachers. Englewood Cliffs, N.J.: Prentice-Hall, 1984.

304. Farr, Roger D., "Reading Tests and Teachers," Address to the International Reading Association, Boston, Mass., April, 1968.

305. _____, and Nicholas Anastasiow, Tests of Reading Readiness and Achievement: A Review and Evaluation. Newark, Del.: IRA, 1969.

306. _____, and Nancy Roser, Teaching a Child to Read. New York: Harcourt, 1979.

307. _____, and Carl B. Smith, "The Effects of Test Item Validity on Total Test Reliability and Validity," in Reading: Process and Pedagogy, pp. 122-134, eds. George B. Schick and Merrill M. May. Milwaukee, Wisc.: National Reading Conference, 1970.

308. Fay, Leo C., et al., Young America Basic Reading Program. Chicago: Rand McNally, 1974, 1981.

309. Fernald, Grace M., Remedial Techniques in Basic School Subjects. New York: McGraw-Hill, 1943.

310. Figurel, J. Allen, "Are the Reading Goals for the Disadvantaged Attainable?" in The First R: Readings on Teaching Reading, pp. 365-374, eds. Sam L. Sebesta and Carl J. Wallen. Chicago: SRA, 1972.

311. Fillmer, H. Thompson, "Roles of the Reading Teacher," in Reading in the Middle School, pp. 45-56, ed. Gerald G. Duffy. Newark, Del.: IRA, 1974.

312. Fitzgerald, Alice Irene, "Literature Approved by Today's Kindergarten Children," Elementary English, XLVIII, No. 8 (December, 1971), 953-959.

313. _____, "Literature Approved by Today's Kindergarten Children," Elementary English, XLIX, No. 1 (January, 1972), 132.

314. Fitzgerald, Gisela G., "Assessing Word-Difficulty in Basal Workbook Vocabulary Exercises," Reading Improvement, XVII, No. 4 (Winter, 1980), 248-255.

315. _____, "How Many Samples Give a Good Readability Estimate in the Fry Graph?" Journal of Reading, XXIV, No. 5 (February, 1981), 404-410.

316. _____, "Why Kids Can Read the Book But Not the Workbook," Reading Teacher, XXXII, No. 8 (May, 1979), 930-932.

317. Fitzgerald, James A., The Teaching of Spelling. Milwaukee: Bruce Publishing, 1951.

318. Flamond, Ruth K., "Critical Reading," in New Perspectives in Reading Instruction: A Book of Readings, pp. 256-261, ed. Albert J. Mazurkiewicz. New York: Pitman, 1964.

319. Fleck, Thomas, et al., "Middle Graders Talk About Reading," in What Is Reading Doing to the Child?, pp. 73-80, eds. Nancy Larrick and John A. Stoops. Danville, Ill.: Interstate Printers, 1967.

320. Flesch, Rudolf, Why Johnny Can't Read and What You Can Do About It. New York: Harper, 1956.

321. _____, Why Johnny Still Can't Read. New York: Harper, 1981.

321B. Focus: Early Education. Princeton, N.J.: ETS, 1977.

322. Focus: Learning to Read. Princeton, N.J.: ETS, 1978.

323. Fodor, M., The Effect of Systematic Reading of Stories on the Language Development of Culturally Deprived Children. Unpublished doctoral dissertation, Cornell University, 1966.

324. Forester, A.D., "What Teachers Can Learn from Natural Readers," Reading Teacher, XXXI, No. 2 (November, 1977), 160-166.

325. Foshay, Arthur W., "What's Basic About the Curriculum?" Language Arts, LIV, No. 6 (September, 1977), 616, 623-624.

326. Frase, Lawrence T., "Purpose in Reading," in Cognition, Curriculum, and Comprehension, pp. 42-64, ed. John T. Guthrie. Newark, Del.: IRA, 1977.

327. Fredericksen, Carl H., "Inference and Structure of Children's Discourse," Paper presented at the Symposium on the Development of Processing Skills, Society for Research in Child Develop- ment, New Orleans, La., 1976.

328. Froelich, Martha, Florence Kaiden Blitzer, and Judith M. Greenberg, "Success for Disadvan- taged Children," in The First R: Readings on Teaching Reading, pp. 388-400, eds. Sam L Sebesta and Carl J. Wallen. Chicago: SRA, 1972.

329. Frostig, Marianne, "Corrective Reading in the Classroom," in Elementary Reading Instruction: Selected Materials, pp. 118-127, eds. Althea Beery, Thomas C. Barrett, and William R. Powell. Boston: Allyn, Bacon, 1969.

330. Fry, Edward, "The Orangoutang Score," Reading Teacher, XXIV, No. 4 (January, 1971), 360-364.

331. Gall, Meredith D., "The Use of Questions in Teaching," Review of Educational Research, L (1970), 701-720.

332. Gambrell, Linda, "Sustained Silent Reading--A Time for Teachers," Reading Teacher, XXXIV, No. 7 (April, 1981), 837.

333. Gans, Roma, "Lectures in Reading," as quoted by Ruth Robinson, Why They Love to Learn. Charlotte, N.C.: Heritage Printers, 1960.

334. _____, "Meeting the Challenge of the Middle Grades," in What is Reading Doing to the Child, pp. 65-72, ed. Nancy Larrick and John A. Stoops. Danville, Ill.: Interstate Printers, 1967.

335. _____, A Study of Critical Reading Comprehension in the Intermediate Grades. New York: Bureau of Publications, Teachers College, Columbia University, 1940.

336. Gates, Arthur, "A Study of the Role of Visual Perception, Intelligence, and Certain Associative Processes in Reading and Spelling," Journal of Educational Psychology, XVII (1976), 433-445.

337. _____, Guy L. Bond, and David Russell, Methods of Determining Reading Readiness. New York: Bureau of Publications, Teachers College, Columbia University, 1939.

338. _____, Interest and Ability in Reading. New York: Macmillan, 1930.

339. _____, Manual of Directions for Gates Reading Readiness Tests. New York: Columbia College, 1939.

340. _____, and David H. Russell, "Types of Materials, Vocabulary Burden, Word Analysis, and Other Factors in Beginning Reading: II," Elementary School Journal, XXXIX, No. 2 (October, 1938). 119-128.

341. Getzals, J.W., "The Problem of Interests: A Reconsideration," in Reading: Seventy-Five Years of Progress, pp. 102-103, ed. H. Alan Robinson. Chicago: University of Chicago Press, 1966.

342. Gibbons, Robert D., "Beware the Home Eye Test for Preschoolers," Reading Teacher, XXVII, No. 6 (March, 1974), 566-571.

343. Gilles, Joanne, "Preferred Picks," The Pointer, XXV, No. 3 (Spring, 1981), 52-54.

344. Gillet, Jean Wallace, and M. Jane Kita, "Words, Kids, and Categories," Reading Teacher, XXXII, No. 5 (February, 1979), 538-542.

345. Gilmore, John V., Manual for the Gilmore Oral Reading Test. New York: Harcourt, 1968.

346. Gipe, Joan P., "Use of a Relevant Context Helps Kids Learn New Word Meanings," Reading Teacher, XXXIII, No. 4 (January, 1980), 398-402.

347. Glass, Gerald G., and Pauline Rea Jarett, "Teacher's Choice: Books for Kids," Reading Teacher, XXV, No. 3 (December, 1971), 257-261.

348. Glass, Patricia A., "Comprehension -- A Vital Skill," in Education for Tomorrow -- Reading, pp. 47-55, ed. Arthur W. Heilman. University Park: Pennsylvania State University, 1965.

349. Glines, Don, "The Status of Year-Round Education," Teacher, XCV (April, 1978), 67.

350. Godfrey, Lorraine L., "Annotated Bibliography for Third Graders," Elementary English, XLIV, No. 1 (January, 1972), 124-133.

351. Goins, Jean Turner, "Visual Perceptual Abilities and Early Reading Progress," Supplemental Educational Monograph 87. Chicago: University of Chicago Press, 1958.

352. Gonder, Peggy, "The Good News in Reading," American Education, XII, No. 10 (December, 1976), 14-17.

353. Good, Thomas, "Teacher Effectiveness in the Elementary School -- What We Know About It Now," Journal of Teacher Education, XXX (1979), 52-64.

354. Goodman, Kenneth S., Address to the Greater Charlotte Council of the International Reading Association and the Association of Childhood Education International, February, 10, 1972.

355. ____, "Reading: A Psycholinguistic Guessing Game," Journal of the Reading Specialist, VI (May, 1967), 126-135.

356. ____, "Reading: A Psycholinguistic Guessing Game," in Theoretical Models and Processes of Reading, pp. 259-271, eds. Harry Singer and Robert Ruddell. Newark, Del.: IRA, 1970.

357. _____, with Catherine Buck, "Dialect Barriers to Reading Comprehension Revisited," Reading Teacher, XXVII, No. 1 (October, 1973), 6-12.

358. Gordon, C., Jane Hansen, and P. David Pearson, "Effects of Background Knowledge on Silent Reading Comprehension," Paper presented at the American Educational Research Association Conference, Toronto, Canada, March, 1978.

359. Goslin, David, Criticism of Standardized Tests and Testing. Washington, D.C.: U.S.O.E., 1967.

360. Gough, Philip B., "One Second of Reading," in Language by Ear and by Eye: The Relationships Between Speech and Reading, eds. James Kavanagh and Ignatius G. Mattingly. Cambridge, Mass.: MIT Press, 1972.

361. Gowan, John Curtis, and George D. Demos (editors), The Disadvantaged and Potential Dropout. Springfield, Ill.: Charles C. Thomas, 1966.

362. Graves, Donald H., "What's New May Not Be Good," Language Arts, LIV, No. 6 (September, 1977), 708-713.

363. Gray, Lillian, Teaching Children to Read, Third Edition. New York: Ronald Press, 1963.

364. Gray, William S., "The Major Aspects of Reading," in Sequential Development of Reading Abilities, pp. 8-24, ed. Helen M. Robinson. Chicago: University of Chicago Press, 1960.

365. _____, On Their Own in Reading, Revised Edition. Chicago: Scott, Foresman, 1960.

366. _____, "Sequence of Reading Abilities," in Sequential Development of Reading Abilities, pp. 3-8, ed. Helen M. Robinson. Chicago: University of Chicago Press, 1960.

367. _____, and Eleanor Holmes, The Development of Meaning Vocabularies in Reading: An Experimental Study. Chicago: University of Chicago, 1938.

368. Greene, Bert I., Preventing Student Dropouts. Englewood Cliffs, N.J.: Prentice-Hall, 1966.

369. Green, Margaret Baker, "Improving the Meaning Vocabulary of Inner-City Children," in Reading Goals for the Disadvantaged, pp. 132-139, ed. J. Allen Figurel. Newark, Del.: IRA, 1970.

755

370. Groesbeck, Hulda G., The Comprehension of Figurative Language by Elementary Children: A Study in Transfer. Unpublished doctoral dissertation, University of Oklahoma, 1961.

371. Groff, Patrick, "Fifteen Flaws of Phonics," Elementary English, L, No. 1 (January, 1973), 35-40.

372. ____, "Phonics in the Middle Schools?" Clearing House, LIV, No. 4 (December, 1980), 160-163.

373. Gunn, B., "Children's Concepts of Occupational Prestige," in Guidance in the Elementary School: Theory, Research, and Practice, pp. 139-148, ed. E. D. Koplitz. Dubuque, Iowa: William C. Brown, 1968.

374. Guszak, Frank J., Diagnostic Reading Instruction in the Elementary School, Second Edition. New York: Harper, 1978.

375. ____, "Teacher Questioning and Reading," Reading Teacher, XXI, No. 3 (December, 1967), 226-234.

376. Guthrie, John T., "Research View: Follow Through: A Compensatory Education Experiment," Reading Teacher, XXXI, No. 2 (November, 1977), 240-244.

377. ____, "Research Views: School Library Circulation," Reading Teacher, XXXV, No. 3 (December, 1980), 364.

378. ____, "Teaching Style and Pupil Personalities," Reading Teacher, XXXI, No. 4 (January, 1978), 468-470.

379. Hagerty, James E. "Individualizing Instruction Through 'Ad Hoc' Grouping," in Readings on Teaching Reading, pp. 166-167, eds. Sam L. Sebesta and Carl J. Wallen. Chicago: SRA, 1972.

380. Hall, MaryAnne, Teaching Reading as a Language Experience, Third Edition. Columbus, Ohio: Merrill, 1981.

381. Hansen, Halvor P, "Language Acquisition and Development in the Child: A Teacher-Child Verbal Interaction," Elementary English, LI, No. 3 (March, 1974), 276-285, 290.

382. Harbiger, Sister Mary Joan, "Comparative Study of the Level of Reading Established by Standardized Tests and Actual Reading Levels Determined by Informal Tests," Research Abstracts, The Cardinal Stritch College, I (1958-1959), 8-12.

383. Harker, W. John, "Selecting Instructional Materials for Content Area Reading," Journal of Reading, XXI, No. 2 (November, 1977) 126-130.

384. Harris, Albert J., "Key Factors in a Successful Reading Program," in Aspects of Reading, pp. 1-8, ed. Eldonna L. Evertts. Champaign, Ill.: NCTE, 1970.

385. _____, "New Dimensions in Basal Readers," in Quest for Competency in Teaching Reading, pp. 124-130, ed. Howard A. Klein. Newark, Del.: IRA, 1972.

386. _____, "Reading Materials for Different Patterns of Grouping for Instruction," in Materials for Reading, pp. 36-42, ed. Helen M. Robinson. Chicago: University of Chicago Press, 1957.

387. _____, and Mae Knight Clark, Enchanted Gates. New York: Macmillan, 1965.

388. _____, and Milton D. Jacobson, "A Comparison of the Fry, Spache, and Harris-Jacobson Readability Formulas for Primary Grades," Reading Teacher, XXXIII, No. 8 (May, 1980), 920-923.

389. _____, and Milton D. Jacobson. "Some Comparisons Between Basic Elementary Reading Vocabularies and Other Word Lists," Reading Research Quarterly, IX, No. 1 (1973-1974), 87-109.

390. _____, and Blanche L. Serwer, "The CRAFT Project: Instructional Time in Reading Research," Reading Research Quarterly, II, No. 1 (Fall, 1966), 27-56.

391. _____, Coleman Morrison, Blanche L. Serwer, and Lynn Gold, A Continuation of the CRAFT Project: Comparing Reading Approaches with Disadvantaged Urban Negro Children in the Primary Grades, Final Report, Project 5-0570-2-12-1. New York: Selected Academic Readings, 1968.

392. _____, and Edward R. Sipay, How to Increase Reading Ability: A Guide to Developmental and Remedial Reading, Seventh Edition. New York: Longman, 1980.

393. _____, and Edward R. Sipay, How to Teach Reading: A Competency-Based Program. New York: Longman, 1979.

394. Harris, Larry, and Carl B. Smith, Reading Instruction: Diagnostic Teaching in the Classroom, Third Edition. New York: Holt, 1980.

395. Hatcher, Thomas C., The Development of Comprehension Skill in Selected Basal Readers. Unpublished doctoral dissertation, University of Northern Colorado, 1971.

396. Hedley, Carolyn, "Reading and Language," in Diagnosis of Learning Difficulties, ed. John Wilson. New York: McGraw-Hill, 1971.

397. Heider, Dorothy P., "Fostering Interest in Reading in Grades Four Through Eight," in Reading: Seventy-Five Years of Progress, pp. 111-114, ed. H. Alan Robinson. Chicago: University of Chicago Press, 1966.

398. Heilman, Arthur W., "Philosophy and Practices of a Sound Reading Program," in Improving Reading Through Classroom Practices, pp. 71-79, ed. Arthur W. Heilman. University Park: Pennsylvania State University, 1966.

399. _____, Phonics in Proper Perspective, Fourth Edition. Columbus, Ohio: Merrill, 1981.

400. _____, Timothy R. Blair, and William H. Rupley, Principles and Practices of Teaching Reading, Fifth Edition. Columbus, Ohio: Merrill, 1981.

401. Herber, Harold, Teaching Reading in the Content Areas. Englewood Cliffs, N.J.: Prentice-Hall, 1970.

402. Heyns, Barbara, Summer Learning and the Effects of Schooling.

403. Hildreth, Gertrude, "Helping Children to Read." in Reading Disabilities: Selections on Identification and Treatment," pp. 467-497, ed. Harold Newman. New York: Odyssey, 1969.

404. Hill, Walter, "Content Textbook: Help or Hindrance?" Journal of Reading, X, No. 6 (March, 1967), 408-413.

405. _____, "Evaluating Secondary Reading," in Measurement and Evaluation of Reading, pp. 126-153, ed. Roger Farr. New York: Harcourt, 1970.

406. _____, Secondary School Reading: Process, Program, Procedures. Boston: Allyn, Bacon, 1979.

407. Hillerich, Robert L., "Accountability and the Teaching of Reading," _Elementary English_, LII, No. 5 (May, 1975(, 681-687, 700.

408. _____, "Continous Assessment of Instructional _Needs_ _in_ Reading," in _Making_ _Reading_ _Possible_ _Through_ _Effective_ _Classroom_ _Management_, pp. 116-145, ed. Diane Lapp. Newark, Del.: IRA, 1980.

409. _____, "A Diagnostic Approach to Early Identification of Language Skills," _Reading_ _Teacher_, XXXI, No. 4 (January, 1978), 357-364.

410. _____, "An Interpretation of Research in Reading Readiness," _Elementary English_, No. 4 (April, 1966), 359-364, 372.

411. _____, "Work Lists -- Getting It All Together." _Reading_ _Teacher_, XXVII, No. 4 (January, 1974), 353-360.

412. Holden, Majorie H., and Walter H. MacGinitie, "Children's Conceptions of Word Boundaries in Speech and Print," _Journal_ _of_ _Educational_ _Psychology_, LXIII, No. 6 (December, 1972), 551-557.

413. Hollingworth, Paul M., "Interrelating Listening and Reading," in _Reading_ _and_ _Realism_, ed. J. Allen Figurel. Newark, Del.: IRA, 1969.

414. Holmes, Eleanor, "Vocabulary Instruction and Reading," _Elementary English Review_, XI (1934), 103-105.

415. Holmes, Jack A., and Harry Singer, The Substrata-Factor Theory: Substrata Factor Differences Underlying Reading Ability in Known Groups on the High School Level. Cooperative Research Project of the United States Office of Education. Berkeley: University of California, 1961.

416. Hong, Laraine K., "Modifying SSR for Beginning Readers," _Reading Teacher_, XXXIV, No. 8 (May, 1981), 888-891.

417. Hoyle, E., _Facing_ _the_ _Difficulties_: _Problems_ _of_ _Curriculum_ _Innovations_. Bletchley, United Kingdom: Open University Press, 1972.

418. Humphrey, Jack W., "The Effect of a Summer Television Reading Program on the Reading Achievement of Children," in _Forging_ _Ahead_ _in_ _Reading_, pp. 533-540, ed. J. Allen Figurel. Newark, Del.: IRA, 1968.

419. Hunkins, Francis P., "The Influence of Analysis and Evaluation Questions on Achievement of Sixth Grade Social Studies," Educational Leadership Journal Research Supplement (January, 1968), 326-332.

420. Hunt, Adrianne P., and Janet R. Reuter, "Readability and Children's Picture Books," Reading Teacher, XXXII, No. 1 (October, 1978), 23-27.

421. Hunt, Lyman, "The Effect of Self-Selection, Interest, and Motivation Upon Independent, Instructional, and Frustrational Levels," Reading Teacher, XXIV, No. 2 (November, 1970), 146-151.

422. Hunter, Carman St. John, with David Harman, Adult Illiteracy in the United States: A Report to the Ford Foundation, n.d.

423. Huus, Helen, "A Total Program of Reading for Children," in Quest for Competency in Teaching Reading, pp. 57-66, ed. Howard A. Klein. Newark, Del.: IRA, 1973.

424. Institute for Development of Educational Ideas, The Influence of Home Environment on the Success of First Graders as Viewed by Mothers of First-Grade Students: A National Study by Gallup International for IDEA. Dayton, Ohio: IDEA, 1969.

425. Irwin, O., "Infant Speech: Effect of Systematic Reading of Stories," Journal of Speech and Hearing Research, III (1960, 187-190.

426. Ives, Josephine P., "The Improvement of Critical Reading Skills," in Problem Areas in Reading -- Some Observations and Recommendations, ed. Coleman Morrison. Providence, R.I.: Oxford Press, 1966.

427. Janz, Margaret, and Richard Thompson, "Reading Research in Action," Florida Reading Quarterly, XVIII, No. 3 (March, 1982), 27-29.

428. Jett-Simpson, Mary, "Reading and the Language Arts: An Interview," Wisconsin State Reading Association Journal, XXVII, No. 2 (Winter, 1983), 9-13.

429. Johns, Jerry, Basic Reading Inventory. Dubuque, Iowa: Kendall/Hunt, 1978.

430. _____, "The Dimensions and Uses of Informal Reading Assessments," in Approaches to the Informal Evaluation of Reading, pp. 1-11, eds. John J. Pikulski and Timothy Shanahan. Newark, Del.: IRA, 1982.

431. _____, "The Dolch Basic Word List -- Then and Now," Journal of Reading Behavior, III, No. 4 (1970-1971), 35-40.

432. _____, "Dolch List of Common Nouns -- a Comparison," Reading Teacher, XXVIII, No. 6 (March, 1975), 538-540.

433. _____, Sharon Gaston, Paula Schoenfelder, and Patricia Skriba, Assessing Reading Behavior: Informal Reading Inventories. Newark, Del.: IRA, 1977.

434. Johnson, Dale D., "Skills Management Systems: Some Issues," Language Arts, LIV, No. 5 (May, 1977), 511-516.

435. _____, "Word Lists That Make Sense," in Classroom Practice in Reading, pp. 39-44, ed. Richard A. Earle. Newark, Del.: IRA, 1977.

435b. _____, and P. David Pearson, Teaching Reading Vocabulary, Second Edition. New York: Holt, 1984.

436. Johnson, Glen R., "A Core Vocabulary Study in the Elementary Grades," Elementary English, XXXIX, No. 5 (May, 1962), 470-473.

437. Johnson, Kenneth R., Teaching the Culturally Disadvantaged: A Rational Approach. Chicago: SRA, 1970.

438. Johnson, K.O., "The Effect of Classroom Training Upon Listening Comprehension," Journal of Communication, I (1951), 57-62.

439. Johnson, Laura S., "Bilingual Bicultural Education: A Two-Way Street," in Reading Interaction: The Teacher, The Pupil, The Materials, pp. 75-85, ed. Brother Leonard Courtney. Newark, Del.: IRA, 1976.

440. Johnson, Marjorie S., "Research and the Reality of Reading," in Children's Prose Comprehension, pp. 133-156, eds. Carol M. Santa and Bernard L. Hayes. Newark, Del.: IRA, 1981.

441. _____, and Roy A. Kress, Informal Reading Inven- tories. Newark, Del.: IRA, 1965.

442. Johnson, Wendell, et al., Speech Handicapped School Children. New York: Harper, 1967.

443. Johnston, Joyce D., "Review of Adult Literacy Education in the United States," Journal of Reading, XXI, No. 6 (March, 1978), 562-563.

443B. Kampwirth, T., and M. Bates, "Modality Preference and Teaching Method: A Reveiw of the Research," Academic Therapy, NV (1980), 597-605.

444. Karlin, Robert, "Evaluation for Diagnostic Teaching," in Assessment Problems in Reading, pp. 8-13, ed. Walter H. MacGinitie. Newark, Del.: IRA, 1973.

445. Kerfoot, James F., The Relationship of Selected Auditory and Visual Reading Readiness Measures to First Grade Reading Achievement and Second Grade Reading and Spelling Achievement. Unpublished doctoral dissertation, University of Minnesota, 1964.

446. Kidder, Carole L., "Choosing a Basal Reading Program," Reading Teacher, XXIX, No. 1 (October, 1975), 39-41.

447. King, Martha L., "Should Critical Reading Skills Be Taught in the Elementary School?" Ohio Reading Teacher, II, No. 4 (May, 1968), 2-6.

448. _____, Bernice D. Ellinger, and Willavene Wolf (Editors), Critical Reading. New York: Lippincott, 1967.

449. Klare, George R., The Measurement of Readability. Ames: Iowa State University Press, 1963.

450. Klesius, Stephen E., "Perceptual-Motor Development and Reading," Proceedings of the College Reading Association, XI (1970), 37-44.

451. Knapp, Clifford E., "Exploring the Outdoors with Young People," Science and Children, XVII, No. 2 (October, 1979), 22-24.

452. Kounin, Jacob, Discipline and Group Management in Classrooms. New York: Holt, 1970.

453. Kravitz, Alvin, and Dan Dramer, "Survival Reading: The Real Life Skills for Real Reading," Address presented at the International Reading Association, Houston, Texas, 1978.

454. Kucera, Henry, and W. Nelson Francis, Computational Analysis of Present-Day American English. Providence, R.I.: Brown University Press, 1967.

455. LaBerge, David, and S.J. Samuels, "Toward a Theory of Automatic Information Processing in Reading," in Theoretical Models and Processes of Reading, Second Edition. pp. 548-579, eds. Harry Singer and Robert Ruddell. Newark, Del.: IRA, 1976.

456. Ladd, Eleanor M., "The Expansion Model for Teaching the Main Idea," Tar Heel Reading Journal, III, No. 2 (Summer, 1983), 3-10.

457. _____, "South Carolina Council of the International Reading Association Study on Main Idea," IRA Speaks, VII, No. 1 (Fall, 1983), 1, 5.

458. Lamme, Linda Leonard, "Reading Aloud to Young Children," Language Arts, LIII, No. 8 (November-December, 1976), 886-888.

459. Landry, Donald L., "The Neglect of Listening," Elementary English, XLVI (1969), 599-605.

460. Lee, Doris, Alma Bingham, and Sue Woefel, Critical Reading Develops Early. Newark, Del.: IRA, 1968.

461. Lefevre, Carl A., Linguistics and the Teaching of Reading. New York: McGraw-Hill, 1964.

462. Letton, Mildred C., "Use and Misuse of Workbooks and Teachers' Guides in Grades Seven and Eight," in Materials for Reading, pp. 81-85, ed. Helen M. Robinson. Chicago: University of Chicago Press, 1957.

463. Lewis, M., "Teaching Children to Listen," Education, LXXX (1960), 455-459.

464. Lezotte, Lawrence W., "Characteristics of Effective Schools and Programs for Realizing Them," Citizen Actions in Education, IX (June, 1982), 1, 10-11.

465. Lillie, David L., Early Childhood Education: An Individualized Approach to Developmental Instruction. Chicago: SRA, 1975.

466. Livingston, Howard F., "What the Reading Test Doesn't Test - Reading," Journal of Reading, XV, No. 6 (March, 1972), 402-410.

467. Lloyd, Helen M., "Progress in Developmental Reading for Today's Disadvantaged," in Elementary Reading Instruction: Selected Materials, pp. 529-533, eds. Althea Beery, Thomas C. Barrett, and William R. Powell. Boston: Allyn, Bacon, 1969.

468. _____, "Reading Instruction for the Disadvantaged: Is It Adequate?" in Current Issues in Reading, pp. 134-147, ed. Nila Banton Smith. Newark, Del.: IRA, 1969.

469. Loban, Walter, Language Ability, Cooperative Research Monograph No. 18 OE 30018. Washington, D.C.: U.S.O.E., 1969.

470. _____, The Language of Elementary School Children. Research Report No. 1. Champaign, Ill.: NCTE, 1963.

471. Lowe, Al J., and John Follman, "Comparison of the Dolch List with Other Word Lists," Reading Teacher, XXVIII, No. 1 (October, 1974), 40-44.

472. Lubway, Raymond, "Promoting Growth in Inter- preting in Grades Four Through Eight," in Reading: Seventy-Five Years of Progress, pp. 85-89, ed. H. Alan Robinson. Chicago: University of Chicago Press, 1966.

473. MacGinitie, Walter H., "Children's Understanding of Linguistic Units," in What Research Has to Say about Reading Instruction, pp. 43-56, ed. S. Jay Samuels. Newark, Del.: IRA, 1978.

474. _____, "An Introduction to Some Measurement Problems in Reading," in Assessment Problems in Reading, pp. 1-7, ed. Walter H. MacGinitie. Newark, Del.: IRA, 1973.

475. _____, "When Should We Begin to Teach Reading?" Language Arts, LIII, No. 8 (November-December, 1976), 876-882.

476. Mackintosh, Helen K., Lillian Gore, and Gertrude M. Lewis, Administration of Elementary School Programs for Disadvantaged Children. Washington, D.C.: U.S.O.E., 1966.

477. _____, Educating Disadvantaged Children in the Primary Years. Washington, D.C.: U.S.O.E., 1965.

478. _____, Educating Disadvantaged Children Under Six. Washington, D.C.: U.S.O.E. 1965.

479. Maeroff, Gene I., in Education Summary (October 15, 1977), 5.

480. Maginnis, George H., "Measuring Underachievement in Reading," Reading Teacher, XXV, No. 8 (May, 1972), 750-753.

481. Malicky, Grace, and Dennis Schienbein, "Inferencing Behavior of Good and Poor Readers," Reading Improvement, XVIII, No. 4 (Winter, 1981), 335-338.

482. Manning, John C., "Assessing Pupil Growth in Language," in Language Arts in the Elementary School: Readings, pp. 461-468, eds. Hal D. Funk and DeWayne Triplett. Philadelphia: Lippincott, 1972.

483. _____, "Ensuring Reading Success," in Improving Reading in the Intermediate Years, pp. 73-83, ed. Helen M. Robinson. Glenview, Ill.: Scott, Foresman, n.d.

484. _____, "Improving Basic Reading Programs in Major American Cities: The Minneapolis Story," in Opportunities for Reading Improvement-Our Responsibility, pp. 20-28, ed. Richard C. Culyer, III. Mt. Gilead, N.C.: North Carolina Council of the International Reading Association, 1974.

485. Manzo, Anthony V., Improving Reading Instruction through Reciprocal Questioning. Unpublished doctoral dissertation, Syracuse University, 1969.

486. Marksheffel, Ned D., "Aspects of Books that Affect Readability and Use," in Forging Ahead in Reading, pp. 136-139, ed. J. Allen Figurel. Newark, Del.: IRA, 1968.

487. _____, Improving Reading in the Secondary School: Principles and Procedures for Teachers. New York: Ronald Press, 1966.

488. Martin, Bill, Jr., Sounds of a Distant Drum, Teacher's Edition. New York: Holt, 1967.

489. Mason, Jana M., and C. McCormick, Testing the Development of Reading and Linguistic Awareness, Technical Report 126. Urbana, Ill.: Center for the Study of Reading, 1979.

490. _____, Jean H. Osborn, and Barak V. Rosenshine, A Consideration of Skill Hierachy Approaches to the Teaching of Reading, Technical Report No. 42. Urbana, Ill.: Center for the Study of Reading, 1977.

491. Mathews, Virginia H., "Making the Right to Read Real," Scholastic Teacher (December, 1970, n.p.

765

492. May, Ann Baldwin, "All the Angles of Idiom Instruction," _Reading Teacher_, XXXII, No. 6 (March, 1979), 680–682.

493. Mazurkiewicz, Albert J., "Comprehension Skills and Developmental Techniques," in _New Perspectives in Reading Instruction: A Book of Readings_, pp. 270–294, ed. Albert J. Mazurkiewicz. New York: Pitman, 1964.

494. _____, Teaching About Phonics_. New York: St. Martin's Press, 1976.

495. McCallister, James M., "Aspects of Books that Affect Readability and Use in Science," in _Materials for Reading_, pp. 174–178, ed. Helen M. Robinson. Chicago: Unversity of Chicago Press, 1957.

496. McCormick, Ethel M., "Language and Number Skills Needed in Reading and Arithmetic," in _Getting Meaning in Reading and Arithmetic_, pp. 29–32, ed. Russell G. Stauffer. Newark: University of Delaware, 1956.

497. McCracken, Robert A., "Basic Principles of Reading Instruction in the Seventh Grade," _High Trails: Teacher's Edition_. Boston: Allyn, Bacon, 1968.

498. _____, The Informal Reading Inventory as a Means of Improving Instruction," in _The Evaluation of Children's Reading Achievement_, pp. 79–96, ed. Thomas C. Barrett. Newark, Del.: IRA, 1967.

499. _____, "Standardized Reading Tests and Informal Reading Inventories," _Education_, LXXXII (February, 1962), 366–367.

500. _____, and Marlene J. McCracken, "Modeling Is the Key to Sustained Silent Reading," _Reading Teacher_, XXXI, No. 4, (January, 1978), 406–408.

501. McCullough, Constance, "The Recognition of Context Clues in Reading," _Elementary English Review_, XXII, No. 1 (January, 1945), 1–8, 38.

502. McDonald, Arthur S., "Some Pitfalls in Evaluating Progress in Reading Instruction," in _Measurement and Evaluation of Reading_, pp. 358–365, ed. Roger Farr. New York: Harcourt, 1970.

503. McDonell, Gloria, and E. Bess Osburn, "New Thoughts About Reading Readiness," _Language Arts_, LV, No. 1 (January, 1978), 26–29.

504. McFeely, Donald C, "Syllabication Usefulness in a Basal and Social Studies Vocabulary," Reading Teacher, XXVII, No. 8 (May, 1974), 809-814.

505. McGovern, Jill, "Auditory Perception: A Review of the Literature," Academic Therapy, XIV, No. 4 (March, 1979), 445-460.

506. McHugh, Walter J., "Indices of Success in First Grade Reading." Paper presented at the Joint AERA-IRA meeting. Chicago, Ill., February, 1962.

507. McKee, Paul, The Teaching of Reading in the Elementary School. Cambridge, Mass.: Houghton Mifflin, 1948.

508. _____, and William K. Durr, Reading: A Program of Instruction for the Elementary School. Boston: Houghton Mifflin, 1966.

508B. McKenzie, Gary R., Facilitating Inferential Thinking with Weekly Quizzes. Paper presented at the conference of the American Educational Research Association, New York, February, 1971.

509. _____, "Helping Students Learn What Teachers Mean to Teach," Education Digest, XLVI, No. 9 (May, 1981), 2-5.

510. McNinch, George, "Awareness of Aural and Visual Word Boundary Within a Sample of First Graders," Perceptual and Motor Skills, XXXVIII (June, 1974), 1127, 1134.

511. Miller, John W., and Frances W. Marshall, "Teachers' Abilities to Judge the Difficulty of Reading Materials," Presentation at the International Reading Association's Annual Convention, 1978.

512. Miller, Virginia, "Treasures for the Telling," Reading Teacher, XXIV, No. 4 (January, 1971), 375-377.

513. Miller, William A., "The Picture Choices of Primary-Grade Children," Elementary School Journal, XXXVII (1936), 273-282.

514. Miller, Wilma H., The First R: Elementary Reading Today, Second Edition. New York: Holt, 1977.

514B. Mills, Queenie B., "Disadvantaged Child," in Read- ing Disabilities: Selections on Identification and Treatment, pp. 434-443, ed. Harold Newman. New York: Odyssey, 1969.

767

515. Mills, Robert, The Teaching of Word Recognition Including Manual of Directions for Mills Learning Methods Test, Revised Edition. Fort Lauderdale, Fla.: The Mills Center, n.d.

516. _____, and Jean R. Richardson, "What Do Publishers Mean By Grade Level?" in Elementary Reading Instruction: Selected Materials, pp. 164-176, eds. Althea Beery, Thomas C. Barrett, and William R. Powell. Boston: Allyn, Bacon, 1969.

517. Mitchell, Ronald W., A Comparison of Children's Responses to an Original and Experimental Form of GS and ND of the Gates Basic Reading Tests. Unpublished doctoral dissertation, University of Minnesota, 1967.

518. _____, Kindergarten Children's Responses to Selected Visual Discrimination Exercises in Reading Readiness Materials. Minneapolis: University of Minnesota, 1965.

519. Moffett, James, and Betty Jane Wagner, Student-Centered Language Arts and Reading, K-13: A Handbook for Teachers, Third Edition. Boston: Houghton Mifflin, 1983.

520. Moore, Jesse, Clarence J. Jones, and Douglas C. Miller, "What We Know After a Decade of Sustained Silent Reading," Reading Teacher, XXXIII, No. 4 (January, 1980), 445-449.

521. "More Money Not Likely to Improve Schools, Study Concludes," Charlotte Observer, March 9, 1972.

522. Morency, Anne, "Auditory Modality, Research and Practice," in Perception and Reading, pp. 17-21, ed. Helen K. Smith. Newark, Del.: IRA, 1968.

523. Mork, Theodore A., "The Ability of Children to Select Reading Materials at Their Own Instructional Reading Level," in Assessment Problems in Reading, pp. 87-95, ed. Walter H. MacGinitie. Newark, Del.: IRA, 1973.

524. _____, "Sustained Silent Reading in the Classroom," Reading Teacher, XXV, No. 5 (February, 1972), 438-441.

525. Morris, Darrell R., "Some Aspects of the Instructional Environment and Learning to Read," Language Arts, LVI, No. 5 (May, 1979), 497-502.

526. Morrison, Ida E., Teaching Reading in the Elementary School. New York: Ronald Press, 1968.

527. Morrow, Yvonne, Personal Correspondence, August 11, 1983.

528. Muehl, Siegman, and Ethel M. King, Recent Research in Visual Discrimination Significance of Beginning Reading," in Vistas in Reading, pp. 434-439, ed. J. Allen Figurel. Newark, Del.: IRA, 1967.

529. Mueller, Doris L, "Teacher Questioning Practices in Reading," Reading World, (December, 1972), 136-145.

530. Mueller, Sandra, "Interview -- Kenneth B. Clark," Reading Newsreport, V, No. 1 (October, 1970), 4-9.

531. A Nation at Risk! Report to the Nation of the National Commission on Excellence in Education, 1983.

532. National Advisory Council on the Education of Disadvantaged Children, Educationg the Disadvantaged Child: Where We Stand, Annual Report to the President and the Congress. Washington, D.C.: By the Council, 1972.

533. "National Assessment of Educational Progress Reading Results," Education Digest, XLVII, No. 1 (September, 1971), 66-68.

534. National School Public Relations Association, Compensatory Education: What Works to Help Disadvantaged Children. Washington, D.C.: NSPRA, 1973.

535. Neill, Shirley Boes, "The Demographers' Message to Education," American Education, XV, No. 1 (January-February, 1979), 6-11.

536. Nelson, Joan, "Readability: Some Cautions for the Content Area Teacher," Journal of Reading, XXI, No. 7 (April, 1978), 615-619.

537. New York City Board of Education, "Developing a Meaning Vocabulary," in Reading Disabilities: Selections on Identification and Treatment, pp. 265-283, ed. Harold Newman. New York: Odyssey, 1969.

538. Newbury, Dorothy J., "Conclusions Concerning Sequential Development of Reading Abilities in Kindergarten Through Grade Three," in Sequential Development of Reading Abilities, pp. 224-225, ed. Helen M. Robinson. Chicago: University of Chicago Press, 1960.

539. "Newsfronts," Reading Newsreport, V, No. 7 (May-June, 1971), unpaged.

540. Nila, Sister Mary, "Foundations of a Successful Reading Program," Education, LXXIII (May, 1953), 543-545.

541. Niles, Olive S., "Comprehension Skills," Reading Teacher, XVII, No. 1 (September, 1963), 2-7.

542. Ninerk, Nedra, "Reading Nits and Bits," Indiana Reading Quarterly, VII, No. 2 (Winter, 1975), 9-12,31.

543. "Non-Graded School: Part I," National Elementary Principal, XLVII, No. 2 (November, 1967), entire issue.

544. Norris, W., Occupational Information in the Elementary School. Chicago: SRA, 1963.

545. North Carolina Department of Public Instruction, Reading: 1974-1975. Raleigh, N.C.: State Department of Public Instruction, 1975.

546. Oliver, Jo Ellen, and Richard D. Arnold, "Comparing a Standardized Test: an Informal Inventory and Teacher Judgment on Third Grade Reading," Reading Improvement, XV (Spring, 1978), 56-58.

547. Ollila, Lloyd O. (editor), The Kindergarten Child and Reading. Newark, Del.: IRA, 1977.

548. Olson, Arthur V., "An Analysis of the Vocabulary of Seven Primary Reading Series," Elementary English, XLII, No. 3 (March, 1965), 261-264.

549. _____, "Reading The Approaches We Use," in Reading and the Elementary School Child: Selected Readings on Programs and Practices, pp. 175-181, eds. Virgil M. Howes and Helen R. Darrow. New York: Macmillan, 1968.

549B. Olson, Lynn, "Reading Skills Up But Leveling Off," Education Week, V, No. 4 (September 25, 1985), 1, 17.

550. Olson, James H., James Childs, and Jeanne Hammond, "The Role of the Administrator," in Handbook for Administrators and Teachers, Reading in the Kindergarten, ed. Lloyd O. Ollila. Newark, Del.: IRA, 1980.

551. Omotoso, Sam O., "Using Wordless Picture Books to Assess Cross-Cultural Differences in Seven Year Olds," Reading Teacher, XXXII, No. 4 (January, 1979), 414-416.

552. Otto, Wayne, "Evaluating Instruments for Assessing Needs and Growth in Reading," in Assessment Problems in Reading, pp. 14-20, ed. Walter H. MacGinitie. Newark, Del.: IRA, 1973.

553. _____, Robert Chester, and Mary Mehling, "Further Validation of the Great Atlantic and Pacific Sight Word List," Journal of Educational Research, LXVII, No. 8 (April, 1974), 363-365.

554. Packer, Athol B., "Ashton-Warner's Key Vocabulary for the Disadvantaged," Reading Teacher, XXIII, No. 6 (March, 1970), 559-564.

555. Painter, Helen W., "Critical Reading in the Primary Grades," Reading Teacher, XIX, No. 1 (October, 1965), 35-39.

556. Paradis, Edward, and Joseph Peterson, "Readiness Training Implications from Research," Reading Teacher, XXVIII, No. 5 (February, 1975), 445-448.

557. Parker, Donald H., SRA Reading Laboratories. Chicago: SRA.

558. Pate, Robert T., and Neville H. Bremer, "Guiding Learning Through Skillful Questioning," Elementary School Journal, LXVII, No. 5 (May, 1967), 417-422.

559. Pearson, P. David, "A Psycholinguistic Model of Reading," Language Arts, LIII, No. 3 (March, 1976), 309-314.

560. _____, and Dale D. Johnson, Teaching Reading Compre- hension. New York: Holt, 1978.

561. Penty, Ruth C., Reading Ability and High School Dropouts. New York: Teachers College Press, 1956.

562. Perez, Eustolia, "Oral Language Competence Improves Reading Skills of Mexican American Third Graders," Reading Teacher, XXXV, No. 1 (October, 1981), 24-27.

563. Perez, Samuel A., "The Effects of Summer Vacation on Reading Retention," Unpublished paper, n.d.

564. Personke, Carl, "Generalization and Spelling: Boon or Bust?" in The Language Arts in the Elementary School: A Forum for Focus, pp. 148-157, eds. Martha L. King, Robert Emans, and Patricia J. Cianciolo. Urbana, Ill.: NCTE, 1973.

565. Peters, Henry B., "Vision Screening with a Snellen Chart," American Journal of Optometry and Archives of American Academy of Optometry, XXXVIII, (September, 1961), 485-505.

771

566. Petre, Richard M., "Reading Breaks Make it in Maryland," _Journal of Reading_, XV, No. 3 (December, 1971), 191-194.

567. Petty, Walter T., Curtis P. Herald, and Earline Stoll, _The State of Knowledge about the Teaching of Vocabulary_. Champaign, Ill.: NCTE, 1968.

568. Pikulski, John, "A Critical Review: Informal Reading Inventories," _Reading Teacher_, XXVIII, No. 2 (November, 1974), 141-151.

569. _____, and Timothy Shanahan, "Informal Reading Inventories: A Critical Anaylsis," in _Approaches to the Informal Evaluation of Reading_, pp. 94-116, eds. John J. Pikulski and Timothy Shanahan. Newark, Del.: IRA, 1982.

570. Poling, Dorothy L., _The Relationship of Auditory Discrimination to Reading Achievement_. Unpublished doctoral dissertation, University of Chicago, 1968.

571. Pow, Beth, "Stimulating Young Children for Creative Writing," in _Translating Theory into Practice_, pp. 43-57, ed. Richard C. Culyer, III. Mt. Gilead,: North Carolina Council of the International Reading Association, 1972.

572. Powell, William R., "Reaprraising the Criteria for Interpreting Informal Inventories," Address to the International Reading Association, Boston, 1968.

573. Preston, Ralph C., "Ability of Students to Identify Correct Responses Before Reading," _Journal of Educational Research_, LVIII, No. 4 (December, 1964), 181-183.

574. Prince, Dorothy, "Step By Step We Grow in English," _Elementary English_, XL, No. 4 (April, 1963), 436-439.

575. Pyrczak, Fred, "Objective Evaluation of the Quality of Multiple-Choice Items Designed to Measure Comprehension of Reading Passages," _Reading Research Quarterly_, VIII, No. 1 (Fall, 1972), 62-72.

576. _____, "Passage Dependence of Reading Comprehension Questions: Examples," _Journal of Reading_, XVIII, No. 4 (January, 1975), 308-311.

577. _____, and Jerome Axelrod, "Determining the Passage Dependence of Reading Comprehension Exercises: A Call for Replications," _Journal of Reading_, XIX, No. 4 (January, 1976), 279-283.

578. Railsback, Charles E., "Consonant Substitution in Word Attack," Reading Teacher, XXIII, No. 5 (February, 1970), 432-435.

579. Ransom, Grayce, "The Barstow Study of Predictors of Reading Success in First Grade: Language, Visual and Auditory Perception Factors." Unpublished manuscript, University of Southern California, 1967.

580. _____, Preparing to Teach Reading. Boston: Little, Brown, 1978.

581. Rauch, Sidney J., "A Checklist for the Evaluation of Reading Programs," Reading Teacher, XXI, No. 6 (March, 1968), 519-522.

582. "Reading Readiness: For Whom? And When?" Reading Newsreport, I, No. 2 (November-December), 13-15.

583. Reeve, Olive R., "The Vocabulary of Seven Primary Reading Series," Elementary English, XXV, No. 4 (April, 1958), 237-239.

584. Reid, J. F., "Learning to Think About Reading," Educational Research, IX (1966), 56-92.

585. Rich, Dorothy, "Underachievement is Developed by Schools," Charlotte Observer, April 8, 1967.

586. Riesman, Frank, The Culturally Deprived Child. New York: Harper, 1962.

587. Rinsland, Henry D., A Basic Vocabulary of Elementary School Children. New York: Macmillan, 1945.

588. Robinson, H. Alan, Reading in the Total School Curriculum," in Reading and Realism, pp. 1-8, ed. J. Allen Figurel. Newark, Del.: IRA, 1969.

589. _____ (editor), The Underachiever in Reading. Chicago: University of Chicago Press, 1962.

590. _____, and Sidney J. Rauch, Guiding the Reading Program: A Reading Consultant's Handbook. Chicago: SRA, 1965.

591. Robinson, Helen M., "Developing Critical Readers," in Dimensions of Critical Reading, pp. 1-12, ed. Russell G. Stauffer. Newark, Del.: IRA, 1964.

592. ____, "Questions, Discussions, and Assignments to Promote Critical Reading," in Improving Reading in the Intermediate Years, pp. 137-153, ed. Helen M. Robinson. Glenview, Ill.: Scott, Foresman, 1973.

593. ____ (editor), Sequential Development of Reading Abilities, Chicago: University of Chicago Press, 1960.

594. ____, et al., More Power. Glenview, Ill.: Scott, Foresman, 1968.

595. Rodenborn, Leo V., "Determining, Using Expectancy Formulas," Reading Teacher, XXVIII, No. 3 (December, 1974), 286-291.

596. ____, and Earlene Washburn, "Some Implications of the New Basal Readers," Elementary English, LI, No. 6 (September, 1974), 885-889.

597. Roeber, Edward C., Counseling the Potential Drop-out. Boston: Research Publishing, 1955.

598. Roehler, Laura R., and Gerald G. Duffy, "Matching Direct Instruction to Reading Outcomes," Language Arts, LIX, No. 5 (May, 1982), 476-480.

599. Rosen, Carl I., "An Experimental Study of Visual Perceptual Training and Reading Achievement in First Grade," Perceptual and Motor Skills, XXII (June, 1966), pp. 979-986.

600. Rosenshine, Barak, "Content, Time and Direct Instruction," in Research on Teaching: Concepts, Findings and Implications, eds. H. Walberg and P. Peterson. Berkeley, Calif.: McCutchan Publishing, 1979.

601. ____, "Recent Research on Teaching Behaviors and Student Achievement," Paper presented at the National International Conference of Research on Teacher Effects, Austin, Texas, 1975.

602. Rosenthal, Robert, and Lenore Jacobson, Pygmalion in the Classroom. New York: Holt, 1968.

603. Ross, Patrecia, "Regression Study--Now the Long Hot Summer," Reading Teacher, XXVIII, No. 1 (October, 1974), 28-30.

604. Rouk, Ullik, "Separate Studies Show Similar Results of Teacher Effectiveness," Educational Research and Development Report, II, No. 2 (Spring, 1979), 6-10.

774

605. Rowe, Mary Budd, "Give Students Time to Respond," School Science and Mathematics, LXXVIII (March, 1978), 207-216.

606. Rowell, C. Glennon, Class presentation on research and the teaching of spelling, Florida State University, Tallahassee, Fla., April 19, 1973.

607. Ruddell, Robert B., "Oral Language and the Develop- ment of Other Language Skills," Elementary English, XLIII (1966), 489-498, 517.

608. _____, Reading-Language Instruction: Innovative Practices. Englewood Cliffs, N.J.: Prentice-Hall, 1974.

609. _____, and Arthur W. Williams, A Research Investigation of a Literacy Teaching Model: Project Delta. Washington, D.C.: U.S. Department of Health, Education, and Welfare, 1972.

610. _____, and Helen Bacon, "The Nature of Reading: Language and Meaning," in Language and Learning to Read: What Teachers Should Know About Language, eds. Richard Hodges and Erwin H. Rudorf. Boston: Houghton Mifflin, 1972.

611. Rumelhart, David E., Toward an Interactive Model of Reading, Technical Report No. 56. San Diego: University of California Center for Human Information Processing, 1976.

612. Russell, David H., Children Learn to Read, Second Edition. Boston: Ginn, 1961.

613. _____, and Elizabeth F. Russell, Listening Aids Through the Grades. New York: Teachers College Press, 1959.

614. Russell, R.D., "A Comparison of Two Methods of Learning," Journal of Educational Research, XVIII (1923), 235-238.

615. Rutter, Florence, "Vocabulary Development," Reading Teacher, XXIX, No. 4 (January, 1976), 402-403.

616. Sadoski, Mark C., "Ten Years of Uninterrupted Sustained Silent Reading," Reading Improvement, XVII, No. 2 (Summer, 198), 153-156.

617. Saily, Mary, "Free the Teacher," Educational Research and Development Report, IV, No. 3 (Fall, 1981), 8-12.

618. Salganik, M. William, "Researchers Team with Reporter to Identify Schools that Work," Educational Research and Development Report, III, No. 1 (Winter, 1980), 2-7.

619. Saltz, Martin, A Comparative Analysis of Selected Basal Reader Series. Unpublished doctoral dissertation, University of Connecticut, 1965.

620. Sample, Gerald T., A Comparative Study of the Scope, Sequence, and Timing of the Introduction of Phonics as Predicted by Some Publishers of Reading Series. Unpublished doctoral dissertation, University of Oklahoma, 1966.

621. Samuels, S. Jay, "Characteristics of Exemplary Reading Programs," in Comprehension and Teaching: Research Reviews, pp. 255-273, ed. John T. Guthrie. Newark, Del.: IRA, 1981.

622. ____, "The Effects of Letter-Name Knowledge on Learning to Read," American Educational Research Journal, IX, No. 1 (Winter, 1972), 65-74.

623. Santa, Carol, "Visual Discrimination: Implications for Reading Readiness and Word Recognition." Paper presented at the IRA, New York, 1975.

624. Sanders, Norris M., Classroom Questions -- What Kinds? New York: Harper, 1966.

625. Sangster, Margaret E., "The Sin of Omission," in Poems That Touch the Heart, comp. A.L. Alexander. Garden City, New York: Doubleday, 1956.

626. Sartain, Harry W., "Administrative Responsibilities for In-Service Training in Combining Sequential and Individual Reading," in Sequential Development of Reading Abilities, pp. 187-190, ed. Helen M. Robinson. Chicago: University of Chicago Press, 1960.

627. Schell, Leo M., Fundamentals of Decoding for Teachers, Second Editon. Chicago: Rand McNally, 1979.

628. ____, "Teaching Structural Analysis," Reading Teacher, XXI, No. 2 (November, 1967), 133-137.

629. Schiffman, Gilbert B., "Corrective Reading and the Total School Program," Perspectives in Reading - Corrective Reading in the Elementary Classroom, pp. 129-138, eds. Majorie Seddon Johnson and Roy A. Kress. Newark, Del.: IRA, 1967.

630. ____, "Total Language Arts Commitment -- Kindergarten Through Twelfth Grade," Reading Teacher, XXII, No. 2 (November, 1968), 115-121.

631. Schnayer, Sidney W., and Leona A. Robinson, "An Analysis of Phonic Systems for the Primary Grades in Eight Basal Reader Series," Journal of the Reading Specialist, IX, No. 2 (December, 1969), 58-72.

632. Schonell, F.J., Essentials in Teaching and Testing Spelling. London: Macmillan, 1955.

633. Schreiber, Daniel D. (editor), Guidance and the School Dropout. Washington, D.C.: NEA, 1964.

634. Schubert, Delwyn G., "An Ounce of Prevention," Elementary English, L, No. 6 (September, 1973), 948-951.

635. _____, "The Role of Interest and Motivation in the Reading Process," in Views on Elementary Reading Instruction, pp. 59-64, eds. Thomas C. Barrett and Dale D. Johnson. Newark, Del.: IRA, 1973.

636. Schultheis, Robert A., "Time to Stop Labeling and Start Teaching," American Vocational Journal, L (October, 1975), 53-57.

637. Seashore, R.H., "The Importance of Vocabulary in Learning Language Skills," Elementary English, XXV (1948), 137-152.

638. Sheldon, William D., et al., Sheldon Basic Reading Series, Centennial Edition. Boston: Allyn, Bacon, 1968.

639. Silvaroli, Nicholas J., Teacher Manual and Classroom Reading Inventory, Fourth Edition. Dubuque, Iowa: William C. Brown, 1982.

640. Simpson, Sara, Ways to Ensure Mastery Learning. Kings Mountain, N.C.: By the author, 1979.

641. Singer, Harry, "Research in Reading That Should Make a Difference in Classroom Instruction," in What Research Has to Say About Reading, pp. 57-71, ed. S. Jay Samuels. Newark, Del.: 1978.

642. _____, 'Resolving Curricular Conflicts in the 1970's: Modifying the Hypothesis, It's the Teacher Who Makes the Difference in Reading Achievement," Language Arts, LIV, No. 2 (February, 1977), 158-163.

643. Sipay, Edward R., A Comparison of Standardized Reading Achievement Test Scores and Functional Reading Levels. Unpublished doctoral dissertation, University of Connecticut, 1961.

644. _____, "Interpreting the USOE Cooperative Reading Studies," Reading Teacher, XXII, No. 1 (October, 1968), 10-16, 35.

645. Smith, Carl B., "Evaluating Title I and Innovative Reading Programs: Problems and Procedures," in Measurement and Evaluation of Reading, pp. 60-79, ed. Roger Farr. New York: Harcourt, 1970.

646. Smith, Charlotte T., "Improving Comprehension? That's a Good Question," in Reading Comprehension at Four Linguistic Levels, pp. 94-103, ed. Clifford Pennock. Newark, Del.: IRA, 1979.

647. Smith, Frank, Psycholinguistics and Reading. New York: Holt, 1973.

648. Smith, Helen K. (editor), Perception and Reading. Newark, Del.: IRA, 1968.

649. _____, "Sequence in Comprehension," in Sequential Development of Reading Abilities, pp. 51-56, ed. Helen M. Robinson. Chicago: University of Chicago Press, 1960.

650. Smith, Irene B., "Methods and Materials for Teaching Word Perception in Kindergarten Through Grade Three," in Sequential Development of Reading Abilities, pp. 31-35, ed. Helen M. Robinson. Chicago: University of Chicago, 1960.

651. Smith, James A., Creative Teaching of Reading and Literature in the Elementary School. Boston: Allyn, Bacon, 1967.

652. _____, Creative Teaching of the Language Arts in the Elementary School. Boston: Allyn, Bacon, 1967.

653. Smith, Madorah E., "An Investigation of the Development of the Sentence and the Extent of Vocabulary in Young Children," Studies in Child Welfare, III. Iowa City: State University of Iowa, 1926.

654. Smith, Mary Katherine, "Measurement of the Size of General English Vocabulary Through the Elementary Grades and High School," Genetic Psychology Monographs, XXIV (1941), 311-345.

655. Smith, Mildred Beatty, "Expectations for Pupil Achievement," in Improving Reading in the Intermediate Years, pp. 9-18, ed. Helen M. Robinson. Glenview, Ill.: Scott, Foresman, 1973.

656. Smith, Nila Banton, "Cultural Dialects: Current Problems and Solutions," Reading Teacher, XXIX, No. 2 (November, 1975), 137-141.

657. _____, Graded Selections for Informal Reading Diagnosis, Grades 1-3. New York: New York University Press, 1959.

658. _____, and Anna Harris, Graded Selections for Informal Reading Diagnosis, Grades 4 Through 6. New York: New York University Press, 1963.

659. _____, and Ruth Strickland, Some Approaches to Reading. Washington, D.C.: Association for Childhood Education International, 1969.

660. Smith, Richard J., and Thomas C. Barrett, Teaching Reading in the Middle Grades. Reading, Mass.: Addison-Wesley, 1974.

661. _____, and Virginia C. Edds, "The Perceptions of Reading Specialists Regarding Their Training and Responsibilities," Wisconsin State Reading Association Journal, XXV, No. 2 (January, 1981), 11-17.

662. Soar, Robert, Follow-Through Classroom Process Measurement and Pupil Growth (1970-1971): Final Report. Gainesville: University of Florida, 1973.

663. Sochor, E. Elona, "The Nature of Critical Reading," Elementary English, XXXVI (1959), 47-58.

664. Solomon, D., and A.J. Kendall, Individual Characteristics and Children's Performance in Varied Educational Settings, Final Report. Rockville, Md.: Montgomery County Public Schools, 1976.

665. South Carolina Word List. Los Angeles, Cal.: Instructional Objectives Exchange, 1980.

666. Spache, George D., Diagnosing and Correcting Reading Disabilities. Rockleigh, N.J.: Allyn, Bacon, 1976.

667. _____, Investigating the Issues of Reading Disabilities. Boston: Allyn, Bacon, 1976.

668. _____, Parents and the Reading Program. Champaign, Ill.: Garrard, 1965.

669. _____, "A Phonics Manual for Primary and Remedial Teachers," Elementary English Review, XVI (April-May, 1939), 147-150, 191.

779

670.   ____, _Toward Better Reading_. Champaign, Ill.: Garrard, 1963.

671.   ____, M.C. Andres, and H.A. Curtis, _A Longitudinal First Grade Reading Readiness Program_. Cooperative Research Project No. 2742. Tallahassee: Florida State Department of Education, 1965.

672.   ____, and Evelyn Spache, "Achievement for Below-Level Readers," _Education Update_, Issue 11 (Fall, 1982), 4-5.

673.   ____, and Evelyn B. Spache, _Reading in the Elementary School_. Fourth Edition. Boston: Allyn, Bacon, 1977.

674.   ____, _et al._, "A Longitudinal First-Grade Reading Readiness Program," _Reading Teacher_, XIX, No. 8 (May, 1966), 580-584.

675.   Spearritt, Donald, "Identification of Subskills of Reading Competence by Maximum Likelihood Factor Analysis," _Reading Research Quarterly_, VIII, No. 1 (Fall, 1972), 92-111.

676.   "Survey Questions for Evaluating Reading Programs," in _Teaching Elementary Reading_, pp. 66-68, author Robert Karlin. New York: Harcourt, 1971.

677.   Stallings, J.A., _Implementation and Child Effects of Teaching Practices in Follow-Through Classrooms_. Monographs of the Society for Research in Child Development, XL, Nos. 7-8, December, 1975.

678.   ____, and D.H. Kaskowitz, "A Study of Follow-Through Implementation," Paper presented at the American Educational Research Association Conference, Menlo Park, Cal.: April, 1975.

679.   Stanchfield, J., Personal Correspondence, March 17, 1983.

680.   Stauffer, Russell G., "Certain Convictions about Reading Instruction," in _Aspects of Reading_, pp. 9-13, ed. Eldonna L. Evertts. Champaign, Ill.: NCTE, 1970.

681.   ____, "Language Experience Approach," in _The First Grade Programs_, pp. 86-118, ed. James F. Kerfoot. Newark, Del.: IRA, 1965.

682.   ____, _The Language-Experience Approach to the Teaching of Reading_. New York: Harper, 1970.

683.   ____, _Teaching Reading as a Thinking Process_. New York: Harper, 1969.

684. _____, "A Vocabulary Study Comparing Reading, Arithmetic, Health, and Science Texts," Reading Teacher, XX, No. 2 (November, 1966), 141-147.

685. _____, and Ronald Cramer, Teaching Critical Reading at the Primary Level. Newark, Del.: IRA, 1968.

686. Stenson, Carol M., "Yes, Workbooks Are Too Hard to Read!" Reading Teacher, XXXV, No. 6 (March, 1982), 725-726.

687. Stevens, Kathleen, "Background Knowledge and Reading Success: Implications for Teachers of Reading," Wisconsin State Reading Association Journal, XXVII, No. 2 (Winter, 1983), 5-8.

688. Stewart, David K., "Values and Limitations of Basal Readers," in Materials for Reading, pp. 51-56, ed. Helen M. Robinson. Chicago: University of Chicago Press, 1957.

689. Stokes, Alan, "The Reliability of Readability Formulas," Journal of Research in Reading, I (February, 1978), 21-34.

690. Stott, D.H., "Some Less Obvious Cognitive Aspects of Learning to Read," Reading Teacher, XXVI, No. 4 (January, 1973), 360-361.

691. St. Pierre, Robert G., and Francis X. Archambault, "Instructional Time: The Crucial Factor in Title I Effects?" Phi Delta Kappan, LXII, No. 5 (January, 1981), 400-401.

692. Strang, Ruth, Diagnostic Teaching of Reading. New York: McGraw-Hill, 1964.

693. _____, Constance McCullough, and Arthur Traxler, The Improvement of Reading, Fourth Edition, New York: McGraw-Hill, 1967.

694. Strickland, Ruth G., The Language Arts in the Elementary School, Third Edition. Lexington, Mass.: Heath, 1969.

695. Strom, Robert D., The Tragic Migration. Washington, D.C.: NEA, 1964.

696. Stroud, J.B., Psychology in Education. New York: Longman, 1946.

697. Sullivan, Joanna, "Receptive and Critical Reading Develops at All Levels," Reading Teacher, XXVII, No. 8 (May, 1974), 796.800.

781

698. Taba, Hilda, "The Teaching of Thinking," Elementary English, XLII, No. 5 (May, 1965), 534-542.

699. ____, S. Levine, and F. Elzey, "Teaching Strategies and Thought Processes," College Record, LXV (March, 1964).

699B. Tarver, Sara, and Margaret Dawson, "Modality Preference and the Teaching of Reading: A Review," Journal of Learning Disabilities, XI (January, 1978), 17-29.

700. Taylor, Stanford E., What Research Says to the Teacher: Listening. Washington, D.C.: NEA, 1973.

701. Thomas, Ellen Lamar, and H. Alan Robinson, Improving Reading in Every Class. Boston: Allyn, Bacon, 1977.

702. Thomas, George I., and Joseph Crescimbeni, Individualizing Instruction in the Elementary School. New York: Random House, 1967.

703. Thomas, Thomas C., and Sel H. Pelavin, Patterns in ESEA Title I Learning Achievement. Menlo Park, Cal.: SRI Research Report, March, 1976. ERIC 4537-12.

704. Thompson, B.B., "A Longitudinal Study of Auditory Discrimination," Journal of Educational Research, LVI, No. 7 (March, 1963), 376-378.

705. Thompson, Martha, "The Purposes of Workbooks and Teachers' Guides," in Materials for Reading, pp. 71-74, ed. Helen M. Robinson. Chicago: University of Chicago Press, 1957.

706. Thompson, Richard A., and Merritt King, Jr., "Turn on to a Reading Center," Reading Teacher, XXVIII, No. 4 (January, 1975), 384-388.

707. Thorndike, Edward L., "The Understanding of Sentences: A Study of Errors in Reading," Elementary School Journal, LX, No. 6 (March, 1960), 325-333.

708. Thorndike, Edgar L., and Irving Lorge, Teachers Word Book of 30,000 Words. New York: Columbia University, 1944.

709. Thorndike, Robert L., "Reading as Learning," Reading Research Quarterly, IX, No. 2 (Winter, 1973-1974), 135-147.

710. Tinker, Miles A., and Constance M. McCullough, Teaching Elementary Reading, Third Edition. New York: Appleton-Century-Crofts, 1968.

782

711. Tomas, Douglas, A Survey of Research on the Teaching of Vocabulary, Unpublished doctoral dissertation, University of Houston, 1977.

712. Tompkins, Gail E., "Young Children's Linguistic Awareness," Ohio Reading Teacher, XVI, No. 3 (April, 1982), 11-14.

713. Torgeson, Hazel M., "Why Not Use the Context Too?" Reading Newsreport, IV, No. 4 (February, 1970), 40-43.

714. Torrance, E. Paul, "Motivating and Guiding Creative Reading," in How It Is Nowadays, Teacher's Edition, pp. 15-21, eds. Theodore Clymer and Robert B. Ruddell. Boston: Ginn, 1969.

715. Tovey, Duane R., "Language Acquisition: A Key to Effective Language Instruction," Language Arts, LIII, No. 8 (November-December, 1976), 868-873.

716. _____, "The Relationship of Matched First-Grade Phonics Instruction to Overall Reading Achievement and the Desire to Read," in Some Persistent Questions on Beginning Reading, pp. 93-101, ed. Robert C. Aukerman. Newark, Del.: IRA, 1972.

717. Traxler, Arthur E., "Sequential Studies of Pupil Achievement," in Sequential Development of Reading Abilities, pp. 100-108, ed. Helen M. Robinson. Chicago: University of Chicago Press, 1960.

718. Trelease, Jim, The Read-Aloud Handbook. New York: Penguin, 1982.

719. Tuinman, J. Jaap, Obtaining Indices of Passage Dependency of Comprehension Questions, Final Report USOE Grant 5-72-0026(509). Blooming- ton: Indiana University, 1972.

720. Turley, Catherine C., "A Study of Elementary School Children for Whom a Second Year of Kindergarten Was Recommended," California Reader, XV, No. 3 (March/April, 1982), 11-12.

721. Tyler, Ralph W., "The Importance of Sequence in Teaching Reading," in Sequential Development of Reading Abilities, pp. 3-8, ed. Helen M. Robinson. Chicago: University of Chicago Press, 1960.

722. _____, "Measuring the Ability to Infer," Educational Research Bulletin, IX (1930), 475-480.

723. Umans, Shelley, New Trends in Reading Instruc- tion. New York: Teachers College Press, 1963.

724. Unfinished Stories for Use in the Classroom. Washington, D.C.: NEA, 1968.

725. Valmont, William J., "Creating Questions for Informal Reading Inventories," Reading Teacher, XXV, No. 6 (March, 1972), 509-512.

726. Vukelich, Carol, "The Development of Listening Comprehension Through Storytime," Language Arts, LIII, No. 8 (November-December, 1976), 889-891.

727. Walby, Grace, S., "Testing and Teaching the Retarded Reader in Grades Four Through Eight," in the Underachiever in Reading, pp. 54-58, ed. H. Alan Robinson. Chicago: University of Chicago Press, 1962.

728. Wallen, Carl J., "Independent Activities: A Necessity, Not a Frill," Reading Teacher, XXVII, No. 3 (December, 1973), 257-262.

729. _____, Word Attack Skills in Reading. Columbus, Ohio: Merrill, 1969.

730. Ware, Kay, "Ways to Develop Reading Skills and Interests of Culturally Different Youth in Large Cities," in Reading Disabilities: Selections on Identification and Treatment, pp. 534-354, ed. Harold Newman. New York: Odyssey, 1969.

731. Wargo, Michael J., "Those Elusive Components That Contribute to the Success of Compensatory Education Projects," Paper presented at the American Educational Research Association, New York: April, 1977.

732. Weintraub, Samuel, "Vocabulary Control," Reading Teacher, XX, No. 8 (May, 1967), 769-775.

733. Wellington, J., and N. Olechowski, "Attitudes Toward the World of Work in Elementary Schools," in Guidance in the Elementary Schools: Theory, Research, and Practice, ed. E.D. Koplitz. Dubuque, Iowa: Brown, 1968.

734. Wepman, Joseph, Auditory Discrimination Test. Chicago: Language Research Associates, 1973.

735. _____, "Modalities and Learning," in Coordinating Reading Instruction, pp. 55-62, ed. Helen M. Robinson. Chicago: Scott, Foresman, 1971.

736. Werner, Heinz, and Edith Kaplan, "Development of Word Meaning Through Verbal Context: An Experimental Study," Journal of Psychology, XXIX (1950), 251-256.

737. Whipple, Gertrude, "A Modern Reading Program for This Season," in Administrators and Reading, pp. 20-40, ed. Thorsten R. Carlson. New York: Harcourt, 1972.

738. _____, "Practical Problems of Schoolbook Selection for Disadvantaged Pupils," in Reading and Readiness, pp. 194-198, ed. J. Allen Figurel. Newark, Del.: IRA, 1969.

739. Whitehead, Alfred North, The Aims of Education and Other Essays. New York: Macmillan, 1929.

740. Williams, Richard P., "Applying Research Findings in Comprehension To Classroom Practice," Address to the International Reading Association, Seattle, Washington, May, 1967.

741. Wilson, Frank T., "Early Achievements in Reading," Elementary School Journal, XLII (April, 1942), 609-615.

742. Wilson, Robert M. Address to a Regional Right to Read Workshop, Panama City, Fla., 1973.

743. _____, Diagnostic and Remedial Reading for Classroom and Clinic, Fourth Edition. Columbus, Ohio: Merrill, 1981.

744. _____, and MaryAnne Hall, Programmed Word Attack for Teachers, Third Edition. Columbus, Ohio: Merrill, 1979.

745. Winkley, Carol L., "Which Accent Generalizations Are Worth Teaching?" Reading Teaching, XX, No. 3 (December, 1966), 219-224, 253.

746. Witham, Anthony P., "Techniques for Identifying the Underachiever in Grades Four Through Eight," in The Underachiever in Reading, pp. 23-27, ed. H. Alan Robinson. Chicago: University of Chicago Press, 1962.

747. Witty, Paul, Alma M. Freeland, and Edith Grotberg, The Teaching of Reading. Boston: Heath, 1966.

748. Wolf, Willavene, Charlotte S. Huck, and Martha L. King with Bernice Cullinan, Critical Reading Ability of Elementary School Children. USOE Project No. 5-1040 (June, 1967).

749. _____, Martha L. King, and Charlotte Huck, "Critical Reading," Reading Research Quarterly, (1968), 435-497.

785

750. Wunderlich, Elaine, and Mary Bradtmueller, "Teacher Estimates of Reading Levels Compared with IRPI Instructional Level Scores," _Journal of Reading_, XIV, No. 5 (February, 1971), 303-308, 336.

751. Wylie, Richard E., and Donald D. Durrell, "Teaching Vowels Through Phonograms," _Elementary English_, XLVII, No. 7 (October, 1970), 787-791.

752. Young, Timothy, "Teacher Time on Task: A Significant Variable," _Phi Delta Kappan_, LXII, No. 1 (September, 1980), 60.

753. Zintz, Miles V., and Zelda Maggart, _The Reading Process: The Teacher and the Learner_, Fourth Edition. Dubuque, Iowa: William C. Brown, 1984.

INDEX